Tax Planning for Farm Land Diversification

Third Edition

CW00923938

Tax Planning for Farm and Land Diversification

Third Edition

Julie Butler (Butler & Co)

with contributions by

Patrick Bidder (Withers LLP)
Allison Broadey (The VAT Consultancy)
Robert Brodrick (Trowers & Hamlins)
James Cleary (Pro Vision Planning and Design)
Imogen Davies (Withers LLP)
Michael Gouriet (Withers LLP)
Judith Ingham (Withers LLP)
Antonia Mee (Withers LLP)

Bloomsbury Professional

Bloomsbury Professional Ltd, Maxwelton House, 41–43 Boltro Road, Haywards Heath, West Sussex, RH16 1BJ

© Bloomsbury Professional Ltd 2011

Bloomsbury Professional, an imprint of Bloomsbury Publishing Plc

A CIP Catalogue record for this book is available from the British Library.

ISBN: 978 1 84592 485 0

Typeset by Phoenix Photosetting, Chatham, Kent
Printed and bound in Great Britain by Hobbs the Printers Ltd, Totton, Hampshire

Preface

The need for a Third Edition of this title has evolved out of the continuing changes to farming, particularly the CAP Reform moving towards 2020. It still holds true that for many farm enterprises the survival of the farming unit can depend upon the ability to diversify successfully. This book accepts the fact that tax planning cannot be looked at in aspect. The farming unit, business and structure must be looked at in the 'round'. Diversification combined with tax planning can be the key to survival for the diversifying farm unit. Proactive practical tax planning has to be embraced by all farming activities.

Since the publication of the Second Edition there have been a number of important tax cases that impact on the farming industry. Examples of these cases are *McCall, Dance, Balfour* and *Atkinson* which focuses on the farmhouse. In 2009 'Chapter 24' of HMRC's Inheritance Tax Manual set about defining what qualifies for Agricultural Property Relief (APR). Since the Second Edition the value of agricultural land has doubled whilst there has been a collapse of farm development land values from around 2008.

Throughout the book there are references to the need for well-drafted legal agreements in all areas, eg partnership agreements, wills, deed of variations, wayleaves, options, share farming, contract farming and all letting arrangements, etc. The need to consider wills and the interaction of trusts deserve their own chapter. Protecting assets on divorce is also considered. All changes will have a potential VAT impact and Allison Broadey of The VAT Consultancy devotes a chapter to this subject. One of the clear developments of client service for the practitioner is the need to look at all angles of added value.

Obvious examples of diversification and profitable land usage are the planning permission opportunities available to the landowner. This is not just the opportunity to sell off land for development, but all angles of diversification. One of the most apparent directions is the use of redundant farm buildings for other purposes, such as commercial or residential lets. James Cleary of Pro Vision Planning and Design explains the current planning policies, how the process works and how to go about achieving the optimal planning consent.

Julie Butler
Butler & Co
April 2011

Contents

Contents

Table of Statutes

Table of Statutory Instruments

[All references are to paragraph number]

Table of Cases

[All references are to paragraph number]

Chapter 1

Farming and the need for diversification

Julie Butler

- **Farming and alternative land use**
  This chapter explains the need for the tax planner to be aware of the subtle (and unsubtle) tax differences between farming and diversification. What is government policy? Farming attracts unique tax reliefs and rules, eg agricultural property relief (APR), farming as one trade, averaging and the five-year rule for losses. It is currently essential to understand what activity is deemed to be *farming* (agriculture) and what is deemed to be *diversification* (alternative use of land) and what direction the complex tax changes are taking.

- **Protecting against the loss of valuable farming tax reliefs**
  With the move to the alternative use of land (diversification), it is essential that all the tax reliefs currently available to the farming industry continue to be used to maximum benefit. The book aims to show how these reliefs can be identified and used effectively and the tax pitfalls of the potential loss of tax reliefs understood.

- **Inheritance Tax Manual (IHTM) Chapter 24**
  HMRC issued guidance in February 2009 which helps define what is agriculture and what is not.

- **Tax planning through change**
  The move to diversification and the massive changes to the farming industry can trigger tax-planning opportunities and tax pitfalls, and this book attempts to identify these. The HMRC 'Rural Diversification Project' highlights the need for full awareness of HMRC interest into the farming and diversification platform.

- **Understanding the single payment entitlement**
  The third edition focuses on farm tax planning and compliance now that the adaptation to the 'single payment scheme' has been made by the farming industry. The full impact of the Common Agricultural Policy (CAP) reform and the Mid-Term Review (MTR) are now understood by farmers and their advisers and the key has to be maximising the tax advantages and avoiding the disadvantages. This is considered such an important subject that it has been given its own chapter (see Chapter 20).

THE FARMING EVOLUTION AND CAP REFORM

1.1   The 'single farm payment scheme' (SFP) was effective from 1 January 2005 within the farming community and the transition from the production-based system to 'land management' system of the SFP is extremely complex.

The principal aim of this book is to aid the tax planner to ensure that, with the adaptation of the farming industry to the fluctuations of the last decade together with the acceptance of diversification, tax reliefs of land ownership and agricultural activity are retained, understood and enjoyed to the maximum.

In January 2003 the detail of the CAP reform was published. It included three main reform points:

- to encourage farmers to produce what the market wants, getting away from 'farming for subsidies';

- to remove the environmentally negative incentives of the current policy; and

- to improve and provide encouragement for more sustainable farming practices.

The CAP reforms seek to separate farm subsidy from output and link it to farm size, other sources of income, quality and environmental functions. The aim is to wean UK farmers off subsidies and to make them more responsive to the marketplace.

The single payment scheme replaced ten major CAP payment schemes.

The aim of modulation (see **1.17**) has been the progressive siphoning by the government of direct payments to the funds of agri-environmental schemes and rural development initiatives and plans.

Whilst the loss of production subsidies is bad news for farming in the UK, it has shown landowners that they need to embrace potential opportunities for alternative land use.

The attitude of the farming community to diversification has evolved over the life of this book. When the first edition was published diversification was something to consider for farms. At the time of writing the second edition, diversification was necessary for survival. Now, the landowning community is much more comfortable with a large amount of alternative land use and the future looks brighter for farming at the time of writing.

For the purposes of income tax, the distinction between farming income and non-farming income could appear to be of little relevance until the 'hobby farming' rules are considered. The impact of the definition of farming on other taxes such as inheritance tax (IHT) and capital gains tax (CGT) means that interpretation assumes considerable importance, and borderline situations can create the most problems. This book looks at all these concerns in depth.

The long-awaited guidance on inheritance tax agricultural property relief (APR) is now contained in Chapter 24 of HMRC's Inheritance Tax Manual (www.hmrc.gov.uk/manuals/ihtmanual/IHTM24000.htm).

Is the farming unit itself generating a 'true commercial profit'? The question of the use of tax losses is dealt with in Chapter 12.

The main tax benefits available to a landowner of trading are that he can obtain income tax, CGT, IHT and VAT reliefs from running his land as a genuine business. This will be explained in greater detail throughout this book and the underlying principle is the need to obtain/maintain business/commercial status as the key to the enjoyment of the tax reliefs currently available.

At the time of writing, with agricultural land values remaining high and some potential for development profits (despite the crash in development land values in 2008), the landowner has a very valuable capital asset which must be protected from attacks by HMRC. In order to preserve business status, it is essential to understand the definitions of farming, diversification, agriculture and business for tax purposes.

The book tries to provide guidance on the key issues but there are constant changes to the role of farming, alternative land use and the need for food and fuel production and there are colourful tax cases in connection therewith. It is essential to look at these changes and adapt accordingly.

RISK OF LOSS OF FARM TAX RELIEFS

1.2   There are a number of tax reliefs that are unique to the farming industry. A move to diversification could put these reliefs at risk. The question is what tax reliefs can replace them or how can they be preserved?

Examples of these specific agricultural tax reliefs include:

- agricultural property relief (APR) for inheritance tax (IHT) on the farmhouse (see Chapter 4). If the farm is no longer surrounded by land in the same ownership that is principally used for farming, then is the house still a farmhouse?

- APR on the farmland and buildings (see Chapters 5 and 13).

- Job-related accommodation. It has always been taken for granted that farm workers will live in cottages 'tax-free' due to the advantages of 'job-related accommodation'. Will farm workers who move from carrying out farm duties to non-farm duties still qualify for 'tax-free', job-related accommodation? (See **1.15.**)

- Five-year loss rule (hobby farming – see Chapter 12).

- Farmers' averaging of profits for tax purposes (see **1.14**).

- Agricultural buildings allowances (ABAs) (now being phased out) (see **7.12**).

Not many pure farming activities are consistently profitable and some form of diversification is necessary in order to achieve overall profitability for the farming unit. This might simply be the letting of redundant farm buildings and cottages, or more radical diversification activities.

The average farm in the UK can be worth several million pounds and the tax risks of not qualifying for IHT reliefs can cost many hundreds of thousands, if not millions, of pounds. This is not monopoly money.

DEFINITION OF FARMING

1.3   'Fiscal farming' is farming that qualifies as farming for tax purposes (see **1.12**). There is a special tax regime for the profits of a trade carried on in the UK under ITTOIA 2005 Pt 2. Whether or not a person is carrying on a trade is a question of fact, but the word 'trade' includes the idea of exchanging goods or services for a reward. The courts have indicated what might constitute trading in a large number of cases – the badges of trade. Under ITTOIA 2005 s 9(1) farming or market gardening conducted in the UK is treated as the carrying on of a trade for income tax purposes.

Under ITA 2007 s 996 and CTA 2010 s 1125(1), 'farming' means the occupation of land wholly or mainly for the purposes of husbandry but does not include market gardening'. Thus, to be a farmer a person must satisfy two tests: the person must be in occupation of the land and the purpose of the occupation must be at least mainly for husbandry. The actual use of the land will normally be indicative of the purpose of occupation, but is not necessarily conclusive. Nor need the occupation be exclusive of others (share farming is an example where two persons may occupy land and each be farmers). 'Husbandry' is specifically said to include hop growing and the breeding and rearing of horses and the grazing of horses in connection with those activities (ITA 2007 s 996(2) and CTA 2010 s 1125(2)). Farming and market gardening, and the intensive rearing of livestock or fish on a commercial basis for the purpose of food consumption count as a qualifying trade, profession or vocation for the purposes of making an averaging claim (ITTOIA 2005 s 221(2)(b) – see **1.14**).

The cultivation of 'short rotation coppice' is specifically described as husbandry, and thus constitutes farming: ITA 2007 s 996(3) and CTA 2010 s 1125(3) (for non-corporate and corporate taxpayers respectively). Short rotation coppice means a perennial crop of tree species (normally willow or poplar) 'planted at high density, the stems of which are harvested above ground at intervals of less than 10 years': ITA 2007 s 996(6) and CTA 2010 s 1125(6).

Farming is further defined in the case of *Lean and Dickson v Ball* (1925) 10 TC 341, where it is stated that for a business activity to be classed as husbandry it must depend to a material extent on the use of the produce of the land occupied by the person carrying on the activity. IHTM Chapter 24 (see **1.1**) has also helped with the definition.

The grey areas of definition are:

- energy crops (see **2.22** and **6.47**);

- market gardening/horticulture;

- certain types of intensive livestock rearing;

- forestry and woodland (see Chapter 6); and

- agri-environment work schemes (see Chapter 2).

A lot of the farm tax planning hinges on the definition of husbandry.

The Capital Allowances Act 2001 (CAA 2001) s 362(1) defines husbandry as 'including any method of intensive rearing of livestock or fish on a commercial basis for the production of food for human consumption'.

It is interesting to note that intensive activity where, for example, livestock is kept indoors or fish are kept in tanks and they are fed on purchased feed, is not considered to be farming. However, the buildings are often considered to be agricultural for APR, ABAs (see **7.12**) and rating purposes. HMRC state that the occupation of land for the purposes of breeding thoroughbred horses is to be treated as farming but this does not extend to any activities involved in training racehorses (HMRC BIM55701).

The sale of farmland is generally not subject to income tax, but to CGT. The benefits that can arise from this are discussed in Chapter 14. However, there may be some instances where HMRC might try to classify land sales as a trading activity.

The difficulty may be in deciding whether the new activity (alternative land use) falls within the definition of farming. For example, some letting activities may qualify as farming such as letting land for grazing or 'grass keep' (see Chapter 11) under an agreement for less than 365 days and with no right of renewal (BIM55065), unless the animals grazing the land are non-qualifying stock, eg racehorses, hunters or children's ponies in which case HMRC may argue that the letting was not farming.

The reasoning in respect of the above is that although the landowner is still occupying the land, he is not occupying the building for the purposes of husbandry. In HMRC's view the grazing of horses, unless it forms part of a commercial stud operation, is not 'agriculture' and therefore not husbandry. Exceptions are made if the grazing forms only an occasional or small part of a larger farming operation (CTO Advanced Instruction Manual L.246.2) and if the grazing is part of the breeding operation which is husbandry.

ACTIVITIES CONSIDERED TO BE FARMING

1.4   Activities considered to be farming would include the following:

- the production and sale of cereals (arable);

- the production and sale of milk and associated products (dairy);

- the production and sale of animals (livestock);

- stud farms (see **6.17**);

- share farming and contract farming correctly structured (see Chapter 11);

- fruit farming (see **19.5**);

- 'set aside' now abolished (see **2.4**);

- growing and selling of turf (*Assessor for Lothian Region v Rolawn Ltd* 1990 SLT 433);

- income from grazing correctly structured (see **11.3**, **11.31** to **11.35**);

- short rotation coppice (see **6.4** and **6.11**);

- hop growing;

- farm shops selling farm produce (see **6.33**);

- normal energy crops (**6.47**);

- sales of turf and depositing soil (**6.23**); and

- certain minor receipts from granting licences over farmland may be treated as farming income (see **15.33**).

There are strong arguments to support the claim that the definition of farming should be expanded to incorporate diversified activities (see **1.6**).

Hop growing is regarded as husbandry, and therefore farming for tax purposes (ITA 2007 s 996(2)(a) and CTA 2010 s 1125(2)).

Growing Christmas trees in specialist nurseries is categorised as market gardening. Where, however, Christmas trees are grown on part of a farm, by HMRC practice the activity may be incorporated in the other farming activities conducted (see BIM 62601). See **6.5**.

IHTM24061 sets out the qualifying uses of land:

'The following land uses should be accepted as for the "purposes of agriculture" within the meaning of IHTA 84/S117

- cultivation to produce food for human and animal consumption,

- use to support livestock kept to produce food for human consumption, such as meat or milk or other products such as wool,

- the keeping of such other animals as may be found on an ordinary farm, for example, horses kept for farm work,

- the breeding and grazing of racehorses on a stud farm. This is not an agricultural purpose (IHTM24068) under general law, but is made one for the purposes of agricultural relief by IHTA84/S115(4),

- land set aside for permanent or rotational fallow (IHTM24064),

- cultivation of short rotation coppice (IHTM24063).

Land that is normally used for agricultural purposes may occasionally be used for other purposes. Provided those other purposes are not the primary reason for the occupation of the land, the land should be regarded as occupied 'for the purposes of agriculture' when considering a deduction for relief. One example is a normal working farm over which an annual point-to-point horse race is run.'

Much help can be gained from Chapter 24 of the IHTM.

ACTIVITIES NOT CONSIDERED TO BE FARMING

1.5   Activities not considered to be farming would include the following:

- property development (see **6.38**);

- parking, mooring and storage of vehicles and vessels (see **9.35**);

- share farming agreements with minimum return (see **11.4**);

- fragile/badly drafted contract farming arrangements (see Chapter 11);

- garden centres selling bought-in items;

- animals kept for exhibition;

- game birds raised for sporting activities (*Cook v Ross Poultry Ltd* [1982] RA 187);

- farm shops selling bought-in items (see **6.33**);

- crops that grow naturally;

- gaming and fishing rights (see **6.51** to **6.54**);

- grazing by horses (see **6.24**);

- letting of sports facilities;

- income from industrial and office units (see Chapter 15);

- land let for 365 days or more (see Chapters 11 and 15);

- letting out redundant farm cottages (see Chapter 15);

- food processing (see **2.5**);

- horse livery and other equine activities (see **6.24** to **6.29**);

- furnished holiday lets and farm tourism (see **6.13** to **6.15**);

- long-term woodlands and forestry (see **6.4** to **6.12**)**;** and

- market gardening.

HELP VIA THE DEFINITION OF AGRICULTURE AND FARMING

1.6 The definition of 'farming' for tax purposes excludes 'market gardening' (ITA 2007 s 996(1) and CTA 2010 s 1125(1)). Market gardening is defined as 'the occupation of land as a garden or nursery for the purpose of growing produce for sale' (ITA 2007 s 996(5) and CTA 2010 s 1125(5)).

If the alternative land use is for a new business activity that falls outside farming, it will be advantageous if the new venture qualifies for the tax reliefs available for a trade. If a particular activity does not, as a matter of fact, fall within the definition of farming, it may still be taxable as representing the carrying on of some other trade (alternative land use), if the land is occupied on a commercial basis with a view to the realisation of profit (ITTOIA s 2005 s 10 and CTA 2009 s 38). This rule could be particularly important for recipients of the SFP where, for example, the land is used for horse grazing in connection with a livery business. Alternatively, the activity may represent casual or occasional profits chargeable as income not otherwise charged (under ITTOIA 2005 Pt 5 Ch 8 for income tax or CTA 2009 Pt 10 Ch 8 for corporation tax.)

7

In trying to understand what is and what is not farming, it is vital to look at the definition of agriculture. The definition of agricultural land is found in IHTA 1984 s 115(2):

> 'Agricultural property means agricultural land or pasture and includes woodland and any building used in connection with the intensive rearing of livestock or fish if the woodland or building is occupied with agricultural land or pasture and the occupation is ancillary to that of the agricultural land or pasture; and also includes such cottages, farm buildings and farm houses, together with the land occupied with them, as are of a character appropriate to the property.'

As mentioned above, agricultural land is further statutorily defined in CAA 2001 s 361(1) and means land, houses or other buildings in the UK occupied wholly or mainly for the purposes of husbandry.

There are many who rightly argue that the definition of agriculture should be widened so as to incorporate non-agricultural diversification. This argument is of particular importance to the agricultural tenant who is bound to carry out pure agricultural activities in accordance with the tenancy (see Chapter 15).

There are large variations in the range and type of enterprises carried out within the definition of agricultural. The choice of agricultural enterprise to date has been largely dictated by the quality and type of land topography, rainfall, proximity to markets and processing facilities and the quota available.

For example the western parts of England and Wales are more suited to grass growth than cropping because of topography and rainfall, therefore livestock enterprises predominate. (The west has also seen the diversification of the 'racing yard' achieve great success.) The better quality grass growing land in these areas usually supports dairy enterprises, with the remainder, including the hill areas, supporting beef and sheep. The drier eastern parts support cropping systems with the land type dictating the type of crop grown. Sugar beet is usually only grown in the proximity of sugar beet processing factories, largely in eastern England.

The best quality land is often used for growing vegetables, particularly where irrigation is available. In general these areas are located in East Anglia, Worcestershire, Lincolnshire, Herefordshire and Kent. There are similar 'drivers' for alternative rural initiatives and they must be able to integrate with the existing agricultural activity.

There are those who argue strongly about the expansion of the definition of farming/agriculture not just because there are currently grey areas and confusion in the tax legislation and guidance but because we are being guided towards alternative rural initiatives and they should be incorporated in a broader definition of agriculture. IHTM Chapter 24 has helped with the definition, but that definition should be expanded.

The basic tax principle is that the IHT relief, business property relief (BPR), is dependent on there being a 'business' or a trade. If a claim for APR fails then there is scope to turn to BPR (see **5.32**) – there has to be a commercial business.

8

FARMING INCOME BY CONCESSION

1.7   There are certain types of income which are treated as farming income by concession, that is where the receipt is included in the farming profits, especially when the amounts have been small compared with the total income from farming. However, should that farming income be greatly diminished, this concession would no longer be available and this type of income would then be considered as a non-farming receipt. Examples of non-farming receipts treated as farming income by concession are:

- leasing quota (see **7.26**);

- contracting income (see **6.35**);

- licences given to treasure seekers (see **19.15**);

- rental income from farm buildings (see **12.6** and Chapter 15);

- wayleaves (see **15.30** and **15.31**);

- Christmas trees (see **6.5**);

- energy crops (see **6.47**)

- biofuels (see **6.48**); and

- alternative agricultural crops.

In 2005, HMRC accepted that the growing of normal energy crops (eg beet, oil seed rape, cereals and miscanthus) was also husbandry (*Tax Bulletin*, Special Edition, June 2005). On the other hand, a farmers' co-operative butter-making business was held not to be husbandry: *CIR v The Cavan Central Co-operative Agricultural and Dairy Society Ltd* 12 TC 1. Land used for market gardening is agricultural land, so it is not necessary to decide whether or not market gardening is husbandry. As already mentioned a total review of the 'agricultural activity' definition is needed.

DEFINITION OF DIVERSIFICATION

1.8   So what is 'diversification'? It has been defined as putting land to a different use – alternative rural initiatives. It is generally considered that pure farming does not always give the required commercial return in the current business climate and the farmer has to look for alternative types of farming or alternative uses for his land and buildings.

Farming as food production is dependent on world food/commodity prices and therefore vulnerable to violent swings in profitability/loss. Diversification can integrate a more constant income/profit stream into the enterprise. At the time of writing corn prices are high and there is a world shortage of some foods (eg rice) but production costs (eg diesel) are very high.

Consideration has to be given to the type of soil (see for example **7.21**) as to the choice of farming.

Diversification is the supply of land for an alternative use moving away from agricultural production, the supply of an activity (not defined as farming) on land. The land supplied could still be used for agriculture but the alternative activity (eg shooting) does not currently come within the definition of farming.

Alternative land and building use

1.9   At **1.5** we looked at activities that are deemed not to be farming; but are they diversification?

Diversification may involve the use of land for other farming uses, or non-farming uses. The main assets of a farm business can be the land and buildings it occupies for the purposes of farming. An inability to generate profits from farming the land, the availability of grants, government direction or some other circumstance, may dictate that:

- a different type of farming should be carried on using the same land and buildings;
- the land and buildings should be used for a non-farming purpose; or
- the land and buildings should be sold and the farmer may then try to make a living outside of farming (see Chapter 14 on property disposals).

Examples of possible diversified activities are as follows:

- energy crops (see **6.47**) (can be agriculture for APR);
- biofuels (see **6.48**) (can be agriculture for APR);
- alternative crops eg winter lupins, sunflowers, borage, pulses;
- diversified livestock eg wild boar, red deer, buffalo;
- cashmere, mohair, angora production;
- agricultural and countryside attractions (see **6.31**);
- recreational fishing (see **6.30**);
- vineyards (see **6.34**);
- plant hire;
- food processing and marketing eg butter, cheese, ice cream;
- opportunities in the food and shopping sector (see **6.33**);
- Christmas trees (see **6.5**) (might incorporate farming);
- farmers' markets (might incorporate pure farming);
- adventure games (see **6.32**);
- trading in land property developments (see Chapter 14);
- bed and breakfast (see **6.16**);
- caravan and camping sites (see **6.18** to **6.22**);
- clay pigeon shooting, including conventional land lasers (see **6.51**);
- furnished holiday lettings (see **6.13** to **6.15**, **12.7** and **15.18**);

- horse liveries, riding schools and horse trekking (see **6.24** to **6.29**, and **15.27**);

- golf (see **6.32**);

- motor sports (see **6.32**);

- water sports (see **6.32**);

- downhill racing (see **6.32**);

- farmland disposals (see Chapter 14);

- car boot sales;

- mobile phone masts (see **6.36**);

- commercial shoots (see **6.52**);

- sites for the music industry;

- commercially exploiting aggregates (see **19.8**);

- property development 'growing houses' (see **6.38**);

- long-term woodlands and forestry (see **6.5** to **6.12**);

- mineral royalties (see **6.37**);

- landfill (see **19.10**); and

- the letting of farm buildings and cottages (see **13.26** to **13.46** and Chapter 15).

As set out in **1.7**, on a small scale these diversified activities could be considered to be farm income by concession and some *will* still count as farming eg diversified livestock farming for human consumption.

The majority of the diversification activities will need legal help and advice and planning permission may be required and cause delays (see Chapter 3).

It is important to look at:

- the effect that such changes may have on the landowner's entitlement to all forms of tax reliefs which are featured throughout the book;

- how the landowner might use the CGT reliefs (eg roll-over relief, hold-over relief, entrepreneurs' relief) to implement the changes forced on him, without incurring a tax liability because of the change (see Chapter 14); and

- how the impact of VAT will affect such changes (see Chapter 9).

FARMING AS ONE TRADE

Alternative land use – new farming activity

1.10   All farming carried on in the UK by any particular person or partnership or body of persons is treated for trading purposes as one trade.

All farming in the UK carried on by a person or company, other than farming carried on as part of another trade, is treated for tax purposes as one trade (see

ITTOIA 2005 s 9(2); CTA 2009 s 36(2)). The same applies to firms, except that the farming carried on by a firm which is treated as one trade is not included in any farming trade of any partner in the firm (ITTOIA 2005 s 859(1); CTA 2009 s 1270(1)).

Farming (which excludes market gardening) has always been considered as one trade: thus, an estate in Scotland, a farm in Yorkshire and a farm in the Home Counties owned by the same legal structure are all treated as one trade. This rule can have a major effect on the computation of farming profits and losses. Its application results in the aggregation of profits and losses (including capital allowances) from more than one farm into a single taxable source of income when more than one farm is operating at the same point of time but in different parts of the country. It is not relevant that perhaps two farms are managed as separate economic units, nor that separate sets of financial accounts are prepared, there should be coterminous year-ends. Likewise, there is no cessation of trade nor any new trade commenced where a farmer ceases trading at one farm, sells up, buys a new farm and starts afresh there.

Tax planning can be complicated where the farms are owned by different legal entities. The trades of diversified activities, as opposed to farming, do not have to comply with ITTOIA 2005 ss 9(2) and 859(1) for income tax and CTA 2009 ss 36(2) and 1270(1) for corporation tax ie all the farms have to be treated as one trade, which presents tax-planning opportunities in respect of the allocation and timing of profits.

If there has been a significant amount of time between the giving up of one farm and the starting of another, HMRC might take the view that a trade has ceased and a new one commenced. This can be an important factor when looking at tax-planning principles surrounding hobby farming and IHT reliefs.

For example, the trade of growing and selling Christmas trees or a bed and breakfast business starting on the second farm would be a new trade within the provisions of ITA 2007 s 72 applying to opening year losses (see Chapter 12).

Since farming is to be treated as a trade it is charged to tax under ITTOIA 2005 Pt 2 or CTA 2009 Pt 3 in the ordinary way, provided the land is in the UK. (If the land is situated abroad, different problems arise.) That also applies to market gardening. The ordinary rules for calculating profits of a trade apply, subject however, to one major exception.

The rule that all the farming carried on by one business is treated as one trade (ITTOIA 2005 s 9(2) and (3) for income tax and CTA 2009 s 36(2) for corporation tax) does not apply to diversified activities and this can have major effects on the computation of farming profits and losses. It is not just the income from the diversified activity that must be removed but also the expenses that relate to that activity – this could include overhead expenses shared with the farming operation.

DIVERSIFICATION: BIG IMPACT ON THE FARM TAX COMPUTATION AND ACCOUNTS

1.11 Diversification could include a whole range of possible trading activities, some of which will fall under new tax regimes and therefore bring potential tax problems and tax-planning opportunities.

The difference between 'farming' and 'non-farming' income and expenditure has to be identified in the preparation of the tax computation. Most farmers look at their diversified farm as 'one unit', one business entity, but the tax rules dictate that there should be division. This is complex, time-consuming and invites error. A farmer's view is generally that all income from farming and farm diversification (including lettings) should be assessed as trading income (ITTOIA 2005 s 9) with no division of source.

When practitioners prepare the farm accounts and/or tax computation, it is important to remove the non-farming income items (see **1.5**) and also to match the expenses. In practice, many practitioners are just preparing a computation, which arrives at a net profit or loss, with little regard for the allocation of expenses and income. It could be that income from items such as quota leasing and grazing by horses are inflating the profit for the purposes of the five-year rule for losses (see Chapter 12) and it is more tax efficient to combine the income as farming.

As a practical planning point, it is important to review all clients who are associated with farming to ensure the correct treatment of income and expenses. It will also be essential to review what future reliefs the client may need to claim, eg considering the 'commerciality' of the farm or the business. It is also useful to ascertain such facts as whether the client intends to claim APR for IHT purposes. If APR is lost, will BPR still be available? (See Chapter 5.)

While reviewing the tax computation, it is essential to see that farmers are still eligible for tax reliefs that are dependent on 'business/commercial' status. Examples of reliefs which could be lost are entrepreneurs' relief and roll-over relief for capital gains tax (CGT) (see **1.13**).

THE FISCAL FARMER

1.12 HMRC *Tax Bulletin* (June 2005 special edition), which discusses the single payment scheme, defines the fiscal farmer. It clarifies that the SP can be taxed in various ways dependent on the underlying factors regarding its receipt as follows:

Fiscal farmer	ITTOIA 2005 s 9
Non-farming trade	ITTOIA 2005 s 10
Non-trading	ITTOIA 2005 Pt 5 Chapter 8

The definition of fiscal farmer will include more than the traditional farmer who continues to farm. As the definition of 'farming' turns upon the purpose behind the occupation of land, HMRC have conceded that those who do not produce anything on the land that franks the SFP will nevertheless be treated as being within this category (see also **20.5** and **20.6**).

Preserving the main farming tax reliefs

Capital gains tax

1.13 It is essential, with the move to alternative use of land or diversification, that all the main tax reliefs available to the farming business are preserved.

The CGT reliefs that might be affected by diversification, or that might be used to assist diversification, are:

- replacement of business assets (roll-over relief) (TCGA 1992 ss 152–159) (see **14.19**);

- incorporation of a business in part or whole (TCGA 1992 ss 162 and 165) (see Chapter 8);

- gifts of business assets and gifts on which IHT is chargeable (hold-over relief) (TCGA 1992 ss 165, 260, Sch 7) (see **14.26** to **14.30**);

- roll-over relief on reinvestment (reinvestment relief) (FA 1998 s 140(2)) and EIS (deferral relief) (TCGA 1992 Sch 5B) (see **14.62**, **8.16** to **8.19**); and/or

- entrepreneurs' relief as introduced by the Finance Act 2008 (see Chapter 14).

Expenditure incurred in the diversification process will be disallowed if it is not deductible in arriving at the true commercial profit calculated on accounting principles. Share farming and contract farming are actually considered to be farming and are taxed as trading income (ITTOIA 2005 s 9) provided they meet all the conditions (see Chapter 11).

FARMERS' AVERAGING OF PROFITS

1.14   Farmers' averaging was introduced in 1977. The system enacted was based upon a simple arithmetic concept of adding together the profits of two successive years and dividing by two. In practice, a variety of limitations are imposed. The rules are now contained in ITTOIA 2005 Pt 2 Ch 16. Only 'farm' profits not diversified profits can be averaged.

The aim of these provisions was (and is) to help ensure that farmers make full use of personal allowances and basic rates available for income tax purposes and do not unduly suffer higher tax rates one year and then fail to utilise these basic allowances and rates another year.

For the purposes of averaging relief, 'farming' includes the intensive rearing of livestock or fish on a commercial basis for the production of food for human consumption (ITTOIA 2005 s 221(2)(b)). Averaging can also be applied to trades of market gardening (ITTOIA 2005 s 221 (2)(a)). Only farming trades carried on in the UK may average profits. Also excluded are farming contractors because their trade does not involve the occupation of farm land, as are cases where farming activity is part of a larger trade that includes substantial non-farming activities (see BIM73110). Averaging only applies to profits chargeable to income tax, so companies liable to corporation tax cannot use these provisions (ITTOIA 2005 s 221(1)).

For the purpose of averaging relief, profits are taken before any allowance is made for trading losses sustained in the year of assessment, or those carried forward or sideways (see Chapter 12) so as to be applied to profits for the period (ITTOIA 2005 s 221(4)). However, profits are computed after any deduction or addition for capital allowances or balancing charges (see Chapter 7).

If there is an adjusted loss for one year, that is treated as 'nil' (ITTOIA 2005 s 221(5)) and the average over the two years becomes one half of the profit for the other year.

It is a precondition for relief that the profit of one of the two consecutive years does not exceed 75% of the profit of the other, or is nil (ITTOIA 2005 s 222(1)). This difference equal to at least 25% of the higher figure is assumed to be needed to justify the relief. However, there is a marginal relief, where the profits of one year exceed 70% but do not exceed 75% of the other year (ITTOIA 2005 s 223(4)). This adds further complication to the calculation.

JOB-RELATED ACCOMMODATION – THE FARMING ADVANTAGE

1.15   The key conditions that need to be in place to achieve the tax-free 'benefits in kind' (BIK) for the farm employees are dependent on proper and better performance of the employee's duties and also the customary provisions (farming is customary). Traditionally farm workers have qualified for tax-free job-related accommodation, but will this benefit still be enjoyed with the move to diversification? The conditions for job-related accommodation in relation to farming are as follows.

- Where it is necessary for the proper performance of an employee's duties that he should reside in the accommodation (ITEPA 2003 s 99(1)).

- Where the accommodation is provided for the better performance of the duties of his employment and he is in one of the kinds of employment in the case of which it is customary for employers to provide living accommodation to employees (ITEPA 2003 s 99(2)).

An individual who lives in job-related accommodation may find on leaving his job that another residence which he has owned has lost the CGT exemption for principal private residence (PPR) relief because he has failed to occupy it continuously. To meet this situation where there has been occupation of the job-related accommodation, for example the farmhouse (after 30 July 1978), it is treated as if it were the occupation of the employee's own house provided he intends to go and occupy it in due course. This is set out in TCGA 1992 s 222(8) (b). Whether the employee does intend to (re)occupy his residence is a question of fact. If the employee has occupied it before the relevant sale, this would clearly represent persuasive evidence. If the sale occurs before occupation, intention can still be demonstrated particularly if the proceeds are applied to buy another home so that the principal private residence relief is endangered.

There is a similar denial of relief for job-related accommodation, where the accommodation is provided by a company for a director, unless he has no material interest and works full time, or unless the company is non-profit making or a charity. The clear tax-planning point here is that farmhouses owned within farming companies and lived in by directors must be given a review to minimise assessable benefit (see **4.13**).

An exemption from the tax benefit in kind for job-related accommodation also requires that the accommodation be provided for the better performance of the duties of the employee. This is most likely sought where employees are provided with accommodation on a rural estate or farm. This requirement is clearly aimed at questioning the employer's reasons for providing accommodation.

The position regarding the kinds of employment created by diversification and the identification thereof for the BIK position does need review. A careful examination is made of the duties of the employment contrasted with both those of similar employees on other rural estates and the duties common to the generic class to determine whether those of the rural estate employee are neither rare nor untypical of the class of employee. So what of the duties carried out as a result of diversification?

Is the provision of accommodation customary? The *Vertigan v Brady* [1988] STC 91 case, helps in this decision where the court determined there were three constituent factors to be examined: the statistical evidence on how common the practice was; evidence on how long the practice had gone on; and whether the practice had achieved general acceptance. So what of the impact of diversification? Will the move away from farming cause problems with regard to the conditions of 'proper performance' or 'customary performance'?

DIVERSIFICATION OPPORTUNITIES

1.16   Examples of diversification ideas are set out in **1.9**. More details are set out below.

- *Equine* – On investigation a farmer might find a local market for horse livery and riding facilities that could provide you with a profitable source of income (see **6.24** to **6.29**).

- *Sport and recreation* – There is great potential for developing sport and leisure enterprises on farms (see **6.32**).

- *Catering* – The catering industry is keen to develop supplies of fresh produce. In some locations there are opportunities for farmhouse restaurants and other types of catering services. Farmers' markets have helped many local food producers sell their produce direct to the consumer, with obvious financial and social benefits (see **6.33**).

- *Provision of pre-school care* – Demand for places exceeds supply in many areas. Some farms have the facilities and a good location for the development of pre-school nurseries.

- *Food and retailing* – Farm shops, direct sales to caterers, farm-based restaurants and cafes, ice cream production, cheese production, linseed oil, essential oil (see **6.33**). 'Farmgate' (see **1.21**) is considered key to the farming industry.

- *Tourism* – Furnished holiday lets (FHLs), B&B, self-catering accommodation, caravanning, camping, visitor attractions, craft centres (see **15.8** to **15.20** and **6.31**).

- *Phone masts and wind farms* (see **6.36**, **6.49** and **6.50**).

- *Sport and recreation* – Horse livery and riding schools, walking and cycling activities, motor sports, water sports, golf, fishing, shooting (see **6.51** to **6.54**).

- *Crop related* – Energy crops, essential oils, herbs, pet foods (see **6.47**).

- *Livestock related* – Goat and sheep milking, buffalo milk and meat, meat processing and direct marketing.

- *Property* – Offices and workshops, engineering works, building trades.

The availability of grants to support these activities is looked at in Chapter 2.

THE 'SINGLE FARM PAYMENT SCHEME' (SFP) – THE JARGON

1.17   The impact of the SFP on farming and diversification is given its own chapter (see Chapter 20).

The jargon that has evolved from the introduction of the SFP will feature throughout the book and needs some explanation.

- *Single farm payment (SFP)* – a payment based on a farmer's claim during a historic reference period 2000–02. It replaces arable aid payments, beef special premium, suckler cow premium, sheep premium etc. For England it is a hybrid of the area-based method and the history-based method (see **20.2** to **20.4**).

- *Decoupling* – payment conditional on keeping land in good agricultural and environmental condition with no obligation to farm the land (see **2.2**).

- *Partial decoupling* – a proportion of the payment is conditional on continuing agricultural production.

- *National reserve* – a national reserve will be established to deal with hardship cases, new entrants and some transitional problems. A linear percentage reduction of the reference SFP is allowed for in order to start a national reserve.

- *Transitional arrangement* – the transition period will create a number of problems for those that fall outside the qualifying criteria. They are complicated and warrant a book in their own right. Suffice it to say that expert advice should be sought when buying or selling land or in changes in tenancy.

- *Entitlement* – the number of tradable hectare rights to a specific annual single farm payment.

- *Modulation* – progressive siphoning of direct payments to fund agri-environmental schemes and rural developments initiatives.

- *Cross-compliance* – conditions of good agricultural and environmental (GAEC) practice which must be met to receive the single farm payment (see **20.17**).

- *Negative list crops* – fruit, vegetables, potatoes.

- *Naked acres* – acres of land, which have no entitlement to the SFP.

- *Non-fiscal farmers* – those farmers whose occupation of land was not principally for the purpose of husbandry (see **1.12**).

- *History-based method* – refers to the farmer's claim in the three years 2000–02 which formed the basis of the calculation of the SFP (see **20.3**).

- *Area-based method* – money available under the scheme is divided by regional agricultural area to yield a standard SFP was based upon 2005 area (see **20.3**).

- *Financial discipline* – replaces the term degressivity and is a mechanism that can be used to reduce direct payments annually if the CAP budget ceiling is in danger of being breached between 2007–13.

- *Farmgate* – The basic principle of 'food chain reconnection', selling direct to the customer and ideally from the front gate of the farm (see **1.21**).

- *Eligible land* – land eligible for the SFP; broadly arable and permanent pastures but excludes permanent crops, forests and land under non-agricultural use.

- *Farmer (under article 2)* – a farmer is someone who engages in an agricultural activity. The latter is defined as 'the production, rearing or growing of agricultural products including the harvesting, milking, breeding animals and keeping animals for farming purposes or maintaining the land in good agricultural and environmental conditions'.

- *Fiscal farmer* – the farmer whose occupation of the land is principally for the purpose of husbandry (see **1.12**).

- *Severely disadvantaged areas (SDA)* – existing designated areas of disadvantaged upland making up most but not all of the less favoured area.

- *National envelope* – England does not use the 'envelope' system. Up to 10% of the total subsidy under the CAP reform could have been transferred into an envelope to find agri-environmental schemes (see **20.16**).

- *The Curry Report – The Future of Farming and Food Report* published in January 2002 (see **1.21**).

- *Entry-level payments (ELS)* – payments under the pilot agri-environmental schemes (see **1.22** and **2.23**).

- *GAEC* – good agricultural and environmental condition, the underlying basics to the 'cross compliance conditions'. The state of the land must be left in good order for farmers to receive the entitlement (see **20.17**).

Subsidies and grants – taxation

1.18   The tax treatment of the subsidy (entitlement) will depend on the purpose for which the payment is made. Where a grant is paid because capital expenditure has been incurred, the capital cost is reduced by the grant when the capital allowances (whether plant or machinery or agricultural buildings) are computed. If it is to reimburse revenue expenditure, it is taken into the profit and loss account for tax purposes.

When farmland is acquired compulsorily for the building of a new road, the compensation may cover the value of the actual land taken, the depreciation in value of adjoining land, the loss of crops, the reimbursement of costs of making good damage to land and fences, the loss of future income, the future additional costs of haulage, the future costs of maintaining new fences and many other items (see **14.57**).

The payments for the capital items mentioned may be liable to CGT and this is considered at **1.23** and in Chapter 14.

Some small compensation payments are included in the 'monthly milk cheques', received by dairy farmers, and this element must be excluded from the profit and loss account. Where a farmer has to make a milk super levy payment, this is treated as a deduction in the profit and loss account.

The principles governing the tax treatment of grants and subsidies, together with examples from case law, are set out in BIM40455, to which reference should be made in any case of doubt or difficulty. The main general principle is the distinction between capital and revenue and the main determining factor is the purpose for which the grant is paid.

Decided cases on farming grants include:

- *Higgs v Wrightson* (1944) 26 TC 73 (ploughing grant held to be a trading receipt);

- *Watson v Samson Bros* (1959) 38 TC 346 (payments for rehabilitation of flood-damaged land held to be capital receipts); and

- *White v G & M Davies* (1979) 52 TC 597 and *IRC v W Andrew Biggar (a firm)* [1982] STC 677 (premiums payable under scheme for conversion of dairy herds to beef production held to be trading receipts) (see **2.25**).

The time at which income should be recognised for tax purposes can be a complex area. Detailed guidance is provided at BIM34010 onwards, to which reference should be made in any case of doubt or difficulty.

A valid basis for determining timing issues is one which is arrived at from the correct application of generally accepted accountancy principles to the particular facts provided it does not offend the taxing statutes as interpreted by the courts. In some cases there may be more than one acceptable basis; but a valid basis, once adopted, should be used consistently unless there is good reason for a change. Where an acceptable basis has been adopted in the accounts, attempts to use some other acceptable basis by means of adjustments in the tax computations are usually resisted by HMRC. Chapter 2 sets out subsidy entitlement. The tax position of the SFP is looked at in Chapter 20.

LAND QUALITY AND DIVERSIFICATION

1.19   The enterprises found in both farming and diversification are largely dictated by the land type and quality. Therefore different enterprises are found in different regions of the country. DEFRA (Department of Environment, Food and Rural Affairs) classifies land in England and Wales into five grades according to its suitability to farming based on soil type, climate and relief. It is essential to understand the land quality before moving ahead with diversification.

- Grade 1 – Soils capable of growing a wide range of crops with high yields. These soils are mostly loams, sandy loams and peats with good drainage and water availability. These soils have a high level of natural fertility or are highly responsive to fertilisers.

- Grade 2 – Soils capable of growing a wide range of crops but with limitations which exclude the land from Grade 1. These limitations restrict the range of crops capable of being grown and their yield potential.

- Grade 3 – (split into A and B) Land which is capable of growing good crops but a more restricted range than Grade 2. At the top of the grade, the less demanding horticultural crops, ie cereals, roots and grass can be grown on the land.

- Grade 4 – This land has restricted potential, the choice of crops being limited, yield moderate and timing of cultivations restricted to times when the weather is favourable. This land is mostly down to grass, with smaller areas of oats, barley and feed crops for animals and has potential for diversification activity.

- Grade 5 – land with very severe restrictions, mostly being rough grazing and again this could be prime for diversified activities.

Arable area payments scheme – before the SFP

1.20   The arable area payments scheme (AAPS) had been integrated into the UK farming industry since 1992 basically unaltered, although it changed radically with effect from the introduction of the SFP.

The AAPS arrangements were designed to limit the amount of farmland used for growing arable crops and required farmers to set aside a proportion of their arable land each year in exchange for a set-aside payment being made (see **13.25**).

Amounts received for set-aside land are treated as farming income and taxed as part of the farm profits under ITTOIA 2005 s 9(1) in the usual way, subject to timing, and expenses relating to the land being deductible.

HMRC confirmed in their *Tax Bulletin* February 1994, p 108, that all arable area payments (including the required level of set-aside) were to be treated as sales subsidies and taken to the credit of the profit and loss account in the accounting period in which the crop has been sold.

With regard to AAPS, HMRC did say that a different treatment would be acceptable to them if it complied with generally accepted accounting practice.

HMRC's interpretation followed their general assumption that the tax treatment should be determined by the purpose for which the payment was intended. If it was designed to supplement the income from a crop, it should have been taken for credit in the period in which the crop proceeds were credited to the accounts; if it was paid to meet certain costs, it was deducted from those costs.

Where the payment reduces the cost of a crop, which was growing at the end of the period in which it was received, then the valuation would be reduced by that payment (see Chapter 7).

The management of set-aside land represents the occupation and use of the land for agricultural purposes, and thus for CGT purposes it will continue to be eligible for roll-over, hold-over and ER (see Chapter 14). Set aside should also be eligible for APR for IHT purposes (see **13.25**).

Direct payments are to be reduced by a set amount each year, with the proceeds to be made available as additional community support for rural development initiatives and agri-environmental schemes.

Farmers have already found applying for grants for diversification initiatives time consuming, complex and in some cases frustrating. DEFRA are working towards making it easier (see Chapter 2).

FOOD CHAIN RECONNECTION ('FARMGATE')

1.21   'Farmgate' can be described as farmers selling direct to customers or attempting to achieve better integration and understanding between farmers and customers.

The DEFRA-funded Forward Farming Project looked at how demonstration farm activities can help people in the farming industry to recognise and adopt best practice, technically, economically and environmentally. This can encourage customers to try and understand where their food comes from and just what it may or may not contain.

The government accepted the recommendation of the 'Curry Report', the Policy Commission of Farming and Food, to set up a project to establish a pilot network of demonstration farms.

The aim of the scheme is to test the effectiveness of different types of demonstration farms and associated activities in improving the economic and environmental performance of farms and their integration into the food chain and rural economy. This can involve farms selling direct to customers and missing out the supermarket, the activity is casually known as the move to 'farmgate'.

The suggestion was and is that farmers need to understand the supply chain better, both upwards and downwards. Reconnection was the central theme of the Curry Report. Red-meat strategy needs to be more balanced – mainstream as well as alternative market.

A broad programme of action might include:

- mapping of significant food chain customers and suppliers within the region as a resource for future work;
- more visits by farmers to customers' and suppliers' premises to promote mutual understanding;

- more information from customers to explain to farmers what the market wants;

- more visits by food chain customers to progressive farmers in the region;

- more marketing awareness programmes by local training groups for farmers and other non-farming decision influencers (agronomists, feed reps etc);

- bringing together farms and rural businesses to promote and market their activities more effectively in the tourism sector (eg local food producers, owners of holiday accommodation, retail outlets etc) and jointly promoting their services;

- more effective and efficient exploitation of new tourism opportunities;

- extending the market for existing tourism activity; and

- improving market awareness and knowledge of farmers and rural businesses.

The accounting and tax treatment of the food chain reconnection will potentially be more complex with possible direct sales. The systems of livestock markets and livestock dealers have the advantage of simplicity and control.

The direction of food chain reconnection is followed through to Chapter 6 with the suggested activity of the 'shopping and food sector'.

One consequence of this has been the development in almost every part of the country of 'farmers' markets'. Most market towns and many larger centres of population will now have such a market on a weekly or monthly basis. Sometimes it will be held in the traditional market place or Town Hall, but it is equally common to find it in a supermarket car park.

Overall, the value of production passing through farmers' markets remains small in terms of national food consumption, and whilst highly visible, they are still mostly niche outlets for small-scale niche producers, and as yet, of little relevance for the larger farm producing agricultural products on an industrial scale. Nonetheless, they make a useful contribution in terms of margins, particularly if the farm is already geared up to retailing.

ACCOUNTING TREATMENT

1.22   There is a constant change in agriculture with regard to subsidies, worldwide food needs and demands and alternative land use and it is essential to review guidance from ICAEW and HMRC together with rural bodies such as the CLA (Country Land and Business Association).

CAPITAL GAINS TAX (CGT) REFORM: CHANGE OF TAX RATE

1.23   Finance Act 2008 reformed CGT for gains made on disposals made by individuals, trustees and personal representatives.

For all disposals made from 6 April 2008 onwards:

- indexation relief was abolished when calculating gains;

- taper relief was abolished when calculating gains;

- all assets owned at 31 March 1982 will be treated as having been sold and reacquired on that date (hence effectively 'rebased');

- a new flat CGT rate of 18% will be applied.

In relation to gains made on or after 23 June 2010, there will be two rates of CGT for individuals – a standard rate of 18% and a higher rate of 28%. The higher rate will apply to individuals whose total taxable income and post 22 June 2010 chargeable gains exceed the basic rate limit for income tax purposes of £37,400 (see F(No 2)A 2010, Sch 1).

Broadly, this means that higher and additional rate taxpayers will pay CGT on gains realised after Budget day at a rate of 28%, whereas for basic rate taxpayers the rate remains at 18%.

All gains realised by individuals before 23 June 2010 are taxed at 18%, regardless of the level of the individual's income (see **2.10** to **2.12**).

Certain technical changes were also introduced, including in relation to disposals of assets acquired by way of gift between 1982 and 1988.

The abolition of indexation relief impacted particularly on individuals who had owned assets for a long time prior to April 1998 (when indexation was frozen and replaced by taper relief) and which had a high base cost. Similarly the abolition of taper relief affected certain entrepreneurs and investors adversely as they saw the effective rate of CGT increase from 10% to a very real 18%. This coincided with the collapse of land development values and the UK recession.

The CGT reform represents an interesting change to the farming community at a time when land prices have soared, diversification projects are working, there is an apparent world shortage of food and resources and no one has a crystal ball. This book tries to look at various alternatives in a dramatically changing world.

COUNTRYSIDE ACCESS

1.24   Farmers have concerns over farm access and potential liabilities (see protection via incorporation – Chapter 8). However a balance has to be reached between risk management and education.

Farming and Countryside Education (FACE) is the joint NFU/Royal Agricultural Society of England's education programme. It is understood that more than 30 industry bodies, agricultural societies and countryside organisations support it. FACE provides a one-stop shop for educationalists, with education co-ordinators working throughout the UK. It helps teachers undertake tailor-made study visits to farms and horticultural units for pupils of all ages. Advice is provided to host farmers on health and safety issues. FACE's website www.face-online.org.uk is the gateway to free curriculum-linked resources on food and farming. Resources are aimed at youngsters from nursery age to further education students. FACE is a stakeholder in the government-led Access to Schools project (www. farmsforschools.org.uk) and the Forward Farming Partnership that sprang from the Policy Commission on Farming and Food.

Soil and how it drives the farming activity

1.25   Soil quality is one of the main criteria for farmers who want to receive environmental payments. Bio-diversity is about farming not just organically but caring for animals and the soil – see Landcare (**1.26**) below.

Soil used for crop production must have a suitable tilth and structure in the surface layer of the seedbed to provide air and water for seed germination. The lower layer of the soil must be free draining and surplus water is usually removed by drains, clay tiles and plastic pipes etc. The tax relief on drainage is dealt with in Chapter 7.

The higher value crops such as potatoes and vegetables are usually irrigated. It is very difficult to obtain licences to irrigate crops, and specialist growers are considering investing in the construction of reservoirs to store winter water for irrigating in the summer. For the tax treatment of reservoirs etc also see Chapter 7.

For optimum crop growth soils should contain the correct balance of the required nutrients. The main nutrients are:

- nitrogen;

- phosphate; and

- potash.

The reason for discussing soil quality is to demonstrate how it drives the choice of farming alternatives and how difficult it is to make changes to adapt to fluctuations in world commodity prices.

Different crops have varying requirements as to soil quality and the required amount of fertiliser to be applied in the seed bed. There are very small reserves of nitrogen in the soil, therefore the crop is provided with the required amount, usually at its active growth state and in two or three applications of artificial fertiliser. Commercially purchased fertiliser is described in terms of its constituent parts eg 20:10:10 signifies 20% nitrogen, 10% phosphate and 10% potassium (always given in that order). Some crops such as peas and beans, being leguminous, manufacture their own nitrogen and therefore do not require any application.

Landcare

1.26   Landcare is about promoting sustainable agriculture and seeking positive changes to soil and water management. Again the commercial cost of compliance must be compared and tailored to the government grant income streams available.

Land management and ecology are now taught at agricultural college, which reflect the changes which lie ahead and which are already taking place. The land management function is incorporated into environmental stewardship.

There are those who argue that livestock represents one of the best forms of land care available when correctly farmed.

SIZE OF HOLDINGS (AND THE NUMBER)

1.27   Each farming business has a 'holding number' enabling a record to be maintained of all agricultural holdings. The size of holdings is measured in 'European Size Units' (ESUs). This is a measure of the financial potential of an agricultural business on standard gross margins. Holdings of under eight ESUs are considered to be part-time holdings.

Over half the holdings in the UK are officially recognised as being unable to financially support a family and are thus considered to be part time. A significant increase in registered units that are under eight ESUs has arisen as a result of the single payment system introduced on 1 January 2005 which has encouraged many smaller and previously unregistered holdings to become registered. This aside, it is a fact that more and more units become less financially viable and the number of full-time farmers decreases year on year with a corresponding increase in part-time farmers.

This clearly has a large impact on the underlying tax planning covered throughout this book.

HMRC RURAL DIVERSIFICATION PROJECT

1.28   HMRC's *Rural Diversification Project* followed on from the previous project on the game shooting industry. It is understood that attention in the rural diversification project will initially focus on the following matters:

- Whether proper regard has been paid to who owns what and whether farm assets are used partly for private purposes or by another entity for its business. One area of interest will be (where no commercial charge is made), whether VAT has been correctly dealt with (whether input tax has been recovered on costs where no output tax has been paid). Overhead costs should not be put through the farm accounts with VAT input tax claimed but not charges raised to, or payment made by, the 'associated' entity.

- Whether the liability of all income, including that from diversification, has been properly considered and declared to HMRC.

- Where diversification grants have been applied for, awarded and paid to a VAT-registered entity and are then used to fund a diversified business whether the grant and new business belongs to the original entity and if not, why not.

- Where business activities are carried on by separate entities whether the VAT disaggregation rules apply. This will particularly focus on holiday enterprises.

- Whether PAYE and benefit-in-kind implications of all payments and non-cash remuneration have been properly considered.

- Close examination of amounts claimed on private or non-business expenses.

The VAT shooting project (see **6.52**) was so successful in terms of 'tax take' for HMRC that it is impossible to ignore the whole area of diversification.

The book will show the potential 'tax take' from HMRC's attempts at denying BPR on non-agriculture values. The advice to both the tax planner and diversified farmer is that there are valuable tax reliefs at stake and waiting to be denied by HMRC – this is a tax minefield and the stakes are high!

Chapter 2

Diversification – alternative land use, grants and impact on the basic tax planning

Julie Butler

- **Tax planning through the choice of business structure**
  The changes brought about by the farming crisis and the need to diversify should encourage the tax planner to review the business structures to ensure that tax reliefs are preserved and tax-planning opportunities are maximised by using the correct business vehicle.

- **Tax planning through obtaining planning permission**
  Various diversification projects, once formally authorised, will not only result in an increased income stream but also possibly add capital value to assets and involve considerable set-up costs. These can present tax-planning opportunities. When the asset is sold or passed to the next generation as a gift, the aim is to ensure it is classified tax efficiently. Favourable capital tax reliefs can then be claimed and the overall tax liability kept to a minimum through maximising the IHT (inheritance tax) and CGT (capital gains tax) reliefs.

- **Maximising government grants and entitlements**
  What grants are available and what are the qualifications? The need for awareness of government direction, grants available, the administration processes and planning permission considerations. Outside help is available and should be enjoyed, particularly in understanding the grants and entitlements.

INTRODUCTION

2.1   This book does not dismiss the benefits of farming, in fact it promotes them. However, the book looks at the tax reality of alternative land use. To quote Mid-Wales Country Land and Business Association (CLA) Regional Director, Julian Salmon:

> 'Farming remains at the core of a vibrant rural economy. It acts as a repository for our national traditions and cultural heritage. It provides us with a sense of identity and a means of delivering the stewardship of our countryside.'

The SFP (see **1.17**) does maintain some form of income support through recognition of appropriate land management.

Farmers have to survive and an objective approach to diversification is the only way forward. In order to be allowed to diversify, planning permission will normally have to be obtained. This matter is dealt with by James Cleary in Chapter 3.

The words to the effect that this scheme is 'now closed' to new applicants appear several times in this chapter.

GRANTS – HISTORICAL TAX POSITION

2.2   The greater detail of the single payment entitlement and its implications are dealt with in detail in Chapter 20.

What about the tax position of other grants? Following provisions of ITTOIA 2005 s 25(1) or for corporation tax purposes CTA 2009, s 46(1) the basic tax principle is that trading receipts are taxed when they are recognised in the accounts (so long as the accounts are drawn up in accordance with generally accepted accounting practice). Thus neither the date of receipt, nor when the receipt is 'earned' can necessarily determine when the receipt is taxable. The accountancy rule is found in SSAP 4 para 24 that a government grant should 'not be recognised in the profit and loss account until the conditions for its receipt have been complied with', ie, until the recipient meets the eligibility conditions attaching to the grant. This was confirmed by the court in the case of *Symonds v Lord Llewelyn-Davies* (1983) 56 TC 630 and in the more recent case of *Johnston v Britannia Airways* (1994) 67 TC 99. Nevertheless, and subject to this, the date at which any amount of grant is accurately quantifiable will normally be a trading receipt for the period of account when the entitlement to the grant is established.

Alternatively, where a subsidy is designed to meet particular costs, it is normally correct for accountancy purposes to match the subsidy with those costs and to reduce them accordingly. If the costs are included in a closing stock valuation the amount of valuation should be net after deducting the relevant grant.

Alternatively, a grant or subsidy may be intended to subsidise (directly) particular sale proceeds. In such circumstances, the correct accountancy treatment is normally to include the grant as income in the period in which the stock is sold, consumed or abandoned.

SINGLE PAYMENT ENTITLEMENTS

2.3   At the time of writing:

- There are now only two different types of entitlements: 'normal' entitlements and 'special' entitlements (the latter generally apply only to very intensive livestock farmers).

- As part of the health check in 2008 set-aside and national reserve entitlements were abolished and replaced with normal entitlements. Authorised entitlements have also now been replaced by normal entitlements.

- Entitlements have been allocated according to the region in England in which the land being claimed is located. There are three regions in England: SDA (severely disadvantaged areas), SDA – moorland, and non-SDA (ie lowland). A farmer may only claim annual payments on land located in the region to which the entitlement relates.

- Entitlements can be transferred by sale, lease, gift or inheritance.

- Entitlements must be claimed at least once every three years or they will be confiscated to the National Reserve. As from 2010 this requirement will change to once every two years.

SET-ASIDE

2.4

- From 1 January 2009 there is no longer a requirement to set-aside land, unless the farmer included set-aside options in an ELS or HLS scheme, in which case sufficient set-aside must be provided to meet the relevant option requirements.

- Set-aside entitlements have been converted to 'normal; formerly set-aside' entitlements, and can be claimed on any land eligible for single payment.

- The payment rate for these entitlements will continue to be at the regional average rate appertaining to the year in question only. (The historic element was allocated to non set-aside entitlements.)

- Set-aside management rules no longer apply and fallow land must be included on claim forms as OT2 or OT1 (if in preparation for a following crop), or as TG1 (if it is grassland).

PROCESSING AND MARKETING GRANT SCHEME (PMG)

2.5   This scheme is closed to new applicants. The grants were for capital investment in processing and marketing agricultural products.

VOCATIONAL TRAINING SCHEME (VTS)

2.6   This scheme is closed to new applicants. The funds were for vocational purposes (ie a person's occupation or work), training those engaged in farming or forestry.

LINKING THE ENVIRONMENT AND FARMING

2.7   Examples of areas of environmental stewardship, which could lead toward conservation grants for farmers are as follows:

- water on the farm;
- managing manures;
- crop protection;

- soils on the farm;

- establishing crops;

- using crop cover;

- using grass, hedges and trees;

- livestock management;

- farm tracks;

- managing ditches; and

- managing bank erosion.

SUMMARY OF MAIN CONSERVATION GRANTS (ENGLAND AND WALES)

2.8   The following grant schemes have been summarised because they can also help to protect soils and water. Some local schemes may also apply, eg in National Parks. They are at the time of writing

Scheme	Summary
Aggregates levy sustainability fund	Aims to minimise demand for primary aggregates, promote environmentally friendly extraction and transport, and reduce local effects of aggregate extraction.
Agriculture development scheme	Grants for industry-led measures in England to improve marketing performance and competition.
CAP reform	Single payment scheme replaces ten major CAP payment scheme. See www.defra.gov.uk/farm/capreform/index.htm
Countryside stewardship scheme	*Scheme now closed and being replaced by* environmental stewardship. Encouraged farmers and land managers to enter into ten-year agreements to manage their land in environmentally beneficial ways.
Energy crops scheme	Grants to establish short-rotation coppice (SRC) or miscanthus; and helps SRC growers set up producer groups.
English woodland grant scheme *	Grants to private landowners to encourage the creation of new woodlands and to assist with the management of existing woodlands. Successor to farm woodland premium scheme and woodland grant scheme. www.forestry.gov.uk/ewgs
Entry-level stewardship	Part of environmental stewardship
Environmental action fund	Grants to voluntary sector groups to further government sustainable development objectives.
Environmentally sensitive areas scheme	*Scheme replaced by* environmental *stewardship;* incentives to agricultural practices to safeguard and enhance parts of the country of particularly high landscape, wildlife or historic value.
Environmental stewardship	Incorporates entry-level stewardship; higher-level stewardship; organic entry-level stewardship

Scheme	Summary
EU structural funds: EAGGF objective 1	Promotes development in certain economically disadvantaged regions
Farm waste grant scheme	*Scheme now closed;* helped farmers in nitrate vulnerable zones (NVZs) install or improve farm waste facilities.
Farm woodland premium scheme	*Scheme now closed;* aimed to enhance the environment through the planting of farm woodlands. See English woodland grant scheme www.forestry.gov.uk/ewgs
Higher-level stewardship	Part of environmental stewardship
Hill farm allowance	Supports beef and sheep producers farming in the English less favoured areas (LFAs).
Land purchase grants	English Nature grants to voluntary nature conservation organisations to acquire and manage important areas of land.
LEADER+	European Community Initiative to help rural communities improve local quality of life and economic prosperity.
Local heritage initiative	Grants for local groups to investigate, explain and care for their local landscape, landmarks, traditions and culture.
Organic entry-level stewardship	Part of environmental stewardship
Organic farming scheme	*Scheme now closed and being replaced by organic entry-level stewardship.* Encouraged expansion of organic production.
Parish plans	Small grants are available to support local consultation to produce parish plans that identify needs and set out how these might be tackled.
Processing and marketing grant	*Scheme now closed to new applicants* – Grants for capital investment in processing and marketing agricultural products.
Rural enterprise scheme	*Scheme now closed to new applicants* – Supports projects aiming to develop more sustainable, diversified and enterprising rural economies and communities.
Sea fisheries grants	Grants to help the fishing industry restructure onto a more sustainable basis.
Sheep and wildlife enhancement scheme	*Scheme now closed as a result of CAP reforms.*
Single payment scheme (CAP)	New single payment replaces ten major CAP payment schemes. See www.defra.gov.uk/farm/capreform/index.htm
Vital villages	*Scheme now closed*; included parish plan grant (see 'parish plans'), community services grant, parish transport grant schemes and rural transport partnership grants.
Vocational training scheme	*Scheme now closed to new applicants* – Funds vocational (ie a person's occupation or work) training for those engaged in farming or forestry
Woodland grant scheme	*Scheme now closed;* aimed to enhance the environment through the creation of new woodlands. See English woodland grant scheme www.forestry.gov.uk/ewgs

THE 'PLANNING PERMISSION' SYSTEM

2.9   The whole issue of obtaining planning permission is dealt with by James Cleary (Chapter 3). Guidance on a range of planning matters is found within the planning policy guidance notes (PPGs).

TAX PLANNING SURROUNDING SUCCESSFUL PLANNING PERMISSION APPLICATIONS

2.10   Chapter 3 makes clear the problems of currently obtaining planning permission. This highlights the value that could be added to land when an application is successful. By definition the application should be for business use, and with the current advantages of entrepreneurs' relief (ER) and roll-over relief. It might be that a subsequent disposal will need to take advantage of entrepreneurs' relief (ER) (see **14.10**).

It is essential therefore to ensure that the asset going into the application is 'clean', ie of correct business status, and does not get caught in the trap of 'tainted' CGT reliefs. It is important to review the business structure of ownership prior to the application and upon commencement of the new project.

There are concerns that the traditional farming unit will be bought by entrepreneurs' experienced in business planning applications etc, who will exploit the opportunity to buy failed genuine agricultural farms and restructure them and make quick tax-efficient profits through the combination of solving farming problems through diversification, the skill of obtaining planning permission and make capital profits as well as income profits (see Chapter 10).

THE SERIAL ENTREPRENEUR (BATR NOW REPLACED BY ENTREPRENEURS' RELIEF)

2.11   BATR has now been replaced by ER under the Finance Act 2008 and 'developed' since that Act.

When business asset taper relief (BATR) was introduced in Finance Act 2000 as CGT relief with a four-year business ownership requirement, it was heralded as the tax relief that encouraged the 'serial entrepreneur'. From 5 April 2002, the business ownership period was reduced to two years. As the capital taxes were so favourable, it has encouraged the opportunist landowner to try and develop projects that will add value to his assets and possibly to dispose of this after the two-year ownership period with a view to obtaining a tax-efficient gain with BATR of 75% and the effective CGT rate being 10% or less. There is still scope to roll over into other projects with the disappearance of BATR.

In a worst-case scenario the lack of profitability in farming has caused traditional farmers who only understand farming and pure agriculture to dispose of all or part of their farms to the profit-seeking entrepreneur. The latter would be able to cope with all the skills needed to organise a diversification project and the relevant planning permission and could take advantage of the favourable tax advantages. The chapter on land disposals (Chapter 14) clearly sets out the tax anti-avoidance provisions. Chapter 10 also deals with the new farmers in farming and direction of the property developer or life-style farmer.

The development of failed farms under the rural development scheme could represent a great opportunity for tax planners to create tax-efficient gains as opposed to harshly taxed business profits. Opportunities still exist under entrepreneurs' relief (ER) rules for tax planning.

Under BATR rules it was essential to ensure that the land and buildings used in all diversified projects qualify for BATR before and after the project, as mentioned previously. One of the major problems of the BATR legislation was 'tainted' taper relief.

It was the disadvantages of tainted taper involved with BATR that have caused many to consider that the combination of ER and the straightforward 18% CGT rate were preferable relief on balance to the complexity of tainted taper relief. With the increase in the rate of CGT to 28% for higher rate taxpayers there has been further re-thinking. Finance (No 2) Act 2010 introduced a new rate of CGT of 28%. For individuals, the rate of CGT remains at 18% where total taxable gains and income are less than the upper limit of the basic rate income tax band (£37,400 for 2010–11). The 28% rate applies to gains (or any parts of gains) that fall above that limit. For trustees and personal representatives of deceased persons, the rate of CGT is increased to 28% (previously 18%).

CAPITAL GAINS TAX (CGT) REFORM: ENTREPRENEURS' RELIEF (ER)

2.12 As mentioned in **1.23**, **2.10** and **2.11**, a new relief from CGT was introduced for disposals occurring after 6 April 2008. Referred to as 'entrepreneurs' relief' (ER) it is intended to reduce the tax payable on business assets which could have previously attracted BATR.

The rules however differ from the taper relief rules, and reintroduce some rules that applied to the old-style retirement relief, which was phased out from 1998 with the introduction of the (relatively short-lived) taper relief.

In order to qualify for the relief the disposal must be of:

- all or part of a trading business carried on by the individual, whether alone or in partnership;

- assets used in the individual's business, whether alone or in partnership;

- shares in the individual's personal trading company; or

- assets owned by the individual and used by his personal trading company.

For the purposes of the relief a personal trading company is a company in which the individual was an officer or employee of the company holding at least 5% of the share capital (which must carry at least 5% of the voting rights), with both conditions having been complied with throughout the 12-month period ending on the date of the disposal. If a trade ceases the disposal must be made within three years of cessation of the trade. The relief can also be claimed by trustees but only if a beneficiary personally qualifies by satisfying the rules including that which requires a minimum 5% personal shareholding.

The relief was restricted to the first £1m of gains arising in an individual's (or aggregated with trustees') gains. It effectively reduces the tax rate to 10% on the first £1m of gains by reducing the chargeable gain by 4/9ths.

The relief was proposed in response to pressure from a number of interested industry groups including farmers and is welcome in as far as it goes. However the limit of £1m is seen as disappointing, particularly at the top end of farming landownership where the value (a maximum tax saving of £80,000) is barely a drop in the ocean.

ER offers nothing in the way of simplification, retaining some elements of the earlier retirement relief. Farmers and landowners should undertake a tax planning review at the earliest opportunity to see how the £1 million 'cap' can be used most effectively.

WHAT BUSINESS STRUCTURE?

2.13   This book does not have the depth fully to review the complete choice of business structure but it does attempt to highlight some clear planning points.

The sole trader is the simplest trading operation for the farmer. Although there is the risk of unlimited liability, there are all the benefits of tax flexibility.

As diversification activities intensify in the farming industry a whole chapter of this book has been given to the subject of the choice of corporate structure (Chapter 8).

So many diversified projects need the protection of a limited company whilst raising finance and using the current low tax rates, Research and Development (R&D) relief and venture capital trusts (VCT).

The partnership is the traditional trading vehicle for the farming family having the advantages of combining resources whilst not risking some of the tax disadvantages of asset ownership and the limited company. One of the risks of partnership is the problem of joint and several liability. The experienced farmland agent, lawyer and tax adviser will be very aware of many other problems of the farming partnership. Many farm partnerships involve the husband and wife, and the protection of assets in a divorce cannot be overlooked (see Chapter 16). Likewise, the need to have the will drafted to match the farming partnership is set out in Chapter 18. The problems surrounding partnerships and gratuitous licences are dealt with in Chapter 11.

The advantages and disadvantages of a limited liability partnership (LLP) are set out at **2.14**. However, before this angle is researched it is important to look at the limited company (see Chapter 8). The latter has become a very attractive trading vehicle for non-farming and non-landowning businesses. Examples of the reasons are:

• low corporation tax rates for retained profits;

• NIC-efficient distribution via dividends; and

• the introduction of a new nil-rate band.

Many of the advantages of incorporation do not apply to the farming and landowning businesses. The problems of agricultural property relief (APR) and business property relief (BPR) for limited companies are set out in Chapter 13. Under the current farming trading position the limited company has other disadvantages:

- trading tax losses are locked in the company and not available to be offset against other income; and

- dividends do not apply if there are no profits.

The position on incorporation and EIS is dealt with in Chapter 8.

LIMITED LIABILITY PARTNERSHIPS (LLPS)

2.14   The Limited Liability Partnerships Act 2000 received Royal Assent on 20 July 2000 and as a result, LLPs became available from 6 April 2001. As the name suggests, members of such a partnership have their liability 'capped' in the event of dissolution, but there is a price to pay: the LLP will have to publish and file corporate-style accounts which will have to follow UK General Accounting Practice and be true and fair. There are different requirements for small and medium-sized LLPs and there is provision for an audit.

The Inland Revenue *Tax Bulletin* No 50 (December 2000) confirms that while an LLP trades it is 'tax transparent' just like a conventional partnership. However, when the trade ceases, the new structure comes into its own when it is no longer regarded as a partnership for tax purposes but is regarded instead as a corporate body.

There will be anti-avoidance legislation targeted at LLPs established for investment purposes, including denial of tax relief for those investing in an LLP.

It is suggested that there may be some uses for an LLP in the context of agriculture. A farmer diversifying might be seeking to let surplus buildings to a small non-agricultural business. He could consider forming an LLP with the other party, instead of granting a tenancy, in order to secure future capital gains tax business asset taper and roll-over relief, together with 50% BPR, without exposing his estate to unlimited liability.

The structure could be of help in the context of a 'retired' partner in a small family business. *Beckman v IRC* [2000] STC (SCD) 59 has demonstrated that the conversion of a partner's capital account to loan account upon retirement results in a loss of BPR, as the 'debt' is not an interest in a partnership (see **5.19**). There are, of course, personal reasons for such a course of action, not least of which is to avoid the burden of 'joint and several' liability. The LLP would allow the farmer to remain a partner (thus benefiting from BPR) whilst not having the farmer's estate exposed over and above the capital left in the partnership.

Broadly, a conventional partnership can be converted to an LLP without any tax implications since the tax regimes are the same. This is intentional, to encourage certain partnerships to convert. There is a restriction of sideways loss relief (ITA 2007 s 64) against other income (see **12.5**), which is limited to the capital that the partner has introduced into the business.

With increased risks of claims against the business eg the Health and Safety at Work etc Act 1974, the LLP becomes very attractive for both farming and diversified activities.

It would be possible to list the comprehensive advantages and disadvantages of all the trading alternatives but this book does not have the scope to go into that amount of detail – there are more important diversification issues to concentrate on.

RESEARCH AND DEVELOPMENT FOR DIVERSIFICATION – TAX CREDITS

2.15   Diversification for many farmers was just a simple move towards supporting farm income with some non-farming income eg cottage lets, redundant farm building lets etc. With the direction of bold diversification projects it is considered that some of the expenses will qualify as 'research & development' and receive the appropriate tax credits.

The Finance Act 2007 allowed more companies to benefit from the research and development (R&D) tax credit.

If a company is liable to corporation tax it is able to claim an enhanced tax credit on its qualifying R&D expenditure. Current rates are 175% for small and medium-sized enterprises and 130% for large companies. For accounting periods ended on or after 9 December 2009, it is no longer necessary for the relevant company incurring the R&D expenditure to own the intellectual property generated by the R&D.

SMALL AND MEDIUM-SIZED COMPANY THRESHOLDS

2.16   Chapter 8 deals with incorporation. SMEs are small and medium-sized enterprises. The Companies Act 2006 defines a company as a small or medium-sized company for its first financial year if it meets two or more of the following requirements in that financial year. Once a company has qualified as a small or medium-sized company, it will continue to be a small or medium-sized company unless it fails to meet two or more of the requirements for two years in a row. Where a large company reduces in size to become a small or medium-sized company it must meet two or more of the requirements for two successive years.

At the time of writing the levels are as follows:

Criteria		Small CA 2006 ss 382–383	Medium CA 2006 ss 465–466
Turnover	Net	£6.5m	£25.9m
	Gross	£7.8m	£31.1m
Balance Sheet Total	Net	£3.26m	£12.9m
	Gross	£3.9m	£15.5m
Employee		50	250

ORGANIC ENTRY-LEVEL STEWARDSHIP (OELS)

2.17 The organic farming scheme, which formed part of the England rural development programme is now closed to new applications. Its purpose was to encourage the expansion of organic production in England in order to help supply the increasing demand for organically produced food.

The hill farming allowances have been replaced by upland ELS and are made in addition to the single payment entitlement.

THE ENVIRONMENTALLY SENSITIVE AREA SCHEME (ESAS)

2.18 The scheme is now closed to new applicants. A new 'environmental stewardship scheme' was launched on 3 March 2005.

FARM WASTE GRANT SCHEME (FWGS)

2.19 This scheme is now closed to new applicants.

The farm waste grant (nitrate vulnerable zones) scheme provided help to farmers in nitrate vulnerable zones (NVZs) installing or improving farm waste facilities. Grants were available, at a rate of 40%, on eligible expenditure up to an investment ceiling of £85,000 for each agricultural business. It is made available to eligible farmers who need to construct or upgrade their manure handling and storage facilities to comply with the NVZ action programme measures.

NITRATE VULNERABLE ZONES (NVZ)

2.20 Following the Nitrate Pollution Prevention Regulations 2008:

- The new nitrate vulnerable zone (NVZ) rules came into effect on 1 January 2009 and will have an impact on most farmers in England, with intensive livestock farmers being affected most. The regulations, which will be enforced by the Environment Agency (EA), now cover 58% of farmland in England. A brief summary is given below, for more details visit www.defra.gov.uk.

- The total amount of nitrogen (N) from livestock manure applied on a holding in any calendar year must not exceed 170kg/ha averaged across the whole farm area (but it is possible to obtain a derogation from the EA to increase this to 250kg/ha in some cases).

- The total amount of N from livestock manure applied to individual fields in any calendar year must not exceed 250kg/ha.

- Anyone intending to spread N fertiliser must prepare a spreading plan for the season. The plan must be produced before the first application each year and must include field numbers, area and type of crop, soil type, previous crop, SNS, anticipated yield, optimum amount of N that should be spread.

- Before spreading any organic manure you must record the area on which manure will be spread, quantity to be spread, date of spreading, N content of manure.

- N max must be complied with. This limits the amount of N that can be applied to a particular crop based on yield potential and other factors. Details of N max can be found at defra.gov.uk.

- By 1 January 2010 a risk map must be produced for all holdings that spread organic manures. These maps must be updated within three months of any change.

- From 1 January 2012 livestock farmers must have sufficient storage capacity to store all slurry and poultry manure produced on the holding between 1 October and 1 March (1 October and 1 April for pigs and poultry). Storage facilities are not required for slurry sent off the holding for example to an anaerobic digester and slurry that can be spread on 'low run off risk' land during the storage period (provided that this is done in accordance with the restrictions on spreading-closed periods). Slurry stores must have in addition to the slurry, the capacity to store all rainwater, washings or any other liquid that enters the store.

LAND NOT IN AGRICULTURAL PRODUCTION
2.21

- Farmland which is not cropped will be classified as 'land not wholly in agricultural production'. Such land will be subject in particular to the cross compliance GAEC 12 rules – as well as other relevant cross compliance rules.

- It is possible to claim on land which is not used all year for agricultural purposes providing the use is one of those listed below and the frequency is restricted to 28 days or less in each calendar year. Such permissible activities are clay shooting, car boot sales, car parking, country fairs, farm sales, equestrian activities, ballooning, festivals, scout and guide camps, TV locations, caravan sites, motor sports and grass airstrips. If the land is used for one of these activities for more than 28 days during the year it cannot be claimed against.

ENERGY CROPS SCHEME
2.22

- Protein crops (peas, beans and lupins) are eligible for a premium of €55.57/ha, subject to an EU maximum guaranteed area of 1.6 million hectares. The protein crop premium is to be withdrawn, probably from 2012.

- Energy crops are eligible for a premium of €45/ha, subject to an EU maximum guaranteed area of two million hectares. It is payable on crops used for transport fuel, heating and electricity generation. The energy crop premium will be withdrawn in 2010 (2009 is the last year of claim for this).

Contacts:

- Organic and Energy Crops National Implementation Team (Organic-energy@defra.gsi.gov.uk);

- Producer groups and bio-energy infrastructure scheme (agri-industrial material branch, London. industrialcrops@defra.gsi.gov.uk);

AGRI-ENVIRONMENTAL STEWARDSHIP SCHEME

2.23

- Agri-environment schemes are administered by Natural England, which was formed on 1 October 2006 to replace the Rural Development Service, the Countryside Agency and English Nature.

- Land in a countryside stewardship scheme (CSS), environmentally sensitive areas scheme (ESA), entry-level scheme (ELS), organic entry-level scheme (OELS), or higher level scheme (HLS) is eligible for single payment in addition to the annual management payments. Likewise hill farming allowances (or their successor uplands ELS) are made in addition to single payment.

- Existing CSS or ESA agreements will continue for their committed term unless agreement is reached with Natural England to surrender the agreement with land rolling over into a new HLS agreement that offers significantly more environmental benefit than the previous agreement.

- The ELS and OELS pay £30/ha and £60/ha respectively each year for five years. For OELS an additional conversion payment of £175/ha will be paid each year for the two-year conversion as long as such land remains in organic production for at least five years from the date of commencement of the agreement. ELS/OELS payments are claimable on the whole farm area, ie including woodland, subject to the farmer entering into options to achieve a value of not less than 30 points/ha for ELS and 60 points/ha for OELS.

- The HLS is a discretionary scheme, which provides additional payments to farmers for implementing targeted annual management and capital works. It is not possible to combine HLS with CSS or ESA agreements, as HLS requires the entire holding first to be entered into ELS or OELS.

ENGLISH WOODLAND GRANT SCHEME

2.24   The aims of the EWGS are to:

- sustain and increase the public benefits given by existing woodlands; and

- help create new woodlands to deliver additional public benefit.

Woodland category	Grant type	What the grant is for
Stewardship of existing woodlands	Woodland planning grant (WPG)	Preparation of plans that both assist with management of the woodland and meet the UK woodland assurance standard.
	Woodland assessment grant (WAG)	Gathering of information to improve management decisions.
	Woodland regeneration grant (WRG)	Supporting desirable change in woodland composition through natural regeneration and restocking after felling.
	Woodland improvement grant (WIG)	Work in woodlands to create, enhance and sustain public benefits.
	Woodland management grant (WMG)	Contribution to additional costs of providing and sustaining higher quality public benefits from existing woodlands.
Creation of new woodlands	Woodland creation grant (WCG)	Encouraging the creation of new woodlands where they deliver the greatest public benefits, including annual farm woodland payments to compensate for agricultural income forgone.

SUBSIDIES – GOOD ACCOUNTING AND RECORDING

2.25   Historically there have been various provisions (eg the Wildlife and Countryside Act 1981) under which farmers may receive payments for managing their land in a particular way. Where the payments under such agreements are made annually, there is no doubt that the sums are income. The tax treatment is set out in part at **2.2**.

The tax treatment of the SFP was established in the June 2005 (special edition) *Tax Bulletin* from HMRC and the concept of the 'fiscal farmer' was created (see **1.12**).

Sometimes, however, farmers receive a lump sum for managing their land in a particular way for a period of years. In this situation it can be argued that the payment is capital because it represents compensation for some sort of sterilisation of the land (ie not able to farm the land).

Under these agreements the farmer is not prevented from using the land for the trade of farming. The management undertaken by the farmer comprises acts of husbandry and, whilst his scope may be restricted by the agreement, there is no doubt that he remains the occupier of the land for the purposes of husbandry and therefore a farmer as defined by ITTOIA 2005 s 876 (this section now repealed). HMRC will therefore argue that this is income and not of a capital nature.

The concept of partial sterilisation was rejected by Browne-Wilkinson J in *White v G & M Davies (a firm)* (1979) 52 TC 597 and the argument that HMRC will use, is by reference to his judgment (see **1.19**).

Farmers may also receive contributions towards specific capital expenditure under such agreements. Such sums are capital receipts deductible from the capital expenditure for capital allowances/ABAs (before they were withdrawn).

The tax planner should work with the client on looking at what grants have been claimed, checking the timing, the accounting and the tax treatment to include the marginal areas of capital versus income.

Ideally, a schedule of all grants and compensations should be kept on the permanent section of the client's file, reviewed and checked. Although it is the client's responsibility to ensure maximum advantage is made of claims, it is more the responsibility of the land agent to help with this and if there is clearly some omission year on year or client on client then this should be highlighted. This permanent record should obviously be regularly updated and would be a very useful document for the accounts department when looking at the correct timing and cut-off treatment for all such compensations. This will obviously include a copy of the SFP application in May each year.

CONCLUSION

2.26   The opportunity for commercial diversification has never been greater. The tax reliefs for businesses, especially farms, are very favourable. Will the suggestions that the definition of agriculture to include diversification is broadened be taken on board?

At the time of writing, against a background of world food shortages, the profitability of pure farming has improved as has the whole farming outlook. The combination of diversification and pure farming is producing a healthy outlook, although many would argue against this.

When the 2nd Edition was written farmers were previously selling a tonne of wheat for £60 to £70, they are now selling the same amount for £150 to £170 which shows a massive leap but costs have also increased, although there have then been drops in price.

Chapter 6 looks at the bold move towards diversification and specific diversification activities.

Chapter 3

Obtaining planning permission

James Cleary MA, DipUD, MRTPI
(Managing Director, Pro Vision Planning and Design)

- **The need for planning permission**
  Review of situations where planning permission may not be required. Feasibility considerations and categories of diversification which normally require planning permission.

- **How to obtain planning permission**
  Review of the current planning system, the application process and considerations for change of use of land or buildings and erection of new structures.

- **Optimising planning consent**
  The planning and development appraisal together with processes of consultation, negotiation and lobbying. The importance of design is considered together with relevant highway or transport issues and the negotiation of planning obligations.

NOTE FROM THE EDITOR

3.1   The British planning system emerged in a consolidated form shortly after World War II. It has been changed a number of times over recent years, most significantly by the Planning and Compulsory Purchase Act which received Royal Assent in May 2004 and again following the publication of Planning for a Sustainable Future: White Paper published by the government in May 2007. The system is now complex and often difficult to understand with national, regional and local policies that can be of vital importance to the owners and developers of land and property.

Attend a planning committee in any part of the country and you will usually see ranks of specialist planners waiting to address the meeting or to hear the debate on a particular proposal. Planning is no longer a subject for amateurs to handle. It is a profession with a range of specialisms.

In this chapter, James Cleary explains how the application process works in relation to the principal forms of diversification. Policy guidelines are summarised and ways in which planning consents can be optimised are discussed.

FEASIBILITY AND THE NEED FOR PLANNING PERMISSION

3.2   Generally speaking, diversification of the use of property is 'development', which is defined as engineering operations, building works or change of use of land or buildings. Development rights within the British Isles were effectively nationalised over 60 years ago and hence planning permission must be acquired before you can proceed with most forms of new development.

The main thrust of this book is the financial and tax-related implications of diversification – its viability or profitability. However, these are matters that should normally only be considered if the project is likely to be feasible or permissible. There is little point in assessing the detailed legal, managerial or financial aspects of a scheme that may never go ahead due to planning obstacles. Unfortunately, there are many examples of well-intentioned and viable projects on which legal and accountancy fees have been incurred that have not been realised because of planning-related problems.

Financial viability is, nonetheless, a matter that should be considered, but within a wider feasibility assessment. The overall feasibility assessment may include a range of non-financial matters and a planning appraisal is essential at an early stage. Some careful consideration of the full range of effects on land use is advisable at the start of any diversification project. The trade name for this task is the 'planning and development appraisal'.

Many diversification projects give rise to factors of which farmers may not at first be fully aware. For example, there can be a considerable management burden of taking on a planning battle or responsibility for a new enterprise. Time and resources may be diverted away from necessary and continuing farming work. Also, the new enterprise may adversely impact on the amenities previously enjoyed by the landowner, farmer or his neighbours. Relations can become soured.

Grants for certain forms of diversification have for many years been available through Regional Development Agencies. These have significantly reduced over recent years. The regional tier of government is now being dismantled by the current coalition government and hence this source of funding is likely to stop altogether.

Within this chapter we seek to outline the planning factors relevant to diversification projects. There is a need to understand what does and does not require planning permission and to appreciate current national planning priorities. These topics are worthy of a book each and hence the coverage here is necessarily brief. The chapter concludes with specific reference to the planning process and techniques for optimising planning consents.

Where planning permission may not be required

3.3   There are some diversification projects for which planning permission may not be needed. If you think you do not need planning permission for an enterprise either in its initial form or in terms of what it is likely to become it is still best to check; better safe than sorry. Be warned, the position is not always clear and is sometimes open to interpretation. Agricultural permitted development rights are frequently changed. Advice from a planning consultant with expertise in these matters may be worth acquiring.

Categories of diversification projects that may not require planning permission include the following.

- Use of farmland or buildings either directly for agricultural purposes or for certain purposes ancillary to agriculture – this includes horticulture and most forms of 'pick your own', shooting, fishing, turf stripping (on a limited scale), agricultural storage, farm shops (selling home-grown produce), food packing and some forms of dairy product processing.

- Activities that constitute development but do not need planning permission by virtue of permitted development rights, such as:

  - temporary buildings and uses – including most moveable structures for animals such as pigs and hens and the use of land for any purpose such as war games, clay pigeon shooting and gymkhanas for not more than 28 days in any calendar year (or 14 days in the case of markets or motorcar and motorcycle racing);

  - caravan sites – for up to three caravans on a site without a licence for up to 28 days each year (on holdings of not less than five acres in size);

  - agricultural or forestry buildings and operations – including the erection of agricultural buildings up to 465 square metres in size, reasonable extensions to existing buildings, replacement plant or machinery, hard surfacing and mineral working for agricultural purposes. In order to benefit from the permitted development right to erect new agricultural buildings the holding must be at least five hectares in size and the building must be reasonably necessary for the purpose of agriculture within that unit. If these conditions are met it is also possible that more than one building (or polytunnel) could be erected at any one time; and

  - forms of renewable energy – such as micro turbines, solar panels and photovoltaic installations associated with dwellings. These are recent changes in response to climate change. Further changes and extensions to permitted development rights are likely in the future following changes in wider government policy.

- Activities that are exempt from enforcement action by virtue of the ten-year rule (established uses) – that is the use of buildings that can be shown to have been continually used for a period of ten years or more for some purpose other than agriculture. The established use may continue without the need for planning permission whether it is for the existing business or another business.

The reader requiring a robust assessment of the need or otherwise for planning permission should refer to the Town and Country Planning Act 1990, the General Permitted Development Order 1995 (SI 1995/418) and the Town and Country Planning (General Development Procedure) Order 1995 (SI 1995/419). Part 6 of the General Permitted Development Order covers agricultural buildings and operations. A summary, albeit detailed, of permitted development rights for agricultural and forestry is set out as Annex E to PPG7. (Note: PPG7 has now been superseded by PPS7 and in part by PPS4 as outlined below, but Annex E to PPG7 remains in force pending the completion by the government of its review of the General Permitted Development Order 1995. This review has been ongoing for several years)..

Legislation is complex; therefore, advice from a qualified, experienced and recommended planning consultant may be the best route to an accurate assessment. Be warned, you may not require planning consent but you may still need Building Regulations approval or consent from the Local Planning Authority as part of the prior notification procedure or Certificate of Lawfulness procedures. Also, depending on the circumstances, it may be necessary to acquire Listed Building Consent, a protected Species Licence or watercourse/drainage related consent from the Environment Agency even though planning permission may not be needed.

CATEGORIES OF DIVERSIFICATION THAT NORMALLY REQUIRE PLANNING PERMISSION

3.4   Diversification is by definition a diversion. In the economic turmoil in which farmers operate it may be the means through which the embattled farmer can survive financially or develop activities that complement his core business. Diversification activities may also enable the farmer to retain ownership or control over property assets.

The degree of agricultural diversification or extent of diversion may vary considerably. It may be a small-scale diversification proposal or a progression from an existing operation, such as the farm shop on the roadside or the cheese-making facility on the dairy farm. Alternatively, it may involve a complete change in direction or a transformation of the farm. It may involve the re-use of cattle buildings for commercial purposes or the change of use of land to a golf course. With these types of development the buildings or land are most unlikely to be available for re-use for agriculture in the foreseeable future. In other words, there is no going back.

Reference to a range of diversification projects is made in Chapter 1 of this book. Within this section we refer briefly to the main categories of diversification projects that require planning permission. One does not need to look far for live examples of each. The full range of options is worth considering before any existing farming operations are discontinued or buildings demolished.

Change of use of land

3.5   Planning permission may be needed whether the change of use of land is permanent or temporary. In some cases, temporary or short-term changes of use may be 'permitted development', but in the cases referred to below, planning permission will normally be needed:

- golf courses and driving ranges – more in vogue 15–20 years ago following the reports from the Royal and Ancient Society and others on demand outstripping supply. Still deemed to be a worthwhile alternative to farming on accessible sites close to centres of population;

- formal outdoor recreation/sports pitches – land may be leased to local sports clubs or district or parish councils for purposes such as football, cricket, rugby, hockey or bowls;

- equestrian use – can include a wide range of grazing, training, trekking and other uses associated with liveries, riding centres, training schools and stud farms;

- fishing lakes – either for commercial fishery purposes or for recreational fishing. If the venue is not for commercial fishing or day visitors alone it is likely that accommodation in the form of lodges or similar will be needed;

- outdoor educational or environmental facilities, interpretation centres or tourist facilities – for local schools or colleges or in areas with large numbers of visitors or holiday makers;

- animal/wildlife centres – for rare breeds or birds of prey, for kennels or catteries, or for animal sanctuaries, animals for scientific testing etc;

- activity centres or recreational events – to meet the continuing demand for corporate hospitality/team building days and venues for children's parties (war games, paintballing, aerial runways, quad biking, clay pigeon shooting, archery, barbeques etc). Events that need planning permission can also include car boot sales, open air markets, motorcycle or motor car racing and riding events except where these uses are temporary and fall within the 'permitted development' tolerances referred to earlier.

New structures or change of use of buildings

3.6   New buildings or structures may sometimes be needed to enable a diversification proposal to proceed. More often than not, these will be small scale or ancillary to other existing buildings or land uses. They normally require planning permission and can include:

- golf club buildings and covered driving ranges;

- ticket kiosks and changing rooms or a café/restaurant ancillary to formal recreational facilities;

- stables, hay stores or tack rooms;

- fishing or shooting lodges;

- interpretation centres or lecture facilities;

- animal cages, kennels, aviaries etc;

- toilet blocks or shower rooms on camping or caravan sites;

- telecommunication masts or aerials; and

- freestanding wind turbines or solar panels.

Permitted development rights still exist for polytunnels but the position had to be clarified following a High Court judgment (*R (on the application of Hall Hunter Partnership) v First Secretary of State and Others* [2006] EWHC 3482 (Admin)) in 2006. Polytunnel complexes exceeding 465 sq m in size (unless they are at least 90m from another building) do require consent.

Diversification proposals involving the change of use of existing or redundant agricultural buildings can include some of the above and:

- visitor accommodation – either general tourist/holiday accommodation or overnight accommodation, for special events or for anglers, shooting parties, golfers, etc;

- arenas or grooms' accommodation/tack stores for equestrian development;

- storage or distribution purposes – ranging from boxed archive stores, facilities for local market traders, craftsmen or other tradesmen to bulk goods storage or winter storage of marquees, caravans, boats and vintage cars;

- workshops or industrial uses – including agricultural engineering, motor repairs, general engineering, craft workshops or other forms of light engineering either with or without related stores and offices; and

- offices or research facilities – ranging in specification from the 'rough and ready' to highly prestigious and suitable for a wide range of small to medium-sized local businesses or large corporate concerns if the accommodation has a good profile, is strategically located, accessible and well fitted out.

CURRENT PLANNING POLICIES

3.7   In November 2000, the government of the day published the Rural White Paper Our Countryside: The Future – A Fair Deal for Rural England. This included statements of support for diversification opportunities including re-use of redundant farm buildings, support for rural businesses and opportunities for new recreational facilities. The general response from the farming community was not positive, because it appeared to say little that had not already been said before. The White Paper placed increased emphasis on the need for control systems to restrict development pressures in the countryside, to prioritise landscape protection, promote tranquillity and steer development toward brownfield sites and urban areas. These have been enduring themes, although there have been continuing revisions to National Policy and guidance which guide and influence Local Authority decision making.

National guidance

3.8   Planning policies and legislation are complex and wide ranging in their effect. There were until recently 25 subject-related Planning Policy Guidance notes (PPGs). Less than half remain and the current coalition government has indicated an intent to create a simplified system. Most PPGs have been replaced by the newer Planning Policy Statements (PPSs). PPGs and PPSs contain guidance that can impact on diversification proposals. (See www.communities.gov.uk for details of all the current planning policies of the government, including copies of all the PPGs and PPSs.)

The relevant guidance or statutory instrument depends on the nature of the proposal, the location of the site and factors such as environmental designations, landscape protection policies, the presence of protected species, listed buildings, ancient monuments or other matters of recognised importance. It should also be noted that the system in England is different to the system in

Scotland. In the past the English and Welsh systems were virtually the same, but with the implementation of the Planning and Compulsory Purchase Act 2004, differences increased.

Following recognition by the government that the system had become inflexible, legalistic and bureaucratic a review was implemented to achieve 'a better, simpler, faster, more accessible system that serves both businesses and the community' (Planning Green Paper: Delivering a Fundamental Change (December 2001)). Priorities for reform included national planning guidance for the countryside, industrial and commercial development including premises for small firms, and also the development plan system that impacts directly upon most types of diversification project.

Changes in the planning system were introduced gradually as the measures set out in the Planning and Compulsory Purchase Act were implemented. The Act received Royal Assent in May 2004. The purpose of this Act was to introduce what the government at the time believed to be a simpler, more flexible and standardised system with increased scope for community involvement. More recently, the Kate Barker (2006) and Killian Pretty (2008) Reviews recommended a streamlined system that is more user friendly.

Following publication of these reports and widespread complaints about the complexity and negativity of the system, the government decided to commit to publish and present to Parliament a simpler and consolidated framework for guidance covering all forms of development. The new framework will set out aspects of the 'localism' agenda with national economic, environmental and social priorities. Specific coalition priorities include the maintenance of Green Belt and environmental protection policy, improved flood defences and prevention of unnecessary building in areas of high flood risk and the consolidation of guidance relating to Tree Preservation Orders and Environmental Impact Assessments.

Most current policy priorities relevant to diversification and the main areas of planning guidance have so far lasted through the ongoing reform period. Probably the overriding priority at the present time is the use of policy to secure forms of development that are 'sustainable'. It is recognised that the environment should be managed in a way that protects it for future generations. This usually means support for proposals that are energy efficient or re-use existing, redundant or under-used property. It also means controls to achieve a reduction in, or limits on, the number and length of private vehicle trips. Re-use proposals may sometimes conflict with traffic minimisation priorities and this is where the planning system seeks to impose various forms of checks and balances.

National planning guidance for Housing (PPS3: November, 2006) sets out guidance on the allocation of land for housing development and includes a definition of brownfield sites or 'previously developed land'. It expressly excludes land that is or has been occupied by agricultural or forestry buildings and was changed in 2010 to exclude residential gardens (as a political response to so called 'garden grabbing' by developers).

Throughout the country there are significant housing requirements because of demographic changes, migration, immigration, house price inflation and the failure of supply to match demand over a long period of time. In the Housing Green Paper (Homes for the Future: more affordable, more sustainable; July 2007) building new housing to meet demand was recognised as a key priority. It went on to set out some of the key challenges that the young and those in rural communities face as they try to get on the housing ladder. In parallel, it stressed the need for better designed and greener homes. The current coalition government is likely to continue to progress this agenda albeit with overall housing targets set locally, not nationally or regionally.

Planning Policy Statement 4: Planning for Sustainable Economic Growth was published in December 2009 and supersedes previous guidance in PPG4 (Industrial, commercial development and small firms) and the economic development sections of PPS7 (Sustainable development in rural areas). However sustainable development priorities remain as the cornerstone of rural planning policy with parallel requirements to address matters of social inclusion, economic development, local distinctiveness, landscape protection, rural enterprise, environmental protection and biodiversity. The basic approach put forward is one that requires good quality, carefully sited and accessible development that is preferably within or close to existing towns and villages. Decisions on developments in more remote areas will depend in part on opportunities to access them by public transport, walking and cycling.

New building development in open countryside away from existing settlements or outside areas allocated in development plans for development are more strictly controlled. The overall aim is to protect countryside for the sake of its intrinsic character and beauty. Priority is, however, to be given to the re-use of previously developed ('brownfield') sites and to the re-use of appropriately located and suitably constructed existing buildings in the countryside. Diversification proposals should, however, seek to maintain the character and qualities of the countryside and any new building should, according to the guidance, be of good quality.

Local planning authorities are told that they should: 'support diversification for business purposes that are consistent in their scale and environmental impact with their rural location' (PPS4 Policy EC6.2f). They are also directed to: '… support rural tourism and leisure developments that benefit rural businesses, communities and visitors and which utilise and enrich, rather than harm, the character of the countryside its towns, villages, buildings and other features' (PPS4 Policy E7.1). Support is specifically given for tourist accommodation, holiday and caravan sites and chalet developments where their scale, appearance and impact on the landscape is appropriate.

National planning guidance also indicates that planning authorities should generally discriminate in favour of re-use proposals for business, rather than for residential purposes. Local Authorities are advised to '…. support small-scale economic development where it provides the most sustainable option in villages, or other locations, that are remote from local service centres, recognising that a site may be an acceptable location for development even though it may not be readily accessible by public transport' (PPS4 Policy EC12.1b).

Guidance for transport generally aims to promote more sustainable transport choices for people and freight, as well as promoting accessibility to jobs and services and opportunities for travel by modes other than the private car (PPG13: March 2001). The good news is that national planning guidance on transport recognises the need for adequate employment opportunities in rural areas and also the increasing trend in diversification of agricultural businesses. Conversion and re-use proposals are referred to specifically. Local authorities are advised not to reject proposals in rural areas where small-scale business development or expansion is likely to give rise to 'modest, additional daily vehicle movements' and where the impact on minor roads would not be significant.

A wide range of other national planning policies may also impact upon diversification proposals. These include policies relating to Biodiversity and Geological Conservation, Climate Change, Green Belts, Environmentally Sensitive Areas, Conservation Areas, Flood Risk, Sites of Special Scientific Interest and National Parks. There is also a raft of guidance specific to proposals affecting coastal areas and listed buildings and proposals for sports and recreation.

The identification of relevant policies is a key part of the normal planning appraisal exercise familiar to most experienced planning consultants.

THE APPLICATION PROCESS

3.9   The process by which planning applications and listed building consent applications are determined is known as the 'development control process'. District councils are generally responsible for the preparation of Development Plan documents and for deciding planning applications. The system is plan-led and hence applications must be considered against Local Plan policy, which in turn should accord with national policy. We are currently in a transitional stage with Local Plans being superseded by Local Development Documents (LDDs) in accordance with the provisions of the Planning and Compulsory Purchase Act (May 2004).

When LDDs are being prepared everyone has the right to object or support local policy initiatives or designations. The right normally extends to a right to submit evidence to or be heard in front of an Inspector when issues are considered at an Examination in Public.

The coalition government intends to alter the system again in line with the 'localism' agenda. Power is to be decentralised and it is proposed that parish councils or neighbourhood groups should have the ability to prepare neighbourhood plans and make decisions locally. However, changes have yet to be fully implemented and at the time of writing the local planning authority or district council is the main plan making body and has principal responsibility for development control matters.

Planning applications submitted to district councils can be decided either by elected councillors (the Planning Committee), or under delegated powers by trained planning officers. The planning officers are accountable to the elected councillors.

Pre-application discussions with a planning adviser and subsequently an officer of the relevant planning authority are important. They are often useful, particularly with proposals that are complex or are likely to give rise to objections. In some cases the pre-application discussions can continue over a longer period of time than the time it takes for the application to be processed. Officer time for pre-application discussions is generally free although Local Authorities do now have the legal right to make a charge. An increasing number of authorities are now taking up this right.

After an application has been submitted (using the national standard 1APP forms and certificates) it is usually checked and registered by administrative staff within the local planning authority. Validation checklists include national requirements (necessary for all planning applications) and local requirements (specific to the district). Applications are often returned if they include insufficient information such as inadequate plans, inadequate details of the proposal or insufficient ownership information or the application fee that has been paid is insufficient.

Once registered, the application is allocated to a planning officer, the applicant is informed and the formal consultation process begins. Consultees can include statutory parties (the Highway Authority, the Environment Agency, Natural England, English Heritage, etc), parish councils, residents' groups, neighbours and other organisations such as the local civic society and the Ramblers' Association.

After a period of several weeks, although in some cases much longer, the planning officer reviews consultation responses, relevant policies and other case specific or site-specific factors and comes to a view on the proposals. With all applications, officers normally make a recommendation for either refusal, approval or deferral. Straightforward proposals are usually determined by senior officers under delegated powers and are only taken to a planning committee if the council's standing orders allow elected members to request that this should happen. Proposals to be considered by elected members are usually subject of a written report on the planning committee agenda and often there will be a site visit by councillors before the application is determined.

In the past, it was normal for there to be discussions between the planning officer and the applicant or his agent if there was a need for amendments to the proposals to make them acceptable. This often delayed the application processing period and the period of time between submission and determination could often extend to several months. Planning authorities now have performance standards and with the advent of 'best value' criteria most officers seek to minimise application stage discussions. Applications can be refused, even though difficulties could have been resolved by negotiation. In this way, pressure is placed on the applicant to engage with officers pre-application and to ensure at the outset that the proposal is carefully conceived and takes account of relevant policies.

Applications that are approved are always subject to conditions. These range from straightforward requirements for agreement on the use of certain building materials or planting species to complex requirements that impose pre-commencement obligations on the applicant. If these conditions are not correctly complied with, the development can be deemed not to have been lawfully commenced. Local Authorities may also impose restrictions on the construction process, or limitations on either hours of use or the scope for further changes under normal permitted development rights.

If an application is refused or subject to a condition that is not acceptable to the applicant, then there is a right of appeal. Clear reasons both for the approval or refusal of an application or reasons for the imposition of conditions should always be stated on the decision notice. The likelihood of success of an appeal depends on the ability of the appellant to argue that the reasons are without justification. The right to appeal only exists for a period of six months following the date of decision.

The appeal process is quasi judicial. It is regularly used for all types of development proposal. Whilst it can be expensive and time consuming it is often the only means of achieving consent and can be cost effective in terms of the overall value of the development proposal. If the actions of the planning authority can be shown to have been unreasonable, a claim for the recovery of costs incurred during the appeal stage can be made. Likewise, if the actions of the appellant are shown to have been unreasonable, a claim for an award of costs may be made by the planning authority.

As an alternative to the appeal process, the applicant may resubmit and seek to overcome reasons for refusal or unacceptable conditions. The nature or form of the proposals may need to be varied. Officers representing the planning authority will often seek to persuade applicants to take this route. Sometimes it may be appropriate. Usually the applicant will be entitled to make the resubmission without having to pay the planning application fee again and it may sometimes be appropriate to pursue an appeal in parallel.

Planning policies, the planning system and reasons why the system operates in the way that it does are becoming ever more complex and difficult for the layman to understand. Clear and appropriate planning strategies should be developed at an early stage. Planning consultancy is a burgeoning profession and good consultants exist in most districts. Chartered town planners have taken over from general practice lawyers and surveyors who used to advise on planning matters before the complexity of law and requirement for sophisticated strategies gave rise to the need for a specialist approach. They are usually known to land agents, solicitors, accountants and bank managers who may all be able to recommend good planning consultants.

WAYS OF OPTIMISING PLANNING CONSENTS

3.10   As outlined at the start of this chapter, there is a need to ensure that diversification proposals are viable and capable of achieving planning consent. At an early stage in any project there is a need to undertake a feasibility study or planning and development appraisal. There may be a need to re-assess costs and values throughout the application stage, as development schemes often change or can be subject to unexpected planning conditions or necessary legal agreements.

The value of a development proposal can often fall during the application stage if the planning authority rules out some element as unacceptable, be it a driving range on a golf course, a café with tourist facilities or an office element of a commercial re-use proposal. Similarly, values may fall if conditions imposed by the planning authority restrict opening hours or the nature of proposed activities.

On other occasions the cost of development can increase significantly as a result of the imposition of planning obligations relating to contributions or planning conditions requiring driveway diversions, extensive landscaping or the use of only local materials and building techniques. The objective should therefore be to achieve the optimum planning consent. That is a consent which accords with relevant policy without incurring excessive delays during periods over which borrowing may be needed, excessive building or other indirect costs or unnecessary operational or other restrictions.

The planning and development appraisal

3.11   A full planning and development appraisal for a diversification proposal would normally contain:

- information on the site or buildings that demonstrates an understanding of key locational factors and the aspirations of the landowner or developer;

- a summary of relevant planning history (or the outcome of earlier planning applications) for the site and its surrounds;

- a summary of relevant national and development plan policies insofar as they are likely to impact upon the development opportunities under consideration;

- a review of key issues and in some cases a discussion of key constraints and principal opportunities;

- some consideration of necessary or appropriate pre-application consultations with neighbours, interest groups or others;

- some consideration of development costs and values and the possible incorporation of sustainable technologies especially where eligible for generous feed-in tariffs; and

- clear recommendations on the course of action that should be followed.

A first appraisal of this type may be prepared by a planning consultant, an architect, a specialist surveyor or another property professional. It is more likely that the appraisal will be value for money if it is prepared by someone who regularly deals with agricultural diversification proposals, who understands national and local planning policy and who can easily access key sources of relevant information.

Necessary surveys

3.12   The planning and development appraisal should help to clarify requirements for survey information. Rarely can a good plan or proposal be devised without thorough analysis of a range of survey information.

Survey information required will depend on the nature of the site and the intended development proposal. However the requirement will usually include a measured site or building survey, photographs, a habitat survey and an initial assessment of drainage matters (possibly including a flood risk assessment). In some instances it may be necessary to acquire more detailed structural, landscape, tree or acoustics surveys, heritage assessment, traffic counts, ground conditions assessments or detailed protected species or other ecological surveys.

The experienced planning consultant should be able to advise on survey requirements and specialists and help advise applicants on which matters need consideration from the outset as opposed to later in the process.

Consultation, negotiation and lobbying

3.13   Beyond the appraisal stage, the scheme must be drawn up and should be subject to a reasonable level of consultation with relevant parties both prior to and during the planning application stage. The consultation process may have begun already at the appraisal stage and it should continue right through to the conclusion of the application stage.

Gauging the appropriate level of consultation can be difficult and it can be costly and time consuming. There is a need to understand when consultation is necessary and when consultation may be inappropriate. In some situations, early consultation may be essential to help determine the course of action to be followed. Parties such as the Highway Authority, the Environment Agency, the council's tree officer, conservation, landscape, archaeological or ecological experts. The parish council may also need to be approached. Their responses may give rise to the need for additional advice from specialist consultants.

Local community and neighbour consultation may also be necessary. It is often wise to enter into pre-application consultation with Parish Councils, local residents, community groups and other potential stakeholders. With 'localism' and the shift of power in decision making to the local level there is an increasing case for investment in this stage of work prior to application submission.

By its very nature, the planning process is a process that often requires subjective assessments. Frequently, a proposal may be deemed to be in the balance or not clear-cut. Should the authority place the emphasis on the need for employment opportunities in the countryside, or restrictions on vehicle trip generation? Should the emphasis be on the need to make best use of redundant land, or the need to protect valuable landscapes or certain types of vulnerable wildlife? These are matters that can often be handled in favour of the applicant by engaging appropriate specialist consultancy advice. Negotiations may need to be with the application case officer or with the specialist officer advising the planning officer on the matter in question.

Sometimes consultees are not experts. They may be parish councillors or representatives of neighbourhood committees or residents groups. Hence it is appropriate to consult with or lobby these parties, either before or during the application period.

Likewise, it may be appropriate to make contact with district councillors within the ward or parish or with district councillors on the appropriate planning committee. In instances such as this, there is a need to understand the make-up of the relevant committee, party politics and the views held previously by elected members. Some councillors can be reluctant to meet or to express a view on a particular proposal. Sometimes information provided may be used against the applicant. If party politics are not taken into account the applicant may be successful in winning over an elected member only to find that he or she is a member of the minority group whose views are likely to be opposed by those holding the balance of power.

Fortunately, we live in a democracy and elected members are effectively performing a public role and should therefore always be contactable. Their addresses and telephone numbers should be disclosed by the district council. Sometimes an approach may be best in writing only, although at other times it may be appropriate to call, speak to or meet with certain councillors. Always remember, you may be providing information to someone who, for whatever reason, may eventually try to use the information against you. Hence, proceed with care.

The lobbying activity can be carried out either by the applicant or his agent. It is often better if the approach can be direct from the applicant who is more likely to be a constituent with voting rights. However, he must be very clear on the purpose of the approach and the nature of the argument to be pursued and, where the case is complex, there may be no alternative but to bring in specialist advisers. In the most complex and political of cases it may even be appropriate to hire a lobbyist.

The importance of design

3.14 Over recent years we have seen an ever-increasing emphasis on good design. Design and the closely related issue of energy efficiency are key issues in the determination of planning applications. Some applications for development that are acceptable 'in principle' fail because of poor design. On the other hand, good design and/or eco-friendly factors can help make a scheme more attractive, more viable and significantly increase prospects for success at the planning stage.

Design can be particularly important in areas with special designations such as National Parks, Areas of Outstanding Natural Beauty (AONB) and Areas of Special Landscape Importance (ASLI). It goes without saying that good design is also important for buildings that are to be located within very open or exposed sites. Even buildings that can be erected under permitted development rights must respect guidance on good design. At the national level, there is extensive advice on the need for new agricultural and forestry buildings to be carefully considered in terms of their setting, size, shape, colour, texture and overall appearance (see PPS4 and PPG7, Appendix E, paras 24–35).

The importance of good design generally is set out in paras 33–39 of PPS1: Delivering Sustainable Development (January 2005). The PPS indicates that good design is considered to be indivisible from good planning and that a 'High quality and inclusive design should be the aim of all those involved in the development process' (para 34, part only).

Applicants for planning permission are now required to provide a short written statement setting out their design principles with reference to the wider context, local distinctiveness, submitted plans and elevations and matters of access. These are called Design and Access Statements and must accompany all applications with only limited exceptions such as applications for small domestic extensions.

Planning policy guidance for rural areas sets good design as a clear objective in order to help achieve local distinctiveness and make new development more acceptable to local people (PPS7, para 12). Where it exists, consideration should be given to relevant supplementary planning guidance such as Countryside Design Summaries, Conservation Area Statements or Village Design Statements.

Generally speaking, there is a need to consider design aspects at an early stage and to take forward design issues in parallel with the initial stages of the planning case. There is a need to avoid the trap of getting an architect or experienced designer who is competent on the design side, but overlooks planning policy matters. Likewise, applicants should not be misled by a planning consultant who focuses on planning policy matters but overlooks design issues. Applicants should either appoint an individual or company who can handle both matters or appoint two people who can work well together.

When handling building conversion matters it is particularly important that the designer understands the need to convert and re-use rather than demolish and rebuild. Local guidance generally requires that buildings in the open countryside should only be given consent for conversion if it is without the need for 'major or complete reconstruction'. A scheme to demolish and rebuild either in part or in whole may be preferred by the owner or proposed occupier as it may be more cost effective. However, unless it is justified by reference to structural reports or other environmental benefits it is more likely to be a non-starter when it comes to planning policy.

Proposals for development within particularly sensitive areas such as Areas of Outstanding Natural Beauty or Environmentally Sensitive Areas may require a special approach to design. To achieve a development that is respectful, there may be a need for design that is sensitive to nature and which requires the appointment of a landscape architect or an ecologist to work alongside the planning consultant and designer.

Dealing with highway or transport issues

3.15   Many diversification schemes fail for highway or transport-related issues. For many years a wide range of schemes have failed because of inadequate visibility splays at the junction of the site entrance with the adopted highway. Over recent years there have been a significant number of planning refusals because of traffic generation concerns, particularly in areas that are relatively remote where compliance with sustainable planning policies is brought into question.

It is important that applicants should not give up on a scheme just because of negative comments at an early stage from a local authority highway engineer or a planning officer. There are frequently ways of presenting a scheme or of altering it to address Highway Authority objections. Further, it is important to note that the local Highway Authority can only advise the planning officer and does not have powers to direct refusal of a planning application.

If the new development gives rise to the need for substantial visibility splays, existing hedges or banks may need to be cut back or kerbs realigned. Visibility splay distances along the main road depend on traffic speeds. It may be possible to show that speeds are actually relatively low (or agree traffic orders to force them to be lower) and hence reduce requirements for splay lengths. Alternatively, traffic calming or traffic management measures may be suggested to bring traffic speeds down.

When the Highway Authority considers development proposals it is mindful of the level and type of traffic that is likely to be generated. It is therefore important that information is obtained on earlier levels of trip generation. Did cattle lorries regularly enter or leave the site, or were there regular milk or egg collections? It may be possible to argue that a scheme with a substandard access should be allowed because of the highway engineer's fallback principle. This requires that development should not generally be resisted if levels of traffic generation for a new use would not exceed the levels associated with an earlier use that may lawfully be recommenced.

In some cases the Highway Authority or the local planning authority may seek to resist commercial development on the grounds that it should not be located in remote or relatively inaccessible rural areas. Clearly, some forms of commercial development may be inappropriate where they give rise to a substantial level of private vehicle trips along small rural roads. However, by devising green transport measures and Green Travel Plans it may be possible to show that private vehicle trip generation will be reduced to more acceptable levels, hence removing the reason for refusal.

Green Travel Plans can be highly complex and expensive. They can include measures such as company-owned minibuses, public transport subsidies or restrictions on parking to limit associated levels of car use. However, there are other elements that may be relatively easy to achieve such as the operation of flexible working hours, display on site of bus timetables and noticeboards for car-sharing opportunities. Other measures that are frequently put forward include provision for secure undercover cycle storage and the incorporation of showers and changing rooms within offices or workshops to encourage cycling to work.

Measures such as these may be the key to a successful planning application. Without them, a building may only be re-used for low-key, low-value purposes or for tenants that are difficult to manage and frequently default on payment rather than the more respectable professional or business user.

Strict controls over the provision of parking spaces have often been used to force the use of green travel measures and more sustainable development. In practice, controls were difficult to manage and often ignored. The coalition government has lifted the strict maximum standards and sought to end what it saw as a 'war against the motor car'.

Negotiating planning obligations

3.16   The Planning Acts make provision for planning obligations to be attached to planning consents. These obligations are normally formalised within

Section 106 Agreements, so-called because the main provision is contained within Town and Country Planning Act 1990 s 106. Planning obligations take various forms. They may be needed to restrict occupancy of buildings or prevent the sale of a building or buildings separate from a wider estate. In other cases, an obligation may require the removal of buildings if they are no longer needed in connection with a specific diversification proposal. In some cases, a planning obligation may require traffic routing or may be used to embrace Green Travel Plans.

The planning obligation may be necessary to persuade the local planning authority or the Highway Authority that the development can go ahead. To be reasonable, the obligation should be deemed to be necessary and clearly related to the development proposed, and it must cover a matter that cannot be dealt with in a standard planning condition. These tests should be applied in each case.

Planning obligations can sometimes take many months to resolve. They can also be onerous and as they run with the land they are likely to bind successors in title. In some cases, an applicant may be required to pay for off-site highway improvements because of forecast traffic generation associated with a diversification scheme. If the measures that have to be underwritten are extensive, the diversification scheme may not be viable. It may be worth finding out what the trigger level is above which contributions may be required.

Once agreed, a planning obligation is difficult to remove. However, in some instances, after a period of five years following the grant of planning permission they can be renegotiated or even removed altogether.

It may be best to take legal advice either at the stage of negotiation or just prior to signing the obligation. Clauses can sometimes be added that may be of considerable benefit to the applicant. For example, if required to contribute to a road improvement scheme it is unreasonable for the Highway Authority to retain the money if the scheme is never implemented. By applying a clause requiring that funds be returned if not used within, say, five years an applicant's interests are more likely to be protected. Other similar clauses will be well known to consultants and lawyers who regularly deal with planning obligations.

These are just a few of the ways in which the value of a planning consent can be optimised. There are others and clearly the relevance of each depends on the nature of the diversification proposal. Planning policy guidance, statutes and development plan policies regularly change and hence the purpose of this chapter has been to give a broad outline of the most relevant matters at the time of writing.

Do not fall into the trap of letting planning matters become the tail that wags the dog. The diversification proposal should be well conceived commercially and should be a workable business venture. At the same time, make sure that planning matters are taken account of and handled professionally to ensure that they do not become an obstacle to success.

James Cleary

James Cleary is a Chartered Town Planner and qualified Urban Designer who has practised for over 30 years. He has experience with the public and private sectors, has lectured at Oxford Brookes and Portsmouth Universities and was a member of the RTPI Development Control Panel for five years. He is the Managing Director of Pro Vision Planning and Design – a company that he helped establish in 1996. Pro Vision is a trading name of P V Projects Ltd. The company now has three offices and handles planning and environmental consultancy and architectural projects throughout the country. Large country estates are one of the company's key client sectors. Over recent years, the company has advised on proposals for numerous diversification projects throughout the country.

Chapter 4

Protecting the tax position of the farmhouse

Julie Butler

- **Protecting the farmhouse against loss of tax reliefs**
  The tax case of *Arnander and others (Executors of McKenna deceased) v HMRC* (2006) SpC 565 23 has shown that HMRC are prepared to continue to attack the right to inheritance tax (IHT) relief on the farmhouse. This is supported by several other cases that are looked at in depth in this chapter, including *Antrobus 1* and *2*.

- **The tax benefits of a principal private residence (PPR)**
  The tax benefits of PPR for CGT relief (TCGA 1992 s 222) must not be under-utilised by the farming community, and the tax planner needs to be aware of the fine balance between business usage and PPR.

- **The tax benefits of a large garden**
  Farmhouses have traditionally enjoyed large gardens with an extensive curtilage and with this comes the opportunity for development. Buildings in the curtilage can qualify as part of the garden. Again, the tax planner must look at maximising both PPR for the garden and business reliefs where appropriate.

- **The danger areas for the farmhouse and APR**
  The structure of the farming unit and the process of land being put to different use other than agriculture by definition could affect the agricultural property relief (APR) on the farmhouse. Examples of risk areas are farm business tenancies (FBTs), land let out, weak contract farm agreements (CFAs), grazing arrangements, ownership in the limited company, reduced land ownership, hobby farming and no history of commerciality.

THE FARMHOUSE – INTRODUCTION

4.1   The assets comprised in the farming and diversification enterprise can principally be divided between farmhouse, farm cottages, farm buildings, farmland, diversified activity and investment in the farming business. The need to preserve inheritance tax (IHT) reliefs, both APR and BPR and main residence relief for CGT is emphasised. There can be no doubt that in recent tax cases it is the farmhouse that has come under the most sustained attack from HMRC for loss of APR for IHT. As house prices have soared over the last decade (at the time of writing), both traditional and diversifying farmers had to protect this asset from the claws of the taxman. HMRC's recent attacks on inheritance tax-planning schemes on general taxpayers' homes set the scene for the negative approach of HMRC on the farmhouse. Are any probate lawyers/tax planners achieving 100% APR on the farmhouse?

Protecting the farmhouse

4.2   With the move from traditional farming activities and structures, for reasons set out in Chapter 1 and Chapter 2, a lot of the previously assured reliefs could be lost without careful tax planning.

The self-sufficient family farm unit could once exist happily with as little as 100 acres. The farmhouse was part of this 'business' unit and achieved many tax advantages such as input VAT claims, business expense claims and, above all, agricultural property relief (APR) for IHT. A very happy scenario then, but where does that leave the farmhouse today? Do these small family farms still exist on a commercial basis? The farmhouse is likely to have a very high value but less likely to achieve all the reliefs it previously enjoyed. At the time of writing, however, house prices have been falling and agricultural land values increasing dramatically.

One of the most valuable tax reliefs at stake is therefore APR for IHT purposes. The first point to consider is the 'character appropriate' test. This is dealt with throughout the chapter. If land is put to a non-agricultural use, or is gifted or sold, then the farmhouse and any land associated with it may no longer be 'of a character appropriate' to the farmland and APR may be restricted.

Is the land still used for agricultural purposes? Has the move to diversification meant that the relief has been jeopardised? With so many advisers seeking the benefits of business property relief (BPR) as opposed to APR, has the farmhouse been overlooked? What chance of success would the farmhouse have with a BPR claim? The same problem arises where the owner lets the land but retains the farmhouse. Reference should be made as to what qualifies as agricultural property and the Inheritance Tax Act 1984 (IHTA 1984) ss 115–117 should be looked at. The adviser must be mindful of the occupational or ownership tests.

In the Income Tax Acts the definition of farming is found in ITA 2007 s 996: 'the occupation of land wholly or mainly for the purposes of husbandry'. See Chapter 1 for more detail. So what does not qualify? Grazing by horses (*Wheatley's Executors v IRC* [1998] STC (SCD) 60), fishing rights, industrial units, farm shops selling only bought-in produce and the farm as a tourist attraction are but a few examples. The case of *Farmer (Farmer's Executors) v IRC* [1999] STC (SCD) 321 provides great potential assistance to the farmer and landowner who diversifies into residential property activity. In this case, several of the properties at the farm were surplus to the requirements of the farm and had been let to tenants on short leases. The letting activities were held to be ancillary to the farm business and the business as a whole was not one of mainly holding investments. The case is dealt with in detail in Chapter 13.

So where does that leave the farmhouse and the professional adviser? One of the first points of concern must be the income tax computation. Is there a clear division of farming and non-farming profits despite the fact they might be all taxed as trading income? Is the adviser mindful of the hobby farming rules (see Chapter 12)? How is turnover divided? What are the hours worked?

Under the strict allocation of farming and non-farming income, would some enterprises be able to demonstrate recent farming profitability? This is not an assumption that the clients are 'bad' farmers, but that for a number of years it has been difficult to show a profit from a small traditional farming unit.

So what planning points are there for consideration by the tax adviser? In addition to looking at the tax computation, all angles of the diversification must be looked at. Farmers are considering (or have been considering) farm business tenancies (FBTs) and various areas of diversification. The angle of FBT, contract farming and share-farming arrangements are dealt with in Chapter 11. At the time of writing, many farms have seen the move back to contract farming. The *Arnander* case focuses on the weaknesses of contract-farming agreements (CFAs).

Perhaps it could be argued that as farming now provides such a relatively small amount of total UK income, such issues are not so relevant, but the land and high asset values still surround us. The land should be put to some commercial use and traditional assumptions will have to be re-thought. There is also the problem of the world food shortage.

Historically, there have been claims of 70% input VAT on farmhouse repairs and one-third claim for business expenses, but the viability of such claims in relation to the newly structured farming enterprise has to be questioned by both the farmer and his adviser, HMRC look at detailed evidence and the actual area used in the business.

Consideration is given to the protection of the matrimonial home (see Chapter 16).

AGRICULTURAL BUILDINGS ALLOWANCES

4.3   The Finance Acts 2007 and 2008 are phasing out agricultural buildings allowances (ABAs) (see **7.12**). Farmhouses have historically been eligible for ABAs.

The general rule is that on each farm, only a single farmhouse is the central controlling point of the farm, ie its use is restricted to the person running the farm. Other houses occupied by individuals working on the farm may be 'cottages'. As the ABA was only 4%, it is now capital allowances queries that are likely to drive the need for clarification of exactly what is a 'farmhouse', however knowledge of the history of ABA claims will be essential.

In *Lindsay v IRC* (1953) 34 TC 289, the taxpayer lived abroad and farmed through agents. The head shepherd occupied the only house. Despite the fact that he was an employee, his dwelling was found to be the farmhouse and expenditure on it was restricted to one-third business use.

In *IRC v John M Whiteford & Son* (1962) 40 TC 379, a house was built for a farmer's son who was a partner in the business. This was held to be an agricultural cottage so there was no restriction for private use.

Where any expenditure is incurred on a farmhouse, not more than one-third can qualify (CAA 2001 s 369(3)). The strict calculation of restriction (as agreed by HMRC) is the exact number of rooms used. This proportion may be reduced if the accommodation and amenities of the farmhouse are out of relation to the nature and extent of the farm. Likewise, if the farmhouse has been used partly for husbandry and partly for some other non-agricultural purpose eg diversification, the expenditure is apportioned for the purpose of the allowance.

One of the features (please excuse the pun) of FA 2008 was the ability to claim capital allowances on the new classification of the 'integral features' of a building (see **7.4**). A farmhouse is an agricultural building and it will be interesting to see how successful capital allowances claims for the likes of electrical systems for the farm office integrated into the farmhouse are with HMRC.

CAPITAL GAINS TAX

Principal private residence (PPR)

4.4   An important tax relief available to farmers and diversifying landowners in respect of the farmhouse is that for a 'principal private residence' (PPR) (Taxation and Chargeable Gains Act 1992 (TCGA 1992) s 222). The relief applies to a gain arising on the disposal of the dwelling-house or its garden and grounds. In the case of the latter relief is restricted to 0.5 of a hectare (inclusive of the site of the dwelling-house) or such larger areas as is required for reasonable enjoyment of the dwelling-house having regard to its size and character dwelling-house (TCGA 1992 s 222(2), (3)). The garden and grounds have to be for the owner's own occupation and enjoyment.

The practical tax-planning point is that the business usage and private residence relief (PRR) must be finely balanced. Strictly, any element of the farmhouse that is used exclusively for business will not be eligible for PRR. Some tax practitioners advocate not dedicating 100% business usage to specific rooms so that the PRR relief is preserved. The owners of the farmhouse must be very mindful of the tax-planning interaction of the potential claim for PRR and APR (see **4.22** to **4.42**). Care must also be taken with the consistency in the claim for business expenditures and the PRR.

The ordinary meaning of dwelling-house can be found in *Batey v Wakefield* [1980] STC 572 (see **4.5** below). Where freehold farms are such useful assets to roll-over capital gains into (see **14.19**), the business element of the farmhouse and the need to roll-over a gain for CGT purposes against that value must be balanced against the position of PRR.

In *Makins v Elson* [1977] STC 46 the dwelling-house was held to include a caravan jacked up and resting on bricks. Contributing facts were that the wheels were not touching the ground and that electricity, water and telephone were connected.

Adjoining houses

4.5   It was held in *Batey v Wakefield* [1980] STC 572 that a chalet bungalow, which had been built to house staff employed for the purpose of providing gardening, housekeeping and caretaking services for the benefit of the main house, was part of the main dwelling. In order to qualify for PRR, the house adjoining the farmhouse (or part of it) must not be acquired for the purpose of realising a gain on the disposal nor must any expenditure be incurred on the property wholly or partly for the purpose of realising a gain from the disposal. This principle is set out in TCGA 1992 s 224(3).

HMRC recognise that anyone who buys adjoining houses will hope that the property will appreciate in value and the taxpayer will benefit from PRR on both properties. A realisation of this advantage is not caught by the anti-avoidance legislation in TCGA 1992 s 224(3) if the property had been genuinely acquired for the use of a residence. The case that sets this out is *Jones v Wilcock* [1996] STC (SCD) 389. HMRC use the anti-avoidance legislation only where the primary purpose of the purchase was for early sale at a profit. However, it is likely that the treatment could constitute 'an adventure in the nature of trade' and if this is so the gain will be taxed as a trading profit, as an income tax charge which must take priority over a CGT charge. Trading profits are dealt with in more detail in Chapter 14 and below.

Currently the main factors that appear to influence HMRC are quality evidence and motive of genuine residence. It is essential that with any PRR claim there is proof of residence ideally in the form of contemporaneous evidence of permanence and fact.

Artificial transactions in land

4.6   HMRC are alive to the reality that PRR relief is open to abuse.

TCGA 1992 s 224(3) most commonly applies where expenditure is incurred on the property to enhance its value prior to a sale. The effect is to deny PRR to part of the gain that is attributable to the particular expenditure. This can most aptly apply in the case of barn conversions. It could be that ITA 2007 s 756 could be applied to the disposal of a main residence which is exempt from CGT – or it would be were it not for the provisions of TCGA 1992 s 224(3). The provision concerning artificial transactions in land is dealt with in more detail in Chapter 14. Issues of permanence and continuity are dealt with in **4.16**.

The scope of ITA 2007 s 756 is broad and catches transactions that have little or no element of artificiality. Therefore the avoidance of this section can be accidental or unwitting. This is of particular relevance to any farmer who is currently considering selling his farmhouse so as to make as much profit as possible, and attempting to obtain planning permission for another property on the same site, or to move to a smaller dwelling connected to the land. It is essential that taxpayers carefully review the implications of TCGA 1992 s 224(3) and ITA 2007 s 756 when looking at any possible restructuring, including the disposal of possibly the most valuable asset, the farmhouse, ideally completely 'tax free' with the benefit of PRR.

Practical examples of s 756 that could come into play would be the farm or estate, where for example the farmer and his wife live in the main farmhouse. The recent poor economics of farming compared with high property prices, have forced the sale of some farmhouses. The farmer can no longer afford a farm manager, so the farmer might move into what was the farm manager's house. Planning permission for conversion of a barn to a dwelling is obtained. The farmer moves into the converted barn and then another converted barn. Each sale could be achieved 'tax free' through PRR, but for ITA 2007 s 756 (see **4.20**) and again the basic question of proof of permanence can be asked for by HMRC.

Curtilage

4.7   The argument as to whether separate outbuildings could be part of the main dwelling-house curtilage was advanced in the apparently conflicting decisions of *Markey v Sanders* [1987] STC 256 and *Williams v Merrylees* [1987] STC 445. However, the conflict was resolved in the Court of Appeal case of *Lewis v Rook* [1992] STC 171, which established the more restrictive curtilage test. A cottage occupied by the gardener was not within the curtilage of the main dwelling-house and therefore could not form part of it. Whilst *Lewis v Rook* [1992] STC 171 appears to offer assistance where outbuildings are within the curtilage of the main house, this is not so because the Crown in that case reserved the right to argue in the future that a 'dwelling-house' can never consist of more than one building.

In CG64245 HMRC have adopted the dictionary definition of curtilage as being 'a small courtyard or piece of ground, attached to a dwelling-house and forming one enclosure with it', which emphasises the smallness of the area involved. Contrast this with *Markey v Sanders* [1987] STC 256 (bungalow 130 metres from the house) and *Williams v Merrylees* [1987] STC 445 (bungalow 200 metres from the main house).

HMRC will not normally regard another building as being within the curtilage of the main house (and hence not part of the dwelling-house) in the following circumstances:

● where the buildings are dispersed, having no geographical relationship between them;

● where a wall or fence separates the two buildings;

● where a public road or stretch of tidal water separates the two buildings; or

● where the buildings pass under separate conveyances or are separately mentioned.

It is considered that a house and outbuildings around a courtyard will comprise a curtilage.

Since PRR includes relief for garden and grounds under TCGA 1992 s 222(1)(b) and there may be opportunities to build another dwelling-house in the garden and grounds, it is essential to understand exactly their definitions for PRR purposes. In the light of the taxpayer's desire to take maximum advantage of the protection of PRR there are lots of helpful tax cases.

The meaning of 'garden'

4.8   A case before the Special Commissioners, *Henke and another v HMRC* SpC 550 (published in May 2006), was a timely reminder for farm tax planners on what is required to achieve the tax-efficient disposal of a large garden (see **4.16**).

For PRR purposes 'garden' takes its everyday meaning, ie 'a piece of ground, usually partly grassed and adjoining a private house, used for growing flowers, fruit or vegetables, and as a place of recreation'. 'Grounds' infers a larger area than garden and may be defined as 'enclosed land surrounding or attached to a dwelling-house or other building serving chiefly for ornament or recreation' (see CG64360).

HMRC are very aware of the development value of gardens and grounds and in the same way that the taxpayer is very keen to try and maximise the tax reliefs so too are HMRC to disallow them. This is clearly shown in the case of *Varty v Lynes* [1976] STC 508. In this case exemption was denied as the land was sold nearly a year after the house because it was no longer occupied and enjoyed with the residence. In practice, HMRC no longer apply this rule unless the land concerned has development value. This shows that it is a concession with virtually no practical value.

It is essential that the garden and grounds must be occupied and enjoyed with the residence at the time they are sold. TCGA 1992 s 222(1)(b) is concerned with the present time, which should be contrasted with s 221(1)(a), which concerns itself with the past tense. It is not sufficient that the garden and grounds have been occupied and enjoyed with the residence at some time during the period of ownership. Land will be excluded from garden and grounds if used for an agricultural or other business purpose, since they would not be chiefly recreational or not occupied and enjoyed with the residence. Land fenced off from the residence to be sold for development is also excluded.

It is, however, not a requirement that the land is used exclusively for recreational purposes. For example, the owner-occupier of a guesthouse may allow guests to use the garden.

Within the provisions of TCGA 1992 s 288, land includes buildings situated on it. Buildings usually qualify for PRR if they are part of the garden or grounds within the permitted area and are not used for business purposes or let out. Under the Interpretation Act 1978 s 1, land includes buildings.

Development opportunities of the garden

4.9   When a landowner has development opportunities on land which is situated very close to the PRR, it is clear that part of the planning advice can be to make sure that maximum use is made of the PRR as far as it relates to the garden and grounds. Some tax practitioners would take this as far as to see development opportunities a long way in advance and to ensure that maximum use is made of the garden and grounds. It has been known for hedges to be planted (usually of the fast-growing fir tree type) and for greater emphasis to be placed on recreational garden space than paddock land.

Property development is looked at in Chapter 6 (see **6.38**) and Chapter 14. The development opportunities on the farmland (and the garden) can lead towards diversification or indeed be termed a diversified activity in their own right eg 'growing houses'.

Various PRR issues arose in the case of *Henke*. In 1982 the Henkes bought a 2.66 acre plot of land with planning permission for one house to be built. Work did not start on the house until February 1991 and was finished by June 1993. Oak House comprised 4,500 sq ft of accommodation and 1,000 sq ft of garage in the same curtilage. The Henkes, having lived elsewhere, moved in to Oak House and had lived there ever since. In July 1995 they obtained detailed planning permission for two separate houses to be built on part of the same plot, with each sub-plot comprising 0.54 acres. Both plots were sold, in 1999 and 2001 respectively and the two houses were built. The Henkes used the proceeds of the first sale to repay the mortgage on Oak House. Until the sales, each sub-plot had been maintained as part of the garden and grounds of Oak House.

The tax-planning opportunities offered by development of a large garden are also looked at in great detail by tax planners for clients who are not farmers and just have a big garden which might get planning permission.

Permitted area for the garden

4.10   What is the permitted area? It is generally accepted that this is probably the most contentious area of tax claims by the taxpayer. If the garden and grounds do not exceed 0.5 of a hectare, which includes the site of the dwelling-house, relief for the whole of the garden or grounds is given automatically. This will include the buildings situated on the relevant land provided that they are not used for business purposes or let out. If the garden and grounds exceed 0.5 of a hectare, relief will only be available for a larger area if that area is required for the reasonable enjoyment of the dwelling-house having regard to the size and character of the dwelling-house.

If the area of garden and grounds is greater than the permitted area, the part that is chosen is the part most suitable for occupation and enjoyment with the residence. This is found in TCGA 1992 s 222(4). Any buildings situated on that part will qualify provided that they are not used for business purposes or let out. Other buildings on the garden and grounds that are not quite as suitable will not qualify.

As set out in **4.5**, it is important to recognise that the dwelling-house can comprise more than one building, as seen in *Batey v Wakefield* [1980] STC 572, and when determining whether additional garden and grounds in excess of 0.5 of a hectare is required for reasonable enjoyment it is important to note that larger houses tend to require larger grounds. This might seem obvious but it is an important tax-planning point.

'Required'

4.11   How is the word 'required' defined? It is an objective test. One clear tax case is *Re Newhill Compulsory Purchase Order 1937, Paynes Application* [1938] 2 All ER 163 in which du Parcq J stated:

'I call attention to the word "required". The use of it raises a question of fact which is necessarily a difficult one. Again, I do not wish to repeat myself, but one has to remember that it is pleasant, and, one must say, both an amenity and a convenience, to have a good deal of open space round one's house, but it does not follow that open space is required for the amenity or the convenience of the house. "Required", I think, in this section does not mean merely that the occupiers of the house would like to have it, or that they would miss it if they lost it, or that anyone proposing to buy the house would think less of the house without it than he would if it was preserved to it. "Required" means, I suppose, that without it there will be such a substantial deprivation of amenities or convenience that a real injury will be done to the property owner and a question like that is obviously a question of fact.'

In the case of *Sharkey v Secretary of State for the Environment and South Buckinghamshire District Council* (1990) 62 P & CR 126 it was held that 'required' meant something more than desirable. One of the most important cases in this respect is set out in *Longson v Baker* [2000] STC (SCD) 244. This case gave a ruling of great importance for landowners looking to dispose of the PRR and the surrounding ground.

In this case the taxpayer claimed that the permitted area (which included a farmhouse, stables and an outhouse all facing a central courtyard) amounted to 7.56 hectares. The claim failed despite the parties agreeing that the stables accommodating 12 horses were part of the dwelling. The Inspector contended that 'required' meant close to necessary. The permitted area was reduced to 1.054 hectares – exactly the same area that the previous owner secured. This appears to set a precedent in that, where the issue has cropped up in the past, HMRC may review earlier disposals of property since 1965.

In the case of *Longson v Baker*, the question must be asked as to what alternative advice could have been given? The stable size was large. What would the chances have been of claiming entrepreneurs' relief on the gain (at the time of the case that was Business Asset Taper Relief)? What business activity or potential for business activity was there? (See Chapter 14.)

As mentioned, HMRC will invariably look at previous conveyance documents for a property. What is the history of garden size?

It is an interesting tax-planning point that, when advising farming clients on their ability to claim PRR for the grounds, they should look at conveyance documents which may have set some form of precedent. For more on PRR see CG64200 onwards. The Valuation Office Agency's CGT Manual, para 8.43 gives an indication of how the District Valuer will approach the objective test.

'In considering the area "required", the most obvious evidence to consider is the extent of the gardens/grounds enjoyed with houses of similar size and character in the locality. Evidence of sale prices is immaterial and should not be used.

The extent of the locality will for this purpose depend upon the proximity of sufficient comparables to obtain a fair impression. It may be necessary to bear in mind:

(i)   that there is a general tendency towards smaller gardens because of cost, convenience, lack of gardeners etc, and

(ii)   that houses in urban localities are generally found to have smaller gardens/grounds than in rural districts.

It follows that houses which were built many years ago and/or are in districts which were once rural, but now urban, may no longer strictly require the area of garden/grounds which they retain. The lower end of the range of areas of garden/grounds occupied with comparable dwellings is evidence of requirement. Larger areas are often accounted for by historic reasons, or the owner's caprice. It should be sufficient to show that there are some closely comparable houses with 0.5 of a hectare or less. No value based test should be used.'

Electing for PRR and period of ownership before the house became PRR

4.12   When looking at PRR for landowners and farmers, it is easy to forget some of the basic principles of this relief and ensure that they do apply to the diversifying farmer. No taxpayer can claim relief on more than one house subject to overlap on elections. If a farmer owns more than one, for example a farm and a town house, he can elect within two years of the date of acquiring the second house which of them is to be his PPR for CGT purposes. If he fails to elect, the issue becomes one of fact for the self-assessment return. No election is required where one of the properties is not owned but merely occupied under licence as, for example, 'job-related accommodation' (see below).

In *Henke* the question was raised as to whether an apportionment was required to exclude the period before the house became Mr and Mrs Henke's PPR. This might not seem obvious, but the garden can only qualify for PRR when the house does, ie in *Henke* after 1993 and not before.

Job-related accommodation

4.13   This was first looked at in Chapter 1 (see **1.15**). In farming it is normal practice for a farm manager and farm workers to be provided with houses and cottages to live in. The owner of a large farm or estate might live in the manor house, or away from the farm. The farm manager will not want to lose the benefit of PRR on another property.

An individual who resides in job-related accommodation may find on leaving his farming job that another residence which he has owned has now lost the CGT relief for PRR because he has failed to occupy the second house continuously. In order to claim the PRR, there must be a time before and after the period of absence when the property was the main residence. The Enactment of Extra-Statutory Concession Order 2009 (SI 2009/730)(previously Extra-statutory Concession D4) allows a period of absence of greater than four years.

To help in the situation of the occupation of the job-related accommodation, for example, the farm employee's house (after 30 July 1978) is treated as if it were occupation of the employee's own house provided he intends in due course to go and occupy it. The provision is set out in TCGA 1992 s 222. Whether he does so intend is a question of fact. If he has occupied it before the relevant sale, this would clearly represent persuasive evidence. If the sale occurs before occupation, intention can still be demonstrated, particularly if the proceeds are applied to buy another home.

For the purposes of CGT the definition of job-related accommodation is set out below and there is a similar denial of relief where the accommodation is provided by a farming company for a farming director unless he has no material interest and works full time, or the company is non-profit making or a charity. The clear tax-planning point here is that farmhouses owned within farming companies and lived in by directors must be given a careful review for tax status for both PPR protection and benefits in kind.

The conditions for job-related accommodation are as follows:

- where it is necessary for the proper performance of an employee's duties that he should reside in the accommodation (ITEPA 2003 s 99(1));

- where the accommodation is provided for the better performance of the duties of his employment and he is in employment where it is customary for employers to provide living accommodation to employees (ITEPA 2003 s 99(2));

- where there is a special threat to an employee's security, special security arrangements are in force and the employee resides in the accommodation as part of these arrangements (ITEPA 2003 s 100).

The most relevant to farming, therefore, is perhaps the second item with emphasis on 'customary'. This is the exemption most likely to be sought where employees are provided with accommodation on a rural estate or farm. One of the requirements is that the accommodation has been provided for the better performance of the duties of the employment: this requirement is clearly aimed at questioning the employer's reason for providing the accommodation eg checking of livestock, the pressures of harvest, protection of farm machinery etc.

The forms of employment and the identification of those forms need review. In *Stanley's Taxation of Farmers and Landowners* (LexisNexis UK) it is stated that it is important to see whether a head gardener on a rural estate is likely to have duties very different from a gardener employed to tend a municipal park. Here, the question arises whether rural estate head gardeners are in a kind of employment distinct from gardeners in general. Stanley suggests that a careful examination is made of the duties of the employment contrasted with both those of similar employees on other rural estates and the duties common to the generic class to determine whether those of the rural estate employee are neither rare nor indistinguishable from the duties of the generic class.

Stanley also looks at this question of the provision of accommodation and whether or not it is customary. The book quotes the *Vertigan v Brady* [1988] STC 91 case, where the court determined there were three constituent factors of 'customary' to be examined: the statistical evidence on how common the practice was; evidence on how long the practice had gone on; and whether the practice had achieved general acceptance. It is also normal practice for farmers to take in lodgers and paying guests who live with the family, sharing accommodation and meals. The PRR is not lost in this case (SP 14/80).

ITEPA 2003 s 105 provides that where an employee is provided with accommodation there is a tax charge on the benefit to the employee of that accommodation. Where rent is paid by the person at whose cost the accommodation is provided the charge is based on the actual rent paid (less any amount made good by the employee), where that is more than the 'annual value'.

Finance Act 2009 s 71 applies in cases where accommodation is provided to employees by reason of their employment through the payment of a lease premium.

Where a lease premium is paid for a lease of ten years or less, the same tax treatment will follow as if the lease premium were actual rent paid (spread over the period of the lease): see ITEPA 2003 s 105A inserted by FA 2009).

Tenant farmers and farm workers – PPR

4.14 The CGT relief for PPR can be of benefit when looking at tenant farmers who have to live in the farmhouse of the tenant farm, but have their own house that qualifies as a PPR. It is vital to consider the whole position concerning occupancy of farm cottages by workers and retired workers, especially with fewer and fewer farms employing farm workers and providing them with their own cottage and the move towards contract farming. This is compounded by a falling workforce due to the reductions in farming income over the last few decades.

Partnerships, trusts and beneficiaries

4.15 As part of any farm tax-planning exercise, it is imperative to see who owns what and who lives where within the farming unit. There are a large number of farms throughout the UK where farmhouses are owned jointly by a partnership, where one partner owns one house and lives in another, where the farm is owned by the limited company that farms the land and also where the house is owned in a trust or settlement.

The case of *Tod v Mudd* [1987] STC 141, does give direction to the joint, but unrelated, owner-occupier. In the case where the owner-occupiers are not husband and wife they will each be entitled to relief. Each one of them is treated as having an undivided share in all the property. This is on the assumption that each has unrestricted access to the whole property, even though some parts may in practice not be used by both the joint owners.

Relief is available to trustees if during their ownership of a property a beneficiary under the trust has been occupying it as his only or main residence (TCGA 1992 s 225). This applies whether he is entitled to occupy or is occupying by permission of the trustee. A similar concession is available to personal representatives who sell a property used immediately before or after the death as a main or only residence by beneficiaries under the will or intestacy who are entitled to the whole or substantially the whole of the proceeds of the sale, whether absolutely or for life. This is set out in CG64240–CG64270. For more details on trusts see Chapter 17.

It must also be noted that, where there are lodgers or paying guests (eg where a paying guest lives with the owner and family sharing accommodation and meals), the relief is not lost. However, where the whole or part of any PRR has been let by the owner as residential accommodation, some relief could be lost.

Preserving PRR relief

4.16   It is important that when carrying out the full exercise of asset ownership the whole question of PRR is not only reviewed but action is taken to make sure that it is preserved and the correct conditions are in place. This is not just with regard to ownership but the period of occupancy, the size of the garden and all the points mentioned previously. The issue of trying to create artificial PRR must be warned against. An example is found in *Goodwin v Curtis* [1998] STC 475, where the taxpayer purchased a farmhouse on 1 April 1985 and personally moved into it. On 11 April the farmhouse was advertised for sale and it was sold on 3 May. The Commissioners found that the taxpayer's occupation lacked permanence and continuity and that the farmhouse had been purchased with a view to realising a gain on its disposal. It was not his PRR and relief was not due. In this case, the finding was upheld both in the High Court and the Court of Appeal.

The question of protection can also be found in *Henke* (see **4.8**). Here it was argued that PRR was due on the sale of two sub-plots. HMRC disagreed and the District Valuer concluded that the plots sold were not part of the 'permitted area' of Oak House as they were not necessary for the reasonable enjoyment of Oak House as a residence (TCGA 1992 s 222(3)). Looking at comparable properties in the area, the permitted area was said to be 2.03 acres.

On the issue of the period of ownership and PRR the Special Commissioner, John Clark, held that as Mr and Mrs Henke did not own the house until 1993, but had owned the land since 1982, an apportionment was necessary under TCGA 1992 s 223(2) to limit the PRR due because they did not meet the 'throughout the period of ownership' condition in s 223(1). There was to be only one period of ownership of the single asset consisting of the land and a house which might be built on it during that period. Where, as in *Henke*, land was held for a period and subsequently a house was built on it and occupied as the Henkes' PRR, an apportionment was required. This was deemed to be very clear. On the question of permitted area the Commissioner found in favour of HMRC, being only the second decision on the permitted area issue (*Longson v Baker* being the other). It is worth noting that the house and the comparables used were all modern properties. The 'permitted area' test in s 222(1)(b) was to be applied by reference to what was required in the particular situation at the time of the disposal and so is an objective one. A house and a garden are subject to two individual tests. For a house, the test for main residence was 'at any time'. The test for land was whether it was a garden or grounds at the time of disposal. The garden would not qualify where a house stopped being an only or main residence. At the time of disposal, if the house and garden satisfied the tests, the grounds would qualify whatever their previous use. In *Henke*, the permitted area was on both occasions 0.82 of a hectare (2.03 acres). Before the sale of the sub-plots the total plot exceeded this; afterwards it was less than 2.03 acres. Thus the sales were partly covered by the PRR and the sales proceeds of the plots should have been apportioned on the basis of the respective non-exempt and exempt areas.

It is possibly more than unfortunate that the Henke family (who represented themselves) did not call upon any expert evidence. Compare this to the two *Antrobus* cases (see **4.31**). The production of expert evidence here, for example of 26 similar farmhouses, was commended.

There are arguments to say that a 2.66 acre plot can historically be shown to be 'required' by a residence of 4,500 sq ft of accommodation and 1,000 sq ft of garage. It would appear that what might have been missing here is expert evidence.

Capital loss on principal private residence

4.17   In the recent climate of rising prices it has always been assumed that PRR will be claimed on disposal. However, there have been cases where capital losses have been made on property and the taxpayer has tried to deny relief saying that the property was purchased for the intention of realising a gain, ie the reverse of ITA 2007 s 756 (see **4.16**).

This principal is set out in *Jones v Wilcock* [1996] STC (SCD) 389. In this case the taxpayer purchased a property in need of modernisation and spent £20,000 on improving it. The property was sold five years later and a substantial capital loss was made, and the taxpayer wanted to set the loss against other gains. In this case HMRC held that the expectation of a gain on the sale had been a hope but not a purpose. HMRC stated that there was no sign of commerciality in the improvement expenditure to suggest an adventure or concern in the nature of trade. Nor was there clear evidence that realising a gain or disposal had been even in part a purpose. The taxpayer had bought the house with a view to providing himself and his family with a home.

At the time of writing, losses on farmhouses seem unlikely; however, they have happened in the past and the property crash of the late 1980s and early 1990s and the recent 'credit crunch' serve as a recent reminder of this. Farmers and their advisers have looked to claim the farmhouse as a business asset with 100% business usage for CGT purposes. The position is complex.

Separate garden

4.18   Another factor that farmers and landowners must consider is the question of a separate garden. The case of *Wakeling v Pearce* [1995] STC (SCD) 96, in which relief was contested by HMRC over the issue of the land, should not be overlooked. Here, the taxpayer had a separate piece of land 30 feet away from the bungalow where she lived. She did not use the land disposed of with the land on which her bungalow was situated. However, it was held that the distance between the two pieces of land did not disqualify relief. The taxpayer had not ceased to use the land disposed of at the time of sale. HMRC sought to clarify this in *Tax Bulletin* No 18 (August 1995) and they set out the following conditions which must be in place for a separate garden to qualify:

●   it must be land of which the owner has occupation and enjoyment with the residence;

●   it must be garden or grounds of the residence; and

●   the area of land must not exceed the permitted area.

Where land is physically separated from a house, HMRC take the view that the fact that it is in common ownership and used for a garden does not automatically secure relief. It must be shown objectively to be naturally and traditionally a garden of the house so as to be normally offered as such to a prospective purchaser. This again is important to many farmers who historically have built additional farmhouses with a separate garden.

House and garden sold separately

4.19   As set out at **4.8** it is also useful to consider the scenario where the house and the garden are sold separately. In the case of *Varty v Lynes* [1976] STC 508 the house was sold first and the garden separately afterwards. The size of the plot, including the house and garden, together constituted less than one acre, but PRR was lost because once the house had been sold, the garden ceased to be occupied and enjoyed with the house. HMRC will not normally take this point unless the garden has development value; but it is clearly this development potential which makes not only a valuable asset for the farmer, but also a tax headache.

Barn conversion and redundant buildings

4.20   An area of complexity for the tax planner is that of barn conversions. There is a risk that the sale of such conversions could be caught under the anti-avoidance rules of TCGA 1992 s 224(3). This section denies the relief on a residence which was acquired wholly or partly for the purpose of realising a gain on its disposal (see **4.6**).

HMRC interpretation R I75 specifically draws attention to barn conversions and other development of outbuildings or land attached to the dwelling-house, which in their view are caught by this subsection. HMRC might try to withdraw relief on that part of the gain which is attributable to particular expenditure.

Generally a garden with planning permission can be sold and PRR obtained. However, where the owner of the residence decides to develop the garden himself, this development will fall into tax.

These matters are discussed in more detail in Chapter 14 but it must be noted that land where a farmer decides to develop a redundant building himself in order to maximise development potential will be taxed as trading profits and not as a gain. The property would be treated as having been appropriated to the trade under TCGA 1992 s 161(1). The effect of this is that the farmer is seen to have disposed of the asset at market value at the time of apportionment and a CGT computation falls to be made. There is, however, a form of hold-over relief contained in TCGA 1992 s 161(3) which has an effect of taxing the gain up to the date of apportionment as part of the trading result rather than as a capital gain. Obviously, only the capital gain element of the transaction is eligible for roll-over relief.

Period of occupation

4.21   In relation to the period of occupation, the extent of relief is proportionate to the extent to which the house has been occupied by an owner during his period of ownership. If he has lived in the house throughout, PRR should be achieved provided the other conditions are met.

In addition to this, as long as the farmer has lived in the house as his PR at any time with evidence of permanence and continuity, then the last 36 months of ownership are exempt. If, for half the period of ownership, he lived elsewhere and let his house, then only half the gain would be exempt. Again, the last 36 months will be exempt in all such cases.

There are a series of exceptions to the general rule designed to meet special circumstances. These include overlapping ownership, breaks in occupation, absences abroad, employer's requirements, occupation delayed use, alterations to use and representative occupation.

INHERITANCE TAX

Farmhouses 'under attack' from HMRC

4.22   HMRC's attacks on the eligibility for 100% APR relief on the farmhouse raise a multitude of problems for the taxpayer. The general public cannot see why a large and valuable farmhouse should escape IHT for the farmer. The farming community who have farmed the same farm for generations cannot see grounds for the attack on their homes. They just want to pass the asset to the next generation with minimal tax liability.

Since the first edition of this book, we have all heard of the *Antrobus* case (see **4.31**), where the farmhouse Cookhill Priory, with its own disused chapel and 126 acres, qualified as a farmhouse for APR.

Many tax advisers overlook the second 'leg' of APR, which restricts the relief to the agricultural property as if it were subject to a restrictive covenant for the use of agriculture only. *Antrobus 2* established at the Lands Tribunal that APR on the farmhouse should be restricted to the agricultural value (see **4.31** and **4.32**). At the time of writing this is often in the region of 70%.

It should be noted that the separate BPR has no such agricultural restriction so that hope value on potential development land farmed in hand should obtain BPR (see **5.33**). However, farmhouses will not qualify for BPR if it cannot be said that they are used wholly or mainly for the purposes of the business. At the time of writing no-one has yet tried to argue that a farmhouse qualified for BPR under the preponderance test for the whole of the business as applied in the *Farmer* case (see Chapter 13).

Rosser v IRC [2003] STC (SCD) 311 (see **4.29**) is a case where a 'genuine' farmer had handed over most of the farm to his children and remained occupying the house, two acres and a barn, but was in partnership with his family. The Commissioners decided that this was not enough for the farmhouse to qualify since on the precedent of *Starke v IRC* [1995] STC 689 (see **4.28**), the house and barn on two acres alone were not an agricultural unit and the adjoining land also occupied in partnership but not owned could not be added to the farmhouse for the purposes of the test. However, it seems to be generally accepted that if the farmer had had a small, undivided percentage in the freehold of adjoining land, he would have qualified and perhaps if he had been a tenant of the adjoining land he would have qualified as well.

What are the tests for the farmhouse?

4.23   In order to maximise the 100% APR claim, every farmhouse should be reviewed with regard to ensuring that it would be deemed to be of a character appropriate to the property. The summary criteria are as follows.

- The primary character test – is the farm essentially a house with some land or an agricultural business incorporating a suitably sized farmhouse? (See **4.31.**)

- The local practice test – is it quite normal for a house of this type and size to be matched with land of this quality of use and size ('character appropriate')? (See **4.36**.)

- The commercial viability or financial support test – is the size and character of the farmhouse in line with the scale of the agricultural operation? To take this further, can the agricultural operation support the owners of the farmhouse?

There must also be the occupation test – the occupation rules apply to a farmhouse as well as to any other land. To reiterate the position, the owner must occupy the property for agricultural purposes for at least two years before the date of the transfer (lifetime or death) or must have owned it for at least seven years prior to the transfer with some person occupying it for agricultural purposes throughout that time.

At this point it is worth looking at the wording of IHTM24036 (see **1.1**).

'A residence must be either a "cottage" (IHTM24034) or "farmhouse" to come within the definition of 'agricultural property' in s 115(2) IHTA.

A number of decisions have impacted on our view of what a – "farmhouse" for the purposes of s 115(2) is. Among the most important are:

CIR v John M Whiteford and Son [1962] TR 157, in which it was stated that "a farmhouse is the place from which the farming operations are conducted".

Rosser v IRC [2003] WTLR 1057, in which the Special Commissioner concluded that "It must be a dwelling for the farmer from which the farm is managed".

Lloyds TSB Banking v Peter Twiddy (Inland Revenue Capital Taxes) [DET/47/2004], in which it is stated "a farmhouse is the chief dwelling-house attached to a farm, the house in which the farmer of the land lives. There is, we think, no dispute about the definition when it is expressed in this way. The question is: who is the farmer of the land for the purpose of the definition in section 115(2)? In our view it is the person who lives in the farmhouse in order to farm the land comprised in the farm and who farms the land on a day to day basis". These statements lead to the conclusion that the occupant of a "farmhouse" must be a farmer. In other words, the person farming the land on a day to day basis. Whether a person is actually a "farmer" of the land will depend on all the facts of a particular case. So, a person with overall control of an agricultural business is not necessarily a "farmer". The key factor is to identify if the occupant of the house has a significant role in the management, or actual operations, of the farming activity being carried out on the land involved. Conversely, it is not necessarily the case that a "farmer" of land is a person whose principal occupation consists of farming the land.

The test is therefore essentially a *functional* one. As the Special Commissioner in *Arnander and others (executors of McKenna, deceased) v Revenue and Customs Commissioners* [2006] STC (SCD) 800 pointed out, "the proper criterion is the purpose of the occupation". Since in that case the day to day farming was undertaken solely by contractors and a land agent was responsible for the management of the land, the deceased's residence was not a "farmhouse".

So, you will need to investigate in detail exactly what the occupier of the residence was doing in the way of agricultural activity in the relevant period prior to the deceased's death, to be able to determine whether their residence could properly be called a "farmhouse". You should be particularly careful in cases where the farmer had retired and let their land on grazing agreements.

However, a temporary cessation of activity (for example, due to ill health) will not, in itself, prevent a residence being a "farmhouse" if, on the precise circumstances of the case, it can properly be considered as *functionally* remaining attached to the farm, along the lines described above. For a house to qualify for agricultural relief as a farmhouse it must also satisfy two conditions. It must

- be agricultural property, (IHTM24030) and

- have been occupied (IHTM24070) for the purposes of agriculture (IHTM24060) for the requisite period.

Both tests can be contentious. The ownership (IHTM24121) test may also need to be satisfied.'

Chapter 24 does help with clarity on the farmhouse.

Financial viability and the economic test

4.24   The question of financial viability is one of great interest in the current climate of very low farming profitability. APR is at risk where there are changes to the business. Examples of this would be as follows.

- When agricultural land is sold, gifted or put to non-agricultural use and the transferor retains the farmhouse to live in.

- Where the owner of the farmhouse lets the land but retains the farmhouse.

Some guidance has been given here by *Rosser* (see **4.29**). It will be necessary to look at economic tests to determine whether the farm can support the respective farming families. This will be very interesting in view of the fall in farming income (and increased income from diversification). Other situations are where there is a large estate where the transferor has an interest in farms in-hand, ie known as home farming, as well as let farms. In this case the farmhouse occupied by the transferor will have to be shown to have a character appropriate to the in-hand farms and not the let farms.

When looking at the primary character appropriate to the farmhouse, use can be made of the Valuation Agency's Practice Notes (Chapter 1B, Practice Note 10) which states 'is the unit primarily a dwelling with some land or is it an agricultural unit incorporating such a dwelling as is appropriate? Is the property as a whole an agricultural unit, ie land albeit amounting to a small hectarage and a few buildings which is not suitable primarily for agricultural use?' This would be important in the case of *Dixon v IRC* [2002] STC (SCD) 53 (see **4.25**).

Other areas that the District Valuer (DV) might look at are how the agricultural unit would be described to the outside world, for example if it were to be marketed by an independent agent. It is also important to consider other comparable farming activities in the local area. It is known that the DV will assess whether the farming operation is commercially viable, ie does it produce sufficient profits to support the occupant of the farmhouse?

In looking at this, they will also look at what income could have been produced on the farm if it had been carried out by a reasonably competent farmer. The DV does take into account the fact that farming profitability can decline due to old age or infirmity, which would often be appropriate to an estate on death.

The Dixon case

4.25   The case of *Dixon v IRC* [2002] STC (SCD) 53 sets the scene for other cases on the farmhouse. Since looking at this case in detail in the first edition of this book, the cases of *Arnander, Antrobus, Higginson* and *Rosser* have appeared before the courts and possibly give far greater direction to the farm tax adviser. *Dixon* is, however, still of importance for smallholdings.

In this case APR was denied on the basis that the cottage was not of a type and character appropriate to agricultural land. In actual fact the opposite was the case. The orchard and garden were of a character appropriate to the cottage, which in truth was a private residence in a rural area and could be regarded by a lay person as being a residential cottage with land.

Although there had been some agricultural activity on the land, it was not enough to encourage HMRC to allow APR in respect of the cottage, garden and orchard on the grounds. The owner of a neighbouring property grew vegetables and fruit commercially and would pick fruit in the orchard of the cottage and sell it with his own fruit. The sale proceeds were about £70 per year. A farmer had at times been allowed to graze sheep on the land and in return his wife carried out general household duties for the deceased. The price received for the fruit had not been included in income tax returns and this is an important point.

The principle appears to be that the purpose of APR was not to provide relief for private residence and gardens but to relieve land and pasture use for agriculture. This decision indicates that it is not simply enough for a person to buy an attractive cottage in the country, keep some form of livestock there and try to avoid IHT on the value of the property. It is essential that the property is first of all truly used for agricultural purposes and then relief should also apply to any cottages and farm buildings occupied with the land, as long as they are of a character appropriate to the property and used as part of the agricultural activity.

The whole question of the validity of APR is something that is causing a large number of agricultural practitioners sleepless nights. At one end of the scale there are some genuine farming activities, which, if looked at in the cold light of day by a harsh Tax Inspector, might result in some loss of APR on certain parts of the asset. At the other end of the scale there are tax practitioners who are actively encouraging anybody who lives in anything like a rural or semi-rural location, with some degree of land, to try and establish some form of business, often of an agricultural nature, on this land, so as to become eligible for not only APR for IHT but also entrepreneurs' relief for CGT.

The case does give practitioners some practical tax-planning points. First, if there is income it should be recorded on the tax return; and, second, if such a valuable claim as APR is to be made it is essential to ensure that the case to be put to HMRC is more valid and the conditions are met to a far greater extent. Many practitioners are aware of clients who are virtually inventing agricultural activities around some small plot of land in the hope of obtaining APR. In the Home Counties and in areas close to them, a small cottage with a small parcel of land can easily be valued at a figure in excess of £1 million. APR can be substantial, as would BPR, on any development value and the benefits of establishing a trading activity for the required period of time is of the utmost importance.

Farm business tenancies (FBT)

4.26   In principle if all the farmland is farmed by an FBT, APR on the farmhouse will be denied. The tax position of FBTs is looked at in more detail in Chapter 11. The period of business activity necessary to obtain APR is two years. In order to claim APR for an FBT the period of ownership is seven years. Therefore, anybody moving to the country with a view to obtaining IHT relief on a large amount of their assets must look carefully at the structure on which they trade.

Dixon v IRC [2002] STC (SCD) 53 shows the need to have the correct conditions in place if a landowner wants to take the farming activity further. With regard to the use of an FBT, the landowner must also be aware of the fact that the FBT is a much slower route to obtaining APR, ie seven years instead of two. A serious planning point with regard to this relief is always to look at the farming activity with a view to the landowner himself farming or using contract or share-farming agreements (see Chapter 11) for the first two years, and *then* taking the route of (the sometimes easier) FBT once the conditions for APR have been established.

It must also be noted that whilst an FBT will allow the farmer APR on the land, generally the asset does not qualify for BPR (see **11.19**) plus business reliefs available in respect of CGT, eg roll-over relief, entrepreneurs' relief, and likewise where there has been no trading activity as such, just an FBT, the APR will only apply to the land and not to the farmhouse in the majority of cases.

Structure of farming

4.27   In a changing farming climate it is essential that practitioners review the structure of the farming activity (see Chapter 11), the tax computation, the commerciality and viability of the operation and assess how potential reliefs for IHT and CGT could be reduced by the current lack of commerciality and farming activities. At the time of writing the first edition, many landowning clients automatically assumed that the asset of their farmhouse would escape IHT and it was essential for the practitioner not only to make sure that the necessary conditions are in place, where possible, but also to warn the client of the potential loss of relief. At the time of writing this third edition, it appears that most farmers are aware of the situation in broad terms but not the detail.

Other areas of concern include a restriction to the provision concerning BPR where relief is restricted to 50% (as opposed to 100%) where the assets are held by an individual and used in the company or partnership of which he is a member. This is explained in some detail in Chapter 13. In some partnerships farmhouses are kept out of the main partnership accounts as the partners feel happier with the ownership of this asset kept in their private names, this can put APR at risk.

With the move towards diversification and more emphasis being placed on BPR as opposed to APR, this could become a very important factor and it is essential for every farming enterprise to review in what business structure the farmhouse should be held.

The Starke case

4.28   This leads on to the tax case of *Starke v IRC* [1995] STC 689. In this instance the claim was for a six-bedroom farmhouse and an assortment of outbuildings standing in a 2.5 acre site – essentially a medium-sized farm which carried on mixed farming. It had several small areas of enclosed land. The appellant tried to use the Interpretation Act 1978 to argue that the farmhouse was included in the interpretation of 'land', as this would include buildings and other structures unless there was a challenge. The rest of the land was mainly owned by a farming company, and it is the fact that the land and farmhouse were in different ownership that demanded careful consideration. This case turned on the character-appropriate position of the farm buildings. The Court of Appeal dismissed the appeal by the executors and refused APR on the farmhouse.

It is not only where the land is owned by a company that *Starke v IRC* [1995] STC 689 could apply. It is also important to look at trusts. It can be argued that for as long as there is substantial unity of ownership between the farmhouse and the land that is farmed, APR can still be claimed on the farmhouse. However, if the farmhouse is placed into a trust it may, once it is within the trust, cease to be of a character appropriate in the context of the ownership. It is mainly with the position concerning a discretionary trust where the most risk lies. If there is an interest in possession trust, the deeming provisions of IHTA 1984 s 49 might protect the position.

The moral in *Starke* is if the farming family give away farmland, whether it is to the next generation, a trust or a limited company, it is important to consider the effect on the APR claim on the farmhouse and what effect 'cutting off' the ownership of the land and buildings from the farmhouse can have.

When looking at the claim for APR, the tax planner must consider situations where there are very large and valuable farmhouses that are not actually being fully occupied. There are cases where parts of farmhouses are being left to 'moulder' and it is difficult to argue that parts of these buildings are occupied for any purpose, agricultural or otherwise. In these instances, it could be argued that APR should be restricted to that part of the building actually being occupied. A tax-planning approach would be to consider a use that might qualify for APR (or even BPR). Examples might include the housing of harvest workers, the housing of farm workers and the letting of the cottage that is made available, or storage. The farmer can, at least, consider the alternatives.

The Rosser case

4.29   In *Rosser v IRC* [2003] STC (SCD) 311 the taxpayer, Mrs Rosser (as executor) lost her claim for APR on the house, but won her claim on the barn. Mrs Rosser's parents had in 1989 given to her 39 out of 41 acres on the farm. Mr and Mrs Rosser farmed both the 39 and the two acres retained by her parents. In 1996 the parents ended their farming partnership and the house thereafter became used for minimal agricultural purposes only. However, they retained a barn in use for agricultural purposes in connection with the two acres of land. The father's death was followed, within a few weeks, by the death of the mother in 2001. The Special Commissioner held that, to secure relief, the house and the barn had to be 'of a character appropriate' to the two and not the 41 acres on the farm (in other words, not applying the *obiter dictum* of Morritt LJ in the *Starke* case, see **4.28**). The house had in 1996 ceased to be a farmhouse and had become a retirement home (although in any event it would, if a farmhouse, not have been of a character appropriate to the two acres). However, the barn was character-appropriate and attracted relief on the basis of satisfaction of the seven-year ownership test in IHTA 1984 s 117.

It could be argued that the barn still owned by Mr and Mrs Rosser senior had been let to Mr and Mrs Rosser junior for more than seven years (date of transfer 1989, date of death 2001), and had been effectively let on FBT and qualified for IHT.

The Higginson case

4.30   On 17 October 2003, the decisions of the Special Commissioner in two substantive cases were issued. In the first case, *Higginson's Executors v IRC* [2002] STC (SCD) 483, a house called Ballyward Lodge was set in an estate in Northern Ireland of 134 acres (of which 63 acres was agricultural land, mostly grassland, with three acres of gardens and 68 acres of woodland and wetland surrounding a lake). Ballyward House was described as 'not the style of house a typical farmer would live' in. The deceased had farmed the estate as a mixed farm until 1985, though from 1985 until his death in 2000 he let the farmland on 'conacre' terms, under which he continued to be the occupier. While the deceased's nephew considered carrying on the farming business himself, he concluded that the profitability would be marginal at best and sold the estate for £1.15 million in 2001. The issue was whether Ballyward Lodge was 'agricultural property' (see **1.6**); the Special Commissioner decided it was not. He said that the definition of 'agricultural property' was intended to give relief only to a unit that was an agricultural unit, *viz* that the land must predominate, which in this case it did not. He found it significant that the estate was sold soon after death. He concluded that: as a farm the estate would represent 'an appalling investment in terms of yield'; within the unit that was the estate, it was Ballyward Lodge which predominated, and therefore Ballyward Lodge was not a 'farmhouse' within the definition of 'agricultural property'. He went on to say (although this is clearly at odds with current Valuation Office practice) that:

> 'the notional restrictive covenant (in IHTA 1984 s 115(3)) would have much less of a depreciatory effect in a case where the property has a greater value than ordinary not because of development potential but rather because of what I might call 'vanity value' on account of its site, style or the like.'

The Antrobus cases (1 and 2)

4.31   These cases have now become written into farming 'folklore' as *Antrobus 1* and *2*. So what are the facts?

In the detail of the first case, *Lloyds TSB (personal representative of Antrobus, deceased) v IRC* [2002] STC (SCD) 468), the estate comprised Cookhill Priory and 126 acres of freehold land and 6.54 acres of let land (all of which was agricultural land or pasture). The house itself was of considerable historic interest (for which it was listed Grade 2) dating back to Tudor times, but with Georgian (and mock Georgian) additions. When Miss Antrobus died in 2001, the priory was in a very poor state of repair and decoration. It is clear that she had been a farmer, both arable and stock, in every sense of the word, for nearly 60 years.

An expert witness described the property as a working farm and produced evidence of 27 comparable buildings in the locality of Western/Middle England to provide evidence of the type of character appropriate to farmhouses occupied with agricultural land of an area not dissimilar to the property at issue. HMRC agreed that Cookhill Priory was a farmhouse, but argued that it was not 'of a character appropriate' to agricultural land or pasture owned by Miss Antrobus; while 'not a rich man's considerable residence' and although a farmhouse, it had a dual purpose as having become the dwelling of a prosperous person and was surrounded by parkland, ie it had become a family home of some distinction. Further, HMRC argued that, on financial or economic tests, the holding was not an economic holding (losses having been made from 1995 to 2001).

In deciding for the taxpayer, the Special Commission said the character-appropriate test could be judged on the basis of five principles (see **4.36**).

The Lands Tribunal decision on *Antrobus 2 (Lloyds TSB Banking (Personal Representative of Antrobus Deceased) v CIR DET/47/2004)* suggested a narrowing of the interpretation of who is a farmer and when a house is a farmhouse for the purposes of IHT. The Lands Tribunal's view was that unless a house was lived in by a farmer who farmed the land on a day-to-day basis, the house should not be regarded as a farmhouse and would therefore be ineligible for IHT relief. This raised concerns that contract-farming agreements as well as some other farming structures might have the effect of preventing IHT relief on the farmer's house.

Antrobus 2 established APR is restricted to the agricultural value of the agricultural property: even if the house does not count, there may be a hefty discount to its market value for calculating the relief. In *Antrobus 2*, this was 30%. In practical situations at the time of writing the tax practitioner is receiving 'offers' from HMRC (CTO) as to what a reasonable percentage should be, ie 60% to 70% of the value (at discounts of 40% to 30%).

Agricultural value (AV)

4.32   It is important to note that the above principle of *Antrobus 2* was that APR is given only on the agricultural value of a farmhouse, ie the value on the assumption that the property is not capable of use other than as a farmhouse. The agricultural value is the value of the farmhouse, the asset, if subject to a perpetual covenant prohibiting its use otherwise than as an agricultural property. AV is set out in IHTA 1984 s 115(3). (See **13.2**.)

It has been suggested that a perpetual agricultural covenant on a farmhouse might reduce its value considerably. Many leading land agents use the figure of one-third reduction, and as mentioned above 30% to 40% is suggested. The difference between full market value and agricultural value will be of particular relevance in areas such as the Home Counties. It is also important to look at the position where there is more than one farmhouse, ie where separate farmhouses are occupied by different members of the farming family in partnership. Agricultural value is a concept not restricted to farmhouses but all agricultural land, buildings and cottages.

WORKING FARMER PROVISIONS

4.33   When trying to look at farmhouses and their eligibility for APR it could be useful to consider the concept of the working farmer provisions. These used to have much greater importance and are therefore not discussed in great detail in this book. However, they do give a guide to whether the farmhouse is seen to be of a character appropriate to the working farmer test. This related to working farmer relief. Before 10 March 1981 working farmers had the benefit of two advantages where they let their land before 10 March 1981. First, that the value on which it could be applied was lower; and, second, because the land was let and the relief was partly available on agricultural property.

It is essential that the practitioner is familiar with working farmer relief in looking at how the DV could apply this in such matters as APR under today's rules. Some help was gained from the former FA 1975 s 8, which defined the main, but not exclusive, test of 'wholly or mainly engaged' by providing that where at least three-quarters of the relevant income of the transferor was derived directly from his engagement in agriculture in the UK then the condition for relief was taken as being satisfied. The relevant income is the aggregate of income in any five of the last seven years of assessment immediately preceding the transfer, including unearned income but excluding income from a pension, superannuation, other allowances, deferred pay or compensation for loss of office. For this purpose, the rules as to aggregation of a wife's income, which were enforced in 1991, are to be disregarded.

Where a transferor fails the 75% test he might still show by other means, such as time spent on other sources of income, that he was a working farmer. In certain situations a farming widow or widower enjoys the benefit of transferred years to help satisfy the seven-year test.

There are those who argue that a farming family who have farmed for a large number of years and meet the type of conditions required in the working farmer relief are far more likely to succeed in a claim for APR on a farmhouse than someone who has other income outside of the farm and has acquired the property relatively recently. Will working farmer provisions return?

FARMHOUSE HELD IN A LIMITED COMPANY

4.34   This is dealt with at **8.3** on incorporation.

The tax questions raised focus on both CGT and IHT. There is the risk of the loss of PRR (see **4.4** to **4.12**) on the farmhouse owned by the limited company as opposed to the individual farmer. The IHT problem was highlighted by the case of *Starke v IRC* [1995] STC 689, CA (see **8.3**). There is also the concern over the benefit in kind for a farming director living in the farmhouse (see **8.1**).

DEATH IN A HOSPITAL OR NURSING HOME

4.35   The IHT reliefs in respect of the farmhouse could be at risk where the farmer dies in a location away from home. A farmer may not be in physical occupation of the farmhouse at his death: he may die in a hospital or a nursing home. However, the CTO are known to grant relief in cases where the farmer had every expectation of returning to the farmhouse had he not died, and have been known to give relief in cases of absence of up to two years (see **4.23**). The case of *Atkinson* (see **4.42**) has now extended that.

There are some tax-planning alternatives to this which do not involve giving the farmhouse away. In what circumstances will the occupation test for APR purposes under IHTA 1984 s 117 (see **13.4**) be satisfied where a farmer fell ill? It is noted that s 117 applies a test of occupation that includes legal rather than actual occupation. Thus, the intention of the farmer was relevant. It would also be relevant if someone else had been allowed (even temporarily) to occupy the house (for other than the management and direction of the farming operations conducted). It is widely suggested that, if the circumstances allow, the planner could advise family members to act as agents of the farmer in continuing to run the business from the farmhouse on his behalf; then IHTA 1984 s 117 could be satisfied. Every case will have to be carefully reviewed.

It is noted that in the case of *Arnander* (see **4.39**), the obituary for Mr McKenna did not mention the fact that he was a farmer. It would be cynical to suggest that upon the death of a farmer, it is essential to ensure that the obituary is tax efficient!

PROTECTING THE 'CHARACTER APPROPRIATE'

4.36   The tax cases of *Antrobus* (see **4.31**), *Higginson* (see **4.30**) and *Rosser* (see **4.29**) have given some direction as to 'character appropriate'. In considering whether a particular farmhouse is of a character appropriate to a given tract of agricultural land, it is important to address the following issues.

●   Ensure that the proper identification has been made of the farmhouse, together with the land occupied with it (ie as garden or grounds). Similarly identify the qualifying property to which the farmhouse will be 'appropriate'.

●   Consider the primary character of the farmhouse. In the Valuation Agency's Practice Notes (Chapter 1B, Practice Note 10), this is formulated: 'Is the unit primarily a dwelling with some land or is it an agricultural unit incorporating such a dwelling as is appropriate? Is the property as a whole an agricultural unit, ie some land, albeit amounting to a small hectarage, and a few buildings, but which is not suitable primarily for agricultural use?' Chapter 24 of HMRC's Inheritance Tax Manual also gives guidance (**4.23**).

The main questions to be asked when considering the appropriate character test for a farmhouse (see **4.31**) include the following.

●   Is the house appropriate with regard to size, content and layout to the land being farmed?

●   Is the house proportionate in size and nature to the requirements of the farming activity?

●   Does it satisfy the 'elephant test' – hard to describe but you know one when you see one?

●   Would a reasonably educated rural layman regard the property as a house with land or as a farm?

●   How long has the house been associated with the agricultural land and has there been a history of agricultural production?

Where there is genuine agricultural use of a farmhouse that fails to qualify for APR because of the 'character appropriate' requirement, a measure of BPR may be available (see **4.22**), but this has yet to be proved in the courts.

THE PARTNERSHIP – SEVERAL FARMHOUSES

4.37   As set out in the early part of the chapter, a number of farmhouse cases have been taken to the Special Commissioners for further clarification on the statutory test. Different problems arise where it is contended that there is more than one farmhouse qualifying for APR. That might be so where separate farmhouses were occupied by separate members of the farming family in partnership. In these circumstances, the test seems to be economic: whether the profitability of the farm was of such by nature as to support the livelihood of the respective farming families occupying the farmhouses, for which relief is claimed.

The reservation of the 'agricultural' value of a farmhouse, ie based on the assumption that the property is incapable of use other than as a farmhouse (IHTA 1984 s 115(3)), will apply to a number of farmhouses. A careful review of APR eligibility is suggested for farms with more than one farmhouse.

The points raised in **4.36** apply particularly where there are a number of farmhouses.

PROTECTING AGAINST THE DANGER AREAS OF AN APR CLAIM

4.38   It is important, therefore, to summarise for tax planners the points which could give rise to problems on the claim for APR on a farmhouse. They are as follows:

- land not of a character appropriate to the house, eg very large house, small unit (eg *Higginson* (see **4.30**));

- no history of commerciality (eg *Dixon v IRC* [2002] STC (SCD) 53 (see **4.25**));

- land used for diversification purposes jeopardising APR/BPR claim on farmhouse;

- farmhouse held outside of farming partnership or limited company (eg *Starke* and *Rosser* – see **4.28** and **4.29**);

- farmhouse held within limited company with question as to qualification in total for BPR (see **8.3**);

- more than one farmhouse on farming unit – character-appropriate review required (see **4.37**);

- hobby farming (see Chapter 12);

- land let for grazing but with the incorrect criteria in place (see **11.3**);

- agricultural value – what will this value be (see **4.32**); and

- *Antrobus* conditions – are they achieved (see **4.31** and **4.36**)?

- *Arnander* – look at strength of the day-to-day farming arrangements (**4.39** and **4.40**);

- *Arnander* – last two years – the two-year rule (see **5.49**); and

- farm business tenancy (see **4.26**).

If it is possible to show that a commercial farmer would buy a particular farm, this will be useful evidence to rebut any suggestion that relief be disallowed on the amount by which market value exceeds agricultural value. In *Antrobus 2* a 30% discount was applied and less discount could be achieved on this argument.

ARNANDER (MCKENNA) – ANOTHER FARMHOUSE CASE

4.39   In *Arnander and others* (*Executors of McKenna deceased*) *v HMRC* SpC 565 23 October 2006 (known as *Arnander*), the question of the land being farmed on a day-to-day basis was raised.

Mr and Mrs McKenna owned a country estate in Cornwall consisting of their residence, the main house with six acres of gardens and domestic outbuildings (the house) and 187 acres of land, most of which was farmland. In 1984, Mr and Mrs McKenna decided to enter into contract-farming arrangements for arable farming. Their agent had approximately five meetings a year with McKenna, sometimes informally, to discuss farm matters either by telephone or in the house. McKenna personally prepared and kept meticulous documents and records for the arrangements and paid income tax under Schedule D Case I (old terminology). In 2003, Mr and Mrs McKenna died within five months of each other. In 2004 the estate was sold, as a residential property, for £3,050,000.

Although HMRC allowed APR in respect of 110 acres of land and some farm outbuildings (see **5.50**), they issued notices of determination denying relief on the house, on the grounds that it was not an interest in agricultural property within the meaning of s 115 IHTA 1984. Applying the law to the facts, Dr Brice found that the house was not the main dwelling from which the agricultural operations over the land were conducted and managed. The day-to-day management and all acts of farm husbandry over the land were solely the responsibility of the contractors who were managed by the agent. The engagement of an agent to manage the land meant that the use of the house for farming matters was very much reduced. The case raises questions over the strength of the contract-farming arrangements (CFAs) (see Chapter 11).

If the farmer of the land was the person who farmed it on a day-to-day basis rather than the person who was in overall control of the agricultural business conducted on the land, it followed that McKenna was not the farmer. He did not occupy the house with the purpose of undertaking day-to-day farming activities. It followed that the house (with its gardens and domestic outbuildings) was not a farmhouse within the meaning of IHTA 1984 s 115(2).

ARNANDER (MCKENNA) – WAS ROSTEAGUE HOUSE A FARMHOUSE (AGRICULTURAL PROPERTY)?

4.40   The Lands Tribunal's definitions of both a farmhouse and a farmer in *Antrobus 2* were considered. The Special Commissioner, although she was at pains to emphasise that each case should be decided on its own facts, felt that the definition of a farmer was helpful. Applying that definition, the Special Commissioner considered that Rosteague House was not a farmhouse because it was 'not the main dwelling from which the agricultural operations over the land were conducted and managed. The day-to-day management and all acts of farm husbandry over the land were solely the responsibility of the contractors and the management of the contractors was carried out by Mr Fletcher (The Agent)'.

The third issue of the appeal was whether the McKennas were in occupation of the farmhouse for the purposes of agriculture for the two years leading to their respective deaths.

Although this matter possibly became meaningless after Dr Brice's decision that the house was not agricultural property, the executors continued their argument. Dr Brice also desired to cover this point in case the executors appealed. The executors contended that the McKennas had been in occupation of the house for agricultural purposes for the two years leading to their deaths. The fact that Lady Cecelia was not physically present in the last few months of her life did not mean the farmhouse was not occupied by her for agricultural purposes as she continued the farming business through the farm contractor; she remained in rateable occupation of the house; and Rosteague House remained fully furnished and was maintained by employees and ready for use by Lady Cecelia at all times. Dr Brice stated 'even if I had concluded that Rosteague House was a farmhouse of a character appropriate to the property it is clear that neither Mr McKenna nor Lady Cecelia were able to engage in farming matters throughout the period of two years ending with the relevant dates of death'.

This statement by Dr Brice is a real cause for concern, especially for elderly clients in poor health. It is in contrast to the approach described in *Antrobus 2* where the Lands Tribunal stated, 'we do not think that a farmhouse would automatically cease to be a farmhouse for the purposes of s 115(2) if, for instance, the farmer who had lived there for many years retired but continued to live in the house or if he died and his widow continued to live there, and the same would go for a cottage and a farm worker. However, it is possible that there could be a point at which, because of the length of time that had elapsed since a retirement or death, the house could no longer be considered to be a farmhouse or cottage.'

Dr Brice's statement appears therefore to reflect a much stricter approach. However, it remains to be seen whether HMRC will take this point and pursue it on a general basis. In *Arnander*, HMRC took a much broader view of matters and looked at the lifestyle of the deceased and also the nature of the property after death.

Dr Brice considered:

- The time spent by the McKennas on farming matters. She asked for details of books that had been kept and reviewed and calculated how much time had been spent by the McKennas on farm business.

- How the property was marketed and presented after death.

- Mr McKenna's obituary which made no mention of him being a farmer.

WAS ROSTEAGUE HOUSE OF A 'CHARACTER APPROPRIATE'?

4.41   Even if Rosteague House had qualified as a farmhouse, applying the five tests from *Antrobus 1*, the Special Commissioner determined that it was not of a 'character appropriate'. Amongst other things, she considered the house 'a rich man's considerable residence' having five reception rooms, seven bedrooms and staff quarters: it was described in the sale particulars following the McKenna's deaths as a 'substantial Manor House' which may have been helpful in marketing terms but was clearly unfortunate in the context of APR; also the farm buildings were not visible from the house.

The estate marketed Rosteague House as a residential property for the asking price of £3,050,000. It was never marketed as a farm with farmhouse. Despite the property being in a poor state of repair, the value of the house still constituted the majority of the asking price, almost 80% of the whole. Rosteague House was described in the sale particulars as 'an historic and substantial Manor House, listed Grade II' and as 'an outstanding manor house and private estate'.

Its accommodation was described as 'long hall, dining room, library, study, drawing room, flower room, main foyer and stairs, cloakroom, rear hall, kitchen, staff sitting room, back kitchen, seven bedrooms, three bathrooms, sewing room, laundry room, staff flat, detached lodge, cottage, music room, garage, gardens, range of outbuildings'.

The executors therefore, did not try to sell Rosteague House and its accompanying land as a farm. This is in contrast to the executors in *Antrobus* where Cookhill Priory was marketed as a farm with the option of buying the property together with some land and an extra lot of land or purchasing the whole farm/estate. HMRC noted this point and used this as further evidence that this was not a farmhouse and the McKennas were not farming. It is unclear how much influence this would have had on the decision, but it is a warning to professionals to make sure any property is marketed as a farm if APR is being claimed.

The clear fact is that we need greater clarity on the farmhouse issue.

ATKINSON – AGRICULTURAL PURPOSE MAINTAINED

4.42   *Atkinson and another (executors of Atkinson deceased)* TC 420. The farmer, Mr Atkinson, lived in a bungalow on farmland which he owned and let on an agricultural tenancy to a family farming partnership. In 2002, Mr Atkinson fell ill and went to live in a care home. Mr Atkinson died in 2006.

While Mr Atkinson was in the care home, the bungalow was unoccupied, although his belongings remained there. During the period of Mr Atkinson's illness he, in his capacity as a farmer, continued to be involved in the decision-making relating to the farm.

On Mr Atkinson's death, the executors of his will claimed APR in respect of the bungalow. HMRC refused the claim saying that the property had not been occupied by the deceased throughout the previous seven years, nor had it been used for agricultural purposes while he was in the care home.

The executors appealed against the HMRC decision.

The First-tier Tribunal set out that while the agricultural property had to be used to accommodate the person engaged in agricultural activities for the seven-year period, the legislation did not state that this had to be continuous. In this instance, the deceased had continued to play a part in farming matters, even while living in the care home, and occasionally visited the bungalow. The bungalow was used to accommodate the reducing needs of the senior partner, so APR was due on the bungalow.

The taxpayers' appeal was allowed.

4.43   Although the facts of *Arnander* are somewhat unusual it provides further evidence of the way that the law is developing on this issue (and if nothing else serves as a reminder that contracting agreements should be properly drawn up and should not look like tenancy agreements, see Chapter 11). It appears that there will be further cases going through the Tribunal and no doubt the position will become clearer as they do so.

It is fair to say that the tax planner has a multitude of helpful tips and advice from case law to call upon to assist their farming and diversifying clients with either a positive action plan or a positive warning. As Dr Brice said, each case has to be dealt with on the specific facts.

Chapter 5

Protecting the farm's assets

Julie Butler

- **The risk of only 50% IHT relief**
  Where farm assets are used in the business but held outside the business, the inheritance tax (IHT) relief can be restricted to 50% instead of 100%.

- **Farm assets not occupied for an agricultural or business use**
  These valuable assets can be at risk from the loss of capital gains tax (CGT) and IHT relief, and the tax position must be protected. Consideration is given to the two-year rule and the seven-year rule.

- **The bold step of gifting assets now**
  In order to maximise the current favourable tax reliefs, there are strong arguments for making gifts now. This must not be undertaken lightly and consideration should be given to avoiding gifts with possible reservation of benefit together with 'failed PETs' . Accurate valuations are an important issue when reviewing tax planning surrounding potential lifetime gifts and the future position on death.

- **Protecting and managing assets**
  There are a multitude of pitfalls and opportunities for the tax planner and landowner, such as where the cash deposits and liabilities are allocated and how best to use related property. With a move from eligibility for agricultural property relief (APR) to eligibility to business property relief (BPR), great emphasis must be placed on understanding the interaction and ensuring the farm is protected from potential loss of tax reliefs. A key area here is cash-flow management. Cash mountains for IHT and the allocation of borrowing to maximise the dual goals of income tax and IHT relief is considered in some depth. BPR claims have been the subject of a number of recent tax cases held in the courts, eg *Balfour, Dance* and *McCall.*

- **Pre-owned assets**
  The FA 2004 imposed a new charge to tax on 'pre-owned assets' from 2005–06 onwards. An election to be outside the charge had to be made by 31 January 2007, but then the asset will be in the donor's estate for inheritance tax purposes. This seems to be an unprecedented attempt by HMRC to introduce an income tax charge to make up for the deficiencies of the IHT legislation.

- **Farmers must keep trading**
  'Business is king', the business reliefs, especially BPR, relate to, yes, 'a business'! Farmers must keep trading and protect the relief. There must be proof of commerciality and business plans – the need for 'active husbandry'.

- **Hope value**
  Hope or 'special' value has to be protected from HMRC's attempts to deny IHT reliefs. Be aware and protect.

INTRODUCTION

5.1   Having looked at the protection of the farmhouse at length (in Chapter 4), let us now look at the protection of other farm assets to ensure maximum tax relief under the inheritance tax (IHT) rules. Many of the points in this chapter are contained in Chapter 13 in more detail, but this chapter is meant to be an *aide-memoire* for IHT problems that can befall farmers – an introduction to the more complex and detailed chapters that lie ahead, especially those farmers embracing diversification. The basic IHT rates, exemptions and reliefs are dealt with in Chapter 18 on wills.

Two very useful 'tools' to protect farm assets are the well-drafted will and trust deeds. These are dealt with in Chapter 18 and Chapter 17 respectively. Farm assets must also be protected from problems such as divorce, and this subject receives serious review in Chapter 16. It is relevant in the current climate to look at how assets can be protected through financial services.

It is considered that the way forward is a 'tax audit' to prepare to deal with the HMRC scrutiny.

- Analyse the farm or estate within its current structure and business management arrangements, ie what assets qualify for APR and what qualify for BPR.

- Produce a report as to the expected taxation outcome in the event of an immediate death of various of the parties involved, or a potential sale if appropriate.

- Make suggestions and give reasons for changes intended to maximise the potential farm assets to qualify for APR or, where appropriate, BPR.

- Give pointers for a review of your business to balance the dangers of ultimate tax pitfalls against the immediate needs of the business and family.

- Woodlands must be reported in detail as the tax treatment is complex.

The report should include a full history with maps, areas of potential development, base costs for CGT, highlighting any areas that might be used for recreational purposes, eg shooting, private home etc. Any areas that do come into the IHT definition of agriculture should be noted.

It is pure speculation, but APR s 115 et seq is currently on a list of over 1,000 reliefs which are under review by OTS (Office of Tax Simplification).

BUSINESS PROPERTY RELIEF (BPR) – 50% RELIEF IS NOT ENOUGH

5.2   When looking at farming tax planning and deciding who should own what and where, it is necessary to see how 100% relief can be maintained and not be reduced to 50% relief. This is dealt with in more detail in Chapter 13 on the interaction of APR and BPR, but a simple summary is set out below.

IHT relief of 100% is available (subject to the correct conditions being met) in respect of a business carried on by a sole trader, a partnership interest and any unquoted shares in a company. IHT relief of 50% is available in respect of land, buildings, machinery or plant owned by an individual and used by a company which he controls, or by a partnership of which he is a partner, or by a quoted company of which he controls shares.

The property must have been owned by the transferor throughout the two-year period prior to transfer, or it must have replaced other relevant business property and the combined period of ownership must amount to two out of the five years prior to the transfer. In respect of replacement business property, BPR is given only on the lower of the value of the original property or replacement property (see **5.18**, **13.13** and **13.17–13.24** where this is discussed in more detail). Below are examples of potential structures that could achieve 100% relief if the correct conditions are in place.

- sole trader business;
- partnership interest;
- shares in an unquoted company;
- business assets held in trust (transferred with the company).

The following are examples of where relief could be restricted to 50%.

- land, buildings, machinery or plant owned by an individual used by a company he controls or by a partnership in which he is a member;
- business assets held in trust (not transferred with business);
- controlling holding of shares in a quoted company.

Is the landowner aware that by holding assets outside of the partnership or company he is jeopardising 100% relief? It could be that there are strong personal, family or control factors that dictate the ownership status. Has the client been warned of the problem? The inheritance tax position on divorcing couples is set out in Chapter 16.

PARTNERSHIP LAND CAPITAL ACCOUNT

5.3   As set out above, BPR has a potential for 100% relief for assets that are part of the business but only 50% for assets used in a business, ie assets not on the balance sheet (see **5.2**). In recent years a lot of time has been spent bringing assets onto the balance sheet in order to ensure the 100% relief. There are prima facie capital gains tax problems in bringing land formerly owned by an individual onto a partnership balance sheet as well as stamp duty land tax (SDLT). However, it is accepted by HMRC that, if capital gains or losses on the land brought into the partnership accrue to the introducer, the transfer of value will not be treated as a disposal for capital gains tax purposes. Some firms of accountants prefer to bring into a partnership a 'land capital account', so that the ownership of the land for capital gains tax purposes is on a balance sheet but remains with the introducer. It is, however, a trading asset available for creditors within the partnership but is entitled to BPR.

EXCEPTED ASSETS FOR BPR – HOW CAN THIS BE AVOIDED?

5.4   For practical tax-planning purposes it is essential that a claim for IHT relief does not fail due to certain farming assets being classified as excepted (IHTA 1984 s 112).

HMRC CTO (Capital Taxes Office) is likely to review the balance sheet for assets which can be excluded from BPR because they are caught under s 112 which states:

'In determining for the purposes of this chapter what part of the value transferred by a transfer of value is attributed to the value of any relevant business property so much of the last mentioned value as is attributed to any excepted assets within the meaning of subsection (2) below shall be left out of account.

An asset is an excepted asset in relation to any relevant business property if it was neither:

(a)   used wholly or mainly for the purposes of the business concerned throughout the whole or last two years of the relevant period defined in subsection (5) below, nor

(b)   required at the time of the transfer for future use for those purposes.'

Historic examples of assets caught under s 112 are 'cash mountains' and investment assets which do not appear to have a 'future use' in the business. The key to protection are business minutes showing future use and contemporaneous evidence that such assets will not fail to be eligible for relief due to the provisions of s 112.

For the purposes of calculating BPR, the value of the relevant business property should exclude excepted assets, which are those:

●   which have not been used wholly or mainly for business purposes throughout the two years preceding the transfer (or since acquisition if acquired within the two-year period); and

●   are not required for future use by the business.

The purpose of the rules is to prevent abuses by denying relief to what are essentially non-business assets. This is achieved by isolating those assets which, at the time of the transfer, either were not used in the business or had been inadequately or too briefly used, and those not actually required for future use in the business, eg surplus cash balances (*Barclays Bank Trust Co v IRC* [1998] STC (SCD) 125). With the farming crisis it is possible that assets can become 'too briefly' used. The tax planner must focus on the words 'inadequately' or 'too briefly used': it is important not to leave assets redundant whilst alternative farming or diversification activities are looked at.

It is permissible for a business asset to replace another business asset provided that both were used for periods comprising at least two years within the five immediately before the transfer.

Where only part of any land or building is used exclusively for business purposes, HMRC will try to argue that part will be treated as a separate asset qualifying for relief with the other non-qualifying part treated as an excepted asset (IHTA 1984 s 112(4)). This can provide assistance for BPR claims where a room in the farmhouse is used exclusively for office purposes, as it would not qualify for APR. It may be possible to argue for BPR for other rooms where there is substantial and genuine business use (eg the kitchen) (see Chapter 4). However, excepted assets include assets used wholly or mainly for personal benefit (IHTA 1984 s 112(6)).

FARM COTTAGES – MAXIMISING THE RATE OF IHT RELIEF

5.5   The tax planner must try to maximise the IHT relief for all farm cottages. We look here at cottages occupied by farm workers and retired farm workers.

Relief of 100% APR will be available (provided the two-year occupation/ seven-year ownership conditions have been satisfied) if:

●   the occupation began on or after 1 September 1995; or

●   the tenancy began before 10 March 1981 and the 'working farmer' tests are satisfied.

Relief may therefore be available in the case of an occupier with no protected service tenancy, perhaps a partner or an occupier with the benefit of an assured agricultural tenancy, so, for example, a farm worker or an occupier who has an assured shorthold tenancy will normally be regarded as occupying the cottage for agricultural purposes.

It is therefore imperative that every farmer and landowner reviews all cottages in their ownership to ensure that they qualify in the first instance for 100% APR and that this is not restricted to a 50% claim. APR at 50% applies where the landowner does not have the right to vacant possession of a farm cottage occupied by an employee with protection under the Rent (Agriculture) Act 1976 or the Housing Act 1988 because the landowner cannot grant 'unimpeded physical enjoyment' of a cottage so occupied. Where farm cottages have protected rights that have existed since before 1 September 1995 then the 50% restriction is applied (see **5.2** and **13.15**). Where a claim for APR fails, a claim for BPR may be eligible under the provisions of *Farmer (Farmer's Executors) v IRC* [1999] STC (SCD) 321. This and *Balfour* are looked at in detail in Chapter 13 (see **13.50–13.52**).

The difficulty arises in relation to cottages first occupied after 10 March 1981, ie without the protection of the old working farmer relief and before 1 September 1995 (when the new rules began to operate). In these cases the nature of the occupation determined the rate of relief. Where there is an unprotected service tenancy or an assured shorthold tenancy, 100% relief is available. Where there is an assured agricultural occupation, whether by a farm worker or by a retired farm worker or by a surviving spouse of a farm worker, the rate is 50% only.

The provision in IHTA 1984 s 115(2) relating to farm cottages is extended by ESC F16. That concession provides that, on a transfer of agricultural property, which includes a cottage occupied by a retired farm employee, or by the widow or widower of such an employee, the condition as to the occupation for agricultural purposes is regarded as satisfied with respect to the cottage if one of two conditions is satisfied, namely:

- the occupier is a statutorily-protected tenant (eg under Housing Act 1988, Rent (Agriculture) Act 1976 or similar legislation in Northern Ireland or Scotland); or

- the occupation is under a lease granted to the farm employee for his or her life and the life of any surviving spouse as part of the contract of employment of the employee. That contract of employment must be by the landlord for agricultural purposes.

The first of these situations arises when someone employed in agriculture for the previous two years has occupied a dwelling house provided by the employer. Depending on the date when the tenancy licence or occupancy began, that employee's right of occupation is normally protected under the 1976 Act or is protected as an assured agricultural occupancy under the 1988 Act or, in Scotland or Northern Ireland, under other legislation giving similar results. That protection can be extended to any living surviving spouse following the death of the employee. The second situation will arise where there is a similar result from any other lease granted to an employee as part of his or her terms of employment for the purpose of agriculture.

Interaction with the income tax position is relevant. It is interesting to turn here to HMRC's BIM55260: on farm cottages.

'Where a cottage is provided rent-free for a farm employee, related expenditure of a revenue nature which is incurred wholly and exclusively for the purposes of the trade and does not otherwise offend the provisions of ITTOIA 2005 s 34 is an admissible deduction in computing farm profits.'

APR – A RELIEF NOT AN EXEMPTION

5.6   The tax planner should bear in mind that for IHT purposes, the beneficial treatment of agricultural and business property is afforded by a relief, rather than an exemption. On death the situation can be quite different if a lifetime gift of qualifying property is made. In the case of a lifetime gift the normal seven-year clock starts to run. If the donor dies within that period, the relief is given only if certain conditions are met as at the date of death. One of these conditions is a requirement that the property still be owned by the donee as at the date of death.

There is a particular pitfall if the property is settled on accumulation and maintenance trusts (see Chapter 17). In that case the original donees are of course the trustees. But once a beneficiary has taken a right to income (often at age 18), HMRC's view is that it is thereafter the beneficiary who owns the property and not the original donee. Relief is thus denied if the donor subsequently dies before the seven years have elapsed from the original gift.

The question of a failed potentially exempt transfer (PET) is looked at in **13.17** and **13.18**.

Tax implications of trying to protect assets by gifting them now feature throughout the book (see **5.9**).

Occupation rules must be considered for APR in IHTA 1984 s 117 (see **13.4**).

DEED OF VARIATION – SURVIVING SPOUSE EXEMPTION

5.7   There are some very basic IHT planning techniques that are often overlooked by the farmer and landowner. These include the use of the nil-rate band, the deed of variation and surviving spouse exemption. The need for a will, the tax planning associated therewith and the problems of intestacy are set out in Chapter 18.

The farmer and landowner will generally own some assets that do not qualify for APR and BPR and the tax planner will have to look to the nil-rate band and the possibility of surviving spouse exemption for IHT relief on these assets. This can be incorporated in will planning, but if this is not achieved then the will can be 'varied' by the beneficiaries within two years of the date of death. For variations on or after 1 August 2002 there will be no need to send in a formal election for exemption from CGT and IHT provided the deed specifies the exemption will apply.

Transfers between husband and wife and civil partners are exempt from inheritance tax (IHTA 1984 s 18). The spouse exemption is not available to unmarried couples and those who have not entered into a civil partnership (*Holland (Executors of Holland) v IRC* [2003] STC (SCD) 43). The Special Commissioners in that case decided also that (even though the transfer of value occurred before the Human Rights Act 1998 (HRA 1998) was applied in English law on 2 October 2000), a wider interpretation of the meaning of the word 'spouse' was not required by that Act and that a surviving cohabitee suffered no breach of human rights. For assets which do not qualify for BPR or APR, there is great potential for 'deathbed' tax planning for unmarried couples through marriage.

The Finance Act 2008 allows any IHT nil-rate band unused on a person's death to be transferred to the estate of their spouse or civil partner who dies on or after 9 October 2007.

Where the value of an asset has been 'ascertained' (agreed) for IHT purposes, that value is normally to be used as the asset's base cost for CGT purposes on a subsequent disposal by the legatee. There are circumstances in which a value will not have been ascertained for IHT purposes, particularly where it is clear there is no IHT to pay. If the value eventually agreed for IHT purposes is higher than the value agreed for CGT purposes, provisions applying to CGT disposals on or after 6 April 2008 will prevent the revision of the CGT calculation. Equally, if the IHT value is lower, HMRC cannot reassess the CGT calculation.

In some cases the changes enforced by the Finance Act 2007 will mean that, to calculate how much nil-rate band can be transferred from the first deceased spouse's estate, the value of assets in that estate will need to be determined when the second spouse dies. In these circumstances, if the value of the asset differs from any already agreed for CGT purposes, TCGA 1992 s 274 would require CGT to be recalculated on the basis of the value agreed for IHT purposes.

This measure will ensure that the requirement under TCGA s 274 to use the IHT valuation for CGT purposes will not have effect where the valuation of an asset does not have to be ascertained for IHT purposes on the death of an individual.

BINDING CONTRACT FOR SALE

5.8   No BPR is given if the property is subject to a binding contract for sale. This will be a particular consideration if buy-out arrangements are in place. See Statement of Practice SP 12/80 Business Relief from IHT: 'buy and sell' agreement for circumstances in which IHTA 1984 s 113 might apply: HMRC's view is that mere options to buy and sell (distinguish obligations) will not trigger s 113. However, there have been recent signs that the issue may not be completely clear cut for CGT (as distinct from IHT) purposes. It may be prudent to have successive (and different) exercise periods for the put and call options respectively.

The other area of concern is partnerships and shareholder agreements. HMRC consider that there is a binding contract for sale where partners or shareholder directors enter into an agreement under which, in the event of the death or retirement of one of them, the personal representative of the partner/directors is obliged to sell and the survivors are obliged to purchase the interest of the deceased in the company or business.

The tax planner should review partnership agreements and structure shareholder agreements in the light of this rule and a large number of tax-planning points are raised in this book. Note the need to structure life assurance arrangements tax-efficiently in the context of shareholder agreements.

THE BOLD STEP OF GIFTING THE ASSETS NOW

5.9   The position of the risk of a 'failed PET' is looked at earlier (see **5.6**) and again under the section on lifetime transfers (see **5.17** and **5.18**).

Where the assets are of significant value and families in the eyes of the donor can be trusted to look after assets, there could be merits in making gifts now. Subsequent sections look at the angles of gifts with reservation and possible clawback within seven years. This is looked at further in Chapters 13 and 14.

Any transfers must be looked at in 'the round': examples are listed below.

- Are there any concerns over the 'mere asset' rule (see **14.12**)?

- Can the transferee maintain trading status for future reliefs?

- What is the CGT position? Is this a good time to consider utilising entrepreneurs' relief (ER) (see **14.10**)?

- Has the hold-over position of gifts to family members been considered (see **14.29**)?

- Does the loss of this agricultural asset affect the trading status of the transferor or the assets he retains, eg farmhouse when land is transferred (see **4.28**)?

- Have the rules relating to POT been considered (see **5.27**)?

- What of GROB (see **5.11**)?

- What protection can be achieved from pre nuptial agreements?

No transfer must be undertaken lightly, or with only one tax relief (namely IHT) in mind. Consideration must be given to CGT (see Chapter 14).

IHTA 1984 s 110 draws a distinction between an interest in the business and the underlying assets (see **5.33**). Section 110(c) states, 'no regard shall be had for assets or liabilities other than those by reference to which the net value of the entire business would fail to be ascertained. The position of the excepted asset is looked at earlier (see **5.4**). When making lifetime gifts, consideration has to be given to the gift of the business or an interest in the business and not the mere asset. This is a matter that now has considerable importance following the confirmation of the Special Commissioners' ruling in favour of the taxpayer in *Commissioners for HMRC v Trustees of Nelson Dance Family Settlement* EWHC 71 CH/2008/APP/0434 (see **5.56**).

It may be useful to make lifetime transfers into settlement where, eg farmhouses, cottages and farm buildings are to cease to be agricultural property and may acquire considerable non-agricultural value before they taint the remaining businesses for BPR, eg by making the remaining business not mainly one of making or holding investments (see **5.22**).

It should be noted that a lifetime transfer of land in a trust should be disclosed under DOTAS.

On large mixed estates, there may come a point where the amount of let property 'tilts' the balance by making the *whole* estate business *mainly* an investment business (and thus losing relief for the whole of the estate property). One strategy would be to remove the 'surplus' let or development property. What *Dance* establishes is that if the removal of the surplus were done by a transfer of value of just the 'surplus' assets then relief would apply to the let property assets transferred. The *Earl of Balfour* case (**5.55**) and the interaction with *Dance* (see **13.52**) show that there is scope for tax planning in this direction.

LAND – SINGLE UNIT OF PROPERTY ON DEATH

5.10   When carrying out a review of all farming assets, their ownership and their tax efficiency, the ruling which values agricultural land as one unit cannot be overlooked.

In *IRC v Gray* [1994] STC 360, CA the deceased owned a freehold interest in land that was farmed with two partners and was subject to certain tenancies granted to the partnership. The CTO attempted to aggregate the freehold interest with the share in the partnership business as a 'single unit of property' for the purposes of IHTA 1984 s 160 (for definition of s 160 see **5.13**). The executors appealed to the Lands Tribunal, which allowed their appeal and the Crown appealed further.

The Court of Appeal held that the two interests must be aggregated for valuation purposes. This follows the House of Lords' decision in *Buccleuch v IRC* [1967] 1 AC 506, HL, which established the principle that the vendor must be supposed to have 'taken the course which would get the largest price for the combined holding' subject to that not entailing 'undue expenditure of time and effort'. The Lands Tribunal had been wrong to have held that the freehold reversion and the partnership share did not form a single unit of property for purposes of IHTA 1984 s 160.

Note that Concession F17 published on 13 February 1995 has reduced the harsh effect of this decision. APR of 100% will be given where (in particular) the interest in property subject to tenancy is valued at an amount broadly equivalent to the vacant possession value. See **13.7** on lotting.

GIFTS WITH RESERVATION OF BENEFIT (GROB)

5.11   Where farm assets or land have been gifted, it is important to ensure that they do not fail to obtain subsequent relief due to being deemed to be a gift with reservation of benefit. As mentioned earlier, many tax advisers worry that the current level of favourable IHT reliefs may disappear and gifts are often considered. From a planning point of view, a gift of a non-business asset which qualifies as a PET could be considered first so as, hopefully, to maximise reliefs.

A gift of an asset other than land falls foul of the gifts with reservation of benefit rules where:

- possession and enjoyment is not at or before the beginning of the relevant period bona fide assumed by the donee; or

- throughout the relevant period the property is not enjoyed to the entire exclusion or virtually the entire exclusion of the donor and any benefit to him by contract or otherwise (FA 1986 s 102(1)).

There are more detailed rules relating to land in FA 1986 ss 102A and 102B with broadly similar effect.

The 'relevant period' is that beginning on the date of the gift or the date beginning seven years before the donor's death, whichever is the later.

If the benefit remains until death, the donor is treated as then entitled to the property (IHTA 1984 s 102(4)), with no pro rata rule. Hence, it is important to identify the subject matter of the gift. If the benefit ends *inter vivos*, there is a notional PET at that time (IHTA 1984 s 102(4)).

From a farming perspective the key issues in order to avoid a GROB, are the possible payment of a full market rent of assets concerned and/or establish 'negligible benefit'. The former is not popular; the latter is set out in *Tax Bulletin* No 9 (November 1993). Negligible benefit includes very minimal use such as dog walking and horse riding. It can be possible to gift the land but exclude the shooting rights so shooting can continue by the donor.

The rules apply only to gifts made on or after Budget Day, 18 March 1986. The 'pre-owned asset' legislation (POT) introduced by the Finance Act 2004 applies to assets 'pre-owned' after 18 March 1986 (see **5.27**).

RELATED PROPERTY

5.12   Related property rules are of wide application and generally serve to increase the valuation of property for IHT purposes. The rules apply to shares and land, and link them to be valued as part of an imaginary larger holding of the individual holding and the related property. The tax adviser and landowner should always be mindful of these provisions. The following sections set out to explain the tax planning associated with this.

The normal rules of valuation

5.13   In general terms, the IHT value is the price that the property might reasonably be expected to fetch if sold on the open market at the date of death, ignoring the costs of sale and without reduction on the ground that the whole property is placed on the market at the same time (IHTA 1984 s 160). Relief is available when sales are made of shares within one year or land within four years after death at a value lower than probate.

Open market value applies even if the property can only be sold to certain people or at a certain price or otherwise subject to restrictions (*IRC v Crossman* [1936] 1 All ER 762, HL). However, if those restrictions will necessarily bind the purchaser, the market price will be lower than it would have been in the absence of restrictions at all. Under IHTA 1984 s 163 where there is a restriction or exclusion on the right to dispose, that restriction or exclusion is to be taken into account only to the extent that consideration in money or money's worth was given for it.

On death, the property is to be valued as it was immediately before the death. However, changes that occur by reason of the death are generally taken into account (IHTA 1984 s 171). Any goodwill in a business that depends directly upon the deceased personally will have less value and, as BPR would apply, it means that this could reduce the value for CGT base cost on subsequent disposal.

HMRC have recently taken an aggressive approach.

This is highlighted by the facts of *Chadwick* (*Linda Frances Chadwick and another (Hobart's Executors) v CRC Land Chamber*), in which the executors of a will disputed HMRC's valuation of the deceased's property.

Shortly after the deceased died, the executors obtained valuations from two local estate agents, both of whom valued it at £250,000. The property was subsequently refurbished and was then used as a holiday home. More than a year later – and after the refurbishment – HMRC visited the property and proposed a value of £300,000. The appellants sent HMRC a detailed report in support of their valuation, in light of which the Inspector said he would compromise at £275,000. The taxpayers appealed against this valuation and were forced to go to a tribunal.

101

The tribunal judge noted that the deceased had bought the property privately, rather than on the open market. Thus, the purchase price, which was £268,450, did not conform to the definition of market value at Inheritance Tax Act 1984 s 160, and should not have been taken into account by HMRC in arriving at its valuation.

The judge decided to use sales of similar properties, also used by HMRC, to reach a conclusion. The more expensive of these was in a different village from the property under appeal, which made a comparison more difficult; however, the sales of two other properties led the judge to agree with the taxpayers' valuation of £250,000. The taxpayers' appeal was allowed.

With this victory for the taxpayer, the IHT at stake must have been £10,000. The calculation is £275,000 – £250,000 = £25,000 @ 40% = £10,000. There are many who might consider that this was a relatively low amount of tax over which to stand firm and debate the matter at Lands Tribunal.

How is related property calculated?

5.14   IHTA 1984 s 161 states 'Where the value of any property comprised in a person's estate would be less than the appropriate portion of the value of the aggregate of that and any related property, it shall be the appropriate portion of the value of that aggregate'. This means that where property is 'related', it will need to be added to the overall value for valuation purposes.

Property is related if it forms part of the estate of the deceased's spouse (including land), or if it is property that has within the preceding five years been property of a charity or other exempt body under an exempt transfer made by the transferor or his spouse after 15 April 1976. If the trust or body disposes of the property, it remains related property for five years.

So far as land and shares qualifying for 100% BPR or APR are concerned, the rules of related property are perhaps of less concern. However, they could still have an adverse impact with, say, a mix of qualification, a property development company, as one example of an investment company, where BPR does not apply. As the probate value will be the subsequent base cost for CGT, there could be advantages in pushing towards a higher value where 100% IHT relief is available.

MANAGING LIABILITIES AND MONEY DEPOSITS

5.15   The rescheduling of debt can be used as part of IHT planning. The focus here for farmers is due to an advantage of APR over BPR. There is insufficient scope in this book to go into the full detail, however, the aim is to highlight this under-utilised but useful tax-planning tool. The basic BPR and APR rules must be understood. Rescheduling liabilities is not a potentially exempt transfer (PET) (see **5.17**) and therefore it does not need to be in place for seven years to benefit.

For BPR where a liability is charged on an asset used in the business, the value of the asset is reduced by the amount of the debt, even if the debt was *not* incurred for the business. Under IHTA 1984 s 162(4), for BPR a 'liability which is an encumbrance on any property shall, so far as possible, be taken to reduce the value of that property'. IHT relief will therefore only be available on the net amount. There is scope to repay debts that reduce IHT reliefs with liquid assets that would be subject to IHT (see **5.35**). The philosophy of taxpayers towards borrowings and cash reserves varies considerably and some might not like debt management to be tax driven. However, this is one of the few tax-planning points that can be dealt with in 'deathbed' tax planning. Farming is different: IHTA 1984 s 110 is restricted to BPR, and for APR s 162 applies. APR is reduced *only* by liabilities charged on the land, and not by debt, which was incurred to buy that land but secured on other property. There is different tax planning therefore between BPR and APR, a diversified activity will probably not be eligible for APR, just BPR, which in this instance gives some protection.

We looked earlier (see **5.4**) at ways of avoiding 'excepted' assets failing in their claim for BPR. Money (cash surpluses) was a specific quote of the excepted assets, and questions that are often asked include the following.

- Are the assets used at all in the business?

- Were they used throughout the whole of the two years prior to the claim?

- Was the asset required at the time of transfer for future use in the business?

The proactive tax planner might try and take this planning further by actively leaving money or minor investments in the business and argue that they are needed in the business. Short-term deposits are more likely to qualify for BPR than long-term fixed deposits. Obviously the favourable tax environment of the business is tempting, but it must have a palpable business purpose. There must be no risk of causing problems under IHTA 1984 s 105(3) 'wholly or mainly holding investment'. The case of *Brown's Executors v IRC* [1996] STC (SCD) 277 showed that tax relief for the 'money box' can be achieved but it must be supported by records.

The allocation of liabilities and debt are an excellent tax-planning tool for both APR and BPR. A review of debts and liabilities should be undertaken. We look at this principle throughout the rest of this chapter.

REDUCING THE TRADING ACTIVITY OR CEASING TO TRADE WITH GIFTED ASSETS

5.16   When an ageing farmer becomes too old to farm he might give away parts of his farm. If these were the result of a gift, a PET, there could be adverse tax consequences if the donor dies within seven years as these are known as 'failed PETS' (see **5.17** and **13.18**). However, protection can be achieved through APR or BPR.

LIFETIME TRANSFERS – CLAWBACK RULES

5.17   The transferor may have gifted agricultural property to family members within the last seven years of death. This is known as a PET and the transferor will need to survive seven years for the gift to be exempt (assuming that there are no retained benefits) from IHT. If the donor dies before the seven-year period is up, the emphasis will be on APR and BPR (see Chapter 13).

APR will be lost where the transferee ceases to use the property for agricultural purposes at any time from the date he received it to the date of the transferor's death. A similar consequence will arise if the property is subject to a binding contract of sale (see **5.8**) at the date of death, as IHTA 1984 ss 114 and 124 effectively convert the property into the proceeds of sale.

On the death of the donor (or donee) within seven years, then in order to avoid a clawback:

● the transferee must have held property until the transferor's death or the earlier death of the transferee – this allows transfer by the transferee to life interest settlement on himself but not to his spouse; and

● the property should be agricultural/business property at the date of the relevant death and, in the case of agricultural property, should have been occupied continuously for agricultural purposes since the date of the gift (with relieving provision for companies) (IHTA 1984 ss 113A and 124A).

Relief is given for replacement agricultural/business property (three years' time limit or such longer period as the board may allow), provided it was an arm's length deal and the whole consideration received on sale is applied in the purchase of new assets. HMRC have confirmed that this can be net of professional fees and incidental costs and of any CGT. This is dealt with in more detail in Chapter 13 (see **13.19–13.22**).

REPLACEMENT OF AGRICULTURAL PROPERTY BY BUSINESS PROPERTY

5.18   With the move to diversification, problems are envisaged where agricultural property qualifying for relief has been replaced by business property that does not qualify for relief at the time the transferor dies. Such a problem is described in HMRC's *Tax Bulletin* No 14 (December 1994). This is dealt with in more depth in Chapter 13.

Where agricultural property, which is a farm business, is replaced by non-agricultural business property, the period of ownership of the former property can count towards the period of ownership for BPR purposes.

Where the transferee of a PET of a farming business sells the business and replaces it with a non-agricultural business, relief will be preserved if the conditions for BPR are satisfied.

RETIRING PARTNERS – SHOULD A FARMER EVER RETIRE?

5.19   It has been said that 'farmers never retire, they just die'. The tax consequences of the retirement of any partner should be very seriously considered, as ceasing to be a partner is the ceasing of his trading status and various tax reliefs that go with it, including the relief on the farmhouse (see

Chapter 4). The position of retirement before death (no matter how unlikely that seems) must be reviewed.

The BPR case of *Beckman v IRC* [2000] STC (SCD) 59, looks at when a retiring partner ceases to have a direct, proprietary interest in any particular partnership asset, including agricultural land. It was decided that the interest in the partnership, qualifying for BPR, had been converted into a debt owed by the sole trader who continued the business that was no longer relevant business property. So what are the tax-planning alternatives?

Where the partnership is to continue to farm the land, it would seem sensible for the land to be taken off the balance sheet and not regard it as a partnership asset (there are various ways in which this could be done) with suitable adjustments being made in the accounts. The debt owing to the retiring partner would therefore be reduced accordingly and he would be left with an interest in agricultural property used for agricultural purposes by someone else.

The above strategy would not work in relation to the farmhouse or cottage in which the retiring partner lives, as the house would no longer be used for the purposes of agriculture. ESC F16 would not be of any help either, since this relates to retired employees, not partners. Again, this is not entirely satisfactory and highlights the need for careful retirement planning. Perhaps the farmer should never retire in order to maximise tax reliefs (see **5.32**)?

'MAKING OR HOLDING INVESTMENTS'

5.20   BPR is not due if a business deals in specific assets such as land or buildings, securities, stocks and shares and the making or holding of investments. This also applies to the shares of a company where the company itself is involved with such activities. IHTA s 105(3). Landowners are particularly vulnerable where land is let for non-agricultural purposes, since APR will be lost and BPR may not be due. Another example is where a tenanted farm is owned by a limited company. This is set out at **5.23**.

It is particularly important for tax practitioners to be aware of what clients might consider to be a business and what will actually qualify for BPR. It must be realised that historically claims for BPR have not been based on how much work is put in by the taxpayer over the years to generate the wealth which is now to be taxed, but what the exact business is at the date of death and, as recent cases show, how much work is carried out at date of death.

Examples of positive cases are *Furness v IRC* [1999] STC (SCD) 232 (see **6.22**) which is considered a victory for the taxpayer and the case of the 'mixed use estate' *Farmer (Farmer's Executors) v IRC* [1999] STC (SCD) 321 (see Chapter 13) and *HMRC v Balfour* [2010] UK UT300 (see **5.55**).

What do other tax cases tell us? There was a 2002 Special Commissioners' case involving a caravan park, *Stedman's Executors v IRC* [2002] STC (SCD) 358. Looking at all the incidents of the business, it was found that those which pointed to an investment activity were far outweighed by those which supported an analysis of trading. The executors' appeal was allowed. The Court of Appeal has upheld the decision, saying that the Special Commissioners' approach had been correct in law (*IRC v George* [2003] EWCA Civ 1763, [2004] STC 147). (See **5.22** and **6.19**.)

It should be emphasised just how significant IHTA 1984 s 105(3) is with regard to the fact that a farming business activity could be deemed to be wholly or mainly holding investments. The actual wording of the Act says, 'consists wholly or mainly of one or more of the following, that is to say dealing with securities, stocks or shares, land or buildings or making a holding investment'. Case history has seemed to focus almost exclusively on the last element of this phrase, ie the making or holding of investments. There is great concern that the diversified farmer could be deemed to be just holding land as an investment, or even dealing in land, thus the claim for BPR could fail. This has proved to be the position in *McCall (McCall v HMRC* SpC 678 and (2009) NICA 12), see **5.22**. This is of particular concern for the limited company featured in **5.23**. The problem there is that when the business is incorporated, the entire value of the shareholding is excluded from relief if it is deemed to be a 'holding investment'. However, for the sole trader the application of rules can be less harsh in that farm assets can be deemed to have failed in their qualification for BPR while the farming business assets can still qualify.

Further recent cases have helped with the guidance on definition of the mixed estate, eg *Balfour*.

AGRICULTURE AND HIGH CAPITAL EMPLOYMENT

5.21   With the current problems in farming twinned with an increase in value of the land and buildings, there has been a tendency towards a trading activity holding a large value investment. The cases of *Martin (Moore's Executors) v IRC* [1995] STC (SCD) 5, *Burkinyoung v IRC* [1995] STC (SCD) 29, *Hall (Hall's Executors) v IRC* [1997] STC (SCD) 126 and *Denekamp v Pearce (Inspector of Taxes)* [1998] STC 1120 are all relevant and need to be looked at to see why they failed and how this can be avoided. It is also important to look at what can be considered the victories for the taxpayer, ie *Furness v IRC* [1999] STC (SCD) 232, as mentioned above, and *Farmer (Farmer's Executors) v IRC* [1999] STC (SCD) 321.

It is interesting to note that in the case of *Furness* it was the sheer quantity of work involved in running the caravan site which was enough to take the business outside the scope of IHTA 1984 s 105(3). In this case the Special Commissioner examined the evidence and the source of net profit. Essentially this book is focusing on farmers and land diversification and, although a caravan park is a diversification the key factors are the provision of both services and activities. The case of *Farmer v IRC (Farmer)*, is of importance as it actually does relate to the activity of farming and diversification. This main area of diversification was the letting out of redundant farm buildings and cottages, which sets the current scene for many UK estates. It is therefore worth looking at in some detail, especially the factors which were reviewed and those which deemed it to be favourable (see Chapter 13).

Many farmers might object to the parallel of the diversification of a caravan park but it does set out a useful comparison to a diversified mixed estate, and *Balfour* aids further understanding.

IS A FARMER TRADING OR HOLDING INVESTMENTS?

5.22 The question of the landowner/farmer trading or holding investments features throughout the book.

The case of a farmer diversifying to a caravan park can be very useful (**6.19**) eg *IRC v George and another (executors of Stedman, dec'd)* [2004] STC 147 (see **5.20**) (*George*).

This an extremely important decision in relation to BPR, as HMRC have been loath to accept that some residential caravan parks trading as businesses came within the qualifications for relief, while contending that in cases where the majority of income and profits came from pitch fees that the business was one of 'holding investments' and therefore disqualified from relief by IHTA 1984 s 105(3) (see **5.20**).

In reversing the decision of Laddie J, Lord Justice Carnwath observed that s 105(3) did not require the opening of an investment 'bag', into which were placed all the activities linked to the caravan park, simply on the basis that they were 'ancillary' to that investment business. Moreover, it was not necessary to determine whether or not investment was the 'very business' of the company.

There is no doubt that farmers can benefit from the *George* decision and this is followed on to the *Balfour* decision. Reference to 'active family business' can be a key point here and one applied to active farming businesses with *very* high capital. The emphasis is on the provision of services and activities.

Where agricultural land has hope or development value, the restriction of APR to the agricultural value of the property may not create additional tax liabilities in a case where an equivalent measure of BPR is available on the non-agricultural value. There are two important cases where BPR will not compensate for the lost APR. First, tenanted agricultural property may not qualify for any measure of BPR, though this recent case of *George* combined with *Farmer* may be helpful where the letting is managed with, and is ancillary to, in-hand agricultural property. Second, where land is made available to a partnership without any tenancy by a partner, business property relief on the non-agricultural value is likely to be restricted to the lower rate of 50% (IHTA 1984 s 105(1)(d)).

As mentioned, there are two further cases first heard in 2009 which help highlight the question of whether the business was 'wholly or mainly' an investment business.

- *HMRC v Balfour* [2010] UKUT 300 (*Balfour*)

The case concerned a Scottish agricultural estate. 'The business was a traditional mix of a Scottish landed estate and consisted of a blend of agriculture (in hand and let farms) woodland and forestry management and related sporting interests and the letting of cottages and other properties within the estate either to estate workers or to others' (para 30).

The case was complicated by a history of the land having been in trust, with the deceased as life tenant until he barred the entail and became sole owner less than two years before death. The tribunal held there had been a single business owned and carried on by the deceased in spite of trusts necessitating administrative and accounting arrangements (*CF Featherstonhaugh v IRC* 1984 STC 261).

The First-tier Tribunal held that business was not 'wholly or mainly' making or holding investments'. Agreed facts suggest that farming and forestry income (ie turnover) exceeded rents. This decision was upheld in the Upper Tribunal (see **5.55**).

- *McCall – McCall and another (personal representative of McClean (deceased)) v HMRC* SpC 678 and (2009) NICA 12

The deceased, Mrs McClean, had inherited grazing land from her husband. After his death she moved away and became mentally incapable of managing her affairs. Her son-in-law Mr Mitchell arranged for land to be grazed, informally, but engaged in little activity. On her death, it was accepted that the modest agricultural value of £165,000 qualified for APR; BPR was refused on the £5.8m development value on the ground that the business was 'wholly or mainly' an investment business.

The Special Commissioner confirmed that BPR was not available, and their decision was upheld by the Court of Appeal in Northern Ireland.

The Special Commissioner and NICA emphasised that the only requirement for BPR was to have owned the business for two years, and that there was no requirement for the deceased to be personally involved in the business if instead the business carried on the role for the deceased. It might be carried on by an agent, employee or even (as in *McCall)* a constructive trustee.

See para 19 of Girvan LJ's judgment for a detailed description of what the son-in-law (on behalf of the deceased) had failed to do to show that the non-investment business of cultivation of the land was being carried on (and by inference how a better advised and organised taxpayer could secure the relief). The claim for BPR failed. For further detail on this case see **10.10** and **13.52**. The key to achieving BPR here was the importance of cultivating the grass as a crop not merely maintaining the land as a landlord.

PROTECTING THE LAND HELD IN THE LIMITED COMPANY

5.23   It might be that agricultural property is the main asset in a limited company. This agricultural property should qualify as relevant business property with APR being applied automatically in the first instance. BPR may apply to the assets that did not qualify under APR.

APR is not available on minority holdings in the shares of a farming company. However, 100% BPR will be available against the minority holding providing the requirements are met. The rules relating to replacement property as set out at **5.18** will apply.

This does lead to the big problem of a tenanted farm being owned in a limited company as IHTA 1984 s 105(3) provisions of 'wholly or mainly holding investments' means that the minority holding fails in its claim for APR and BPR. Clients must be made aware of this potential failure of a claim for BPR/APR.

A majority holding may seek the benefit of 50% APR if it can be shown that the company has owned the farm for seven years and the majority holding has been held for a minimum of seven years (see Chapter 8).

LIFE ASSURANCE – WHEN ALL ELSE FAILS

5.24   Life assurance can be a useful IHT planning tool for farming families. The classic problem of the farming family is that there is often a large valuable asset (especially with the increase in land value at the time of writing), but sometimes low income. Equality of succession can be very difficult to achieve and life assurance can assist. It can be used to provide for cover for IHT liabilities which would otherwise fall upon members of the family who do not work on the farm or in the business. Also, where the inheritance structure is such that one farming child inherits the business and has to buy out the siblings at the market value of the land, this can be financed by the remaining child taking out an insurance policy. Obviously the specialist advice of an independent financial adviser (IFA) is needed in this regard.

THE 'CLASSIC' FARMING FAMILY – PROVIDING FOR THE FUTURE

5.25   The section looks at how a classic farming family has tended to structure its assets through the generations and how it will need to deal with the problems that arise. The farming community has long had a reputation for continuing to work well past normal retirement age. With the recent history of falling investment returns, less profits to shelter, and no spare cash to invest, today's farmers are much less likely to be financially independent from the farm when they reach retirement age.

There are currently many farm partnerships where the land is owned by one partner, often the father, but farmed by the partnership with no formal tenancy agreement, and probably no partnership agreement. If the tenancy commenced before 1 September 1995 (see **11.15–11.17**), and there is no clause in the partnership agreement enabling the 'landlord' to obtain vacant possession of the land within 24 months of his death, it is likely that HMRC will limit any claim for APR to the 50% (see **5.2**) rate available for tenanted property outside the provisions of the Agricultural Tenancies Act 1995. The same situation could arise if the father ceases to be a partner but continues to let the land to the partnership, perhaps at a nominal rent to provide him with some retirement income.

Where there is a partnership agreement, in particular an old agreement, care should be taken to ensure that there is not a binding agreement for the deceased's share of the partnership to be sold to the remaining partners, as this can result in no relief being available at all. Similarly, if the father retires from the partnership, but leaves his capital in the business as a loan, perhaps to draw on to provide income in retirement, the loan is not eligible for BPR, even if left to one of the partners in his will (see Chapter 18). This is emphasised in the case of *Beckman* (see **5.19**). However, if the capital had been gifted on retirement, or if the father had remained a partner, 100% relief should be available.

APR is only available on the agricultural value of the property (see **4.32**). This is not normally a problem where the deceased is still a partner in the business, as any difference is eligible for BPR, although the conditions for 100% relief are tighter. If, however, a number of buildings have been developed and let out, it should be borne in mind that the letting of property is not a business for tax purposes, and relief may well not be available, unless it can be argued that it is a minor part of the business as a whole. The tax planning is set out in *Farmer (Farmer's Executors) v IRC* [1999] STC (SCD) 321 (see **13.25**).

A warning is needed where property eligible for either APR or BPR has been gifted during the father's lifetime (see **5.6**). The gift does not escape inheritance tax until seven years have elapsed, and, on death within seven years, relief is only available if the property has continued to qualify in the hands of the donee for the appropriate APR or BPR throughout the period between the gift and death. See Chapter 13 for the consequences of a PET. Development of part of the property during this period, or its sale without replacement with qualifying assets, would count as a failed PET (see **5.17** and **13.17**).

The longer therefore that financial circumstances require farmers to retain their farming interests (see **5.19**), the more important it becomes to obtain good tax-planning advice to ensure that as much benefit as possible is obtained from the available APR and BPR at the date of death.

RETIRED FARM WORKERS

5.26 Farm cottages are often occupied by retired farm workers under a protected occupancy, eg under the Rent (Agriculture) Act 1976 or under the equivalent provisions of the Housing Acts 1988. We have already looked at the IHT position (see **5.5**). The occupants of these cottages are not employed; therefore they are not considered to be used for the purposes of the farming for CGT purposes and do not qualify as business assets for entrepreneurs' relief (ER) (see **14.10**).

With planning, the cottage should qualify for IHT relief, particularly after the *Farmer* case (see Chapter 13) but again the facts should be checked very carefully.

So what proactive advice can be taken? It might be appropriate to consider part-time employment for the retired worker rather than full retirement to preserve both potential IHT and CGT reliefs (although the restrictions of ER must be noted – see **14.10**).

INCOME TAX CHARGE FOR 'PRE-OWNED ASSETS'

5.27 An income tax charge has been imposed from 2005–06 onwards on the annual benefit of using or enjoying an asset that was once owned by the user (and has not been sold by him at an arm's length price for cash), where such use is enjoyed free of charge or at below market rent. The charge will also apply to assets, which the user did not formerly own but which were purchased with funds provided by him. Both tangible and intangible assets (eg shares) will be within the charge. The rules will quantify the annual taxable value of the benefit – modelled on the existing rules for taxing benefits in kind provided to employees (but the precise details have still to be finalised). Relief will be given for any amount paid by the taxpayer for the benefit (eg rent). No income tax charge applies where the total taxable value for any tax year is less than £5,000. If the asset in question still forms part of the taxpayer's estate for inheritance tax purposes, whether under general principles or under the 'gifts with reservation' (GROB) rules (see **5.11**), the asset will not fall within the income tax charge. In addition, the charge will not apply where the asset ceased to be owned before 18 March 1986; or the asset is now owned by the taxpayer's spouse; or the taxpayer was formerly the owner of the asset only by virtue of a will or intestacy subsequently varied; or the use or enjoyment is merely incidental. Arrangements derived from cash gifts made at least seven years previously are also exempt.

The charge applies to UK residents. For those not domiciled in the UK, the charge is being restricted to their UK assets. For those becoming domiciled in the UK, the charge will not thereafter apply to any non-UK assets, which they ceased to own before acquiring UK domicile.

Pre-existing arrangements will escape the new charge if they are dismantled, or the user begins paying full market rent before the start date of 6 April 2005. Alternatively, a taxpayer had to elect, by 31 January 2007, to remain outside the income tax charge (in relation to the asset(s) specified in the election), but in that case the asset in question will be treated as part of his estate for inheritance tax purposes while he continues to enjoy it.

Tax-planning checks, which interact with work on IHT planning surrounding GROB (see **5.11** and **13.14**), will be essential.

THE RIGHT OF 'UNIMPEDED PHYSICAL ENJOYMENT' – VACANT POSSESSION

5.28 This title is taken from the case of *Cumberland Consolidated Holdings Ltd v Ireland* [1946] KB 264, CA. It was used to assess whether vacant possession had been achieved or not in the purchase of a warehouse which was found to have its cellars full of rubbish on completion date. The analogy of 'unimpeded physical enjoyment' is a useful summary for vacant possession.

The theme of this chapter is about protecting the assets. It is ironic that the case used to determine vacant possession should use the phrase 'unimpeded enjoyment'. Farming is not just an income source, a way of feeding the family, a business venture solely for the purpose of profit. It encompasses a large number of other issues, which cannot be overlooked, such as tradition, way of life, responsibility and environmental awareness. Many people who undertake farming as a vocation cannot suddenly change direction. Many do not want to change direction and for the most part it is a way of life following a long family tradition.

Looking at trying to trade profitably and to protect the assets from unnecessary tax is something that is imperative if this way of life is to continue. One of the clear tax-planning points is that the clients must involve the tax planner, and often the land agent, before an action is taken, rather than after it has happened and then asking what is the tax position. This should involve close links with the land agents, who should naturally be seeking tax advice on agreements entered into. There are many circumstances where the tax treatment will totally depend on the wording of agreements. It can be marginal whether something is of a capital or an income nature. It can be marginal as to whether it is taxed as trading income or non-trading income, but the long-term effects in tax saving can be quite dramatic and should be considered in advance.

At the risk of stating the obvious, planning ahead with farmers and landowners involving their land agents at an early stage is the key to strong tax planning. It is hoped this book shows why.

LET AGRICULTURAL LAND WITHOUT VACANT POSSESSION

5.29   Land subject to an FBT qualifies for APR. However, there is possible fallback to BPR for hope value and incorporated let property (eg the *Farmer* case) if market value exceeds agricultural value. Land let subject to FBT after 1 September 1995 achieves APR qualification where vacant possession can be achieved in 24 months (see **11.15–11.19**). For BPR to apply a business must be the predominant activity (see *Balfour* **5.55**).

REPAIR TO FARM PROPERTY BEFORE AND AFTER DEATH

5.30   A Lands Tribunal case, *Tapp v HMRC* 2008 EW Lands TMA/284/2008, highlights the importance of the market value of property at the date of death, and its interaction with the state of repair.

In the *Tapp* case the District Valuer (DV) only visited the property two years after the date of death.

The basis of valuation for IHT is market value (IHTA 1984 s 160), ie the price that would be paid by a willing buyer to a willing seller.

Clearly the valuation should be undertaken as soon after the date of death as possible. If a professional valuation is not undertaken, photographic evidence of the property and the state of repair should be obtained. Clearly beneficiaries and/or executors who do arrange to have repair work carried out should keep records of work done ready for the valuation.

The valuation is important for IHT planning and establishing IHT liability. The tax relief on the expenditure must also be considered – is this a CGT expense for the improvement, or is this a cost to offset against income?

The fact that repairs to farms may attract 100% APR and/or BPR, whilst non-business property does not benefit from these reliefs, could be the subject of some deathbed planning or planning in the years leading to death. For example:

- Farmer A owns a farm worth £2 million including a farmhouse worth £500,000. It is anticipated HMRC could accept agricultural value of 60% so £200,000 of the farmhouse may not qualify for APR. Farmer A has recently sold development land and has £400,000 cash due to savings and this sale. The obvious tax planning is to roll-over the gain into more land. Entrepreneurs' relief would not be available as a material sale has not been made. The cash is clearly 'IHT vulnerable', ie it will not be covered by the nil-rate band. Roll-over can save CGT and ensure the replacement property for IHT. The roll-over could be improvements to the farm prior to death which would achieve APR and BPR.

- Farmer B owns a farm worth £3 million including a farmhouse that could be subject to restriction. Farmer B has savings and investments of £600,000 and the farm is in a bad state of repair due to the deteriorating health of Farmer B. If cash is used on repairs and improvements the value of the farm should increase and be subject to APR and BPR as appropriate at 100%. Income tax relief could be achieved on the repairs.

The *Tapp* case shows an example of late DV visits and questions over repairs indicating the need for photographic evidence at various stages post death. There are tax-planning opportunities for the use (and timing thereof) of 'inheritance tax vulnerable' cash. There is also the question of the complexity of what exactly is 'market value'.

There is no doubt that 'repair and market uncertainty' can be used as tax-planning tools when trying to agree values with the DV that could be to the taxpayer's advantage, but spending surplus cash before death on the farming enterprise has to be tax efficient when correctly structured.

DEVELOPMENT VALUE AND IHT

5.31   At the date of death, the 'hope value' of land has to be valued and subject to IHT like any other asset in the estate of the deceased. Prior to the current 'credit crunch' it was argued that all the land had some 'hope value', but what now of the crash of development land values and subsequent recoveries?

How is hope value ascertained? It must be valued at market value under IHTA 1984 s 160 (as mentioned above). The land agent acting for the deceased has to apply the 'Red Book' guidelines in accordance with his or her Royal Institution of Chartered Surveyors (RICS) qualification. Concerns and caveats must be documented and, if necessary, a range of values presented. The estate cannot be finalised until the value and the resulting IHT liability is agreed.

There are arguments to say that the beneficiary of the development land would like as high a value as possible as this will be the CGT base cost for any future disposal. Obviously the executors would only want to endure a high hope value if the land achieves IHT reliefs, eg BPR on farmland.

There have been some quite high-profile attacks on BPR on farmland and grazing agreements which protect high development values through the *McCall* case (see **5.22**). In *McCall* the development value was £4.8 million when the agricultural value was only £165,000.

The *McCall* case raises a number of tax-planning questions if the taxpayer died prior to the development land crash, or if after death, the planners move the 'planning goalposts' to another area of land, eg the next door farm or another part of the country, then what tax relief can the executors obtain?

There could be a situation where hope value exists at date of death, but collapses after death, eg change of development plans.

So what action can the farm tax adviser take to try to prevent these problems?

113

- Where there is any hint of development value, look to ensure BPR can be achieved via share farming or partnership rather than grazing agreement and ensure full warnings are given to living clients to manage their expectations.

- If there is a large drop in value post death, the executor should look at a third party or in-house sale so that the sale proceeds can be substituted within four years.

- Fight the DV on the hope value figure if appropriate. Hope value is very difficult to ascertain: try to force the DV to disclose method and basis of valuation. The valuation is what the market value and planning conditions were at the date of death and not what happened to the market afterwards. The post-death negatives can be used in a constructive and objective manner – hope value is based on *'hope'*.

This is another clear example of planning ahead and where the land agent and tax adviser must always work together. The land agent must warn of hope value and must work with the tax adviser on robust tax-efficient trading structures (see **5.33**).

FARMERS NEED TO KEEP TRADING

5.32   The recent tax cases have emphasised the need for 'active husbandry' and 'active' diversification where appropriate in order to achieve BPR. The post 2013 CAP reform proposals also point towards 'active' farming (see **20.1**).

All tax advisers acting for landowners, farmers and landed estates must be very careful to check the position concerning the robustness of the trading activity, whether it is farming or some other form of alternative land use which would still qualify as a trade. The tax treatment would be seen to be driving farmers, who can no longer economically or physically farm themselves, to move towards contract farming arrangements or share farming arrangements with local farmers or large contract farming organisations. A carefully worded contract that protects the trading status and the preservation of some very important tax reliefs for VAT, income tax, CGT including ER and IHT (APR/ BPR) should be considered.

For contract or share farming arrangements to pass trading status tests, there must be all the basic 'badges of trade' both within the wording of the contract and in the factual operation thereof. Many farmers are supporting the contract/ share farming arrangement with elements of 'in-hand' farming, eg some livestock rearing, so as to ensure greater protection of the trading status.

PROTECTING THE 'HOPE' VALUE FROM HMRC ATTACK

5.33   The 'hope' value of farmland is the market value of the land over and above the agricultural value (see **4.32**).

IHT is a tax on values – specifically on the diminution in value caused by a transfer of value in the transferor's estate. The distinction is crucial to why various reliefs and exemptions are statutorily expressed, for example why the spouse exemption (IHTA 1984 s 18(1)) is expressed to be limited to what the transferee gains in terms of assets or value. HMRC have always proved to be very keen on drawing the distinction between the business and the assets.

The first question is whether the land with 'hope value' qualifies as 'agricultural property' for the purposes of IHTA 1984 s 115(2). The 'agricultural value' is to be calculated on the value of the land as agricultural land only. It disregards any value which may be attributable to the 'hope' or prospect of obtaining planning permission. The definition is provided by IHTA 1984 s 115(3) which states that the agricultural value of any agricultural property:

> 'Shall be taken to be the value which would be the value of the property if the property were subject to a perpetual covenant prohibiting its use otherwise than as agricultural property.' (See **4.32**.)

The second question is does the property qualify for BPR? The full reduction of 100% in the value transferred which, attributable to the farmland, could be obtained if the value transferred qualified for BPR under IHTA 1984 s 104. 'Business' is liberally defined. However, the business which qualifies for these purposes does not include the business of 'making or holding investments' (IHTA 1984 s 105(3)).

It is hoped that this book will explain through tax cases that have been won by the taxpayer, (eg *Earl of Balfour* (see **5.22** and **13.50**)) and lost by the taxpayer (eg *McCall* (see **5.22** and **10.10**)) what the key factors are required for success.

If BPR could be made available, it does not matter that a major part of the market value of the farmland may reflect the hope or prospect of obtaining planning permission. That 'hope' value will attract BPR, for so long as the land was held in exactly the same way as land which does not attract such permission, ie the land qualifying for APR and BPR must all be farmed in the same way.

So under what circumstances would the Capital Taxes Office (CTO) contend that the hope element farmland was not eligible for BPR? Well, we have already looked at s 105(3). What if the farming business has been overtaken by an investment business, ie the capital value of the farmland was far in excess of the value of the rest of the farm? The case of *Prosser v IRC* [Lands Tribunal] (see **13.49**) looks at the question of the quantum of hope value.

CASH-FLOW MANAGEMENT – THE *PHILIPS* CASE

5.34   Every farm will have to look carefully at cash-flow management throughout its business life, dealing with 'cash mountains', controlling distributions and commercial borrowings. Each individual sole trader, partner, shareholder or investor has to look at their own tax position and this includes IHT relief. Although the focus of the farming business has to be commercial, the recent case of *Executors of Rhoda Philips v HMRC* [2006] WTLR 1280 has illustrated the need to ensure that all loans are ideally IHT efficient for BPR, while also achieving maximum corporation and income tax relief. Can this present a conflict of interest?

When Rhoda Philips died in June 2001, she owned 245,000 shares in PPI Investments, but HMRC determined that they did not qualify for BPR. Mrs Philips' executors appealed and the Special Commissioner was called on to determine whether PPI's business consisted 'wholly or mainly of ... making or holding investments' under IHTA 1984 s 105(3).

Ms Philips was a widow and she held a majority of shareholding in PPI, a company that lent money to related companies. Her executors claimed BPR. HMRC rejected the claim on the basis that PPI's business consisted mainly of making or holding investments under s 105(3).

The case emphasised that for BPR purposes in such circumstances, it is important to look at the activity of the farming business at the date of death and two years before and not at the activity the business undertook in the past. Thus, the fact that until 1989 the company had been a property investment business was not relevant to the current claim for BPR.

The ultimate finding of this case was that money lending is a trading activity. The Commissioner did not regard the activities of a money lender as investment and allowed the executor's appeal, finding that PPI was a banking arm for in house transactions. On the evidence, PPI was in the business of making loans and not of investing in loans. The loans were not investments for their own sake but the provision of a finance facility to the other companies. Accordingly the shares in PPI qualified for BPR.

DEATHBED LOAN PLANNING

5.35   The allocation of secured borrowing is essential planning to protect against the potential IHT liability that might arise if the borrowings are not allocated correctly. When reviewing the potential IHT liability of property and the related borrowings at the date of death, there is no requirement for a liability to have been secured on a particular asset for any particular length of time. The appropriate arrangement of borrowings can lead to 'deathbed' tax planning, though of course any rearrangement of borrowings must be completed before death. It must be remembered that APR is reduced only by liabilities charged on the land, but BPR is reduced by debt to buy the land but secured on other property (see **5.15**)

'WHOLLY AND EXCLUSIVELY' LINKING WITH SECURITY

5.36   The aim of every business is to achieve maximum tax relief on borrowing.

Income tax relief and corporation tax relief is given for interest paid on borrowings incurred 'wholly and exclusively' for the purpose of a trade. Similar rules apply for borrowings to finance a rental business. This tax relief on interest payments is therefore given according to the purpose of the loan, whereas for IHT purposes a loan is matched with the assets on which it is secured or charged.

An anomaly of the different taxes is that the loan can be for the purpose of purchasing one asset and it can be secured against a totally separate asset. It is often beneficial for IHT purposes to secure a loan on assets that do not qualify for any IHT reliefs rather than business assets. Thus the business assets' value is increased and therefore so is the BPR claim, while the IHT vulnerable assets are reduced by the borrowings. The tax planner must consider whether a conflict in interest arises in trying to juggle income tax, corporation tax and IHT relief. Who is the client? Who is seeking advice? Who is giving the instruction? Sole traders do not present such a problem, but companies and partnerships can require either disclosure of the potential conflict or that alternative independent advice be sought.

PRE-DEATHBED LOAN PLANNING

5.37 Deathbed loan planning certainly has a part to play in farm IHT planning, but clearly long-term restructuring and possible refinancing should be put in place at an early stage to ensure that maximum tax reliefs are achieved. For example, it might be that corporation or income tax relief is available on loan interest where tax relief might not have been previously allowed or might have been disallowed because it was not wholly and exclusively for the purpose of the trade. In an ideal world all clients should undergo a 'loan management' tax review or tax audit. The obvious choice of the lender is the security over the house but for income tax relief the key is the purpose of the loan.

REALLOCATED BORROWINGS: APR V BPR

5.38 A review of the tax efficiency of loans that would result in the reallocation of borrowings should not give rise to CGT problems. There are important differences between APR and BPR in the context of borrowings. Under IHTA 1984 s 110, for the purposes of BPR the value of a business or an interest in a business is to be taken as the net value, ie the value of the assets used in the business reduced by the aggregate amount of liabilities incurred for the purposes of the business, regardless of the security given. There is IHT planning to secure the loan against a non-business asset that does not qualify for BPR or APR.

APR is restricted to 'agricultural property' and reduced by loans secured on the property. As defined by IHTA 1984 s 115(2), agricultural property means agricultural land or pasture and also includes such cottages, farm buildings and farmhouses, together with the land they occupy, as are of a character appropriate to the property.

When looking at reallocating borrowings it is also imperative to review excess cash balances (the 'cash mountain') – see **5.15** and **5.30**. The potential future claim for BPR or APR must therefore be assessed when looking at the borrowings structure to ensure maximum benefit is achieved.

THE IHT REQUIREMENT FOR THE CASH MOUNTAIN

5.39 It is equally important to ensure that any excess cash deposits are protected by an IHT claim. It has to be shown to be for future use. *The Barclays Bank Trust Company Limited v IRP* [1998] SSCD 125 (SPC C158) highlights this.

The question was whether a £300,000 'cash mountain' that a company held was an excepted asset under IHTA 1984 s 112(2) and therefore did not qualify for IHT relief. The facts were that the deceased died in November 1990, holding 50% of the shares in a company; her husband held the other 50%. The company sold bathroom and kitchen fittings, mainly to the trade. The cash position was strong. The company did not tie up working capital either in premises (which were occupied rent free and which belonged to the deceased) or in stock. The company's cash at bank and in hand in 1990 was more than £450,000. Cash was invested for periods of up to 30 days. Turnover was around £600,000.

In February 1990 the company approached a similar company and expressed an interest in buying that company's properties. The other company did not reply and was later liquidated, In 1997 the original company spent more than £335,000 on a venture in the purchase of goods imported from China.

HMRC accepted that the company needed £150,000 in cash at the death of the deceased, but subsequently issued a notice determining that £300,000 was not so required. The appellant, executors of the deceased appealed.

The decision was that on the evidence of the facts presented, the £300,000 was not required for the purposes of the business. An asset did not cease to be an excepted asset because at the time of the deceased's death it might be required at any time in the future. 'Required' in IHTA 1984 s 112(2)(b) did not include the possibility that the money might be required should an opportunity arise to make use of it in two, three or seven years' time for the purposes of the business. Some imperative was implied that the money would fall to be used on a given project or for some palpable business purpose. There was no evidence on the facts that the company was to be the purchaser of the other company's assets. The money was not 'required'. The appeal was dismissed.

The message to the farm tax planner is that for IHT relief to be achieved, cash surpluses must be required for future use and there must be evidence to support this. If there is no argument to support future use then an alternative use for the cash should be considered (see **5.30**).

ALTERNATIVE USES FOR THE CASH MOUNTAIN

5.40   What are the alternatives? For example, to repay family or group borrowings if appropriate, loan planning must also incorporate a review of cash balances to see where repayment can be achieved and improve potential IHT relief for the owners of the business. Cash mountains could be taken from the incorporated business and invested in 'IHT-efficient investment products' to prevent them being caught under IHTA 1984 s 112 (see **5.4**).

There are schemes available that effectively allow the donor some measure of income stream without apparently contravening pre-owned assets or gifts with reservation of benefit legislation.

Repaying, borrowing or even achieving IHT relief as a money lender as in the *Philips* case appears high risk. It is perhaps essential where there are cash mountains or complex borrowings that written confirmation by tax counsel of the availability of IHT relief is obtained and ideally a copy of the supporting tax counsel's opinion kept safely on file.

LOANS TO TRADERS – THE INSPECTOR'S CAT

5.41   Loans to traders that are not repaid can achieve CGT relief. When organising loan management, it is also essential to understand the ability to claim this CGT relief under TCGA 1992 s 253. The tax case of *Crosby v Broadhunt* [2004] STC (SCD) 348 showed that the claim does not have to be made at the point the loan is waivered and released.

The facts were that H Ltd was a trading company that had been lent money on two occasions by the trustees of a settlement that E had made. By 1991 it had total debts of over £2 million, including the aggregate £250,000 owed to the settlement. The (then) Inland Revenue accepted that the loans were irrecoverable. The shareholders were able to secure a sale of the company to its then managing director and an outsider, neither of whom was a member of the settler's family. The sale was completed in March 1992. One condition of the sale was that the trustees should execute a deed of waiver and release of the loans and this was done. However, H Ltd continued to decline and it entered in to receivership in 1993.

The settlement's 1992–93 tax return included a claim for a capital loss of £250,000. The Inspector refused the claim, based on the view that, at the time of a claim for relief, the loan must still be in existence, ie it must not have been at this point written off, waivered or released. The trustees appealed.

The taxpayers' argument was based on the purpose of legislation, which related only to a limited class of loan, ie those made to traders. It could be deduced that it was intended to encourage such loans by allowing the lender relief if the borrower became unable to repay the loan. The Revenue's interpretation of s 253(3), that the loan must still be in existence at the time the claim is made, was unwarranted. It was clear in this case that at the time the claim was made the loans had become irrecoverable and the waiver did not affect that position. It did not cause the irrecoverability; nor would the loans have become recoverable again had there been no waiver.

HMRC's opinion was that the statutory words were clear. The use of the words 'has become irrecoverable' necessarily implied a continuing state of affairs. They gave as an analogy the sentence 'My cat has become ill': one would not use that form of words if the cat had since recovered, or died, but only if the cat was alive and unwell.

The Commissioners returned to the Revenue's cat (pre HMRC). While it is right that one would not say 'My cat has become ill', one might say 'My cat has become ill and has recovered several times'. The latter sentence implies no continuing state of affairs. The semantic subtlety on which the Revenue's argument depended had to be treated with some caution.

The Commissioners agreed instead with a point the taxpayer made: that if parliament had intended that a loan must be both subsisting and irrecoverable, it would have been simple to say so. The appeal was allowed.

It is hoped that, now the Revenue and Customs have merged, the cat is still alive and well. The tax-planning key is to review all loans that farming clients have made to traders that might not be recovered and ensure that maximum CGT relief is obtained if appropriate.

PROFESSIONAL LOGISTICS OF FINANCIAL PLANNING

5.42   There are a number of logistical problems surrounding tax planning, planning around the subject of borrowings, money lending and 'cash mountains' in the form of the Financial Services Act.

First, many small businesses do consider it appropriate to involve their tax adviser in the borrowing arrangement and sadly seek tax advice in a retrospective manner. Second, the advice can be defined (or considered to be defined) as the provision of financial services and some firms are concerned over the understanding of their professional code of conduct and the problems this might create. Third, at large firm level the corporate finance departments are totally dedicated to corporate efficiency but not so aware, for example, of the IHT considerations. There could also be a conflict of interest between the corporate tax-planning advice where the client giving the instructions is the company and the shareholder (who needs the IHT advice) is a conflicting client interest. Likewise, in a partnership where the tax adviser is appointed and instructed by the partnership to advise on the income tax efficiency of loans, the adviser has to consider the individual partners' IHT position. If they are conflicting, the tax planner must identify the conflict or suggest alternative independent advice.

A code of ethics issued by the ICAEW identifies for accountants (and tax advisers bound to this code) who they can refer their clients to.

Members of the ICAEW received a professional code of ethics from September 2006, which now takes into account changes in the provision of financial services advice and the introduction of the Insurance Mediation Directive. The updated code, which is available on the ICAEW website, highlights the need for members fully to understand the nature of the referral they are making and whether or not their authorisation means they can actively make a referral or whether they are restricted to a more passive referral style by providing information only.

The tax-planning work regarding business cash flows can move over to the domain of investment advice and with this move, complying with the appropriate code of ethics is essential.

So many angles of financial planning for the diversified farming enterprise are based on immediate need – 'asset needed now: obtain instant borrowings'. The 'cash-flow tax audit' is an essential way forward subject to the restrictions set out above and should form part of the 'BPR audit'.

'SIZE DOES MATTER' – FARM VALUATIONS

5.43   The publicity surrounding *Antrobus 2 (Lloyds TSB Private Banking (Personal Representative of Antrobus Dec'd) v CIR* DET/47/2004) (see **4.31**) and other valuation cases eg *Chadwick* and *Tapp* has highlighted the need for accurate valuations and the importance of the role of the professional valuer, the District Valuer (DV) and the Lands Tribunal. Likewise the case of *McCall* with such high development value (see **5.22** and **5.31**).

It has been said that tax planning is based on fact and the interpretation of statute and that variations in property values should not impact upon the tax advice that is provided by the tax planner. So does size or quantum matter to the tax planner? Does the approach of the tax planner vary with different values? What about the simple matters of 'risk assessment' and the calculation of future tax liabilities?

Clearly one obvious example with regard to the importance of accurate property values is that of the probate value of the farmhouse for both market value and agricultural value. The latter is the value of the asset used in the trade of farming as if the asset is subject to a perpetual covenant prohibiting its use otherwise than as agricultural property (IHTA 1984 s 115(3)) (see **4.32**).

The emphasis of the use of 'agricultural value' in the tax press has been heavily focused on the farmhouse but the agricultural value is also of prime importance with regard to farmland and the difference between farm and potential 'development' values. It can be argued that all land has some 'hope value', ie some hope of future development.

DEVELOPMENT (HOPE) VALUE – THE VALUATION

5.44   The question of 'hope' or 'special' value was looked at earlier in this chapter (see **5.33**). Likewise, the diversification to the trade of a developer is looked at in Chapter 6 (see **6.38**).

'Development' is not defined by statute. HMRC's interpretation is 'any physical adaptation or preparation for new use of land'. Development value is the increase in value created by planning consent or the anticipation of planning consent. This difference in value is of particular importance for IHT whether as a probate value or as a lifetime transfer. The agricultural value should attract APR and the difference with market value (hope value) should achieve BPR under IHTA 1984 s 110 (see **5.33**).

To achieve BPR under s 110 the land with development potential must be held in *exactly* the same way as land which does not attract such hope value. Evidence of the development land being used in the farming business in the same way as the other farmland would be imperative and must be retained.

But what is the quantum of the hope value? How is it determined? Note that development land values collapsed in 2008 and, at the time of writing, are recovering particularly on small developments.

As agricultural values had remained fairly static over the last 20 years or so, although they are rising at the time of writing and are thought to have doubled in the last five years, the correct valuation of hope or development value either before death to facilitate tax planning or for probate purposes is going to be of vast importance to the tax planner. At the time of writing, there has been a turnaround with general property prices falling, agricultural land prices staying strong, but development land values trying to recover. What would happen if the calculation of hope value quantum is wrong by, say, several millions of pounds? Does quantum matter, ie if the DV includes a high value, are there tax problems ahead? The answer has to be yes.

The probate value will potentially be the future base cost for capital gains tax (CGT). Clearly where large development values are involved, if full BPR can be achieved on the hope value then the IHT liability will be lower and the future CGT liability will be reduced due to a higher base cost. There are two questions that must be asked here. First, how certain is it that BPR will be achieved? Secondly, what codes are the valuers bound to try and help the taxpayer and the farm tax planner ensure total independence at all times? Obviously the answer must be 'Red Book'.

The apportionment of the total value between the element that achieves, say, full ER and the element that does not is critical to the farm tax planner (see below).

THE 'RED BOOK' VALUE

5.45   What guidelines are there with regard to property values? As from 2002–03, all tax property valuations that are used for all Tax Returns should be conducted within the standards governed by the 'Red Book' (the RICS valuation guide). Professional standards require comprehensive and thorough reports. The 'Red Book' *directs* both the taxpayer's valuer and the DV. The expectations should be that they are all performing to the same professional standards. Both have to apply themselves to the same definitions of market value. The probate valuation represents a document upon which the executor bases their IHT Returns dealing with market value and the quantum of agricultural value. The executors and tax advisers rely heavily upon the quality of the opinions and the accuracy of such valuations contained within probate valuation reports. The drafting of the probate valuation should be seen as an opportunity to give clear and independent advice to a client as to the issue of agricultural property relief. The probate and lifetime transfer valuation should be prepared with a great deal of precision and research and should clearly set out the taxpayer's position so that the executors can truly rely on it in terms of potential tax liabilities that may or may not be payable.

A well-prepared report is going to be more favourably received by CTO/DV than a report that lacks this professional duty of care, and they are more likely to be persuaded of the taxpayer's position by the application of such professional excellence. The DV's office is broadly exempt from 'Red Book' compliance due to the internal nature of their practice. However, there is no visible difference between chartered surveyors who act in private practice and those working within DVs' offices in so much as they will both be bound by the technical definitions found in statutes and the 'Red Book'.

If cases become contentious, requiring the need for the submission of expert witness type reports, then both types of valuer will be bound by the Civil Procedure Rules which have helpfully been set out in the RICS practice statement of 'Chartered Surveyors Acting as Expert Witnesses'.

A valuation, especially when dealing with complicated references, tends to be based upon thorough research. This suggests that only valuers with the relevant degree of experience in valuing certain property should attempt to provide probate valuations and/or expert reports and such valuers must have a detailed understanding of the complicated areas of tax case law that have evolved in recent years. This will require a valuer to work closely with the taxpayer's adviser and understand a lot of the basic tax principles and cases.

FUTURE LITIGATION – THE VALUER

5.46 With the potential for future litigation, high professional standards of valuers working in conjunction with their clients' legal and tax advisers are essential. Valuers will need to be independent and capable of providing documentation to support their valuations. In the property climate at the time of writing there can be huge variances in property values and therefore huge variances in the exposure to tax liabilities. Are valuers prepared to give evidence of valuation and for that evidence to be tested before the Special (Tax) Commissioners or the Lands Tribunal?

This is the procedure with regard to the unagreed land valuation. The Lands Tribunal applies to valuations on lifetime sales, lifetime transfers and probate.

To quote HMRC at CG74502:

'The Lands Tribunal is a Court equivalent in status to the High Court and with the power to award costs, which may be substantial. If a reference to the Lands Tribunal is necessary we are represented by the Board's Solicitor.'

Obviously where property will be subject to varying reliefs for either CGT or IHT, the apportionment of total value between individual values will impact upon the calculation of current and future tax liabilities.

CG74503 states:

'Following the introduction of Self-Assessment TMA70/S46D extends the jurisdiction of the Lands Tribunal to:

Amendments to self-assessment.

Amendments to a partnership statement.'

CG74160 declares:

'If agreement cannot be reached about an apportionment of any consideration between different assets that include land it may be necessary to refer the dispute to the Lands Tribunal.

TCGA92/S52(4) requires that any necessary apportionment is to be "just and reasonable". Where land is involved any judgement about what is just and reasonable must take into consideration the value of that land, therefore the Land Tribunal has authority to consider any land valuations within its jurisdiction needed to come to a judgement about an apportionment. You should follow the instructions at CG74500.'

TAX-PLANNING PROPERTY VALUES

5.47 For those tax planners who are about to undertake future CGT/IHT planning for their clients who have a sensitive IHT position, the accuracy of the property valuation is of prime importance and 'size does matter' with regard to assessing the mitigation and prediction of future IHT liabilities. An example of this would be where there is potential development land. The client and land agent must provide the tax adviser with the correct tax tools of their trade – accurate and reliable valuations with clear indicators of problems and uncertainty.

The quality of property valuations for tax-planning purposes is as important as the probate value. Is the client willing to pay for the cost of a Red Book valuation? Has the tax planner carried out the full risk assessment of the valuation being wrong? Is the tax planner happy to work with a value that is not 'Red Book'?

Should the taxpayer 'audit' the valuation before carrying out the tax-planning work?

Guidance can be obtained from the Auditing Practices Board's Statement of Auditing Standards 520, *Using the Work of an Expert*, which states that:

- 'When using the work performed by an expert, auditors should obtain sufficient appropriate audit evidence that such work is adequate for the purposes of the audit;

- When planning to use the work of an expert the auditors should assess the objectivity and professional qualifications, experience and resources of the expert;

- The auditors should obtain sufficient appropriate audit evidence that the expert's scope of work is adequate for the purposes of their audit; and

- The auditors should assess the appropriateness of the expert's work as audit evidence regarding the Financial Statements assertions being considered.'

Clearly some review/checking of the valuation should be undertaken for expert witness work but what of basic tax planning at the early stages? Can the tax adviser rely on these valuations?

THE TWO-YEAR TEST

5.48   One of the most frequent areas of attack by HMRC against a claim for IHT relief (IHT) is whether or not the agricultural property has been occupied for the purposes of agriculture for the two years prior to death (see **5.6**). The recent *Arnander* case (see **4.40**) was not restricted to the farmhouse. In deciding whether Rosteague House qualified for APR, Dr A N Brice (Special Commissioner), stated 'that Rosteague House was not occupied for the purposes of agriculture throughout the period of two years ending with the relevant dates of death within the meaning of section 117(a)'.

Whilst the *Arnander* case adds to the legal principles established in a string of IHT authorities which have looked at APR and the farmhouse, a significant point is that the Commissioner determined that the farmhouse and certain outbuildings had not been occupied for the purposes of agriculture throughout the period of two years ending with the relevant dates of death within the meaning IHTA1984 s 117(a).

Practitioners are finding that more and more emphasis is placed on the two-year rule established by s 117(a) by HMRC. Has the property been occupied for the purposes of agriculture in the two years prior to transfer?

A significant problem in achieving the APR appears to be where there is a reduction of physical presence by the owner through age or infirmity (see **4.42** *Atkinson*). Although the occupation requirement of s 117 does not require physical presence, there are problems where there is an absence for more than a minimal period. The key to a successful claim for APR is being able to show evidence of the taxpayer engaging in farming activities. It can be argued that the 'physical presence' can be evidenced and demonstrated with greater ease with regard to the farmland and buildings than the farmhouse through contract farming arrangements which involve genuine decision making and input by the landowner.

Are former agricultural buildings (buildings whose purpose was agriculture but is no longer) capable of failing in the claim for APR? Will BPR under IHT 1984 s 110 need to be called upon and will the BPR claim succeed?

Probate practitioners are receiving numerous questions over what agricultural business had actually been taking place over the two years before their client's death. This is not just limited to the history of agricultural activity. Questions are being raised with regard to proof of what was happening. The approach cannot be 'well she was farming it 50 years ago so she must be farming it now'. Historical documentation helps to give background and insight but it does not override the need to satisfy IHTA 1984 s 117(a). There are many farmers who will not just lose APR on the farmhouse, but may also lose eligibility to APR on farmland buildings.

The seven-year test is also of importance in the case of *Atkinson*.

It was emphasised that to qualify for agricultural property relief (APR) the agricultural property (in this case a farmhouse) has to be used for an agricultural purpose for seven years, but the use does not have to be continuous.

Mr Atkinson, who owned the farmhouse (actually a bungalow), died in 2006. In the four years prior to that he lived in a care home but he did visit the bungalow which still contained his belongings. The bungalow, plus other farm property and land owned by Mr Atkinson, was let to the family farming partnership. He was still involved in farming decisions as the senior partner.

His executors claimed APR but HMRC refused the claim on the grounds that the bungalow had not been occupied by Mr Atkinson throughout the previous seven years and had not been used for agricultural purposes while he was in the care home. The tribunal decided for the executors, on the grounds that the bungalow was occupied by the farming partnership and, in relation to the 'purposes of agriculture' test, it was used to accommodate the diminishing needs of the senior partner.

This case gives guidance to those elderly farmers in a similar situation, and perhaps the action plan of the relatives is not to rush out and let the farmhouse the day after the farming partner moves into a care home! This could be quite difficult for some farming partnerships which would need the rental income to pay for the care home. Equally the property should be kept available for use by the elderly partner and not emptied of his possessions. The case is being appealed by HMRC.

THE OUTBUILDINGS – THE BURDEN OF PROOF 'FOR THE PURPOSES OF AGRICULTURE'

5.49   In practice the outbuildings often have a high probate value and therefore a high potential IHT liability. There is often scope for planning permission and some form of development of the buildings.

The *Arnander* case also placed focus on the outbuildings. For the appellants Mr Massey QC argued that all the outbuildings were occupied for the purposes of agriculture as they were used or kept ready for use predominantly for the purposes of the storage of farm machinery and utilities. His argument was that they were not used for any non-agricultural purposes.

For HMRC Mr Karas accepted that the Dutch barn (building area 1) and the grain silo (building area 9) were used for the purposes of agriculture. The Dutch barn and grain silo passed the test, but what of the others?

It was stated that 'the burden of proof in these appeals is on the appellants to show that the outbuildings were used for the purposes of agriculture throughout the period 2001 to 2003' and that 'the appellants have not discharged the burden of proving that these buildings were used for the purpose of agriculture for the two years prior to the dates of death'.

What were the outbuildings? Which of the outbuildings were disallowed APR on the basis of not being used for the purposes of agriculture?

1.	Dutch barn	Allowed
2.	a dung stead	Disallowed
3.	informal tack room	Disallowed
4.	horse stabling	Disallowed
5.	storage for seasoned timber for rent	Disallowed
6.	storage-field troughs, gates, fencing stakes	Disallowed
7.	storage-creosote, hand tools, farm tools	Disallowed
8	storage-cement and block for construction	Disallowed
9	grain silo	Allowed
10	storage of agricultural machinery	Allowed
11	no evidence	Disallowed

What was Dr A N Brice's conclusion and reasoning with regard to the above? She stated, 'my conclusion on the fourth issue in the appeal is that the farm buildings numbered 1, 9 and 10 were occupied for the purposes of agriculture throughout the period of two years ending with the relevant date of death within the meaning of s 117(a) but that the farm outbuildings numbered 2, 3, 4, 5, 6, 7, 8 and 11 were not occupied for the purposes of agriculture throughout the period of two years ending with the relevant date of death within the meaning of s 117(a)'.

What is to be learnt here? It can be argued that this again emphasises that horse liveries are not an agricultural activity (IHTA 1984 s 115(2)). Would there be evidence in place to support the claim for BPR on outbuildings 2, 3, 4, 5, 6, 7, 8 and 11? The BPR position was not discussed in *Arnander* but the adviser must be prepared for the claim for BPR where APR claim fails.

'BARTER'– THE REALITY

5.50   The rural community has thrived on the concept (and reality) of the practice of 'barter' for centuries. In the majority of rural communities, most of the population have known each other for generations and a large number of the inhabitants are related to each other and with that comes trust – or bitter disputes – but let's concentrate on barter and trust.

It is quite normal for ferreted rabbits to be swapped at the local butchers' shops for pork chops, or for grazing to be exchanged for field maintenance. Hay bales can act as currency in return for building work, home made cakes or repairs to vehicles. All very innocent and rustic, as well as tending towards a paper-free environment, but this can underpin what can only amount to potential income tax, corporation tax or VAT non-disclosure – or even fraud.

That might sound harsh but it is the hard fact. The dream of a paperless rustic society has to be shattered when simple tax legislation and the self-assessment requirement to keep good books and records intervenes. The enquiry specialists will explain the need to keep 'contemporaneous' records.

Barter is not exclusive to rural communities; it occurs in urban and suburban communities as well, for example painting and decorating work in exchange for motor repairs, or even building work in return for legal services. Another well-documented area is bartering in the advertising industry, where customers provide free advertising space to their suppliers. The opportunities are endless.

'BARTER' – THE NEED FOR PAPERWORK

5.51   Clearly the service or product provided must be recognised at market value (*Sharkey (Inspector of Taxes) v Wernher* (1955) 36 TC 275) and a 'contemporaneous' sales invoice must be made out with sequential sales or fee invoice number and date. The business records must show how the invoice was settled, perhaps via a drawings journal or by the settlement of a purchase ledger invoice. Advice regarding the recording of such revenue is given in the HMRC booklet Self Assessment – A General Guide to Keeping Records. To quote direct from the booklet:

'Even if you do not record these through a till, you will need to make a record at the time the transaction takes place of the goods taken or supplied and their retail selling price.'

It is important here to refer to paragraph 45020 of HMRC's Business Income Manual, headed Specific deductions: Entertainment: Expenditure which is not Allowable. This quotes:

'Expenditure on business entertainment is not allowable as a deduction against profits, nor may a deduction be made for any expenditure which is incidental to business entertainment …

Traders may obtain entertainment through barter arrangements in which their own goods or services are exchanged for hospitality. The amount to be disallowed is the larger of:

(1)   The value at which the transaction is recognised in the profit and loss account; and

(2)   The cost of the goods or services exchanged for business entertainment.'

The correct VAT invoices must not only be recorded in the correct VAT quarter but the correct amount of output VAT must be charged and reclaimed.

The Institute of Chartered Accountants in England and Wales (ICAEW) summarise the accounting treatment under IAS 18 as follows:

'Revenue is measured at the fair value of the consideration received or receivable. The consideration is usually cash. If the inflow of cash is significantly deferred and there is no interest or a below market rate of interest, the fair value of the consideration of determined by discounting expected future receipts. If dissimilar goods or services are exchanged (as in barter transactions), revenue is the fair value of the goods or services received or, if this is not reliably measurable, the fair value of the goods or services given up.'

Further to this the International Accounting Standards Board interpretation SIC-31 Revenue – Barter Transactions Involving Advertising Services states:

'However, a swap of cheques, for example, for equal or substantially equal amounts between the same enterprises that provide and receive advertising services does not provide reliable evidence of fair value.'

'BARTER'– THE RISK OF LOSS OF TAX RELIEFS

5.52   In the farming community (with the average age of a farmer being high) it is possible for (in all innocence) the majority of farming activities to be dealt with via a simple barter arrangement, for example grassland exchanged for farm maintenance. If the barter transactions are not reflected, the farm accounts might show almost no activity: how would this reflect a claim for APR under IHTA 1984 s 115? Could it be proved that the land qualifies for APR or BPR? Could it be proved that the trade of farming was being undertaken? Is there enough of a business to support BPR?

What if part of the above farmland was to be subject to development? Would the land qualify for ER for CGT mindful of the restrictive nature of ER?

In order to claim roll-over relief or ER, it is essential to show that the farming assets are business assets, that is to say, assets used in the business. If all the activities are sheltered via barter, it is difficult to prove that the farm is a trading activity. If for example a parcel of the land were to become available for development, it could be very tempting for HMRC to challenge whether this is actually a business asset used in the business, because that is not supported by the business accounts and 'contemporaneous' records, although the restrictions of ER for the disposal of mere assets must be considered, the

CGT reliefs or hold-over and roll-over must also be considered. This is another example where unrecorded barter could work against the taxpayer in the claim for tax reliefs.

IHT – DO NOT LEND IT OR GIFT IT – DOCUMENT IT

5.53   HMRC guidance which applied from 31 March 2008 stated that there will be greater scrutiny of lifetime transfers. In 'IHT and Trusts Newsletter' HMRC included a note that it intended to pay close attention to such transfers. The HMRC theme for the documentation of all estates above and below the nil-rate band is similar to the record keeping of the self-employed. There was further indication of this need to document with both the transfer of the unused nil-rate band and jointly owned property.

(a) Lifetime transfers

The HMRC August 2007 'IHT and Trusts Newsletter' states:

'From now until 31 March 2008, when looking at forms IHT200 received on a death, we will be paying particularly close attention to lifetime transfers. Not only will we be looking at estates where a form D3 has been completed giving details of gifts or other transfers of value but we will be reviewing other aspects of estates which we know can give rise to a lifetime transfers.

These may include:

- Joint assets – gifts can arise on a transfer into joint names or where a joint owner receives the benefit of withdrawals from accounts funded wholly by the deceased;

- Loans – gifts can arise on the forgiveness of a debt or part of a debt;

- Movement of funds between multiple bank accounts – this can lead to gifts being overlooked;

- Inheritance – gifts can arise if there have been redistributions of property inherited by the deceased;

- Business or partnership – transfers from a business or partnership will not necessarily qualify for business relief;

- Rights under a pension scheme – a gift may arise if acts or omissions by a member of a pension scheme have the effect of increasing the value of benefits passing outside the member's estate at the expense of his own estate.

Where the information provided about these aspects is unclear, or incomplete, there is an increased likelihood that we will ask for further information or seek an explanation of what has occurred.

In appropriate cases we will open an enquiry and ask you for further information to satisfy ourselves that all gifts have been included. We will tell you if the estate is one that has been selected for enquiry in this way. Where it appears that the accountable persons have been negligent in not disclosing a gift in the IHT200 we will consider whether a penalty is appropriate.'

So is this HMRC behaviour intimidating or just HMRC doing what they should be doing (ie checking information submitted and collecting the correct amount of tax)?

The self-employed taxpayer realises they have to keep business records; so too must the taxpayer whether the estate falls below the nil rate band or above. Clearly incorrectly recorded transfers could place the estate above the nil rate band and hence cause a need for review and now there are games to be played with two nil rate bands.

(b) Estates below the nil-rate band

It will be necessary to keep records of estates below the IHT threshold so that the appropriate relief may be claimed when the surviving spouse dies.

HMRC have confirmed that:

'Where someone dies after 9 October 2007 with a nil rate band discretionary trust in their Will, an appointment of the trust assets in favour of the surviving spouse or civil partner (before the second anniversary of the death, but not within the three months immediately following the death) would normally be treated for IHT purposes as if the assets had simply been left to the surviving spouse or civil partner outright. Ending the trust in this way could mean that the £nil rate band was not used in the first death, and so the amount available for eventual transfer to the surviving spouse or civil partner would be increased accordingly.'

(Inheritance Tax: Transfer of Unused Nil Rate Band from www.hmrc.gov.uk/pbr2007/supplementary.htm)

So from 9 October 2007 were all those 'nil-rate band protection wills' torn up and started again?

The answer is that all wills should be looked at in a timely (but unrushed) manner, and the basic angles of loans, gifts and joint property should periodically be reviewed.

HMRC's Brief 71/07 announces that henceforth, when valuing land or buildings jointly owned by husband and wife (or by civil partners), HMRC will assume that IHTA 1984 s 161(4) applies. This means that the shares of the husband and wife will no longer be separately valued; instead, the overall value of the shares of both spouses will be determined (using the value of the whole property, if they are the only joint owners), and then divided between them, according to their fractional shares.

This change of practice follows a review of the decision in *Arkwright v Inland Revenue Commissioners* [2004] STC 1323 since when it has been assumed that s 161(4) applies only to assets held as a number of separate units (eg shares in a company). The background to *Arkwright* was that a Special Commissioner had held that s 161(4) did not apply to jointly owned land or buildings. That decision was not challenged in the High Court, either by the Inland Revenue or the judge. However, the judge allowed the Revenue's appeal 'to the limited extent' that the Special Commissioner should not have gone on to consider questions of fact – rather, she should have remitted such questions to the Lands Tribunal. HMRC have now received 'legal advice' that s 161(4) does apply to jointly owned land and buildings.

The new practice applied where the inheritance tax account was received by HMRC on or after 29 November 2007 (the day after the Brief was published).

There may be cases where s 161(4) treatment is advantageous to the taxpayer (eg to establish a higher base cost for CGT purposes). HMRC state that they will, at the taxpayer's request, re-open any valuation concluded on or after 16 July 2004 (the date of the decision in the *Arkwright*), on the basis that s 161(4) did not apply.

(c) Loans

Making or receiving a commercial or family loan can have implications with regard to wills and IHT. Not all loans can be deducted from a person's estate.

It is common for an individual to either loan or receive money as a loan and there are complicated rules in notifying HMRC that judge whether that the loan is allowable as a deduction against the value of the estate or not. In family situations where a loan is made or received it is often done on an informal basis with little or no documentation.

IHTA 1984 ss 162 and 164 broadly provide that a debt is to be valued for IHT purposes on the assumption that the obligation will be discharged and this would include any accrued interest.

In the case of a mortgage or bank loan HMRC will normally accept the deduction claim on Form D16 (part of the IHT 200) and it will first be set against the property against which it is charged; but where the property is being passed on to a spouse or civil partner and is exempt, the loan will not be allowed as a deduction against the deceased estate.

A family loan or a commercial loan secured against family assets must periodically be reviewed, as what may seem 'a good idea at the time' may have the potential to cause problems with the calculation of the net estate, the IHT liability and family entitlement. A meeting with the family's tax adviser and lawyer beckons with the following issues possibly being on the agenda.

● Loan planning for IHT (see **5.35**).

● Jointly owned property.

● Lifetime transfers.

● Don't just lend it or gift it, document it!

● Loans, jointly owned assets and lifetime transfers – is documentation robust enough?

SALE OF PROPERTY WITHIN FOUR YEARS WHERE NEITHER BPR NOR APR AVAILABLE

5.54   If, within four years of death, the property is sold for less than the agreed probate value for IHT, then the earlier IHT liability can be reduced by substituting the lower sale proceeds instead of the agreed value, therefore hopefully saving the estate IHT.

If it was originally planned to hold on to the property, the sale will obviously trigger the full payment for IHT where previously it was due in instalments over ten years, ie as instalment option property.

Where the property is passed by the personal representative to the residuary beneficiary, the personal representative must be mindful of the fact that if the beneficiary sells the property the full IHT liability will become due immediately and the ten-year option lost. The personal representative should therefore either retain an IHT fund or an 'indemnity' from the beneficiary.

It is only the personal representatives who can make this four-year claim. If the property is transferred to the beneficiary and they then dispose of the property within four years they cannot take advantage of the election.

If the beneficiary sells the property (or part of a portfolio of properties) within four years (or after four years) to produce a loss, the IHT value cannot be taken advantage of, *but* a CGT loss can be created by the beneficiary.

It has been said that the IHT planner and adviser has to deal with the IHT planning prior to death – tax planning for 'the dead and the nearly dead'. These are changing turbulent times and the opportunities must be taken to use, for example, the election to replace original valuation at death with subsequent sale proceeds where values have dropped, and to use the opportunity to promote strong arguments for tax-efficient values.

EARL OF BALFOUR – NOT AN 'INVESTMENT BUSINESS'

5.55   The first judgment of the *Balfour* case was delivered on 14 May 2009. This recorded a successful BPR claim for a mixed agricultural estate in Scotland. The First-tier Tribunal (Special Commissioners) ruled that the business in question was not 'wholly or mainly making or holding investments' under the interpretation of IHTA 1984 s 105(3). This is seen as great news for the farming world and the case is regarded as reinforcing the decisions of *Farmer* and *George*. This has been taken further by the Upper Tribunal. The decision was endorsed by the Upper Tribunal in *HMRC v Balfour* [2010] UKUT 300.

The emphasis of *Brander (Representative of Fourth Earl of Balfour) v HMRC Comms* [2009] UKFTT 101 was that in order to see if a business was in fact an 'investment business' there was a need to establish where the 'preponderance of the business activity' was (para 42).

The relevant factors that have to be looked at are 'turnover, profit, expenditure and time spent by everyone in carrying on the various business activities'.

With incomplete evidence as we have here, and probably in most cases, it is a matter of more general assessment and impression as to where the preponderance of business activity lies. This means looking at the activities being carried on at the estate in the round (an approach by the Court of Appeal in *IRC v George* 2003 at 152c).

This case is looked at in more detail in chapter 13. Whilst this is considered good news for the mixed estate, death and the allowability of BPR are absolute and whilst reasonable investment activity can be allowed in the 'one overall business', there must be caution about where the 'preponderance of business lies'.

As mentioned, the decision in the case of *HMRC v Balfour* [2010] UKUT 300 has been endorsed by the Upper Tribunal. They found that the First-tier Tribunal was correct to conclude that Lord Balfour operated the estate as one business before November 2002, even though the in-hand farms were run from a farming partnership, which did not include the trustees, and separate accounts were prepared for the partnership and the trust.

The factors used in the case of *Farmer* were considered to determine whether or not the composite business carried on by Lord Balfour was mainly one of the making or holding of investments so that BPR could not apply (IHT Act 1984 s 105(3)). The overall context, turnover, net profit and time spent all pointed towards this not being the case, but the capital value of the let properties exceeded the value of other property in the ratio 1.88:1. The Upper Tribunal was satisfied that the First-tier Tribunal was entitled to attach little weight to the capital value and as such was also entitled to conclude that s 105(3) did not apply because Lord Balfour's business did not consist mainly of holding investments.

The appeal by HM Revenue & Customs was therefore refused.

DANCE – LOSS TO DONOR

5.56   In *HMRC v Trustees of Nelson Dance Family Settlement* [2009] EWHC 71 Ch the taxpayer succeeded before both the Special Commissioner and in the High Court. HMRC are not appealing the High Court decision. There has been no attempt at reversing or changing the decision in the subsequent Finance Acts. The relevant facts are as follows:

The settlor had owned and farmed a number of farms part of which he subsequently gifted to a discretionary settlement. This gift was an immediately chargeable transfer for IHT purposes and the question was whether 100% BPR was available on the occasion of the transfer. HMRC were trying to argue BPR did not apply to the transfer.

It was accepted that the farms, in the hands of the settlor (Nelson Dance), were relevant business property (as required in the legislation), being property that was a '… business or an interest in a business …' (IHTA 1984 s 105(1) (a)) because the settlor was carrying on the farming business. This creates tax-planning opportunities regarding transfers of non business farm property.

It was also accepted that, in the hands of the trustees, the farms were not *relevant business property* because the trustees were not farming the land immediately. HMRC argued that BPR should not be given because the property which had been transferred to the trustees was not in itself a business at the point of transfer.

The Special Commissioner accepted the taxpayer's argument that the terms of the IHT legislation made it necessary to look only at the transferor (in this case the settlor, Mr Dance) and what he had lost. Therefore, what had lost value in Mr Dance's estate was *relevant business property*. What the transferee (here the trustees) had, or had not, received was irrelevant.

The High Court confirmed the approach of the Special Commissioners, emphasising that the general principle of the 'loss to the donor' governed the operation of IHTA 1984 and that the objective of BPR was to encourage the use of assets in a business.

This case can aid tax planning with regard to both gifting assets now and protecting the mixed estate (see Chapter 13). As with all IHT planning on the diversifying farm or mixed estate there is high risk involved and the quantum of tax at risk is high. Therefore, the protection afforded by 'BPR audits' and the advice of Tax Counsel must be considered by both the tax planner and the client.

Chapter 6

Diversification – the reality

Julie Butler

- **Specific diversified activities and environmental stewardship**
  As farming possibly moves away from production and rural diversification becomes a reality, the tax treatments of various alternatives are considered, along with a review of what grants are available for dedicated diversified activities.

- **Woodland and forestry**
  Long-term woodland and forestry is not strictly agriculture (see **1.5**) and has its own set of rules. The interaction between short- and long-term woodland activities, and the tax-planning implications are reviewed below. The IHT relief on long-term woodlands is possibly a deferral of the charge to IHT and the possibility of APR/BPR as an alternative needs consideration.

- **Furnished holiday lets (FHL) or furnished holiday business (FHB)**
  FHBs is a diversified activity. The alternative use of farmland and buildings for FHLs which is currently supported by a favourable tax regime and possible grants. Restructuring from 6 April 2011 is proposed.

- **The equine issue**
  Stud farming is farming for tax purposes, but what about other equine activities? Do they constitute farming or diversification?

- **Caravans**
  There is much case law to help give guidance for other diversified activities.

- **Heritage property – a deferral of the charge to IHT**
  For assets which do not qualify for the generous APR and BPR, an alternative could be a review of the heritage property reliefs. They are, however, a deferral of IHT tax and must be given consideration as such.

- **Property development**
  Property development is a diversified activity. Sheltering development profit in farmland (and agri-environmental schemes) features throughout the book, but what of the collapse of development land values?

- **Wind farms and energy crops**
  Tax-planning considerations.

WHAT CAN BE ACHIEVED?

6.1   Chapter 1 introduced the need for diversification, with Chapter 2 explaining the bold move towards diversification. It has been said that diversification is not new. What is new is the need for farmers to seek profitability from an activity other than husbandry and the amount of grant funding that is possibly now available to help finance diversification schemes. This funding is looked at in Chapter 2.

The business structure available (or chosen) to deal with the diversified activity will be of prime importance. A lot of the activities featured here carry a high degree of risk, eg equine activities, recreational fishing and shooting, tourism, farm exhibitions, activity leisure pursuits etc. The owner of the land may remain a farmer for business and tax purposes and separate the risk activity into a separate legal entity. The farmer can retain the generous farming tax reliefs (see **1.13**), whilst still working toward the activity. However, the legal and tax position of the new separate business and the farmer must be established (see Chapter 15).

GRANT FUNDING FOR DIVERSIFICATION AND STEWARDSHIP

6.2   Chapters 1 and 2 introduced grants available for diversification and rural initiatives. There are other grants available, but these are for agri-environmental schemes and they are assumed to be farming, not diversification/rural initiatives.

The emphasis of grant funds is now on environmental stewardship, energy crop schemes, stewardship of existing woodlands and the creation of new woodlands.

TYPES OF RURAL INITIATIVES

6.3   Chapter 1 set out a table of what can be considered farming (**1.4**) and what cannot be considered farming (**1.5**). Alternative land uses were listed in **1.9**. Let us now look at the reality of rural initiatives:

- woodlands (see **6.4–6.12**);
- furnished holiday lets (see **6.13–6.15**);
- bed and breakfast and caravanning and camping (see **6.16, 6.18–6.22**);
- the stud farm – this is farming (see **6.17**);
- sales of turf and depositing soil (see **6.23**);
- equine and riding schools (see **6.24–6.29**);
- fishing (see **6.30**);
- shooting (see **6.51–6.55**);
- activity leisure pursuits and walking and cycling holidays (see **6.32**);
- agricultural and countryside attractions (see **6.31**);
- visitor attractions and craft centres (see **6.15**);
- farm shops, restaurants and cafes (see **6.33**);

- the farm contractor (see **6.35**);

- mobile phone masts (see **6.36**);

- extracting minerals (eg gravel, sand) beneath the land (see **6.37**);

- the property developer (see **6.38**);

- ice cream and cheese production;

- meat processing (reconnecting the food chain);

- energy crops and biofuels (see **6.47** and **6.48**);

- review of heritage property relief (see **6.39–6.44**);

- agri-environmental schemes (see **6.45**);

- fruit orchards (see **6.46**);

- wind farms (see **6.49–6.50**);

- Christmas trees (see **6.5**);

- letting redundant buildings (offices and workshop) (see Chapter 15);

- residential lets (Chapter 15);

- self-catering holiday accommodation (furnished holiday lets see **6.13–6.15**);

- pet foods;

- pre-school nurseries;

- engineering works;

- buffalo; and

- vineyards.

WOODLANDS

6.4   The woodland found on most farms is often grown for amenity or conservation value. The prospects of timber production can be a commercial reality. Grants are available for woodlands. To quote Stephen Judd of Independent Woodland Management:

> 'The idea of planting new native woodlands on the farm is ever growing in popularity. The current farming recession adds to this appeal because substantial grant aid is available from the first year and profitability measured over a fifteen year period is often substantially better than a stock or arable comparison.'

The occupation of commercial woodlands (or land being prepared for forestry purposes) in the UK is exempt from being taxed as trading income or property income. The exemption from income tax includes land being prepared for forestry purposes (ITTOIA 2005 s 10(3)(b)).

ITTOIA 2005 ss 11 and 768 ensure that income from the commercial occupation of woodland is neither trading income nor income not otherwise charged; however, ITTOIA 2005 s 267(b) now makes explicit that no charge as profits of a property business can apply to the occupation of commercial woodland (via ITTOIA s 10(3)).

This chapter (see **6.4–6.12**) looks at whether farms want and need the current apparent tax advantage of woodlands, the income tax exemption and IHT deferral. Are there better alternatives? The exemption does not include Christmas trees or short-rotation coppice cultivation, which are treated as farming not forestry. Coppicing is defined as a perennial crop of tree species planted at high density, the stems of which are harvested above the ground level at intervals of less than ten years (ITA 2007 s 996(6)). Examples are willow or poplar, which are being used for new 'green' power stations as an energy crop (see **6.47** and **6.48**).

The annual stock valuation for Christmas trees (**6.5**) and short rotation coppice (SRC) cultivation should include direct costs of weeding, disease prevention, harvesting and the cost of the first cut. The initial cultivation of the land includes spraying, ploughing, fencing and planting of the cuttings as capital expenditure.

Where an owner of woodlands lets the woodlands and receives income in the form of rent, that rental income is charged as profits from a property business (under ITTOIA 2005 Pt 3 or CTA 2009 Pt 4). This would also apply to income derived from other uses of the woodland, for example, profits from the exploitation of sporting rights or income from picnic and camp sites.

Christmas trees, the sale of timber and timber merchants

6.5   Generally, Christmas trees and the sale of timber are not exempt from being taxed as trading income under ITTOIA 2005 ss 11 and 768. The position concerning Christmas trees is at HMRC's BIM55210:

> 'The growing of Christmas trees is not covered by the exemption for commercial woodlands (see *Jaggers v Ellis* [1996] STC (SCD) 440). Nowadays most Christmas tree production is from specialist Christmas tree producers or from farmers who grow the trees as a crop. Where Christmas trees are grown on an ordinary farm the income may be included in the farm profits. Specialist "Christmas tree farms" are nurseries and thus fall within the definition of "market gardening" … Some poor quality Christmas trees are produced by selling the tops of felled trees from commercial woodlands or the thinnings from land being prepared for forestry. In those cases the profits are covered by the woodlands exemption.'

Likewise, the position concerning receipts from sales of timber etc is found at BIM55205.

OCCUPATION OF WOODLANDS

6.6   Identifying the occupier on whom tax is chargeable may present problems. There is no definition of who is the occupier for this purpose. The same problem exists for the definition of farming. Generally, the person who has paramount use of the land will be the occupier (*Dawson v Counsell* [1938] 22 TC 149) and that user will normally be the occupier to the exclusion of others, though there is authority to suggest that there may be more than one occupier (see *Beck v Daniels* [1924] 9 TC 183).

It is now generally established that a person who enters land for the purposes of felling, processing or removing timber, or clearing land for replanting, is not treated as being in occupation of the woodlands and hence would be taxable on any profits made. This is notwithstanding *Russell v Hird* [1983] STC 541, which accordingly is of limited authority.

BIM55205 states:

'Commercial woodland is not within the statutory definition of farming (see BIM55051). Profits from the sale of timber from commercial woodland are outside tax, although annual payments received by farmers under certain grant schemes in respect of such woodland may be taxable (see BIM55165). Some guidance on the distinction between woodland and farm land may be derived from *De Poix v Chapman* [1947] 28TC462 (see, in particular, Atkinson J's comments on page 470 about definite separation of woodland and farm land with permanence of purpose and use).'

If the land is predominantly occupied for other purposes the receipts from felled timber may fall outside the exemption. For example, BIM55205 continues: 'Receipts from the sale of trees planted on a farm should be included as part of farming profits (see, for example *Elmes v Trembath* [1934] 19 TC 72)'. Short-rotation coppice is specifically brought within farming. Many farms focusing on diversification activities should note the importance of the 'predominant occupation' for woodland.

The generally held view is that the occupation of woodland ceases and the processing of timber begins when processing goes beyond turning felled timber into planks. For example, in *Collins v Fraser* [1969] 46 TC 143 it was held that if the activity was simply to make the produce of the soil marketable, the profits of it could be treated as franked by Schedule B (and hence be within the scope of the current exemption). However, in that case the timber was felled, planked and trimmed, and manufactured into packing cases. The court suggested a liability to trading income would arise on the manufacturing profit as this represented additional 'taxable capacity'. Unfortunately the exact outcome in *Collins v Fraser* is not reported, but in practice, the value of the planked timber is brought into the accounts of a timber processing business at market value at that stage in the processing and profits thereafter become taxable as profits of a timber merchant.

Woodlands – capital gains tax

6.7 Under TCGA 1992 s 250(4)–(6) the part of the cost and sale proceeds of woodlands in the UK which is attributed to underwood or trees growing or felled on the land, is disregarded for CGT. Under TCGA 1992 s 250(1)–(2) where woodlands are managed on a commercial basis with a view to the realisation of profits the proceeds are also disregarded. The proceeds could be the right to fell standing timber, the proceeds of felled timber or the insurance proceeds from their destruction.

These two provisions, in principle, ensure that where the woodland income is exempt from income tax under ITTOIA 2005 ss 10(3)(c),11 and 768 the woodland is also exempt from CGT.

The problem arises on the disposal of the land as the sale and purchase price needs to be apportioned between the land and the growing timber. The former is taxable, the latter is not. Although the occupation of woodlands on a commercial basis is exempt from income tax it is still a business for CGT. It is still possible to roll-over for CGT purposes with the sale of business assets.

Land used for commercial forestry is not a 'business' asset although it can qualify for roll-over relief and gifts hold-over relief under TCGA 1992 s 165.

Woodlands – short rotation coppice

6.8   IHTM24063 states:

'In relation to transfers of value or other events occurring on or after 6 April 1995, the cultivation of short rotation coppice is regarded as an agricultural purpose (IHTM24101), and land on which it is cultivated is regarded as agricultural land, and buildings used in connection with its cultivation are regarded as farm buildings.

For this purpose, "short rotation coppice" means

a perennial crop of tree species planted at high density

the stems of which are harvested above ground level at intervals of less than ten years.

One use for such a product is to produce renewable fuel for biomass fed power stations. Willow or poplar cuttings are planted on farmland and, after the first year, are harvested every three years or so. The cuttings are made into chips that are used as fuel.'

In conclusion cultivation of SRC is farming for IHT purposes.

Woodlands – commercial considerations

6.9   The choice of diversifying into woodlands might be grant led. However, it is not something that should be undertaken lightly – there is no room for error due to the long-term nature of the decision and lack of flexibility. Woodland planting can result in a loss of value of the land. However, a small percentage of woodland can help increase the value of the farm/estate with increased sporting rights as a benefit. SRC as an energy crop is looked at under **6.47**.

The increasing awareness of the environment makes woodlands very attractive. In theory, there is a market for wood, as approximately 90% of the UK's needs are currently met by imports.

The grants are complex, and the management and economics associated therewith need careful review. Like all diversification projects they need detailed research; and professional assistance with grants and quality management is essential. Additional training and equipment may be required if undertaken on a large scale.

Woodlands – inheritance tax deferral relief

6.10   There is a deferral relief for woodlands by which an election can be made within two years after death to leave the timber (but not the land) out of account when valuing the estate (IHTA 1984 ss 125–130). The deceased must have owned the woods for at least five years before death unless he became beneficially entitled to the woodlands by gift or inheritance without consideration. However, when the timber is subsequently disposed of, whether by sale or by gift, IHT is charged, with a deduction for allowable expenses (including replanting costs within three years). Much more favourable, however, than this deferral relief will be outright exemption at 100%; either APR where woodlands are occupied with agricultural land (and are 'ancillary' to it) or BPR where the woodlands are managed on a commercial basis. The planning around this is looked at below (see **6.12**).

Woodlands can qualify for BPR, providing, of course, they are run as a business on a commercial basis. This may need to be evidenced by the presentation of separate woodland accounts showing profitability.

Where the person liable has elected to take the relief under IHTA 1984 ss 125–130, IHT will become payable if there is a disposal of the timber before the next death, whether by sale for full consideration or not. Since the tax has merely been deferred since death, the tax will become payable on a subsequent disposal whether or not that disposal is itself a chargeable transfer. The only exception is that a disposal by a person to his spouse will not cause the charge to be triggered (IHTA 1984 s 126).

If the timber is sold, tax becomes payable on the net proceeds of the sale. The person exclusively liable is the person who is, or would be, entitled to the proceeds of sale. The IHT liability is calculated by adding the sale proceeds to the estate of the deceased and calculating the IHT liability thereon. No change is made to any tax liability in any other asset in the estate. The proceeds that are brought into charge are the net proceeds of sale or the net value. For the net proceeds of sale, one must deduct from the proceeds certain expenses, namely those incurred in the disposal, in replanting within three years or such longer time as HMRC may allow, and in replanting to replace earlier disposals so far as not allowable on those previous disposals (IHTA 1984 s 128). These deductions, however, are not allowed if they are allowable for income tax, a phrase that presumably means theoretically allowable and so excludes deduction for IHT, whether or not there is sufficient income to absorb its expense. The net value is the value of the timber after allowing for these deductions.

Where the disposal is itself a chargeable transfer, two sets of liability to tax will arise: the first by reference to the previous death, the second by reference to the disposal. It is then provided that in computing the value transferred on the second transfer a deduction is made for the tax chargeable on the first (IHTA 1984 s 127). The deduction is simply in valuing the transfer. It is not a credit of tax against tax. Where the second transfer is an occasion for business relief, the reduction under that relief is applied to the value as reduced by the tax paid in respect of the first death (IHTA 1984 s 114(2)).

SRC is a perennial crop. The land on which it is cultivated becomes 'agricultural' and buildings used in connection with the cultivation become 'farm buildings' (FA 1995 s 154). Therefore, APR applies to land used for SRC and there is also the possibility of BPR to be considered (see **6.10**).

Chapter 24 and greater definition of woodlands

6.11   Chapter 24 of HMRC's Inheritance Tax Manual helps give clarity on 'ancillary' woodlands and the availability of IHT relief.

IHTM24030 states:

> 'Agricultural property is defined in IHTA84/S115 (2). It means agricultural land or pasture (IHTM24031) which includes woodland (IHTM24032) and any building used in connection with the intensive rearing of livestock or fish (IHTM24033), if the woodland or building
>
> • is occupied with agricultural land or pasture, (IHTM24031) and
>
> • the occupation is ancillary to that of the agricultural land or pasture.'

Provided the woodland is occupied by the same occupiers as the agricultural land and that occupation is part of the agricultural operation then it seems appropriate to make a claim for APR. The woodland should be supplementary and/or supporting to the main activity of agriculture.

IHTM24032 goes into more detail on the ability to claim APR on woodland:

> 'Woodland is only agricultural property if it is occupied with, and that occupation is ancillary to, agricultural land or pasture. It will include woodland shelter belts, game coverts, fox coverts, coppices grown for fencing materials on the farm and clumps of amenity trees or spinneys.
>
> Woodlands occupied for purposes that are not agricultural, such as amenity woodland or woodland used for the production of commercial timber will not be agricultural property. However, they may be eligible for woodlands relief (IHTM04371) or business relief (IHTM25251).
>
> This will also be true of agri-environmental schemes (IHTM24067).'

What about new plantation under the agricultural/environmental schemes? IHTM24067 gives guidance on new woodland:

> 'There are many other agricultural/environmental schemes that can apply to agricultural land.
>
> The Farm Woodland Premium Scheme is administered by DEFRA, and exists to promote the establishment of woodland by offering annual payments to compensate for the agricultural income foregone. It is only available to farmers who must at the same time apply for grants under the Woodland Grant Scheme (WGS), as the environmental and silvicultural

standards of the WGSr must be satisfied before an FWPS application can be approved.

The Scheme is open to farmers who, either personally or through a manager, run an agricultural business that includes the land to be converted to woodland. Agriculture is defined in the Rules and Procedures and is broadly in line with that included in s.96(1) AHA 1986; keeping horses for recreational and/or sporting purposes is specifically excluded, as is fish farming.

Once accepted into the scheme the woodland must be maintained in accordance with good forestry practice and not returned to agricultural use for at least

- 30 years after planting in the case of woodland receiving payments for 15 years (generally more than 50% by area with broadleaves);

- 20 years in the case of woodland receiving payments for 10 years (generally 50% or less by area with broadleaves).

Agricultural relief cannot be available as the whole purpose of the Scheme is to take land out of agriculture.

You should refer any cases involving schemes not covered by these instructions where it appears that the land is not occupied for agricultural purposes (IHTM24060) to TG.'

General tax planning for woodlands

6.12   With farming in crisis and so many forms of diversification being considered, the commercial and income tax benefit of woodlands can be very advantageous. The ability to have the relevant element of income (see **6.5**) (and related expenses) removed from the business tax computation is a very attractive proposition as indeed is any 'tax-free' income. The problem arises that with the high value of land APR could be put at risk.

In order for land used for growing 'woodlands' to classify as eligible for APR it must be occupied with agricultural land and be ancillary to it. As more land is used for non-agricultural purposes, the emphasis of IHT reliefs moves from APR to BPR and the picture becomes more complicated. As a general planning point, whilst the taxpayer should look to minimise income tax through exempt income from woodlands, the finer points of future IHT planning should not be overlooked. As with all land ownerships in these changing times of diversification, it is imperative to look at the total ownership 'in the round' and to review the total interaction of income tax, CGT and IHT reliefs.

As mentioned above, the ability to leave income from some woodland activities out of the taxable profits of a farming business is very attractive to many farmers and landowners. However, the IHT position of the very high value of the land is a pertinent factor. For example, it would be a shame to jeopardise the claim for future IHT relief by a relatively small saving of income tax.

Finance Act 2009 s 122 extends the IHT agricultural property and woodlands relief to property outside the UK but within the European Economic Area

(EEA). This new relief which is backdated to allow tax due or paid since 23 April 2003 (ie six years before Budget Day 2009) to be reclaimed, is required to comply with the UK's obligations under EC law, as clarified by the decision in *Persche v Finanz-ampt Ludenscheid* (Case C-318/07). That case in fact concerned tax relief for charitable donations made by an individual in Germany to a charity in Portugal, but the European principle of free movement of capital covers both charitable donations and taxes on inheritances. Having considered representations made by the European Commission, the government decided that the reliefs should be extended to property in the EEA.

FURNISHED HOLIDAY LETS (FHL)

Furnished holiday lets – the changing tax position

6.13   FHLs have become a dedicated and positive diversified activity for the farmer and landowner. With the reduction of the workforce and the conversion of redundant livestock buildings to accommodation, FHLs are considered in Chapter 15.

As machinery has taken over rural labour, workers' cottages on traditional farms have become available to let. Redundant farm buildings can also be converted for letting. Now that rental income is high, it is not just farmers wanting to maximise their income from property who see furnished lets as a good investment.

The current rules

The rules for FHLs prior to 6 April 2011 are that for income tax loss relief, ER, capital allowances and other CGT reliefs to be achieved certain conditions must be met. To benefit, the property must be available for commercial letting as holiday accommodation for at least 140 days a year and actually let for at least 70. It must not be in the same occupation for a continuous period of more than 31 days for at least seven months in any 12-month period. The government consultation document published in July 2010 proposes that the dates available for commercial letting increase from 140 days to 210 days and the period that the property is actually let is increased from 70 days to 105 days.

If these conditions are met, the letting of furnished holiday accommodation is treated as a trade for tax loss relief purposes. Many property owners will want to maximise returns by moving from furnished long-term letting to furnished holiday lets. The tax loss situation is looked at in **12.7**.

Wear and tear allowances cannot be claimed in respect of holiday lets where capital allowances are available. If a house is let long term, however, expenditure on furniture and fixtures qualifies for wear and tear allowances. These are calculated on 10% of the rents, less any expense that the landlord meets that would normally be paid by a tenant (such as council tax). The wear and tear allowance is meant to cover furniture and fixtures that, in unfurnished lodgings, a tenant would provide (eg cookers, washing machines, etc). It only applies to residential property that is furnished in such a way that the tenant does not have to provide any furnishings. Instead of wear and tear, the cost of renewing furnishings can be claimed, as long as there is no deduction of the original expenditure, no claim is made for any cost of any improvement when the old asset is discarded. The farmer can also claim the cost of renewing fixtures that are not usually removed if a property is vacated or sold (eg baths, toilets, etc).

The current advantages

It must be borne in mind that the FHL rules only present advantages in terms of income tax and CGT relief *and* they had to be commercial. IHT relief via BPR was, and is, a separate subject. So consider the concept of a hotel business and the provision of services for BPR.

What tax reliefs are in place until 6 April 2011?

1.   (a)   ER (which reduces the taxable gains on the sale of a business to an effective 10% rate from an 18% or 28% rate);

    (b)   roll-over relief (which allows gains arising on the sale of business assets to be deferred if the proceeds of sale are reinvested into other business assets); and

    (c)   specific hold-over relief for business assets (which allows the accrued gains arising on a lifetime gift of property to another individual to be deferred and assumed by the donee).

2.   Losses from FHLs can be set against other income (eg other trading or employment income).

3.   Entitlement to plant and machinery capital allowances on furniture and furnishings etc which are not available to normal non-FHL residential lettings.

Future proposals

The government consultation document published in July 2010 proposes that from 6 April 2011 the change to the above is that losses from FHLs are *carried forward* against the profits of future FHLs.

The tax-planning point is perhaps to consider immediate repairs that will need to be made prior to 6 April 2011 when any excess of expenses over income will only be allowed to be carried forward per the consultation document.

The standard rate of VAT applies to rents from holiday lets as long as they are advertised as such, ie the supply of the accommodation is subject to standard rate VAT as opposed to qualifying for exemption to VAT. If they are offered at lower rates in the off season, they can be treated as residential accommodation if they are let for that purpose for more than four weeks and the property is situated in a resort where trade is clearly seasonal (see **15.11**).

Furnished holiday letting – the inheritance tax viewpoint

6.14   It is important that farmers who own holiday cottages should try and ensure, as far as possible, that they qualify for IHT relief. With property prices remaining high, the need to shelter these assets from IHT is greater than ever.

IHT relief will depend on the 'level and type of services' provided to holidaymakers, eg provision of meals, cleaning and hotel type services. See IHTM25278 which confirms that HMRC are scrutinising claims for BPR on holiday lettings.

As part of farm enterprise, holiday lettings may be eligible under *Farmer v IRC* principles and now *Earl of Balfour* as part of a larger business. Beware a separate 'person', eg the farmer's wife carrying on business for VAT reasons ie avoid charging VAT on the holiday service.

Case law suggests that in order to qualify for BPR, it might be necessary to own a number of properties.

IHTM25278 states:

'In the past we have thought that business property relief would normally be available where:

- the lettings were short term, and

- the owner, either himself or through an agent such as a relative, was substantially involved with the holidaymakers in terms of their activities on and from the premises.

Recent advice from Solicitor's Office has caused us to reconsider our approach and it may well be that some cases that might have previously qualified should not have done so. In particular we will be looking more closely at the level and type of services, rather than who provided them. Until further notice any case involving a claim for business property relief on a holiday let should be referred to the Technical Team (Litigation) for consideration at an early stage.'

As usual, whether this IHT test will be satisfied will depend on the facts. The question is whether or not such businesses would be excluded by the Inheritance Tax Act 1984 (IHTA 1984) s 105(3) and the criteria are not that dissimilar to the points raised in *Farmer (Farmer's Executors) v IRC* [1999] STC (SCD) 321. 'Is there a business or is there a holding of investments?' (See Chapter 13.) Risk areas which might jeopardise the IHT claim are:

- where no services are provided to holidaymakers;

- where lettings are to friends and relatives; and

- longer term lettings (including assured shortholds).

If it is considered that an 'adventure in the nature of trade' and 'business' can be established for an elderly taxpayer is the opportunity to pass the property to the next generation now?

There are possibly many FHL IHT tax cases waiting to be heard by the Tax Tribunal. Will this be a farm FHL?

HMRC would no doubt like to choose a hopeless BPR claim that can be 'walked all over' and show why FHLs qualify as a 'non-investment business'. It is therefore essential that the FHL case that goes before the Tribunal must be strong. HMRC would like to see FHLs placed firmly within the confines of s 105(3), but this insults the real holiday cottage businesses that exist in the

UK. If any BPR case looks like appearing before the Revenue Tribunal the UK tourist authorities must put all their energy into fighting the case.

There are a large number of holiday businesses in the UK which need to be recognised as businesses now. Rethink, restructure and register the business with HMRC/Contributions Agency as a trade, using form CWF1 (check HMRC website), if appropriate.

Furnished holiday business – not furnished holiday lets?

6.15   So has all the tax 'fuss' over FHLs and consideration of turning the operation of FHLs into a business been unnecessary since 22 April 2009? The answer has to be no if one of the main concerns for the owner of the property is IHT relief.

From the practical commercial viewpoint the farmer/owner of the accommodation has to decide what direction they want to take their holiday business in – landlord or viable, economic commercial undertaking (trade)?

So what are the problems of the adventure in the nature of a trade?

- A true commercial business is as 'it says on the tin' an adventure – an undertaking that involves risks and service to the client.

- Class 4 National Insurance (NIC). As a business, when the profits exceed a certain level then Class 4 NIC is due, although there are deferments for those with Class 1 earnings through employment and retirement age advantages.

BED AND BREAKFAST

6.16   UK tourism depends on farming not only for preserving the countryside but also for the provision of cost-effective, homely places to stay. Farming clients looking for tax reliefs may find setting up bed and breakfast (B&B) accommodation or FHLs very useful (see **6.13–6.15**).

The inheritance position on the diversified business of B&Bs is interesting and it should be handled with care by the tax planner. It is not an agricultural activity and therefore will not qualify for APR. In the current climate the IHT position on the farmhouse should be reviewed regardless of the B&B diversification. (See Chapter 4.)

The correct procedure should be to claim APR on the agricultural element in the farmhouse and BPR on that part carried out by the B&B business. The exact distinction could prove ifficult and the relative size of the operation and the size of the farmhouse should be considered. Tax planners could argue that with the claim for full APR on the farmhouse being at risk, then the B&B business should help in the claim for BPR. As with any BPR claim, there must be clear evidence of a genuine business being carried on. In order to qualify for relief, part of the farmhouse must be used 'wholly or mainly' for the purpose of a business.

Another problem area is if the B&B is a partnership; if the asset is held outside the business there could be a restriction to 50% relief (see **13.5**).

There are a multitude of permutations and combinations of complexity, eg the farm partnership, which does not include the member of the family who carries out the B&B. The supply of B&B accommodation is standard rated for VAT (whereas the supply of accommodation with service is an exempt supply).

The planning point is that the move towards diversification such as a B&B should not be entered into lightly without a review of all the IHT considerations. Sometimes the desire to minimise the VAT at the standard rate could involve more complexities than originally envisaged. If the diversifying farmer is already registered for VAT, then this registration will apply to the B&B. Attempts to avoid charging VAT could be caught by the 'anti-fragmentation' rules (ie splitting the business for the purpose of avoiding charges to VAT).

A B&B business carried out in a property other than a farmhouse should qualify for 100% BPR provided the business conditions are met, along with the ownership requirements that ensure the 100% and not 50% relief is available. Again, for maximising IHT reliefs, the tax planner must review asset ownership and the interaction to the business structure and other farming business activities (see **5.2**).

Any letting is only likely to amount to a trade if the owner is still in occupation of the property and services are still provided beyond those normally offered by a landlord. For long-term lets, HMRC tend to argue that there are two sources of income: rent (property income), and other, relating to the provision of services if significant, including meals (trading income). HMRC's Property Income Manual is helpful on this subject (see **15.12**) although with the changes to FHLs the whole question of reliefs is being considered.

STUD FARMS

6.17   The whole area of equine tax planning is dealt with by the author's *Equine Tax Planning* (Bloomsbury Professional). Stud farming counts as farming for tax purposes (see **1.4**). It would be impossible to look at diversification without considering the tax-planning angles of stud farms and racing. The positions concerning stock valuation and losses are considered elsewhere (see **7.29** and **12.8**).

BIM55701 states:

'Stud farming, which in these paragraphs is taken to mean the occupation of land for the purpose of breeding thoroughbred horses, is a very expensive and high-risk activity. In some cases it may be carried on by wealthy individuals essentially as an adjunct to their racing activities. Nevertheless, for tax purposes it is treated as farming and thus – by virtue of ITTOIA/S9 and ICTA88/S53 (1) for companies – as the carrying on of a trade regardless of its commercial viability (but see BIM55725 as regards relief for losses).

Horse racing however is not a taxable activity. Where, as is often the case, a stud farmer also races horses, considerable care may therefore be needed to ensure that the division between the two activities has been correctly made. In particular, attention should be given to any transfers of animals from the stud farm to training (that is, being kept for the purpose of racing) or vice versa (see BIM55715).'

BIM55715 states:

'If a breeder transfers an animal to training and it is then returned to stud at a higher value after a successful racing career then the uplift in the market value whilst it was in training is tax free. Furthermore the value at which the animal is returned to stud is relieved over the rest of its life (see BIM55710). The valuations of animals at the dates of transfer to or from training are, therefore, significant. (See BIM55705 as regards open market valuations).'

It is essential for diversifying farmers to understand the difference between racing and stud farms. The racing adjustment is fairly complex from the angle of accounting and tax. The tax-free uplift in value when a racehorse returns to stud is important in tax planning. The other side of the coin is that the drop in value does not attract tax relief. BIM55715 states further:

'If the occupier of a stud farm races animals bred by him or her –

- The stud farm accounts should be credited when animals are transferred to training with the then market value of the transferred animals, as if they had been sold at that value (Sharkey v Wernher [1955] 36TC215) or with effect from 12 March 2008 (ITTOIA/ S172D for income tax and FA08/Sch 15/para 6 for Corporation Tax).

- When animals return to the stud farm after racing, the stud farm accounts should be debited with their market value, at the time of return, as if they had then been purchased at that value.

- If an animal purchased and not bred on the stud farm is brought into the stud after racing by the occupier, the stud farm accounts should similarly be debited with the then market value of the animal as if it had then been purchased at that value.

The same treatment should be applied to a person who is a dealer in thoroughbred animals bred by him or her but on a stud farm occupied by some other person.'

Another form of diversified income can be stallion syndicates. The tax position on the sale of the share in a stallion together with the sales of nominations must be considered. BIM55730 says:

'Since the cost of buying a successful stallion outright is prohibitive for some bloodstock breeders, ownership may be shared in a syndicate. The usual form of syndication is into forty equal shares, representing the number of mares which, traditionally, was regarded as the standard for a stallion to cover in one season. Each syndicate member contributes towards the costs of keeping the stallion and is entitled to one "nomination" each season per share owned. The member may use the nomination to cover one of his or her own mares, or it may be sold on the open market. The shareholders appoint a committee that deal with the day to day management of the stallion.

149

Where the occupier of a stud farm owns a share in a stallion for the purpose of obtaining services for his or her own mares, the tax treatment will depend on whether he or she has made an election for the herd basis:

- If no election for the herd basis has been made, the share in the animal should be treated as stock in trade and sale proceeds brought into account in the normal way. The cost of the share may be written off in line with the practice described in BIM55710.

- If an election for the herd basis has been made, the share in the animal may be treated as part of the herd. In that case, any adjustments necessary on the sale, purchase etc of the share should be dealt with as if that share were a whole animal (see BIM55635)

Whichever treatment applies, it should be applied consistently for all shares owned.

In either case, the proceeds of any sales of nominations are treated as trading receipts. Any contribution by the stud farmer towards syndicate expenses will be an allowable trading expense.

If either:

- the owner of the stallion share is not carrying on a trade of stud farming or horse breeding; or

the owner is carrying on such a trade but does not use the stallion share for the purpose of obtaining services for his own mares;

then the proceeds from the sales of nominations are assessable under ITTOIA/ Part 5/Chapter 8 or Case VI of Schedule D for companies. An allowance for depreciation, computed on the lines described in BIM55710 may be given but if a share is sold any excess allowances should be recovered.'

The situation on losses in stud farming is dealt with in **12.8**.

STUD FARMS – COMMERCIALITY

6.18   IHTM24068 sets out HMRC's understanding of the stud qualification for APR: 'One difficulty is that there is no definition in the Act of what constitutes a stud farm, but it is considered that an essential requirement is for an element of horse breeding carried on in a systematic manner, with proper record keeping.'

The starting point is commerciality. There must be gain and the easiest way of proving this is a profit in the accounts – the stud must be commercial.

Among other factors that HMRC will consider are:

- 'the number of horses held at the date of death and the breeding record in recent years;

- details of advertising and publicity for the stud, plus full particulars of sales.

- accounts of the enterprise, and details of the precise nature of the trading activity, including purchases and sales of horses'.

A client the author acted for said with genuine respect and love of her horses 'I don't sell my horses in the same way I don't sell my friends'. It is difficult to establish a business with no sales.

Clearly there must at some point be proof of profit potential; sales and advertising.

The claim for APR will come under scrutiny as to the precise nature of the business.

HMRC are capable of accessing the racing and particularly the breed websites for stock performance, 'Google Earth' for location and Google for the name of the owner, stud and image. This information will provide HMRC with a very clear picture within a few minutes. There is a huge amount of independent information available to HMRC.

Quotes by well-meaning stud owners to *Horse & Hound* correspondents (not necessarily as adorable and uninformed as Hugh Grant in *Notting Hill*) to the effect that 'we breed for fun', 'we bought the stud as an investment', 'our horses are our family and we hate to part with them', 'we turned down £x million because it cannot all be about profit' might reappear and be quoted by HMRC.

Commerciality and 'purpose of gain' are essential for IHT reliefs to be achieved. There are vast sums to be saved and so the running of the operation for profit should be implemented accordingly.

There are a vast number of commercial, well-run, professional studs but the perception of HMRC that it is a 'rich man's hobby which is not carried on for gain' can be difficult to shift.

CARAVAN PARKS – IHT

6.19   The diversifying farmer can receive three types of income from 'caravans'. Income from caravans in a caravan park, income from letting fields to touring caravans and camping, and storage fees for the storing of caravans in the winter (and possibly throughout the year). The caravan park can be further divided between 'residential' and 'holiday'. We first look at the IHT position on a caravan park.

IRC v George (executors of Steadman) [2003] EWCA Civ 1763, [2004] STC 147 (see **5.22**) is a Court of Appeal decision. The late Mrs Steadman owned a company, Dunton Park Caravan Sites Limited, where the caravans belonged to the residents and not to the company. The company made a profit by supplying water, electricity and gas and charging a site fee. The company also took commission on sales of caravans on the site, sold caravans to the residents, ran a club for residents and non-residents, stored touring caravans when not in use, let a warehouse and a shop, held some fields on grazing licences and ran an insurance agency from which the company received commission on insurance sold. Most of us would have been deeply pessimistic of their chances of success in getting BPR on all these activities. IHTA 1984 s 105(3) excludes BPR where the business consists' wholly or mainly of making or holding investments'. Their Lordships decided that the preponderance of activities was that of a trade not consisting of making or holding investments. The moral is always to increase the number of trading activities, such as a restaurant/club house, and purchase and sales of caravans whenever the farmer possibly can, irrespective of 'park' or 'pitch'. This establishes a BPR principle of activity or the provision of activities. This will feature throughout the book.

Caravan sites – the income

6.20   Income from letting caravan 'pitches' is chargeable as letting income subject to the provision of activities. Where the site proprietor carries on associated activities (eg shops), which constitute trading and account for a substantial part of the income, the letting income may be included as receipts of the trading income. This applies regardless of whether the letting is for permanent or touring caravans.

Caravan sites – capital allowances

6.21   With regard to caravan sites, capital allowances can be claimed on plant. This will depend on the definition of plant as follows:

- caravans occupying residential sites do not qualify as plant (caravans on a residential park);

- expenditure on the provision mainly for holiday lettings of a caravan (as defined in Caravan Sites and Control of Development Act 1960 s 29(1)) on a holiday caravan site qualifies as plant; and

- caravan park swimming pool – held to be plant (*Cooke v Beach Station Caravans Ltd* [1974] STC 402).

Caravans and BPR

6.22   The question of BPR has already been looked at in **6.18** but the supporting history of tax cases is useful. There have been a number of cases on this subject in relation to caravan sites, as there is inherently a mixture of trading and letting activities. It is a question of whether the business as a whole constitutes one of mainly holding investments and how this impacts on the farming business.

- *Furness v IRC* [1999] STC (SCD) 232 – relief allowed (see **13.35**). The activities of the owner and his staff were greatly in excess of what would be the norm in a business concerned wholly or mainly of the holding of investments.

- *Weston v IRC* [2000] STC (SCD) 30 – relief denied – sales of caravans were ancillary to the pitch fees. The employees spent 111 hours a week on park maintenance and 37 hours on sales activities.

- *Hall v IRC* [1997] STC (SCD) 126 – relief denied (see **13.35**) – almost 84% of the income from the park consisted of rent and standing charges.

- *Powell v IRC* [1997] STC (SCD) 181 – relief denied even though income had been assessed under Sch D Case I (old terminology now trading income).

- *IRC v George (Executors of Steadman)* [2003] EWCA Civ 1763, [2004] STC 147 – relief allowed (see **6.19**)

SALES OF TURF AND DEPOSITING SOIL

6.23   The largest market from the sale of turf is for landscaping and sports turf. Receipts from sales of turf should be treated as part of the farming receipts assessable as trading income. However, these can be treated as receipts arising from a right over land (ie the right to take turf from the land) assessable as rental income (ITTOIA 2005 ss 12 and 262).

A borderline situation is illustrated by *Lowe v J W Ashmore Ltd* (1970) 46 TC 597. The company carried on the trade of farming but sold to business contractors the right to cut and take turf from the land. It was held that the profit was part of the farming trade because of the fact, 'that grass is sold together with the earth in which it is rooted'. However, this did not prevent the transaction from falling under the head of farming. The court held that alternatively the profits were assessable as rental income. The taxpayer had contended that he was selling part of his ownership, that is a grant of fee simple of an area of 26.5 acres, and two inches thick. This argument was rejected on the grounds that what had been sold was a *profit à prendre* for a limited period. It is worth nothing that this case was litigated before the introduction of capital gains taxation, and is of limited authority.

Lowe v J W Ashmore Ltd was carefully distinguished in *McClure v Petre* [1988] STC 749. In this case, the taxpayer received from contractors £72,125 under two agreements licensing them to enter onto land and deposit subsoil. There was a supplementary payment of £4,000 under a licence to use a disused railway cutting on similar restorative terms. These payments were held to be not liable under Schedule A (old terminology), principally because the land once used for dumping could never again be used for that purpose. There was nothing in the dumping agreement to compensate the taxpayer for lack of the use of land or loss of income from the land. Indeed the tenant had continued to pay rent to the taxpayer throughout the agreement period. The principle was that where a transaction realised permanently the capital value of one of a number of valuable characteristics, the proceeds of that transaction could be in the nature of capital (*Haig's Trustees v IRC* (1939) 22 TC 725). It is worth nothing that HMRC now accept that tipping receipts will normally constitute a part disposal of land. Often the turf is sold to a specialist company which deals with the entire cutting, lifting and transport; if not, specialist mowing and harvesting equipment is required. See **19.10** on landfill tax.

LIVERY YARDS

6.24   Reference should be made to the author's *Equine Tax Planning* (Bloomsbury Professional).

In the UK over the last ten to 20 years there has been a large increase in the number of livery/DIY yards for horses as a consequence of an expanding equine leisure industry. The recent need for agricultural diversification will probably increase the number of new livery yards even further.

At present, all cat and dog boarding kennels have to be inspected and licensed by law, as do riding schools, whilst livery yards fall outside the licensing requirements. There is currently no control over the standards of care offered or the experience of the staff in charge of these yards.

It is of concern to some members of the British Equine Veterinary Association (BEVA) that if there is no registration system for livery yards and no control over the standards of care then the ability to maintain proper disease control within the horse population in the UK is inadequate. Many liveries are run as part of a larger equine or agricultural business and this will impact upon the tax position.

Livery yards obtained a potential boost when VAT charged to clients with minimum service (Business Brief 21/2001) was deemed to be exempt. However, it comes with the downside of the 'exempt' supply – not being able to claim back input VAT and the possible complexities of partial exemption. Problems can arise in deciding whether schooling and breaking in are provided. If the yard is mainly a specialist breaking yard, then any supply relating to breaking in will be standard rated. On the other hand, if the main purpose of the yard is livery, with schooling or breaking as an add-on, then the entire supply will be exempt. Where a horse is sent to a yard that has the specific purpose of breaking in or schooling horses, rather than as somewhere to keep them, then the supply will be standard rated.

Provision of grazing is zero rated (as food) – if there is a significant degree of care then VAT is standard rated.

Horses are not farming, and the business should be separate from farming in the accounts and tax computation.

The advantage of the complete horse livery service (as opposed to DIY) is that it is a business for tax and full ER and BPR should be achieved. However, it is labour intensive, involves payroll, PAYE concerns and tight margins (see **6.25** below). Alternative equestrian establishments are:

- riding schools (see **6.26**);

- horse tourism (see **6.27**); and

- polo and integrated sports (see **6.28**).

THE FULL LIVERY QUESTION

6.25 Under the interpretation of the *Business Brief,* where there is a grant of a right or a supply over land, then the supply of livery will be exempt regardless of whether it is full livery or DIY livery, as the supply is somewhere for the horse to live. This brief seems a contradiction to the basic principle of the grant of right over land, for the supply of land is exempt, as the 'full' livery by definition means that the service is not ancillary to the supply of land. Full means a horse being 'fully' looked after. The result is that there is a variance in the interpretation of 'full'. In many establishments, DIY and part liveries are treated as exempt, but full liveries are charged standard-rated VAT, as it is considered that by definition the volume of the services provided does not fulfil the basic principle of exemption criteria.

Part livery is where the horse owner, for example, rides the horse five days a week, but the livery provider rides and looks after it the other two days. It is likely that the livery provider will be responsible for mucking out and looking after the horse generally. Provision of hay and turnout may also be provided.

The livery provider will be fully responsible for maintaining the premises and the grass. The livery provider will be responsible for feeding. However, full livery is where the livery provider is responsible for the complete care of the horse. The owner will come and go and the livery provider should act in accordance with the owner's wishes, but will be fully responsible for the full care of the horse. The provision of full livery will be a trade.

Finding out that their DIY livery operation is not trading income can be a shock for many landowners and farmers. If it is not trading income, then on the sale of the underlying property it will be very difficult to claim ER under CGT legislation, or on death, or a gift, business property relief for the purposes of IHT. Hold-over relief from CGT on gifts may also be restricted. The VAT complexities on the supply of land are a clear example of how all tax planning surrounding farms and lands has to be comprehensive and looked at in the round.

THE RIDING SCHOOL

6.26   Riding schools generally offer a wide range of equine-related activities and training, including lessons at all levels, holiday accommodation, trekking and hacking, show-jumping tuition, dressage, etc. They may also offer ancillary facilities such as an all-weather or indoor sand school, full, part or DIY livery, holiday accommodation and tack and equine supplies. Some riding schools are small-scale and offer only basic facilities, whilst, at the other extreme, others may have a whole team of British Horse Society (BHS)-qualified instructors and quality horses/ponies. Once the VAT-registration limit has been exceeded, however, the VAT-registered business will often have to charge VAT inclusive prices roughly equal to its non-registered competitors. This means that margins are often reduced, with the effect that larger organisations often have a lower gross profit than smaller ones. Apart from the relatively few cases where a customer is VAT registered and can recover the extra, prices have to remain competitive.

Proprietors have to be willing to work long hours, since many people, particularly in spring/summer, like to take riding lessons in the evenings. Whilst whole courses of lessons may be paid for by cheque, individual lessons are usually paid for in cash, making this business an ideal target for HMRC who historically mistrust 'mainly cash' businesses.

Any riding school will come under the BHS licensing provisions.

Historically, most livery operations (see **6.24**) did not come within the operation of the licensing provisions of riding schools, but are now being encouraged to join the scheme. The chief object of the licensing provisions is to ensure that the horses are properly fed, accommodated and cared for. However, there are also provisions about the supervision by responsible persons of horses hired out for riding unless a rider is competent to ride without supervision. The licence holder must hold an insurance policy covering him for liability for injury suffered by persons hiring horses for riding. The licence holder must also keep a register of all horses aged three and under kept on the premises, and these must not be let out on hire for riding or used for riding instruction on payment. The Acts provide for issue of provisional licences in certain cases.

The combination of the costs of the compliance with the BHS licensing provisions, business rates and the insurance costs associated with protecting against risk have caused a decline in the traditional riding school. Many have been loss making and unable to compete on price with the smaller unlicensed operation.

The structure of the equine business world has moved away from riding schools over the last 30 years. The casual rider has almost disappeared, as there are so many other forms of leisure activities available. There has been a growth in general ownership, with many horses being kept at home or at a small livery yard. Lessons are given by freelance instructors and generally everything is dealt with below the VAT-registration limit. The decline of farming has meant paddocks have been sold at high prices to large houses in order to facilitate the keeping of horses. Small farms have been sold as potential equine establishments, but not necessarily riding schools.

The riding school is not necessarily where pupils learn to ride anymore, they may learn on a friend's pony. There has been a restructuring of the industry and this gives diversification opportunities to the farming industry.

HORSE TOURISM, TREKKING AND RIDING HOLIDAYS

6.27   These activities are not farming; nor are they agriculture, but they are a useful diversification activity for farming. The equestrian industry is now a major economic factor in many rural areas. No comprehensive survey of the sector has been undertaken, so reliable statistics are not easy to find. However, it is estimated that there may currently be some 800,000 horses in the UK. The number of riders is much higher with estimates in the range of 2.4–3.2 million. Thus there are many opportunities to offer equine recreational facilities – both to those who do not own a racehorse of their own, and also to those who can provide their own mount.

Trekking is more suited to hill and upland areas, and legal access to suitable riding country must be available. As with livery and riding schools there are very tight margins.

The average price of a one-hour trek is likely to be in the range £10–£20 (average £15). The number of hours that can be sold per horse per year is likely to vary considerably – depending on location, the season, marketing, etc. An average of 150–200 hours per horse per year might be considered reasonable.

The risks are high, as are the costs of insurance.

The range of establishments offering riding holidays is large. Details are available from the British Horse Society (www.bhs.org.uk). This can be an additional attraction of the FHL market (see **6.13**).

Many farms offering bed and breakfast (see **15.20**) or cottage accommodation will also have suitable buildings to accommodate owners' horses. In locations with good riding facilities this can be a strong selling point and higher charges can be made. Customers will expect certain minimum standards in any horse accommodation (see Redlands Equestrian at www.redlandsequestrian.co.uk).

Trail rides lasting for a number of days are becoming popular. This usually involves trekking between co-operating farms.

POLO

6.28   Polo has been brought into the diversification limelight through a VAT tribunal case. The letting of sports facilities and sporting rights is normally standard rated. An example of sporting rights is the right to take game which is standard rated. However, there are debates over the element of land supplied with the facility and the split between exempt and standard rated. There are special rules for the use of sports facilities where there are lets in excess of 24 hours or for the hire of facilities to the same user for a regular series of events (both then become eligible for exemption but can be opted).

Within the definition of sports facilities HMRC include swimming pools, tennis courts and croquet lawns and areas of land that have been specifically designed or adapted for sporting activities. However, if the sporting facilities are let for non-sporting purposes then the exemption will apply. An example of this will be the letting of a swimming pool for a fashion shoot. The exemption will also apply if the supply is a horse livery with minimal care – which can cover full livery.

Allowing access to recreational and sports activities is usually standard rated, but there is a provision that exempts the supply in respect of a series of lettings, subject to tight criteria. One of these conditions is that each particular letting must not be less than one day apart. Clearly where VAT leads so does business status.

POLO FARM

6.29   A VAT tribunal case, *Polo Farm Sports Club* VTD20105, has highlighted the fact that the whole area of VAT, the supply of land, the supply of sports facilities and horse liveries could benefit from clarification by HMRC.

It suited the Polo Farm Sports Club to make standard-rated supplies. It had not opted to tax the land in question. A dispute therefore arose with HMRC, which said the club was making a series of lettings which should therefore be exempt. In this case the lettings were daily for several hours each day and there was never a whole day between each letting. HMRC argued that this was nonetheless sufficient to fulfil the exemption criteria, since there was still 'a day' between each letting. But the tribunal preferred the appellant's view which was that there had to be at least a clear day, or 24-hour period, in order for the rule to apply. The Polo Club won this case and achieved their standard-rated supply.

FISHING

6.30   IHTM24039 states:

'The value of fishing rights does not form part of the agricultural value of agricultural land. Accordingly agricultural relief is not due. However, fishing rights may qualify for business relief (IHTM26001).'

157

Fishing is a broad category and can include letting fishing rights on existing rivers, lakes and ponds, or creating a new business. The market can be segmented into different types of fishing (trout, carp, etc). Different business models are possible such as letting to a club (letting non-trading income), individual fishing licences, or pay-and-fish system. Extra income from supplying consumables (bait, etc) might be possible.

Fishing is one of the most popular participation sports in the UK. The activity is usually divided into 'game fishing' – trout and salmon; and 'course fishing' – roach, bream, perch, carp, rudd, tench, etc.

Various marketing approaches can be adopted:

- Day tickets for one-off visits by the general public – this approach has the potential for the greatest income but requires more management (to collect fees and market the site). It also relies on a strong local demand (near a centre of population) to generate trade, and may require higher investment in infrastructure such as access, car parking, toilets, etc. Returns are more viable – dependent on the particular season. The tax relief on the infrastructure needs careful review.

- Season tickets or permits for individuals – these have the advantage of providing a known income stream through advance permit sales and should also require less management.

- Letting the entire fishery on an annual basis to a club/syndicate, etc – in many cases such clubs will undertake all stocking and maintenance, etc.

Often it is possible to combine fishing with other leisure enterprises to add value – eg with bed and breakfast accommodation to create 'fishing breaks'. For example FHL income can be enhanced (see **6.13**).

It is vital to establish who owns the fishing rights – particularly on rivers/ streams.

Building new ponds will require planning permission and consent from the Environment Agency. EA approval is also needed before stocking ponds, lakes, rivers, etc. Again tax planning around the costs of improvements and repairs needs to be reviewed.

For tax purposes, the provision of recreational fishing is not farming. Small amounts of income for providing fishing facilities can be incorporated into farm accounts. Classification as non-trading income will have to be considered. The business of recreational fishing should be established as a separate business activity. The choice of business structure should be considered (see incorporation Chapter 8). The tax relief for set-up costs could be delayed with classification as CGT improvements as opposed to repair.

The European Court of Justice (ECJ) recently helped define 'immoveable property'. The case reinforced an earlier decision that a piece of land is immoveable property even if it is underwater. This test was applied in relation to permits to fish in a river.

In *Rudi Heger GmbH v Finanzamt Graz-Stadt* (Case C-166/05) a German company had purchased permits to fish in Austria and then sold those permits on to customers in other EU countries. The company later applied to the

Austrian tax authorities for a VAT refund under the Eighth Directive, on the grounds that it was a taxable person not established in Austria and that its onward supplies of fishing permits had not been made in Austria.

The Austrian tax authority did not allow the refund of VAT, claiming that the onward supply by the company of the permits was a supply of services connected with immoveable property, within Article 9(2)(a) of the Sixth Directive. This provides that: 'The place of the supply of services connected with immoveable property … shall be the place where the property is situated.' The place of the onward supplies was deemed to be Austria, where that property (the right to fish) was located.

An earlier case, *Fonden Marselisborg Lystbadehavn v Skatteministeriet* (Case C-428/02) had established that a section of land was actually immoveable property even though it was underwater. This case related to mooring fees for boats. The court ruled that, as fishing rights could only be exercised on particular stretches of river, they were attached to certain areas of land and so the transmission of fishing rights by means of fishing permits, granted for a consideration, did constitute a supply of services connected with immoveable property.

The court ruled that an essential characteristic of immoveable property was that it was attached to a specific part of the Earth's surface. It follows that the decision should therefore also apply to shooting rights – indeed, perhaps this concept is easier to understand than fishing rights?

The permit to fish, or the right to shoot, is deemed to be located in the country where the fishing or shooting rights are situated, the country indeed where the fish or game are to be found. It does not matter where the person who buys the rights lives. With the current 'tax attack' on shooting spearheaded by the Norwich Shoot Project Team (see **6.53**), this will have some interesting impacts upon the shooting rights in the UK (see **6.54**).

AGRICULTURAL AND COUNTRYSIDE ATTRACTION

6.31   An increasingly urban population seems to regard farming itself as a novel and interesting attraction. Some of these enterprises may not be highly lucrative in themselves, but do have the associated benefit of increasing the awareness of farming, and its methods, among the general population. Examples under this heading are farm open days or school visits (ie a normal farm that only opens to the public on a small number of defined days); farm attractions, including working farms, farm museums, rare-breeds centres etc, and more general countryside activities such as rural craft centres, sheepdog or gundog trials, corn mazes, adventure playgrounds.

Whilst farms which have occasional open days will still be taxed as 'farmers' involved in agriculture, farms which are dedicated to exhibition can be a trading activity assessable to tax, but not 'farming'.

The risk of public access and the cost of protection insurance together with the costs of health and safety compliance, can make these alternatives less attractive.

ACTIVITY LEISURE PURSUITS

6.32   New leisure and sporting pursuits are being created all the time so this list is never exhaustive and the risks often need the protection of limited liability (see Chapter 8). Such pursuits might include:

- *Motor sports* –– this can involve hiring out the land to clubs for rallies, races or meets (alternatively, the landowner may put on his own event – such as tractor pulling). Other businesses may offer the racing of vehicles – for example go-carts, buggies, off-roaders, and even hovercraft.

- *Watersports* – obviously a suitable area of water is needed on, or adjacent to the farm. This could evolve from the pit left behind on gravel extraction (see **6.37**).

- *Downhill racing* – a broad term, which includes such activities as grass skiing, mountain boarding and 'zorbing'.

- *Golf* – this varies from the relatively cheap provision of driving ranges up to the large investment in a full course. Farmers should consider carefully whether to embark on such a development themselves. High levels of investment are needed to achieve a good course. Frequently, outline planning permission is sought (see Chapter 3) and then the site is sold on – often to the growing number of golf chains. Specialist agents operate in the golf market and are able to advise on the suitability of individual sites. The tax treatment of set-up costs needs to be reviewed. Those looking to enter this market at lower capital costs might consider the following options:

  - standalone driving range;

  - pitch-and-putt course;

  - nine-hole par three course.

- *Adventure games* – otherwise known as 'paint-balling':

  - Most farmers rent a site to a games operator (sometimes franchised) rather than running the operation themselves.

  - The implications of income being taxed as property income should be considered. The facts will dictate whether it can be farm income by concession.

  - Sites are rented throughout the country, some on a monthly basis, some annually (again good sites have become established and there would appear to be only limited opportunities to develop new sites).

  - Planning permission is required if activities occur more than 28 days in a year (see Chapter 3).

  - Set-up costs are high with possibly additional costs such as changing rooms, portable lavatories and advertising.

  - The tax relief on the set-up costs must be analysed between capital gain improvements, allowable trading expenses and plant and machinery eligible for capital allowances (see **7.4**).

- *Letting to clubs or for events* – clubs of model aircraft enthusiasts or even balloonist or gliding/hang-gliding clubs may be more interested in renting suitable land on a periodic basis. It might be possible to let land for concerts or similar events. Whether the income is assessed as trading income or rental income will depend on fact. The provision of services with the letting will move the assessment towards trading income and should be part of the tax planning.

OPPORTUNITIES IN THE SHOPPING AND FOOD SECTOR

6.33   There is increasingly a divergence between the main weekly supermarket shop which is seen as a chore, and other shopping activities (be it for clothes, consumer goods, or luxury foods) which is now regarded by many as a leisure activity. These trends represent an opportunity for some farmers to supply such 'lifestyle' retail, such as:

- Farm shops – particularly attractive to consumers if they sell home-produced, speciality, or local goods. Customers may be prepared to travel some distance if they see such shopping as a 'trip out'. As set out in Chapter 1 selling bought-in items is not farming.

- Pick-your-own enterprises – can still be farming, just with a different retail outlet.

- Garden centres.

- Farmhouse teas.

- Restaurants – this could also include providing facilities for conferences, weddings and other occasions.

- Car boot sales – obviously 'retail' enterprises, but they probably fall more readily into the category of 'events'.

- Farmers' markets.

All of the above carry associated risks and separate legal entities should be considered.

It was explained in Chapter 1 that farm shops that sell produce from the farm count as farming and farm shops that sell bought-in items count as non-farming. This instantly shows a need for very careful book-keeping as a lot of farm shops would have a combination of own produce and bought-in produce. The question will then be raised on the share of overheads such as wages, heat and light and, once again, this makes for complicated accounting and gives a clear example of why many accounts staff find the preparation of accounts and the associated tax computation of diversifying farms very complicated.

Essentially, the bought-in produce element of the farm shop should be shown as a separate trade and should qualify as a business within the provisions of the capital gains tax and inheritance tax reliefs. The advantage of a farm shop not qualifying for farming status is that it could qualify as an EIS activity. Within the rules it should qualify as a non-prohibited activity because under the section dealing in goods, other than in the ordinary trade of retail or wholesale distribution, it should qualify as the trade of retail.

From a practical accounting point of view it is likely that the accounting requirements of a farm shop are far different from that of a farming unit and they should operate separate clear records, even a separate bank account.

The question of marketing is looked at in Chapter 19 (see **19.37**).

VINEYARDS

6.34 Vineyards are a specialist diversification enterprise, needing specialist accounting and tax treatment. Vine growing is a very old enterprise (dating back to Roman times), but it is in the past 30 to 40 years that this activity has seen a revival, with the emergence of a new breed of wine grower. The following factors are significant:

- Climate severely limits the areas suitable for vines in the UK and can make even the most favourable parts borderline in an average summer.

- Soil is less critical than the location but it must be well drained and preferably south facing, sloping, and well sheltered.

- Fencing against rabbits and deer is essential.

THE FARM CONTRACTOR

6.35 Many farming families are forced to contract hire either their services or their equipment. It is not unusual to find that farmers receive income for the use of their equipment either with or without an operator, although BIM55090 says categorically that the contractor is not farming and is taxable on his profits as a contractor. If this is occasional and the amounts are small, the practitioner will need to consider the merits and risks of including this in the farming self-assessment, rather than treating it as a separate trade.

It is quite usual for one member of the farming family to try and obtain the majority of their income from contracting work. It could be that the contracting work is separate. In practice many farms can only survive with the contracting income. The structure of these trading activities can make it very difficult to extract the farm profits in accordance with BIM55090 above. Many contracts take the form of share-farming arrangements (see Chapter 11), which, by contrast, are treated as farming. In many circumstances it is the contracting income which secures profitability for the farming unit and without which the farmer would have a loss, which could question the five-year profitability rules (see Chapter 12). The position concerning capital allowances and planning are looked at in Chapter 7 (see **7.17**).

MOBILE PHONE MASTS

6.36 Locations for mobile phone masts have been and still are in high demand. The tax-treatment principles are essentially similar to those of wayleaves and will very much depend on the agreement that is entered into. The difference is that there is a far greater chance of selling the land that the mobile phone mast is on and therefore realising a capital sum (see Chapter 15) and there can be capital advantages.

The key to the tax planning lies in the agreement that is negotiated, the wording thereof, and the tax treatment that results. It is advisable to use a land agent to negotiate the alternatives and it might well be that the interest in a mobile phone mast has arisen due to seeing an advert in the farming press and therefore an agent is already involved. It is possible to re-negotiate existing arrangements and the tax consequences should not be overlooked. For further consideration of the tax treatment see also the section on wayleaves (see **15.28**).

MINERAL ROYALTIES

6.37 Not everyone may be aware of the taxation of mineral royalties, which is still treated as if half income tax and half capital gains tax. However with the CGT reform of Finance Act 2008, particularly the introduction of ER, the whole matter is under review. The review of the taxation of mineral royalties has become even more relevant with the introduction of aggregates levy from 1 April 2002.

The extraction of minerals generally results in the creation of a 'pit' or a hole, which can be used for a diversification activity or income stream in its own right, eg recreational fishing (see **6.30**) or landfill (see **19.10**).

One of the most common commercial minerals is gravel, and there are a number of ways of organising the extraction to be taxed as efficiently as possible.

The land could be sold containing the pit. It is to be hoped that this would be claimed as capital gains tax with all the business relief associated therewith, such as roll-over relief and business taper up to 5 April 1998. This assumes that business status can be shown, ie farmed in hand. The disadvantage is that many landowners do not want to lose ownership, and this leads to the next point.

The land could be sold containing the pit with an option to buy back the land afterwards. The sale of the gravel pit, with the option to buy it back after exhaustion, means that normally most of the extracted proceeds will be liable to income tax (ITTOIA 2005 s 284). This forgoes most of the advantage of CGT relief.

Capital tranches of gravel may be sold without selling the land itself. The problem was that HMRC claimed that unless the surface is sold, the tranche of gravel will not be a business asset for taper relief purposes – this will all be under review with the introduction of ER.

The treasury route is a well-tried method where the landowner sells a capital tranche of gravel with the licence for the aggregates company to enter the land for the purpose of extraction. The key is to establish a capital gain in-house, for instance put the land into settlement or gift it to a member of the family. This should result in use of ER however the restrictive nature of ER now makes the treasury route almost impossible to work in practice. If the calculation is correct, there should be no further tax. It is a good idea to put a restrictive covenant on the number of cubic metres. The downside is that for the aggregates company under CAA 2001 s 418, capital tranches are subject to capital allowances at only 10% a year. However, when the tranche is exhausted, the company is entitled to claim a balancing allowance for the balance amount spent (CAA

2001 s 428), ie the aggregates company will not receive 100% relief until the end of the tranche.

Again it should be remembered that the hole created by the extraction presents a diversified activity in its own right (see **6.32**). Sometimes the mineral royalty price includes the value of waste disposal. Sometimes it includes a reduction for landscaping. The tax alternatives of the 'deal' with the extraction company must be scrutinised. The extraction of mineral royalties are looked at in more detail in **14.35–14.37**, planning property disposals tax efficiently.

NEW TRADE AS A DEVELOPER OF LAND

6.38 As mentioned in chapter 5 development is not defined by statute. HMRC interpretation is any physical adaptation or preparation for new use of land. The increase in value created by planning consent, representing the difference between agricultural value and development value can raise problems if matters are not thought through first.

The development by the farmer himself of houses for sale will be an adventure in the nature of trade as a developer or property dealer. The question of whether or not there is a trade should be dealt with as part of the tax review when planning permission is obtained and the alternatives considered.

If the landowner becomes a developer, land previously held as a farm asset will be appropriated to the trading stock of the new trade. On this change of status, CGT arises on a deemed disposal at market value (TCGA 1992 s 161). An election under TCGA 1992 s 161(3) will normally be sensible. This avoids upfront tax, but increases the eventual income tax profits. However, a farmer who has owned land with no intention of selling does not necessarily become a property developer merely because he takes steps to enhance the value of the property in the eyes of a developer who might want to acquire the land for development (*Taylor v Good* [1973] STC 383).

There are circumstances where it must be accepted that the trade of property developer has started and the eligibility to CGT reliefs ceases. As mentioned previously, this must be planned accordingly.

For a well-established farmer to move to property development for growing houses as opposed to growing crops, there is a risk of having profits taxed at the top rate of 50% compared to the exceptionally beneficial CGT rates helped by ER and the 18% and 28% under the CGT reform. It must be noted ER does not apply to the mere asset.

See **10.15–10.17** for a discussion of the question of sheltering development profits in farmland.

HERITAGE PROPERTY

6.39 It might be questionable as to why heritage property features in a book on tax planning for farmers and landowners. Clearly, the heritage property includes land and buildings and the landowner might seek to claim IHT deferral relief in the appropriate manner. Obviously, tax-planning exercises which include a claim under BPR and APR would be much more satisfactory, as it is not a deferral. However, there would be circumstances where BPR/APR fail and the property might qualify as 'heritage'. The tax relief opportunities should not be overlooked if this occurs. Farms and landed estates are going through a lot of change and must adjust accordingly. It can be considered that such a move, particularly with the need to allow 'reasonable access' for viewing, counts as a diversified activity. This can be integrated with other diversified activities such as tourism.

Heritage property – what property qualifies?

6.40 Relevant property should be one of the following (IHTA 1984 s 31(1) as amended by FA 1998):

- pictures, prints, books, etc which (or collections of which) appear to the Board to be of pre-eminent value for their national, scientific, historic or artistic interest;

- land, which, in the opinion of HMRC, is of outstanding scenic or historic or scientific interest;

- any building for the preservation of which special steps should, in the opinion of the Board, be taken by reason of its outstanding historic or architectural interest;

- any area of land, which, in the opinion of HMRC, is essential for the protection of the character and amenities of such as a building;

- any object which, in the opinion of HMRC, is historically associated with such a building.

Heritage property – what is the relief?

6.41 As with woodlands relief, the relief for heritage property is a deferral of the charge, rather than the abolition of liability that arises from 100% BPR/APR. Unlike woodlands relief, relief for heritage property is available on lifetime transfers of value and transfers of value made by trustees, as well as the deemed transfer made by death.

The relief operates to make a transfer of value an exempt transfer to the extent to which the value is attributable to property accepted as 'heritage property' (IHTA 1984 s 30). In order to obtain this exemption, a claim must be made. A claim can be made in respect of:

- any transfer on death; and

- any other transfer of value provided that the transferor or his spouse or civil partner, or the transferor and his spouse or civil partner between them, have been beneficially entitled to the property throughout the six years ending with the transfer; or the transferor acquired the property on death and the property was then the subject of a conditionally exempt transfer (IHTA 1984 s 30(3)).

In the case of a PET (see **5.6**) of heritage property, no claim for conditional exemption can be made until the death of the transferor and no claim at all can be made if the property has been sold before then (IHTA 1984 ss 30(3)–30(3)(c). However, if the property has been transferred to the government in satisfaction of IHT (IHTA 1984 s 230), the transfer becomes exempt (IHTA 1984 s 26A).

A similar exemption applies where there is an occasion giving rise to tax in relation to property held on discretionary trusts (IHTA 1984 s 78). Exemption may be claimed in respect of both the ten-year charge (IHTA 1984 s 79A) and the exit charge.

Heritage property – the undertaking

6.42   Undertakings are required for the maintenance of a building designated as heritage property for the repair and preservation of its character, for the retention of objects associated with the building concerned and, also, for reasonable access to allow viewing of the heritage property by the public (IHTA 1984 s 31(4)).

Heritage property – the disposal

6.43   Where there is a disposal of property that has been designated as heritage property for the purpose of the IHT relief, the conditional exemption is reviewed. Current practice is that if the disposal does not materially affect the heritage entity, the designated heritage property status remains in force.

When a chargeable event occurs and the conditional exemption ceases, tax is charged on an amount equal to the value of the property at the time of the chargeable event (IHTA 1984 s 33(1)). The value will be measured by the sale proceeds or market value as appropriate (IHTA 1984 s 33(3)).

The tax is calculated by reference to the circumstances of the 'relevant person'. This will be the person who made the last conditionally exempt transfer, save that where there have been two or more such transfers within the last 30 years HMRC may select whichever of the transferors they choose (IHTA 1984 s 33(5)).

Heritage property – breach of undertaking

6.44   On a breach of undertaking (or expiry without a new undertaking, unless a disposal occurs to a defined heritage organisation), a charge to IHT crystallises on the basis of the then value of the property, but (broadly) by reference to the rate applicable to the person who made the last conditionally exempt transfer. However, where there has been more than one such transfer since 7 April 1976, HMRC can choose any of the transferors. It is understood that in applying this rule, HMRC do not have to regard conditionally exempt transfers before 7 April 1976 (when the current regime broadly took effect).

DIVERSIFYING INTO ACTIVITIES THAT GO BEYOND OCCUPATION OF THE WOODLAND

6.45   The owner-occupier of woodlands may also carry on a trade by making and selling wooden items, marketing firewood or even selling processed timber. Is this agriculture?

The occupation of woodland is essentially the growing of timber and the normal preparation for marketing timber as timber. Once processing progresses beyond the planking stage it is not regarded as being part of the occupation of the woodlands, ie it is not agriculture; however, it may well qualify for BPR. See further **6.6** et seq.

FRUIT ORCHARDS

6.46   Diversification projects into orchards need to be monitored carefully.

Initial expenditure on the planting and staking of a new orchard is treated as capital expenditure, according to the principle that payment for a right to obtain trading stock does not qualify as a payment for that stock itself (see *IRC v Pilcher* (1949) 31 TC 314). It was held in this case, where a fruit grower purchased a freehold orchard at a price inclusive of the trees' current fruit crop, that no part of the purchase price was deductible as revenue expenditure.

After trees have been planted in an orchard, subsequent expenditure on cultivation is deductible (*Vallambrosa Rubber Co Ltd v Farmer* (1910) 5 TC 529). Expenditure on the grubbing up (digging up) of an old orchard and subsequent planting of new trees (whether or not of the same kind) is normally allowable on a renewals basis principle, providing the replanting takes place within a reasonable time of the grubbing up (see BIM55275) (see **2.22**).

The tax treatment for grubbing up an old orchard is set out in Chapter 19.

ENERGY CROPS

6.47   The production of energy crops raises interesting tax arguments as to whether the activity is farming and an agriculture activity (see **1.3**). This was looked at with the availability of grants (see **2.26**). It could be that some crops are grown by farmers and subsequently purchased as energy crops and the income in relation to the total farm income is very small. However, energy crops would be undertaken as a large-scale operation involving research and development costs and the associated tax reliefs (see **2.15**).

The concept of using crops like oilseeds, wheat and sugar to produce the raw materials for fuel is long-established and, until relatively recently, was seen as non-controversial. It seemed to make obvious sense, as the world's reserves of fossil fuels ran down, to switch from relying on the products of ancient sunlight for the bulk of our energy supplies to the products of present-day sunlight, particularly if you happened to live in a country with few if any reserves of coal, oil or gas and were concerned for the security of your energy supplies.

Climate change was another potent factor in the equation. Using bio-diesel made from oilseed rape, or bio-ethanol, manufactured from wheat, maize or sugar, involves the emission of significantly lower volumes of carbon dioxide over the full cycle of production and use than using the equivalent volumes of fossil fuels. And, unlike most other forms of renewable energy, biofuels can be used in transport fuels.

Waste straw is being used, and there is also potential for switch and reed canary grasses. However, most interest is centred on short-rotation coppice (see **6.5** and **6.11**) with willow being the favoured species, and miscanthus (elephant grass).

BIOFUELS

6.48   Biofuels are transport fuels produced from plant material. They can also be made from organic waste such as used cooking oil and paper. Their production could help British farming by providing new markets for current crops such as cereals and sugar beet, and for oil seed rape.

Biofuels and energy crops can qualify as farming income by concession. The tax treatment will have to be reviewed for each and every farming/diversified operation. Does it qualify as husbandry? The debate surrounding the tax treatment is almost as hot as the political debate surrounding biofuels themselves.

It is generally considered that the land which grows these energy crops and biofuels will qualify for APR for IHT. There will also possibly be a fallback to BPR. Chapter 1 (see **1.7**) explains that energy crops and biofuels can qualify as farming income by concession as mentioned above. In 2005 HMRC accepted that this activity was husbandry. The cultivation of short-rotation coppice which is an energy crop (see **1.3**) is farming (ITA 2007 s 996 and FA 1995 s 154).

Biofuels could encourage production of new energy crops, and provide an environmentally friendly use for certain waste products. They are supported by the NFU, CLA, British Sugar, the Institute for Food Research attached to the University of East Anglia, Friends of the Earth and many others.

Bio-ethanol, which is made from starch and sugar crops, can be used to run petrol engines. Bio-diesel, made from plant oils, is used in diesel engines. The fuels can be either wholly or partially substituted for petrol and diesel.

There is sometimes confusion between biofuels and energy crops. The NFU has warned that Britain could lose out unless more encouragement is given to the country's biofuels industry. DEFRA have said that support would be given for bio-fuel production where it is most effective and affordable. World biofuel production is more advanced than in the UK and it is considered that part of the world food shortage (at the time of writing) is attributable to utilisation of biofuels.

WIND FARMS – A BLOT ON THE LANDSCAPE?

6.49   Wind farms are a very controversial subject; they have been described as an 'horrendous blot on the landscape'. However, many people consider wind turbines graceful and think that they represent a cleaner sustainable source of energy for the future. This is all very well, but what of the tax position? To date there is no specific direction from case law and there are no clearly presented rules contained within HMRC guidelines. Wind farms are of interest to investors, developers and landowners. Venture capital trusts have been set up to invest in companies that develop, construct and operate wind farms. So what are the facts behind the operation?

- Landowners have the opportunity to receive regular income for up to 25 to 30 years with no additional labour expense required.

- Once in place, normal farming can go on around them with no requirement to fence off.

- Arable farming can continue right up to the base of the tower. The turbines are connected by cables that are below ploughing depth which will usually run along the boundaries to minimise disruption.

- A developer will choose the site and discuss terms with the landowner. Planning permission can be obtained in six months for small projects and in two to three years for larger projects. In this planning period, the landowner could receive a nominal income of several thousand pounds a year. Once planning permission has been obtained, the landowner is either paid pence per kilowatt hour produced by the wind turbines or a fixed sum per year.

- After a wind farm has been built, over 99% of the land can still be used for farming.

The basic assumption is that the income is non-trading. For BPR the income should be considered in the context of *Farmer* and *Earl of Balfour* (Chapter 13) as part of the whole business. The problem that is emerging is that the income is very substantial and therefore likely to exceed the farming income and therefore put BPR at risk.

WIND FARMS – TAX PLANNING

6.50   Essentially, the income from the wind farm lease is non-trading income from land and property in the hands of the landowner. Income should be included within the landowner's accounts, but identified separately. With the unprofitable state of many farms, the income will be used to support the farming enterprise and to make the overall operation profitable.

If a farming or market gardening enterprise has sustained losses computed without regard to capital allowances in each of the five preceding years of assessment, ITA 2007 s 67 denies the offset of the losses against other income in the current year under 'hobby farming' rules.

Non trading income from the wind turbines cannot stop the farm from falling within the hobby farming rules but, with careful structuring, the income could help, ie overheads could be allocated against the income.

General farm expenses can be allocated against the income from the wind turbines. This will include direct costs and a justifiable proportion of farm overheads that relate to this income. It could be that the ITA 2007 s 64 loss relief will not be denied under s 67 due to an accounts profit being achieved.

Tax planners may set themselves the task of seeking to treat the money received by the landowner for allowing the wind farm on his land as a capital sum derived from the asset. Can the grant of the licence by the landowners to the wind farm developer be treated as a part disposal of land? Very difficult.

6.50 *Diversification – the reality*

HMRC quote *Chaloner v Pellipar Investments Ltd* 68 TC 238, which in turn depends upon *Marren v Ingles* 54 TC 76, as authority for the statement that the grant to a right to a *profit à prendre* or a licence is not a part disposal of the land. It states that the profit deriving from the granting of the licence arises from the creation of the licence.

Once the developer is interested in the site or indeed once the planning permission is obtained, it could be possible to sell the land to a third party for a value which reflects the potential (as opposed to the actual) income stream. On the assumption that the land qualifies as a business asset and has been farmed up to the date of sale, ER can possibly be utilised subject to its restriction, or the straightforward 18% rate under the CGT reform rate of CGT is achieved.

It could be that the landowner would like a right to buy back the land should there be a change of energy policies. A right to buy back documented in writing could be caught under ITTOIA 2005 s 284. This section is a further anti-avoidance provision which seeks to tax the difference between the sale price and the lower purchase consideration as a deemed premium. Essentially, the increase in value is taxed as income.

The landowner could sell the land to the wind farm developer/operator and lease back part of the land to farm. Such a sale could be caught, in part as income and not capital under ITA 2007 s 756 and, therefore, part of the disposal will not be eligible for ER.

The landowner might have concerns as to ascertaining the value of the land and the value of future energy generation. Where the land is sold and there are rights to further monies depending on the amount of energy generated, the uplift should be a capital disposal for CGT. The wording of the contract will be of paramount importance.

If the land is owned in a limited company, the income should be taxable at the company's marginal rate of corporation tax. In practice, few farms trade through a limited company because of the risk of trapping losses in the company and potential IHT disadvantages.

Extracting the profits from the limited company via the dividend route will result in the eventual capture of the income in the hands of the individual. There can be a greater spread of the income to family members and shareholders resulting in personal tax savings. Retaining the profit within the company at lower corporate tax rates can be attractive.

Transfer of the land into a limited company could be a useful tax-planning tool, although consideration of the possible question of ITTOIA s 625 problems with regard to the gifting of shares to family members should be taken in to account.

Land used by the wind farm is subject to a lease and we have to look at a number of issues:

- Does the lease qualify as an FBT (see **11.15**) in accordance with the Agricultural Tenancies Acts 1995?

- If the lease to the wind farm developer is not a farm business tenancy, will the land qualify for agricultural or business property relief?

170

- What are the terms of the lease?

- Can vacant possession be achieved within the required 12/24 months?

- Is the activity agriculture?

- Will the wind farm be an excepted asset under IHTA 1984 s 112 or will relief for the whole enterprise be achieved through the recent case law set by *Farmer (Farmers Executors)* (1999) STC (SCD) 321 or *Marquess of Hertford* (SpC 444)?

For BPR purposes, the aim is to achieve IHT relief on the whole of the farming activity, including the let land. Much will depend on the wording of the lease/licence, as well as on case law as it evolves. There is every possibility that the tax planner should be able to achieve 100% relief on the enterprise. The 'unified management' of the farming business will be essential to achieve BPR. Where it can be demonstrated that the wind farm is part of the business, the case for the availability of business property relief will be much stronger. Key factors will be to ensure:

- that the wind farm is incorporated into the farm as one unit;

- integrated accounts, ie treating all the income from farming and wind farms as one integrated unit; and

- that the business consisted 'mainly of farming'. If the land used for the wind farm is sold so as to capture the advantage of full roll-over relief (TCGA 1992, s 155) and reinvested into another business asset, agricultural and business property relief should apply.

Agricultural property is defined in IHTA 1984 s 115(2) as follows:

'agricultural land or pasture and includes woodland and any building used in connection with the intensive rearing of livestock or fish if the woodland or building is occupied with agricultural land or pasture and the occupation is ancillary to that of the agricultural land or pastures.' (See Chapter 1.)

Agricultural land will include any interest, servitude or right over land.

APR is restricted to agricultural value (see **4.32**). This is defined as the value which the property would have if it were subject to a perpetual covenant prohibiting its use other than as agricultural property (IHTA 1984 s 115(3)). Where the claim for APR is restricted, then provided the conditions are met (see above), business property relief should apply to any balance not attributable to agricultural value.

Many landowners want to receive regular income without the responsibility for maintaining the turbines, but the landowner can act as developer. There is also scope to have one grid-connected turbine to help provide the farm's own fuel.

If the landowner acts as developer, this is a new trade and has all the complexities of such a course of action, such as what should the trading vehicle be and what is the arrangement between the trading vehicle and landowner. This would give rise to many new tax-planning opportunities and the facility to pass income to other family members, whether via a company or partnership.

SHOOTING – THE BEATERS

6.51   While the 'tax attack' on shoots has focused on VAT, many shoot organisers are also worried about the position concerning payments to beaters, who are typically engaged for a day's shoot as occasion demands. HMRC and CLA reached an agreement effective from July 1985 (yes, it has been in existence for over 25 years) and the CLA issued a briefing note to its members on 1 September 1997. The situation is principally: 'Please do not bury your heads in the sand, a reasonable agreement has been reached with all parties.'

The treatment provided by the agreement can only be applied to those beaters who are truly engaged on a casual basis. To be eligible they should not have any other more permanent connection with the estate, as any regular employee who chooses to do some beating cannot be treated as a daily casual. The same can be said for a person who does a significant amount of other casual work for the estate.

The agreement does not affect the way in which the employer record is treated with HMRC and there is a similar arrangement in place for casual harvest workers.

Practical problems will arise in trying to operate PAYE procedures for a short-term arrangement and HMRC recognise this. Most estates will not have more than a maximum of 10 or perhaps 15 days in the whole year on which there will be shooting on a scale requiring beaters and, moreover, the shooting will be taking place at distinct intervals.

The agreement is that where a beater is engaged for one day or less and is paid in cash at the end of the day with no agreement for further days' work, PAYE is not applicable.

National Insurance contributions are a different matter. If a beater's casual earnings equal or exceed the National Insurance lower earnings limit in any earnings period, the shoot will be required to keep National Insurance records, deduct primary and pay secondary National Insurance contributions and complete forms P11 and P14.

At the end of the tax year a P35 return giving details of any person who has received in excess of £100 may be required.

All payments made to casuals, irrespective of the amount, should be recorded. These records will be useful anyway to satisfy the authorities that no PAYE liability arises.

Some local Inspectors of Taxes and PAYE Audit or Compliance Officers are unaware of the national agreement, which means employers are targeted for direct settlement of tax and National Insurance contributions. The local Tax Office should be reminded of the agreement if anyone comes across such problems (the official reference is PAYE23015).

Key factors revolve around the keeping of names and addresses, but with the pressure of health and safety regulations, together with insurance requirements, this is necessary in any event.

The other side of the coin is, how can those beaters who are 'truly engaged on a casual basis' deal with their individual tax liabilities?

THE 'TRUE COUNTRYMAN'

6.52   This is someone who devotes the whole of the shooting season to beating and picking up and probably spends the whole of the non-shooting season helping with the harvest. Whilst day rates are low and this is emphasised in torrential rain, such a person can enjoy not only great camaraderie, hospitality and a good income stream, but also some fine 'cock' days at the end of the season.

If all the badges of self employment are there, this lucky fellow (or woman) should consider registering as self-employed. The role of beater is essentially a contract for services and there are a number of masters (each shoot organiser) and some essential tools of the trade, such as a 4x4 vehicle, a faithful black Labrador and a large stick. Whilst the beater is not employed and does not have to turn up to every day's shooting, the 'substitution' clause is very important as most serial beaters will provide a substitute.

SHOOTING – THE NORWICH HIT TEAM

6.53   In April 2006, HMRC revealed that they would be looking closely at commercial shoots. The focus is on VAT, but all areas of income tax, corporation tax and PAYE must be considered.

Gameshooting is a prosperous and thriving rural industry. This country sport provides healthy employment in rural environments, including remote outposts of the British Isles. Many farms and estates integrate the sport of shooting into their farming activities and the 'selling off' to the outside world of days' shooting can provide a nice income.

HMRC continue to carry out a programme of visits to shoots across the UK and this has moved to all diversified income.

The apparent prime objective of HMRC is to improve the extent to which individuals and businesses pay the amount of tax due and receive the credits and payments to which they are entitled.

What are HMRC really looking for? The list is considered to be as follows:

- 'Shoots that have previously escaped the HMRC 'net'. Commercial shooting that has been variously misdescribed, in the opinion of HMRC, as private shooting, non-profit making club activity or the supply of zero-rated birds.

- Barter. Exchanging supplies of VATable shooting for zero-rated or other supplies, by way of barter, with neither transaction recorded in business records.

- Not registering. Failure to register for VAT if the turnover of the shoot exceeds £70,000.

- Dividing to escape. Artificial separation of business activities to stay below VAT registration limits.

- What is everything really worth? Under-recording of sales values.

- Paying VAT and tax on your private enjoyment. VAT and income tax irregularities on claims for private expenditure.'

173

In April 2006, HMRC wrote to members of the Country Land and Business Association (CLA) and shooting authorities saying it would be paying particular attention to game shooting. It suggested that those shoots with problems should contact the HMRC National Advice Service (tel 0845 010 9000). The author's advice, however, is to seek professional, sensible, damage limitation advice from those experienced in providing positive help, as opposed to adopting the principle of letting HMRC tell you how to protect your position while making yourselves vulnerable.

As with so many country sports, a passion for shooting involves a range of emotions. There are family shoots that want to respect their private nature and sometimes avoid any involvement with the notion of commercial shooting, but in so doing must respect the need not to claim the costs of the shoot as either an income tax or input VAT-allowable expense. If the core of the shooting expenses is paid by the farm or estate, then the tax computation and VAT return must disallow, for example:

- the rearing costs of birds;
- the gamekeeper's wages and benefits in kind;
- refreshments for shoot lunches.

The only allowable costs are those attributable to the control of vermin.

The private element of the family shoot should already have been addressed in the annual farm/estate accounts, but it is worth discussing this matter with your accountant in the very near future – perhaps they have forgotten to raise the question or you have omitted to provide the information.

Commercial shoots where a shoot's turnover is more than £70,000 per annum must register for VAT and register as a business.

HMRC are placing great emphasis on barter, because failing to record the offsetting of standard rated and zero rated supplies to avoid accounting for VAT is an offence – if the day's shooting has VAT attached and is 'swapped' for, say, a supply of corn that is zero rated, there will be an underpayment of VAT.

Where 'commercial' and 'private' shooting are run in parallel, HMRC state that the whole will be treated as a single taxable activity.

Syndicate and private shoots that sell a few days to help cover costs are making supplies that would be taxable, but, depending on the circumstances, whether such supplies are being made 'in the course of furtherance of a business' may be open to question. If the syndicate regularly allows non members to participate, however, or regularly supplies other goods or services, then it will be regarded as carrying on a business and will be required to charge VAT on supplies made to members and non members alike. If your shoot is in this position and you are uncertain as to whether or not you should register for VAT then you should seek professional advice.

Though many property rentals are exempt from VAT, rents paid for sporting rights, whether for a day or for a longer period, are not exempt from VAT. They are taxable at the standard rate, ie 20% (from 4 January 2011) must be added to the supply.

Goods imported from overseas are subject to special VAT treatment. Goods imported from the EU, in particular, if they are for private use or for the use of the business that is not VAT registered, are chargeable to VAT in the member of state from which they are despatched.

Eggs, chicks and poults can only be imported free of VAT by VAT-registered shoots.

Dead game sold to guns is food and therefore zero rated; this implies even when the sale is made at a price that is higher than the general market price.

There are VAT exemptions for certain non-profit making sporting clubs, but these depend upon there being no commercial element. If they have not done so already, clubs that provide shooting will need to seek professional advice regarding their VAT position.

SHOOTING – THE OVERALL TAX PROBLEMS

6.54   IHTM24039 continues:

'The circumstances in which other sporting rights may be treated as agricultural property are primarily matters for the District Valuer (DV). [23002] You should draw the DV's attention to existence of any sporting rights on which agricultural relief has been deducted. The exploitation of sporting rights such as commercial shoots may qualify for business relief if agricultural relief does not apply.'

Many farms and landed estates integrate the sport of shooting in their farming activities and the 'selling off' of days shooting to the outside world can provide lucrative income.

The activity is currently suffering various areas of 'tax attack' or further scrutiny. For example, the payroll compliance department appears to be focusing on a number of issues, such as:

● Tips paid to gamekeeper(s). These should be declared and subject to income tax (PAYE).

● Gamekeeper taxable benefits in kind – the question of whether the vehicle used has private use and is therefore a benefit in kind. The 'tax-free' status of the gamekeeper's cottage. Where is the vehicle kept?

● Beaters – all names should be kept and the correct PAYE treatment applied. This could cause problems on claims for tax credits, unemployment benefit etc.

Some shoots are purely private, although this is quite a luxury. Where there are no days sold to the outside world then the costs that genuinely relate to vermin control or conservation disallow the proportion of:

● gamekeepers' wages and benefits in kind;

● refreshments for shoot lunches;

● beaters' wages and tips;

● the rearing cost of birds.

175

The VAT implications are also receiving attention. Are 'sold' days subject to the correct output VAT? If there is private use, ie days retained for the family, is the appropriate input VAT disallowed?

More long-term problems on CGT and IHT could arise on the possible private use of assets. For those conversant with the running of a game shoot, it will be understood that the activity of shooting is integrated in the activity of farming. Most of the shooting activity will take place in woodland (for the rearing and 'housing'). The woodland is used to provide timber for use on the farm.

The taxation of woodland does of course have interesting tax considerations. The use of 'game strips', ancillary woodlands and hedgerows does raise possibly complex issues for CGT and IHT and the identification of areas of 'complex' use should be identified.

If the income from the sale of days' shooting is declared in the accounts of the farm/landed estate there are much stronger arguments for no private use to be charged provided that it can be demonstrated that this is a commercial activity and there is an add-back for private use in relation to the number of private days or private guns on a commercial shoot.

The taxation of the shoot is something that many tax advisers (preparers of farm accounts) ignore, sometimes through lack of knowledge owing to clients deliberately keeping information away from their advisers. For example, is part of the arable production used to feed game? If so, is the correct private use recorded in the accounts?

To those advisers who do not understand the organisation and running of a game shoot it could be very difficult to ensure that the correct questions are asked. But these queries must be raised. The key must be to warn clients and to look at solutions before the enquiry 'hits' the client. The notes must be on the file and consideration must be given to the points raised. Can the activity show commerciality, or will this again be deemed to be private or as having a high proportion of private use?

As mentioned in April 2006 HMRC issued a letter to the shooting authorities to say that they are looking closely at commercial shoots who consider themselves outside the scope of tax. They are trying to bring such shoots within the scope of tax and they must register for VAT.

This was followed by shooting hitting the front page of HMRC in November 2006, with the Norwich-based shooting project team making claims of an extra tax take of £19,000 a visit. So what positive steps have to be made? Please see Chapter 9 for further VAT developments.

SHOOTING – THE ACTION PLAN

6.55   So what action can the farm tax adviser/accountant take?

- Ascertain the facts. Ask every farming client what the shooting arrangements are on the farm and keep a copy on a permanent file which is updated regularly.

- On farm maps, note areas of woodland that are used for game rearing and also note other areas of woodland and what they are used for.

- When the annual books and records are received, ask how much private shooting there has been.

- When the annual accounts and income tax computation based thereon are sent to the client, note any private usage for the shooting activity in writing and ask them not only to confirm that relevant figures are correct, but also that they accord with the VAT treatment.

- Risk management. If a client were to undergo a payroll, VAT or tax return enquiry, will this unearth irregularities with the farm shoot? The adviser would have greater protection against potential claims, if warnings have been given.

CONCLUSION

6.56   Diversification is a reality. There are lots of profitable alternative land uses for farmers to explore. Obtaining planning permission might prove a larger 'hurdle' than tax planning but the commercial tax-efficient alternatives are waiting to be taken advantage of.

Chapter 7

Tax planning for fixed assets and stock incorporating the phasing out of quota

Julie Butler

- **When is a building plant?** – Integral fixtures and features can be plant and machinery, as can elements of new (and old) farm buildings.

- **Goodbye agricultural building allowance (ABAs)** – tax planning around the loss of ABAs.

- **Annual investment allowance** – taking advantage of the window of £100,000 until April 2012.

- **Changes in trade** – Diversification can result in the cessation of a farming business or changing the nature of a business; it can also mean plant being used in more than one business and agricultural buildings allowance (ABA) status changing. The tax planner must look at the consequences of all these permutations and combinations.

- **HMRC's Business Economic Note 19** – BEN 19 is reproduced in BIM55410. It was thought that this would be replaced/updated with the introduction of the SFP but it was not. How does it apply to diversified trades and the Mars adjustment?

- **Herd basis** – The principal advantage of the herd-basis election has been that the increase in the value of the herd was effectively achieved 'tax free'. With farms undergoing restructuring of the business, the need to make a fresh election on the change of the partnership must not be overlooked.

- **Everything green** – continued support of the 'green' tax regime.

- **Appropriation of farming stock** – in order to understand the basis of the stock valuation and the 'cut-off' point it is essential to understand basic farming principles, the FA 2008 moves 'GAAP' to *Sharkey v Wernher* for appropriation of trading stock.

- **The Mars adjustment** – The much forgotten mandatory adjustment and the impact on farm tax computation.

- **Quota** – the phasing out of quota – when is the negligible loss claim due?

MAXIMISING THE CLAIM FOR PLANT AND MACHINERY

Definition

7.1 There is no statutory definition of plant or machinery, although the latter usually takes its everyday meaning. In *Yarmouth v France* (1887) 19

QBD 647, the plant was described as 'apparatus used by a businessman carrying on his business ... which he keeps for permanent employment in the business'. One dictionary definition of 'apparatus' includes 'a collection of equipment used for a particular purpose; a machine having a specific function'. Over the years case law has been developed on the principle which seeks to distinguish property that has a functional purpose, having the characteristic of apparatus, from property that is merely part of a setting in which the business is carried on. Whereas for 'long life assets' eg where the life of the asset is anticipated to be in excess of 25 years then be prepared for writing-down allowance of 10% reducing to 8% from April 2012 (see **7.4**).

It might be wondered why a book on tax planning for farmers and landowners pays so much attention to the definition of plant and machinery. There are a number of reasons for this, the first being the relatively generous and complicated tax allowances available in certain situations. So, for example, can part of a building be redefined as plant (see **7.7**)? There is also the possibility of writing expenditure off against revenue as an expense and obtaining 100% relief, eg on repairs and renewals, and a clear understanding of the definition is important and something to which HMRC pay close attention. The identification of 'green' expenditure is important for both tax compliance and tax planning for diversified farmers.

The function and durability test

7.2   The case of *Yarmouth v France* (see **7.1**) in fact concerned a vicious horse (defined as plant because it was used for haulage). A full consideration of what constitutes plant for capital allowances is outside the scope of this book but reference should be made to the following cases:

- *IRC v Barclay Curle & Co Ltd* [1969] 1 WLR 675: a dry dock;

- *IRC v Scottish and Newcastle Breweries Ltd* [1982] STC 296, HL: light fittings, bagpipes and deerskins;

- *Haigh v Charles W Ireland Ltd* [1974] 1 WLR 43, HL: not a safe; it was stock; and

- *Benson v Yard Arm Club* [1979] 1 WLR 347, CA: not a ship used as a restaurant.

In the cases listed above, the issue of whether an asset might be plant concerned the identification of the function of the asset. A separate line of cases considered whether the item was for long-term or short-term use ie its durability. The principle has emerged that articles with a working life of two years or more may qualify as plant if they are of the right type. In *Rose & Co (Wallpaper and Paints) Ltd v Campbell* [1968] 1 WLR 346, wallpaper pattern books failed the 'durability' test which had previously been established in *Hinton v Maden & Ireland Ltd* [1959] 1 WLR 875, HL, which rejected as plant articles which might be consumed quickly or worn out after only being used a few times.

Annual investment allowance (AIA)

7.3   The Finance Act 2008 introduced annual investment allowance (AIA) at 100% for the first £50,000 of a business's expenditure on most plant, machinery and commercial vehicles.

In April 2010, the annual ceiling on qualifying purchases was doubled, from £50,000 to £100,000 (FA 2010 s 5). But in the coalition government Budget the Chancellor announced that from April 2012 it will be reduced to £25,000.

One complicating factor is that, where the trader's accounting year is other than the year to 5 April (or 31 March for companies) the allowance was apportioned when it was increased, and it is thought that it will similarly be apportioned when it is reduced. As an example, a company makes up its accounts to 30 September annually.

AIA ceiling will be:

Year to 30 September 2010	6/12 × £50,000	£25,000
	6/12 × £100,000	£50,000
		£75,000

(However, of that £75,000, only £50,000 – expenditure up to the old ceiling – could be incurred before April 2010)

Year to 30 September 2011		**£100,000**
Year to 30 September 2012	6/12 × £100,000	£50,000
	6/12 × £25,000	£12,500
		£62,500
Year to 30 September 2013		**£25,000**

AIA is available to:

- Any individual carrying on a qualifying activity (this includes trades, professions, vocations, ordinary property businesses and individuals having an employment or office);

- Any partnership consisting only of individuals;

- Any company (subject to certain limitations).

The taxpayer has the freedom to allocate the AIA between different types of plant and machinery. Expenditure that qualifies for 100% allowances under separate capital allowances codes will be unaffected by the introduction of the AIA and likewise cars do not qualify.

Generally, where one or more companies or unincorporated businesses are under common control, one AIA will be available between all, total to be allocated as required. Smaller farms may benefit from AIA provisions, claiming accelerated allowances on all qualifying capital spend. There is a distinct window of opportunity before the reduction to 25% in April 2012.

The advantage to the small diversified enterprise cannot be understated however some of the complications anticipated are identifying how to maximise AIA where there are many trading relationships eg the partnership and the individual.

Where a person or persons control(s) one or more unincorporated businesses or companies, (but not a combination of the two, as the entitlement to an AIA for companies is considered totally separately from that for unincorporated businesses, and vice versa) then the entitlement to one or more AIA will depend on whether either 'the shared premises' or 'similar activities' condition is met. If either of these conditions is met then the companies or unincorporated businesses will be 'related' and so only entitled to a single AIA between them.

For businesses under common control, the two conditions are considered on a financial year basis for companies and on a tax year basis for unincorporated businesses. The summary is that the matter is complex for a farming partnership and needs careful planning.

Capital allowances – the rates

7.4

- Writing-down allowances are available for capital expenditure incurred on the provision of plant and machinery. Qualifying expenditure is added to the asset 'pool', and writing-down allowances at a rate of 20% pa on a reducing balance basis are given on the residue of expenditure in that pool.

- From April 2012, the rate of annual writing-down allowances (for expenditure not written off at once by the annual investment allowance) will reduce from 20% to 18%, and from 10% to 8% for 'special rate' items (see below). This will be especially significant for purchasers of motor cars which, generally speaking, do not qualify for the annual investment allowance and which, if their carbon dioxide emissions rating exceeds 160g/km, count as 'special rate' items.

- For expenditure on certain long-life plant and machinery, writing-down allowances are restricted to 10% pa (these reduce to 8% from April 2012). The rules apply broadly to assets whose expected working life is at least 25 years.

All expenditure within the classification of 'integral features' of a building, as described in the list below, will attract the 10% 'special rate' of WDAs:

- electrical systems (including lighting systems);

- cold water systems;

- space or water heating systems, powered systems of ventilation, air cooling or air purification, and any floor or ceiling comprised in such systems;

- lifts, escalators, and moving walkways;

- external solar shading; and

- active facades.

The 10% rate will have effect for both initial and replacement expenditure on the designated integral features, preventing a revenue deduction in those cases where this might otherwise have been claimed.

Clearly with farmers and diversifying farms improving farm buildings there are substantial tax advantages.

100% FIRST-YEAR ALLOWANCES (FYAS) ON GREEN EXPENDITURE

7.5   100% FYAs are available to businesses that purchase equipment required to refuel natural gas and hydrogen powered vehicles. The scheme ended on 31 March 2008 for companies and 5 April 2008 for unincorporated businesses. However, legislation was introduced in the Finance Act 2008 to extend this scheme for five years, to 31 March 2013, and from 1 April 2008 to extend its scope to include biogas refuelling equipment for vehicles. Biogas is a non-fossil fuel substitute for natural gas.

The 100% FYA for expenditure on cars with CO_2 emissions not exceeding 120g/km was due to end on 31 March 2008, however legislation was introduced in the Finance Act 2008 to:

- extend the scheme for an additional five years until 31 March 2013;

- reduce the qualifying emissions threshold so that only expenditure on cars with CO_2 emissions not exceeding 110g/km driven will attract the 100% FYA.

Low emission cars are not subject to the special rules restricting the hire charge for leased cars costing over £12,000. In the coalition government Budget it was stated that the government will need £200bn of investment by 2020 to provide secure low-carbon energy. It will publish its proposals to reform the climate change levy to 'provide more certainty and support for the carbon price'. There will also be proposals on the creation of a green investment bank to help the UK meet a low-carbon investment challenge.

ENHANCED CAPITAL ALLOWANCES (ECA)

7.6   The energy efficient and water saving (environmentally-beneficial) enhanced capital allowances (ECA) schemes allow businesses investing in designated technologies that reduce energy consumption, save water or improve water quality to write off 100% of the cost against the taxable profits of the period during which the investment was made.

The result is:

- the water technology criteria list will be revised to include one new technology, waste water recovery and reuse systems; and

- the energy technology criteria list will be revised to include four additional sub-technologies, compressed air master controllers, compressed air-flow controllers, heat pump dehumidifiers and white LED lighting.

The qualifying criteria for good quality combined heat and power technology within the energy efficient technologies scheme, has also been reviewed to ensure that it includes all the necessary equipment to enable such facilities to use solid refuse waste as a fuel.

The lists of qualifying expenditure are available on the internet at www.eca. gov,uk.

- 100% FYAs can be claimed for expenditure incurred on designated energy-saving and environmentally beneficial technologies and products, known as the ECA scheme.

- For expenditure by loss-making companies a payable ECA is available of 19% of the loss that is surrendered. The upper limit of payable ECA is restricted to the greater of (a) the total amount of the company's PAYE and NICs liabilities for payment periods ending in the chargeable period and (b) £250,000 (see **8.32**).

ADVANTAGES OF DEFINITION OF PLANT NOT BUILDING

7.7   A large amount of expenditure in relation to a modern building relates to items that can constitute plant or machinery. The farmer or landowner may identify such expenditure and claim the appropriate capital allowances in accordance with the rates as set out in **7.4**. All appropriate conditions must be met. This applies as much to a second-hand building as a new one. The apportionment depends on the valuation techniques and requires knowledge of building construction. The bold tax planner might look at building works carried out for their clients over the last six years to see if claims have been overlooked.

The 'after-tax' cost of funding a new diversified venture will be affected by whether expenditure is treated as buildings or plant. There may well be borderline cases where planned expenditure could be regarded as plant. However, there are certain items of expenditure where the legislation is clear as to what it deems to be plant alterations to buildings incidental to the installation of plant (CAA 2001 s 25).

This identification of 'integral features' ie long-life assets as set out in **7.4**. increases the need to review a building and check for fixtures and features. There are complicated times ahead and such identification is easier carried out in advance when costings are available.

As mentioned in the introduction to this chapter, buildings are not plant but there is often difficulty in distinguishing one from the other, especially where items are incorporated into buildings or the building has a functional purpose.

In *Gray v Seymours Garden Centre (Horticulture)* [1995] STC 706, a claim for plant and machinery allowances was denied in respect of a greenhouse with no mechanical controls, used to display plants for sale to the public. However, Vinelott J stated that a specialised glasshouse with integral heating, temperature and humidity controls, automatic ventilation, shade screens and other equipment could be considered plant.

HMRC have agreed that silage clamps and slurry pits qualify as plant and machinery. With nitrate vulnerable zone legislation (see **2.20**) placing more pressure on the farmer to have increased storage capacity by 1 January 2012, this is obviously a useful area of tax planning.

PLANT AND MACHINERY FOR INHERITANCE TAX (IHT)

7.8   Plant and machinery are not specifically defined for IHT. The capital allowances definition is used in practice, qualified slightly so as to exclude items that would qualify for capital allowances only on the renewals basis. However, that rule is not absolute: some latitude may be given. Thus, plant includes anything that the businessman uses to carry on his business, other than his stock-in-trade. It will include goods and chattels, fixed or movable, which he keeps for permanent employment in his business. It does not just mean 'machinery'. Provided that it is used in the business it should be eligible for 100% APR or BPR, as appropriate (see **5.2**). It has been argued that 'deathbed' IHT planning is to use spare cash to increase the plant and machinery held by a farm.

FARMING BUSINESS CEASING WITH PLANT BEING SOLD, SCRAPPED OR TAKEN OVER PERSONALLY

7.9   What is the situation where a farm ceases to trade? Balancing allowances or charges will arise upon cessation of farming activities, usually based on the actual consideration limited to original cost, where disposal is at or above market value.

Assets taken over personally are accounted for at market value.

The same rules are applied to value assets on hand at the date of cessation even though the events take place after cessation (unless there is likely to be a long delay between date of cessation and the above events, in which case HMRC take market value at the date of cessation as being the disposal value (CCAB Memorandum, June 1971)).

FARMING BUSINESS CEASING WITH PLANT BEING TRANSFERRED TO NEW BUSINESS

7.10   The date a farming business ceases and a new diversified business starts is of prime importance. Certain items of the old trade might be used in the new trade (eg a tractor for contracting). Such items will be treated as a disposal at market value in the old trade with the same amount representing qualifying expenditure in the new trade (assuming no proceeds change hands; otherwise the price paid will be substituted if capital allowances will be claimed). It would appear that no FYAs are available in these circumstances. The proactive tax planner should look at maximising the tax reliefs on cessation or transfer. The allocation of allowances between the businesses can change subject to realistic price or market value and there could be the opportunity to claim allowances in the right business. It could be that the value of the plant and machinery has been virtually written down to nil, which would then create a balancing charge in the old business which could be used efficiently as capital allowances in the new business.

PLANT USED BY MORE THAN ONE BUSINESS

7.11   If the farming trade continues, certain items of plant and machinery may be used by more than one business (eg a digger used on the farm and in a plant hire business). For new acquisitions, the cost can be apportioned on a reasonable basis (usually based on initial usage), with capital allowances being claimed by the respective businesses in the usual way. For existing items included in the farm's general pool, the proportion relating to usage of the new business can be treated as a disposal at market value, with a corresponding entry as an addition in the new business.

Alternatively, the farm could invoice the other businesses for the use of the plant, which would potentially enable full capital allowances to be claimed by the farm, although the method of giving the capital allowances will differ. If plant is first let otherwise than in the course of trade, the expenditure is treated for capital allowances purposes as having been incurred for the purposes of a notional trade, and therefore included in a separate pool. An apportionment will be required where the farm also uses the item of plant. Relief for such an item of plant and machinery is only available against the leasing income from that item, and cannot be claimed against other income, with excess allowances being carried forward for offset against letting income of later periods.

Another alternative could be to form a separate entity and transfer the plant and machinery into it, for the purposes of leasing the plant and machinery to respective businesses. The problems surrounding the financing of plant and machinery are dealt with at **7.13**.

The VAT position in the above situations will need to be considered carefully.

AGRICULTURAL BUILDINGS ALLOWANCES (ABAS)/ INDUSTRIAL BUILDINGS ALLOWANCES (IBAS)

7.12   Prior to FA 2008 agricultural buildings allowances (ABAs) have been available to owners or tenants in respect of capital expenditure on agricultural buildings and works, including farm buildings, fences, drainage, power supplies, etc. Agricultural land is defined by statute (CAA 2001 s 361(1)) and means land, houses and other buildings occupied wholly or mainly for the purposes of husbandry. Therefore, ABAs will not be available for new buildings not put to agricultural uses. New buildings put up for a diversified activity that is not husbandry do not qualify for ABAs.

Industrial buildings allowances (IBAs), introduced in 1945 to encourage post-war reconstruction by productive industry and ABAs are to be phased out over four years.

The measure withdraws balancing adjustments and the recalculation of writing-down allowances in respect of balancing events occurring on or after 21 March 2007, unless:

● in pursuance of a relevant pre-commencement contract; or

● in respect of qualifying enterprise zone expenditure.

Previously capital expenditure on new buildings and structures that met the criteria set out in legislation qualified for tax relief on that expenditure at 4% a year with tax relief being available to subsequent purchasers within a 25-year period of first use of the building. This relief is to be phased out so that by 2011, industrial buildings allowances will be abolished leaving companies with industrial assets unable to claim tax relief on these assets other than if they qualify for plant and machinery allowances. The phased introduction meant that in 2008–09 three-quarters of the normal agricultural buildings allowance was available, in 2009–10 half and for 2010–11 a quarter. From 2011 no relief will be available.

Previously a sale of an agricultural building at a profit could result in a clawback of tax allowances previously given. This will no longer happen; although the taxpayer can no longer claim allowances on an asset he does not own, he keeps the relief previously given. However, if the building is sold or demolished at a loss, a balancing allowance will not arise on expenditure that has not yet been the subject of relief. Although there are minor small exceptions to these transitional rules, the new rules will catch the majority of agricultural buildings and structures.

There might be some happy farming tax clerks who sigh with relief about not having to deal with the administrative strain, problems and complications of calculation especially with tracking the historic expenditure, but overall this is a further loss of incentive to invest in the infrastructure of farming and the phasing out is going to be just as complex for that clerk.

FINANCING PLANT AND MACHINERY

7.13   The purchase of farm plant and machinery can be a large financial outlay. There is no doubt that the financing of plant and machinery is complex. It is useful if all farms keep a fixed asset register and retain all the documents that support the associated borrowings. The alternatives for purchase are:

- outright purchase;

- hire purchase;

- finance lease; and

- operating leases (also known as contract hire).

The Statement of Standard Accounting Practice 21 (SSAP 21) gives guidance on the difference between finance and operating leases.

The first three alternatives are the same as a purchase and qualify for capital allowances. Generally, operating leases are a lease arrangement with low rentals (usually including a maintenance element) during the period of hire, with a large balloon rental as the final payment. For accounting purposes the rental payments of operating leases are treated as rentals, which are accounted for when they fall due.

Historically, finance agreements on the purchase of plant and machinery have been a cheap source of finance. It can sometimes be difficult to try and ascertain exactly what the purchase price is and what is the trade-in value. This can all be tied up with discounts on new machines.

From a tax-planning point of view, the farmer or adviser should review the tax status on the new addition, and the commercial viability of the alternatives should be linked to tax status. If the machinery is used in the new diversified activity, then the machine and the associated machinery should be allocated accordingly.

COMPANY CAR BENEFIT TAX FOR EMPLOYEES

7.14   Company cars – cash equivalents as taxable benefits in kind

For 2011–12 the cap on car benefits for expensive cars will be removed. Prior to 6 April 2011 the list price of a car for calculating the car benefit is capped at £80,000.

- For 2010–11, the taxable benefit is 15% of list price for CO_2 emissions of 130g/km, 09/10 135g/km or less. This charge increases by 1% for each additional full 5g/km up to a maximum charge of 35% for emissions of 235g/km or more. Second cars are taxed in the same way as first cars.

- For 2010–11, the minimum benefit is 5% for emissions of 75g/km or less.

- There are reduced percentages for cars running wholly or partly on alternative fuels, eg hybrid, LPG, electricity, dual-fuel cars.

- From 2008–09, cars which have been manufactured to run on E85 fuel receive a 2% discount from the appropriate percentage.

- Where there is no CO_2 figure, and for cars registered before 1 January 1998, the taxable benefit is based on the engine size.

- Diesel supplement: for cars registered on or after 1 January 1998 a 3% supplement applies, but the maximum charge will not exceed 35%. This supplement does not apply to Euro IV compliant cars registered before 1 January 2006.

- There are no adjustments for business mileage.

  Example (2009–10)

  Price of car £15,000; CO_2 emissions 188g/km; benefits percentage 25% (28% if diesel); taxable benefit £3,750 (£4,200 if diesel).

Fuel for private use – cash equivalents

- The fuel scale charge is determined by reference to the CO_2 rating of the car, applied to a fixed amount, which was increased to £16,900 from 6 April 2008. Thus a CO_2 rating of 25% would lead to a taxable benefit of £4,225.

EMPLOYER-PROVIDED VANS: FUEL BENEFIT RULES

7.15

- The standard benefit for private use of a company van increased to £3,000 from 6 April 2007, with no reduction for older vehicles. Furthermore, since 6 April 2007, there has been an additional private fuel charge of £500.

- If private use of the van is restricted to (in essence) home-to-work journeys, then no benefit will apply. These rates apply at the time of writing. There are distinct advantages of providing farm employees with vans and not cars – there is no benefit if the restricted private use condition is met.

187

CARS USED IN THE UNINCORPORATED FARMING BUSINESS

7.16 The green car has already been looked at in **7.5**.

Finance Act 2009 also amends the capital allowance code for motor cars. In the past, there has been a special rule limiting the capital allowances that can be claimed on motor cars costing more than £12,000, to £3,000 a year (and also restricting tax relief for lease rental payments on such cars).

For cars purchased on or after 6 April 2009 (1 April 2009 for companies) this rule is replaced by one restricting capital allowances on cars with CO_2 emissions above 160g/km to 10% a year (instead of the usual 20%). Lease rental payments on such cars will be subject to a flat-rate restriction of 15%. Importantly, these new restrictions will apply to taxis and hire cars, which were exempt from the old rules.

Finance Act 2009 also changes the status of motor cycles. In the past, they have been classed as 'cars', but when purchased on or after 6 April 2009 (1 April 2009 for companies) they will be taken out of the class and so qualify for the 100% annual investment allowance and the new, temporary 40% FYA.

ENTERPRISE ZONE ALLOWANCES (EZAS)

7.17 On 17 December 2007, it was announced that enterprise zone allowances (EZAs) would also be withdrawn from April 2011 and that EZAs (which primarily provide a 100% incentive allowance) will not be subject to the phasing-out rules applying to industrial and agricultural buildings allowances. Where the full initial EZA has not been claimed, a WDA of 25% per annum is given on a straight-line basis. This will continue to be given in full until April 2011.

Parts 3 and 4 of CAA 2001 dealing with IBAs will be repealed with effect from 1 April 2011 for corporation tax purposes and 6 April 2011 for income tax purposes. Although EZAs will no longer be available, balancing charges, in respect of qualifying enterprise zone expenditure, under CAA 2001 ss 314 or 328, will be retained for a limited period. This is because where a business disposes of a building within seven years of first use, in respect of which either an initial allowance or WDA(s) have been claimed, then the business is potentially liable to a balancing charge.

CAPITAL ALLOWANCES PLANNING

7.18 With the variable farming profits experienced in the last decade, the timing of the claim for capital allowances can turn a profit into a tax loss (see Chapter 12). This could be utilised efficiently; however, it could mean the loss of personal allowances and the benefits of the income tax basic rate band. This links to farmers averaging (see **19.1**), but with the move away from farming and towards diversified income not qualifying as farming income, there will be less chance to use this and the timing of capital allowances could be critical to ensure personal allowances are used or tax refunds claimed.

Likewise, in difficult times it might be efficient to waive (ie not claim) some capital allowances so as to ensure that personal allowances are utilised. It can be seen that a lot of new building work can classify as plant, and again the tax planner must be involved before the building is built to ensure maximum tax efficiency from both a timing viewpoint and also the classification of plant and machinery. In an ideal situation, farm management accounts will be reviewed prior to the year-end, to look at fixed asset needs and the planning carried out accordingly. It is understood that the response in the practical world of farming is likely to be reluctance, but we should be training clients to treat their farming and diversified business like any normal commercial activity with management accounts and pre-year-end decision making.

LIVESTOCK FARMING – DAIRY AND LIVESTOCK

7.19   In order to understand diversification and the need for the move to diversification it is essential to have some knowledge of the basic origins of livestock farming. Most diversification is integrated into traditional farming.

The Friesian and Holstein breeds dominate the UK markets to maximise yield, with many herds being a cross between both breeds. Where higher butter fat output is required, Channel Islands breeds predominate. Considerations must be given to the value of stock at the year end, and this is often used in tax planning for farming. 'Zero grazing' is when the herd is kept inside throughout the year and grass is cut and fed fresh to the animals. This can raise issues of diversification use of the fields and also the definition of farming. With the phasing out of ABAs and variable livestock prices, intensive livestock rearing might become less popular.

The area of land required per cow per annum is in the region of one to one and a half acres (0.4 to 0.6 hectares).

Silage is made by eliminating air and fermenting fresh grass. Self feeding of silage is common involving rationing of the silage by an electrical fence at the silage clamp face, again the tax treatment of the clamp must be reviewed. For the capital allowances on the silage clamp see **7.7**. A cow will typically require eight to ten tonnes of silage per winter. Complete diet feeding is popular, being the mixing of silage, concentrates and feed supplements mixed in a special trailer called a 'feeder wagon', which can be towed by a tractor into the buildings housing the cattle where it discharges the feed along the manger. The stock valuation is complex. For NVZ position see **2.20**. For Mars adjustment see **7.32**.

LIVESTOCK FARMING – SHEEP, PIGS AND POULTRY

7.20   There is an old saying in farming, 'up corn, down the horn' meaning that when corn prices are high the livestock industry suffers.

Sheep systems are based on the production of meat and wool from grass. There is a varying dependence on concentrate feeding, temporary leys, permanent grass, hay, silage and forage crops. The system adopted depends upon the farm type and location, weather conditions, other farm enterprises and the markets supplied.

To supplement grassland, forage crops may be grown either as an annual crop such as kale and swedes, or as a catch crop such as rape and stubble turnips. The valuation of these forage crops at cut-off can often be overlooked by the accountant. Forage crops have good dry-matter yields, and are most valuable in the period from October to February when little grass is available and when it is important for ewes to be on a rising plane of nutrition. Rather than planting forage crops specifically for sheep it may be possible to utilise arable by-products. These include sugar beet tops, pea straw and so forth. Many hill and upland farms send sheep to lowland farms for winter grazing.

Feed for pigs varies from carefully formulated concentrate rations through to by-products such as milk, whey and potatoes. Waste products must be cooked prior to feeding in order to prevent the spreading of disease. There can be liability issues here.

See **2.20** for NVZ details – by 1 January 2010 a risk map must have been produced for all holdings that spread organic manures.

ARABLE, DIVERSIFICATION AND STOCK

7.21   Crops are commonly rotated around the farm to maintain soil nutrients and structure and to control weeds, pests and diseases. These objectives can mostly be achieved by the use of disease-resistant varieties, artificial fertilisers and chemicals and some farmers grow continuous cereals. However, because of the costs and environmental considerations, most farms rotate different crops around the farm at some stage. Diversification can be entered into this rotation. Poorer grades of land are less able to support continuous cereals and are more suitable to diversification. Winter wheat currently has the potential to produce the highest margin, therefore this crop predominates.

The inputs used to grow crops are:

- seeds of a correct variety dressed in chemicals;
- fertilisers (looked at in **1.25**);
- chemicals.

Wherever possible, winter varieties of cereals are grown. These are sown from mid to late September to mid to late October. Spring cereals are sown from late February to the end of March. One of the main determinates of yield is the time of sowing. Generally, the earlier the sowing the greater the yield. Because of the longer growing season, yields from winter crops are up to about 30% higher than spring varieties.

The valuation of tillages at farm year end varies substantially with the difference between winter and spring crops and has cut off profitability concerns, ie concerns over year end valuation (see **7.22**).

Cereals may be grown for the following:

- feed wheat;
- milling wheat;

- seed grown under contract;

- malting barley;

- feed barley;

- biofuels and energy crops (biofuels are looked at in Chapter 6).

Energy crops are a big discussion point at the time of writing – there are those who consider that biofuel utilisation 'steals' food from world food resources and others who consider biofuels the salvation of world resources. Time will tell.

The tax position, especially APR, on whether all arable crops are considered as agriculture is looked at in **1.4–1.7**.

Milling wheat and malting barley varieties produce less yield than feed varieties. However they command a premium if the required quality is achieved. Spring crops usually yield less and result in a lower margin but they become necessary where the previous crop cannot be harvested early enough to allow autumn cultivation and sowing to proceed. Potatoes, sugar beet and forage maize are three crops which are harvested from October to December and sometimes in January. With the world shortage of food and the increasing use of wheat as a biofuel, the whole arable industry could be subject to change. Farms that have heavy soils usually only have a relatively short time period after harvest to sow the following year's crops before the ground becomes too wet and unworkable. In wet autumns these farms have to resort to spring crops on land not sown in time.

The position of the advantages and disadvantages with heavy and light soils also has to be reviewed for the purposes of diversification projects as to how the soil will lend itself towards diversification and away from pure agriculture. The question of soil is looked at in **1.25** and the matter of land quality in general is looked at in **1.19**.

BEN 19 AND THE HERD BASIS

7.22   The correct accounting for stock in farming business has become increasingly important with HMRC regularly requiring details of the basis and verification of quantity and value. If stock valuations have been incorrectly accounted for, HMRC have the power to seek adjustment of financial accounts from the preceding six years with the possibility of imposing interest and penalties.

Business Economic Note 19 (BEN19 – now BIM55410) was published in March 1993 by HMRC as an authoritative statement of acceptable methods of valuing farm stock and it remains in place at the time of writing although it now needs to be carefully considered in the light of the single payment regime (SFP) (see **2.3**). The basic principle is that stock is valued at the lower of cost or net realisable value, which is a standard accounting policy that has not altered.

This principle applies for taxation purposes and in financial statements prepared under the historic cost convention and is not applicable to management accounts where stock may be included at market value or estimated selling price.

Farmers normally seek the assistance of an agricultural valuer in the computation of annual stocktaking. However this is not compulsory for any trading medium and some farmers prepare their own valuation. Farmers not using professional valuers need to justify their basis of valuation carefully and, above all, be consistent with the method used.

In general, actual costs of production should be used unless it is not possible to ascertain them, with reasonable accuracy, from the farms records. It can, however, prove difficult to identify actual costs, particularly forage costs in livestock enterprises, and deemed cost is then acceptable.

Stocks can be divided into two distinct areas for the two main farming systems: arable crops (see **7.21**) and livestock (see **7.19** and **7.20**). Herds basis obviously applies to livestock only.

For non-farming stocks it will be important to value them at the basic principle of the lower of cost and net realisable value. Alternatively farmers may elect for quite a different treatment: the herd basis (ITTOIA 2005 Pt 2 Ch 8 and ITTOIA 2005 s 111(1)). Herd basis is very complex and there is not the scope here to look at it in detail. The effect is that valuations of production herd animals are excluded from the computation of trading profits: the cost of the original herd, and additions to it, are not deductible in computing profits. Nor are the proceeds of sale included, so that a profit is not taxed, nor a loss relieved. Herd basis allows the chosen classes of mature animals to be treated as assets and excluded from the trading stock valuation. The advantage of the herd basis is that changes in the value of the production animals do not distort taxable profit. If they are eventually sold without replacement, the proceeds are effectively free of tax. That is, they are not included in the computation of taxable trading profits for income tax purposes.

The decision as to whether to elect for the herd basis or not will depend on the individual. One of the disadvantages of electing is that there will be no tax relief on any reduction in value of the animals. The time limit for making the election is within 12 months after the fixed filing date of the year of assessment in which the production herd is first kept. The election is irrevocable. Any new livestock enterprise should think hard about making the election. There are detailed notes in HMRC's manual at BIM55500–BIM55640.

If within five years of the sale of the herd the seller begins to acquire a new production herd of the same class, then they are treated as 'replacements' of the whole herd.

Where the difference between the cost of animals in the herd is much less than their ultimate market value, the election is more beneficial. Likewise in periods of inflation, the herd basis helped keep unrealised profit out of the tax computation. Changes in a partnership need a fresh election, and with farmers looking at restructuring, this is important. An election for the herd basis is complicated in a share-farming arrangement (see **11.4–11.9**).

'Flying flocks', that is herds of cows and flocks of sheep, are sometimes kept with individual animals sold at the end of their production cycles. These are not eligible for the herd basis election.

Whether treated as trading stock or on the herd basis, farm animals are exempt from CGT. They are regarded as wasting assets, which are 'tangible moveable property' (TCGA 1992 ss 44–45).

Horses working on a farm may be treated as either trading stock or as a fixed asset, providing the treatment is consistent (see **7.28**).

HERD BASIS – *TAX BULLETIN*

7.23   Various concerns regarding livestock farming have resulted in some small reduction in herds. This has included a move to diversification. BIM55550 clarifies the interpretation of a situation where there is a small reduction within a herd.

There has been some uncertainty as to how the 'cost of the disposal' should be taken out of the herd and hence how much profit will fall into tax on the disposals. HMRC revised their view of the situation so that where a farmer sells part of the herd without replacement, the profit should be computed with reference to the actual cost of the animal disposed of rather than on a 'first in, first out' basis. An example of the practical effect of this can be found in BIM55550.

STOCK VALUATION ADJUSTMENTS ON CESSATION

7.24   With a move to diversification it could be that part of the farming activity has to cease. It is therefore worth considering the position of what happens to stock at cessation.

When a farm business ceases, the general rule is that stock is valued at market value (ITTOIA 2005 ss 173(1), 175(3) and (4)). But this is not necessarily so, if the business is ceasing because the farmer has died (ITTOIA 2005 s 173(4)). Where stock is to be sold to another UK trader, the general rule is that the price paid is adopted for tax purposes provided that the parties are not connected with each other. The farmer ceasing to trade treats the monies as a trading receipt and the incoming farmer treats the amount as a trading expense.

Where the parties are connected (ITA 2007 s 993):

- stock is valued at open market value;
- however, where open market value is greater than:
  - (a)   the actual price agreed; and
  - (b)   the amount which would be taken into account when calculating profit as representing cost of the stock as sold in the ordinary course of trade,

  the parties can jointly elect to substitute the greater of (a) or (b) and must do so not later than two years from the end of the chargeable period in which the trade is discontinued (ITTOIA 2005 s 178(3)).

Stock taken for personal use or use in another business before cessation of trading shall be treated as a sale at market value (*Sharkey v Wernher* (1955) 36 TC 275, HL) (see **7.31**).

ANIMALS' ELIGIBILITY FOR CAPITAL ALLOWANCES

7.25   In certain circumstances a claim for capital allowances is available on working animals and production livestock kept for the purposes of a business, and includes live animals kept for permanent employment in farming and which serve to produce saleable products. CA21200 accepts that a horse used in a school or show jumping business is plant, as is a guard dog or circus animal. In practice horses are rarely capitalised as fixed assets in this way.

Animals that are kept mainly for sale to provide a saleable product after slaughter are outside the description. Thus, there is a distinction between dairy cattle, which qualify as 'production livestock', and beef cattle, which do not. Laying poultry are plant, but not broilers. Young animals not yet ready for use as production livestock do not qualify. CA21200 requires a dog to be working to qualify. Farm animals are normally trading stock such that their cost is a revenue item, thus barring a capital allowances claim.

QUOTAS

7.26   Introduced by European Economic Community Regulations in 1984 (EC Reg 857/84), milk quota is an arrangement which allows the wholesale milk producers to produce milk up to the quota threshold without attracting liability to supplementary levy. A quota is allocated to a particular holding of agricultural land.

Regarding IHT, it has been HMRC's practice in the case of dairy farmers to combine the value of quota with the value of the agricultural land for APR purposes. In any event APR and BPR will not be due on milk quota where dairying activities cease, that is, the quota is held without a trading activity and leased out.

Quotas are being phased out (see **7.30**), so the most important issue now is potential 'negligible' loss claims on purchased quota, but there follows a history of the quota so that there is greater understanding of the tax planning and action that needs to be taken.

Quotas came into being when the regulatory system of which they are a part was introduced. Normally, a total quota for the UK is subdivided among existing producers according to their level of production at a certain date. A pool of reserve quota may also be created and held centrally for allocation to special cases, such as new entrants. Each eligible producer thus receives an initial allocation of quota without payment. The quota is immediately of value to farmers because it enables them to carry on the particular farming activity more profitably than they would be able to do without quota. One effect of the introduction of a quota system has been the creation of a new capital asset in the hands of farmers.

Quotas may be transferable between farmers by outright sale and purchase. As the quota is normally a fixed capital asset of a farmer's trade, such transactions normally have no income tax consequences for the farmers concerned. In particular, there can be no question of farmers who have bought quota claiming a deduction for the amount of any expenditure such as levies or leasing charges, which they would have incurred if they had not bought it. That is, the sale is a CGT disposal and the purchase represents the CGT base cost for a future sale.

Quota is a fixed capital asset. BIM55305 describes quotas as follows:

> 'A farmer holds a quota primarily in order to make a profit from carrying on the particular farming activity which it covers. She or he does not ordinarily buy and sell quota in the course of the farming trade. The quota has the character of an enduring asset of the farmer's business similar to the buildings or farm machinery. Quota is normally therefore a fixed capital asset of a farmer's business.'

Quotas treated by HMRC as capital assets are subject to CGT and IHT in the normal way. Examples are:

- suckler-cow quota – allowing a producer to claim headage payments on suckler cows; or

- ewe premium quota – allowing a producer to claim headage payments on ewes and ewe lambs.

For clarity, **20.2** sets out the subsidies that the SFP replaces. It is essential to understand the difference between quotas and subsidies. The whole of Chapter **20** is devoted to the SFP.

All quotas can be leased or sold (see above) between farmers. For tax purposes there are two types of transaction: temporary or permanent. 'Back-to-back' transactions are increasingly used whereby 'dirty' (used) quota is sold and 'clean' (unused) quota purchased on the same day. A temporary transaction is known as leasing: the cost to the purchaser is a trading expense.

From 1 April 2002 new quota owned by a company will qualify for write-off against profits either at 4% or at a preferred rate (see **8.25**). As the future of quotas is not guaranteed beyond 2012, it could be prudent and tax efficient to write it off over a period to that date. This could have large benefits to farmers trading through a company. There are a number of anti-avoidance provisions including the exclusion of relief on quota purchased from a connected party.

From a tax-planning viewpoint, potato quota now has nil value, therefore a claim for the capital loss should be considered under TCGA 1992 s 24(2). The timing of the claim, as in all such claims, should be made where possible in the year of a gain above the annual exemption for CGT. The future value of milk quotas will be nil and similar tax planning should be contemplated (see **7.30**).

For quotas in a limited company see Chapter 8.

Milk quota – as a 'fungible' asset

7.27   At the time of writing quota is being phased out (see **7.28**).

Fungible assets are assets that are movable or perishable and are of a sort that can be estimated by weight. The disposal of quota is generally a capital disposal taking advantage of CGT reliefs. But what is the base cost? If no milk quota has been purchased, it is nil, but what if further quota has been bought? How is the cost allocated between the total holding? Prior to the fungible asset rules it was 'pooled' with the total holding, therefore giving a low CGT base cost.

It should be noted that the fungible asset rule does not apply to a limited company.

Where possible the farmer should contact his tax adviser before the disposal of any quota and as mentioned at **7.29** quotas are being (or have been) phased out.

It is understood that HMRC will not take the unreasonable view that milk quota is a fungible asset. It is worth considering what benefit this could have to the farmer.

CG77821 states that a producer primarily holds milk quota to produce and sell milk profitably and not to run the risk of financial penalty for over-production. The Manual states that such producers do not ordinarily buy and sell quota in the course of their day-to-day trade. Quota is an enduring capital asset of the business in the same way as buildings or farm machinery. Thus, where some of a producer's quota was allocated without cost in 1984 and some was subsequently purchased, HMRC originally considered that the acquisition cost should be apportioned under TCGA 1992 s 52(4) by reference to the total holding.

This could seem unreasonable to the producer who has had to buy and sell quota to reach production targets. The result could be a high sale price matched with a relatively low acquisition cost. The Capital Gains Manual now confirms that milk quotas are regarded as fungible assets, under TCGA 1992 s 104(3), and the same identification rules will apply as for shares and securities. For milk quota disposals before 6 April 1998, it could be said that the share pooling rules may be analogous with the apportionment rule in TCGA 1992 s 52(4), but disposals on or after that date should be identified with acquisitions under the share identification rules.

There are many who think that the application of TCGA 1992 s 54(4) was unfair on those producers who, from time to time, had to purchase and dispose of quota and the disposal was matched against the much reduced cost due to the inclusion in the apportionment of the 1984 allocation with nil base cost. In these cases the disposal proceeds largely represented the gain, which was produced by what could be said was transitional, and better matched with the purchased quota. It is hoped that applying the current 'fungible asset' rules will help to present a 'fairer' position and also a clearer representation of the correct position.

It could be argued that the taxpayers could use both methods. The earlier method could produce gains to offset against any unused annual exemption, whilst keeping the base cost higher for future disposals. However, the latter treatment could produce gains, which would not otherwise have been taxed.

And the good news is this all disappears when quotas disappear – parties will erupt in farm tax departments.

PHASING OUT OF QUOTAS

7.28   Quotas were abolished before 1 January 2005 and will be treated as having been disposed of on the date on which they ceased to exist. Capital losses may arise in respect of quota acquired other than for nil consideration which were held as non-wasting assets (HMRC Tax Bulletin Issue 78 August 2005).

Milk quota is not officially 'dead' (at the time of writing) until the milk quota market ceases – it still has a small value. All dairy farmers with purchased quota must ensure they identify the amount paid for the quota and when. The value of milk quota is falling but it is still not completely redundant but what of a negligible value claim?

Negligible value claims

The rules for negligible value claims are found in TCGA 1992, s 24 with further guidance being given in HMRC's Capital Gains Manual at CG13118 onwards.

'Negligible' is not defined in TCGA 1992. CG13124 says that negligible means 'worth next to nothing'. But of course this is just HMRC's view.

If a taxpayer owns an asset which has become of negligible value (ie it is worth next to nothing) the taxpayer can make a claim to be treated as if they had disposed of the asset and then immediately reacquired it for its value at the time the claim is made. The deemed disposal of the asset will result in a capital loss. There is no time limit for making a negligible value claim but the taxpayer must still own the asset when they make the claim. When a taxpayer makes a claim he or she can, if they wish, specify that the deemed disposal took place on another date during the two years before their claim is made, provided the asset was also worthless on the earlier date and he or she owned it on that date. The resulting loss is then treated as arising in the tax year in which that date fell. The claim can be made by companies as well as individual owners of assets.

In the specific case of purchased milk quota, it is possible to make a negligible value claim provided the conditions are met. The quota must have been purchased in order for there to be a loss of value and those details must be ascertained.

Farmers can use the loss arising from their negligible value claim on purchased milk quota against capital gains arising in the same year, or carry it forward to be used against future capital gains. There are specialist milk quota and entitlement brokers who will provide a letter confirming market value at a selected date. The law does not specify the form of claim but it may be advisable to accompany it with a professional valuation. While the definition of negligible is vague (in that it is not defined), the conditions and detail of the potential for the claim are explained clearly in TCGA 1992 s 24(2):

'(2) [Where a negligible value claim is made:]

(a)   this Act shall apply as if the claimant had sold, and immediately reacquired, the asset at the time of the claim or (subject to paragraphs (b) and (c) below) at any earlier time specified in the claim, for a consideration of an amount equal to the value specified in the claim.

(b)   An earlier time may be specified in the claim if:

(i)   the claimant owned the asset at the earlier time; and

(ii)   the asset had become of negligible value at the earlier time; and either

(iii)   for capital gains tax purposes the earlier time is not more than two years before the beginning of the year of assessment in which the claim is made; or

(iv)   for corporation tax purposes the earlier time is on or after the first day of the earliest accounting period ending not more than two years before the time of the claim.

(c)   Section 93 of and Schedule 12 to the Finance Act 1994 (indexation losses and transitional relief) shall have effect in relation to an asset to which this section applies as if the sale and reacquisition occurred at the time of the claim and not at any earlier time.'

With so many asset values in turmoil, now is clearly the time for a review of all farming assets, especially property, with regard to values and possible tax planning. The potential utilisation of the loss claim on milk quota must not be overlooked when other capital gains are in prospect.

EQUINE STOCK AND STUD FARMS

7.29   Stud farming is farming (see **6.17**). Other equine activities are not farming (see **6.24–6.29**). The valuation of stock is set out at BIM55705 and BIM55710. This is summarised as follows:

'Specialist advice on open market valuations of thoroughbred horses is available from the Bloodstock Section, Shares and Assets Valuation, Nottingham. Requests for advice should include

●   the name(s) of the horse(s) to be valued

●   the valuation dates

●   any opinion of open market value together with reasoning, if supplied.

Except where the herd basis has been adopted, both stallions and mares should be dealt with as stock in trade and valued individually at the beginning and end of each year on the usual basis of cost or net realisable value (see BIM55705), whichever is the lower. Stock valuations should also include any foals and, where appropriate, stud fees paid (see below).

In the case of stallions (but not mares) we accept a rule of thumb method of valuation, whereby the cost of the animal is written off by equal annual instalments until it reaches the age of 10 (15 for valuations as at dates up to and including 31 December 2000). This rule of thumb method is an attempt to arrive at an acceptable figure for net realisable value where this is less than cost. It is not appropriate

●   where a better figure is available because the animal is valued at the balance sheet date or

- where it would give an unreasonable result. For example, in those exceptional cases where the value of an animal increases, or drops at a rate significantly slower than that used in the rule of thumb, because, for example, of very successful progeny, the figure computed using the rule of thumb should be increased to an amount not exceeding cost.

STUD FEES PAID

The stud fee or "nomination" fee paid by the owner of a mare for the services of a particular stallion can be a substantial sum. Unless

- the mare has already given birth to the foal, or is known not to have conceived, or has aborted, by the accounting date; or

- an "adjusting event" (see BIM33140) occurs – for example, the discovery between the balance sheet date and the date the accounts were finalised of a congenital defect rendering the foal valueless;

the fee paid should be reflected in the balance sheet by one of the following methods:

- including the fee in a stock valuation of the embryo or foetus of the foal

- increasing the value of the mare while she is carrying the foal by the amount of the fee

- carrying forward the fee as a prepayment

FOALS

When the foal is born the stud fee becomes part of its cost.

Foals should normally be included in the stock valuation at cost.'

It is HMRC who have the use of the valuations office at Nottingham. The stud farmer normally has to engage the services of a bloodstock agent especially for transfers in and out of the stud into racing.

Tax planning around equine stock values

7.30   The equine industry is unique. It could be said that stud stock values are more volatile than teenage fashion. Outside factors such as the racing achievements of animals from associated bloodlines can have a dramatic impact. Keeping stock fit and healthy and injury free is a real problem. Some may view the equine stock valuation as an unimportant paper exercise, but they can, in fact, produce tax refunds resulting from the tax losses that arise. If potentially valuable equine stock is held at cost, the timing of the profit can be planned around the date of sale. However, if a disaster waits in the form of a valuation fall, it can be realised as soon as possible by means of being reflected appropriately in the stock valuation, therefore accelerating the tax loss (or reducing the taxable profit).

The stud farmer and all equine activities must therefore take full cognisance of the importance of year-end valuation for his profit/loss. The timing of the sale of good and bad stock is critical, as is the timing of any transfer to racing and owners and tax advisers alike need to give appropriate weight to this subject. It will frequently determine exactly when a profit is achieved. As with all tax-planning issues, however, commercial common sense should take priority such that when a good sales price can be achieved, the adviser may need to accept that the owner will very likely ignore the tax-planning advice given previously.

Mares and stallions will have been purchased or transferred from training, ie racing. Those purchased in the market will have been brought in at cost, while those transferred in from training will be brought in at market value. The accounts will reflect these amounts unless the current market value of the animal is lower, in which case this will be substituted. A number of factors can influence the market value of a horse, including its past performance, racing career, market conditions and breeding prospects etc.

As stock values considerably affect the taxation position, HMRC tend to examine them closely if they consider they are being used for 'focused tax planning', and so it may be worth seeking a written independent valuation in certain cases.

APPROPRIATION TO/FROM TRADING STOCK

7.31   ITTOIA 2005 s 25 provides that trading profits must be computed in accordance with generally accepted accounting practice (GAAP) subject to any adjustment required by law. Where a person disposes of stock otherwise than by way of trade (eg where an individual appropriates stock for personal use, eg farm and diversification goods), then under UK GAAP such a transaction would normally be accounted for at cost.

However HMRC insist that the decision in *Sharkey v Wernher* means that an adjustment to the computation of trading profits is required by law, such that the taxable profits of the trade should be computed as if that stock had been disposed of at market value. This could have a big impact on the diversified farmer.

Legislation has been introduced to extend the view of *Sharkey v Wernher* and to put it on a statutory basis, ITTOIA 2005 ss 172A–172F (income tax) and CTA 2009 ss 156–161 (corporation tax). It applies to transactions on or after 12 March 2008 in relation to land and other property appropriated into or from trading stock other than in the course of trade. The new rules will apply to both individuals and companies.

The scope of this legislation is wider than the principle that was established by *Sharkey v Wernher.*

Historically the farmer has taken produce (eg milk, eggs, meat, hay and straw) for private use etc.

The transactions to which the open market value rules apply include:

- appropriation of trading stock by a trader/farmer for a non-trading purpose;

- other disposals of trading stock by a trader/farmer (eg where trading stock is disposed of to another person), other than in the course of trade;

- where goods belonging to a person were not trading stock but then become trading stock of that person's trade; and

- other acquisitions of trading stock by a person otherwise than in the course of a trade (eg this might be where a farmer purchases a relative's cattle and then proceeds to sell it as part of his farming activity).

For these purposes 'trading stock' means land or other property that is sold in the ordinary course of the trade (including partially manufactured stock), but does not include:

- materials used in the manufacture, preparation or construction of any such trading stock;

- services performed in the ordinary course of a trade; or

- articles produced or materials used in the performance of any such services.

THE MANDATORY 'MARS ADJUSTMENT' AND FARMING STOCK

7.32   In the last century the Mars bar was promoted as being capable of helping the purchaser 'work, rest and play'. By the same token any tax adviser who 'buys in' to this March 2007 House of Lords decision (see below) can save their clients tax (reduce the tax liability or increase the tax refund). However it appears that the benefits of the tax saving are being ignored. Is this because the case is not understood or the calculation is too complex or the taxpayer does not want to pay for the work and the revision to the tax returns?

The case *Small v Mars UK Ltd* and *HMRC v William Grant & Sons Distillers Ltd* provides the guidance for the 'Mars adjustment'. As depreciation is added back in the tax computation then a mirror adjustment must be made for depreciation included in stock to comply with GAAP ie adjustments to tax computations for depreciation carried in stock. The adjustment is mandatory and this has been reiterated by HMRC and that this applies to 2007–08 onwards.

For farm stock valuation guidance BEN19 (set out in BIM55410) is used which bases the valuation on 'deemed cost'. From 2009 CAAV identify depreciation within their tables. But what is the amount of depreciation carried in stock?

The production of corn by an arable farm can be likened to the production of a Mars bar:

- The process involves large expensive machinery with heavy depreciation – eg combine harvesters cost over £350,000.

- At year end there is likely to be a possible range of corn in store (the finished Mars bar) or tillages (the Mars bar in production).

The starting point in order to try to calculate the depreciation 'carried' in stock is to take the depreciation from the accounts. This has to be allocated between growing crops, harvested crops and non-productive work. The sum of the depreciation allocated to growing crops and a percentage of the depreciation allocated to the harvested crops (in proportion to the percentage of the harvested crops still in store) would be the tax adjustment figure used.

2007–08 is the start year as this is after the date of the decision

BIM 33190 states:

> 'Business should use the method approved by the House of Lords in the first computations accompanying accounts prepared and submitted after the date of the decision.'

The question of 2007–08 was agreed in correspondence dated 17 September 2008 from HMRC, from Alison Bull, of HMRC Technical Advisor, Tax and Accountancy issues. In this letter Miss Bull wrote 'it will of course be the responsibility of individual inspectors to consider whether the precise allocation method actually used is acceptable depending on the facts and their assessment of risks'. Obviously there are the concerns of the complexity of the calculation, the cost and client understanding. It can be argued that the Mars calculation is not restricted to arable stock figures. It can also apply to livestock. Calves and lambs are a production process involving machinery and the year end figure for stock at deemed cost does carry depreciation of this machinery. The Mars bar can help the tax adviser 'work' on behalf of their clients, 'rest' knowing that all is in order and 'play' with a more relaxed approach with the benefit of this adjustment in tax-planning terms. Please excuse the Mars bar parallel to attract attention, but for some reason this appears to have missed the radar of a large number of practitioners and non-compliance would cause very bad indigestion!

CONCLUSION

7.33   For stock valuations, a move to diversification will mean a move away from the agricultural tax and accounting standards of BEN 19. More straightforward accounting standards of the 'lower of cost' and net realisable value will be important for the purposes of valuing stock.

With possible falling stock values, previous assumptions might be challenged, especially by a harsh bank manager. Changes in the basis of valuation will have to be considered carefully for the contravention of consistency principles of diversification, and rural initiatives will mean increased capital expenditure in plant, improvement and repair. Great care will have to be taken in regard to classification, accounting and tax treatment, consistency and of course tax planning. HMRC seek consistency of treatment in all these matters.

These are difficult times and the valuations must be given the due care they deserve for business assessment, consistency and tax planning. Likewise tax-saving opportunities can be achieved through the identification, addition and disposal of plant and machinery as opposed to improvement to freehold.

Chapter 8

To incorporate or not to incorporate?

Julie Butler

- **Limited companies are considered not 'farm friendly'**
  The tax disadvantages of incorporation for farmers have moved the farming fraternity away from the corporate structure over recent decades due to tax losses being 'trapped' in the company, also the complexity of securing IHT reliefs on land farmed by a limited company together with the tax cost of removing development gains out of the company.

- **Diversified activities might seek benefits of incorporation**
  A move to diversification has brought the limited company back into 'fashion' as a protection against risk and a way of enjoying the current specific fiscal advantages of incorporation. It is for this reason that the company deserves a whole chapter.

  With the top rate of income tax of 50% there can be distinct advantages of the lower rates of corporation tax on retained profits for the diversified business.

- **Choice of business structure**
  Incorporation of a specific diversified activity can have fiscal advantages. Each business and/or trade needs to have 'tailor-made' decisions. Comparisons are presented in this chapter.

THE PROBLEMS WITH INCORPORATION AND FARMING

8.1   Many farms own their land in the limited company or trade on the land through a limited company. This presents some tax problems:

- the trapping of losses within the limited company, no sideways offsetting of losses (see **12.5**);

- companies cannot use averaging of farmers' profits;

- the problems over the loss of private residence relief (PRR) for a farmhouse owned by a limited company (see **8.3**);

- the problems over benefits in kind of assets used in the company;

- IHT planning complexities of 'tax marriage and the trading vehicle';

- the problems of taking money out of the company generated through development gains.

There are risks to trading status for IHT and very complex IHT considerations surround the choice of business structure. The family farm that is owned within the structure of a limited company is currently very vulnerable to loss of IHT reliefs.

USING THE LIMITED COMPANY FOR THE DIVERSIFIED ACTIVITY

8.2 Over the last few decades, the farming industry and the HMRC tax rules that help influence the choice of trading vehicle have not embraced incorporation and there are many sections throughout this book that point out the disadvantages.

When a farm moves into a risky, diversifying operation, incorporation could be considered, with the land possibly not being owned within the limited company. It is important for farming tax practitioners to look at what diversified activities qualify for the enterprise investment scheme (see **8.16**), and which activities have not qualified and the reasons given.

With the 50% rate of income tax applying from 6 April 2010 (see **8.8**) the limited company has the advantage of being able to help the shareholder determine when the income arises via the dividend route.

The company will be taxed at the small companies rate (see **8.6**) and the shareholder pays higher rate income tax when the dividend is taken. Thus if a limited company is used as the trading vehicle for a diversified activity the business can accumulate profits at the lower corporation tax rates as opposed to the higher income tax rates of a sole trade or partnership (see **8.8**).

Chapter 6 gives a clear indication of the risks involved with equine activities, recreational fishing and shooting, tourism activity, leisure pursuits etc, and incorporation might be sought. There could be some VAT advantages of a split business, that is to hive off the activity into the limited company, but the potential for a challenge from HMRC over business 'disaggregation' must be kept in mind, ie a small diversified farming operation could fall below the VAT registration limit. If the customers of the separate business are not VAT registered, this could have distinct immediate advantages.

For very risky diversification projects that might involve R&D expenditure, the corporate structure might be the natural choice to achieve tax advantages (see **2.15** and **2.16**).

THE FARMHOUSE IN THE LIMITED COMPANY

8.3 No IHT relief is available for shares in a company if the business of that company consists wholly or mainly of dealing in shares or securities, land or buildings or making or holding investments (IHTA 1984 s 105(3)). The question of whether a qualifying business was carried on or whether the assets concerned were merely being exploited as investments has recently been given a lot of attention by HMRC. Where the farmhouse is held in a limited company it may be given special attention; all farming companies must be mindful of these provisions and the possibility of jeopardising APR and BPR claims (see **13.3–13.16**).

Agricultural property including the farmhouse may be the underlying assets of the company. This property then qualifies for relevant BPR. APR will be applied automatically through the operation of IHTA 1984. APR and BPR will be available on the value of the underlying assets reduced by those qualifying for APR. APR will not be available in respect of minority holdings of shares in a farming company but 100% BPR will apply where, as will often be the case, the holding is in unquoted shares.

If the farmer does not own the farmhouse personally then there will be a loss of private residence relief (PRR) on the farmhouse (see **4.4–4.12**) held in the limited company. The *Starke* case (see **4.28**) shows problems where the land is held in the limited company and the farmhouse outside the company. There are also concerns over benefits in kind.

THE OWNERSHIP OF THE FARM IN THE LIMITED COMPANY

8.4 The question of land held in the limited company was first looked at in **5.23**.

A significant limitation of BPR is that where a company owns a tenanted farm, BPR may not be available on the taxpayer's shareholding, because the company may not be trading. The company could be wholly or mainly holding investments within IHTA 1984 s 105(3). Thus, if a farmhouse were in this company there would be problems with a claim for APR and BPR. With the move to diversification and more land failing in its claim for APR but succeeding in its claim for BPR it will of course make the claims for the farmhouse more vulnerable.

Another problem can arise under the hobby farming rules (see Chapter 12) whereby a farm is treated as uncommercial and therefore has losses restricted under ITA 2007 s 67. This means the losses are 'trapped' in the limited company and not offset against total income. However, there are differing schools of thought, as set out in Chapter 12, as to how ruthless the Inspector can be in disallowing the claim if there has been a previous period of strong profitability or a long history of farming etc.

There are also potential benefits-in-kind problems regarding use of the farmhouse. However, if the farmhouse is included in the limited company there is a problem of whether it qualifies as a business asset or as an investment within the meaning of 'making or holding investments' found in IHTA 1984 s 105(3).

Only controlling interests qualify for APR (IHTA 1984 s 122), although a minority interest may attract BPR.

Section 122 allows APR on the value of shares in or securities of a company if, and only if:

- the agricultural property forms part of the assets of a company and part of the value of the shares or securities can be attributed to the agricultural value of that agricultural property; and

- the shares or securities gave the transferor control of the company immediately before the transfer.

A diversified activity might qualify as a 'business' not 'agriculture' for inheritance tax purposes and it might be considered a risky enough activity to put into a new limited company. Chapter 24 has helped with the clarification. If there are high levels of profits the limited company can present distinct advantages.

Where land is held in the limited company, there is less chance of being able to claim APR on the farmhouse as in *Starke v IRC* [1995] STC 689 (see **4.28**).

Further alternatives could include a share-farming agreement (see **11.9**) between the landowner and the limited company.

COMPANIES ACT 2006

8.5   Under the 1985 Act, companies were required to include the following details: name, place of registration, registered number and address on their letterheads. The 2006 Act extended this requirement, from 1 January 2007, to cover websites, e-mails and other electronic documents. These measures also apply to limited liability partnerships.

The other changes which may affect rural companies are as follows:

- A company is no longer required to have the two governing documents commonly referred to as the memorandum and articles of association. Instead there is just one governing document, the articles, with the memorandum reduced to a snapshot of the situation at the company's formation.

- The company's share capital need no longer be stated, or limited, by its constitutional documents.

- Private companies are no longer required to have a company secretary.

- Private companies can pass any resolution as a written resolution, save one for the removal of a director or auditor before their term expires.

- Private companies are no longer required to hold an annual general meeting.

- Directors' duties are now laid down in statute and include the duty to promote the company's success for the benefit of the members. In doing so the director should have regard to a number of specific areas such as the affect of the company's operations on the community and the environment; employee interests; and the likely long-term consequences of a decision.

- Directors do not need to give home addresses for the public record; a separate register of home addresses must be kept, but with restricted access.

- Shareholders need to approve directors' long-term service contracts in excess of two years.

206

- The prohibition on providing financial assistance for acquiring the company's own shares has been abolished for private companies.

Existing companies may need to alter their articles if they want to take advantage of some of these measures.

CORPORATION TAX RATES

8.6   The corporation tax rates are reduced from FY 2011 as follows:

	FY 2010	FY 2011
Small profits rate	21%	20%
Marginal rate	29.75%	28.75%
Main rate	28%	27%

It is proposed to reduce the main corporation tax rate to 24% over four years, reducing the rate by 1% a year out to 31 March 2015.

To summarise:

Tax year	Small co	Large co	Marginal rate
FY 2010	21%	28%	29.75%
FY 2011	20%	27%	28.75%
FY 2012	20%	26%	27.50%
FY 2013	20%	25%	26.25%
FY 2014	20%	24%	25.00%

- The marginal rate of tax between £300,001 to £1,500,000 is 29.75%.

- Closely controlled investment holding companies are always taxed at the main rate – currently 28%. Note the small companies rate limit of £300,000 is reduced for each 'associated company' (see **8.27**).

CORPORATION TAX PAYMENTS

8.7

- Small companies – tax due nine months and one day after end of accounting period.

- Large companies – tax due in quarterly instalments from six months and 13 days after start of accounting period.

THE 50% RATE OF INCOME TAX

8.8   As set out in **8.2** there is a top rate of income tax of 50%.

From 6 April 2010 a 50% income tax rate applies for income over £150,000. From 6 April 2010 the personal allowance reduces by £1 for every £2 of income above £100,000 irrespective of age. The limited company provides choice as to when the dividends are taken and therefore potentially what rate of tax is paid. Dividends for income between £37,400 and £150,000 are taxed at 32.5%. Dividends for income over £150,000 are taxed at 42.5%.

For farmer shareholders who are trading through limited companies for the whole or part of the activity they are able to decide when to take dividends from the limited company. Retained profits which could reflect stock, fixed assets and general working capital will only be taxed at the higher rate of tax when the dividend is taken by the shareholder.

SO WHY A LIMITED COMPANY FOR DIVERSIFICATION?

8.9   The whole area of tax planning surrounding the choice of trading vehicle has to be looked at in the 'round'. The possible advantages of a limited company could be:

- protection via limited liability (comparison to the sole trader or partnership);

- the ability to raise outside funds via EIS (subject to qualification) (see **8.16–8.19**);

- the current tax advantages for small profitable companies (see **8.6** and **2.16**);

- the ability to 'spread' ownership through share capital in a range of shareholdings;

- a clearly defined separate business for subsequent sale;

- the ability to claim R&D tax credits (see **2.15**);

- the ability to claim contaminated land relief;

- the ability to plan the 50% income tax rate for shareholders via the timing of dividends;

- in FA 2008 tax credits for companies in respect of enhanced capital allowances (see **8.33**).

BENEFITS OF SOLE TRADER/PARTNERSHIP/LLP

8.10   The unincorporated business plays a vital role in the farming world. Many, if not most, small businesses start their life as a sole trader or partnership. The key initial tax planning point for the diversified business is that an unincorporated structure is also preferable if the early years are likely to produce trading losses. A sole trader/partner would normally be able to claim prompt repayment of income tax by making a loss relief claim against their other current or prior income (of the three previous years) under ITA 2007 ss 64 and 572(1) respectively. If such losses fall within a company they could not be relieved until it generated profits.

There are no legal formalities in establishing a partnership (other than under the Partnership Act 1890, the Limited Partnerships Act 1907, or the Limited Liability Partnerships Act 2000) (see **2.14**) and a written agreement is not necessary although advisable. The mutual rights and duties of partners, whether ascertained by agreement or defined by the Partnership Act 1890, may be varied by the consent of all the partners, such consent being either express or inferred from their actions (Partnership Act 1890 s 19).

Whether or not a partnership exists is a mixed question of fact and law, and it is obviously more difficult to prove the existence of a partnership if there is no written agreement. HMRC may require proof that there is a partnership by requesting sight of contracts, agreements, VAT-registration details and bank accounts. However, the mere existence of a written agreement is not proof, and it must be supported by the facts. In *Dickenson v Gross* (1927) 11 TC 614 there was no substance behind the deed of partnership and it was held that for income tax purposes a partnership did not exist.

One of the main disadvantages of the sole trader and partnership structures is unlimited liability (see **2.13** and **2.14**), which many claim are rectified by the LLP.

CHOICE OF COMPANY NAME FOR DIVERSIFIED BUSINESS

8.11   In broad terms, those forming a company are free to choose any name for it provided that:

● it is not too similar to an existing company name;

● it does not infringe another's trade or service mark;

● it is not offensive; and

● its use would not be a criminal offence.

Some words and expressions may be used in company names only with official consent. Examples of such 'sensitive' words include 'British', 'international', 'holding', 'group', 'royal' and 'United Kingdom'. This could be of relevance to many equine businesses.

A UK company may also use a business or trading name under which it conducts its business. The only restrictions on a business name are that it:

● is not too similar to another business name; and

● does not require prior official approval because it contains 'sensitive' words.

As a safeguard for customers, suppliers and others, a company must show its company name on all business letters and contracts, including invoices.

DIRECTORS' DUTIES AND RESPONSIBILITIES IN A DIVERSIFIED BUSINESS

8.12   One of the problems of a limited company for farmers who are diversifying is the complexity of directors' duties and responsibilities.

The directors of a UK company are appointed by the shareholders and are typically entrusted with the day-to-day management and conduct of the business and to represent the company in its dealings with the outside world. Various legal safeguards prevent any abuse of power by company directors. Directors have both statutory and common-law duties and are subject to a large number of restrictions and controls.

Directors must exercise due skill and care in carrying out their duties but no specific qualifications are required. Certain personal information must be disclosed to the company and to Companies House to be kept with the public records of the company, for example, date of birth, residential address and other directorships.

Like the shareholders, directors of a limited company are generally protected from personal liability. In extreme cases, directors may be personally liable for any wrongdoing on their part. A director's duty is first and foremost to act honestly and in the best interests of the company itself rather than individual shareholders. A director also owes a duty to the company's creditors and must have a regard to the interests of the company's employees. Directors must not make a secret profit from their position as directors (ie without the company's consent) nor show bad faith towards the company.

Directors are not appointed for any fixed period and may be removed by the shareholders at any time. In small private companies, the directors are typically all executive directors. They are, therefore, employees of the company and may enjoy the benefit of service agreements (employment contracts) which will govern the company's ability to remove them with or without compensation. In larger companies or in subsidiaries, it is typical for some, if not all, of the directors to be non-executive.

Meetings – directors and shareholders of diversified business

8.13 The directors should hold regular board meetings to make important decisions concerning the company. It is difficult for directors to establish that they have acted properly unless they meet regularly.

Whilst the management of a company is, in effect, delegated by the shareholders to its directors, a company must generally hold an annual general meeting of its shareholders to deal with the regular shareholder business (such as presentation of the annual accounts). Other specific types of transaction or business require the directors to obtain shareholder approval and to call extraordinary general meetings as required.

Records of all directors' and shareholders' meetings should be kept in the form of formal minutes. It is argued that it is as important to keep minutes of partners meetings – in case of dispute and also to prove the use of the farmhouse (see Chapter 4). Indeed for IHT purposes the involvement of the farmer in the business is often called into question for claims for BPR (see *Earl of Balfour* case).

ADMINISTRATION AND RECORDS OF THE COMPANY

8.14 All UK companies must (unless they are dormant) keep accounting records and prepare annual accounts, which require them to prepare a profit and loss account and balance sheet for each financial year.

In addition to accounting records, a company must keep statutory registers recording details of directors and company secretaries, directors' interests in shares or debentures of the company, shareholders, charges and mortgages affecting the company's assets and debenture holders. Whilst this might seem a disadvantage to a diversifying farmer, in practice the administration of a partnership or LLP is equally onerous.

REAL ESTATE INVESTMENT TRUST

8.15 Under CTA 2010 Pt 12, a special regime may apply to companies whose main business is property investment. This special regime is available by election and has operated from 1 January 2007. Companies under the regime are referred to as real estate investment trusts (or 'REITs').

The purpose of the special regime for REITs is to shift the main tax burden from the REIT to shareholders. Only a brief summary of the special regime is provided here.

In the coalition government Budget of 22 June 2010, the Chancellor announced proposals which will allow UK REITs to issue stock dividends in lieu of cash dividends in meeting the requirement to distribute 90% of the profits from the property rental business of the REIT. Currently, stock dividends do not count as property income distributions and so are not able to be used by UK REITs to meet the distribution requirement.

A company may qualify to elect to be a REIT if all of the following conditions are satisfied (CTA 2010 ss 528–531, 543):

- It must be UK resident and its shares (which must be of only one class of ordinary shares and fixed rate non-voting preference shares) must be listed on a recognised stock exchange.

- It must not be a close company, nor an open-ended investment company.

- It may not borrow money from a lender on profit-related terms.

- The company's rental business must involve at least three properties and no one property must represent more than 40% of its rental property portfolio by value. For this purpose any property occupied by the company is excluded from its rental business.

- The rental business of the company must account for at least 75% of the company's whole business activities, measured by both assets and income.

- A ratio of more than 1.25:1 must exist between the company's taxable property profits (before deduction for interest and capital allowances) and the company's interest on loans taken out to fund the rental business.

If a company makes an election to become a REIT it must pay a special charge of 2% of the market value of its investment property portfolio at the entry date (CTA 2010 ss 538, 539).

The benefit to the company of establishing itself as a REIT is an exemption on its rental profits – broadly, its rental income from rental property in the UK that would be taxed under rental income and its capital gains on the disposal of any rental property. However, to remain within the special regime the company must distribute at least 90% of these rental profits to shareholders every year. The company must deduct basic rate income tax from distributions out of its rental profits and these distributions are treated as income from a property business in the hands of the shareholder. The special regime does not apply to distributions out of non-rental profits.

THE ENTERPRISE INVESTMENT SCHEME (EIS)

8.16   The EIS has been introduced to encourage business investment.

Currently farming does not count as a qualifying trade for EIS and there are those that argue that the rules need to be changed. Obviously diversification presents an opportunity where the diversified trade qualifies for EIS. With the phasing out of the single farm payment emphasis must be placed on alternative land use.

The EIS is looked at again in **14.62** with regard to the deferral of CGT through EIS.

There is not the scope in this book to go through the full position concerning EIS, however, this section tries to set out the tax reliefs that are available, what trades qualify and how diversifying businesses can try and attain tax relief. The purpose of EIS is to help certain types of small higher risk unquoted trading companies to raise capital. It does so by providing a range of tax reliefs for investors and qualifying shares in those companies. However, one of the trades excluded from the rules is that of farming (ITA 2007 s 192). In addition, market gardening, holding, managing or occupying woodlands or other forest activities or timber production and property development, managing hotels, leasing or letting assets on hire together with dealing in land are also excluded from EIS.

A larger list of those trades that do not qualify is set out in **8.18**. In principle, this means that the farmer cannot benefit from EIS as farming is an excluded trade; however, some of the forms of diversification that are mentioned in this chapter could qualify and it is important to take professional advice to see whether a diversified trade does fall within the EIS qualifications. With the availability of EIS for diversified activities, the farming industry will need to take a complete review of the business structures available to the enterprise. This could result in a greater use of the limited company in order to achieve the EIS relief. It is not necessary to have the asset of the land owned within the limited company.

There are also those who argue that the rules for EIS should change. Farming and agricultural land use needs a commercial approach. It can be argued farmers need help from the government and making farming an 'included trade' in the EIS rules could be a good move. It is assumed that farming is not allowed because the trade is not considered to have a high enough risk. However, all those currently involved in farming and in diversification will appreciate that at the moment there are some very high risks and tax reliefs should be of assistance.

In summary, it could be that the new diversified trade seeks the protection of limited liability, seeks the separate legal identity of a limited company and tries to attract outside investors through EIS. If potential investors are to be attracted into the investment it is important to understand briefly what the tax reliefs are.

In the coalition government Budget, the Chancellor announced the final five changes to the EIS and venture capital trusts (VCT) schemes agreed with the European Commission as a condition for their approval by the Commission as approved state aids. These are included in Finance (No 3) Act 2010.

The changes will generally have effect on and after a date to be appointed, with the exception of the definition of eligible shares for VCTs, which will not affect monies raised by the VCT before that date.

In summary, the changes are:

- An increase in the minimum amount VCTs must hold in 'eligible shares'. At present eligible shares in unlisted companies must represent at least 30% of a VCT's qualifying investments (which in turn have to be at least 70% of the VCT). The eligible shares minimum holding will more than double to 70%.

- Revision of the definition of VCT 'eligible shares' to include shares which may carry certain preferential dividend rights.

- Allowing a VCT to be listed on any EU/EEA investment market rather than be restricted to a UK listing.

- Preventing shares in companies that are 'in difficulty' from qualifying for the purposes of the VCT and EIS rules.

- For both EISs and VCTs, the existing requirement that an EIS company or a company in which a VCT invests must have a qualifying trade carried out wholly or mainly in the UK is changed to one that it need only have a permanent establishment in the UK.

The tax reliefs

8.17 An individual (the taxpayer) who subscribes for shares in a company that qualifies under the scheme, may be able to get an income tax reduction based on the amount invested (income tax relief).

Individuals and trustees of certain trusts who subscribe for shares in qualifying companies may be able to postpone the charge to capital gains tax on gains arising on the disposal of other assets around the time that they make their investments (deferral relief).

If the taxpayers obtain income tax relief the taxpayer may also be eligible for one of the following reliefs when the taxpayer disposes of the shares in question:

- if the disposal takes place after five years and gives rise to a gain, the taxpayer may not have to pay capital gains tax on it (capital gains tax exemption); or

- if the disposal gives rise to a loss (irrespective of when the disposal takes place) the taxpayer may be entitled to deduct the loss (less income tax relief attributable to the shares) from the taxpayer's income for tax purposes (loss relief). The taxpayer may of course set the loss (less income tax relief attributable to the shares) against chargeable gains in the usual way instead of claiming loss relief.

The taxpayer may also be eligible for loss relief if the taxpayer makes a loss on disposing of shares to which deferral relief, but not income tax relief, is attributable.

Do all trades qualify?

8.18   In order to qualify, throughout the company's 'relevant period' the trade must be conducted on a commercial basis with a view to making profits. A trade will not qualify, however, if, at any time in the relevant period, one or more excluded activities together amount to a substantial part of the trade. The main excluded activities are as follows (ITA 2007 s 192):

- dealing in land, in commodities or futures in shares, securities or other financial instruments (see Chapter 14);

- financial activities such as banking, money lending, insurance, debt factoring and hire purchase financing;

- dealing in goods other than in ordinary trade of retail or wholesale distribution;

- leasing or letting assets on hire, except in the case of certain ship-chartering activities (assume plant hire);

- oil extraction activities, except where the qualifying business activity for which money is raised through the scheme is oil exploration leading to oil extraction;

- receiving royalties or licence fees, other than, in certain cases, such payments arising from film production or from research and development;

- providing legal or accountancy services;

- property development (see **6.38**);

- farming or market gardening (see **1.4–1.9**);

- holding, managing, or occupying woodlands, any other forestry activities or timber production (see **6.5–6.12**);

- operating or managing hotels, guest houses or hostels in which the company carrying on the trade has an interest or which it occupies under licence or any other form of agreement;

- operating or managing nursing homes or residential care homes in which the company carrying on the trade has an interest or which it occupies under licence or any other form of agreement; or

- providing services to another company in certain circumstances where the other company's trade consists, to a substantial extent, in excluded activities.

Whether excluded activities amount to a substantial part of a company's trade is a question that can be decided in any particular case only by reference to the relevant facts and circumstances. HMRC will generally consider that they do where they amount to more than 20% of the trade.

It is hoped that the government will help the farming community, who are having to diversify, to take advantage of the generous EIS tax relief, hopefully encouraging more outside investment and interest. Interesting examples are vineyards (see **6.34**), opportunities in the shopping and food sector (see **6.33**), activity leisure pursuits (see **6.32**) and energy crops (**6.47**). See Chapter 6 generally for activities that might qualify, eg equine activities that are not stud farms, eg livery yards and riding schools (**6.27–6.29**); fishing and shooting (**6.30**); leisure pursuits (**6.32**); retail element of shopping and food (**6.33**); and farm contracting (**6.35**).

EIS – investment limits of £500,000

8.19   The limit on the amount invested on which an investor can claim EIS income tax relief in any one year was increased from £400,000 to £500,000 from 6 April 2008 and still remains at that level. Capital gains tax (CGT) deferral relief was also available and there is CGT deferral.

COMPANIES IN PARTNERSHIP

8.20   One of the trading structures that has evolved from diversification is a 'diversified company' as a partner in the original farming partnership. Whilst at first sight this seems to add complications it has some interesting possibilities. In England and Wales (the position is different in Scotland) the partners do not own a particular share of partnership assets; they own a share of the partnership as a whole. This means that the financial statements of the company will be straightforward, showing the interest in the partnership as an asset at cost, and the partnership share of income as a one-line entry for revenue. The only expenses will be those specific to the company (Companies House fees etc) and anything that is deliberately put through the company because it is more tax efficient (eg a mobile phone in the company's name).

'STUCK WITH A LIMITED COMPANY FROM A FORMER LIFE'

8.21   The problems of asset ownership in the limited company have been well documented. The limited company is eligible for roll-over relief on assets that it owns.

Some tax-planning problems can arise when a farm purchaser has the business assets being sold within a limited company. The purchaser of the old business perhaps wants to buy assets, not a limited company. In these days of risk avoidance and the pressures of due diligence, the desire for the purchaser to avoid the risks inherent in a share purchase is obvious. The vendor of the business (the investor in the new farm business) is therefore stuck with the limited company, which holds all the proceeds from the sale of the company's business.

The problem is that the gain on the asset has to be rolled over into the assets of a new business, which may be another farm or diversified business, although this is not a requirement of the tax provisions for roll-over relief. The end result is a farm in the limited company and possibly being 'stuck with a limited company from a former life'.

It is therefore important to consider whether the assets of the new farm should stay in the limited company or be taken out.

REORGANISATION OF THE SHARE CAPITAL OF A FARMING COMPANY

8.22 Where there has been a reorganisation of the share capital of a farming company within the APR qualifications, or where the property held at the date of death consists of shares of a farming company for which the original property was exchanged, the shares held at death are treated as if they had been the subject of the PET (IHTA 1984 s 124A(6)) (see **5.6** and **13.17–13.19**). APR is made available by deeming the owner of the shares to be the owner of the original agricultural land.

GRANT OF SHARES IN A LIMITED COMPANY

8.23 Another common situation arises where the director of a farming company wishes to gift some of the shares in that company if the director might have control and there are concerns therefore of gifts with reservation of benefits coming into play. Here HMRC will not regard the gift as being with reservations (GROB (see **5.11**)) subject to the correct conditions being in place.

AGRICULTURAL QUOTAS FOR COMPANIES

8.24 With effect from 1 April 2002, agricultural quotas for new companies (but not partnerships or sole traders) came under the new rules for the taxation of intangible assets contained in FA 2002 s 84, Sch 29 and 30 (what is now CTA 2009 Pt 8). These treat amortisation properly charged in the profit and loss account of farming companies as an allowable deduction, with sales being taxed as income.

Transitional rules ensure that assets held at commencement will be taxed on the old (chargeable gains) basis. However, disposals thereof will not qualify for capital gains roll-over relief except where reinvestment under the capital gains rules has taken place before 1 April 2002 and within the 12-month period prior to the disposal.

However, with the SFP provisions, questions must be raised as to the value of quotas to be included in a company balance sheet, arrangements for the alignment of accounting standards and tax. Limited companies can consider negligible loss claims for milk quotas.

Aligning tax and accounting

8.25   The law was amended to ensure that companies choosing to adopt International Accounting Standards (IAS) will receive broadly the equivalent tax treatment to those that continue to use UK Generally Accepted Accounting Practice (UK GAAP).

The revision applies to accounting periods beginning on or after 1 January 2005. It amends the legislation on loan relationships, derivative contracts, intangibles and R&D to accommodate accounting changes under both IAS and UK GAAP.

The detailed changes were as follows.

- Intangible fixed assets: where tax relief for amortisation of goodwill has been claimed, it will not be allowed again if goodwill is written up to original cost under IAS.

- R&D: claims will be allowed for revenue expenditure treated for accounting purposes as added to the cost of the asset, rather than when amortised in the profit and loss account over later periods (see **2.15**).

- Derivative contracts: separate authorised accounting methods will no longer apply. Exchange gains and losses on certain currency contacts can be matched. Fair value gains and losses on certain hedging instruments can be deferred for tax purposes until gains and losses on the underlying item are recognised. There will be a coherent tax treatment for the derivative contract element of convertible and asset-linked loans and interest-linked gilts.

Capital allowances: buying and acceleration

8.26   Under CTA 2010 Pt 22, Ch 2 where a loss-making company sells its trade, if the assets sold include plant or machinery with a value lower than their tax written-down value, then the disposal will give rise to a balancing allowance in that company. To the extent that the balancing allowance increases a tax loss, the company can then surrender the balancing allowance to another group company.

However, if the relevant group is unable to utilise those deductions, the loss-making company could first be sold to a profitable third-party group and the trade then sold to a different third party. The balancing allowance thereby generated can then be surrendered to the profitable third-party group.

The inclusion of a motive test is important because there will be situations in which a loss-making company will be sold to a third party as part of a larger transaction, with the purchaser then on-selling non-core assets that might include the relevant trade. Prima facie we would not expect such a transaction to be caught by the new rules. However, if the pricing of the transaction reflects the potential benefit of the balancing allowances then there is still a risk that HMRC will seek effectively to disallow those balancing allowances.

Finance Act 2010 (FA 2010) introduced targeted anti-avoidance legislation that applies where there is a change in ownership of a trade carried on by a company at a point where the tax written-down value (TWDV) of its plant and machinery exceeds the balance sheet value of those assets.

The legislation only affects instances where the main purpose, or one of the main purposes of the change in ownership, was the obtaining of a tax advantage.

Where the legislation has effect, the amount by which the TWDV of a pool exceeds the balance sheet value is transferred to a new pool and future losses generated by allowances on that new pool are restricted. These provisions generally have effect from 21 July 2009, although certain elements only apply where the change in ownership occurred on or after 9 December 2009.

If a company has excess trading losses, it has been an established tax-planning method to disclaim capital allowances in order to reduce the amount of any unutilised current year trading loss carried forward. The result of this is that the company is able to claim higher capital allowances in a future period, which in turn can lead to the creation of, or increase in, a current-year trading loss at that time. Such treatment can give the company a tax advantage, as the current-year trading loss can be set against other profits of the company in that year or could be group relieved, whereas a brought-forward loss would only be able to be set against future profits of that same trade. HMRC's concern was that this well-used plan was then developed into various tax-planning schemes to create a pool of unclaimed capital allowances that were then sold to a profitable company in order to reduce their tax liability.

Section 26 and Sch 4 of FA 2010 insert a new Chapter 16A (made up of ss 212A–212S) into CAA 2001. This new chapter contains provisions that target these types of schemes where there is a change of ownership of a company and the main, or one of the main, purposes of the change in ownership was the obtaining of a tax advantage. HMRC issued a technical note on this area on 9 December 2009, which can be viewed on its website (see PBRN12).

Simplification of associated companies

8.27 When a farming organisation decides to trade through a limited company it can also decide to trade through multiple companies or groups of companies. This can cause problems of inadvertently creating associated companies and the division of the £300,000 small company rate.

This can be of particular importance for a diversifying farm which decides to put each alternative land use project under a separate company.

In order to determine the rate of corporation tax which applies to a company's profits, it is necessary to compare profits with upper and lower limits, currently set at £300,000 and £1,500,000 respectively.

These limits must be reduced pro rata where the company has one or more associated companies. CTA 2010 s 25(4) states that:

'a company is an associated company of another at any time when—

(a)   one of the two has control of the other, or

(b)   both are under the control of the same person or persons.'

In establishing control, shareholdings owned by a person's associates are also attributed to that person. CTA 2010 s 448(1) defines an associate to include a relative or partner.

New provisions were introduced with effect from 1 April 2008 to simplify the rules determining whether companies are 'associated' for the purposes of applying the small companies' rates of corporation tax. Current tax rules (CTA 2010 s 24(3)) say that if two separate companies are owned or controlled by the same person or persons then the amount of profits that each company can earn at the small companies rate is proportionately reduced. The purpose of this rule is to prevent trades owned by the same person being split up between different companies so each company has the benefit of its own small companies rate of corporation tax.

When applying the control test, persons who are associated for tax purposes are treated as one. The definition of 'control' for these purposes is so widely drawn that individuals who are partners in a partnership are treated as one person for the purpose of this test. This leads to an anomaly whereby any company controlled by a partner in an individual capacity is treated as associated with every other company owned by the other partners in their personal capacity, even if there is no commercial interdependence between them.

New provisions were introduced in FA 2008 to clarify the position in respect of 'business partners'. Essentially the rights and powers held by business partners will only be attributed for the purposes of being 'associated' when 'relevant tax planning arrangements' are in place. 'Relevant tax planning arrangements' is taken to mean a tax advantage designed to obtain the small companies rate (CTA 2010 s 27).

As mentioned, the relevant limits for corporation tax are reduced proportionately where a company is associated with other companies.

The coalition government Budget confirms that, following a period of consultation on proposals to introduce a new fragmentation test, the associated company definition will be relaxed from 1 April 2011 with new legislation to be introduced in Finance Bill 2011. The consultation document stated that the rule will 'attribute rights held between linked persons only in circumstances where actual links between the companies make it appropriate to do so'. It should also ensure that companies cannot be associated by an attribution of rights by mere 'accident of circumstance'.

It should be noted that the proposals do not disturb the status of companies within the same group or under the control of the same person or persons. The new test would only amend the circumstances in which rights held by linked persons are attributed between them to establish control.

COMPANY LOSSES – GROUP RELIEF

8.28   This is looked at in Chapter 12 (see **12.5** and **12.17**).

INCORPORATION OF EXISTING DIVERSIFIED BUSINESS

8.29   The farmer might have diversified into a vibrant activity, eg equine trade such as a tourism riding centre (see Chapter 6 for example) and the benefits of incorporation would be needed part-way through the business's life. But what are the CGT implications of transfer into the new legal structure? What are the IHT implications (see **13.16** and **13.17**)?

For CGT purposes, deferral of whole or part of the liability is usually obtainable under TCGA 1992 s 162, when deciding whether or not to transfer to agricultural land.

Where a business is carried on by a company and ownership of the land is retained by a shareholder or director, the entitlement to roll-over relief on the sale or gift of the land is now not lost merely because the land will have ceased to be an asset of the business. Where, similarly, an individual lets land to a family partnership, in which he is a partner, roll-over relief is also given.

Consider the farmer's situation where the transaction concerns the sale of a farming or diversified asset by an individual in a s 162 transfer to carry on the diversified/farming business (TCGA 1992 s 162). The advantages of such a company are discussed throughout this chapter and for the present purpose it is sufficient to note that a special form of roll-over relief is available, designed to meet the circumstances of this transaction and no other. This form of roll-over relief must be applied unless, exceptionally, an election is made to specifically waive the relief. The framework of the relief is as follows:

The disposal of the asset must take place as a transfer to a company by an individual or individuals, not another company (TCGA 1992 s 162(1)). If the shares of individuals in a partnership do not match the ultimate shareholdings in the company, liability will arise.

It is not enough that a single asset be transferred; a whole business must be transferred as a going concern (TCGA 1992 s 155). That means all business assets must be transferred with the exception only of cash. Where liabilities are transferred, it is HMRC practice not to treat them as consideration, for the purpose of relief. That is, if liabilities are not taken over, relief is not lost (Extra-statutory Concession D32).

However, where land does not appear in the business balance sheet, it may not fail to be regarded as a business asset for this purpose.

What is meant by, 'going concern' was considered in the case of *Gordon v IRC* [1991] STC 174. HMRC contended that because a second sale was immediately in prospect, the farm business was not being transferred 'as a going concern'. It claimed no right of property in the farm was ever legally transferred to the company. These arguments were rejected. It was held that the correct test was whether the business was operative at the date of transfer. Moreover a farming business could change its place of operation without breaking continuity of operation.

The transfer must be wholly or partly in consideration for shares newly allotted by the company to the transferor. It is these shares that carry the deferred capital on the sale of the farm business. When the shares are later disposed of, their historic cost and acquisition date will be those of the assets in consideration for which they were issued. If the consideration is partly shares and partly cash, the chargeable gains are apportioned rateably between shares and cash in the proportion of respective market values. The part attributed to the shares is not immediately chargeable but is deferred as described above. The part attributable to the cash is chargeable forthwith to CGT in the normal way.

It is considered by many that relief on transfer to a company applies only to trading farmers and not to landowners who let land. However, there is a strong case for claiming that the letting of agricultural land, in certain circumstances, is a business for the purposes only of this relief. 'Business' is what is required to be transferred according to the wording of the section, and there is no reference to trades or vocations as elsewhere in the Taxes Acts. There is useful authority for this position in *American Leaf Blending Co Sdn Bhd v Director General of Inland Revenue* [1978] STC 561, PC.

RESEARCH AND DEVELOPMENT

8.30   The tax advantages of R&D are considered at **2.15** and **2.16**.

NOTIFICATION OF TRADING

8.31   FA 2004 introduced an obligation on a company to notify HMRC when its first corporation tax accounting period begins, and again when any subsequent accounting periods begin, ie to oblige companies to notify HMRC when they start in business again and if they restart after a period of being dormant. The time limit is three months from when the accounting period began and there are penalties for failure to comply.

INTRODUCTION OF FIRST-YEAR TAX CREDITS FOR COMPANIES ON ENHANCED CAPITAL ALLOWANCES

8.32   Finance Act 2008 included provisions to enable loss-making companies to surrender losses attributable to 100% first-year allowances (ECA) (see **7.6**) in respect of designated energy-saving or environmentally beneficial plant and machinery in exchange for a cash payment (a first-year tax credit) from government, see CAA 2001 ss 45A and 45H.

The ECA credit applied to qualifying expenditure by companies incurred on or after 1 April 2008.

In order for companies to be eligible there must be unrelieved losses from a trade, an ordinary property business, an overseas property business, a furnished holiday lettings business or from managing the investments of a company with investment business (CAA 2001 Sch A1 Pt 1).

The company will receive a first-year tax credit of 19% of the loss surrendered subject to an upper limit of the greater of:

• the total of the company's PAYE and National Insurance Contributions (NICs) liabilities for the period for which the loss is surrendered; or

• £250,000.

(CAA 2001 Sch A1 para 2)

Where the loss could be used by the company to offset its own other taxable profits in the same period or surrendered as group relief then it may not be surrendered for a first-year tax credit. Any losses available to carry forward will be reduced by the amount of the loss that has been surrendered under the new rules.

A company must claim first-year tax credits in a return or amended return.

As part of the claim a company must provide:

- a description of the ECA qualifying plant and machinery; and

- the amount of expenditure on this plant and machinery; and

- the date on which the expenditure was incurred.

Where the plant and machinery is of a type that requires certification by Defra under CAA 2001 ss 45B or s 45I in order to qualify for ECAs, then the certificate must also be enclosed with the claim (FA 1998 Sch 18 para 83ZA).

The rules contain a mechanism for clawing back first-year tax credits if the ECA qualifying plant and machinery is sold within the claw-back period (CAA 2001 Sch A1 paras 24–27). This begins on the date the expenditure was incurred and ends four years after the end of the period for which the tax credit was paid.

ENTREPRENEURS' RELIEF (ER) AND COMPANY SHARES

8.33   Entrepreneurs' relief (ER) is available inter alia where there is a disposal of shares in or securities of a company (TCGA 1992 s 169I). Note that the rules do not require a disposal of all the shares or securities held.

A disposal is a material disposal if condition A or B is met:

'(6) Condition A is that, throughout the period of 1 year ending with the date of the disposal–

   (a)   the company is the individual's personal company and is either a trading company or the holding company of a trading group, and

   (b)   the individual is an officer or employee of the company or (if the company is a member of a trading group) of one or more companies which are members of the trading group.

(7)   Condition B is that the conditions in paragraphs (a) and (b) of subsection (6) are met throughout the period of 1 year ending with the date on which the company–

   (a)   ceases to be a trading company without continuing to be or becoming a member of a trading group, or

   (b)   ceases to be a member of a trading group without continuing to be or becoming a trading company,

and that date is within the period of 3 years ending with the date of the disposal.'

A *personal company* is one in which the individual has at least 5% of the voting rights represented by a shareholding of at least 5% of the ordinary share capital (TCGA 1992 s 169S(3)). For joint holdings, for example, shares held jointly by spouses, each joint owner is treated as having an appropriate proportion of the voting rights and ordinary shares. Note that the particular shares disposed of do not have to be held throughout the year prior to disposal. For example, a shareholder may have held, say a 10% shareholding for more than a year and then acquired a further 4% shareholding six months before disposing of the entire 14% holding: provided the 5% rule above is satisfied throughout the year, relief may be due on the entire 14% holding.

Various definitions are contained in TCGA 1992 s 165A. A trading company is defined as a company carrying on trading activities whose activities do not include to a substantial extent activities other than trading activities. For this purpose trading activities include activities carried on by the company preparatory to carrying on a trade or with a view to its acquiring a trade or starting a trade; they also include the acquisition of an interest in a company that becomes a trading subsidiary (or the holding company of a trading group). The acquisition of a trade or starting to trade must be made as soon as is reasonably practicable in the circumstances. A trade includes any trade, profession or vocation within the meaning of the Income Tax Acts provided it is conducted on a commercial basis with a view to the realisation of profits. A holding company is defined as a company with one or more 51% subsidiaries.

Although the individual has to be an officer or employee of the company (and this will include, for example, non-executive directors and company secretaries) there is no requirement in relation to the number of hours the officer or employee is required to work. Where the company is a member of a trading group, the individual may satisfy this condition in relation to any company or companies within the group.

There is a relaxation to allow an individual time to make a disposal of shares where the company ceases to be a trading company (with mirroring provisions for groups). Provided all of the above conditions have been satisfied for at least one year, relief remains available for three years if the company then ceases to be a trading company. For this extended period to apply, the company must not be a member of a trading group within this three-year period (even if it was one before) nor, if it was a member of a trading group, must it become a trading company.

In the cases of a company reorganisation of shares where there is a paper for paper exchange of shares or debentures, it is possible for an individual to elect for the exchange to be a disposal for the purposes of entrepreneurs' relief. An election should be considered where the old shares, etc., qualify for relief but the new shares, etc, do not (perhaps as a result of a change of voting rights or an exchange of ordinary share capital for another sort of paper). The election has to be made within the same time limits as a claim for relief.

Special rules apply where there is a company reorganisation which results in the receipts of qualifying corporate bonds (TCGA 1992 s 169R). Also it is possible to apply relief on such an exchange where gains arose before 6 April 2008. A claim for relief can also be made in respect of gains arising before 6

April 2008 where such gains have been deferred until after 5 April 2008 by use of enterprise investment or venture capital schemes.

ER was originally limited to chargeable gains of £1million made during the taxpayer's lifetime, which have been entered into a claim for the relief. The lifetime limit was doubled to £2 million effective for disposals on or after 6 April 2010 and then increased to a further £5 million from 23 June 2010 (see Chapter 14).

CONCLUSION

8.34 The choice of business structure is a very serious decision-making process subject to numerous considerations. The decision cannot be made in isolation, and every diversification project must be 'tailor-made' to the needs of the business.

Chapter 9

Planning for VAT

Allison Broadey ATII
(The VAT Consultancy)

- **Diversification – a VAT shock for the farmer**

  Historically, farmers have had relatively straightforward VAT registration and return issues with output generally being zero-rated and an ability to claim input VAT. Greater consideration towards the charging of VAT must now be considered with such matters as annual accounting, flat-rate schemes for small businesses, partial exemption, capital good schemes and transfer of a going concern (TOGC). The emphasis has to be that VAT must be planned ahead in the same way as tax.

- **Land and property – maximising the VAT position**

  Areas that are most commonly encountered are options to tax, urban regeneration measures, listed buildings and land and property diversification activities. The VAT issues surrounding property can be very high value and it is imperative to plan in advance and look at all the alternatives.

- **Equestrian activities**

  The VAT case of *John Window* is discussed and VAT-planning ideas to assist in minimising VAT on livery and stabling are considered. The registration scheme for racehorse owners is discussed.

NOTE FROM THE EDITOR

9.1   It is impossible to consider land use and ownership of assets without considering the VAT position. This is a comprehensive chapter on VAT and the effect that this tax may have on the various diversification activities and organisational structures being considered.

Not only are the VAT issues discussed in plain English, but they have been written to highlight the hidden pitfalls and promote areas in which advance planning can bring real savings. VAT remains an extremely complex and ever-changing subject, but Allison Broadey shares her technical knowledge with great enthusiasm and an understanding of the impact that this indirect tax burden has on us all.

INTRODUCTION

9.2   It is assumed that the VAT issues of day-to-day activities are likely to be understood and it will be the norm to complete VAT returns and deal with the input and output VAT in a routine way. However, with the need for farmers and landowners to diversify their activities and to seek alternative sources of income, the business will find itself moving into uncharted waters in many areas. The pressures faced by a business wishing, or having, to diversify its activities are huge. Considerations such as whether the proposed trade is financially viable, whether planning permission is required or will be granted, the cost of diversification and the tax implications of doing so are all necessary well before the proposed plans can be put into practice. As if this is not enough, there is also the often forgotten indirect tax implication of VAT.

VAT is, unfortunately, often an afterthought in the planning stages and, consequently, can be the downfall of many business ventures. As with all taxes, little can be done to mitigate a tax burden after the event but much can be done to prevent its cost by a little forward thinking and planning.

The aim of this chapter is to highlight the impact of VAT on the diversification of a business and to consider its effect on some of those activities that the reader may be considering.

VAT RATES – THE BASIC PRINCIPLES

9.3   Business supplies will be subject to VAT at the standard (20%), reduced (5%) or zero rate. These rates are known as taxable rates and give the right to recover input VAT on any related purchases. The standard rate of VAT was reduced to 15% for the period from 1 December 2008 to 31 December 2009 and reverted back to 17.5% on 1 January 2010. With effect from 4 January 2011 the rate increased to its current rate of 20%.

There are also exempt supplies which do not carry VAT but which do not give the right to recover any VAT on related costs unless such VAT is beneath a *de minimis* limit. When a mixture of exempt and taxable supplies are made the business will usually be 'partially exempt' and the best method of apportioning input VAT on overhead costs will need to be considered. The issue of partial exemption is considered in further detail at **9.38**.

One of the greatest VAT dangers is to confuse the making of zero-rated supplies with the making of exempt supplies. Whilst both are not liable to VAT on sales income received the exempt supply will not give right to VAT recovery on costs and may even mean that a VAT registration is invalid.

There may also be other sources of income, such as grants and compensation payments, which are 'non-business' and are outside the scope of VAT. HMRC are often quick to associate the receipt of non-business income with an automatic disallowance of some of the input VAT incurred by the business. This should be resisted as this disallowance should only follow when non-business supplies are actively undertaken or if VAT is borne on costs that wholly and directly relate to the receipt of non-business income.

One of the initial hurdles when changing business activities is to ensure that the correct VAT rate is applied and that the VAT implications are fully understood.

DIVERSIFICATION – IS A VAT REGISTRATION REQUIRED?

9.4   If the new business is to be carried on by the same legal entity as that already VAT registered, then there is no need to inform HMRC of a change – all supplies will automatically be covered by the existing registration. This is an important point to remember: if a business is VAT registered then any business activity undertaken by that entity will be covered by the existing registration. How diverse those activities are does not matter.

Following this line of thought, if the activity is to be undertaken by a new legal entity – a partnership rather than a sole proprietor – then it should consider whether a new registration is required. If the income generated from the new activities is taxable, and exceeds the current VAT registration limit of £70,000, then a compulsory VAT registration is required. A voluntary registration can, however, be sought if this limit is not exceeded and can be beneficial if the sales are largely at the reduced rate or zero rate, or if significant VAT on set up costs has been incurred.

There is also a further category of registration, which is an 'intending registration'. For a business that is not yet trading but which will incur costs relating to intended future taxable supplies, it can register for VAT and recover input VAT on those costs to assist with its cash flow. A classic example is woodland farming. A business will prepare the land and plant trees for felling and sale in 20 years' time. No income will be received until such sales are made but VAT registration can be sought and VAT recovered on the costs of the enterprise from the outset. With any VAT registration it is normal for the business to be on quarterly VAT returns, but if the activities will result in input VAT exceeding output VAT each quarter then consider asking for monthly returns to help the cash flow.

The voluntary and intending registrations are ideal if the business wants to recover VAT on costs but what if the business has little by way of taxable costs and wants to avoid registering and accounting for VAT until it absolutely has to? It is possible to arrange the business activities to keep legitimately below the threshold providing that each is a genuinely separate commercial enterprise. If the existing business trades as a partnership then the new activities could be routed through a different legal entity. This could have the advantage of keeping exempt and taxable activities separate to allow for individuals to maximise their personal tax allowances or to ensure that the new venture is kept out of the VAT net for as long as possible. There are several important considerations in creating separate legal entities and both VAT and tax planning feature most highly on the list. There is no point in creating a different entity for VAT purposes if the direct tax implications outweigh the VAT benefits and vice versa.

However, if the new activities are best carried out by the creation of a new or different legal entity then the simple rule is to ensure that these activities are operated and run on commercial lines and that it is a clear and distinct business in its own right. The greatest danger with family businesses is that what starts off to be a separate business activity often tends to merge back to the original business after a period of time. Costs start to be 'shared' and sales income is paid into joint or main accounts 'for ease'. Beware!

HMRC are well aware that businesses will seek to split their activities in order to avoid VAT. This is known as disaggregation and legislation was introduced to enable HMRC to direct that businesses should be treated as one legal entity. They will also critically review businesses to see whether, despite the use of two or several legal entities, there is in fact only one business activity which should always have been covered by one VAT registration. Should such a decision be made by HMRC then this will have a catastrophic effect on the business; HMRC will assess for VAT on previous income and a VAT registration can be backdated by as much as 20 years. In order to successfully challenge a ruling the business must ensure that it is financially, economically and organisationally independent from any other business.

GRANTS AND COMPENSATION PAYMENTS – ARE THEY TAXABLE?

9.5   Where grants are received then these will be outside the scope of VAT providing that nothing is given in return. Should the donor require a report on how the grant has been spent or to inspect premises as a condition of the grant then this is not considered to be consideration for the supply. However, if there is an expectation or requirement that something will be provided to the donor, or to a third party, in return for the payment then this is likely to be viewed as a supply and the consequent VAT treatment should be considered very carefully. A compensation payment is outside the scope where it is given only as recompense for injury, inconvenience, loss or damage. It is important to identify whether the compensation is in return for a supply as, like grants, a VAT charge could then arise.

VAT on costs incurred directly in connection with the receipt of grants or compensation payments will not be recoverable as input VAT. However, such VAT is likely to be relatively small and might only include the costs of seeking professional advice in submitting a claim. The fact that grant monies are used to support a fledgling business venture or are used to modernise an existing business should not affect that business's overall right to recover VAT.

SPECIAL VAT SCHEMES – THE BENEFITS AND BURDENS

9.6   Assuming that the business will remain in the VAT net then there are several schemes which HMRC have introduced in order to reduce the burden of VAT upon certain activities. These include cash accounting, annual accounting, the flat-rate farmers' scheme, the registration scheme for racehorse owners, and the flat-rate scheme for small businesses.

Cash and annual accounting

9.7   Most businesses will be familiar with the cash and annual accounting schemes and these can be used by any business with a taxable turnover of less than £1,350,000 pa. The cash accounting scheme allows for VAT to be declared on sales only when the income is received (thereby assisting with cash flow) although VAT can only be recovered on costs when the purchases are paid for (Value Added Tax Regulations 1995 (SI 1995/2518) regs 56–65).

Annual accounting allows for a business to complete an annual VAT return rather than quarterly returns (Value Added Tax Regulations 1995 (SI 1995/2518) regs 49–55(2)). The business is required to make nine interim payments equalling 10% of the previous year's VAT liability with a balancing payment made on submission of the annual return. With prior agreement from HMRC it is possible to make quarterly payments of 25% of the liability but the more generous rules for deferment of all payments for smaller businesses has now been removed. There are, of course, conditions placed upon both schemes and whilst the cash accounting scheme is a popular choice there are relatively few who decide to use the annual accounting scheme.

Flat-rate farmers' scheme

9.8   The flat-rate scheme for farmers was introduced as an optional scheme for businesses (Value Added Tax Regulations 1995 (SI 1995/2518) regs 202–211(3)). The scheme refers to supplies made by farmers, but the nature of activities included within the scheme means that any business supplying farming and agricultural goods and services could be eligible. By registering under the scheme the 'farmer' receives certification and is no longer VAT registered. The scheme can only be used for designated supplies and its use means that VAT is no longer due on sales and that there is no VAT recovery on costs. Instead, the farmer is able to add a 'flat-rate' charge of 4% on sales of designated produce to VAT-registered customers. The farmer can retain this 4% addition and the VAT-registered customer can recover it on his normal VAT return. As the farmer is able to sell to the public without the addition of either VAT or the flat-rate 4%, he can increase his sales price in order to make a little more profit whilst these prices still remain below his VAT-registered competitors.

Unfortunately, the scheme has never been popular, but for those farmers using the scheme, a diversification of business activities will require an overview of its continued use. For businesses that are diversifying into supplies covered by the scheme then its use may mean that a VAT registration can be avoided without the creation of separate legal entities.

The designated supplies covered by the scheme include crop production, stock farming, forestry, bee keeping and silkworm farming, fisheries, certain processing of farm products and supplies of agricultural services. For supplies not covered by the scheme the normal VAT rules apply. This means that once the non-scheme supplies exceed the VAT threshold then the farmer must leave the scheme and a VAT registration is required to cover all supplies. The only exception to this is where the non-designated activities are either wholly zero rated or exempt. There are of course always conditions to the use of the scheme and the farmer is not entitled to use the scheme where his retention of the flat rate 4% means that he is recovering 'substantially more' as a flat rate farmer than he would under the normal VAT rules.

An example of where planning and the use of the scheme may be of benefit is shown below.

Example

A business currently lets 50 acres of land to a tenant farmer (an exempt supply) and has 150 acres of arable land, which he farms. The sales of the produce are a mixture of zero-rated cereal and standard-rated linseed (grown for its oil). Currently, the farmer is VAT registered and wants to increase his income by offering bed and breakfast accommodation and to sell nursery plants and cut flowers to guests and to the public. By using the flat-rate scheme the farmer could de-register from VAT until such time as the B&B income exceeded the current VAT threshold. He would need to charge VAT-registered customers 4% flat rate on the linseed sales and on any of the nursery plant sales. However, he can avoid accounting for 20% VAT on the B&B and on the nursery sales to the public. He needs to consider the loss of recoverable VAT on assets and overheads but, if these costs are low, and his nursery sales to the public are successful, then the benefits could be very welcome.

Registration scheme for racehorse owners

9.9   The registration scheme for racehorse owners was introduced following discussions between HMRC and the horse racing and breeding industries. It has always been recognised that businesses were entitled to register for VAT where their activities were economically geared to the care, breeding and showing or riding of horses. However, the increase in the purchase of shares in, or the whole ownership of, bloodstock by individuals, partnerships and companies brought into question whether the investment was of an economic or private nature. The scheme is not a 'scheme' in the truest sense but more a statement of practice for the procedure adopted by HMRC for the VAT registration of owners of racehorses.

Under the scheme it is accepted that a racehorse owner can register for VAT as long as he is registered as an owner with Weatherbys. He also needs to have a sponsorship agreement registered with Weatherbys or to have the benefit of continuing business income from the exploitation of the horse, such as appearance monies.

The part ownership of a racehorse requires VAT registration as a partnership with the other owners where the share is less than 50%.

The scheme only covers those entities that are not currently VAT registered. If a business is VAT registered and wishes to purchase an interest in a racehorse then, for VAT purposes, it will be entitled to VAT recovery only if it can demonstrate the 'business' sponsorship or use as mentioned above. The business must remember that, once included within the VAT registration, the income received from the horse, such as prize money, sponsorship or sale proceeds will need to be declared and VAT accounted for where appropriate.

For a business diversifying into the horse racing industry it is vital to ensure that there is sufficient evidence of the intention to treat the activities as a commercial enterprise. This will secure VAT recovery on costs and avoid arguments with HMRC over the activity being one of mere pleasure or recreation (see **19.3**).

Flat-rate scheme for small businesses

9.10   In the Finance Act 2002 the flat-rate scheme for small businesses was approved and was introduced on 25 April 2002.

The scheme is designed for businesses with a taxable turnover of less than £150,000, although the inclusion of exempt supplies increases the threshold to £187,500. The aim of the scheme is to enable businesses to declare a flat-rate percentage of their turnover as VAT rather than having to calculate VAT on a transaction-by-transaction basis for both sales and purchases.

The business remains VAT registered and is required to complete and submit its regular VAT returns. Invoices can still be issued to VAT-registered customers and show VAT as normal. When the VAT return is completed the output VAT is calculated by taking the gross turnover in the period and multiplying it by the flat-rate percentage determined by the main activity of the business. As an example, the flat rate for agricultural services is 11%, forestry and fishing is 10.5% and the boarding and care of animals is 12%. The differing flat rates are designed to take account of businesses whose sales are not all at 20% and to compensate the business for the lack of input VAT recovery.

There have been several changes to the flat-rate percentages since the scheme was first introduced and businesses need to ensure that the flat rate being applied is still at the correct rate.

With effect from 1 January 2004, HMRC offered a further incentive to newly registered businesses in that they are able to deduct 1% from the flat rate for sales within their first year of VAT registration. A new agricultural business that registers for VAT on 1 May 2011 will therefore pay a flat rate of 10% (rather than the normal 11%) on gross sales until 30 April 2012.

A business will benefit under the scheme because, where before it has accounted for VAT at 20% on all supplies, it only needs to declare VAT to HMRC on the flat-rate percentage of the gross sales. The difference between the flat-rate value and the VAT actually charged is retained by the business to compensate for VAT incurred on expenditure that is not recoverable under the scheme.

It should be noted that the flat rate is calculated on all sales even where these sales would normally be liable at the reduced and zero rate or would be exempt. The business is also unable to recover input VAT on costs unless they are goods of a capital nature with a value in excess of £2,000 inclusive of VAT.

Each business must consider whether the scheme use is of benefit to it and for many the loss of input VAT may mean that there is more of a cost than a saving to its use. As with many tax schemes the business will need to consider its own status, customer base and activities before making a decision on its application.

LAND AND PROPERTY – A SUMMARY OF VAT ISSUES

9.11   One asset which the business is likely to want to exploit as fully as possible is that of its land and buildings. The value of these assets can create enormous financial gains to the owner when sold or leased but the danger of hidden taxes always follows closely on its heels. VAT is no exception to this.

In general terms property can be split into those that are commercial in design and use and those that are domestic. The sale or lease of commercial properties and land can be subject to VAT at the standard rate or be exempt whilst residential properties can fall into the zero rate or exempt categories. Work to commercial properties will almost certainly be standard rated whereas work on residential properties could be at the zero or reduced or standard rate. The VAT legislation governing the rates of VAT applicable to land and property transactions can be found in Value Added Tax Act 1994 (VATA 1994) Sch 8 Group 5 (concerning zero rating for the construction of residential buildings), Group 6 (concerning the zero rating applicable to protected buildings), Sch 9 Group 1 (concerning the exemptions for land), Sch 10 (relevant residential and charitable buildings, option to tax and anti-avoidance legislation) and, most recently, Sch 7A Groups 6 and 7 (concerning the reduced rate for conversion, alteration and renovation of dwellings).

The disposal, leasing or improvements of land and buildings is one of the most complex areas of VAT and specialist advice should always be taken before entering into any contract or supply. The following paragraphs are designed to assist in the planning stages but the exact VAT treatment will usually also be influenced by the VAT status of the vendor and purchaser and of the building or land in question.

The tax implications of property disposals and property letting are set out in Chapters 14 and 15 respectively.

Option to tax

9.12   The option to tax gives businesses the opportunity to standard rate a supply of an interest in commercial property. Normally such an interest would be exempt, but the option enables the business to charge VAT on supplies of the property and then to recover input VAT on costs associated with such supplies – thus potentially avoiding partial exemption issues.

Legislative references to the option to tax can be found in VATA 1994 Sch 10 paras 2(1)–3A(14). VAT Notice 742A, entitled 'Opting to Tax Land and Buildings', also provides more information on the option and how to apply.

When the option to tax was introduced it was not possible to opt to tax specific parcels of land and HMRC insisted that an option was effective in respect of all adjoining land under the same legal ownership. However, with effect from 1 March 1995 this rule was relaxed and options were accepted on specific parcels of agricultural land.

It is a misconception that the option to tax stays with the land or property once it has been made. The option only binds the VAT-registered entity that makes the election. A business can therefore opt to tax on individual properties or on parcels of land which are registered separately under land registry. It is therefore possible for a business to own three commercial properties of which two are opted and one is exempt.

The following paragraphs highlight the most common issues affecting the option and some points that businesses may not be familiar with.

Who can make an option?

9.13   The option can be made by any VAT-registered business over land and buildings for commercial use.

How do I make an option?

9.14   The option must be made in writing to the Option to Tax National Unit, HM Revenue & Customs, Cotton House, 7 Cochrane Street, Glasgow, G1 1GY. In the case of a business that is applying for VAT registration because of the taxable supply of a property, the option should accompany the VAT application form and be sent to the relevant VAT Registration Unit.

Following the Tribunal decision of *Blythe Ltd Partnership v Customs and Excise Comrs* [1999] BVC 2224 HMRC recommend that the letter notifying an option and any accompanying list or schedule of properties, is signed as appropriate by a director, two or more partners (or trustees), an authorised administrator, or by a sole proprietor.

A third party can notify an option on a business's behalf but HMRC will require written confirmation that this person is an authorised signatory.

When is an option valid?

9.15   An option must be notified within 30 days of the decision to opt to tax. HMRC have no discretion to backdate an option but they will generally accept that an option has been validly made in cases where a business has evidence to show that it made a conscious decision to opt and has charged and accounted for VAT on the relevant supplies.

In cases of a property transferring as a transfer of a going concern (TOGC), HMRC now accept that the option is notified on the date that a notification is posted to them. This was established in the Tribunal case of *Chalegrove Properties Ltd v Customs and Excise Comrs* [2001] BVC 2279.

Once made an option can only be revoked within the first six months, providing no related input VAT has been recovered or supplies have been made, or after a period of 20 years, or where no interest has been held in the property for over six years.

Once it has been made the option applies to that legal entity and not to the property itself. If a partnership opts to tax a barn then any interest in that property will also be taxable. Should the partnership sell the barn to a limited company then that limited company can either opt to tax or can let the barn as an exempt supply. It does not inherit the option made by the partnership.

There are some supplies upon which the option, even when notified to HMRC, has no effect. This means that the supplies will remain exempt:

●   if land or buildings have previously been used by the business for exempt supplies then an option is not effective unless the business first asks HMRC for permission to opt to tax;

●   on any supply of a building intended for use as a dwelling, number of dwellings or relevant residential purpose where the taxpayer has received a VAT 1614D from the buyer;

- on any supply of a building to be used for relevant charitable purposes (on receipt of a certificate from the charity);

- on any supply of land for a residential caravan pitch, moorings for a residential houseboat or for land to be used by an individual for construction of his dwelling;

- on any supply of land to be used by a housing association for the construction of dwellings or for relevant residential purposes (on receipt of a VAT 1614G from the housing association).

In addition to the above, there are anti-avoidance rules which block an option to tax being made on certain supplies of land and buildings to connected parties, or persons responsible for financing the development of land and buildings, where it is the expectation or intention for that land or buildings to be used for exempt purposes. It is outside the scope of this chapter to give detail on these anti-avoidance measures (VATA 1994 Sch 10 paras 2(3AA)–2(3AAA), 3A(1)–3A(14)) but very great care should be taken to ensure that land and property transactions that fall within the scope of the capital items scheme are not affected by these rules.

Do I need permission before opting?

9.16 If a property has previously been used for making exempt supplies then HMRC must normally be approached to ask for written permission before an option can be exercised. HMRC do accept that in certain circumstances permission is not required but this is restricted to those situations outlined in HMRC Notice 742A (June 2010 edition) s 5.2, which has legal force.

Where permission is required the business must write to HMRC and disclose full details of the previous use of the property, why the option is now sought and how much input VAT is likely to be recovered once the option is accepted. Providing that HMRC are satisfied with the proposals then they will give written permission and the business must then write and formally opt the property. If permission is not obtained when it should have been, then any subsequent option will be deemed invalid.

Is there a need to opt to tax?

9.17 There is no need to make an option on supplies that are automatically standard rated. These supplies are listed in VATA 1994 Sch 9 Group 1 Item 1 and include the following:

- the sale of new commercial properties, ie properties which have been constructed within the last three years;

- gaming and fishing rights unless the fee simple in the land is given;

- the provision of hotel or similar sleeping accommodation;

- caravan, tent pitches and camping facilities held out for holiday use (see **15.19** and);

- parking facilities;

- the right to fell or remove timber (see Chapter 6);

- the grant or right to store, moor or house aircraft, ships and other vessels;

- the right to occupy a box or seat at a sporting event or place of entertainment; and

- sports facilities.

As the above are likely to be areas in which a farmer will consider diversification, each has been discussed in further detail later in this chapter.

If a business acquires land or buildings upon which VAT has been charged then this VAT can be recovered in full, providing that the business uses the asset for its fully taxable trading activities. There is no need for it to opt to tax. An example of this is the purchase or construction of a new barn for storage of its farming goods. If the business is fully taxable then the VAT incurred in purchasing the barn can be recovered automatically.

Why opt?

9.18   By opting to tax the business must charge 20% VAT on the letting or disposal of the opted property although (as mentioned above) there are some exceptions. As the option is largely irrevocable it must be exercised with great care.

The main benefit of the option is that it reduces the need for the business to make exempt supplies and therefore the need to carry out complex partial exemption calculations. The consequence of an exempt supply is a loss in the amount of input VAT that can be recovered. By opting the input VAT is secured and thus it does not become a cost.

The disadvantages of the option are that the prospective purchaser or tenant must pay VAT. His ability to recover this VAT will then depend upon whether he is VAT registered and whether he is fully taxable. In selling an opted property it should be borne in mind that the purchaser is required to pay the VAT and this is therefore a cash-flow issue as well as an actual cost in that stamp duty is calculated on the gross not the net cost of the purchase price.

Before an option is made the farmer must consider whether the making of an exempt supply will give rise to significant VAT loss on costs and administration. If it does then he should consider whether the option will put off prospective tenants or purchasers or whether, in his chosen market, this is not an issue.

Urban regeneration measures – the 5% reduced rate

9.19   With effect from 1 May 2001 a reduced rate of VAT of 5% was introduced for certain supplies of construction services. The reduced rate was a measure introduced under the banner of 'urban regeneration', but the title is misleading as the reduced rate has nothing to do with inner city rejuvenation. Instead, the measures apply across the board to dwellings, and conversions of properties to dwellings, throughout the UK.

The reduced rate lessens the cost of VAT for private individuals and businesses that are renovating, converting and extending dwellings either for own occupation or for letting. This is particularly relevant for farmers and landowners who wish to create new dwellings or to renovate old properties to let for residential purposes. As these lettings are exempt, and the VAT incurred on costs would therefore be irrecoverable, the reduction from 20% to 5% must help to make such ventures more economically viable.

The reduced rate applies to renovations of existing dwellings, residential conversions, houses for multiple occupancy and to relevant residential and charitable buildings. As the first three of these areas are likely to be the more relevant to the diversifying farmer and landowner, the measures are highlighted in further detail below. HMRC leaflet 708 Construction Services was reissued in February 2008 and includes details of all the urban regeneration measures including changes to domestic, relevant residential and charitable buildings.

Renovation of dwellings

9.20   The 5% rate is appropriate for the cost of renovation of dwellings that have been empty for at least two years. Renovation services includes any works of repair, maintenance or improvements carried out to the fabric of the building. The reduced rate will apply to the services of redecoration, annexes or extensions, including conservatories, provision of all utilities and construction of new garages.

The property must have been empty for at least two years prior to the works commencing. As the property owner you will be required to obtain such evidence to satisfy the contractor that the works are liable to the reduced rate.

It is interesting to note that HMRC will accept confirmation from an 'empty property officer' who is apparently located in each local authority division, but if this cannot be obtained then they will require other evidence such as electoral role and council tax information.

Note that the 5% rate applies to the services of the builder or contractor and the building materials supplied in the course of these services. The purchase of goods only will result in a 20% VAT charge. Wherever possible, contracts should be on a 'supply and build' basis. Landowners intending to buy materials and carry out the work themselves will not benefit from the urban regeneration measures.

The reduced rate will also apply where an empty property is purchased and the new owner starts to occupy it whilst renovation services are carried out. However, the two-year 'empty property' rule must still be met, the occupier must be the recipient of the services and no renovations should have been carried out within two years prior to the occupier purchasing the property. It is also a condition that the services are supplied within one year of the date of completion of the property purchase.

Under these rules a contractor must ensure that no previous renovations have been carried out within the two years prior to the date of purchase. It is also important to note that the services provided by the contractor must be completed within one year of the date that the property has been purchased not within one year of the building work commencing.

Where contractors carry out work on a property that is unoccupied then this one-year grace period does not apply.

Residential conversions

9.21   The reduced rate applies to the conversion of a non-residential building into a dwelling or the conversion of a residential building to change the number of single household dwellings. Essentially, this means that the reduced rate will apply to conversion services where the number of dwellings either reduces or increases when compared to the original number of dwellings. This will assist a landowner who is considering the conversion of a barn (which is treated as a commercial property) to a new dwelling or number of dwellings. The services supplied in the course of the conversion will be at the reduced 5% rate.

The reduced rate will apply to all works of repair, and maintenance or improvement to the fabric of the building where the work forms a fundamental part of the change in the number of dwellings. The creation of new garages, annexes and extensions to the property will also be covered by the reduced rate providing that they are carried out at the same time.

HMRC also consider that a property designed as a dwelling that is then converted for commercial purposes should be treated as a non-residential building. The conversion back to a dwelling will now qualify for the reduced rate.

For a landowner that is converting a property from commercial to residential use for his own occupation, the 5% VAT charge can be recovered by the submission of a DIY house builder's claim. However, if the conversion creates a dwelling that is to be sold as a freehold or a major interest (a lease in excess of 21 years), then the sale will be zero rated and full VAT can be recovered on the normal VAT return.

If a new conversion is to be let as investment income, then consider the grant of a major interest or freehold to a connected third party first (thus crystallising the right of VAT recovery) and then the third party can let the properties as an exempt activity. As well as giving an absolute VAT saving this planning then removes a partial exemption issue from the original owner. However, do consider the costs of stamp duty and capital gains tax issues before proceeding!

House in multiple occupancy dwelling conversion

9.22   Where a property is converted from a dwelling, or several dwellings, into a property of multiple occupancy the reduced rate will apply to the costs of conversion. This will include for instance the conversion of a house into bedsits or a bed and breakfast establishment.

HMRC have confirmed that the reduced rate for conversions does not include a conversion to a hotel, a dwelling with a granny annexe or accommodation for guests or lodgers so great care needs to be exercised in these areas.

Extension of zero rating

9.23   The urban regeneration measures also introduced zero rating for the freehold sale or grant of a major interest in residential properties that have been renovated but were unoccupied for at least ten years prior to the grant. This will enable full VAT recovery to be made on properties such as abandoned farm cottages that have been left empty for at least ten years. The renovation costs will be liable to 5% VAT, but this will now be recoverable providing that the cottage is then the subject of the grant of a major interest.

Listed dwellings – zero rating

9.24   HMRC have always allowed a partial VAT recovery on the costs of maintaining the working farmhouse. This is usually allowed to a maximum of 70%, but will depend upon the taxable level of business activities being carried out. However, for those businesses that are partially exempt or where the maintenance or construction costs are not related to business activities the VAT recovery will be much lower or even non-existent.

In these circumstances it is important to ensure that maximum use is made of the reduced rate and, for listed dwellings, the zero rate.

Works to a listed building which is, or will become as a result of the work, a dwelling can be zero rated providing that the work required, and received, listed planning consent and that the work amounts to alterations to the fabric of the building (VATA 1994 Sch 8 Group 6). Unfortunately, repairs and maintenance are not eligible for zero rating, but it is often arguable whether the works are repairs or alterations so careful consideration needs to be given for the purpose of the works and the extent of the listed planning consent required.

The zero rating does not apply to commercial properties or separate structures in the curtilage of a listed dwelling where those structures are not themselves self-contained dwellings.

Where work does qualify as an approved alteration then the zero rating will also apply to the making good of the area surrounding the alteration. It is usual to find that works will comprise of a mixture of alterations and repairs and therefore an apportionment of the build contract should be made. A review of the nature of the work carried out will help to ensure that the lower VAT rates are applied wherever possible.

It should be noted that a contract builder will often err on the side of caution and charge standard-rated VAT on the majority of contracts. Only when provided with sufficient evidence of the applicability of the reduced or zero rate will they usually be willing to review the VAT position. Where possible, the VAT treatment of the alterations or repairs should be established before the work begins.

Land and property diversification activities

9.25   Whilst it is impossible to outline all the activities in which a farmer or landowner may seek to diversify, the following paragraphs highlight those that are likely to require the most VAT planning.

Commercial properties – sale

9.26   The sale of a commercial property ie barns or land, will be exempt from VAT unless the owner has 'opted to tax'. One notable exception is that a commercial property constructed within the last three years is automatically standard rated on disposal.

Assuming that the sale is exempt then the VAT-registered entity will not be able to recover VAT on the sale costs (legal fees, estate agency costs) unless this VAT is below a *de minimis* amount of £625 per month on average and that this is less than 50% of all input VAT incurred (see **9.38**).

If the owner has opted to tax then the sale of any commercial land and buildings will be standard rated. This means that 20% must be charged and accounted for on disposal and will increase not only the cash-flow cost to the purchaser but also the cost of stamp duty (see Chapter 14).

Commercial properties – letting

9.27   Similar to the sale of property and land, the letting of any buildings or land will also be exempt from VAT if the option to tax has not been made. The VAT implications on the letting costs are also the same in that there can be no VAT recovery on costs unless these fall within the *de minimis* limits. The main difference is that the letting of a new property remains exempt unless the option is made – there is no automatic standard rating.

If the letting is an exempt supply it should be remembered that VAT on the costs of maintenance and repairs to the property will also potentially be blocked so a tenant repairing lease becomes a strong recommendation (see Chapter 15).

Residential properties – sale

9.28   The sale, ie freehold or leasehold interest in excess of 21 years, of a new residential property will be zero rated. This means that any VAT incurred on the construction or development will be recoverable, but no VAT will be due on the value of disposal.

'New' means either a new construction from foundations upwards or where no more than one wall has been retained as a condition of planning permission. Take care with the renovation of existing residential properties, as the disposal of such a property will still remain exempt unless the property has not been lived in or occupied for ten years or more – and note that evidence is required to support this. If the property has been empty for this period then the sale after refurbishment will be zero rated. The conversion of a commercial property to residential use will result in a new dwelling and its sale as new will therefore be zero rated. The costs of conversion will be liable to the reduced rate of 5% (see **9.19**), but this VAT will be recoverable as long as it relates to the zero-rated disposal. This will apply particularly to barn conversions.

The zero rating for new residential houses only applies where the dwelling is self-contained, there is no direct internal access between connected dwellings and there is no restriction on occupation or disposal (statutory or otherwise). The construction of a new dwelling in the curtilage of an existing property often gives rise to VAT issues. If the new dwelling does not meet the above requirements, then its construction costs are standard rated and the disposal exempt – thus the VAT becomes a cost (see Chapter 14).

Residential properties – letting

9.29   The letting of residential accommodation is exempt from VAT and, as mentioned previously, you cannot opt to tax a residential property. A distinction is drawn between a residential let and a holiday let – both having different VAT treatments.

A holiday let will be advertised as such and will normally only be available for short, ie weekly or monthly, durations. There may be a planning restriction on the occupancy of a property available for holiday let and the rates or council classification may also be different. By contrast a residential tenancy will be for any period of time, but should be the main or only private residence of the tenant.

As residential lets are exempt, the VAT incurred on the cost of refurbishment, capital expenditure and overheads will be subject to partial exemption rules and it is unlikely that this VAT will be recoverable. In order to reduce this cost the business should check whether it could take advantage of the reduced rate or zero rate for supplies in connection with certain dwellings (see Chapter 15).

Bed and breakfast and holiday accommodation

9.30   The provision of bed and breakfast and holiday accommodation is always standard rated. For VAT purposes there is a difference between residential lettings and holiday lettings and it is important to recognise this both in terms of setting prices and for recovery of VAT on costs. Where guests stay for a continuous period of four weeks or more then a reduced rate of VAT applies. This reflects a taxable charge for the catering and 'serviced' element, but an exempt supply of letting accommodation. With effect from day 29, an apportionment must be made and VAT is only declared on the taxable part.

The conversion of a farmhouse to accommodate B&B guests is a business expense for VAT purposes so VAT on the purchase of linens, decorations and on a proportion of capital expenditure can be recovered. Equally, the conversion of a barn or the construction of a new property for holiday lets will incur considerable amounts of VAT and this should be recovered on the normal VAT return.

Do not overlook the fact that only the legal owner of the property can recover VAT on the capital costs. If the B&B business has been structured so that a wife runs the B&B and registers for VAT, then no VAT will be recoverable on property conversion costs if the farmhouse is in the name of the husband and wife. Even if the husband and wife are VAT registered as a partnership then the costs will still not be recoverable as the partnership is not the entity supplying the B&B accommodation.

The sale of a holiday home will be standard rated within the first three years of construction and exempt at any time after the three years have elapsed. If the property sale is exempt then consideration will need to be given to any capital goods scheme adjustments which may be required (see **9.41**, **15.10–15.13** and **15.14**).

Camping and caravan pitches

9.31   Camping and caravan pitches are also included within the definition of holiday accommodation so are automatically standard rated. However, the legislation refers to seasonal pitches, so that any pitches which are provided for 12 months or more and are not held out for holiday use are exempt. The provision of pitches for residential use and for travellers are considered to be exempt as long as they can be used for a person's principal private residence (see **15.15–15.18**).

Gaming and fishing rights

9.32   The granting of fishing and shooting rights are standard rated but any additional charges for the actual taking of game or fish can be zero rated as long as the produce are edible in nature.

If the fee simple in land includes the right to take game or fish then there must be an apportionment between the exempt land element (subject to the option to tax not having been made) and the taxable gaming and fishing rights. HMRC accept that this apportionment will not be required where the rights are less than 10% of the value of the land.

The VAT liability of shooting rights does depend upon the status of the landowner and HMRC accept that a charge by a landowner to guests in order to cover the costs of the shoot can be treated as a private and therefore non-business activity. However, it will be treated as a business activity if the shoot makes a profit at year-end, the shoot is advertised to the general public or where it is run on a similar commercial basis.

Grazing rights are zero rated if the principal purpose is for animal feeding; where care is the principal purpose then the supply becomes standard-rated (but see further **9.37**).

Letting of sports facilities

9.33   The letting of sports facilities and sporting rights are automatically standard rated. There are special rules for the use of sports facilities where there are lets in excess of 24 hours or for the hire of facilities to the same user for a regular series of events (both then become eligible for exemption but can be opted).

Within the definition of sports facilities HMRC include swimming pools, tennis courts and croquet lawns and areas of land that have been specifically designed or adapted for sporting activities. However, if the sporting facilities are let for non-sporting purposes then the exemption will apply. An example of this will be the letting of a swimming pool for a fashion shoot.

Boxes and seats at events and admissions

9.34   Admissions to events, ie car boot sales and concerts, are standard rated. There are exemptions available if such events are organised by a charity for charitable purposes but otherwise the supply remains taxable.

However, land leased or let to a tenant remains exempt (subject to the option) even if the tenant then organises and runs an entertainment or event.

The farmer may consider opening the farm for tours as an additional source of revenue. Such tours are likely to be attractive to schools and to tourists. However, the charges for such tours, for tractor rides or other similar entertainments will all be standard rated.

Parking, mooring and storage of vehicles and vessels

9.35   Charges for the right to store, park or moor are standard rated. The exemption will be available if a lease is given in a particular area of land. If a landowner allows people to park on his land for a charge then this will constitute a standard-rated supply.

If the mooring, storage or parking forms part of a residential lease then it always remains exempt as it is seen as incidental to the residential use.

Timber rights

9.36   The right to allow a person to fell timber is standard rated. However, the sale or lease of land containing woodland is exempt subject to the option to tax. A distinction is drawn between the rights to the timber afforded by the landowner and the rights of the land (see Chapter 6).

EQUESTRIAN ACTIVITIES

9.37   The VAT Tribunal case *Window v Customs and Excise Comrs* [2001] VTD 17186 confirmed that the stabling of horses will remain exempt from VAT unless the option to tax has been made. Where any livery is provided as an incidental part of that stabling charge then the whole supply can remain exempt. Before 2001, HMRC treated the supply of livery and stabling as a single standard-rated supply so businesses should ensure that they are taking advantage of the exemption for DIY livery services and that the VAT liability of other stabling supplies are reviewed.

Care should be taken in determining the VAT liability, however, as the nature of the supplies made will vary from client to client – some clients may only require DIY livery services (clearly exempt subject to the option to tax) whereas others will request full livery such that the level of care becomes the most predominant part of the supply and therefore remains standard rated. The supplies made by racehorse trainers, stud farms and breaking-in are therefore not considered to be exempt in nature.

The exemption gives rise to opportunity for keeping the charges at a competitive level, but businesses must remember that the ability to recover VAT on costs is also lost.

The provision of grazing rights is a zero-rated supply providing that the right is for a specific area of land for the purposes of allowing animals to feed. If a significant element of care is provided then the supply will be standard rated.

Commercial supplies of horse-riding lessons and tuition are considered to be educational and will qualify for exemption when provided by a partner, sole proprietor or non-profit-making organisation. Corporate entities should treat the supplies as standard rated unless they are also non-profit making and plough any 'profit' from this educational activity back into the furtherance of those activities.

Hacking and treks remain standard rated unless they can be directly linked to an educational supply.

With the increasing exemptions available for stabling and educational tuition the business will need to consider the benefits of structuring these activities to maximise the VAT position. Whilst exemption will bring savings to the consumer, the business must consider the loss of VAT on related and overhead costs (see **15.19**).

PARTIAL EXEMPTION – CALCULATING THE COST OF EXEMPT SUPPLIES

9.38 Legislation governing the application of partial exemption can be found in Value Added Tax Regulations 1995 (SI 1995/2518) Part XIV and HMRC's interpretation of this in Notice 706.

When a business makes a mixture of exempt and taxable supplies it will suffer a restriction on the amount of input VAT that it can recover. This restriction is known as partial exemption. VAT cannot be recovered on the costs of making an exempt supply unless this VAT is beneath a *de minimis* limit.

Whilst the making of exempt supplies means that no VAT is chargeable to the customer there is a cost to the business in that it restricts the VAT recovery on directly related costs and also on a proportion of overhead costs.

Any business making a mixture of exempt and taxable supplies should carefully consider the impact of partial exemption so that it can determine how much VAT is likely to be lost as a result of making exempt supplies – or what planning can be put in place to ensure that any loss is mitigated.

For a farmer seeking to diversify his activities his biggest resource will be land and property. These are normally exempt from VAT so that a move into increased land and property transactions – be it selling or letting, may well give rise to a VAT cost. In some cases early planning can mean that an option to tax can be made or that a transaction is structured to ensure it remains taxable. However, most businesses will have a partial exemption issue at some time in its existence and advance knowledge of it will ensure that any cost is factored into the sale value of exempt supplies.

The basic rules for partial exemption are that all input VAT must first be attributed either directly to a taxable supply, directly to an exempt supply or to an overhead cost (such as telephone, professional costs and running costs). Having identified the overhead VAT it must be apportioned so that only the proportion relating to taxable supplies is recoverable. Any costs directly relating to an exempt supply and the exempt proportion of the overhead cost are added together and are known as exempt input VAT. If the total amount of this exempt VAT is less than the *de minimis* limit (£625 per month and less than 50% of all input VAT) then all VAT is recoverable. If this limit is exceeded then none of the exempt VAT can be claimed in the VAT quarter.

The apportionment of the overhead VAT is the key issue and often forms one of the best planning opportunities. The 'standard method' is the most common method and does not need the prior permission of HMRC. It is the method that must be used if no other method is requested or granted. The amount of overhead VAT that can be recovered is determined by the percentage that taxable supplies bear to total (taxable plus exempt) supplies. This percentage is rounded up to the next whole number. An example of the standard method is given below.

Example

A business has taxable sales of bed and breakfast accommodation and cereal crops and exempt income from the letting of barns and a residential cottage.

1. Identify all input VAT wholly attributable to taxable (ie standard rated, lower rate and zero rate) supplies – say £2,000 on B&B and agricultural costs.

2. Identify all input VAT wholly attributable to exempt supplies – say £550 on the letting agreements and repairs.

3. Identify the rest (ie overheads etc) as being attributable to both taxable and exempt supplies – say £4,800.

The amount of input VAT that may be recoverable under point 3 above can be calculated by reference to the percentage of taxable supplies to total supplies in the period concerned.

Taxable supplies	£5,000
Exempt supplies	£15,000
	£20,000

Amount of overhead VAT recoverable under point 3 is therefore 25% (£1,200) and the amount of VAT which is therefore deemed to be attributable to exempt supplies is 75% (£3,600).

The total amount of exempt VAT in the period is therefore £550 plus £3,600 a total of £4,150. The VAT recoverable in the period is £2,000 plus £1,200 a total of £3,200.

The business should then check whether the value of exempt VAT is beneath the *de minimis* limit – if it is then all the VAT can be recovered. However, in our example £4,150 is above the £625 per month on average (£1,875 per quarter), and is more than 50% of all input VAT. As neither test is met, then none of the exempt VAT can be recovered.

However, at the end of the year (usually March, April or May dependent upon the VAT return periods) an annual adjustment is carried out and the quarterly calculation is repeated but using the year's figures. This may give the opportunity to recover exempt VAT which might have been irrecoverable in a previous VAT return, as the *de minimis* limit is multiplied to a threshold of £7,500 and less than 50% of all input VAT.

Alternative methods

9.39 If the standard method does not produce a fair and reasonable result, then a business can apply in writing to HMRC for approval to use a special method. Once accepted the special method can be applied to the start of the current partial exemption year or from the start of the next year.

A special method can take any form – some of the most common are inputs based, but others can be staff time spent on taxable activities or floor space used for the making of taxable supplies. In the example above the letting activities generate a high value of sales but the business does very little to achieve them. Under the standard method the value of exempt supplies restricts the proportion of recoverable overhead VAT considerably. By opting for a special method based on the percentage that wholly taxable input VAT represents of wholly taxable plus wholly exempt input VAT, the percentage will increase from 25% to 79%. An alternative would be to consider the number of staff or hours involved in the taxable business against the total staff or hours used in the whole business.

Exclusions

9.40   There are some activities which, although exempt in nature, should not be included in the denominator of any value-based calculations (Value Added Tax Regulations 1995 (SI 1995/2518) reg 101(3)).

Examples include the sale of capital assets. If an exempt property is sold, and that property was a capital asset of the business, then any VAT on costs incurred in making the exempt supply are still treated as exempt input VAT. However, the sale value of the property need not be included within the denominator of a value-based apportionment calculation as to do so would be distortive. Other supplies which can be excluded from the denominator include those which are incidental to the main business activity are specified in reg 101(3), such as the sale of a business or part of a business, self supplies and reverse charge services, supplies involving finance and certain grants in relation to land and buildings.

CAPITAL GOODS SCHEME – THE EXEMPT USE OF CAPITAL ASSETS

9.41   The capital goods scheme applies where a VAT-registered business purchases certain computers, computer equipment, land or buildings for use in his business. The scheme requires the business to review the use of the assets on a year-by-year basis over a given period of time (Value Added Tax Regulations 1995 (SI 1995/2518) regs 112–116 Pt XV and VAT Notice 706/2 (January 2002 edition) gives more detailed information).

The scheme only covers computers and items of computer equipment with a tax-exclusive value of £50,000 or more, and land and buildings of a tax-exclusive value of £250,000 or more where the business acquires these for use in the business. The adjustment intervals are five for computers and ten for land and buildings (approximately five and ten years respectively). The 'use' clause means that businesses buying and selling properties are excluded: only those goods that are retained as capital assets in the balance sheet are to be included. With effect from 1 January 2011 purchases of ships and boats costing more than £50,000 plus VAT are also to be included within the capital goods scheme.

A land or building acquisition is covered by the capital goods scheme if:

- it costs more than £250,000 and tax has been charged on its purchase, or it has been the subject of a self-supply charge; or

- the building has been constructed by the person using it and the aggregate value of the land and the standard rate of construction costs is £250,000 or more; or

- it has been altered, enlarged or extended so as to create 10% or more additional floor area, and the value of the standard-rated works in connection with the alteration, extension or enlargement is £250,000 or more.

Refurbishments or fitting out costs where the value of capital expenditure is in excess of £250,000 will also fall within the capital goods scheme.

Unfortunately, the £250,000 limit for land and buildings now means that any business purchasing such a taxable asset is likely to have to consider the impact of the capital goods scheme. The scheme requires the business to monitor the use of an asset and to pay VAT back to HMRC, or recover additional VAT from HMRC, if the use of that asset varies from the use when first purchased.

Example

A landowner has several barns on his property and wishes to convert one of them so that he can use it for his own office accommodation. The renovation and refurbishment of the barn costs £275,000 plus VAT. As the landowner makes no exempt supplies, he can recover all the VAT on the costs incurred. Four years later he decides to let part of the barn to a tenant. He has not opted to tax so the rental income is exempt. Under the standard method of partial exemption his level of taxable activity is now 83%.

As the barn conversion cost in excess of £250,000 it has become a capital goods scheme item. This has no effect whilst he continues to use the barn for taxable purposes, but now that exempt income has commenced, HMRC will require a proportion of the VAT originally recovered to be repaid to them. The amount of VAT to be repaid will be calculated on the taxable percentage determined under the partial exemption calculations but HMRC can also be asked to base the calculation on the actual use of the barn. If the business originally claimed 100% of the input VAT it will be required to pay back to HMRC the difference between the 100% recovery and the current 83%, although the adjustment is restricted to one-tenth for each year.

£48,125 divided by 10 = £4,812.50 × (100% − 83%) = £818.12

The calculation needs to be carried out on a yearly basis until the item is sold or the ten-year period has elapsed. In our example £818.12 must be repaid in the year that the letting commenced although allowance will be given for lettings part way through the year. If the level of exempt and taxable supplies remained constant at 83%, then £818.12 would need to be repaid each interval for approximately the next six years.

If the barn was sold in year 4 then the calculation would be the same except that the remaining six years are treated as being for wholly exempt use so that a payment of £4,908.72 (£818.12 × 6) would need to be made in the adjustment period following the sale.

In the above examples the landowner has to repay input VAT to HMRC and this becomes a cost to him. Advance planning will enable the landowner to build this cost into either his rental charges or sales value. Alternatively, by opting to tax the barn the landowner can avoid the adjustments under the scheme as his use would remain fully taxable.

Should the barn continue to be used as the landowner's office then the capital goods scheme will also bite if the general business of the landowner becomes partially exempt. In our above example if the barn continues to be used as an office the costs will be treated as an overhead of the business. If the landowner's business becomes partially exempt, perhaps he receives rent from the letting of residential properties, then a proportion of the VAT on overhead costs must be restricted in accordance with his partial exemption calculations. Even if he remains within the *de minimis* limits he is still required to carry out a capital goods scheme adjustment.

TRANSFER OF A GOING CONCERN (TOGC) – IS VAT DUE ON THE SALE OF A BUSINESS?

9.42   The sale, or purchase, of business will not be subject to VAT if the TOGC conditions are met. This can benefit both the purchaser and the vendor and should be used wherever possible. The TOGC conditions are as follows, ie that:

● the purchaser is VAT registered, or required to be VAT registered, at the time of purchase;

● the purchaser will continue to carry out the same business activities as the vendor;

● what is transferred is a 'business' in its own right;

● there must be no significant break in trading; and

● the transfer must not be one of consecutive transfers.

For instance, the sale of land planted with crops can be sold as a transfer of going concern ie outside the scope instead of exempt, provided that the purchaser is VAT registered and that he will continue to farm the crops. The 'business' does not need to be a whole business – as long as what is sold can be operated as a separate business then this condition will be met.

The advantage of the going concern provisions is that the purchaser will not have to fund any additional VAT thus also making an absolute cash saving on stamp duty. The VAT incurred on the costs of selling the business should be recovered in accordance with the nature of the business being transferred. Thus, the sale of our farmed land would have given rise to a zero-rated supply if the crops were sold and the costs of the sale can therefore be recovered in full as relating to a wholly taxable supply. If the business was exempt, then no VAT on costs would be recoverable and if the business was partially exempt then the costs should be treated as overhead.

Opted land

9.43 If the business being transferred includes land on which the vendor has opted then the purchaser must also opt in order for the TOGC requirements to be met. This is especially important and the purchaser should ensure that his option is submitted to HMRC prior to the payment of a deposit on exchange if such monies are available to the vendor ie held by a solicitor as agent. If the solicitor acts as stakeholder then the deposit does not create a tax point and the option should be submitted to HMRC prior to the completion date. If the option is not made in time then the transfer will not be a TOGC even if all other conditions are met (*Higher Education Statistics Agency Ltd v Customs and Excise Comrs* [2000] STC 332).

The 2004 Budget announced anti-avoidance legislation aimed at ensuring that partly exempt or fully exempt purchasers of opted land and buildings under the TOGC rules must now apply strict rules to identify whether the purchaser is able to opt to tax. The extent of the new rules is wide but will, hopefully, not bite on the normal TOGC transactions that are referred to above. However, it is recommended that any business looking at moving property via a TOGC through an SPV or using a specific planning scheme are advised to seek careful VAT advice before proceeding.

TOGCs and auctions

9.44 If an opted property is sold, then the sale may qualify to be treated as a TOGC providing that the normal TOGC rules are met and that the 'business' transferring is one of property rental. In addition to the normal rules the purchaser must make an option to tax as mentioned above.

In the case of an auction it is important for a purchaser to be aware of the VAT status of a property prior to making any bids. If the property can be transferred as a TOGC then the purchaser should make an option and post it prior to bidding. HMRC now accept that written notification of the option to tax will be 'made' when it is put in the post (*Chalegrove Properties Ltd v Customs and Excise Comrs* [2001] BVC 2279). If unsuccessful, the bidder can rescind the option by writing to HMRC within the six-month deadline. If successful then the purchaser will gain not only a cash-flow advantage as there will be no VAT to pay, but also a real saving in the reduction of stamp duty.

Allison Broadey

Allison Broadey has over 25 years' experience as a VAT practitioner, initially as a VAT Inspector with HM Customs & Excise, and then as 'gamekeeper turned poacher' in commercial practice. Having qualified as a Chartered Tax Adviser specialising in VAT with Coopers & Lybrand, she is now a director with The VAT Consultancy. She has a diverse range of clients in the farming and private sector and specialises in planning for land and property. She lectures to associations, practitioners and private businesses on all VAT matters. Allison Broadey and The VAT Consultancy can be contacted via www.thevatconsultancy.com or Allison.broadey@thevatconsultancy.com.

Chapter 10

The 'reluctant' and 'lifestyle' farmer

Julie Butler

- **The traditional farmer changes**
  Diversification, SFP, falling farm profits and increasing property values
  can result in a move away from the traditional farmers – towards lifestyle
  farmers, asset strippers, and even those reluctant to farm but keen to
  obtain the tax reliefs.

- **Reluctant farmer – farming for tax reliefs**
  The tax reliefs available to both the farming and diversifying businesses
  are potentially so beneficial that it is worth all landowners considering
  whether or not they should ensure that the activity carried out on
  their land qualifies for future business tax reliefs regarding IHT, CGT
  and income tax. The CGT reform included in the Finance Act 2008
  replaced BATR with ER (entrepreneurs' relief) but still provides scope
  for business tax planning especially with the increase in the lifetime
  limit to £5 million.

- **Lifestyle farmer**
  The reluctant farmer is now joined by a multitude of new diversifying
  farmers – the 'grant grabber', 'the asset stripper' and the 'lifestyle'
  farmer. The weaknesses of grazing agreements for both reluctant and
  lifestyle farmers have been clearly highlighted by the *McCall* case.

- **Reluctant farm practitioner**
  There are many general practitioners who act for only a few agricultural
  clients but they do have a number of landowners (possibly 'lifestyle'
  or potential developers) who could benefit from a careful review
  of the business tax advantages of the land being used for farming or
  diversification activities. The tax reliefs for farms and alternative land
  use could be used to shelter development profits wealth for IHT by a
  'reluctant' farmer.

INTRODUCTION

10.1   A large number of farms sold in the UK are to 'new farmers' (with
little or no background in agriculture). The percentage of existing farms held
by non-traditional farmers varies. Here are some suggested headings under the
restructuring:

- 'Lucky traditional farmer' – traditional farmer with development
  opportunities in farmland.

- 'Unlucky traditional farmer' – traditional farmer with no development opportunities on farmland or traditional farm with development opportunities with too complex tax structures or family ownership positions to enjoy the development opportunities.

- 'Asset stripper' – the development opportunities and high value of amenity/ paddock land that can be achieved encourage the purchase of farms that are 'stripped' or divided into small developments and amenity units at high gain/return with great tax efficiency through the advantageous farming tax reliefs.

- 'Diversified farmer' – farmer who has diversified and (ideally) managed to make the farming enterprise profitable.

- The 'environmental steward' – (see Chapter 2).

- 'The fiscal farmer' – (see **1.12**).

- 'Reluctant farmer' – landowner pursuing (or continuing to pursue) farm activities to take advantage of the beneficial tax reliefs, eg the sheltering of capital gains and removing wealth from the estate free of IHT.

- 'Lifestyle farmer' – purchases a farm or small holding to enjoy the country way of life, perhaps to follow an interesting 'niche' farming market where commercial return is not the main direction of the enterprise.

The current UK farming business tax reliefs that are available to landowners are very attractive and place a lot of emphasis on farmers and landowners to ensure that business status is achieved and maintained. This creates a position both of complexity and opportunity. The complex issues are discussed at length throughout the book, as are the tax-planning opportunities. There is also an opportunity to create business status from barren and redundant land and buildings, which has obvious advantages.

There are those accountancy and tax practitioners who 'love' farming, the countryside, agriculture and all that goes with it and those practitioners that do not. There are those practitioners who see it as a complex, unprofitable industry to be avoided at all costs.

Most practitioners act for clients who own land but have no interest in farming and this must be integrated to the very favourable tax reliefs available for involving the land in a trading business. Various chapters of this book show the rules that need to be followed to ensure a farming activity qualifies as a business. Chapter 11 is devoted to explaining the ways of establishing the 'business' of farming without too much involvement in the day-to-day management, eg contract farming and provisions to establish grazing agreements as business (see **11.35**). Although the recent case of *Arnander* has shown the problems of not being involved in the day-to-day management, this is a constant focus of HMRC attention.

MAXIMISING 'RELUCTANT' TAX RELIEFS

10.2   The trade of farming or the trade of alternative land use should exist where there is any profit arising from the occupation of land on a commercial basis and maximum use of the tax reliefs is needed.

'Reluctant farmers' are seeking the valuable reliefs to secure any potentially beneficial CGT reliefs (see Chapter 14) on any future disposal and the beneficial IHT reliefs – see Chapter 4, Chapter 5 and Chapter 13 and the former in Chapter 14. There can be some very beneficial income tax and corporation tax reliefs for landowners to take advantage of. These are set out in Chapter 12, with the main focus on tax losses and any landowner must maximise tax reliefs available.

The scene has been further set in Chapter 2, which explains that the government direction is towards environmental stewardship and not direct farm subsidy. ITA 2007 ss 775 and 776 sets out the problem where HMRC would like to define a landowner or diversified farmer as trading in land (see Chapter 14).

The backdrop of tax losses is set against an increase in the income tax rate to 50% from 6 April 2010 for taxable earnings over £150,000. It becomes more attractive for HMRC to capture profits from property as 'income' as opposed to 'capital'.

RELUCTANT TRADITIONAL FARMER

10.3   Imagine the situation where the happy landowner decides to venture into the mysterious world of farming to try and achieve a commercial return thereon whilst benefiting from associated tax reliefs.

The first step has to be to engage the professional services of a good land agent who can explain the alternatives and help with choice, grants and local contacts. If the traditional routes are chosen the alternatives generally are:

- contract farming (see **11.10–11.14**);
- grazing agreements established as business (see **11.31–11.35**);
- share farming (see **11.4–11.9**); or
- farm business tenancies (although these have to do with restricted tax reliefs) (see **11.15–11.24**).

These business alternatives are all explained in more detail in Chapter 11. It must be emphasised that whether the ultimate goal of the reluctant farmer is to achieve beneficial tax reliefs (although possibly less attractive from 6 April 2008) through possible development or other sale proceeds, any arrangement must be well drafted and subject to scrutiny by HMRC. The arrangement must not be artificial and if development proceeds are involved it must not insult the intelligence of a keen Tax Inspector. Professional help is essential.

An experienced agricultural solicitor must draft any agreement with help from the land agent/tax adviser. The ownership structure should be reviewed jointly with solicitor/tax adviser and the whole project must have a full tax report in 'the round' which covers all areas of the income tax/capital gains tax/ inheritance tax/VAT together with commercial budget business plans, advice on proper record keeping, etc. If 'tax protected development gains' are the long-term aim it is well worth the effort and attention to detail to achieve the beneficial tax reliefs.

There are arguments to say that easier tax protection can be gained via relatively simple contract-farming arrangements or share-farming agreements than all the complexity of a separate diversification package – this is something that must be considered in 'the round'.

RELUCTANT DIVERSIFYING LANDOWNER

10.4 It might be that the traditional trade of farming (even if neatly packaged in a well-drafted and structured contract farming agreement) might not be so attractive to the landowner and the benefit of schemes under the rural development packages would be more appealing. These alternatives could be more commercial and in theory produce a more profitable return, especially on a smallholding of land. Again, the first point of call is the progressive land agent well versed in diversification projects, planning permission (see Chapter 3) and government grants and support, as mentioned in Chapter 2 and Chapter 20. The same requirement for ownership structure, a complete tax report and business plans apply to any diversified project.

It has been argued that a positive practical point is to try and obtain some bank borrowings to fund the project. A well-chosen business bank manager should be able to help review the plan and add value to different areas of commerciality. However, with the recent credit crunch, borrowings might be more and more difficult to achieve and the need to prove commerciality more and more important.

RELUCTANT FARM PRACTITIONER

10.5 Abuse of the tax provisions is foolhardy in the extreme. Reluctant farmers must not become 'lets see how far we can push it' landowners. The case of *Dixon v IRC* [2002] STC (SCD) 53 gives an interesting ruling in this area (see **4.25**).

In the same way that there are landowners who 'love' farming and the countryside and those who do not, there are also practitioners who love working with agricultural and rural industries and those who do not. There are many practitioners who would actually actively try to avoid agricultural clients because they know the complexities surrounding farm and land management from a tax viewpoint. Unless practitioners act for a large number of farming clients they feel that it is not worthwhile having a one-off client. Farmers averaging, the herd-basis election APR, BEN 19 for stock valuations, SFP, defining agriculture and loss claims together with the complexities of trying to sort out farming income from non-farming income make it commercially unviable to act only for a handful of farming clients.

However, land ownership is something that is common to all accountancy firms and with the move from farming to diversification the problem is likely to impact far more practitioners than previously. The fact that so many agricultural properties are being bought by people with no previous agricultural experience and that the government direction is towards a revival of the rural economy, rather than farm subsidies point towards a new type of landowner and a new type of practitioner.

Many practitioners might find that their existing clients are buying land and they are forced to embrace the farming tax rules reluctantly. It could be that a new business venture is only semi-agricultural but there is still a need to understand the complexities. It could be that a reluctant farming practitioner has a reluctant farming client who owns land, which needs to establish genuine business status in view of some future development or potential CGT and IHT reliefs – establishing business usage of land could be more common to general practices than first considered.

Right to vacant possession

10.6   This is an obvious tax-planning tool for a reluctant farmer to maximise farming tax reliefs. In this instance, provided the landowner has the right to obtain vacant possession within 24 months (if ESC F17 applies in non-tenancy cases, it may not), he may qualify for APR at 100%, but if the landowner grants an FBT then in relation to the farmhouse he is no longer a farmer but merely a landlord. If the landowner is not occupying the farmhouse for the purposes of agriculture, the right to APR on the farmhouse could then be lost (see Chapter 11 and Chapter 13).

Grant to right of herbage

10.7   The alternative is to grant a right of herbage to a grazier. The landowner must be very careful when trying to ensure that this alternative choice of farming succeeds. In *IRC v Forsyth Grant* (1943) 25 TC 369, the owner was considered to be occupying the land for the purposes of husbandry and it was accepted for the purposes of income tax and IHT that there was 100% relief due on both farm and farmhouse. In this instance the income will be taxed as farming income.

Farming and diversification are complex activities requiring capital and experience. A grazing agreement can give the reluctant or lifestyle farmer trading status and tax relief without some of the headaches of the 'full-blown' farming activity. It might be considered that grazing rights (**11.3**), grazing tenancies (**11.32–11.34**) and grazing agreements (**11.35**) have received too much focus in this book. It is essential when looking at a grant of right of herbage that the responsibility for any manuring, seeding or fertilising the land is retained by the landowner. The CLA have prepared a form of deed to grant a right of herbage and this has obtained approval from HMRC. There are essentially seven criteria which must be fulfilled. This whole area is discussed in some detail in Chapter 11 and it is worth noting an observation of the Financial Secretary to the Treasury when looking at agreements in the context of trading income that 'owners wishing to enjoy the generous tax reliefs that trading status brings should take care to ensure that they comply with the statutory definition of farming' (see **1.3**) and *Arnander* has shown the approach of the Special Commissioners to fragile contract farming agreements (see **4.39**).

The principal seven points recommended by the CLA deed are as follows:

1   The owner must harrow and roll the grass as necessary.

2   The owner must cut or spray all weeds to prevent seeding.

3   The grazier must covenant not to mow or cut the grass.

4   The owner must cultivate, sow and establish the grass crop.

5   The owner must fertilise the grass crop in the spring and through the season as necessary.

6   The owner must do all mowing that may be required for whatever reason or purpose on the ground to be grazed.

7   The owner must do any hedging, fencing and ditching needed and any other work of a proprietorial nature.

It should be noted that not all owners of the farmhouse will have the required machinery to deal with the fertilising, hedging and ditching and they might wish to employ a contractor to deal with the task. It would be unwise for the contractor to be the same person who has the right to graze, or if needs must it is wise that there should be a separate contract fee under a separate agreement to the herbage agreement.

There is a fundamental principle that for grazing income to be accepted as farming income with trading status the landowner must be able to show that he is the 'paramount occupier'. Thus, the owner must be able to show that he is in paramount occupation and that he will be regarded as the trading farmer. It must always be remembered that HMRC will look behind the wording of a legal deed to see what the actual facts of the case are.

In *McCall* it was deemed in the circumstances of that case that the grazing agreement constituted 'the management of lettings' and BPR was claimed but denied (see **10.9** and **10.10** below). The grazing agreement must be the management of a business, not of a letting.

THE MOVE FROM TRADITIONAL FARMING

10.8   The farming industry can be a very complex subject for accountants and tax advisers. It is an industry surrounded by tax cases and tax jargon only used in the farming world.

The single farm payment scheme (see Chapter 20) announced the definite direction of government grants away from farm production and towards environmental stewardship schemes and rural development initiatives. Chapter 2 shows, however, that there are few grants available for rural initiatives and it seems to be more a question of applying for planning permission and then being left to the full, immediate test of economic reality.

To the accountancy profession, lifestyle farmers have emerged and farm property developers have started to take advantage of farming tax reliefs. These impact on nearly every accountancy practice. Apparently the new entrants into the farming industry (with no previous experience of farming) account for over 50% of farms purchased, this could represent a lot of potential new tax-planning advice. Will this trend continue, however, in the aftermath of the credit crunch and CGT reform?

The importance of a business

10.9   Many lifestyle farmers enter the world of farming for the IHT benefits but the case of *McCall* emphasises a common false assumption that because farming is trading it is *automatically* a business. The correct position, however, is that farming is *treated* as being a trade for income/corporation tax purposes and for CGT purposes but this does not necessarily mean that farming activity is a business for BPR purposes.

The concern of the grazing agreement as an investment business

10.10   In order to achieve BPR many lifestyle farmers have opted for grazing agreements but the case of *McCall* has raised questions as to eligibility.

The basic facts of *McCall* (*McCall v HMRC* [2009] NICA 12) are as follows:

- Eileen McCall inherited 33 acres of land in Country Antrim on her husband's death in 1983. She lived in a house next to the land and next door to a house occupied by one of her daughters and her son-in-law, Tom Mitchell.

- The land was a rectangle of 2.8 furlongs by one furlong. Along one of the shorter sides were some watering troughs and on the other shorter side, a sheugh (a ditch with water). Along one of the longer sides ran a road with houses on the other side; along the other longer side was a dry stone wall. The perimeter is about one mile in length of which about three furlongs had barbed wire fencing.

- The land was subject to agistment agreements – something which in Northern Ireland falls short of a conacre agreement. The essential feature of a conacre is that the paramount occupier of the land is not the landowner but the conacre tenant. This normally operates on grassland because there is no change of ownership of any crops on the land once full payment under the agreement is made. The agistment agreement thus has the characteristics of a profit à prendre in that the grazier does not have exclusive possession of the land (but does have a right to exclude others from using the land for a purpose that competes or interferes with the grazing).

- In 1992 Eileen McCall went to visit another daughter in County Tipperary and never returned. She died in 1999 and on her death the 33 acres of land was worth £5.8m compared with an agricultural value of £165,000.

- From departure in 1992 to her death in 1999 Tom Mitchell agreed the agistment agreements over the 33 acres. During this period it was found as fact that:
    - Tom Mitchell spent about 100 hours a year tending the land by doing some weed control, fence maintenance, litter and damage control, and tending to drainage and water works.
    - That each grazier had exclusive grazing rights over the land and could fertilise the land (the landowner and her agents could not).

255

The Special Commissioner accepted that Eileen McCall was the owner of a business being run on her behalf by Tom Mitchell since her departure in 1992 but that the business was excluded from BPR because it was an investment business principally because '... the income arises substantially from the making available of the asset not from other activity associated with it or from selling separately the fruits of the asset'.

In the Court of Appeal (Northern Ireland) Lord Justice Girvan confirmed the Special Commissioner's decision and amplified the reasoning in a very useful paragraph 19. He noted that as a matter of fact the land was not cultivated and then:

- '...The grass was not sown or grown in the manner of a crop...'. Thus, there were no acts of husbandry commensurate with growing the grass as a crop, ie this confirms, rather than cuts across the Forsyth-Grant decision.

- '...The activities of Tom Mitchell were...in the nature of maintenance work necessary to enable the landowner to successfully let the grazing in the growing season ... the work done was aimed at maximising the return from the grazing which represented income of the landowner by way of a return from the land...'. – ie there were no sufficient additional activities conducted to show that the income came from the growing of the grass as a crop but rather from the exploitation of the land.

- '...The graziers rather than the landowner fertilised the land maximising the growth of the grass...'. – ie if grass is to be grown as a crop then *fertilising* the land is a requisite act of husbandry and it must be performed by the person claiming to grow the crop of grass. Note that the most frequently used model profit à prendre agreement makes the landowner responsible for fertilising the land.

- '...The absence of a full and exclusive right of occupation of the land for the grazier and the existence of a right by the owner to enter the land during the period of the agistment does not prevent the business being regarded as an investment business ...'.

Lifestyle farmer

10.11 Many of the recent acquisitions of farms have come from new entrants to the industry, ie those seeking a lifestyle purchase. The task of the tax practitioner is to ensure that the trading activity results in the protection of potential IHT reliefs (APR/BPR), CGT reliefs eg roll-over and hold-over together with the ability to use entrepreneurs' relief if required and to offset losses against total income (ITA 2007 ss 64 and 72(1)), (see **12.5**) ideally without restriction under the hobby farming rules (see **12.9**). Work can often involve sheltering CGT on the way into the farm, ie on the purchase of the new farm via roll-over (see **14.16**).

There are many who consider that the 'lifestyle farmer' was an invention of the 1960s – wild 'hippy' parties down on the farm with no neighbours to interrupt the fun. The fact that it was in the sixties that the well-known and well understood tax legislation of 'hobby farming' was introduced would support this idea. However, 'lifestyle farmers' are a creation which span centuries of history and tradition. The sole aim of land ownership has not always been commercial return and this is reflected in the 'lifestyler'.

A clear example of history repeating itself is the 'industrial revolution' and the purchase of landed estates from the vast wealth that this created. While the purpose behind the acquisition might have been more driven by status than lifestyle and tax planning, there are many parallels that can be drawn from that period of history to current times.

So what are the tax reliefs currently available to the lifestyler that make the acquisition of a landed estate, large or small, considered to be so tax driven?

The farming industry has historically been a 24 hours a day, seven days a week vocation and a number of expenses which might in other industries be seen as private expenditure have for a large number of years justifiably achieved acceptance as a business expense. Examples of these are:

- farmhouse expenses;
- the cost of vermin control;
- the cost of four-wheel drive vehicles to achieve farm inspections etc; and
- repairs to cottages occupied by family members living on the farm.

The question of duality is looked at in Chapter 12 at **12.19** – Duality of purpose and personal benefit.

The key issue of vermin control ties in to HMRC's letter to the Country Landowners' Association (CLA) and representative shooting associations in April 2006. The guide talks of tax irregularities and complying with these.

Farm trading losses can be offset against total income in the year of the loss under ITA 2007 s 64 provided there is profit every sixth year as provided by the 'hobby farming' rules. The reality is that tax refunds generally at a 40% rate of income tax and now 50% rate of income tax help support what is deemed to be the 'lifestyle' farming operation.

The 'lifestyle farmer' – the non-commercial business

Help with the definition is found in IHTM25153 'Meaning of a business'.

IHTA 1984 s 130(3) excludes a business carried on otherwise than for gain. IHTM25153 states that: 'Many stud farms are carried on otherwise than for gain and the Tax Inspector should refer cases of doubt via Technical Group TG to Shares and Assets Valuation (SAV) (Livestock) for advice.

In the VAT case *Commissioners of Customs and Excise v Lord Fisher* (1981) STC 238 at page 245 Gibson identified six indicators, some or all of which should be satisfied to identify an activity or activities as a business. These indicators are equally applicable as a test for IHT purposes.

Gibson said a business will exist where the activity:

- is 'a serious undertaking earnestly pursued' or 'a serious occupation, not necessarily confined to commercial or profit making undertakings';

- is 'an occupation or function actively pursued with reasonable or recognisable continuity';

- has 'a certain measure of substance as measured by the quarterly or annual value of … supplies made';

- was 'conducted in a regular manner and on sound and recognised business principles';

- is 'predominantly concerned with the making of … supplies to consumers with consideration'; and

- whether those supplies 'are of a kind which subject to differences in detail, are commonly made by those who seek to profit by them'.

The asset stripper

10.12   Many new farms are purchased with a view to 'stripping' the prime elements of the property for high commercial return and minimum tax liabilities. With land in the UK in short supply and property prices currently very high there are opportunities to establish the farming trade to maximise entrepreneurs' relief and then to dispose of various assets at uplifted values very tax efficiently, eg barns converted to residences, paddocks sold to neighbours for high value, redundant agricultural buildings developed for letting etc. With the combined impact of the CGT reform in the Finance Act 2008, the credit crunch, the collapse and the part recovery of the development land value, it is difficult to predict if the 'asset stripper' will continue with the same success as in earlier years.

Attacks on the 'asset stripper' will come from HMRC under ITA 2007 s 756(3) (see **14.48**) under the 'dealing in land' provision, ie to develop 'with the sole or main object of realising a gain from disposing of development land'.

Many parcels of land are owned in the UK in the hope of some future development. Farming may not be the main aim or love of the owner but it can be used for tax efficiency or tax shelter (see **14.58**).

ER was increased to a limit of £2 million from 6 April 2010 and to £5 million from 23 June 2010 *but* it is in essence like 'retirement relief'; it does not apply to the disposal of mere assets. At the time of writing, the greatest development opportunities for landowners are the small farm developments (see Chapter 14).

Reluctant farmer

10.13   Landowners wanting to take advantage of the attractive farm tax benefits including ER and the 18% rate of CGT could have problems with ITA 2007 s 756(3) (see **14.48**), ie will they be deemed to be 'dealing in land' as opposed to farming.

SHELTERING DEVELOPMENT PROFITS IN FARMING

10.14   When BATR applied to let farmland from 6 April 2004 (subject to conditions), there were even more opportunities to shelter development gains via the activity of countryside and environmental stewardship (also known as farming). From 6 April 2008 there are restrictions of ER and a whole new approach.

The tax on land disposals is looked at in Chapter 14 (see **14.46** and **14.58–14.61**).

Usually, the mere mention of the word 'farming' warns off most practitioners. It is easy for most practitioners to rest easy thinking that farm tax is something they do not have to be involved with. However, there are arguments to say that this escape route has disappeared.

There has been a lot more jargon to absorb (see **1.17**). Practitioners will have to embrace such words as 'modulation', which is the progressive siphoning of direct subsidy payments (previously production based) to fund agri-environmental schemes and rural development initiatives (diversification). The latter are not farming but they are the direction of the CAP reforms and grants are available to fund them.

As stated throughout, diversification is not new but it is quite alarming.

So, back to the task of sheltering development gains on the disposal of land. With BATR legislation resulting in an attractive effective maximum CGT rate of 10% from 6 April 2004, the farming community have enjoyed (and should still enjoy) some very attractive tax shelter from the trade of farming when farmland has been sold for development. The 10% rate is still available with ER but there are restrictions. With high potential development values, there is a lot of commercial drive to achieve development gains and there are still valuable tax reliefs to be achieved.

Since the loss of BATR, the farming community have now been forced into having to use roll-over relief for CGT (see **14.19**) in an attempt to reduce high CGT liabilities. The traditional farmer can keep the high net return (after paying the relatively small CGT liabilities) for a number of other positive uses:

- to repay the bank borrowings to reduce interest charges and increase profitability;

- to invest the monies to produce a 'return for old age' not previously enjoyed; or

- to gift monies now via a PET (potentially exempt transfer) to try and pass wealth to the next generation tax efficiently without burdening them with land or complex ownership.

The alternatives are endless for a diversifying farmer who wants to continue to be able to shelter future development gains and use the current tax reliefs. So what have the problems been and what problems need to be avoided in the future, particularly for reluctant or lifestyle farmers and ever mindful of the 'asset stripper'?

'Sheltering developments profits in let land'

10.15   Let land does not qualify for ER with the exception of FHLs. What was the history?

From 6 April 2004 (under FA 2003 s 160) let land qualified for BATR. In principle this meant 10% CGT rate (75% of 40%). This is looked at in detail in Chapter 14 (see **14.16–14.18**).

In order to claim the 75% BATR (100% BATR eligibility), the assets must have business use only from 6 April 1998. Until 6 April 2004 let land did not count as the trade of farming. Let land that qualified between 6 April 2004 and 5 April 2008 could still be 'tainted'. It will have mixed use since it did not qualify for the 75% relief before 6 April 2004.

The history of the tax position of let farmland prior to 6 April 2004 is complex. From 6 April 1998, the landowner had to be in partnership with the tenant to qualify for BATR. From 6 April 2000 it was sufficient for the land to be let to any unlisted trading company. The aim of the tax planning has to be to achieve 'pure' taper relief so as to minimise the capital gains tax payable. The good news is that BATR applied to let farmland from 6 April 2004, but ceased from 5 April 2008. The proactive tax-planning point was to change 'let' status.

Therefore from 6 April 2004 following FA 2003 s 160 nearly all tenanted land and buildings used in a trade profession or vocation qualified as business assets for BATR purposes but this ceased on 6 April 2008. However, land used for commercial forestry did not qualify as a 'business asset' for BATR, although it did and still does qualify for roll-over relief.

Farmers trading in land

10.16   Where land is sold for development realising a capital gain, HMRC may seek to apply ITA 2007 s 756(3) (see **14.48**) rather than CGT. HMRC are not saying that the farmer is trading in land, but developing with 'the sole or main object of realising a gain from disposing of development land'. Prior clearance can be obtained from HMRC before or after the transaction – the dangers are obvious. This is dealt with in detail in **14.45–14.54**.

How much more advantageous to HMRC it would be for the profit from the land to be subject to income tax. The tax planner must take steps to ensure that the farmer is not classified as a developer with top rate of income tax without the benefits of the CGT regime.

Should the landowner become a 'developer' for tax purposes (voluntarily or non-voluntarily), land previously held as a farm asset will be appropriated to the trading stock of the new trade (see **6.38**). On this change of status CGT arises on a deemed disposal at market value (TCGA 1992 s 161). Tax planners should try and ensure that all the CGT reliefs are utilised.

Stamp duty land tax (SDLT)

10.17   SDLT at a maximum of 4% on land transactions came into effect from 1 December 2003. It has been described by the farming community as 'the new tax nobody told us about'. The rates of SDLT from 6 April 2010 are:

- £0 to £125,000 - 0%
- £125,001 to £250,000 1%

- £250,001 to £500,000   3%
- Over £500,000   4%

ENVIRONMENTAL STEWARDSHIP AND RURAL DIVERSIFICATION INITIATIVES

10.18   The move to environmental stewardship schemes (see **2.18**) and rural development initiatives (see **10.8**) should ensure the diversified land still qualifies as a business.

Perhaps it can be said that the mention of the word farming will no longer force the town-based practitioner into apathy, as they can now equate this activity with the sheltering of development profits and wealth from IHT. Will they ever become used to the trendy new direction of farming, environment schemes and rural development initiatives? The reality could be that most farms will be a mixture of traditional farming, positive environmental activities and diversification. So yes, that makes it even more complex – necessitating an understanding of all the farming and diversification rules.

NOTIFICATION OF SELF-EMPLOYMENT

10.19   Reluctant farmers will have to notify their new business. In order to ensure maximum IHT (should this be applicable) they should ensure that the start date is the date of the exchange of contracts. There will also be the one-year ER time limit to consider.

HMRC issued guidance on the late notification of self-employment in their February 2004, 'Working Together'. It is worth quoting direct from the text:

> 'From 31 January 2001, anyone who becomes liable to pay Class 2 National Insurance Contributions (NIC) must register within three months from the end of the month in which their liability commenced in order to avoid a penalty of £100. Some of you have told us that you feel that this period is too short. Some of you have said that this is causing difficulty and would prefer a period of twelve months. Furthermore that the three month deadline may deter people from registering at all and is particularly problematical for those in the construction industry who may be self-employed for some weeks, then employed, then self-employed again, etc. Do they need to register each time they become self-employed again?

> You can find out more about the Class 2 NIC late notification penalty in *Tax Bulletin* 53A (August 2001), which is available on the Revenue website at www.inlandrevenue.gov.uk/bulletins/index.'

This could be useful for those who are self-employed in some capacity, eg a partnership and start another self-employed activity but found the registration period 'too short'. Examples of this could be 'lifestyle farmers' or 'reluctant farmers' who embrace farming to achieve tax advantages (ever mindful of ITA 2007 s 756 and concerns over artificiality) if they are already registered as self-employed through other business activities.

The other key point here is that the starting of a business has attached to it a number of time restraints in order to achieve the tax reliefs and these are mentioned throughout the book eg the one-year rule for ER and the two-year rule for IHT (see **5.48**). The date of starting the business is critical and must be able to be supported by fact and contemporaneous evidence.

CONCLUSION

10.20   It has been argued that the 'simplest taxes are the easiest to apply'. The current farm tax regimes offer huge potential advantages for CGT, IHT and income tax. There could be huge benefit to be obtained from ensuring that landownership is surrounded by farming tax reliefs.

Chapter 11

Share farming, contract farming, farm business tenancies and other farming business agreements

Julie Butler

- **Casual and formal lettings**
  The tax disadvantages of land being let as opposed to being utilised in a trading business has been emphasised throughout the book. By definition in order to achieve BPR and ER the key word is 'business'. Some tenancies such as farm business tenancies (FBTs) and grazing can still attract restricted tax reliefs. This chapter emphasises the need for all letting arrangements to be reviewed and formalised for maximum tax reliefs and protection mindful of all tax advantages and pitfalls including stamp duty land tax (SDLT). Grazing agreements are looked at in the context of the *McCall* (*McCall v HMRC* [2009] NICA 12) case.

- **Contract farming**
  Contract farming can be a very tax-efficient method of farming the land without some of the complications of share farming. The tax advantage of contract and share farming is that they are a trading activity for tax purposes. The advantage over an FBT is that 'untainted' CGT reliefs are still preserved. A well-drafted agreement supported by facts that would stand up to HMRC scrutiny is essential. Matters have been highlighted by the *Arnander* case (*Executors of McKenna Deceased v HMRC* SpC 565).

- **The need for an agreement**
  It is important that the landowner carefully reviews all the options and chooses the one which best suits their specific financial and tax requirements. Whatever choices (or complex series of choices for each area) are made it is essential to ensure that current and future arrangements are reviewed for tax efficiency and protected by a robust formal agreement.

- **Distinguishing land ownership and farming**
  One needs to look closely at the difference between trading income and the profits of a property business. This is closely linked to letting activity. There needs to be evidence to support a claim to be an 'active farmer'.

INTRODUCTION

11.1 With the recent history of fluctuations in farm profitability it has been important to try to control costs and keep overheads to a minimum whilst trying to achieve tax efficiency. With the move away from 'farming in-hand', farmers have been reviewing the methods by which they farm. One way of achieving greater profitability has been through share farming and contract farming agreements. Since 1 September 1995 advantage has also been taken of the farm business tenancy (FBT) provisions. The aim of these agreements is to be not only commercially viable but also IHT efficient. The drafting of the correct agreement is all-important. This is set out very clearly in the author's article entitled 'Casual Lettings' published in *Taxation* on 11 April 2002. Some of the points of the article are further emphasised in this book. The problems surrounding casual lettings are set out in **11.2** below and still apply a number of years after the article was written.

CASUAL LETTINGS

11.2   In an effort to overcome the uncertainty of farming incomes, many landowners are engaging in casual letting or grazing agreements. Likewise, farming units are trying to take on more land under management in order to take advantage of economies of scale.

Many tenancy arrangements have arisen without the appropriate legal advice having been taken, and this can have unpleasant tax consequences. The introduction of the FBT from 1 September 1995 has placed the landowner in the apparently happy position of having 100% agricultural property relief (APR) available for inheritance tax (IHT) purposes (see **11.15**). It must be remembered that an FBT did not attract CGT reliefs before 6 April 2004 and this was subsequently lost from 6 April 2008. There can also be restrictions for expenses, as essentially it should be taxed as non-trading income. Furthermore, the farmhouse will probably not qualify for expenses of trading or claims for IHT relief where the farm has been let. This is currently very important with the strong value of farmhouses in the UK and is looked at in **4.26**.

It is often overlooked that the FBT (subject to previous tax status) will have to be in existence for seven years in order to qualify for APR. However, a contract farming arrangement which is properly constructed will give the landowner the ability to show that he is the main occupier and, therefore, bring himself within IHTA 1984 s 117(a). The result is that the minimum period of occupation or ownership required to be eligible for APR is two years rather than seven. This is looked at in more depth in this chapter.

GRAZING RIGHTS

11.3   Rupert Brooke wrote: 'Breathless, we flung us on the windy hill, laughed in the sun and kissed the lovely grass'. Perhaps it appears that this author has an over-enthusiastic interest in grasslands but the potential for tax relief has a big impact on the tax planner and farming (see **10.7**).

Where a landlord grants an FBT in relation to farmland, he is no longer a farmer of that parcel of land but a landlord. This can apply with grazing rights unless he carries out the seven functions as set out in **10.7** but see also **10.9** and **10.10**.

The question of trade or farming is looked at throughout the book. The grazier must also covenant not to mow or cut the grass and the owner must do any hedging, fencing and ditching needed and any other work of a proprietorial nature.

If the landowner manages to achieve proof of the functions referred to above he should then be deemed to be trading with paramount occupancy and, therefore, eligible for not only APR on the land, but also on the farmhouse. The required period of occupancy could then also be reduced for tax planning. There is also greater potential to claim business expenses and qualify for CGT entrepreneurs' relief (ER).

The tax case of *McCall* has questioned whether grazing agreements are a business for BPR or the 'management of lettings' (see **10.10**).

Historically, many written and unwritten tenancies have evolved within farming partnerships and farming arrangements between members of the family, and these could jeopardise the tax shelter the farmland should present. Likewise, diversification could move towards a claim for BPR and not APR and, again, jeopardise the claim for APR on the farmhouse (see Chapter 4).

Another problem facing the farming community arises where members of a farming arrangement with the advantage of a pre-1 September 1995 tenancy then wish to change it. This could give rise to serious tax consequences and problems, such as the surrender of the tenancy (see **11.29**). Even before the *Arnander* decision HMRC would look closely at grazing licences (and contract farming) to see whether it was the farmer or the grazier who was carrying out husbandry activities on the land. If the farmer was doing little or nothing to produce the grass crop then the farmer might be treated as not occupying the land for agriculture himself or that the licence was akin to a tenancy – both interpretations could result in the farmhouse failing to qualify for APR. It can be argued the *Arnander* decision 'raises the bar' and requires the farmer to be farming on a day-to-day basis. Others would say that the case just gave greater clarity that active grassland management by the farmer will be needed in the future to limit the chances of a grazing licence prejudicing APR on a farmhouse.

SHARE FARMING

The concept

11.4   The farming community has been forced to look more closely at contract and share farming arrangements, which will provide great opportunity to claim available trading tax reliefs, eg the associated APR/BPR, and CGT reliefs. It is essential that these farming arrangements are carefully drafted so as to protect the landowner. The Country Land and Business Association (CLA) has a draft agreement for share farming and all landowners and farmers should look at the current structure of the farming agreement in place and ensure that they are not jeopardising very valuable tax reliefs (see www.cla. org.uk).

The number of farmers who die intestate is alarming and while looking at all matters such as partnership agreements, tenancy arrangements and their tax consequences, and ensuring that all major tax reliefs are protected, it is essential that this review is linked in with a well considered tax-efficient will (see Chapter 18).

The need to review all legal agreements currently in place with the farming family is of paramount importance as a starting point.

The question that presents itself most regularly in the review of the share farming agreement is that of who is the user or occupier of the farmland. We will now review more of the detail of each of the alternatives.

The arrangement

11.5   The principle of share farming should be to try and take advantage of the economies of scale in the farming operation. Where smaller farming units only need utilisation of part of a machine it is possible to share equipment. It has also evolved into an arrangement whereby a landowning farmer 'shares' the farming and has time to seek other profit alternatives.

Each party should be conducting a separate business. There should be separate bank accounts for each business and a separate one into which gross takings are paid and then divided into agreed shares. Each party must keep their own accounting records. When there are meetings, as there should be, to decide farm policy there should be minutes of those meetings. Without such minutes it may well be very difficult to show that the landowner has taken any active part in the farming operation at all. Whilst this might be seen to be over-protective, the size of the CGT and IHT reliefs must not be overlooked.

In a share farming agreement the landowner and the farming operator agree to split the sale proceeds in a particular ratio based on the relative values of their contribution to the venture. Examples of the contributions are as follows.

- The share farmer provides:
    - labour;
    - machinery – moveable plant and equipment;
    - management – liaison on the farm policy with the landowner;
    - working capital in the form of a share of variable costs; and
    - a share in the livestock.
- The landowner provides:
    - farmland and buildings;
    - farmhouse;
    - fixed equipment such as milking parlours or grain dryers;
    - major property repairs;
    - working capital in the form of a share of variable costs;
    - a share in the livestock; and
    - involvement in the decision-making of farming policy.

Accounts and tax

11.6   The share farming agreement should ensure that the two businesses are separate with their own VAT and tax returns. It is essential to try and ensure that the arrangement is not constructed as a partnership; otherwise the parties will be joint and severally liable for each other's debts. If there was a deemed partnership there will also have to be partnership accounts prepared with a partnership and the related self-assessment tax returns and all the problems that are associated with this. There are of course many tax advisers who promote the partnership as opposed to the share farming arrangement as the tax-efficient protection of the available tax reliefs but there are business risks associated with this.

It is also noted that no tenancy is created providing the operator does not enjoy exclusive possession of any part of the land and buildings.

It is not always considered necessary to produce a full set of accounts for a share farming venture as both parties' tax returns will include the proportion of output rather than it just being linked to a profit figure. Generally, the annual accounts to be drawn up by the landowning share farmer will only include a proportion of the gross margin and will exclude the items of the overhead paid for by the share farmer (unless separately billed as agreed).

It is considered that the growing crops will be the property of the landowner whilst in the ground, but the cultivation, which is carried out by the share farmer up to the end of the accounting period will have been carried out by the share farmer's own labour and machinery. The value of tillages will also be the property of the landowner at this stage with a corresponding amount owing to the share farmer.

It is prudent to review the position regarding the annual investment allowance (AIA) as introduced by Finance Act 2008 (see **7.3**). To recap on the AIA, the workings are as follows:

The AIA will be available to qualifying persons (CAA 2001 s 38A), ie:

- an individual;
- any partnership of which all the members are individuals (ie a partnership of which a company is a member, for example, is not eligible to claim: see CA23082); or
- a company,

carrying on a qualifying activity (this includes trades, professions, vocations, ordinary property businesses and employments or offices: see CAA 2001 s 15).

A business will be able to claim the AIA on the first £50,000 spent on plant or machinery or long-life assets, but not cars. Where businesses spend more than £50,000 in any chargeable period, any additional expenditure will be dealt with as usual in either the special rate (10%) or main pool (20%), where it will attract WDAs at the appropriate rate.

The maximum allowance is £100,000 in relation to expenditure incurred on or after 1 April 2010 for corporation tax purposes, and 6 April 2010 for income tax purposes: CAA s 51A(5) (amended by FA 2010 s 5). It was announced in the coalition government Budget of June 2010 that this would drop to £25,000 from April 2012.

Inheritance tax and capital gains tax planning

11.7   The aim is to establish that all parties to the share farming agreement are trading as farmers with trading income. In practice, the amount of income assessable will be similar whether it is trading or non-trading income, but it is the reliefs from CGT and IHT that must be preserved.

In order to be sure that APR (and in some cases BPR) is not lost, the landowner must show that the purpose of occupation is for agriculture and, therefore, brings himself within IHTA 1984 s 117(a), with the result that the minimum period of occupation or ownership required to earn relief is two years rather than seven. Such valuable reliefs as APR and BPR are worth the effort to comply strictly with statutory requirements. An attack on BPR will probably argue that the farming arrangement involves 'making or holding investments' (see **5.20**). The success of the use of farmland as a tax shelter is dependent on the care with which the arrangements are drawn up.

Another important factor is that if the share farmer is genuinely 'trading' then the farmhouse is treated as being part of the farming unit and it should be a case that the tax relief on the farmhouse will be preserved (see Chapter 4). A similar position concerning cottages will also apply and the use of this agreement is important (see Chapter 13).

The risks

11.8   The advantage of the above approach to share farming is that the landowner can retain a genuine interest and involvement in the farm. However, if the arrangements are not set up correctly there are risks involved:

- the risk of classification as a partnership;

- the risk of tenancy status; or

- the risk of loss of trading status for IHT and CGT and income tax reliefs.

There is not enough room in this book to explore the full risks of partnership and tenancy status, and these would be best explained by a legal practitioner. The key points would be the problem of joint and several liability associated with partnership and the loss of trading status when a tenancy is created. However, there are those who argue that partnership is the ultimate risk for tax.

The above points emphasise the need to have a correctly drafted legal agreement. Alternative ways of farming could be reviewed, such as contract farming. With the current emphasis on HMRC looking at the 'true facts' and being concerned over 'fragility' and 'artificiality' of arrangements, sound legal drafting is not enough – the correct facts must be in place. HMRC take as much notice of what is actually happening as to what is supposed to be happening.

The need for an agreement

11.9   Whilst share farming is generally acceptable to HMRC to prove 'trading as a farmer', there have been occasions when the whole principle has been questioned. Again, it is very important that the agreement is correctly constructed to ensure that there is no partnership for legal purposes and that it will pass HMRC scrutiny and be established as a trade for tax purposes. It is recommended that share farming agreements follow the model agreements from the CLA, which have had HMRC approval, and that legal advice is looked for when drafting the agreement. Complications might arise as to who is eligible for the receipt of the SFP and the landowner should check that they are protected from enthusiastic HMRC scrutiny.

HMRC have agreed that under an agreement based on the model set out by the CLA the landowner may establish trading status. Provided the landowner takes an active interest in the operations conducted, he must show that he concerns himself with the details of farming policy. The farmer must go on to the land for a material purpose, eg to inspect crops or stock and decide the farming policy in the light of that inspection. The CLA have undoubtedly undertaken much good work in this area and this is reflected in their publication *Share Farming: The Practice*. Model forms of agreement can be obtained from the CLA (www.cla.org.uk).

Under share farming arrangements both the landowner and operator farm the land. The tenancy problem is avoided if neither the landowner nor the operator has exclusive possession. The landowner must retain occupation of the land and any buildings to protect the future claim for entrepreneurs' relief purposes. The operator should have a mere licence to occupy. A difficulty could arise where, for example, animals on the land are owned by one party or the other subject to agreement rather than shares. The occupation of the land by the animals might lead to the owner of the land being regarded as the occupier of the land. Again, the risk of inadvertently entering into partnership should be avoided for legal reasons.

In reality the complexity of share farming compared to contract farming has made the latter very attractive but subject to attack by HMRC.

CONTRACT FARMING

The concept – 'farming with contractors'

11.10   A contract farming arrangement is essentially a landowner using the services of a contractor or another farmer to farm the land. The landowner supplies variable costs of seeds, fertilisers and sprays for growing the crops. The contracting farmer supplies labour, machinery and management. It should be genuine farming with the use of contractors.

Examples of when a contract farming arrangement can be used effectively would be at the time of retirement of a farm manager; or when a tenanted farm has fallen vacant due to the departure of the tenant and the landlord does not wish to farm the land himself – he may lack the capital or the inclination to do so but nonetheless wishes to retain vacant possession, having in mind that one of his family might wish to have a farming career in the future. Sometimes the contract farming arrangements are entered into following farming losses when the landowner will take the view that they cannot continue to incur losses and would want to try and make the outfit more productive, effectively sharing in economies of scale and reducing employment costs.

Generally, the contractor will receive a set fee for the services provided and a bonus as a percentage of the calculated surplus from the venture. The arrangement is suitable for both livestock and cropping enterprises. The contracting income received by the contractor must be reviewed carefully. Whereas it will qualify as trading income for the contractor, it will often not qualify as farm income.

Contract farming arrangements became even more attractive under the introduction of SDLT on leases (see **11.37**). However the recent case of *Arnander* (see **4.39** and **4.40**) showed the weakness. For example:

> All the contracting agreements reserved sole responsibility for providing machinery and farming policy decisions to the contractor. Day-to-day management was also to be reserved to the contractor after consultation with Mr McKenna.
>
> However the manner in which the agreements were drafted and run was similar, in many respects, to a tenancy. For example during negotiation over the last contracting agreement there was talk of the contractor paying 'rent'; Mr McKenna's return was paid to him quarterly (like many farm rents); in later years the contractor made the claim and kept the arable area aid payments; the contractor bought the crop (sometimes standing); the contractor was a co-signatory to a Woodland Grant Scheme application as 'occupier'.
>
> On the other hand Mr McKenna walked the farm and inspected it on a regular basis. He kept the cash book and records and composed and submitted the farm census. However the involvement of an agent meant that the use of Rosteague House for farming matters was much reduced.
>
> In other words the contracting agreements at Rosteague were conducted on the basis that much of the responsibility for farming decisions fell to the contractor. Also, although this is not entirely clear from the judgment, it seems some of the financial risk of trading may have passed from Mr McKenna to the contractor also.
>
> The Commissioner found that the house was 'primarily a rich man's residence rather than a farmhouse'. Mr McKenna did not occupy the house to undertake day-to-day farming activities, as the day-to-day management was carried out by a contractor. The contract farming arrangement was not considered robust. In addition, the fact that Mr McKenna was a farmer was not mentioned in his obituary.

Accounts presentation

11.11   Contract farming agreements generally centre on a memorandum joint venture account, which is an arithmetical calculation to establish how much the contractor should be paid for the services. It is often advisable in a contract farming agreement to set up a separate bank account in the landowner's name with all transactions relating to the agreement going through the account. This would also automatically divide the interest calculation on working capital as the account becomes overdrawn to fund variable costs.

The contracting farmer can provide the funding of the variable costs in a cropping agreement. In this instance the contracting farmer is providing an interest-free loan to the landowner as the legal title to the crops always remains with the landowner. It is essential that a correctly drawn-up agreement should aim to enable a landowner to carry on the trade of farming and provide a reasonable return for both parties, even within the current falling income position in the UK. This should then ensure that the landowner preserves the business reliefs. Additionally, the IHT reliefs on the farmhouse are also preserved, as this is one of the assets occupied by the landowner for farming (see Chapter 4).

Businesses with financial year-ends prior to the calculation of a memorandum account will not know how much to provide for the amount owing to the contracting farmer for the final profit share. There are two options available:

- delay the preparation of the final accounts until the creditor is known (this would depend upon the time delay involved); or

- include an estimated amount for the profit share, which will have to be adjusted the following year in the contract charge.

Many contract-farming arrangements include an annual valuation of grain for sale, variable costs and cultivations in September.

Unless the financial year-end of the business is the same time as the valuation it has no practical use or relevance to the preparation of the annual accounts.

The total remuneration of the contractor consists of supplying the following services:

- labour;

- machinery; and

- management.

The total amount is normally invoiced as contracting fee plus VAT. It must be noted that each party is treated as a separate business for VAT and tax (see Chapter 9).

As current farm cottage rents that can be achieved are high the overall cost of a farm employee becomes greater and the employment law problems surrounding this become greater still. The burgeoning cost of farm workers has resulted in some radical redundancies and some sharp contract farm agreements. Sometimes contract farming arrangements are entered into out of the pure necessity that the landowner physically cannot continue to farm commercially with the more conventional method of employing a farm manager and staff living in farm cottages.

Inheritance tax and capital gains tax planning

11.12   The advantage of contract farming is that provided the conditions are met for income tax purposes the landowner preserves trading status and the ability to offset any losses against other income under ITA 2007 s 64 (see **12.5**). There is also a greater ability to claim for general overhead farming expenses than under an FBT as an example (see **11.15**).

Ideally, if both owner and contractor are carrying on genuine separate farming businesses, then BPR at the rate of 100% will be available on the business assets of both parties. The owner should be regarded as farming the land and, therefore, APR at a rate of 100% should be allowable. However, it must be noted that the relief will depend upon whether it can be said that the landowner has a right to vacant possession, which will in turn depend upon the construction of the contract farming agreement. There are many who argue that the tax-efficient way forward is through a partnership.

This is another clear example of where a farmer who provides contracting services must check their tax computation and the practitioner must give very careful consideration to the position (see **12.4**). Clients with substantial contract farming income should be warned that a proportion of their income may not be treated as the trade of farming and that contracting income may have to be excluded in any averaging calculation (see **11.14** and **19.1**).

The risks and practical solutions – 'farming with contractors'

11.13   The landowner involved in a contract management agreement will inevitably be exposed to an element of risk as the result of fluctuating production and prices. In essence the landowner will continue the trade of farming and the degree of risk will depend upon the structure of the actual agreement. In many contract management agreements, the contractor is not paid a fixed fee in profit share until all crop proceeds have been received by the landowner. At this stage the contractor is exposed to substantial risk, particularly if the variable cost has also been funded by the contractor.

Ideally the contractor should simply be a replacement for direct labour and the management and control of the farming business should remain in the hands of the landowner. Even if a contract farming agreement is in order, the landowner must ensure that it is adhered to and it does not gradually slip into being a quasi-tenancy arrangement under which the contractor does everything and the landowner simply receives his first charge and a nominal share of any profits. The landowner must be personally involved and bear the financial risk of the farming business. Meetings to decide policy should take place in the farmhouse and be minuted as evidence of the landowner's input. All the farm records and paperwork should be kept at the farmhouse.

Practical suggestions are to retain a mix of 'real' farming eg suckler herd, separate grazing agreement where the landowner is responsible for hedges, ditches, mowing, fertiliser and spraying. Another alternative is to ensure that the contract farming agreement requires real physical input and genuine commercial risk and there is no 'guaranteed' income.

In *Arnander* the contractor claimed the farm subsidy payments and the landowner (McKenna) received quarterly payments, which could be presented as weak factors in the argument for retaining genuine trading status with HMRC.

It must be mentioned that in the current farming climate it is critical for commercial viability to ensure that a return will be made under the contract farming arrangements and some are obviously making losses. This is a double edged sword – the landowner undertaking a contract farming arrangement is being asked to be seen to be taking risk (eg losses) and yet seen to be commercial (ie profits). It can be reported that the landowner feels somewhat confused by achieving all these demands. This is pushing clients towards the more attractive return in FBTs. The merits and problems associated therewith are reviewed at **11.15**.

Many argue that the term 'contract farming' should be changed to 'farming with contractors' to ensure greater understanding and tax efficiency.

The need for robust agreements – IHT audit

11.14   In practice, there are a multitude of official and unofficial agreements operating in the agricultural industry in the UK. Many of these agreements are inadequate or have no written documentation. Unless the written agreements and their operation are very similar to the structures required to establish a trade then practitioners must warn clients that their farming business status may be questioned by HMRC. All clients should be encouraged to ensure agreements are reviewed by a good agricultural lawyer/land agent.

A correctly constructed agreement for contract farming is more straightforward than with share farming. Essentially, one party is supplying contracting services to a landowner. In practice, most contractors involved in these arrangements also farm in their own right. Therefore, their contracting income in addition to their income from their farming trade (depending upon the relative amounts) will be accepted as farming income. However, in the case where contractors do not farm land and derive all their income from contract farming, they will be treated by HMRC as contractors and not farmers (see **11.12**).

As with share farming, complications could arise as to SFP entitlement.

It is important that the contract farming arrangement will not be construed as a tenancy agreement. For this reason it might be best not to stipulate three-year reviews as creating an obvious analogy with the three-year reviews of agricultural rents (in England and Wales). It is desirable that the agreement operates for a limited period only so that this rental equivalent can be reviewed in line with current market rents. With regard to the latter it is possible to arrange to share out the profits of the enterprise in a variety of ways, but it is usual to reserve a slice of the profit for the owner corresponding to the amount he would have received had he let the farm in the normal way.

Care will be needed so that the arrangement is not construed as a partnership agreement because of legal risks or as creating the relationship of employer/employee, all of which might create tax consequences other than those intended. It is also important that the contract is drafted so that the owner does not inadvertently purport to transfer ownership of or an interest in the farm property to the contractor.

With regard to contract farming it is essential to receive good legal advice to ensure a correct agreement can be achieved. Generally the land agent will play an important part in ensuring tax efficiency.

It has been argued that contract farming arrangements should be audited for tax efficiency, indeed the whole of the land ownership should be treated to such a tax audit. An IHT audit should ideally be carried out on the farm property to check the availability of future IHT reliefs and establish what rescue work can be undertaken in order to protect future relief. Will the assets comply with the requirement in IHTA 1984 s 117(a) of being occupied for the purposes of agriculture for the two years prior to death?

Would the assets qualify as agricultural property under s 115(2)? This provision states that agricultural property is 'agricultural land or pasture … and also includes such cottages, farm buildings and farm houses, together with the land occupied with them as are of a character appropriate to the property'. If the assets fail to achieve APR, would BPR be achieved on the other assets? Would *Farmer and Another (Executors of Farmer Deceased) v IRC* (1999) STC SSCD 321 SpC 216 apply? (See Chapter 13.)

Does the contract farming arrangement need review? Does clear evidence of activity need to be documented?

FARM BUSINESS TENANCIES (FBTS)

The concept

11.15   Farm business tenancies, also known as FBTs, were introduced on 1 September 1995 under the Agricultural Tenancies Act 1995. Any land let for agricultural purposes after this date will be subject to an FBT. The advantages are that FBTs give greater freedom of contract and tenancies of any length without security of tenure. Also, there are open-market rent reviews (unless no review of formula) and compensation for improvements added to the land. In simple terms, the FBT may replace any of the following arrangements:

- seasonal cropping agreement;

- Ministry licences (usually five years);

- 'Gladstone and Bower' arrangements (usually 23 months);

- land let under the Agricultural Holdings Act 1986 (AHA 1986), which provided lifetime rights; or

- pre-AHA 1986 tenancies, which contained the right to succession.

However, it is noted that they cannot replace the following arrangements:

- grass keep arrangements;

- share farming; or

- contract management agreements.

The history of the FBT has been a tax rollercoaster. In 1995 the APR advantages of the FBT had a high profile and BATR for CGT was very attractive from 6 April 2004. However, this disappeared from 5 April 2008. The lack of BPR on an FBT is explained below.

An FBT is a lease and as such will be subject to SDLT (see **11.37**). Questions over entitlement to SFP do arise.

Accountancy treatment and farming lifestyle expenses

11.16   Farm accounts should clearly show the rental income and record the allowable expenses. Income under an FBT is treated as rental income for tax purposes, whereas the income of contract farming and share farming is assessable as trading income providing the badges of trade are in place. Any trading losses brought forward cannot be used against this income and can only be carried forward to be used against any future 'trading' farming income. The expenses that will be allowed against this rental income will be restricted to the costs directly attributed to the land ownership; therefore many costs will not be eligible for tax relief, such as expenses relating to the farmhouse and motor vehicles of the landowner etc.

Farming has been described as a way of life. There are certain 'lifestyle' expenses inherent in the nature of the trade, the location of the farm, historic claims for business expenses, etc. Examples of these types of expenses would be the running costs of the farmhouse and of four-wheel drive vehicles. It is unlikely that the move to an FBT will result in a significant reduction in this expenditure, but will the outlay still qualify for income tax relief?

Whilst 'lifestyle' expenditure would in practice be justified as a trading expense, it is unlikely that it will be allowed as an expense against the FBT income.

Farmer and landowner – what is the difference?

11.17   It is important to consider why the FBT relates to land ownership and not the business of farming. The two activities of farming and land ownership are distinguished for tax purposes respectively as trading income (ITTOIA 2005 Pt 2 or CTA 2009 Pt 3 for corporation tax) or property income (ITTOIA 2005 Pt 3 or CTA 2009 Pt 4).

Both income tax and corporation tax legislation contain rules to ensure that property income cannot also be taxed as trading income (ITTOIA 2005 s 4(1); CTA 2009 s 201).

In summary, the landowner is taxed on profits arising in respect of leases of land and other receipts arising from or by virtue of an ownership of an estate or interest in or right over land. The farmer, on the other hand, is taxed on profits arising from the occupation of land. Taxpayers in the former category are described as 'landowners' and those in the latter as 'farmers'. In the latter category a trade or business is carried on; in the former it is not. One taxpayer may concurrently operate in both capacities in respect of different land. The taxpayer may at the same time be a tenant of other land.

One of the best practical examples of where the 'border' (please excuse pun) lies between farming and landownership is the treatment of income from the grazing of grasslands (see **10.7**). The owner of grasslands who manages to secure that the income therefrom be treated as farming income can obtain several tax advantages. These will include the treatment of the grazing income as 'earned' income from a trade, rather than as 'unearned' profits from a property business. An FBT is not a trade but a correctly drafted grazing agreement can be. This has proved to be a source of great confusion in farm taxation.

Inheritance tax and capital gains tax planning

11.18   The introduction of FBTs on 1 September 1995 was heralded as a positive IHT decision for the landowner in that he had an opportunity to secure 100% APR where previously this had not been available. When land is let under an FBT the landowner is deemed to be no longer trading. Roll-over relief on any capital gain that may arise will usually be restricted on a time-apportioned basis.

The creation of a new FBT is a relatively straightforward matter. Much greater complications arise where there is an existing tenancy under the AHA 1986 or there is no right to vacant possession within 24 months. In order for the landlord to achieve 100% APR the tenancy should come to an end. In order to achieve this there must be a clear surrender of the old tenancy and a grant of the new. In his book *Business and Agricultural Property Relief* (Bloomsbury Professional), Toby Harris goes to some length to explain the provisions of IHTA 1984 s 116(2) and explores the position where the tenant of an old tenancy dies and a new tenancy commences. For a landlord currently bound by the tenancy arrangements, there are lots of useful details contained within this book.

To summarise: provisions of IHTA 1984 s 116 apply 100% APR relief to all land subject to an FBT. In addition, it would apply to land let subject to any succession tenancy granted on or after 1 September 1995 under AHA 1986. This is extended so that it can include cases where the land transferred is let under a tenancy granted before 1 September 1995 but where either:

- a valid retirement notice for succession has been made after that date; or

- the tenant has died after that date and the tenancy has become invested or obtained by another person as a consequence.

The full details of the tenancy logistics are outside the scope of this book but the aim of this section is to set out the worries and concerns so that they can be looked at in more detail.

Inheritance tax position

11.19   In deciding when a tenancy commences regard must be had to the old and new tenant legislation. Obviously the starting point is 1 September 1995, so tenancies falling under the new legislation will qualify for 100% APR. Some tenancies governed by the old legislation will qualify for 100% APR because the tenancy began on or after 1 September 1995, for example, a succession tenancy following the serving of a retirement notice or death of tenant in occupation on 31 August 1995. In succession cases it may be possible to qualify for 100% APR where the new tenancies have not yet begun at the date of transfer, for example, where the landlord dies before the commencement of the new succession tenancy but after the death of the tenant or the serving of a retirement notice.

At this stage it is wise to look at any cases where 100% APR was already available before 1 September 1995 for certain qualifying tenancies. These situations were where the landlord had the right to vacant possession or the right to obtain it within the following 12 months (IHTA 1984 s 116(2a)). Also, by February 1995 let land had the right to qualify for APR where the landowner had the right to vacant possession within 24 months (HMRC Extra-statutory Concession F17) (see **11.21**), and double discount cases under s 116(2)(b).

Here it is convenient to deal separately with (a) farm land and buildings still used for agricultural purposes; (b) the farmhouse itself; and (c) farm cottages, barns and other buildings put to new uses.

Since 1 September 1995 the FBT has ensured that the relevant land and buildings included within the scope of the FBT qualify for APR. The key to the qualification for APR is the clause contained within the FBT, enabling the landowner to obtain vacant possession within 12 or 24 months. Consideration must be given to any development or hope value of the land as it is extremely unlikely that BPR will apply.

The IHT disadvantage of the FBT focuses on the potential loss of APR on the farmhouse (assuming it is to be retained for occupation by the landowner and not included in the FBT). The tax profession accepts that farmhouses are anyway under attack for their eligibility to IHT relief (see Chapter 4).

As already mentioned, with a large number of farms the potential IHT relief on the farmhouse (see Chapter 4) is significant and is at great risk should there be a move from farming 'in hand' or by way of a share or contract farming arrangement. Clearly, how can the APR on the farmhouse be argued if there is no business? Whilst the finding of *Antrobus 2* dictated that the IHT relief on the farmhouse is restricted to the agricultural value, this is still a significant potential tax saving for those farmers who continue to farm their land as opposed to entering in to the FBT.

Most farms of a significant size have a number of let farm cottages included within the business or enterprise – these are often the cottages where the farm workers used to live when farming was much more labour intensive. Alternatively, the let property is often farm buildings converted into dwellings available for rental – literally converted pig sheds, milking parlours and the building where the cart horses used to stand. The IHT position is included in Chapter 13.

Tax planning and the period of ownership

11.20   APR at 100% is available for land let under an FBT but in order to qualify the land must either have been owned for seven years or have been farmed in hand, ie under trading status, for at least two years ending at the date of transfer. Therefore, new owners of agricultural land should ideally farm the land themselves for two years or contract farm the land for the first seven years before letting it on an FBT to secure APR at the earliest opportunity.

Double discount

11.21   The average age of farmers is high and many were farming before 1981 – hence the case of the 'double discount' is still of interest. This will be where the pre-1981 full-time working farmer relief provisions would have applied had they not been abolished and the transitional provisions are satisfied. The main example will be land continuously let to a partnership or a company since before 10 March 1981, which the transferor has previously farmed in some capacity.

Capital gains tax and the 2008 reform

11.22   From 6 April 2004 under FA 2003 s 160, FBTs qualified as business assets for BATR which caused a big move to the FBT in the farming community. However, BATR has been abolished from 6 April 2008 and the FBT does not qualify for entrepreneurs' relief (see **14.10**). It is likely that many will reject the FBT in favour of farming in hand.

Provided that the FBT would qualify for APR (see **11.19**) then the gain can be 'held over' (see **14.29**) when it is moved into new ownership so that the land can be 'clean' for future roll-over relief and ER.

FBT – For the purposes of agriculture and the claim for lifestyle expenses

11.23   In order for a lease to qualify as an FBT it is essential that the land is farmed as a trade or business and that the use of the land and character of the tenancy is primarily and wholly agricultural. Fixed farm tenancies of two years or less will expire automatically at the end of the term but fixed tenancies of two years plus will continue as yearly tenancies until notices between one or two years expiring on the contractual term date have been served. Rents may be determined by agreement between the parties.

The tax risks of an FBT are the potential loss of ER, the loss of claims for trading expenses and concerns over IHT complications. The other risks are the complexity of tenancy rules as set out above. The question of FBT and the IHT problems on hope value etc are set out in **11.19**.

The need for a well-drafted agreement to achieve tax relief

11.24   This chapter highlights the need for well-drafted agreements and this advice has been repeated regularly. It is hoped that the value of the potential tax reliefs shows the need to use an agricultural specialist to draft the agreement and to employ a tax specialist to ensure the tax treatment is correct.

In summary, with the introduction of the SFP scheme, many farming enterprises have moved away from the complexity of contract or share farming to the FBT. However, with the loss of BATR for CGT the FBT is less attractive but that does not remove the need of those who still use an FBT to have a well-drafted agreement. The answer is that any change in business structure in any farming activity must be reviewed in advance, taking account of all areas of tax planning. The loss of BPR and the potential APR on the farmhouse have reduced the attractiveness of the FBT.

FAMILY FARMING PARTNERSHIPS, FARMING THE LAND AS A LICENSEE AND/OR TENANTS

The history

11.25   Historically, many family farming partnerships have actually farmed the land that they jointly owned under a tenancy. This may present substantial tax problems. The tax planner must carefully review the IHT and CGT implications of all tenancies.

Participants in farming partnership are often blissfully unaware that a tenancy/ licence exists between the 'trading vehicle' and the landowner. Farming partnerships are being promoted more and more as a result of a loss of confidence in the tax-effectiveness of FBTs. Tax advisers are promoting the 'tax safety' of the partnership, but what of the legal risks?

Tenancy compared with licence

11.26   The landowner must understand not only the concepts of contract farming, share farming and tenancies but also the concept of the licence.

There are those who would argue that where there is an existing family farming tenancy with adverse tax consequences it should be brought to an end. If this is the case it is not just the tax costs of making the change that should be considered but a valuation of the advantages of the existing structure and what new structure could be substituted. It is, therefore, important to look at the tax consequences of having any form of agricultural tenancy in place as opposed to a licence. In order for 100% APR to be secured the owner's interest in the land must carry the right to vacant possession. Entrepreneurs' relief (ER) must be considered along with SDLT. There is no SDLT on licences with no consideration.

The tax disadvantages of farm tenancies

11.27   The tax disadvantages of any form of tenancy are as follows.

- The creation of a tenancy can give the tenanted land a lower base cost for CGT purposes where there is a death intervening. This is because on the first death the IHT value will be reduced by the tenancy and this will be the base cost of CGT. Obviously, the age of the landowners for proposed future sales should be considered and the whole matter is extremely complicated.

- Potential loss of APR on the farmhouse.

- APR might be put in jeopardy because of a failure to complete the stipulated seven-year ownership requirement for tenancies.

- Potential loss of BPR on hope value and cottages.

- CGT reliefs of roll-over relief and ER could be lost.

- SDLT compliance by tenant.

Changing the current business structure

11.28   A lot of farmers who are working within a family farming trading structure will be reluctant to change arrangements which are currently working well, both from a farming and a business standpoint, simply to try and obtain better tax reliefs. Who knows when the tax rules might change again? Nevertheless, it is essential that tax drawbacks and risks are pointed out, at the very least to ensure protection under professional indemnity insurance. Likewise, it should be noted that any change in the partnership arrangements is likely to involve legal costs. It is a bold tax planning move to change a structure with a high quantum of value and the risks for the client must be clearly set out.

Consideration must be given to the changes in the legal structure of the partnership, which could in themselves give rise to CGT. It should also be considered that there is a possibility of CGT arising on the termination of a tenancy. The tenant will be making a disposal of an asset, which may be regarded as of significant capital value. It could be deemed that the tenant has potential IHT problems. The tenant will need to consider whether, on a surrender of his tenancy, he is making a transfer of value for IHT purposes and, if so, what is the value of such a transfer and whether the transfer qualifies for APR.

Surrender of old tenancy

11.29   It should be noted that the surrender of the old tenancy by a tenant certainly does diminish the estate by value. Clearly, from case law such as *Baird's Executors v IRC* [1991] 1 EGLR 201 a non-assignable agricultural tenancy has a value for IHT. It must be questioned, therefore, that where a landlord and tenant are in negotiations to surrender an old tenancy, with a view to bringing in an FBT, HMRC might argue that the old tenancy has a significant value, due to the landlord and the tenant wanting to extinguish it, and consideration must be given to the value of the land being greater once the old tenancy has been removed. The Capital Taxes Office has indicated that it intends to construe IHTA 1984 s 124A(3)(a) strictly.

A solution would appear to be that it is the surrender of the tenancy made for no consideration. Any gain should be capable of being held over. The tenancy is a qualifying asset within TCGA 1992 s 165(2)(a). The problem arises where there are monies paid for the transfer, as the surrender of an existing tenancy for consideration is the disposal of a chargeable asset for CGT purposes. The tenant will be deemed to receive the open market value of the tenancy as consideration (TCGA 1992 ss 17–18) and possible transfer for IHT.

Consider tenancy changes

11.30   There has been coverage in the farming press about landowners wishing to change to FBTs from the old tenancies, and the tenants receiving quite a considerable sum of money for this change, ie the surrender of the old tenancy. The action has helped some parties considerably in that the landlord has a chance for improved APR and greater security over his own land, and the tenant receives a considerable sum, which in these difficult farming times can be the difference between failing or surviving. Where there is potential development value this is a route to be considered.

It is essential in any circumstance to weigh up the tax consequences and it is advised that all landholding operations involving third parties, that could in any way be considered a tenancy situation, be assessed as part of the current review of assets. What if the landlord is able to negotiate the grant of a new tenancy with his established tenant?

This will have the immediate result of securing APR at the rate of 100%, rather than the rate of only 50% that would normally apply to a tenancy, granted before September 1995. The objection, from the tenant's point of view, is that the result of entering into a new tenancy could have been a loss of the security of tenure which he enjoyed under the Agricultural Holdings Acts. A modification to the Agricultural Tenancies Act 1995 would enable a new tenancy to be granted following a surrender of the original tenancy, with the new tenancy conferring the same rights to security of tenure as applied under the original tenancy. The tenant's principal object will invariably be to ensure that he preserves his security of tenure, while assisting in an improvement to the landlord's tax position. However, the tenant will also wish to ensure that he does not suffer any unexpected tax liability.

An agricultural tenancy is, of course, a form of property conferring valuable rights (and perhaps onerous responsibilities and liabilities), and therefore an asset for CGT purposes. The surrender of the tenancy is therefore prima facie, the disposal of an asset which may give rise to a chargeable gain. Since it is unlikely that the arrangements being considered would be 'lubricated' by a transfer of cash, what is happening, from the tenant's point of view, is effectively the disposal of the old tenancy in exchange for the new one. The size of any chargeable gain will depend, therefore, on the value of the new tenancy.

Unless there is some change in the terms on which the replacement tenancy was granted, or there was some unusual term in the original tenancy, the Court of Appeal decision in *Walton v IRC* (1996) STC 68, should be helpful. This case confirmed that the value of the customary, non-assignable agricultural tenancy would usually only be very modest reflecting the difference between the rent currently being paid and the rent which might be obtainable on a review. *Walton* specifically concerned capital transfer tax, and must be regarded as effective for IHT, but in practice, the valuation criteria are the same for CGT. The same approach has even been applied by the court in a partnership case which did not involve tax at all (see *Greenbank v Pickles* (2000) EWCA Civ 264).

It is, of course, highly unlikely that there will be a significant acquisition cost, so to the extent that there is a capital value at the date of the surrender, there may well be a chargeable gain. An arrangement of the type discussed, in practice, may only be made with a tenant who had been actively farming the land. Part of the gain might, in any event, be attributable to the farmhouse which may very well be the tenant's principal private residence, and therefore obtain full PRR relief from CGT. This will not, of course, prevent the tenant from claiming the relief for another owned house which he has purchased as a retirement home if the tenancy agreement requires him to live in the farmhouse (see TCGA 1992 s 222(8) and 222(8A)(b)).

As the tenancy will have been used by the tenant for the purposes of his farming trade, roll-over relief will be worth consideration. The tenancy agreement would invariably contain express terms requiring the tenant to occupy the land and to farm it in accordance with the requirements of good husbandry. The other condition that could, of course, be regarded as raising a query would be whether a 'new asset' would be acquired, but this could be resolved by applying ESC D16 – land splitting for CGT. Assuming that no cash has changed hands, the consideration for the disposal of the 'old asset', the original tenancy, will be its value and no doubt be accepted as being the same acquisition cost of the new asset, the new tenancy. It would, however, be necessary for the tenant to claim roll-over relief, and on mature consideration he might decide it preferable not to. Depending on the age of the tenant – and therefore his expectation of life – it is highly likely that the new tenancy will be a wasting asset or within 10 years will become one. In this event, TCGA 1992 s 154(2)(c) will cause the rolled-over gain (described as a *'held-over'* gain in the legislation) to become taxable after 10 years have elapsed. In reality s 154 is far stricter than the normal roll-over relief provisions, since it brings the gain into charge to tax automatically if the new, depreciating, asset ceases to be used in the trade, as well as after 10 years. In this particular context, therefore, roll-over relief may be regarded as something of a trap.

CASUAL LETTING, GRAZING TENANCIES AND INCOME FROM GRASSLANDS

Casual letting of land

11.31 This subject has already been reviewed throughout the book and is considered again here. The casual letting of land does not spoil the qualification of the landowner to be regarded as the occupier for APR, however it can cause problems. The cases of *IRC v Forsyth Grant* (1943) 25 TC 369 and *Mitchell v IRC* (1943) 25 TC 380 are examples of this. Problems can arise when there is a significant interval between one casual letting and another and whether the land has been used for the purposes of agriculture in the intervening time. When one 'Gladstone and Bower' agreement follows one after another or has been entered into over a period of time, it could be argued by HMRC that the taxpayer has effectively let the land. It could well be argued by HMRC that the taxpayer has effectively let the land. Care must be taken with the drafting of agreements and the structure of the arrangement so as to ensure tax efficiency.

Grazing tenancies – the trade of farming?

11.32 Grazing rights have already been considered (see **10.7** and **11.3**) and featured throughout the chapter. The *McCall* case (see **10.10**) has influenced the whole area of grazing agreements. The Court of Appeal view was that it was clear that a landowner who derived income from land would be treated as having a business of holding an investment, regardless of the fact that he had to carry out some maintenance work and management, and find tenants. In this instance, the deceased's business consisted of earning a return from grassland, the real value of which lay in its grazing potential.

The position of grazing tenancies needs to be looked at very carefully to see whether it is actually the trade of farming or rental income. The example was used as a 'borderline' example between farming and landownership in **11.17**. If the latter applies there is jeopardy to all the tax reliefs that have been discussed previously. Obviously, the owner of the land which is let for grazing and who manages to secure that the income be treated as farming income can obtain many of the tax advantages of ER, of both APR and BPR, together with income tax expenses. The CLA has recommended a form of deed to grant a right of herbage, which has been approved by HMRC (see www.cla.org.uk). Post the *McCall* case there are many who consider that the eligibility for BPR on the land and APR on the farmhouse are at risk with a grazing agreement.

With regard to IHT HMRC have agreed that a landowner who continues to occupy a farmhouse on a farm which is grazed by tenants may still be in agricultural occupation of the farmhouse, provided the income from grazing is farming income, and hence will potentially qualify for APR (see Chapter 4). If, on the other hand, grazing income is purely ITT01A 2005 Pt 3 income and there are no other farming activities undertaken, there is a considerable risk that the APR on the farmhouse will be lost. There are also VAT advantages on grassland, which is deemed to be a zero-rated trade supply and VAT input tax can be claimed against it (see Chapter 9).

It is essential that a landowner who wishes to secure these tax advantages is meticulous in their approach to the nature of the grazing agreement and the activities they agree to undertake. It is important that, under ITA 2007 s 996(2) (see **1.3**), the farmer is proved to be occupying the land for the purposes of husbandry so as to preserve APR. In reality HMRC also look for the farming work carried out.

Paramount occupier

11.33 In order to achieve the maximum tax relief for the landowner it is vital to establish who the paramount occupier of the land is. The courts have approved the view that the occupier for tax purposes will normally be the same as the occupier for rating purposes. This is found in *Dawson v Counsell* [1938] 3 All ER 5, 22 TC 149. In the case of grazing of grassland the courts have been prepared to accept that the landowner can be the person who is occupying the land for this husbandry. In *IRC v Forsyth Grant* (1943) 25 TC 369, it was noted by Lord Carmont that the laying down of grass in suitable parts, the manuring of land so as to produce a good crop and the arrangement for the seasonal grazing of the grass by cattle brought to the land are operations of husbandry. The parks are being used for the purposes of husbandry by the proprietor who is occupying them. The tax advantages of this are obvious.

It was also noted that the growth of grass in a grass park does not require cultivation in the same sense as grain crops do, as such agricultural operations on the land as are necessary to promote its growth, namely manuring, are performed by the landowner and not by the grazier. On the assumption that the landowner is the occupier the agreement between him and the grazier may be regarded as the sale of growing crop rather than the let of land.

Grazing as a tenancy

11.34 There are two Scottish cases, *Mitchell v IRC* (1943) 25 TC 380 and *Drummond v IRC* (1951) 32 TC 263, which held the landowner was not farming the grasslands. The *Drummond* case put forward the point that the owner did not apply the top dressing to the land. It was found that the landowner was not a farmer, primarily because the grazing agreements were in reality a type of tenancy rather than merely a seasonal let for grazing. Obviously, if the courts regard a grazing agreement as a tenancy it will result in the landowner not being regarded as a farmer. In the case of *Bennion v Roper* (1970) 46 TC 613, the court was influenced by the fact that the grazing agreement was seen to be 'a perfectly ordinary tenancy agreement'. The essential ingredient of a grazing agreement is to ensure that the landowner qualifies as a farmer. The landowner and not the grazier should be responsible for growing the crops of grass.

As featured throughout the book the *McCall* case (see **10.10**) has influenced both the farming and the tax world view of grazing agreements and tenancies.

The argument presented on behalf of the executors was that Mrs McCall's son-in-law Mr Mitchell's work was not work associated solely with the letting of land but was similar to 'dog boarding kennels'. In this case it was argued that the cows were being cared for by Mr Mitchell's work, ie 'akin to holiday accommodation for cattle'. The Special Commissioners had decided that the distinction was that Mrs McClean's land was used to make a living *from* (part of) it, ie it was used as an investment as opposed to business where the land would be used to make (part of) a living *on* it. It was considered that Mrs McClean's farmland was not used to create a product or to provide any service distinct from the use of the land (other than the provision of the water).

Provisions to establish grazing agreements as business

11.35   The position on grazing 'rights' has been looked at, see **10.7** and **11.3** and grazing 'tenancies', at **11.32–11.34**. The key now is to look at the specific grazing 'agreement' to establish a business.

Some landowners have thought to employ contractors to perform all the acts of actual husbandry, who are distinct and totally at arm's length from the grazier, in order to establish the trading status of the income and not the letting status. At this point the distinction between trading and letting becomes very borderline, as do all the associated tax reliefs. This was explained at **11.17**.

It is generally considered that where the landowner is actively farming other land and provides only some of his land for seasonal grazing he will be regarded as the farmer of the grasslands, even where he contracts others to fertilise, weed, seed etc, particularly if these people are working on his own land. However, a landowner who only owns grasslands would be in a much stronger position if he carries out all the duties himself.

It goes without saying that in every case it would be more robust if the duties are physically carried out by the landowner but the next best thing would be an independent contractor.

TAX PLANNING ON NEW AND EXISTING AGREEMENTS

11.36   The message of this chapter has to be that all landowners and farmers (once they understand the difference between landowner and farming – see

11.17) should enter into all new agreements and arrangements with a view to tax planning. All existing agreements must be reviewed and all verbal arrangements should be made formal, in writing, and tax efficient. Legal help should be sought and the role of the land agent can be very useful.

The tax reliefs associated with genuine farming status are too generous to overlook. Review all assets and arrangements, as the tax reliefs could mean the difference between surviving or not. What does the future hold for farming arrangements?

If the land is farmed under contract farming arrangements is the landowner an active farmer who is eligible for BPR under IHTA 1984 s 104?

The *McCall* case (see **10.10**) needs to be considered when a claim for BPR may be needed on hope/development value on the land or on the market value which exceeds the agricultural value. The agricultural value should still qualify for APR but will BPR be available on the excess/development value? If the landowner is not actively involved with the land then it is unlikely BPR will be available. If he is simply making the land available to the contractor and does not retain a substantial residual use there is now a real argument that his business is one of holding an investment (ie the land). If the landowner's priority is to maximise the return he can obtain from this land rather than make a living on the land himself then BPR is at risk.

The landowner needs to look at the business as a whole. The landowner must not simply have control of the land, he needs to retain his occupation, have obligations in respect of the land and fulfil these obligations. He must not simply be making the land available to someone else. The landowner will have to be involved in the husbandry of the land. This emphasises the need for robust contracting agreements. The landowner must understand his role under the agreement and the importance of performing his duties.

If the land is farmed in hand, the landowner will be making his living on the land as opposed to from the land and BPR could then be possibly available on any excess market/hope/development value.

THE FUTURE FOR FARMING ARRANGEMENTS

11.37   Many farmers are dependent on their professional advisers, eg land agents, lawyers, tax advisers for advice regarding farming arrangements and they have never had such a complex time.

What evidence is there to support the active farmer?

●   How often are farm meetings held? Where were the meetings – in the landowner's office? Who was present? What was discussed? How long do the meetings last? Minutes must be kept.

●   Does the landowner sign cheques and approve all expenditure?

●   Does the landowner sign HMRC documents such as P11Ds, P35s (Employer Annual Return), Returns of class 1A NIC?

●   Does the landowner approve bills, invoices, stock prices?

- Does the landowner walk the farm, check stock and boundaries, attend sales/auctions?

- Does the landowner deal with the vet, bank manager etc? If so, how often, where did they meet, what did they discuss? Was a note kept?

- Does the landowner claim the single farm payment, hill farm allowance, entry-level stewardship?

Whatever happened to simple discussions and decisions across a farmer's kitchen table? Those times have gone – the complexities are too great. But the farmhouse table is still a good venue for the start of the discussions (the case of *Arnander* told us so – see Chapter 4). Tax advisers must be prepared to look at farm tax planning 'in the round', to work with land agents and solicitors in these very trying times, and to highlight the risk of a loss of tax reliefs.

Chapter 12

Hobby and lifestyle farming and use of farming losses

Julie Butler

- **Hobby and lifestyle farming and the need for commerciality**
  If the 'five-year' loss rule applies to a farming operation, ie it is deemed non-commercial, it is not just the income tax loss relief that is at risk but also potential future IHT and CGT reliefs (see **1.13**). The need to review the tax computation, identify diversification income and areas of commerciality are of utmost importance to the tax planner. There is a lot at stake. HMRC have been very vigilant in checking the correct application of the hobby farming rules.

- **Loss restriction for lack of activity in the business**
  Legislation has been introduced to prevent partnership loss manipulation on 'sideways loss relief'. This was effective from 10 February 2004. This has been further endorsed by the Revenue & Customs Brief 18/07 dated 2 March 2007. FA 2008 introduced loss relief for individuals carrying on a 'non-active' trade.

- **The use of losses by the individual**
  There is great flexibility with farm losses – they can be carried forward or carried back in the opening years and offset against total income; they can also be offset against capital gains. Farm losses can be claimed independently of the averaging claim and there is great scope for the tax planner to use losses carefully but the matter is complex.

INTRODUCTION – UNDERLYING PURPOSE AND COMMERCIAL ADVANTAGE

12.1   This chapter looks at the use of farm tax losses, their computation, the risk associated therewith and the interaction of hobby and lifestyle farming, but the starting point is to ask whether the expenses are allowable.

There is a wide-ranging general prohibition against the deduction of expenditure not incurred wholly and exclusively for the purposes of trade (ITTOIA 2005 s 34 (1)(a)). This rule is frequently invoked in a whole variety of contexts, has been many times interpreted by the courts, yet is still capable of reinterpretation. The key is the underlying purpose of the expenditure.

Money may be spent in the course of the farming business; the expenditure may be connected with the business; business cash may be used; the item may be entered in the business books; but none of these are sufficient. Nor is it relevant whether the money be paid under legal obligation, or not. Instead, attention needs to be directed towards the underlying purpose, as to whether the expenditure is made to promote the business and earn profits from it. Neither the moral intent, nor the sense of duty prompting payment is relevant; the test is always commercial advantage.

The 'hobby farming rules' should be considered, amongst other things, (see **12.9** test of commerciality) and how these could affect, at some time in the future, or even now, a history of farming losses.

It is imperative that the tax computation is reviewed for the correct allocation of farming and non-farming income and direct expense (see **12.4**) with possible apportionments of overheads etc. A large number of farming tax computations now include a significant amount of diversification income which should, strictly speaking, be extracted from the tax computation, thus possibly increasing the farming loss and the profit from other activities (see Chapter 1). In many cases the diversification income has become so significant that separate accounts or enterprise accounts are essential. The allocation of expenses and overheads can be complex.

The definition of farming income is found in Chapter 1 (see **1.3**).

INTERACTION OF HOBBY FARMING AND COMMERCIALITY

12.2   Farming has its own set of 'hobby farming rules', which historically have stated that a profit must be made every six years, 'the five-year rule', ie there can be five years of losses but there must be a profit in the sixth year. This again can be seen as an over-simplification and must be looked at carefully.

The hobby farming rules were introduced in the 1960s due to concerns over taxpayers farming for recreational purposes and not for commercial reasons. The original intention was to restrict loss relief in 'extreme cases' where the trading activities bore no relationship to the criteria of a commercial trade. The so-called 'five-year rule' was introduced as an extension to the original rules, ie as a further test it must be shown that the business is capable of making a profit (CTA 2009 s 48 for corporation tax purposes and ITA 2007 s 67 for income tax). Similar provisions for the restriction of corporation tax relief are included in CTA 2010 ss 37, 44. There are provisions to prevent the formation of a company or a change of partnership being falsely used to break the five-year rule. In the latter case, husband and wife are treated as the same person.

Business Income Manual at BIM75620 states the position as follows:

> 'The five year rule only applies to trading losses arising from farming or market gardening activities. ITA2007/S67 (or ICTA88/S397 for CT) denies relief against general income etc (see BIM75605) where a loss computed without regard to capital allowances was incurred in each of the five years of assessment preceding that in which the claimed loss was incurred (see BIM75625). Section 67 does not apply to any other trades.'

This provision was introduced in 1967 to complement what is now ITA2007/S66. Section 67 provides a more objective test and should be applied, subject to BIM75640 and BIM75645, in all cases where the conditions are satisfied.

While only farming in the UK is deemed to be a trade the five year rule is not restricted to UK based activities. Prior to 6th April 2005 the definitions of those trades were extended, by subsection (5), to include activities carried on outside the UK. For IT purposes from the 6th April 2005 the definition of farming was rewritten to exclude the UK restriction (ITA2007/S996) and consequently the extended definition for the five year rule is no longer required and has been omitted from ITA2007/S67-71.'

It is also worth referring to BIM75601.

'Farmers do not control the two main factors affecting the results of their businesses; market prices and the weather. These and other factors (for example, the 2001 outbreak of foot and mouth disease) may cause even the most efficiently managed farms to show losses from time to time. Various forms of loss relief are available to help in such cases (see BIM75000 onwards). In a minority of cases, claims for tax relief in respect of farming losses can present particular difficulty because:

- All UK farming is treated as the carrying on of a trade by virtue of ICTA88/S53 (1) and ITTOIA/S9 – and is thus eligible for the loss relief provisions applying to trades – whether or not it meets the normal commercial criteria of trading (see BIM55110).

- People with income from other sources sometimes take up farming for the sake of recreation or the lifestyle or status which it offers rather than for genuinely commercial reasons.

- Because of this, Parliament has enacted rules which prevent some farming losses being offset against non-farming income.

Restrictions to relief under ITA2007/S64 (previously ICTA88/S380)

Where losses are sustained in farming activities of an essentially uncommercial nature, relief under ITA2007/S64 may fall to be restricted under either:

- ITA2007/S66 – which restricts relief (see BIM75605) where the trade was not run on a commercial basis and with a view to the realisation of commercial profits (see BIM75615 and BIM75201), or

- ITA2007/S67 – often known as the five year rule restricts relief (see BIM75605) where tax adjusted losses before capital allowances were incurred in each of the five previous years of assessment (see BIM75620 onwards). ICTA88/S397 operates in the same way for CT purposes.

The five year rule is generally more straightforward to use as it involves a mechanical test. It should be applied, subject to BIM75640 and BIM75645, in all cases where the conditions (see BIM75620 onwards) are satisfied. Cases where Section 67 does not apply, but where the activities appear clearly uncommercial, should be considered for challenge under Section 66, subject to BIM75615 and BIM75201 onwards.

Restriction to relief under ITA2007/S72ICTA88/S381

Where relief by way of carry back in respect of losses sustained in the commencing years of a trade is claimed under ITA2007/S72 the test of commerciality is provided by Section 74. This test is stricter than that of Section 66 (see BIM75450).

Companies

As regards companies within the charge to CT, see CTM04000 onwards.'

Outsiders looking at the tax position of a farm or estate held as a pleasure activity, rather than as a genuine working farm, would say that all that has to be achieved is a profit every six years and there is great scope for claiming what could only be termed as 'quasi-business expenses', to subsidise an enjoyable country life. However, anybody contemplating undertaking the purchase of a country estate or following in the steps of the TV comedy *The Good Life* must embrace the hobby farming rules with their eyes wide open. With the move to diversification they must also look at standard commerciality rules. Diversified activities do not benefit from the hobby farming rules.

Tax planners must be aware of what would happen if a farm, or holding, were deemed to be trading as a hobby. Not only would income tax losses no longer be available under ITA 2007 s 64 but it could lead to a large potential denial of other tax reliefs. If the farm is deemed to be a hobby then the assets used therein would not have business status, which could put in jeopardy previous roll-over claims for CGT, and future claims for CGT and IHT relief. The loss of BPR for IHT, where income tax loss relief has been denied under the hobby farming rules, is a matter on which opinions differ. The CGT reliefs and IHT reliefs are a separate regime to income tax and tax arguments can protect these reliefs but in marginal cases the tax argument of profitability and commerciality are strong support for the claim of these reliefs.

A large number of farming enterprises have had to look seriously at diversification in order to ensure that there is a profit. Some of these diversification activities do not come under the farming definition. As a result, HMRC have a right to apply to some or the whole of the trade not just the hobby farming rules but the normal commerciality rules. In the current climate, those involved with the farming industry are painfully aware that it can be difficult to make a profit from pure farming and it has been difficult for a number of years. As set out in Chapter 1, strictly the accounts and the tax computation of the business should be separated between farming and non-farming (see **12.4**) and the tax implications of the hobby farming/commerciality rules dealt with accordingly. If a diversified activity does not make a profit it does not have five years to do so – the claim for losses and commerciality could be questioned well before that.

It is vital, therefore, that anyone contemplating entering into such a venture, or advising clients about entering into such a venture, should look carefully at the definition of what is and what is not farming (see **1.4** and **1.5**) and what is farm income by concession (see **1.7**).

Anybody contemplating the purchase of a farm should do everything in their power to ensure that the hobby farming rules do not apply. Review of farming methods such as the choices between share farming, contract farming and farm business tenancies (FBTs) (as set out in Chapter 11) is a prime example: whereas the FBT does not qualify for business reliefs for CGT and IHT, it can result in a higher return. It is a question of commercial choice.

HOBBY AND RECREATIONAL FARMING – THE GOOD LIFE OR A NIGHTMARE?

12.3   The desire for many people to return to 'the country' has, over the years, been given much media publicity. The recent re-runs of the TV comedy *The Good Life* create an image at one end of the scale, while celebrities of the music and TV industries (and City workers) buying very expensive estates in beautiful parts of the West Country present a picture at the other. Likewise, with the recent fashion for tracing family roots back several generations via the Internet, people are more aware than ever of the UK's strong agricultural history. Prior to the Industrial Revolution, which in the grand scheme of things is not that long ago, over 70% of the UK population earned their living from the land. Hence, the desire to own a small farm or estate is a dream of many hardworking town and country dwellers alike.

The above factors could link quite closely to the interesting current position in the UK whereby, despite the recent recession, land prices are still maintaining their high levels and in some instances increasing in value. A number of factors, including world food shortages, underpin the current level of land prices.

For farmland in the Home Counties where a large percentage of the workforce is based in the City or the prosperous large towns surrounding London, the increase in land prices is not that surprising. There are the underlying factors of 'hope value' for development, the laws of supply and demand and the desire for privacy. There is an undeniable shortage of houses, and the proposals to build on the 'green belt' increase the demand for farm land.

At the risk of repetition from other chapters, a summary of the farm tax advantages is set out below:

- the ability to roll-over gains from business assets into another business asset, and the potential for ER for CGT.

- BPR and APR for IHT;

- the ability to claim 'sideways' income tax loss relief where losses are sustained and include some 'lifestyle' expenses;

- the ability to repair and improve the property whilst claiming maximum allowable input VAT and, where possible, maximum income tax relief.

All tax reliefs must be carefully scrutinised by the tax planner and it is essential that all the relevant conditions are met so as to take full advantage of each and every one of them. As with any business all expense claims must be wholly, necessarily and exclusively for the purpose of the farming trade or estate enterprise and the operation must be commercial and must be shown to be commercial. The terms of any contract or share-farming agreement must be carefully reviewed (see Chapter 11). Some agreements are no more than tenancies 'dressed up' as farming arrangements. Some arrangements are fragile and could fail HMRC scrutiny. It is imperative to have a well-drafted agreement.

Another area of concern is where 'recreational activities' are blatantly incorporated into the farming activities and subjective decisions have to be made between the allocation of expenses between business and private. Clear examples are shooting estates and farms that incorporate the stabling of private horses. The position of 'duality' must be given consideration eg horses being ridden around the farm to inspect crops, livestock, fencing etc, and recreational horses.

There can be examples where the owners/taxpayers can be greedy in their claim for business expenses, such as those creating large losses for income tax purposes but jeopardising the five-year rule and future CGT and IHT reliefs. The expenditure and income of recreational activities, eg shooting should be excluded except for the element of controlling vermin. Professionals must not only warn their clients of the potential problems of trying to claim such expenses, the professional must also provide evidence that the expenses that have been claimed show an underlying business purpose and a commercial advantage. The restriction of losses for farmers with a non-active trade is explained at **12.17**.

THE NEED TO REVIEW THE ACCOUNTS AND TAX COMPUTATION

12.4   With the farming industry moving towards greater diversification there is a need to consider carefully how business tax computations are prepared and to plan for protecting future tax reliefs.

When practitioners prepare the farm tax computation, the correct procedure is to remove non-farming income items and also to match the non-farming expenses to the income for classification (see Chapter 1). In practice, a lot of accountancy and tax practitioners are simply preparing a computation, which arrives at an accurate farm trading net profit or loss, and which has little regard to the allocation of expenses and income. It could be that income from items such as quota leasing and grazing by horses are inflating the profit to assist with the avoidance of the hobby farming rules. Diversified activities could form a separate activity so that separate accounts should be considered – enterprise accounts are a suggested alternative. Nevertheless, abuse of the 'hobby farming' provisions is foolhardy in the extreme, partly in view of the current high values of the farmland and farmhouses and the associated IHT reliefs.

As a practical tax-planning point, the affairs of all clients who are associated with farming must be reviewed to ensure the correct treatment of income and expenses. It will also be essential to review what future reliefs the client may need to claim. For example is there a question of the 'commerciality' of the farm or the business? It is also useful to ask such questions as does the client intend to claim APR for IHT purposes? If APR is lost will BPR still be available? (See Chapter 13.)

Another reason to check the tax computation is clearly to show the division between 'farming' and 'non-farming profit' because of the farmer's average claims (see **1.14**). The latter only relates to farming income. The importance of the classification of diversification as opposed to farming income and expenses is mentioned in a number of chapters. Whilst reviewing the tax computation it is essential to ensure that the trade is still eligible for tax reliefs that are dependent on 'business/commercial' status.

Another problem is that hobby farming loss relief rules are calculated on the fiscal basis (to 5 April) and this is often overlooked (see **12.5**).

It is worth considering the position where taxpayers might try to trigger notional cessations and recommencements in order to preserve the use of the losses. BIM75635 sets out the effective anti-avoidance position as follows:

'ITA2007/S67 does not deny relief where the trade was set up and commenced within the five years prior to the year of claim. This includes a notional commencement when a person enters the UK (ITTOIA/S17) and under ITA2007/S69(2) where there has been a complete change in the persons carrying on the trade. However, it is worth noting:

- The application of ITTOIA/S852(2) (notional trade) for a new partner joining a firm is not a deemed commencement for the purposes of Section 67. In other words it is necessary to look before that date of joining the partnership to determine whether a particular partner's loss relief needs to be restricted under this section (ITA2007/S69(2)).

- Husband and wife, or civil partners, are to be treated as if they were the same person. Any transfer of the trade between them will, therefore, not affect the operation of Section 67. A widow, widower, or surviving civil partner, is not, however, to be treated for these purposes as a wife, husband or civil partner, so that when a trade passes to a widow, widower, or surviving civil partner on death, a new run of losses must accrue before Section 67 becomes effective to deny loss relief.

- If a husband and wife, or civil partners, or either of them, control a farming or market gardening company and succeed to the company's trade, or if they, or either of them, carry on a trade which is taken over by the company (they and the company are regarded as the same person and the trade is treated as a continuous trade without regard to any discontinuance). (In this connection, 'control' has the meaning given by ICTA88/S416. See CTM60200 onwards.)'

Note: 'Control' has now the meaning of CTA 2010 ss 450 and 451 (ITA 2007 s 69(7)).

HOW CAN TRADING LOSSES BE USED?

12.5 The first point is to identify the genuine farm trading loss. Expenditure will be disallowed if it is not deductible in arriving at the true commercial profit on business or accounting principles. Attention needs to be directed towards the underlying purpose. Does the expenditure promote the business and earn profits from it? The test is always a commercial advantage, not moral interest. It is essential to establish the validity of the loss and to ensure that it is not restricted. Once the exact amount has been confirmed the destination must be decided.

A large number of farming reliefs can be overlooked by non-farming accountants, such as the ability to exclude woodland income (see **6.4–6.12**) when appropriate.

Loss reliefs that can be available to the farming business are as follows:

- set-off against total income in the year of the loss or total income of the preceding year (ITA 2007 s 64 (previously ICTA 1988 s 380));

- relief for losses in earlier years of trade carried back to the three years of assessment preceding the year of loss (ITA 2007 s 72 (previously ICTA 1988 s 381)). Earliest years are taken first;

- carry forward against subsequent profits of the same trade (indefinitely) (ITA 2007 s 83 (previously ICTA 1988 s 385));

- terminal loss relief on cessation, applied against earlier profits for the three years of assessment (ITA 2007 s 891);

- relief where pre-trading expenditure is set against income of year of assessment in which trade is newly set up (ITTOIA 2005 s 57) (incurred not more than seven years before);

- relief for losses on unquoted shares in trading companies (ITA 2007 s 131 (previously ICTA 1988 s 574)); and

- temporary extension of loss claim facility. The ability to claim the loss where ITA 2007 s 64 applies for 2008–09 and 2009–10. The extension adds a further two years to the existing facility to set a loss against profits of the preceding year. There is a cap of £50,000 in respect of each of the years 2008–09 and 2009–10 (ie £100,000 in total).

Trading losses suffered by the limited company are trapped in the limited company and only carried forward against future profits or carried back one year (CTA 2010 s 36) extends this to three years (see Chapter 8).

Income tax losses can be set against CGT of the individual under ITA 2007 s 71, formerly FA 1991 s 72 (see **14.7**). It is only the trading losses for the year of sale or preceding the year of capital disposal which are available to offset against the capital gain. In-depth planning is required in respect of the timing of the disposal of assets to coincide with difficult years of trading. ITA 2007 s 71 effectively brings unincorporated businesses in line with companies which can set trading losses against income and capital gains under TCGA 1992 s 8. Any trading loss which is not set against income or gains for current or preceding years is available to carry forward and set against future trading profits.

Income tax loss relief against gains is given in priority to relief for CGT losses brought forward from earlier years and in priority to annual exemption, which is therefore sometimes lost. So-called hobby farming losses do not qualify for relief against CGT, ie if they are disallowed for offset against total income and only carried forward against future profits (ITA 2007 s 83) then likewise they are not allowed under ITA 2007 s 71.

There is obviously great scope for the tax planner to utilise losses efficiently with regard to farm disposals and structure timing of expenditure to maximum use. Clearly, as part of the review of asset ownership, and tax efficiency, there is a need to review all proposals and plans to utilise the timing of the losses. From 6 April 2010 with the introduction of the 50% rate of income tax, loss planning is of key importance where loss relief can be at 50% not the 40% rate of income tax. The timing of property disposal for CGT is of prime importance as, under TCGA 1992 s 28(1), it is the date the contract is entered into, not the date of the conveyance, which is significant. If the contract is conditional it is the date the condition is satisfied under TCGA 1992 s 28(2), and hence this conditional element is vital when reviewing the exercise of an option (see Chapter 14). Chapter 14 looks at capital gains tax planning with the interaction of trading losses being set against capital gains and options.

It is essential that 'tax loss memoranda' are kept for all farmers with division between farming and non-farming to ensure the six year, 11-year rules are highlighted before HMRC attack the loss claim. The fiscal basis (to 5 April) of the hobby farming rules must be recalled – the calculation of profit in the sixth year is on an actual basis to 5 April, not an accounts basis.

LETTING INCOME ASSESSABLE AS TRADING INCOME

12.6   Chapter 11 sets out the tax advantages of contract farming over letting income.

Chapter 15 sets out the practical considerations of letting income with the associated IHT angles.

It is appropriate to deal with letting income losses in this chapter. However, before this is looked at in depth it is necessary to see how rents can be assessable as trading income. This is of prime importance for tax-loss management and links closely to the hobby farming rules. The ability to reclassify rents as trading income can be the difference between making or not making a trading profit in a year and therefore not being caught under the hobby farming rules.

So when is rent trading income? First, when a trader's business premises is sub-let and secondly where services provided by the landlord are of sufficient substance that the landlord is carrying on the trade of providing serviced accommodation. This would be a vital tax-planning tool to the diversifying farmer who is looking to maximise income from buildings. To qualify for a sub-let of farmer's business premises, the accommodation must be temporarily surplus to business requirements and the property must be used partly for the business and partly let. In addition, the rental income must be comparatively small, although the definition of this is not clear.

A prime example would be the subletting of part of a barn or building for another trade. Most farmers currently have this type of income in their accounts and the tax planner should ensure that it is assessed as trading income (see **15.2**).

The next stage is to look at the provision of serviced accommodation. Generally, following the decisions in *Gittos v Barclay* [1982] STC 390 and *Griffiths v Jackson* [1983] STC 184 HMRC try to move the status from trading income to other income. The VAT treatment of serviced accommodation cannot be overlooked, as rents from letting residential accommodation are normally exempt from VAT but serviced accommodation could be liable to VAT at the standard rate (see Chapter 9).

There is the dilemma, as so often, of choosing between a possibly more beneficial tax treatment and a possibly disadvantageous VAT position (see Chapter 15). Likewise trading income could be penalised by National Insurance Contributions.

LOSSES FROM RENTS RECEIVED AND FURNISHED HOLIDAY LETTING (FHL)

12.7   Furnished holiday lets (FHLs) are looked at as separate diversified activity (see **6.13–6.15**). Non-holiday letting income tax losses are carried forward against any future income from the letting income business (ITA 2007 s 118).

A company's losses from carrying on a UK property business can be set against total profits for the accounting period (CTA 2010 s 62). If not all the loss can be deducted in that accounting period it can be carried forward and deducted in the next accounting period (CTA 2010 s 62(4), (5)). The loss can be surrendered to another group company under the group relief rules but it cannot be surrendered as group relief in that later period. The restriction to loss relief in the opening years is set out in chapter **6.15**.

However, it will possibly all change for FHLs (see **15.37–15.40**) from 6 April 2011.

Losses from FHLs are currently allowable under the provisions of ITA 2007 ss 64 and 71 until 5 April 2011. This means that, in principle, they can be offset against total income in the year of the loss and the following year. In the opening years they can be offset against total income of the three years of assessment preceding that in which the loss was suffered (ITA 2007 ss 64 and 72), but this could cease from 6 April 2011.

Many diversifying farmers have sought to maximise their returns by moving from furnished letting income to furnished holiday lets. The advantage of the latter is the ability to claim losses under ITA 2007 ss 64 and 72, ie against total income in the year of the loss and the following year with all the advantages of the opening year's losses as set out above which could cease on 5 April 2011. Where furnished holiday accommodation was first let as furnished accommodation there can be a restriction under s 72, ie the holiday accommodation is deemed for s 72 to start when furnished lettings began, not when lettings as holiday accommodation began. (See also Chapter 15.) FHLs also qualify for entrepreneurs' relief (ER).

The government proposal as set out in their consultation document published in July 2010 is that from 6 April 2011 losses arising from FHLs are carried forward against the profits of FHLs. The aim of this suggestion would be to try to eliminate what is perhaps seen as abuse where, say, loan interest and repairs create losses which are offset against total income.

LOSSES IN STUD FARMING

12.8   Stud farming is farming for tax purposes (see **1.4**). The definition 'agricultural' is specifically extended to include the breeding and rearing of horses: IHTA 1984 s 115(4).

BIM55725 states:

'Following discussions with the Thoroughbred Breeder's Association (TBA) in 1982, Policy Division wrote to the association as follows:

"it has always been recognised that some ventures are by their nature unlikely to show a profit by the sixth year of trading and section 397(3) provides for loss relief to be continued after the fifth year where the claimant is engaged in a particular farming activity of an intrinsically long term profit making nature. We have long accepted that the breeding of thoroughbred horses is such a long term venture, and provided that a stud farming business is potentially profit making, we would not normally seek to invoke section 397(1) until after 11 years from the start of the business".

The Thoroughbred Breeder's Association have circulated this text to their members.

This letter does not mean, however, that all stud farming losses are relievable against other income up to 11 years from commencement. The requirement that the business should be potentially profitable (in other words, the question of whether Section 397 (3)(a) is satisfied) is important and should be checked in suitable cases. Nor should the letter be interpreted as meaning that the five year period is extended in cases where a run of losses arises in periods after a year in which a profit has been made, or in cases where a business is taken over as a going concern. Such cases should be dealt with individually on their merits.

Where the enterprise is clearly not being carried on on a commercial basis and with a view to the realisation of profits, a challenge under ITA2007/S66 (ICTA1988/S393A(3)) should be considered.'

Note: ICTA 1988 s 397 is replaced by ITA 2007 s 67.

Stud farms as a separate trading activity are looked at in **6.17**. Claims for IHT relief will also depend on the ability to prove commerciality.

FARMING LOSSES – TEST OF COMMERCIALITY

12.9   The tests for commerciality are very well set out in HMRC Manual BIM75615:

'ITA2007/S66 denies relief against general income etc (see BIM75605) unless the taxpayer can show that, during the period when the loss was sustained, the trade was being carried on on a commercial basis and with a view to the realisation of profit. For guidance on the meaning of "not on a commercial basis" see BIM75705; and with a view to the realisation of profits see BIM75710.

The provision was first introduced in 1960. The Chancellor of the day stated in the course of a Parliamentary debate on the Section:

"we are after the extreme cases in which expenditure very greatly exceeds income or any possible income which can ever be made and in which, however long the period, no degree of profitability can ever be reached".

These words should be borne in mind when considering the application of the Section to farming cases. The small farmer and the farmer farming marginal land genuinely trying to make a living from their farms in difficult circumstances are not caught.

Nor can the Section be used to deny relief to a farmer who incurs temporary losses while establishing an enterprise, for instance by building up a production herd or bringing land back into fertility, provided the enterprise in which he or she is engaged is likely in due course to become an economic undertaking. For example, it may take a farmer five years to clear and work land infested with bracken before there can be an expectation of profit. Relief under ITA2007/S64 should not be refused on the initial losses in such a case.

General guidance on Section 66 may be found at BIM75700 onwards.'

There is a let-out where farming is part of a large undertaking. This is set out in BIM75645 as follows:

'ITA2007/S67(3)a provides that relief is not to be denied where the loss-making farm or market garden is part of, and ancillary to, a larger trading undertaking. The subsection is designed to meet cases such as that of a butcher who makes a practice of fattening bullocks for his business, or a manufacturer who grows his own raw materials, or a seedsman or chemical manufacturer who runs a farm for testing or improving his products. Many farmers in current times will have diversified and this may give rise to claims for extended loss claims by virtue of being ancillary to and part of a larger undertaking. Such claims will need to be carefully examined and are unlikely to succeed unless the diversified activity has become the major part of the business and the original farming activity now supports and serves in a functional way the new diversified operation. For example if a working farm has been converted into a tourist attraction where the existence of farm animals including perhaps some exotic creatures is an integral part of the attraction. Tourist income (gate receipts, shop and café sales etc) is likely to exceed traditional farm receipts and farm labour is now more directed towards looking after the customer and enhancing the customer experience rather than maximising agricultural efficiency.

The phrase, 'part of, and ancillary to' should be interpreted strictly. 'Ancillary' means 'subservient and annexed to', 'part of' does not simply mean part of the business. It implies a close operating link with and contribution to the larger undertaking. (See Croom-Johnson J in *Cross v Emery* [1949] 31TC198.)

A review of the case law will show that these cases will turn on their own facts and it is suggested that useful areas to examine in this context are:

1.   The method by which the holding as a whole is run.

2.   The purpose of the operation.

3.   The strength of the links between the two.

4.   The contribution one makes to the other.

A very useful and more recent analysis on the meaning of ancillary can be found in the IHT case of *Williams (Personal Representative of Williams deceased) v HMRC* (SpC 500) by Special Commissioner Charles Hellier.'

BIM75650 sets out the principle on how HMRC look for avoidance with regard to tax losses.

'Taxpayers may attempt to avoid the operation of ITA2007/S67 by ensuring that the farming enterprise periodically makes an isolated profit. The most obvious year to pick for this purpose would be the sixth year, and then every sixth year thereafter.

Obviously there is nothing to say that a farm which has been unprofitable for five years could not make a profit in the sixth year. Furthermore, it may be possible for a taxpayer to arrange his or her affairs in a way that leads to the making of a genuine one-off profit.

But, especially in a case where substantial farming losses have been relieved against the income of a wealthy taxpayer, it may be worth checking to ensure that the profit has not been manufactured by means of artificial transactions or devices. These may, for example, include:

●   charging business expenses (especially interest paid) to the farmer's capital account or not including them in the accounts at all;

●   recognising sales and/or expenses in the wrong year;

●   manipulating opening or closing stock valuations.

●   These and similar methods are unacceptable and enquiries should therefore be made, in worthwhile cases, to ensure that the accounts include all the business income and expenses for the period concerned but only the business income and expenses for the period.'

STUD FARMING AND FARMING COMBINED

12.10   Where a taxpayer has losses from a stud farm and from a general farm business, for tax purposes there could be one business (ITTOIA 2005 s 859(1)). But HMRC apply an 11-year rule for stud losses and a five-year rule for farm losses. How does one apply that practice in this situation? Where is the preponderance of the activity?

It could be possible of course to try segregating the two trades and losses. There is nothing to stop the taxpayer producing separate accounts for the stud and the farm and then amalgamating them for tax purposes, with the stud losses being claimed for up to 11 years.

There is a view however that the loss is restricted to five years where farming is dominant. BIM55725 (see **12.8**) makes it clear that the 11-year rule is not a concession but simply the application of ITA 2007 s 67. Section 67 overrules the five-year restriction if there is an expectation of profit and the stud business could not reasonably have been expected to be profitable before the 11 years is up.

Most importantly however ITA 2007 s 67 is applied with regard to the 'whole of the activities' and 'the way in which the whole of the activities were carried out in the current tax year' (ITA 2007 s 68(4)). In this case only the stud satisfies the subsection, the farm does not. There is nothing in s 67 (previously ICTA 1988 s 397(3)) to allow it to apply where any part of the farming activities carried out satisfies the subsection. Separate accounts and trades seem to be the answer with a careful review of expenses where there are the two separate activities.

How to prevent a real farmer being classified as a hobby farmer

12.11   There is no doubt that in the current economic climate it has been difficult for a landowner to produce a profit from true farming after all overheads have been correctly allocated. This is particularly so if a farming unit has borrowings, staff commitments or rent to pay. Unless the word 'agriculture' is broadened it could be that a lot of farming units will be showing profits from diversification such as let property but losses on the actual farming activities. If these losses continue on the farming activity then the hobby farming rules might have to come into play. At the time of writing increased corn prices have helped but costs have also increased dramatically.

It is imperative that costs are allocated correctly and that non-farming income such as let property has its full share of overheads allocated against that enterprise. The CLA are lobbying for a broadening of the definition of agriculture to prevent this, but in the meantime the tax planner must take care when reviewing tax computations and enterprise accounts to ensure correct allocation.

At the other end of the scale is the recreational landowner who enjoys the lifestyle and would like to embrace the tax reliefs as a side issue. The tax planner must point out all the benefits, but at every stage warn of the need for commerciality and the prospect of attack by HMRC against the claim for expenses.

PROPERTY AND FARMING LOSSES AND TAX CREDITS

12.12   Many farmers and diversifying farmers with low earnings and losses are eligible for tax credits but often do not realise that this is the case. The complex area of tax credits is outside the scope of this book, but it is something that should be considered and reviewed.

HMRC have given some clarification regarding the relief for property losses. In their Tax Credits Helpsheet 825 HMRC confirm that if part of the loss a tax credit claimant has made in his property business 'arises from capital allowances or from agricultural land, that part of the loss may be set against other income which you (but not your spouse or partner) may have, either in the tax year in which the loss was made or in the following tax year.'

Partnership loss manipulation – 'sideways' loss claims

12.13   FA 2004 contained legislation with effect from 10 February 2004 to counter tax avoidance arrangements that exploit relief for trading losses through partnerships, which individuals can claim against their other income or gains. The rules only affect partners who do not spend a significant amount of time working in the trade when losses arise. This has been developed further through the Finance Act 2008.

The new rules involve the following loss claims.

- ITA 2007 s 64 – relief for trading losses against general income of the same or the preceding year of assessment (see **12.5**).

- ITA 2007 s 72 – relief for trading losses incurred in the early years of trade (see **12.5**).

- ITA 2007 s 24 – relief for loan interest paid.

- ITA 2007 s 71– trading losses relieved against capital gains (see **12.5**).

The provisions above are collectively referred to as 'sideways loss relief' (see **12.5**). A person (a non-active partner – ITA 2007 s 103B) who could get caught by the 'loss manipulation' provisions is someone:

- who is not a limited partner or a member of a limited liability partnership; and

- who does not devote a significant amount of time (at least ten hours per week on average) to the trade.

Where losses are incurred in any of the first four years in which the partner carries on the trade, 'sideways' relief will be allowed to that partner only on an amount of losses up to the amount contributed to the trade by him/her.

The time spent by the partner playing an active and personal role in the operations of the trade will be relevant, excluding activities such as:

- considering information to decide whether and how much to invest in a trade;

- considering reports and information provided largely by others about the progress of the trade; or

- taking decisions concerning the trade based largely on information provided by others.

Any loss, which a person cannot set against their other income or gains because of the new rules may be carried forward and set against later profits from the same trade, ie they will not be able to claim the 'sideways relief' but they may be carried forward under ITA 2007 s 83 (previously ICTA 1988 s 385).

The restrictions apply after any existing rules which restrict losses or interest that may be set off against other income or chargeable gains. The restrictions will apply to trading losses derived from expenditure incurred on or after 10 February 2004 (IR Press Release 8/04, 10 February 2004 and IR Notice, 10 February 2004).

What impact will this have on contract farming arrangements? (See **11.10–11.14**.) What are the practical implications for farming? The losses of non-active partners is restricted to the amount that partner actually contributed to the business. Questions have to be asked. How will this affect the non-active farmer? New farmers? What is 'active'?

The partner must spend a 'significant amount of time' contributing to the business, ie a minimum of ten hours per week on *average*. The partner must be personally involved in the activities of the trade. This may include a management role, eg instructing staff and accounting, but this does not include time spent deciding whether or not to invest and/or how much to invest, in the partnership or its trade. There will also be a similar restriction on the amount of interest relief that such partners may obtain. The answer at the time of writing is to review each situation and encourage farmers to record the amount of time they spend.

The tax planning key is to ensure that there is documentary evidence of the activity, diary, minutes of meetings, record of the involvement etc.

True commerciality

12.14   The twist of ITA 2007 s 72 is that relief should not be given, unless the trade was carried on throughout the relevant period, on a commercial basis and in such a way that profits in the trade could reasonably be expected to be realised in that period, or within a reasonable time thereafter.

This was tested in *Walsh v Taylor* [2004] STC (SCD) 48. Although HMRC denied relief on the normal 'hobby' rules, the Commissioner held that the trade had been set up to generate income and a profit. A planning point arising from this case is the need to keep sufficient evidence as to the business-like nature of his activities to be able to persuade the Commissioner.

Losses to be offset against gains (possible farm development gains)

12.15   Relief under ITA 2007 s 71 can only be given after losses have first been set against the claimant's other income under ITA 2007 s 64. It is thus not possible to claim loss relief against capital gains only, and it is inevitable that the personal allowance for the year will be lost.

The maximum amount of the claim is the amount chargeable to CGT in any year before deducting the annual exemption, so it may well be that the annual exemption is also unused. Losses can be set against gains on any type of asset, but relief is not available in a tax year beginning after the cessation of the trade in which the losses were incurred. The amount of loss relief to be set against income must be finally determined before relief against gains will be given. With the CGT rate of tax now at 18% and 28% (see **1.23**) and the top rate of income tax at 50% the use of losses in this way is possibly less attractive. Capital losses can be created via 'negligible loss' claims and also set against capital gains (see **7.30**).

Losses in the limited company – group loss relief

12.16   Chapter 8 looks at the limited company and the problems that farms encounter through trading as a limited company and they have been well documented.

As farming and diversification move forward in the twenty-first century, there is the possibility of new and varied structures. Groups of companies are a possible alternative and the ability to claim loss relief for farming or diversified activities against the current year's profits of other group companies is a consideration for the tax planner. For this purpose 'group' implies 75% or more common ownership.

It might be that a very successful business person trading through a separate company or group of companies chooses to purchase a farm and a diversified activity in separate companies which become part of the group and eligible for group loss relief.

Restriction of loss relief for individuals with a non-active trade

12.17   An individual who carries on a trade can currently offset losses arising in that trade against other income and gains, under provisions known as 'sideways loss relief' (see **12.5**).

HMRC believe that tax is being avoided by certain individuals using trades to intentionally create losses which can be used to offset their other income. Finance Act 2007, introduced measures to limit the amount of sideways loss relief available in the case of a non-active or limited partner (see **12.9**). The Finance Act 2008 extends this restriction to individuals, other than partners, carrying on a non-active trade. A non-active trade is broadly one on which the individual spends less than ten hours per week.

In these circumstances, the sideways loss relief available will be limited to £25,000 annually, although this restriction will not apply to qualifying film expenditure. No relief will be available where the loss arises in connection with any arrangement where one of the main purposes of the arrangement is to reduce the individual's tax liability by means of sideways loss relief. The changes applied from 12 March 2008, with transitional arrangements for periods straddling that date.

Sideways loss relief – Revenue & Customs Brief 2 March 2007

12.18   Revenue & Customs Brief 18/07 set out proposals for additional restrictions on amounts that a relevant partner may claim as relief for trading losses under ITA 2007 ss 64 and 72 (ICTA 1988 ss 380, 381) and ITA 2007 s 71 and these became effective from 2 March 2007. HMRC's approach is now set out at BIM72640.

Previously, the amount of trading losses for a tax year for which a non-active partner could claim sideways loss relief was restricted broadly to the amount of capital that the partner had contributed to the partnership.

Two changes affect the amount of trading losses for a tax year for which a relevant partner can claim relief:

- a purpose test for capital contributions by a relevant partner to a partnership when applying the existing restrictions based on capital contribution in ICTA 1988, ss 117, 118ZB and 118ZE;

- an annual limit of £25,000 (or, if lower, the amount of trading losses for that tax year for which the relevant partner can claim relief after applying existing restrictions in ss 117, 118ZB, 118ZE and 118ZL).

A relevant partner for this purpose will be an individual who, on or after 2 March 2007:

- carries on trade as a partner in a partnership at any time during the tax year; and

- is a limited partner, or any other partner who does not devote a significant amount of time to the trade in the relevant period for the tax year.

So what is a 'significant' amount of time? And what of the traditional farmer who has been forced to diversify in to 'paid employment'?

Personally engaged in activities carried on for the purpose of the trade

What is meant by a significant amount of time in the brief?

- An individual does not devote a significant amount of time to a trade in the relevant period for a tax year if, in that period, the individual spends an average of less than ten hours a week personally engaged in activities carried on for the purpose of trade.

How is significant time defined in real terms eg bookkeeping, VAT returns, meeting with land agents, accountants and solicitors will all be part of carrying on the trade. Work must be carried out to ensure all work is documented.

In summary the restriction on sideways relief for partnership losses is designed to block relief for investments made as a tax shelter, but is clearly capable of affecting genuine family businesses (especially, perhaps, in agriculture, because farms are more likely than other large businesses to be carried on by partnerships, and even a successful farm is likely to see the occasional large loss).

A family which has a portfolio of businesses, for example, may find that a member who is a partner in a business which makes a loss for a year, does not work for the requisite ten hours a week in that particular business. Or it may be that the older generation contributes capital and expertise, but a limited amount of time, to the family business due to ill health. Accordingly, it may be that business structures need to be re-examined.

It is fair to say that there is a connection between the statement above 'personally engaged in activities carried on for the purpose of the trade' and some of the recent IHT cases. For example, the *Earl of Balfour* case (see **13.50**) – another key point from the case being the amount of involvement by the deceased in managing the business.

Duality of purpose and personal benefit

12.19   HMRC have difficulty in accepting that expenses related to areas of farming are incurred wholly and exclusively for the benefit of a trade. In tax law this goes back to the concept of 'duality of purpose', where HMRC effectively try to argue that if someone enjoys what they are doing, any expenses associated with the activity are disallowable. They generally believe that such a trade is an attempt to achieve tax relief on the costs of a hobby and try to deny expenditure on the grounds that the taxpayer obtains private enjoyment from the expenditure.

HMRC are always concerned about duality of purpose and personal benefit.

The concept of duality is best explained by *Mallalieu v Drummond* (1983) 57 TC 330 where black clothing needed for an appearance in court was held to be needed for the more conventional use of clothing the body as well.

The legislation is contained in what is now ITTOIA 2005 s 34 which states:

'(1)   In calculating the profits of a trade, no deduction is allowed for –

    (a)   expenses not incurred wholly and exclusively for the purposes of the trade, or

    (b)   losses not connected with or arising out of the trade.

(2)   If an expense is incurred for more than one purpose, this section does not prohibit a deduction for any identifiable part or identifiable proportion of the expense which is incurred wholly and exclusively for the purposes of the trade.'

Problems arise where HMRC believe that personal pleasure is being derived from elements of the farm. Examples of this are escalating costs of vermin control, the horse or even the quad bike to inspect the farmland and farm/diversified activity, farm clothing and farmhouse expenses.

A thorough review of possible areas of 'duality' is recommended for all farmers and landowners.

Chapter 13

Planning the best use of APR and BPR for inheritance tax

Julie Butler

- **Maximising agricultural property relief (APR) and business property relief (BPR)**
  This chapter goes into more detail on this subject following on from Chapter 4 and Chapter 5. The problems of agricultural value and the risk of IHT relief being reduced to 50% are looked at in some detail. The complex issue of replacement property is also considered.

- **Avoiding failed potentially exempt transfers (PETS)**
  The subject of 'gifting now' is mentioned in Chapter 5 and this chapter looks in detail at, for example, how to avoid 'failed PETS'. With farming in decline and going through significant transformation with diversification there are worries that business gifts might 'fail' if the transferor dies within seven years and there is a change of business status with regard to the gift.

- **The case of *Farmer* – looking at the farm enterprise in 'the round'**
  The author considers this a significant case for the purposes of the diversifying farmer and landowner. The business of letting cottages and redundant farm buildings can be an integral part of the business of farming, land management and diversification. The successful claim for BPR against the whole of the farm business has to be reviewed in detail.

  One of the principles arising from the *Farmer* case is not just the potential ability to claim BPR on the business of letting farm properties when integrated with the main farming business but the need to look at every case 'in the round'.

- **The case of the *Marquess of Hertford***
  The case of the *Marquess of Hertford* – further endorsement of the 'net business' principle for BPR. The 'diversification' into opening a stately home to the public helped show the benefit of looking at the value of the business at its net value. 'No regard shall be had to assets or liabilities other than those by reference to which were 'used in the business.'

- **The case of *Balfour* – the 'investment business'**
  This case was successful for the taxpayer. *Balfour* is an extension of many of the principles of *Farmer* and the attempts by HMRC to disallow BPR through IHT 1984 s 105(3).

Looking at ways of protecting the mixed estate; the need to look at the involvement of the deceased; where the preponderance of the business lies; and tax planning through the interaction of *Dance*.

TOO VALUABLE TO PUT AT RISK

13.1   As mentioned, an introduction to the issues discussed in this chapter has been approached in Chapter 5. In addition, the inheritance tax (IHT) reliefs on farmhouses have been set out in Chapter 4. It is hoped that this has emphasised the benefits to the landowner that can be attributed to IHT reliefs for the farm and surrounding land. The case of *Dixon v IRC* [2002] STC (SCD) 53 gave an interesting insight into an attempt to claim agricultural property relief (APR) on a farmhouse linked to a very small holding of land.

There are considerable complexities surrounding BPR and APR. The purpose of this chapter is to emphasise how IHT reliefs are at risk with a move towards diversification. The tax planner must be aware of how to maximise APR and BPR, their interaction and also the major pitfalls surrounding the reliefs.

This chapter looks at the case of *Farmer (Farmer's Executors) v IRC* [1999] STC (SCD) 321, as it involved a successful claim for BPR on a diversified farm, which in this case was the farming business which included let property as part of the overall business. This case has featured throughout the book. This is followed by the case of the Earl of Balfour, *HMRC v Balfour* [2010] UKUT 300.

AGRICULTURAL VALUE

13.2   Agricultural value is first looked at in Chapter 4 (**4.22** and **4.32**) regarding the subject of the agricultural value of the farmhouse. When reviewing APR claims, an understanding of the definition of agricultural value is vital. It is limited by Inheritance Tax Act 1984 (IHTA 1984) s 115(3): 'The value which would be the value of the property if the property was subject to a perpetual covenant prohibiting its use otherwise than as agricultural property.' Priority is given to APR under IHTA 1984 s 116(1) before BPR (ie when property qualifies for both reliefs, APR is given first). Development value is considered at **5.44** and tax-planning values are considered at **5.47**.

District Valuers (DVs) have been known to argue for a discount of between 30% and 40% from market value in determining the agricultural value of a farmhouse (see **4.32**). However, the circumstances in each case will determine the 'natural unit' (per the House of Lords decision in *Duke of Buccleuch v IRC* [1967] 1 All ER 129) for valuation purposes (ie the importance of 'lotting' (see **13.7**) the appropriate area for valuation cannot be over-emphasised). Further, DVs tend to apply the s 115(3) definition by assuming that the property was subject to an agricultural tie; however, this is thought to be unduly restrictive, in that the statute refers to 'use' rather than to agricultural 'occupation' (see **13.15**).

The first point that any tax planner would worry about (as indeed would their clients) is the fact that the market value of agricultural property might well exceed its agricultural value and there could, therefore, be a differential which would be chargeable to IHT over and above the APR claim. It is useful at this point to look at the scope of the claim for BPR, as it may be that the relief could be claimed against the difference. (See **5.44**)

Differences in value could be caused by such factors as the granting of sporting rights, which would have a considerable influence on the value of agricultural land. As the raising of pheasants is not deemed to be (in most instances) for the purpose of the production of food, then this would not qualify as 'agricultural' activity, and so a BPR claim could be pursued. In these instances, as with any form of diversification, it will be necessary to examine exactly how the shoot is run and how it is managed as a business. Thus, the landowner might not secure APR on the value of the sporting rights, but it could well be that BPR would be claimed on the business element of the shoot, ie the exploitation of those rights. It is vital that there is evidence that the business has been commercial in this instance.

As a practical planning point, it is advisable to see that every asset owned by landowning clients is reviewed and consideration must be given to whether APR can still be claimed. If APR is going to be lost due to diversification, careful consideration must be given to ensure that BPR can be claimed. The BPR claim depends on the existence of a commercial business. HMRC do not just look to see that it was a business, but a business carried on for commercial gain. The previous chapter (Chapter 12) on recreational hobby farming gives direction with regard to commerciality, and case law should be reviewed when considering the BPR claim.

The problem with defining 'agricultural value' is that there has been very little market evidence of the value for property subject to such a covenant. Any restrictive covenant must make that property worth at least 'one bid' less than an unencumbered property.

WHEN AND WHERE DOES APR APPLY?

13.3   APR does not just apply on death. It also applies to lifetime transfers, for example settling on discretionary trusts (see Chapter 17), transfer of value by a close company and lifetime potentially exempt transfers (PETs).

BPR applies to worldwide business assets.

APR was originally limited to agricultural property situated in the UK, the Channel Islands or the Isle of Man (IHTA 1984 s 115(4)). The Finance Act 2009 s 122 extended relief to agricultural property situated in EEA states where inheritance tax would be due. This became effective from 22 April 2009.

What categories of property attract 100% relief?

13.4   Protecting 100% relief is first discussed in **5.2** on protecting the farm assets. The following categories for APR can be considered in more detail here:

- Property where the transferor has the right to vacant possession, or can obtain vacant possession within 12 months (IHTA 1984 s 116(2)(a)) extended to 24 months by Inland Revenue Extra-statutory Concession (ESC F17). Where there are joint owners of the land, the conditions are held to be satisfied where the aggregate of their interest carries the right to vacant possession (IHTA 1984 s 116(6)).

- Property let on a tenancy that began on or after 1 September 1995, irrespective of the terms of that tenancy (IHTA 1984 s 116(2)(c)). This date was the date on which the provisions of the Agricultural Tenancies Act 1995 came into effect. In repealing the Agricultural Holdings Act 1986, a landlord is entitled, from that date, to give a tenant farmer a farm business tenancy (FBT), with whatever security is agreed between the parties and without an automatic right for the tenant farmer to renew the lease or pass the tenancy to his successor.

- Let agricultural land where the terms of the tenancy are such that the value of the land is not diminished by the tenancy, notwithstanding the freeholder's inability to obtain vacant possession (ESC F17).

- The land has been owned since before 10 March 1981 and satisfies the conditions for APR that applied under the pre-1981 rules (IHTA 1984 ss 116(2)(b) and 116(3)). This gives relief for a 'working farmer' where the tenant is a company controlled by the taxpayer or a partnership of which he was a member, or the tenant was an employer or relative. However, relief is restricted to the lower of £250,000 of agricultural value or 1,000 acres of land (FA 1975 Sch 8 para 5(1)).

The period of ownership and occupation for APR must be considered under IHTA 1984 s 117. One of the following two rules must apply:

- The required occupation must exist throughout the two years before the transfer and must be by the transferor.

- The required occupation must exist throughout seven years before the transfer, during which period the transferor must own the property (see **5.5**).

What categories of property attract 50% relief?

13.5   The risk of 50% relief was first looked at in **5.2**. Relief at 50% is given against the agricultural value of land that is let on a tenancy that commenced prior to 1 September 1995 and does not allow the landlord vacant possession within 24 months (IHTA 1984 s 116(2)). Where the lease commenced before 1 September 1995 but the current tenant did not become entitled to the lease until after that date (perhaps as a result of statutory succession to an old Agricultural Holdings Act tenancy), relief is provided at 100% (Inland Revenue Interpretation IR21).

Where a tenancy is acquired by succession, succession is treated as taking place at the death of the tenant from whom the succession occurs (FA 1996 s 185(5)–(6)).

BPR of 50% is given against the value of the following categories of business property:

- any land, building, machinery or plant used wholly or mainly for a business carried on by a company controlled by the transferor (IHTA 1984 s 105(1)(d));

- any land, building, machinery or plant used wholly or mainly for a business carried on by a partnership in which the transferor is the partner (IHTA 1984 s 105(1)(d)):

- land, building, machinery or plant held by trustees in which there is an interest in possession and the asset and the property was used wholly or mainly for the purposes of a business carried on by the beneficiary entitled to the interest in possession (IHTA 1984 s 105(1)(e));

- quoted shares in a company that does not carry on an excluded business (IHTA 1984 s 105(1)(cc));

- quoted securities in a company that does not carry on an excluded business (IHTA 1984 s 105(1)(cc)).

Definition of 'agricultural property'

13.6   In order for the tax planner to make use of the maximum IHT reliefs it is essential that there is a clear understanding of what the definition of agricultural property is for APR. APR is a 'property'-based relief and in most farm businesses it must be clear where BPR will apply when APR does not apply.

'Agricultural property' is defined as:

- agricultural land or pasture (IHTA 1984 s 115(2));

- buildings occupied with agricultural land or pasture and use for arable farming, livestock rearing or intensive fish farming (IHTA 1984 s 115(2));

- such cottages together with land occupied with them as are of a character appropriate to the property (see **5.5**);

- such farm buildings together with land occupied with them that are of a character appropriate to the property;

- such a farmhouse together with land occupied with it which is of a character appropriate to the property (see Chapter 4);

- short rotational coppice (FA 1995 s 154(2)) (see **6.11**);

- land used for growing energy crops and biofuels – farming by concession (see **6.47** and **6.48**);

- stud farms (IHTA 1984 s 115(4)) (see **6.17**);

- land in habitat schemes (IHTA 1984 s 124C) (see **13.24**); and

- land within conservation schemes (dedicated to wildlife habitats) (see **13.24**).

As mentioned earlier, the granting of sporting rights is generally considered as a non-agricultural activity and therefore BPR is required. The case which gives clarity to this is *Earl of Normanton v Giles* [1980] 1 WLR 28.

Lotting

13.7 A farm can be sold as a whole or in natural lots. Lotting is the consideration for the valuation of agricultural property where different areas would be sold as separate lots. If one or more of the lots is wholly exempt from IHT then it is unnecessary to value that lot. However, where a lot is partially exempt, this gives rise to an interesting tax-planning point with regard to valuations of the parts that are not exempt, eg surviving spouse exemption.

When considering valuations, it must be assumed that the seller marketed the property in a way which produced the best selling price. If appropriate, it must be divided into lots, or the items assembled to sell them together. This can be of importance in relation to farmhouses and in light of the case of *Earl of Ellesmere v IRC* [1918] 2 KB 735. In *Duke of Buccleuch v IRC* [1967] 1 AC 506, the general principle is that there is no obligation that there should be lotting into natural units, but the property should be marketed in such a way as to produce the largest price provided that it did not involve excessive time or effort (see **5.10**).

Inheritance tax (IHT) – interaction with capital gains tax (CGT)

13.8 Death is not a chargeable event for capital gains tax (CGT) purposes but lifetime transfers are. It is generally accepted that values which attract 100% APR vary enormously due to different circumstances. It is essential that a tax planner is involved in the tax implications of the valuation together with the client's circumstances and, above all, future plans are given consideration.

The restrictive nature of entrepreneurs' relief (ER) introduced in the Finance Act 2008 should be taken into account when looking at the CGT position of lifetime transfers.

Concerns over future CGT liabilities can be overcome when it is clear that the client wants to hold on to the family property (hopefully) forever. However, if it is obvious that the beneficiaries cannot afford to maintain the estate as it stands and might have to dispose of certain assets, then the whole interaction with CGT and IHT relief is of prime tax-planning importance.

Where future disposals are intended after death it can be argued that the tax planner should try to argue high values for IHT relief on death and therefore high CGT base costs, provided IHT relief is available. Whilst there are those who argue that there is only one value (ie market value), there can often be a vast difference as to what this value is considered to be by the DV and the professional valuer/land agent. Examples to test the tax planner are as follows:

- 'Hope value', that is land used for farming that has planning potential. Ideally, BPR can be claimed on the difference between the agricultural and hope values (see **5.33**).

- The valuation of related property. As defined by IHTA 1984 s 161(2), the concern here is that an artificial assumption can be made in order to determine the value of property for tax purposes. Related property rules are of wide application and must be given consideration by the practitioner in a large number of cases (see **5.12–5.14**).

- Restrictions on disposal of the asset.

- Unquoted shares and securities.

- A lease being treated as a settlement.

- The interaction of debts (see **5.15**).

- Farm cottages (see **5.5**).

It has often been argued that the concept of an open market is a hypothetical one. It is generally considered that the market which is perceived is one where the property is offered for sale to the world at large and that all potential purchasers have an equal opportunity to make an offer and it is widely known the property is for sale. Reference can be found in *Lynall v IRC* [1972] AC 680, HL.

Assets not qualifying for APR

13.9   The tax planner should identify what assets might not qualify for APR to see if they in turn would attract other forms of IHT relief such as BPR. Some of these points were touched upon in Chapters 4 and 5. Problem areas for APR are listed as follows:

- farmhouses, the ownership of which has been separated from the land or where the land is not held by a company controlled by the owner of the house (see Chapter 4);

- very large farmhouses or mansions occupied with small let acreages (see Chapter 4);

- non-commercial agricultural units (see Chapter 12);

- land used for non-agricultural purposes as set out in Chapter 1. Examples of this are grazing by horses, income from industrial units, share-farming agreements with minimum return, non-agricultural activities, etc;

- buildings used for rearing birds or fish (does not qualify as the use of the 'land' for agriculture unless it is ancillary to the farm (IHTA 1984 s 115(2)));

- farm cottages that are not occupied by farm workers or former farm workers nor their dependants (see *Farmer (Farmer's Executors) v IRC* [1999] STC (SCD) 321 at 13.26); and

- 'hope value' (see **5.33**)

If the APR claim could fail then a BPR claim should be researched for support protection, this is looked at in **5.56** with the question of a 'BPR audit'.

INTERACTION OF AGRICULTURAL PROPERTY RELIEF (APR) AND BUSINESS PROPERTY RELIEF (BPR)

Priority of APR

13.10   As mentioned previously, under IHTA 1984 s 116(1) APR takes precedence over BPR. Thus, in a situation where both of these are available in respect of a single asset, APR is given first and BPR second. This can often happen in the case of farmland left in the estate of a deceased person where there are assets that do not qualify for APR. If the relevant conditions are fulfilled, APR will remove from charge the value of the land, valued for agricultural purposes, and the balance could form a claim for BPR provided the relevant conditions are satisfied. It is therefore essential to see how and when BPR can be claimed.

Claiming BPR

13.11   Further to Chapter 5, which showed examples of where BPR can be claimed (see **5.2**), further detailed conditions to achieve BPR are as follows:

- a business carried on as a sole trader or the partners' interest in a business carried on in partnership (IHTA 1984 s 105(1)(a), (3));

- any unquoted shares in a company that does not carry on an 'excluded business' (IHTA 1984 ss 105(1)(bb), (3)); or

- unquoted securities (opposed to shares) in a company that was controlled by the transferor before the transfer (IHTA 1984 s 105(1)(b)).

For BPR to be available, the business concerned must not consist 'wholly or mainly' of any of the 'excluded businesses', which are:

- dealing in securities, stocks or shares;

- dealing in land or buildings;

- making or holding investments (IHTA 1984 s 105(3)) (see **5.20**).

For tax-planning purposes these definitions are of great importance for the diversifying business including the limited company. As the nature of farmland and buildings moves from trading property to possible investment properties with diversification, eg let industrial buildings, there is a risk of not qualifying for BPR; likewise, the farmer who decides to move from 'growing crops to growing houses' (see Chapter 14). In recent years the greatest attack on the BPR claim has been under s 105(3) – see **5.22**.

BPR more favourable than APR

13.12   In what circumstances is BPR available because APR does not fully cover the liability?

- Businesses or shares attributable to agricultural property where the ownership requirement is not yet sufficient for APR but which replace non-agricultural business assets (so that the assets qualify for BPR under the replacement property rules).

- Non-controlling unquoted shareholdings in a farming company.

- The assets of a farming business other than land and buildings.

It should also be noted that BPR does not have the territorial limits of APR, ie it is not restricted to the UK, the Channel Islands and the Isle of Man and now EEA states; it applies worldwide (see **13.3**).

There has been a trend in the UK farming community to expand overseas to try to use superior markets, interact with UK operations etc, and the eligibility for BPR/APR should be considered in each case.

Replacement property – business property with agricultural property

13.13   The tax planner should be aware of the definition of replacement property in the context of IHT planning. In order to understand these rules it is necessary to review the rules regarding the period of ownership. No BPR is available unless the property or replacement property has been owned by the deceased throughout the two years immediately preceding his death or by the transferor throughout the two years immediately preceding a chargeable lifetime transfer (IHTA 1984 s 106).

The property concerned can satisfy the period of ownership if it is a replacement for a property which has previously qualified for BPR (IHTA 1984 s 107). The test that is applied is whether BPR would have been available on the property previously owned if there had been a transfer of value immediately before it was replaced (IHTA 1984 s 107(1)(b)). It is interesting to note that there can, in principle, be any number of replacements that together make up the two-year qualifying period of ownership. The eligibility for BPR on a property that has been replaced necessitates a two-year period of ownership for that original property (IHTA 1984 s 107(2)), unless it would itself qualify as replacement property for the property transferred on an earlier disposal.

Agricultural property or the landed estate can provide practical choices for replacement property. There are real-life situations which can require the practical use of agricultural/landed estate, eg:

- sheltering development profits in farming/the landed estate;
- sheltering business gains in farming/the landed estate;
- sheltering wealth from IHT.

The classic 'hope value' shelter is where farmland is sold for development and the gain is rolled over in to an agricultural property as an eligible business asset for CGT (thus sheltering the CGT liability) and potentially sheltering the asset for IHT via the replacement asset rules but will agricultural property/the landed estate qualify as replacement property?

It is not uncommon for a successful entrepreneur to turn to agriculture late in life. The fondness of the English for farming as a pastime is well documented. Whilst the assets of the entrepreneur remain within his business, he may pass them to the next generation with the benefit of substantial tax relief – BPR. On a successful sale of the entrepreneur's business he now faces a new problem. The substantial value which has been protected by BPR is represented by cash, which, unless invested in qualifying property, will be taxed very heavily in the event of his death without having distributed it among his family and survived seven years.

An attractive option for the retired entrepreneur might seem the purchase of landed estate including, typically; a home farm in hand, some let farms and local facilities such as part of a village. The estate will be run as a composite whole. The question arises as to how far the entrepreneur has succeeded in reinvesting into property which provides IHT relief. Generally APR will be allowable but problems will arise where let properties are not occupied for the purpose of agriculture. Depending on the location of the estate such properties might command a premium value because of their setting. BPR will not be available on such properties if, taking the estate as a whole, IHTA 1984 s 105(3) applies to treat it as consisting wholly or mainly of making or holding investments. BPR could apply to these cottages under IHTA 1984 s 110 and the case of *Farmer (Farmer's Executors) v IRC* (1999) STC (SCD) 321 helps explain the successful claim for BPR on let cottages; likewise the case of *Balfour* (see **5.55**).

What guidance can be obtained to help explain the problems of the movement of replacement assets between BPR and APR? What guidance is given by the HMRC IHT manuals?

IHTM25303 states:

'The Ownership Test: Changes in the nature of the business – For the purposes of the ownership test (IHTM25301) the nature of the business carried on by (or on) the business property need not be the same throughout the two year period. But there must have been a business throughout that period.'

IHTM25312 provides a very useful replacement property chart.

IHTM25313 sets out a limitation of relief for replacement property. There is an anti-avoidance provision which prevents a business owner from buying a much more expensive property shortly before death or transfer. Clearly it can be quite special tax planning to predict the exact date of death.

IHTM25313 however quotes as follows:

'When the replacement property (IHTM25311) provisions apply, IHTA84/S 107(2) restricts business relief by providing that the relief shall not exceed what it would have been had the replacement or any one or more of the replacements not been made. For this purpose a replacement resulting from the formation, alteration or dissolution of a partnership, or from the acquisition of a business by a company controlled by the former owner of the business, is to be disregarded, IHTA84/S 107(3).

IHTA84/S 107(2) is an anti avoidance provision and its purpose is to prevent a person who has qualified for relief from purchasing a much more expensive property shortly before death or making a transfer.

Your approach to IHTA84/S 107(2) should be practical. If there is any indication that the deceased's/transferor's resources were being rearranged into considerably more extensive business property to obtain increased relief on the death/transfer, you should refer the case to Technical Group (IHTM01081). Otherwise you should adopt a reasonable approach aimed at quantifying and agreeing the restricted relief in a practical way. The approach you should adopt is illustrated by two examples: one of which deals with the equivalent provisions for replacement property in an agricultural relief case (IHTM24136) and another which involves agricultural and business relief (IHTM24137)'.

Careful planning must be taken with switching replacement assets between those qualifying for BPR and APR.

Gifts with reservation of benefit (GROB)

13.14 With concerns over the ability to achieve IHT relief on death the diversifying farmer might want to gift the farm now but still reserve possession and enjoyment.

This is first looked at in **5.11**. The rules have been highlighted in *Lyons PRs and Alloro Trust v HMRC* (2007) SpC 616 before the Special Commissioners.

In this case, the power of Finance Act 1986 s 102 was considered. This provision is drafted in wide terms to catch gifts with reservation of benefit, and to ensure that the gifted property is subjected to IHT by being treated as part of the donor's estate. There are, in fact, two limbs of s 102. Section 102(1)(b) is the one which receives the most attention. This is the provision which catches the gifted property if, at any time, it is not enjoyed to the entire exclusion of the donor. It is this provision which requires clients to be advised that, for example, a rent paid by the donor to the donee for the occupation of gifted land must not only be commercial at the date of the gift, but must also remain an up-to-date commercial rent. But s 102(1)(b) is the second hurdle. Section 102(1)(a) may be regarded as the first hurdle, requiring the gifted property to be regarded as subject to a reservation unless possession and enjoyment of the gifted property has been bona fide assumed by the donee. The Special Commissioner held that the taxpayer had fallen at both hurdles in *Lyon's PRs and Alloro Trust v HMRC* (2007) SpC 616.

It is now impossible to look at the GROB rules without having some regard for the pre-owned assets (POT) legislation (see **5.27**).

Obviously, a certain amount of judgement is required in ascertaining the existence of a reservation of benefit in relation to a gift. It is probably sensible to err on the side of caution, however, if in any doubt. Farming clients should be warned so they can advise if they want action to be taken.

This situation has been emphasised with the introduction of the POT legislation (see **5.27**). No POT charge will be made if the assets fall into the individual's estate under the GROB rules. This is a good opportunity to consider market rent charges for assets, where there could be deemed to be any retained benefit.

Agricultural occupation

13.15 The property must have been occupied for agricultural purposes throughout the relevant period in order to qualify for APR (see **13.4**). There can be a problem with farmhouses where the farmer becomes ill, goes into a nursing home or hospital, expecting to return, but does not do so by the time of this death, in which case technically the farmhouse does not attract APR. In such cases, HMRC are known to give relief provided there was every expectation of return and that, for example, the house had not been let or put on the market in the interim. Periods of up to 24 months of non-occupation in such circumstances have been known (see **4.35**). The case of *Atkinson* (see **5.48**) raised issues around this question – HMRC are appealing.

Inland Revenue Extra-statutory Concession F16 allows farm cottages, which are not occupied, for agricultural purposes at the date of death, but nonetheless they have to be treated as so occupied, if occupied by an ex-employee or his spouse and provided that the occupation is protected either under a contract of employment or by statute (see **5.5**). This is where the case of *Farmer (Farmer's Executors) v IRC* [1999] STC (SCD) 321 comes into play (see **13.25–13.45**) as a possible protection to obtain IHT relief.

Dance – loss to donor

13.16   This case was looked at in Chapter 5 – (see **5.56**) for consideration of loss to donor principle.

There are tax-planning opportunities to transfer surplus 'investment assets' from a mixed estate to ensure that the core preponderance of activities lies with the farming and the active husbandry (see **13.53**).

Dance considers BPR at the date of transfer on assets transferred. The tax planner must also look at the business status of the asset transferred at the date of death.

The current restructuring of the ownership of farmland and farming business units under diversification can include gifting to the next generation. This largely involves making a gift now under the PET rules. Consideration must be given not only to CGT on this gift, or potential CGT, but whether there will be BPR or APR on a 'failed PET'. These are sometimes just known as the clawback rules (see **5.17**).

WHAT IS A 'FAILED POTENTIALLY EXEMPT TRANSFER' (PET)?

13.17   Where there has been a PET followed by the donor's death within seven years, no tax would have been payable at the time of the transfer, but IHT may become due by virtue of the death. This is known as a 'failed potentially exempt transfer' (a 'failed PET'). BPR is available against the PET if the conditions for obtaining a relief were fulfilled at both the date of the PET and the date of the subsequent death (IHTA 1984 s 113A(1)). Similar rules apply to transfers to discretionary trusts (IHTA 1984 s 113A(2)).

In order for BPR to be available on the failed PET, or the recalculation of the lifetime chargeable transfer, two conditions must be satisfied:

- the property must qualify as a 'relevant business property' for BPR at the time of the death (IHTA 1984 s 113A(3)(b)); and

- the recipient of the lifetime gift must have retained the property given until the death of the transferor or, if earlier, his own death (IHTA 1984 s 113A(3)).

The conditions are applied strictly. Although property moving between an individual and a settlement in which he has an interest in possession is ignored for this purpose, as for all other purposes of IHT (IHTA 1984 s 49), any other change in ownership denies the relief. Hence, a transfer of property between spouses, whilst an exempt transfer for IHT purposes, could cause any BPR on a PET to be removed if the donor dies within seven years.

An example is where a farmer transfers part of the farm, say development land, to his son. The transfer is eligible for BPR, but the son sells the land two years after the date of transfer and does not replace the business asset. The father dies three years after the transfer, so there is a risk of a failed PET or clawback.

How can a failed PET be avoided?

13.18 In the same way that BPR is available on a PET that becomes chargeable by virtue of the death of the donor within seven years, APR is also available (IHTA 1984 s 124A).

Obviously, one factor that cannot be planned exactly is the date of death of the donor. Carrying out tax planning around ill or very ill clients requires great sensitivity. Practical work can involve a regular review of the lifetime gifts and, of course, warning the transferor and transferee at the point of transfer. There are a large number of changes to the gift that can take place over the seven years and not all landowners and donors may be aware of them. The aim of this section is to highlight the fact that, where gifts that should qualify for BPR or APR are made, it is vital that any predictable changes to the assets transferred over the next seven years are planned out for tax purposes and by the same token actual changes are reported to the tax planner.

Agricultural property replaced by agricultural property

13.19 In a similar position to BPR, there is provision to cover the situation in which the agricultural property that was gifted is sold and replaced by other agricultural property that is owned at the date of death (IHTA 1984 s 124B). APR and BPR reliefs are only available where both the disposal of the original property and the acquisition of the replacement are made in a bargain at arm's length, or on such terms as would be contained in such a bargain (IHTA 1984 s 124B(2)). Clearly, this means that disposals and subsequent purchases must be carefully monitored between family members and associates. The time limit of three years or such longer period as HMRC may allow is also the same (IHTA 1984 s 124B(2)(a), (5)(b)). The conditions for the relief are then applied to the original, and replacement, property so that the transferee must have owned the original property at the date of the disposal and the replacement as from the date of the acquisition. The properties must have been occupied for purposes of agriculture during these times and the replacement property must be agricultural property immediately before the death (IHTA 1984 s 124B(3)). As with BPR, where the donee dies before the donor the rules are applied at the death of the donee (IHTA 1984 s 124B(5)). The similar position is when business property replaces agricultural property. The donee should ideally check with the donor's tax adviser about all prior replacements on acceptance of the gift.

Length of occupation or ownership

13.20 There are provisions for BPR where the conditions as to length of occupation or ownership are not satisfied, but the farm was acquired on a previous transfer that did qualify for relief. It is further necessary that it should be only these conditions that prevent relief on this occasion and that one of the transfers should be on death (IHTA 1984 s 121). Provision is made for the replacement of property between the two transfers. As with the general replacement rule, relief is restricted to the lower of the agricultural values of the replaced and present farms (IHTA 1984 s 121(2)). Where, on the previous transfer, only a part of the value qualified for relief as where the earlier transfer was a part purchase, only a like part can be reduced on the present transfer (IHTA 1984 s 121(3)).

Transferee retaining ownership

13.21   In a similar position to BPR, there is a condition that the original property transferred must be owned by the transferee from the time of the transfer to the death of the transferor (or the earlier death of the transferee) (IHTA 1984 ss 124A(3)(a), (4)). Where property is settled on trusts in which there is no interest in possession, the trustees are to be treated as the transferee (IHTA 1984 s 124A(8)). It is imperative that transferees keep the transferor and their tax adviser fully aware of all changes of ownership and occupation, and ideally before the change.

Continuing agricultural use by the transferee

13.22   It is essential that, where the original property is agricultural property prior to the death of the transferor or, if earlier, that of the transferee, it should have been occupied by the transferee (or another) for the purpose of agriculture throughout the relevant period (IHTA 1984 s 124A(3)(b)). Care must be taken where the original property consists of shares in a farming company and so, in this instance, it will suffice that the company that owned the land and farm was occupied for the purposes of agriculture throughout the period (IHTA 1984 s 124A(3)(c)). The replacement by agricultural property is mentioned above. Satisfaction of the tax rules should also be achieved by replacement with business property (see **13.19**). BPR criteria are essential.

What happens when a gift of a BPR property is sold and an agricultural property purchased? If the donor then dies within seven years of making the gift, is any relief available on the failed PET? In HMRC's view, BPR is available if the agricultural property satisfies the requirements for business property (eg if it is farmland farmed by the donee), but neither relief is available if it does not satisfy the BPR criteria (eg if it is farmland let to another person) (Inland Revenue Interpretation RI 95).

The tax planner must review all gifts in the last seven years of any farming client to ensure that any potential risk of the loss of BPR/APR is highlighted to the parties concerned and such rescue action as is required is taken. Once again this highlights the need for agricultural property to continue to embrace all 'business' not 'letting criteria'.

Gift of a share in a farm

13.23   When gifts of shares of property are made, this could impact upon the size of the PET. These gifts are always calculated using the 'discrimination of the estate' concept. This principle was looked at in the case of *Arkwright Williams' Personal Representatives v IRC* [2004] STC (SCD) 89. This involved the gift of a half-share in a farm to the daughters of a farmer, Mr Williams. The Special Commissioner decided that the value of Mr Williams' share should be discounted to take into account the right of occupation of Mrs Williams. For example, when a father gifts half of his house to his daughter (tenants in common), as she also lives there, this should take father and daughter into the exemption from gifts with reservation of benefit (see **5.11**) (IHTA 1984 s 102(4)). Under the circumstances, a 15% discount is applied to the mathematical half of the vacant possession value of the farm immediately before Mr Williams' death which he could not have sold without consent.

LAND WITHIN CONSERVATION SCHEMES AND SET-ASIDE

13.24   Farmland and related buildings which have been dedicated to wildlife habitats on or after 26 November 1996 qualify for 100% APR, where the normal ownership tests have been satisfied. Land used in such a scheme must be managed in accordance with the scheme. Whether or not this type of diversification arises from genuine concerns over conservation or the attraction of the grant, it is encouraging to know that it does attract full 100% IHT relief through APR (IHTA 1984 s 124C).

As the explanation of the jargon listed at **1.17** shows, it can be considered a logical progression that as decoupling and modulation both refer to 'environmental' conditions and agri-environmental schemes, more and more land will fall under this heading. However, with corn price at the time of writing this has not been the case (see **20.15**).

Set-aside land is still regarded as 'farm land' for APR; it is merely that part of the land is fallow whilst the remainder of the land continues in production. If there are buildings on the set-aside land they will qualify for APR if used in the *farming* business. If they are converted for other use, it could be possible to regard them as having a retained agricultural value on which the relief is due, and a non-agricultural value over and above the agricultural value on which a claim for BPR would be made if appropriate (see **13.2**). For more detail on set-aside land, see **2.4**.

FARMER (FARMER'S EXECUTORS) v IRC

13.25   *Farmer (Farmer's Executors) v IRC* [1999] STC (SCD) 321 has been mentioned throughout this chapter and the book and it is worth looking at the case in full detail. The interaction of *Balfour* is also considered important and it is considered that the points made in *Farmer* underpin some of the principles of *Balfour* (see **13.51**). Not only is the case considered to be very helpful to the diversifying farmer wanting to protect IHT reliefs, but it also gives the reader an example of how an appeal is dealt with. It highlights sections of the Taxes Act and other cases that are relevant to the important interpretation of IHTA1984 s 110, the net value of the business.

Areas that are focused on are the basis of appeal, the facts and the issues of the case, together with the evidence and arguments produced by the executors.

In addition, the history and structure of the farm and lettings are looked at. Finally, there is an examination of HMRC's arguments and the reasons behind the final decision.

This case has already been looked at briefly in **5.5** and it is again mentioned in **15.2**.

Considering the position 'in the round'

13.26 One of the principles arising from the case is that when the factors have been considered, it is necessary to stand back and consider the position 'in the round'. In this case this included deciding on whether the business was trading or consisted mainly of making or holding investments.

Let us look at the basis of the appeal. Mr A B Farmer and Mr C D E Giles, the executors of Frederick Farmer (the deceased), appealed against a notice of determination dated 30 April 1998 that the business known as Home Farm, which formed part of the estate of the deceased at his death on 17 February 1997, consisted mainly of making or holding investments within the meaning of IHTA 1984 s 105(3) and so was not relevant business property for the purposes of s 104 of the Act.

Chapter 1 of Pt V of IHTA 1984 (ss 103–114) gives relief for relevant business property by providing for a percentage reduction in the value transferred. At the date of the death of the deceased, the relevant parts of ss 103, 104, 110 and 114 provided:

> '103 ... (3) In this chapter "business" includes a business carried on in the exercise of a profession or vocation, but does not include a business carried on otherwise than for gain.

> 104 ... (1) Where the whole or part of the value transferred by a transfer of value is attributable to the value of any relevant business property, the whole or that part of the value transferred shall be treated as reduced – (a) in the case of property falling within section 105(1)(a) below, by 100%.

> 105 ... (1) Subject to the following provisions of this section ... in this chapter "relevant business property" means, in relation to any transfer of value – (a) property consisting of a business or interest in a business ... (3) A business or interest in a business ... are not relevant business property if the business ... consists wholly or mainly of one or more of the following, that is to say, dealing in securities, stocks or shares, land or buildings or making or holding investments ...

> 110 ... For the purposes of this chapter – (a) the value of a business or an interest in a business shall be taken to be its net value; (b) the net value of a business is the value of the assets used in the business (including goodwill) reduced by the aggregate amount of any liabilities incurred for the purposes of the business ...

> 114 ... (1) Where any part of the value transferred by a transfer of value is reduced under chapter II of this part of this Act by reference to the agricultural value of any property ... such part of the value transferred

as is ... so reduced under that chapter shall not be reduced under this chapter.'

Chapter II of Pt V of IHTA 1984 (ss 115–124) gives relief for agricultural property by providing for a percentage reduction in the value transferred.

The facts and issue of the case

13.27   At the date of his death, the deceased owned the freehold of Home Farm at which he carried on a farming business. He also let properties at Home Farm, which were surplus to the requirements of the farm. The Inland Revenue accepted that the business carried on by the deceased did not consist wholly of making or holding investments but argued that it did consist mainly of making or holding investments, with the result that relief for relevant business property was excluded by IHTA 1984 s 105(3). The executors accepted, on the authority of *Martin (Moore's Executors) v IRC* [1995] STC (SCD) 5, that the letting of property consisted of making and holding investments but they argued that the business carried on by the deceased consisted mainly of farming with the result that the relief given by IHTA 1984 s 104(1)(a) applied, and was not excluded by IHTA 1984 s 105(3).

Accordingly, the issue for determination in the appeal was whether the business carried on by the deceased consisted mainly of farming (as argued by the executors) or mainly of making or holding investments (as argued by the Inland Revenue). The net value of the business, as referred to in IHTA 1984 s 110, had not been formally agreed and the parties requested a decision in principle. The position on s 110 is looked at in Chapter 5 (**5.33**).

Evidence presented by the taxpayer

13.28   A bundle of documents was produced by the executors. It included copies of the accounts of the business for the seven years ending on 31 December 1995 and for the period from 1 January 1996 to 17 February 1997 (the latter being the date of death of the deceased). The bundle also included a plan of Home Farm. In addition, Mr A B Farmer produced a large framed aerial photograph of Home Farm at the hearing. Mr A B Farmer the son of the deceased, and one of his executors, and Mr Gerard Hanley Carter, the farm manager of Home Farm, oral evidence on behalf of the executors.

Structure of the farm

13.29   In about 1969 the deceased purchased the freehold of Home Farm. At that time the deceased was about 60 years old and had already succeeded in a number of other businesses. He continued to be involved with at least one other business, a countryside park, but no business other than that carried on at Home Farm was in issue in the appeal.

Home Farm had a total area of about 449 acres, broken down as follows.

Breakdown of total area on Home Farm

Arable land	274 acres
Grassland	60 acres
Farmhouse, farm buildings, their curtilages, etc	9 acres
Woodland	98 acres
Rented properties and their curtilages and tracks	8 acres

Total 449 acres The area of Home Farm remained unchanged during the eight years prior to the death of the deceased. At the time of its purchase by the deceased, Home Farm had the benefit of a planning permission for a dwelling house and the deceased subsequently built the dwelling house. The deceased managed Home Farm on a businesslike basis. He instructed a firm of agricultural consultants and had regular meetings with them. Representatives of the agricultural consultants visited the farm and looked at the crops and machinery. The deceased had a business plan and budgets were produced to monitor profitability. He was also registered for VAT. The deceased liked his farm to be well equipped with machinery, which was maintained to a high standard and replaced regularly. He also let out any buildings which were not required for use by the farm. He treated the whole of Home Farm as a single business of which he was the sole proprietor. He operated one bank account into which all receipts were paid.

Each year a firm of chartered accountants prepared a 'Balance Sheet and Trading and Profit and Loss Account' for 'F Farmer Esquire trading as Home Farm'. These were unaudited accounts compiled from records, information and explanations supplied to the chartered accountants. They related to the single business, which included the farm and the lettings. In this decision they are referred to as 'the business accounts'.

History of the farm

13.30 Home Farm is on sand and so needs treatment to make it productive as a farm. It is, however, good for root crops. At the relevant time, the main crop was wheat but some root crops (potatoes and carrots) were grown as well. In evidence Mr Carter said that one-fifth was potatoes from which it was assumed that one-fifth of the acreage that was farmed was used to grow potatoes. Because yields were low, the farm aimed at the quality market.

Although Home Farm employed a number of employees in earlier years, by 1989 there were only two full-time employees, namely a farm manager and an assistant farm manager. Mr Carter was appointed as farm manager as from 10 April 1989. The terms of his appointment were set out in a letter to him from the agricultural consultants which said that, in addition to his salary, he would be paid a percentage of the farm profits, which included the estate rentals. An assistant farm manager was appointed in 1992 on similar terms. Casual labour was employed for seasonal tasks such as bagging and grading potatoes and for estate maintenance work, such as fencing. In evidence Mr Carter estimated that there would be four or five casual staff in a year.

Before his appointment as farm manager at Home Farm, Mr Carter had had a lifetime's experience in farming and had been employed as assistant farm manager at another estate of 250 acres which had grown vegetables and seed crops and which had a staff of ten. At Home Farm, Mr Carter's responsibilities included everything that happened on the estate including cropping, selling, buying in seed vegetables, seed contracts, liaison with markets, overseeing the shoot, safety, tracks, fences, cottages, and 'keeping the tenants happy'. If a tenant had a problem, he went to Mr Carter to sort it out. In evidence Mr Carter estimated that he spent 90% of his time on the farm and 10% of his time on the lettings; the assistant farm manager spent 95% of his time on the farm and 5% on the lettings; and the casual staff did not spend any time on the lettings with the possible exception of 'a bit of painting or mowing'.

The deceased and Mr Carter used to meet once a week and go around the estate. Mr Carter prepared a weekly report, which mentioned matters such as the weather, prices, etc. The deceased and Mr Carter had meetings with the agricultural consultants three times a year. There was one such meeting at the end of each year when they discussed results and forecasts; there was another meeting in May; and another at harvest time. At each meeting the budgets were checked and rechecked and the agricultural consultants advised on European Union provisions.

Facts and history surrounding the lettings

13.31   Mr A B Farmer (the son of the deceased) has a BSc degree in estate management. In 1971 he qualified as a solicitor and thereafter practised in a firm of solicitors. In 1989 his firm merged with another firm and Mr A B Farmer then retired from practice as a solicitor. In the same year his mother died. The deceased was then about 80 years of age and so Mr A B Farmer assisted his father with his business interests. He was not employed by his father, but rendered monthly invoices for his services as a consultant. These payments were shown in the business accounts as professional fees. In 1989 Mr A B Farmer reviewed all the lettings and ensured that future lettings were on a commercial basis. Later, he looked after the renewals of the leases and licences and completed forms for the Ministry of Agriculture, Fisheries and Food (now DEFRA). He spent about a day and a half each week on work connected with Home Farm and, of that, about 30% was spent on the farm and about 70% on the lettings.

At the date of the death of the deceased, there were 23 tenancies. One was an agricultural tenancy of a farm cottage occupied by a former farm worker and it emerged at the hearing that the value of that property was probably entitled to APR. Of the remaining 22 tenancies, six were of original farm cottages; four were of original farm buildings or barns converted for use by small businesses; four were of original farm buildings used for storage; three were of mobile homes placed by the deceased; two were of stable blocks, one of which was let with some grazing land; one was of a staff bungalow which was let with some stables and grazing land; one was of a pre-fabricated bungalow built by the deceased; and one was of redundant land for the storage of timber. The plan of Home Farm showed that the buildings which were let were grouped in two main clusters towards the centre of the estate, and the grazing areas which were let were contiguous with the clusters of let buildings.

Most of the residential lettings were shorthold tenancies for either six months or one year; the other lettings were either by licence by letter for one year, or by leases for one year which excluded the provisions of the Landlord and Tenant Act 1954 ss 24–28. There was one licence of a converted barn for commercial use which was, exceptionally, for five years. This longer term was granted because, although the deceased had provided the materials for the conversion, the tenants had provided the labour to produce a purpose-built gymnasium and the deceased therefore wished to give them a longer licence than usual. In evidence Mr A B Farmer said that he and his father did not want to grant long-term leases, which might affect the future use of the estate. The cottages had not been let to individual tenants until the shorthold legislation had come into force.

In respect of the let properties, the deceased was responsible for landlord's repairs as required by statute and also provided water for which tenants paid. If a tenant had a problem which required immediate attention, such as a blocked drain, then the tenant approached Mr Carter or the assistant farm manager. Mr A B Farmer dealt with the renewals of the leases and licences.

Contents of the business accounts

13.32   The business accounts related to the activity of a single business carried on by the deceased. The following details have been extracted from the business accounts.

Details from the business accounts of Home Farm

Year ending	Total turnover	Non-rental turnover		Rents received	
31.12.89	£216,065	£142,254	(65.84%)	£73,811	(34.16%)
31.12.90	£210,421	£115,134	(54.72%)	£95,287	(45.28%)
31.12.91	£270,108	£175,488	(64.97%)	£94,620	(35.03%)
31.12.92	£182,928	£87,264	(47.71%)	£95,664	(52.29%)
31.12.93	£258,168	£139,791	(54.15%)	£118,377	(45.85%)
31.12.94	£340,089	£218,612	(64.28%)	£121,477	(35.72%)
31.12.95	£386,289	£258,802	(67.00%)	£127,487	(33.00%)
01.01.96 to 17.02.97	£285,280	£134,113	(47.01%)	£151,167	(52.99%)

The non-rental turnover includes sales of farm produce, revenue grants received from the Ministry of Agriculture, Fisheries and Food (now DEFRA), and profit on the sale of fixed assets used in the farm.

The business accounts showed separately the direct cost of farm sales but the overhead expenses did not differentiate between expenses relating to the farm and expenses relating to the lettings. Mr A B Farmer stated that his father had not been interested in breaking down the expenses between the farm and the lettings.

Probate values

13.33   The deceased died on 17 February 1997 and Home Farm was included in his estate at the date of his death. The probate value of Home Farm was agreed at £3.5 million. Of that, £2.25 million related to the farmhouse, farm buildings and farmland and it was agreed that that value qualified for 100% APR. The sum of £2.25 million included £600,000 for the farmhouse, which was used as an office for the entire estate and £145,000 for the house occupied by Mr Carter, the farm manager. The other £1.25 million related to the let properties.

Arguments put forward by the executors

13.34   For the executors, Mr Tallon QC first argued that, in reaching a decision, it was necessary to consider all the circumstances over a period of time and not to take an arbitrary date or a 'snapshot': he cited *FPH Finance Trust Ltd v IRC* [1944] AC 285, 26 TC 131, HL and also *Martin (Moore's Executors) v IRC* [1995] STC (SCD) 5.

Next, Mr Tallon argued that the word 'mainly' in IHTA 1984 s 105(3) was used in its ordinary everyday sense of 'chiefly' or 'principally' and involved no more than deciding whether the letting activities predominated. He cited *Miller v Owners of the Ship Ottilie* [1944] KB 188, CA, at 190 and 191; *Minister of Agriculture, Fisheries and Food v Mason* [1969] 1 QB 399, at 404, and *Hall (Hall's Executors) v IRC* [1997] STC (SCD) 126, at 129 and 131 (see **6.22**). He also cited *Furness v IRC* [1999] STC (SCD) 232 (see **6.22**) as authority for the view that it was necessary to look at the business in the round. He distinguished *Sywell Aerodrome Ltd v Croft (Inspector of Taxes)* [1942] 1 KB 317, 24 TC 126, which, he argued, was not concerned with the meaning of the word 'mainly'.

In deciding which of two activities of a single business constituted the main part of that business, Mr Tallon proposed four relevant tests, which he placed in order of priority.

- The first test was the extent to which the proprietor and his employees were engaged in each activity. In this appeal there were only two full-time employees and Mr Carter spent 90% of his time on the farm and the assistant farm manager spent 95% of his time on such activities.

- The second test was the amount of income or turnover produced by each activity; in this appeal the farm turnover exceeded the letting turnover for six out of eight years.

- The third test was the amount of capital employed in each activity. In this appeal £2.25 million of capital was employed in the farm and £1.25 million in the lettings; although the figure of £2.25 million included the dwelling house it was used as an office and so was used for agricultural purposes; the figure of £2.25 million also included the sum of £145,000 for the farm manager's house and that was also used for agricultural purposes.

- The last test was the contribution of each activity to the overall profit of the single business. Mr Tallon argued that one reason why profit was the least important test was because different activities could have different profit margins and profits from some activities, such as farming, could be very volatile.

In *Furness v IRC* [1999] STC (SCD) 232, the court had considered both gross and net profit but Mr Tallon argued that gross profit was a better indicator, especially in this appeal where farm prices were so volatile. In *Hall (Hall's Executors) v IRC* [1997] STC (SCD) 126 there had been no mention of profits, just of turnover. IHTA 1984 s 103(3) merely provided that the business had to be 'carried on for gain' and did not provide that there was no relief if there were losses.

Mr Tallon concluded by arguing that the single business carried on by the deceased at Home Farm qualified for 100% BPR, although the provisions of IHTA 1984 s 114(1) operated to restrict the BPR to that part of the value which was not entitled to APR.

Arguments put forward by the Inland Revenue

13.35   For the Inland Revenue, Mr Twiddy accepted that it was necessary to look at the business over a period of time and he also accepted that the period from 1989 to 1997 was representative.

However, Mr Twiddy went on to argue that IHTA 1984 s 103(3) defined a business for the purpose of the relief as a business 'carried on ... for gain', which, in the present context, meant profit. Accordingly, the whole thrust of the legislation was geared to looking at profits and so, in considering what a business 'mainly' consisted of, it was primarily necessary to have regard to the profits. In *FPH Finance Trust Ltd v IRC* [1944] AC 285 at 303, 26 TC 131 at 149 Viscount Maugham indicated that 'mainly' related to more than half the income. In *Hall (Hall's Executors) v IRC* [1997] STC (SCD) 126 at 129 the Special Commissioner had directed his mind to profit and not to turnover and had asked whether the activity made a profit. In *Furness v IRC* [1999] STC (SCD) 232 at 237, although the Special Commissioner had said that he had looked at the business in the round, he had then gone on to base his decision on the allocation of the net profits. Mr Twiddy also cited *Sywell Aerodrome Ltd v Croft (Inspector of Taxes)* [1942] 1 KB 317 at 328, 24 TC 126 at 137 and went on to argue that certain figures which he had produced demonstrated that the net profits (or losses in four years out of eight) of the farming business were swamped by the net profits of the lettings.

Finally, Mr Twiddy argued that, in applying the capital test, it was necessary to look at the use of the capital. He argued that, although the sum of £2.25 million had been granted APR, it included the dwelling house built by the deceased which was valued at £600,000 and that was not capital employed in the agricultural activities. There was also the farm manager's house valued at £145,000, and a cottage valued at £60,000 and neither represented capital employed in agricultural activities.

Reasons behind the decision

13.36   In considering the arguments of the parties, it is convenient first to consider the point made by Mr Twiddy that, because IHTA 1984 s 103(3) refers to a business carried on for gain, the principal factor to be considered, when deciding if a business consists 'mainly' of making or holding investments, is the net profit of each part of the business. In this connection the decisions in *Miller v Owners of the Ship Ottilie* [1944] KB 188 and *Minister of Agriculture, Fisheries and Food v Mason* [1969] 1 QB 399 are of assistance.

The issue in *Miller* was whether a cook employed on board a fishing trawler, who suffered an injury by accident, was entitled to compensation under the Workmen's Compensation Act 1925. Section 35(2) of that Act provided that it did not apply to such members of the crew of a fishing vessel who were remunerated 'wholly or mainly' by shares in the profits. The appellant was paid a weekly basic wage of £2 3s 9d, risk money of £1 5s 0d and food valued at 18s, making a total of £4 6s 9d. In addition, he was entitled to a share in the profits which amounted in his case to £7 9s 0d per week. The Court of Appeal held that as three-fifths of his remuneration was derived from a share in the profits, the only possible conclusion was that he was remunerated 'mainly' by shares in the profits and so the Act did not apply to him.

From this authority the principle can be derived that the word 'mainly' has to be considered within the statutory context in which it appears. In *Miller* the statutory context required a decision as to how a person was remunerated and the fact that more than half of his remuneration came from a share in the profits meant that he was 'mainly' remunerated by shares in the profits.

The issue in *Minister of Agriculture, Fisheries and Food v Mason* [1969] 1 QB 399 was whether an employer was entitled to a repayment of selective employment tax. The Selective Employment Payments Act 1966 s 2 provides that a repayment is due if the establishment was engaged by way of business in certain activities and if more than half the employees were employed 'wholly or mainly' in connection with those activities. The employer owned a house and employed a gardener to look after the flower garden and the vegetable garden. As more vegetables were grown than the owner could use, some were sold. The gardener spent between 10% and 15% of his time on the commercial side of the vegetable garden. In deciding that the repayment was not due, the Divisional Court held that the requirement that an employee should be employed 'wholly or mainly' in connection with certain business activities meant that the employee must devote more than 50% of his time to those activities.

Again, in *Mason* the word 'mainly' took its meaning from the statutory context in which it appeared. The statute required that the employee had to be employed 'mainly' in connection with certain business activities and that meant that he had to spend more than half of his time on them.

Applying the principles in *Miller* and *Mason* to the facts of the present appeal, the statutory context of IHTA 1984 s 105(3) requires a decision to be made as to whether a 'business consists' mainly of making or holding investments. Section 105(3) does not limit the decision to one particular factor of a business, for example whether the gains of a business are derived mainly from making or holding investments; the decision must be of what 'the business consists'. That indicates that all the relevant factors of what a business consists require consideration.

If IHTA 1984 ss 103(3) and 105(3) are considered in their statutory context, it appears that s 103(3) defines the type of business which can obtain relief for relevant business property, namely, a business carried on for gain; whilst s 105(3) provides that, where there is such a business, it is not relevant business property if it consists wholly or mainly of making or holding investments. Hence, it does not appear necessarily to follow that, because the making of net profits is part of the definition of a business, the level of net profits is to be the only, or principal, test for determining whether 'the business consists' mainly of making or holding investments.

Neither party argued that s 110(a), which refers to the net value of a business, was relevant for the purposes of interpreting s 105(3); but if s 103(3) were thought to be relevant then the same could be said for s 110(a).

Factors surrounding definition of 'the business consists'

13.37   Having considered the statutory context of IHTA 1984 ss 103(3) and 105(3), the conclusion is that the level of net profits is not the only, or even the principal, factor in deciding whether a business consists mainly of making or holding investments: all the factors of which a 'business consists' require consideration.

That leaves open the question as to what factors should be considered in deciding whether a business consists mainly of making or holding investments and to answer that question a reference is now made to the other authorities cited by the parties to see what principles they establish.

The decision in *Sywell Aerodrome Ltd v Croft (Inspector of Taxes)* [1942] 1 KB 317, 24 TC 126 is of limited assistance in this appeal because it concerned the issue as to whether profits which arose wholly from the ownership and occupation of land, which was assessed under Schedules A and B, were also assessable under Schedule D. The decision that they were not was reached on the grounds that Schedules A and B taxed the deemed income from ownership and occupation of land by reference to its annual value and no further tax was payable in respect of any income referable to the same property.

In *FPH Finance Trust Ltd v IRC* [1944] AC 285, 26 TC 131, HL the issue was whether the income of a company 'consisted mainly of investment income' because that determined whether it was an investment company for surtax purposes. The company dealt in stocks and shares and in earlier years profits from its business were very much larger than its income from investments. Later, however, it had trading losses and its investment income was its only income. Viscount Maugham stated ([1944] AC 285 at 305, 26 TC 131 at 150) that it was wrong to take a period of great losses in trade without also considering the results of the preceding periods: if the periods when the company had trading income were also considered, the conclusion must be that the company was not an investment company.

Authority given by the case

13.38   That decision is, therefore, authority for the view that consideration should be given to the overall picture. Also, the phrase requiring interpretation in that appeal was 'the income whereof consists mainly of investment income'. That is not the issue in the present appeal where the phrase requiring interpretation is whether 'the business consists mainly of making or holding investments'.

The decisions in *Hall (Hall's Executors) v IRC* [1997] STC (SCD) 126 and *Furness v IRC* [1999] STC (SCD) 232 were both concerned with the same issue as this appeal, namely whether a business consisted wholly or mainly of making or holding investments. They were both decisions of the Special Commissioners and were, therefore, decisions on their own facts. In one the appeal failed, but in the other the appeal succeeded.

In *Hall* the deceased had owned and managed a caravan park. Lots for caravans were let to tenants who owned the caravans, but the caravans had to be bought and sold through the deceased, who received commissions on the sales. There were also some holiday chalets let on leases for 45 years. The rents and standing charges totalled a little less than 84% of the total income of the business and the Special Commissioners held that the activities of the business consisted mainly of making or holding investments.

It is interesting that in *Hall* the leases were for 45 years, which can be distinguished from the short leases in the present appeal. Also, the Special Commissioners considered what 'the activities of the business consisted of' and regarded income as the relevant factor on the facts of that appeal.

Furness v IRC [1999] STC (SCD) 232 also concerned a caravan park, which was licensed for 218 static caravans and eight touring caravans. There were also about seven rallies each year. The static caravans were owned by the residents but had to be purchased from, and sold to, the owner of the site. Various facilities were provided at the park for entertainment and amusement. The owner of the park, and three full-time employees, carried out a considerable amount of office and maintenance work including the cleaning and repairing of caravans, maintenance of the grounds, and servicing of the drains. The profits from the sales of the caravans, together with sundry sales and rally charges, exceeded the profits from the rentals from the caravans.

The Special Commissioner held that the business did not consist 'wholly or mainly of holding investments' because the net profits of the caravan sales exceeded the caravan pitch rentals. Also, the owner and his employees undertook a very considerable amount of work in maintaining the park and its structures, a level of activity not normally found in a business, which consisted wholly or mainly of the holding of investments. From that decision, the principle can be derived that it is necessary to look at the business and its activities in the round and to consider all the relevant factors.

Factors relevant to the decision

13.39 Applying the principles derived from the authorities to the facts of *Farmer (Farmer's Executors) v IRC* [1999] STC (SCD) 321, the following factors can be identified as being relevant when determining of what the business consists:

- the overall context of the business;
- the capital employed;
- the time spent by employees in making the business function;

- the turnover; and

- the profit.

These factors will now be considered in turn.

Overall context of the business

13.40   In considering the overall context of the business, it is relevant that the business of Home Farm is that of a landed estate and that most of the land is used for farming. The area occupied by the let properties is a small proportion of the total area. Also, most of the let properties are of buildings, which were formerly used by the farm but are now superfluous to the requirements of the farm. They are located towards the centre of the land, which comprises the estate: most of them would not exist if it had not been for their previous connection with the farm. To that extent it could be said that the let properties are subsidiary in function to the main function of the estate, which is its use as a farm. In this connection it is also relevant that the terms of the leases and licences are short and that is unusual for properties that are used for investment purposes. It is also relevant that the farming business was conducted in a businesslike way with the help of agricultural consultants, professional farm managers, business plans and budgets. By contrast, the lettings appear to have been conducted personally by the deceased, with the assistance after 1989 of Mr A B Farmer.

Capital employed in the business

13.41   The next relevant factor is the capital employed in the business. It was agreed that, of the total probate value of £3.5 million, £2.25 million obtained APR and £1.25 million represented the value of the let properties. However, Mr Twiddy sought to argue that the value of the dwelling house (£600,000) and of the farm manager's house (£145,000) should be deducted from the amount of capital employed in the farm for the purposes of the present calculations. As the farm manager's house was occupied by Mr Carter, who devoted 90% of his time to the farm, it would appear that, at the most, 10% of the value of his house might be treated as capital employed in the lettings. As far as the dwelling house was concerned, the evidence was that the value included some woodland, which was managed on a commercial basis; also that it was used as an office for the whole business. It may be that some reallocation of the capital value should have been made for such part of the office use as related to the lettings, but there was no evidence as to the extent of such use. On the other hand, it emerged at the hearing that one of the cottages valued at £60,000, and included in the figure of £1.25 million for let property, was occupied by an agricultural tenant and might therefore be entitled to APR.

It was decided that the evidence was not sufficient to establish that any alteration should be made in the probate values. That means that, for the purposes of this appeal, £2.25 million was the capital employed by the farm and £1.25 million was the capital employed by the lettings.

Time spent by the employees

13.42   The third relevant factor is the time spent by the employees and consultants in making the business function. Here the evidence was that Mr

Carter spent 90% of his time on the farm; the assistant farm manager spent 95% of his time on the farm; and the five casual workers spent all their time on the farm. Mr A B Farmer spent one-and-a-half days each week on estate business of which about 70% was concerned with the lettings. The exact time spent by the agricultural consultants was not known but the evidence was that it was all connected with the farm.

Turnover

13.43 The fourth relevant factor is the turnover. In two years out of the eight (1992 and the last period) under consideration, the non-rental turnover exceeded the lettings turnover. The evidence of Mr A B Farmer and of Mr Carter that the explanation for the fluctuations in the farming turnover, and for the very low farming turnover in 1992, was primarily related to the volatility of the potato market was accepted. Mr Carter mentioned that the price of potatoes ranged from £150 per tonne in 1995 to £30–£50 per tonne in 1996. Another factor was that the price of cereals fluctuated with the weather. The last period (1 January 1996 to 17 February 1997) was not typical as there was an oversupply of potatoes in October 1996 and prices became depressed. Also, that period included rents for 14 months, whereas there would have been little in the nature of farm sales in January and February 1997.

Profit

13.44 The final factor is profit. The business accounts showed the farming sales separately from the rental income and also showed the direct cost of the farming sales from which it was possible to calculate the gross profit of the farming sales. However, because the business accounts did not distinguish between the overhead expenses relating to the farm on the one hand and the overhead expenses relating to the lettings on the other, the business accounts did not give figures for the net profit of the farm and the net profit of the lettings.

At the hearing, Mr Twiddy produced some figures which assumed that all the depreciation and vehicle expenses were incurred by the farm and that one-quarter of the professional fees related to the farm and three-quarters to the lettings. The result of these assumptions was that the farming activities either made a net loss or a small net profit, whereas the letting activities made a substantial net profit.

An extract from Mr Twiddy's figures

Year ending	*Agricultural gross profit*	*Agricultural net profit (loss)*	*Lettings net profit*
31.12.89	£46,600	(£1,120)	£70,637
31.12.90	£38,541	(£7,684)	£89,298
31.12.91	£65,757	£28,470	£86,602
31.12.92	£11,189	(£30,250)	£86,185
31.12.93	£46,895	£16,313	£107,699
31.12.94	£132,537	£88,475	£105,435
31.12.95	£162,560	£112,276	£114,576
01.01.96 to 17.02.97	£16,256	(£46,680)	£132,901

Deducting the cost of farm sales from the figure for farm sales, and then adding revenue grants received and the profit on the sale of fixed assets, derived the agricultural gross profit. Deducting all the depreciation, all the vehicle expenses, and 25% of the professional fees from the agricultural gross profits derived the agricultural net profit. The lettings net profit was derived by deducting 75% of the professional fees from the rental income.

The agricultural gross profit as a percentage of total gross profit (Mr Twiddy's figures)

Year ending	Agricultural gross profit as a percentage of total gross profit
31.12.89	38.7
31.12.90	28.8
31.12.91	41.0
31.12.92	10.5
31.12.93	28.4
31.12.94	52.2
31.12.95	56.1
1996–97	9.7

The lettings net profit as a percentage of total net profit: for these purposes any loss is ignored (Mr Twiddy's figures)

Year ending	Lettings net profit	Lettings net profit as a percentage of total net profit	Total net profit
31.12.89	£70,637	100	£70,637
31.12.90	£89,298	100	£89,298
31.12.91	£86,602	75	£115,072
31.12.92	£86,185	100	£86,185
31.12.93	£107,669	87	£124,012
31.12.94	£105,435	54	£193,910
31.12.95	£114,576	50.5	£226,852
1996–97	£132,901	100	£132,901

When Mr Twiddy's figures were put to Mr A B Farmer in cross-examination, he accepted that they were feasible and that he could not dispute them. However, the assumptions on which the figures were based did not accord with the oral evidence of Mr A B Farmer, which was more probable. Mr Farmer said that some of the depreciation related to the let buildings and he also said that about 70% of his fees related to the lettings.

Mr Twiddy's figures only gave deductions for depreciation, vehicle expenses and professional fees and not for the other overhead expenses which included bank charges, rates, insurance, heating, lighting, telephone, repairs, renewals, upkeep and other sundry expenses. Also, Mr Twiddy's figures did not give any deduction for depreciation of the let buildings; they assumed that Mr A B

Farmer spent 75% (and not 70%) of his time on the lettings; and they made no allowance for the fact all the fees of the agricultural consultants (which were also professional fees) probably related to the farm. There were one or two computational errors in Mr Twiddy's figures (in particular the transposition of the depreciation figures for 1991 and 1992 which made the net profit of 1991 look better than it should have been and the loss in 1992 look worse than it should have been) which meant that his figures could not be treated as wholly accurate. Nevertheless, even bearing in mind those reservations, the figures did show that the lettings were more profitable than the farm. In only two years out of the eight did the agricultural gross profit exceed the lettings gross profit and in all years the net profit of the lettings exceeded the net profits of the farm. In some years (eg 1994 and 1995) the difference was small but in other years (eg 1992 and 1996) the difference was large. The explanations for the low performance of the farm in 1992 and 1996 have already been considered.

The decision and the way forward

13.45   Mr A B Farmer gave evidence that the farm was run for a profit but that it is very difficult to make a farming profit without subsidies from the European Union. The evidence of Mr Carter was that the farm could have been run at a profit if there had been no lettings; there would not be a large profit but the farm could be self-supporting and there would be a healthy profit in some years. Over a ten-year period the farm would be viable.

It is now time to stand back and to consider the business in the round. Of the five relevant factors four, namely the overall context of the business, the capital employed, the time spent by the employees and consultants and the levels of turnover, all support the conclusion that the business consisted mainly of farming. The profit figures, and more particularly the net profit figures, on the other hand, support the opposite view. Taking the whole business in the round, and without allowing any one factor to predominate, the conclusion is that the business consisted mainly of farming.

The decision on the issue for determination in the appeal was that the business did not 'consist mainly of making or holding investments'. The appeal was, therefore, allowed.

However it is anticipated that a decade (plus) later it would be difficult to meet the same criteria of turnover and profit due to the further decline in farming income and profit and the percentage rise in returns from rental properties. Would the farming enterprises consist mainly of farming? The *Balfour* case seems to endorse this (see **13.46** and **13.52**).

The theme of *Farmer* and the significance to the tax planner is that of 'unified management' with all aspects of the business being examined. The consideration of the fact that surplus properties were let is relevant. Until further cases emerge it will be essential for the tax planner advising mixed rural estates to work very closely with the land agent and the farmer. The action to be taken could be beyond tax advice and linked to the reality of good land management. Key factors appear to be:

- ensuring that the letting of surplus farm buildings is incorporated into the farm as one unit;

- ensuring integrated accounts of one unit;

- recording time spent on let properties;

- using organisations such as the CLA, the National Farmers' Union (NFU) and the farming and rural business group of the Institute of Chartered Accountants to monitor APR/BPR claims and to report back on successes and failures.

Mr Carter's statement that it 'could have been run at a profit if there had been no lettings' is of interest. Could this statement still be made in 2010? Also, the business 'consisted mainly of farming'. Is this still the case? Hopefully, direction from case law or the government will provide some clarity in future, but in the meantime the tax planner should utilise the main points as far as possible and work together for a common aim of achieving maximum tax reliefs.

DOES *FARMER* STILL APPLY IN THE THIRD EDITION?

13.46   The Special Commissioner held that the decision has to be made looking at all relevant factors including profits, turnover, the time spent and the value of the assets concerned. These all help to establish the fundamental nature of the business, which in *Farmer* was 'farming' – 'active husbandry'.

Mr Frederick Farmer died in 1997. At **13.32** the non-rental turnover and the rents received are split up to 1997 and the 'farming business' turnover is greater than the rental business ie more than 50%. Would that still apply more than a decade later? Will the criteria of trading profits, turnover and time spent still be met?

It is interesting to note that *Farmer* is still considered relevant in the third edition as it is the foundation of the *Balfour* case (see **5.55**). The capital value of the let property was far greater than the farming activity and the upper Tribunal held that this was not of significance (see **13.50**).

MARQUESS OF HERTFORD (DEC'D) – NET VALUE OF THE ENTIRE BUSINESS

13.47   The case *Marquess of Hertford (Dec'd)* SpC 444, decided on 11 November 2004, has brought more hope for claims for BPR on 'in hand' farms and the concept on the 'whole'.

This case looked at whether the whole of Ragley Hall qualified for BPR, notwithstanding that part of the interior was in private occupation. This case looked very closely at IHTA 1984 s 110 – the value of a business (or an interest in a business) shall be taken to be its net value and for this purpose and 'no regard shall be had to assets or liabilities other than those by reference to which the net value of the entire business would fall to be ascertained'. One of the key words here is 'entire'.

Oliver LJ in the earlier Finch case (in the Court of Appeal it became *Fetherstonaugh and others v IRC* [1984] STC 261) said when looking at the overall picture it is not the net value of some interest less than the whole, but the value of 'the business'. In such a case there is no such thing as an asset of the business. All the assets of the estate, to the value of which the tax is attributable are assets 'of the decedent'. There is only one practicable test – were they assets which were 'used in the business'? The question was whether the building was wholly or mainly used for business. There was no provision for apportionments and the fact that the building was a vital backdrop to the business was a key factor in the taxpayer's favour.

Marquess of Hertford (Dec'd) – The facts

13.48 So what are the facts? On 18 November 1991 the eighth Marquess transferred by way of gift to his son (now the ninth Marquess) a business of opening a historic house to the public. This business was referred to as the 'Ragley Hall Opening'. This gift was made by various deeds of gift, one of which dealt with the transfer of land and buildings known as Ragley Hall, another with the contents of the house and a third with the goodwill of the Ragley House 'opening business', eg copyright in the catalogues/brochures, book debts, cash in hand and at bank, benefit of contracts, motor vehicles, foodstuffs, beverages and all other chattels used in the business and not already given.

Ragley Hall is an historic grade 1 listed house and prior to the transfer to the ninth Marquess the freehold was vested in the eighth Marquess. Both before and after the transfer, the same parts of the interior of Ragley Hall were open for the public. There was consistency throughout.

The value transferred in 1991, to the extent that it was attributed to the business of the eighth Marquess, was eligible for BPR under IHTA 1984 s 104. The value transferred to that extent fell to be treated as reduced by 100% as a consequence of the effect of s 105 (1)(a). It was accepted that:

- The eighth Marquess had owned the business for at least two years prior to the transfer in 1991, so that the required period of ownership before BPR was available in respect of any transfer of business property (IHTA 1984 s 106) was satisfied.

- IHTA 1984 s 113A(3) was satisfied by the fact that the ninth Marquess carried on the business from and after the transfer until the death of the eighth Marquess as required for BPR to be available.

- The exterior was accessible to the public to view as a whole. Only a part consisting by volume of some 78% was open to the public. Part of the interior consisting by volume of 22% was not open to the public. This area was occupied by the eighth Marquess and the ninth Marquess (then the Earl of Yarmouth) and their families as their living quarters prior to the gift and part was let at a rent of £10,000 per annum to the eighth Marquess after the gift on 18 November 1991.

The appellants (the executors of the eighth Marquess of Hertford) contended that so far as the value transferred by the transfer of value in 1991 was attributed to the value of the freehold of Ragley Hall, the value transferred was eligible for 100% BPR under s 104.

PROSSER V IRC (LANDS TRIBUNAL)

13.49   'Hope' value is looked at in Chapter 5 (see **5.33** and **5.44**).

The case of *Prosser v IRC* (Lands Tribunal) has helped define values where there is no planning permission at the date of death but planning permission is obtained by the executors.

Hope or development value is not part of 'agricultural value' defined in IHTA 1984 s 115(3).

'Hope value' prior to the grant of planning consent may be less than expected when taking guidance from this case:

- no planning consent granted or applied for before death;

- executors applied for and got planning consent (close to death);

- DV originally allowed 20% deduction from development value to allow for uncertainty immediately before death;

- Tribunal thought any purchaser in the open market would only offer 25% of full market value before death on basis of 50/50 chance of obtaining consent, and would expect profit if successful to outweigh loss if planning application failed.

All useful to consider when there are debates over hope value. The DV was pushing for 80% of development value. The Tribunal accepted 75%.

EARL OF BALFOUR – 'INVESTMENT BUSINESS'

13.50   The first judgment of the *Balfour* case was delivered on 14 May 2009. This recorded a BPR claim for a mixed agricultural estate in Scotland. The First-tier Tribunal (formerly Special Commissioners) ruled that the business in question was not 'wholly or mainly making or holding investments' under the interpretation of IHTA 1984 s 105(3). This was regarded as great news for the farming world and it is seen as strengthening the decisions in *Farmer* and *George*. HMRC are, however, appealing.

The emphasis of *Brander (Representative of Fourth Earl of Balfour) v HMRC Comms* [2009] UKFTT 101 was that in order to see if a business was in fact an 'investment business' there was a need to establish where the 'preponderance of the business activity' was (para 42).

HMRC appealed the case and lost – *HMRC v Balfour* [2010] UKUT 300. An appeal by HMRC to the House of Lords was denied.

The relevant factors that have to be looked at are 'turnover, profit, expenditure and time spent by everyone in carrying on the various business activities'.

With incomplete evidence as we have here, and probably in most cases, it is a matter of more general assessment and impression as to where the preponderance of business activity lies. This means looking at the activities being carried on at the estate in the round (an approach by the Court of Appeal in *IRC v George* 2003 at 152C) (see **6.19**).

Earl of Balfour – need to take more protection for the mixed estate

13.51 The victory for the mixed estates and endorsement of the ability to claim BPR on ancillary rented property that forms an integral part of one farming business unit or enterprise. Para 42 goes on to say:

> 'Most estates of the type under discussion are heavily based on farming and to some extent on forestry and woodland management and related shooting interests. The letting side was ancillary to the farming, forestry, woodland and sporting activities. The farming activities, albeit they include agricultural tenancies, occupied by far the greater area of the Estate (see for example *Farmer v IRC* 1999 STC (SCD) 321 especially at paragraphs 6, 22, 40, 41, 43, 47, 52–4)'.

It can be argued that the important point of this case is that HMRC's appeal was defeated.

For all those advisers of mixed agricultural estates who are taking comfort from this case, there are arguments to say that they should consider actually taking more protective action around IHT safeguards now than before. The only time the 'investment business' question is actually tested is death. Failure to achieve BPR is therefore absolute. If the guidance of *Farmer* and *Balfour* encourages greater diversification into the investment business as opposed to the farming and trading activity are there risks of s 105(3) becoming engaged and the estates being determined not to be a business activity?

Chapter 24 of the IHTM manual which was published in February 2009 now gives much greater clarity to the issue of which activities qualify as agriculture and qualify for APR and which do not, so there is improved understanding of what activities qualify for APR and do not necessarily need BPR as support. However, what if the position is say the agricultural land and buildings need to protect development hope value? How do the values compare? Is the result of the good news of *Balfour* actually the trigger to reduce some of the excessive or 'surplus to requirements' activities from the main trade? For CGT consequences see Chapter 14.

Is the guidance the positive feedback that BPR can be achieved on mixed estates but this is so useful in the round that greater tax safeguards must be contemplated? The question is, does the investment business taint the remaining business BPR by making the remaining business not mainly one of making or holding investments? Does the amount of let property and other investment property tilt the balance by making the whole estate vulnerable to s 105(3) attack?

Earl of Balfour – tax-planning interaction with Dance

13.52 Passing to the next generation to remove the surplus investment assets has been considered by many to be 'franked' by the *Nelson Dance* case.

HMRC v Trustees of Nelson Dance Family Settlement [2008] SpC 682 where the taxpayer's appeal was successful in CH/2008/APP/0434 (see **5.56**).

The Special Commissioner held in *Dance* that what mattered was the loss in value to the transferor's estate and that the loss to the estate was attributable to what left the estate, not what the transferee received. BPR can therefore apply to transfers of 'surplus to requirements' activities to the main trade subject to all the conditions being in place. For the CGT implications see Chapter 14.

Paragraph 30 of the first hearing of the *Balfour* case provides help in assessing the factors to take into account. The case applies to Scotland and England.

> 'The traditional mix of a traditional Scottish landed estate consisted of a blend of agriculture (in hand and let farms, woodland and forestry management and related sporting interests and the letting of cottages and other properties within the estate either to estate workers or to others). The letting of some of the cottages provides a good illustration of the fact that the management of the various activities on the estate was integrated and strategically prudent, eg the provision of accommodation at reasonable or low rent to attract good workers or occupants who had skills which might one day be displayed on the estate ...'

Another key point arising from the case is the strength of involvement by the deceased in managing the business. There are complexities around trusts and partnerships which are not looked at for the purpose of this chapter. The summary has to be to look at all the recent guidance given by Chapter 24 on the definition of agriculture.

The *Balfour* case perhaps gave guidance on grazing. This should be considered in the light of the fact that the further appeal re *McCall v HMRC* [2009] NICA 12 has been declined by the House of Lords. In *Balfour*, the grazing rents were regarded as investment activity as opposed to trading turnover. Paragraph 19 of the judgment in *McCall* helps explain the importance of cultivating the grass as a crop and not merely maintaining the land as a landlord. There is a difference between landlord and trader activities.

There is no doubt that in the light of the value of most diversified farms or mixed estates which are worth millions of pounds, a BPR audit should be carried out to ensure that BPR is protected. If there is any doubt or worries regarding say the age and health of the landowner, then advice of tax Counsel should be sought.

Chapter 14

Planning property disposals tax efficiently

Julie Butler

- **Capital gains tax (CGT) reliefs**
  On the assumption that the disposal of farm or diversified land is classified as a capital disposal, this chapter looks at maximising all the CGT reliefs that are available to the farmer/landowner with a close look at entrepreneurs' relief (ER) and the extension of the relief to £5 million.

- **Sheltering development gains**
  The current business tax breaks combined with the farm tax reliefs can mean that the trade of farming presents opportunities to shelter development gains. Does this hold with the loss of BATR from 6 April 2008? What of the impact of the coalition government Budget on 22 June 2010?

- **Trading in land**
  There could be situations where the disposal of farm or diversified land is deemed to be trading in land or an artificial transaction in land. This chapter warns against the problems whilst showing how they can be embraced by the tax planner. Should the development route be followed?

- **General tax-planning opportunities relating to land**
  Consideration for the sundry points of options, reinvestment relief, enterprise investment scheme (EIS) and deferral relief.

- **Who is buying land?**
  It is said that as well as lifestyle investors, farmland is attracting keen interest from land managers and city investors but what of the recession and collapse and then minor recovery of development values at the time of writing?

LOOKING AT TAX-PLANNING OPPORTUNITIES

14.1   The CGT annual exemption for individuals for 2010–11 is £10,100. From 6 April 2008 onwards the rate of CGT above the annual exemption was 18% (see **1.23**). CGT rose from 18% to 28% for taxpayers with total income and gains above the higher rate threshold from midnight 22 June 2010. For basic rate taxpayers, the rate of 18% remains. The threshold remains unchanged at £10,100 for 2010–11 but will rise in line with inflation. The effective 10% lifetime limit for entrepreneurs' relief rate will be extended from the first £2m to the first £5m of gains made over a lifetime.

Many farmers and landowners have had to sell parts of the farm in order to boost the struggling farm income. It might well be that part of the farm or estate is very suitable for a diversification project that would add considerable value to the land or buildings in question but the landowner does not feel able to see the project through himself, and would do better to dispose of the site and use the funds to support the farming enterprise.

Planning consent details are dealt with by James Cleary in Chapter 3, and the rural development details (as far as they are known) are set out in Chapter 2.

Reform of capital gains tax (CGT)

14.2   The capital gains tax regime was 'simplified' with effect from 6 April 2008 and further adjusted in the coalition Budget on 22 June 2010.

There was a single rate of 18% applicable to individuals, trusts, and estates but not companies (these continue to be liable as under existing rules) from 6 April 2008 to 22 June 2010. This was the lowest ever headline rate of CGT since its introduction in 1965.

The previous rules for tapering gains according to how long an asset has been held have been repealed.

Indexation relief which was introduced with effect from 31 March 1982 ceased from 6 April 2008. This relief gave an allowance for inflation between that date and April 1998.

If an asset was acquired before 31 March 1982 at a higher cost price than the value of the asset on 31 March 1982, gains could be calculated by reference to that higher cost price. This no longer applies from 6 April 2008 and the 1982 value will apply in all cases.

Disposal of non-business assets

14.3   The previous generous taper relief for business assets (which includes farmland, furnished holiday lets and shares in unquoted trading companies) has been swept away.

The loss of indexation relief for assets acquired before 1998 could in some cases be of significant consequence. Where the asset was originally purchased in 1982, indexation was, in approximate terms, double the actual capital gains tax base cost. As a result the loss of this relief on assets acquired in the 1980s has had a major impact on capital gains calculations.

14.4   Entrepreneurs' relief (ER) was introduced in response to the outcry about the unfair effect on those losing out from 6 April 2008. Under this relief, these assets have an effective 10% tax rate for gains up to £5m. The original limit was £1m from 6 April 2008 to 5 April 2010, this increased to £2m from 6 April 2010 to 22 June 2010 and from 23 June 2010 the limit has been increased to £5m. This is a lifetime allowance and so it may be used to cover a number of different smaller disposals. However to qualify as a business asset it must either be one used by an individual for the purposes of his/her own trade or profession, or else, in the case of shares in a trading company, the shareholder must be an officer or employee of

341

the company with 5% or more of the ordinary shares; this will mean that most AIM shareholdings will not qualify. ER, however, follows the basic retirement relief rules and it does not apply to part or small disposals of a farming enterprise.

Considering the right to secure future value – 'overage'

14.5 'Overage' is securing the rights to future development value. 'Overage' is the vendor making a statement in the sale agreement as follows: 'You may realise additional value and if you do, you will pay me for it.'

At first glance, overage might appear just to apply to farmland that might be developed at a future point. It can however include a much wider range of property – for example, private dwellings with large gardens or low-key farm and residential property that might at some stage enjoy development value.

Types of overage

14.6 Overage can take the form of a restrictive covenant, a reverse option, a lease with an option to purchase the freehold or a 'ransom strip'. The key is to put a structure in place to ensure a tax-efficient overage payment. Every person involved in property disposals must consider the need for clauses which protect the vendor's right to a share in the future development profits. There have been cases where solicitors, land agents and estate agents have been sued for negligence for not bringing the opportunity for overage to the vendor's attention.

It is therefore important that all land and property sales not only include the protection of a right to future profits but also recognise the need to ensure that, when the monies are received, they are taxed efficiently. First, the key is to capture the 'profit' as a capital asset subject to capital gains tax, with all the potential tax advantages (eg the annual exemption, PRR and ER (if applicable)).

Overage can be in the form of a restrictive covenant over the property. It derives its value from the land and therefore a payment for release from a covenant should be assessable to CGT at 18% or 28%. On disposal the vendor receives consideration, which is the purchase price. Clearly, this is an improved tax position on the top rate of income tax – currently 50%.

In 'slice of the action' cases the vendor is to receive an agreed percentage of the future development profits. The initial consideration is for the disposal of capital assets and may therefore be subject to capital gains tax. However, the subsequent consideration is for the disposal of a new asset – the right to the contingent consideration (the 'slice of the action') – at a later date. This could be caught under ITA 2007 s 756 (previously s 776) because the vendor's rights under the contract were acquired with the sole or main object of realising a gain from the development of the land. It will therefore be taxed as income at the higher rate of income tax (see **14.48**).

Trading losses set against gains

14.7 In order to maximise tax-planning opportunities on property disposal, the rules for the offset of losses and the interaction of the annual allowance should not be overlooked.

Under ITA 2007 s 71 a claim to set trading losses against general income may be extended to cover capital gains as well as income. The 'sideways' income tax relief will be at 40% or 50% whereas the CGT relief will be at 18% and a calculation of maximising relief must be carried out before 'wasting' the loss on a mere 18% or 28% rate of CGT.

The timing and interaction of disposals to maximise reliefs

14.8 Concerns over the availability of ER on part disposals might influence decisions affecting CGT on farmland and property disposals. Of particular importance may be the timing of transactions. For example, where a gain or gains have arisen in a year of assessment and a loss is anticipated, it may sometimes be advisable to review the loss-making disposal to maximise the availability of offset loss relief.

With the restrictive nature of entrepreneurs' relief (ER) and the 18% or 28% rate the use of capital losses brought forward might also be of importance. For loss planning and CGT see **12.5** and **12.16**.

Difficult decisions may be required before making a claim for roll-over relief on such disposal.

Tax date of disposal

14.9 It is well known that the date of disposal of an asset is the time when the contract is made, and not when the asset is conveyed or transferred. This generally means exchange of contracts rather than completion is the tax point for CGT. TCGA 1992 s 28 states as follows:

> '… where an asset is disposed of and acquired under a contract the time at which the disposal and acquisition is made is the time the contract is made (and not, if different, the time at which the asset is conveyed or transferred).'

The case of *Underwood v HMRC* SpC 614 examined s 28 in some detail. The facts in this case were not straightforward. There was a contract for sale and an option for the taxpayer to repurchase the property; there was subsequently a sale back to the taxpayer which was treated as the exercise of his option to repurchase.

The taxpayer argued that a disposal took place on the exchange of the original contract but HMRC claimed that s 28 only applied when the vendor disposed of the asset and the purchaser acquired it, that is to say he became beneficially entitled to it under the contract.

Mr Underwood claimed that although there was no movement in the legal title, none was necessary, but the Special Commissioners concluded that there must be a time (no matter how short) when the purchaser became the beneficial owner. Acquiring an equitable interest under the contract prior to performance did not represent a disposal or a part disposal of the property. Because the purchaser never acquired the beneficial ownership there was no disposal. When looking at the loss memorandum for maximising the efficiency of CGT mitigation this should be considered.

Need to review potential disposals for entrepreneurs' relief eligibility

14.10   ER should be claimed when available until the £5 million lifetime allowance is fully utilised. Claims can be made for disposals on or after 6 April 2008 providing the gains qualify for the relief.

ER will be available in respect of the held-over gains that become chargeable on or after 6 April 2008 when the qualifying corporate bonds are redeemed (or otherwise disposed of) if the original sale of the shares would have met the conditions of the relief if it had taken place after 6 April 2008. Gains on disposals of let residential properties will not qualify for ER. The exception is FHL (see **6.13** and **15.37–15.40**).

By itself a disposal of let property will not qualify for ER. There must be a disposal of the whole or part of a trading business and commercial property letting is not a trading activity. However, if the property is let to a trading partnership of which the taxpayer is a member, or to a trading company of which the taxpayer is an officer or employee, the taxpayer may be entitled to a measure of relief on disposal of the property if that disposal is associated with a disposal of their interest in the partnership, or of their shares in the company and that other disposal meets all the conditions for the relief.

Shares in unquoted company – 'wholly' for the purpose of carrying on a trade

14.11   The whole area of incorporation is dealt with in Chapter 8. Diversification could move a trading company into a company holding investments.

This could impact on the eligibility for ER which is set out in detail at **8.33**.

The sale of an asset in isolation

14.12   In order to qualify for ER there must be a disposal of the whole part of the trading business, 'a qualifying business disposal'. The sale of an asset in isolation will not qualify for ER.

HMRC's Capital Gains Manual CG64010 et seq discusses what constitutes the disposal of the whole or part of a business.

A business of commercial FHL in the UK will be treated as a trade for the purposes of ER. However, the FHL rules potentially change from 6 April 2011 (see **15.37–15.40**).

Qualifying business disposal

14.13   For each category of 'qualifying business disposal' capital gains and losses are computed for all assets comprised within the disposal but excluding gains or losses arising on assets which are not 'relevant business assets'. Any capital losses arising have to be fully utilised, ie, they must be set against the full amount of gains arising on the same disposal before relief is applied. A claim for ER must be made and can only be made if a net gain results.

Dependent upon the category of 'qualifying business disposal' additional rules may then need to be followed to achieve ER.

Alternative land use – non-trading activity

14.14   Farmers have traditionally looked to roll-over relief (see **14.19**) to assist them in CGT saving on farm and land disposals, and the interaction must be carefully reviewed. Roll-over relief may still be the best relief to use, unless there is a further sale of the new assets, without further reinvestment. With the 18% and 28% rate of CGT there is now an opportunity to sell assets with no business use without the complexity of BATR. The section on roll-over relief looks at a tax-planning opportunity through separating land and buildings (see **14.21**).

Tenanted farmland

14.15   Tenanted farmland does not qualify for ER.

ROLL-OVER RELIEF

Alternative land use

14.16   Where the new diversified activity involves the cessation of the farming business and the commencement of a new non-farming business, there may be a change in the use of the farmland or the farm buildings.

A common solution where a farm business cannot make a profit is for the farmland to be farmed by contractors, for example by a neighbour, or even let to a neighbour, and for the farm buildings to be put to some other non-farming business use (see Chapter 11). A point that needs to be considered is whether the buildings used in the new business, if sold at some point in the future, would then qualify for roll-over relief. The tax-planning point is that non-farming does not necessarily mean non-trading.

Relief is not lost if the buildings were originally used for a farming purpose, but have become assets of a new non-farming business after the cessation of the farming enterprise (TCGA 1992 s 152(8)). The test is that the assets disposed of must have been used throughout the period of ownership only for the purposes of 'a business'. However, this rule is relaxed where a person carries on two businesses 'successively' and they are treated as one.

If there is an interval between the cessation of one trade and the commencement of another, the two trades are treated as being carried on 'successively', providing the interval does not exceed three years. If there is a disposal of assets, and reinvestment in new assets, for roll-over relief purposes it will not matter if the old trade and the new trade are different in nature, as long as both the old and new assets fall within the headings at classes 1–8 of TCGA 1992 s 155.

The farmer must be careful, though, if the disposal of the old assets and the acquisition of the new assets takes place during the interval between the old business ceasing and the new one starting. Roll-over relief is not lost provided the asset is not used for any other purpose before the commencement of the new business and is used for the new business after it has commenced.

The time limits are of course subject to the overriding rule that the acquisition of the new asset must take place within a four-year period starting one year before and ending three years after the disposal of the old asset. There is a 2003 tax case which questions this three-year period, see *R (on the application of Barnett v IRC* [2003] EWHC 2581 (Admin), [2004] STC 763. The issue of this case was whether the Board of Inland Revenue was bound to exercise its discretion to extend the three-year period for acquisition in favour of the claimant taxpayer.

The facts are that for purposes of roll-over relief from CGT, the acquisition of the new assets must, under TCGA 1992 s 152(3), be made within one year before or three years after the disposal of the old assets or at such earlier or later time as the Board of the Inland Revenue might allow. Mr Barnett applied to the Board to exercise its discretion to allow him roll-over relief in respect of the sale and purchase of property. The Board refused. Mr Barnett appealed to the Commissioners, who made certain findings in a written decision, on the basis of which Mr Barnett reapplied to the Board, which again refused to exercise its discretion. Mr Barnett sought judicial review of that decision.

It was not the function of the Commissioners to make findings regarding the exercise of the TCGA 1992 s 152(3) discretion, since that power was expressly vested in the Board. While the Board was under a duty to take into account relevant findings by the Commissioners in exercising its discretion, the Act conferred the discretion on the Board with no right of appeal. It followed that the Board had been entitled to exercise its discretion as it had done. The application was dismissed (*R (on the application of Barnett) v IRC* [2003] EWHC 2581 (Admin), [2004] STC 763).

This is an area of the law which is completely within HMRC's power without a right to appeal! Moral: make sure the business plan clearly recognises the need to reinvest within three years for roll-over purposes after the farm or diversified asset has been sold.

Replacement of business assets

The whole proceeds

14.17   One of the most frequently utilised CGT reliefs by the landowner is that of replacement of business assets. However, a common problem for the unwary arises in that the owner of the old asset is not the owner of the new asset. This is a particular problem on setting up or disbanding a partnership, or where a new partner is added or leaves a partnership. If the asset is owned by the partnership, these changes can trigger a loss of relief. Another problem arises in that a requirement for full roll-over relief to be allowed is that the entire proceeds of the old asset must be reinvested in the new qualifying asset. This is set out in TCGA 1992 s 153. It must be noted that any proceeds not so applied will be charged to CGT.

The principle of replacement of business assets is that the gain arising on the disposal of the land may be rolled over and subtracted from the cost of acquiring the new asset. Additionally, both the disposal and the corresponding acquisition must be made by the same person and with the assets being used for the purpose of a trade or other qualifying activity. Due to this relief, land sales used in the business can be rolled over into non-farming activities. This can be a diversified farming activity or a completely separate business activity.

Separate land and buildings – tax planning

14.18   Having to roll-over the whole of the sale proceeds can be restrictive for the farmer.

For roll-over relief purposes, 'buildings' and 'land' are the most widely used class of assets (TCGA 1992 s 155). They are defined as the following.

- Building: any building or a part of a building and any permanent or semi-permanent structure in the nature of a building occupied (as well as used) only for the purposes of the trade.

- Land: any land occupied (as well as used) only for the purposes of the trade. The Interpretation Act 1978 Sch 1 requires that unless the contrary intention appears, the word 'land' includes 'buildings and other structures, lands covered with water and any estate interest, servitude or right in or over land'. This approach is somewhat modified by TCGA 1992 s 288(1) which defines 'land' as including 'messuages, tenements and hereditaments, houses and buildings of any tenure'.

There is a tax-planning advantage identified here in that buildings and land are separate, ie there are people who strongly argue that land should not be given an extended meaning and must exclude buildings together with permanent or semi-permanent structures in the nature of buildings. It can be extremely useful with matching acquisitions, disposals and support of the claim for roll-over relief. If land is sold with a building erected on that land, the sale proceeds may be apportioned between two different assets, ie the building and the land separately. A similar approach may be used when land and buildings are purchased.

It may, therefore, be possible to roll over the gain arising on disposal of only one of the two assets, leaving the gain on the other asset to absorb the annual exemption or perhaps losses or just to pay tax on so that cash is relieved.

Roll-over relief – What are the requirements?

14.19   The requirements to qualify for roll-over relief are set out in TCGA 1992 s 152(1) and can be summarised as follows:

- the old assets and new assets must fall within the classes of assets listed in TCGA 1992 s 155;

- the person must be carrying on a trade;

- the person disposing of the asset (the old asset) must obtain consideration from the disposal of that asset or an interest in an asset;

- the consideration obtained must be applied in acquiring other assets or an interest in other assets (the new asset); and

- on acquisition, the new assets must be taken into use and used only for the purpose of the trade.

The old asset must also have been used and used only for the purpose of the trade.

Let property

14.20   Let property does not in principle qualify for either roll-over relief or ER and there are a number of definitions that must be looked at, such as the difference between trade and income derived from property that is let out. Although it has been defined previously, some further direction has been given in the case of *Griffiths v Jackson and Pearman* [1983] STC 184. The decision in this case confirmed that the profits derived from property which is let out (in this case furnished) are not the profits of a trade and assessable under Schedule A or Schedule D Case VI (old terminology). It was stated that:

> 'income derived by the owner of a property from letting the property furnished whether for a short or a long term and whether in small or large units and whether in self-contained units or to tenants who share a bathroom or kitchen or the like is not income derived from carrying on a trade.'

There are some exceptions: the letting out of industrial units and distinct office complexes converted from farm buildings are not the profits of a trade; the other exceptions are dealt with in the section on FHLs (see **6.13**) under TCGA 1992 s 241(3). The activity must be carried on commercially (see Chapter 15).

Many farming organisations are lobbying for let property to be an asset that qualifies as an asset for roll-over purposes. It has been suggested that provisions should include low-cost residential accommodation in rural areas. The advantage of roll-over into refurbished farm buildings, which are used for either commercial or residential lets, would have obvious advantages for the rural economy.

Partial business use of farm assets

14.21   One section of the replacement of business assets which is important to the farming and landowning community is where there is partial business use of an asset. This is dealt with under TCGA 1992 s 152(6) where, over the period of ownership or any substantial part of that period, part of a building or structure is not used for the purposes of a trade. There is no direct definition of the word 'substantial'. It is agreed that if part of a building is not used for purposes of trade throughout the whole, or substantial part, of the period of ownership the asset must effectively be divided into two parts for roll-over relief: there must be the part which represents the business use, and the other representing the non-qualifying use. Each part will then be treated as a separate asset with roll-over being confined to the chargeable gain allocated to the business use element.

Mixed use of farm assets

14.22   In order to qualify for the relief of the replacement of business assets another point to check is where the old asset was not used for the purposes of the landowner's trade throughout the period of ownership. This is covered in TCGA 1992 s 152(7). It is accepted that this deals with the situation where at some stage within the ownership period there was no qualifying use whatsoever. For disposals taking place after 5 April 1988, the period of ownership cannot commence earlier than 31 March 1982. When this situation is in existence, the old asset is effectively divided into two different parts as follows:

- the element representing the non-trading use; and

- the element representing the use for the purposes of the trade.

It is generally accepted that the apportionment of costs and disposal proceeds will be undertaken on a just and reasonable basis, as there will be periods of both use and non-use. Time apportionment may well produce an acceptable solution to this problem.

Further, where there is prior cessation of use, ie the asset ceases to be used in the business prior to disposal, there are concerns that the ability to claim roll-over relief will be lost because the old asset ceased to be used for the purpose of a continuing trade before being sold. There is a clear decision in the case of *Richart v J Lyons & Co Ltd* (1989) 62 TC 261 which shows that the relief is not lost, but it might be restricted. It confirms that an asset need not actually be used for a qualifying purpose at the time of disposal before a claim for roll-over relief can be made.

Is it worth making the roll-over claim?

14.23   With the disappearance of both indexation and BATR and the replacement by the restrictive ER the roll-over claim appears to look very attractive again at a general level.

Detailed 'what if' calculations are essential if it is known that there is a proposed sale of the new assets within four or five years. The real difficulty of course arises where roll-over relief has been claimed because no sale was contemplated within four or five years, but the new venture does not take off and the new assets have to be sold. The interaction of ER or just paying CGT at 18% or 28% now rather than risk higher rates in the future has to be contemplated.

Roll-over into a depreciating asset

14.24   It is possible to postpone a gain by holding it over into a depreciating asset (eg plant and machinery). This would appear in the balance sheet as fixed assets. This is found in TCGA 1992 s 154. A non-depreciating asset can be acquired within the ten-year period and again held in suspense and the gain can be rolled over.

A depreciating asset is one with a useful life of 60 years or less at the date of acquisition. The standard roll-over rules bring the deferred gain back into charge on the earliest of:

- ten years elapsing;

- the second asset being disposed of; or

- the second asset being used for the purposes of the trade.

Commerciality test

14.25   One of the clear factors to be considered is that difficulties may be experienced in securing entitlement to CGT reliefs following a change of trade if the new or the old trade were not carried on commercially and with a view to profit. The existence of a commercial trade is an essential requirement before any entitlement to roll-over relief or claim for ER can be made.

HOLD-OVER RELIEF

Gift to family members

14.26   A gift of a farm asset to a family member may trigger a CGT charge. The provisions of TCGA 1992 s 165 may be used to hold over the gain arising on a gift made directly to a family member. If the gift is made into a discretionary trust, TCGA 1992 s 260 will achieve the same result (see **17.6**). It should be noted that these hold-over provisions could apply equally to the gift of let land if it falls within the definition of agricultural property for IHT purposes (TCGA 1992 Sch 7).

Note, however, that when making gifts that separate the ownership of buildings from the ownership of land with which they have been historically associated, the right to APR and BPR on the buildings may be lost.

Hold-over relief is preserved if the asset continues to be used for the purposes of a trade carried on by the transferor. This means that it has to have been in trade use just before it is gifted. The fact that there may be a change in the nature of the trade should not affect the operation of the relief. However, if there is a period of non-business use (including any gap period between successive trades), or part of the asset is not used for business purposes, apportionments will have to be made, so that only part of the gain will qualify.

Whereas gifts and transfers to a trust do not attract SDLT, as there is no consideration, transfers to a limited company do.

Agricultural property qualifying for APR for IHT purposes also qualifies for hold-over relief where it is not used for the purposes of trade carried on by the transferor, or his personal company (TCGA 1992 Sch 7 Pt I). This effectively means that relief is available on the gift of let agricultural land even where the transferee does not actually use the property. Switching to non-agricultural lets, eg industrial units, will mean hold-over relief is lost. It is the gift of let agricultural property that can be the most beneficial.

The conversion of a barn for residential use, which was previously used for trade purposes by the transferor, will not qualify as it would neither be used for the purposes of trade nor be occupied for the purposes of agriculture at the time of a subsequent gift.

Qualifying assets

14.27   Under the current rules for transactions carried out after 13 March 1989, a claim for hold-over relief can be made under TCGA 1992 s 165. In order to make a claim for hold-over relief, it is important to identify persons involved that are eligible and also the assets which are capable of supporting a claim for hold-over relief.

There are principally three groups of qualifying assets, as discussed below.

Assets used for the purpose of trade

14.28   The first group that qualifies is under TCGA 1992 s 165(2) which is an asset or an interest in an asset used for the purpose of a trade, profession or vocation, by the transferor's personal company or a member of the trading group of which the holding company is the transferor's personal company. This also includes shares or securities of a trading company or the holding company of a trading group where:

●   shares or securities are not listed on a recognised stock exchange; or

●   the trading company or holding company is the transferor's personal company.

Agricultural property – hold-over relief

14.29   The second group of assets that qualify for hold-over relief is agricultural property. This is limited to disposals by an individual otherwise than by way of a bargain at arm's length. In order to qualify as an asset for the hold-over provision, agricultural property must come within the meaning of IHTA 1984 Ch II Pt V. In addition, it must be shown that the disposal does not otherwise fall within TCGA 1992 s 165(1).

For this purpose IHTA 1984 s 115(2) defines agricultural property (see **1.6**) as meaning:

> 'agricultural land or pasture and includes woodland and any building used in connection with the intensive rearing of livestock or fish if the woodland or building is occupied with agricultural land or pasture and the occupation is ancillary to that of the agricultural land or pasture; and also includes such cottages, farm buildings and farmhouses, together with land occupied with them, as are of a character appropriate to the property.'

The land used for the breeding and rearing of horses on the stud farm and the grazing of horses in connection with those activities is treated as agricultural property, and any buildings used in connection with those activities are also treated as farm buildings. It can also be noted that land and buildings used for the cultivation of short rotation coppices can be treated as agricultural property from 6 April 1995.

IHTA 1984 s 115(2) means that agricultural property can be divided into three different categories:

●   agricultural land or pasture;

●   woodland and any building used in connection with the intensive rearing of livestock or fish if the woodland or building is occupied with agricultural land or pasture and the occupation is ancillary to that of the agricultural land or pasture; and

- such cottages, farm buildings and farmhouses together with the land occupied with them as are of a character appropriate to the property.

In the case of *Starke v IRC* [1995] STC 689 it was defined that 2.5 acres added on to a six-bedroom farmhouse which had previously been an agricultural holding did not comprise agricultural land or pasture and it was not agricultural property within the meaning of s 115(2).

Transfers by trustees – hold-over relief

14.30   The third class of assets which can qualify for hold-over relief are transfers by trustees into discretionary and life interest trusts. In order to qualify for inclusion in this group, it must be demonstrable that the trustees undertake the disposal of specific assets otherwise than by way of a bargain at arm's length. This is covered by TCGA 1992 Sch 7 para 2(1).

The assets must comprise:

- assets, or an interest in assets, used for the purpose of a trade or professional vocation carried on by:

    – the trustees making the disposal; or

    – a beneficiary who has an interest in possession in the settled property immediately before disposal; or

- shares or securities of a trading company or a holding company of a trading group where:

    – the shares or securities are not listed on a recognised stock exchange; or

    – not less than 25% of the voting right exercised by shareholders of the company and general meeting are exercisable by the trustees at the time of the disposal.

The claim for hold-over relief is not mandatory and a formal claim is required. The transferor and the transferee must make the claim jointly, unless the transferees are trustees of the administering of the settled property when the transferor may make the claim only.

RETIREMENT RELIEF

14.31   The 'sell-by' date for retirement relief as a CGT relief against disposals was 5 April 2003. The case law surrounding this relief could be relevant for deciding if ER applies (see **14.4**).

MINERAL ROYALTIES

14.32   The traditional taxation of mineral royalties is still half income tax and half capital gains tax (ITTOIA 2005 s 157). The review of the taxation of mineral royalties has become even more relevant with the introduction of aggregates levy from 1 April 2002 (see **19.8**).

The most common commercial 'minerals' are gravel, sand, and stone, and there are a number of ways of trying to have the extraction taxed as efficiently as possible. Essentially, capturing the monies as capital rather than income will be important.

Selling the land

14.33   An obvious tax-planning tool is the sale of the land including the minerals, which captures the 'income' as capital. The problem is that many landowners do not want to lose the land itself and look for alternatives. Obviously the 18% and 28% rate of CGT is less attractive than the previous 10% when BATR applied. There will be a question whether eligibility for ER can be achieved in view of the complex conditions.

If the owner were involved in a number of transactions whereby he sold the land and the minerals, the sale could fall under the speculative transaction rules and be deemed to be an adventure in the nature of trade. The six badges of trade would be:

● the subsequent matter of realisation;

● the length of period of ownership;

● the frequency or the number of similar transactions;

● supplementary work on assets sold;

● reason for sale; and

● motive.

This is looked at in more detail at **14.41**.

The sale of land including minerals with the right to buy back the land is a disposal for CGT. Provided it has been farmed, the land should qualify as a business asset and be eligible for roll-over relief and possibly ER. The income element is calculated under the normal premium rules, and is assessable as income in the period in which the sale occurs. The term of the lease for the purposes of computing the income element is the period between sale and repurchase. If there is no one particular date, but a series of possibilities arising from the sale contract, the repurchase is treated initially as taking place at the lowest possible price under the terms of the sale. The vendor then has six years from the reconveyance to make a claim, to recover any excess tax paid once the actual date of the reconveyance is known.

A right to buy back, documented in writing, could be caught under ITTOIA 2005 s 284. This section is a further anti-avoidance provision, which seeks to tax the difference between the sale price and the lower purchase consideration as a deemed premium. Essentially, a sale with the right to lease back will be caught in part as income and not capital, and is, therefore, not eligible for CGT reliefs and rates.

Where an owner of land (or any other description of property) enters into a transaction whereby he becomes the lessee of that property, eg sale and lease back, and there is a subsequent adjustment of rights and liabilities under the lease (whether or not involving the grant of a new lease), which is on the whole favourable to the lessor, such an adjustment is a disposal by the lessee of an interest in the property (TCGA 1992 s 29(4)).

With sale and lease back, the proportion of capital sum received is taxed as income in certain circumstances. Where the lease when sold has no more than 50 years to run and the period for which the premises are leased back is 15 years or less, a proportion of the capital sum received is to be taxed as income. There is a let out for leases entered into within 30 days.

Where land is sold and there are rights to further monies depending on the amount of minerals, the uplift should be a capital disposal for CGT. If the contract includes subsequent payments for uplift in value subject to gravel extraction, the uplift in value could be eligible for 18% and/or 28% rate of CGT. Provided that this is a genuine disposal and not a trade in gravel, it will be subject to CGT. The wording of the contract will be important.

It might be that a capital gain arises on sale, but the contract for sale has a few worrying clauses, such as the vendor retaining the shooting rights and agreeing to keep the land 'tidy', the purpose being to protect the vendor's other land. Such conditions, if genuine and correctly drafted in the contract, should not prejudice the CGT position

The gravel extraction company leases the land and pays a premium for this (ITTOIA 2005 s 341); the income element is determined by reducing the premium by 2% for each year of the lease less one. The resulting figure will be assessable to tax as letting/property income as additional rent.

Treasury route or arrangement

14.34   The treasury route is a well-tried method where the landowner sells a capital tranche of gravel with a licence for the aggregates company to enter the land for purposes of extraction. The aim is to achieve the profits as a capital gain. This takes the sale of gravel in capital tranches one stage further by including the surface of the land so that the capital tranche is a business asset for further CGT reliefs and rates. Should a connected person take ownership of the land, the disposal of gravel is subject to CGT. The key is to establish a capital gain in-house. For instance, the land could be put into settlement or gifted to a member of the family.

If the calculation is correct, there should be no further tax. It is a good idea to put a restrictive covenant on the number of cubic metres. The downside is that for the aggregates company, under the CAA 2001 s 418, capital allowances are given at only 10% a year. However, when the tranche is exhausted, the company is entitled to claim a balancing allowance for the balance of the amount spent (CAA 2001 s 428), ie the aggregates company will not receive 100% relief until the end of the tranche.

The aim is, by using the treasury arrangement, to have the profit arising from the sale of mineral rights treated as a capital gain, rather than as partly income tax and partly capital gains tax.

With the removal of indexation and BATR from 6 April 2008 the treasury route will need very careful review as to the benefit of the 18% and/or 28% rate of CGT against the possible 50% rate of income tax.

HMRC quote *Chaloner v Pellipar Investments Ltd* (1996) 68 TC 238 (which in turn depends upon *Marren v Ingles* (1980) 54 TC 76) as authority for the statement that the grant to a right to a profit (à prendre) or a licence is not a part disposal of the land. It then says the profit deriving from the granting of the licence arises from the creation of the licence. This is not an asset used in the farming business, and as such business asset taper relief is not due.

Chaloner v Pellipar was about a landowner who leased two pieces of land in central London to a developer, in consideration of his developing a third site for the benefit of Pellipar. It was about the time that re-basing came in, and the date of the disposal was critical.

Pellipar argued that the gain was taxable under TCGA 1992 s 22(1)(d), which meant that the date of the disposal was the date that the development was completed (and handed over to Pellipar), rather than the date of the original contract. TCGA 1992 s 22 deals with cases where a capital sum is received, but the payer does not necessarily receive a capital asset in exchange. Having said that, the judge made the point that nothing in TCGA 1992 s 22 excluded situations where there was a capital asset that changed hands.

The judge concerned himself with whether he had authority from *Marren v Ingles* for the granting of a lease to fall within TCGA 1992 s 22(1)(d). Although Lord Wilberforce, in *Marren v Ingles*, gave example of transactions in land that would qualify for taxation under TCGA 1992 s 22(1)(d), these examples were a licence or a profit (à prendre, presumably), not a lease. While admitting that it was not authority for his statement, Mr Justice Rattee said that it was consistent to omit reference to a lease. Although he had previously said that there was nothing in TCGA 1992 s 22 that prevented it from being used to tax a transaction in which no capital asset changed hands, he said:

> 'the words of paragraph (d) are apt to include the former, ie licence/ profit, but not the latter, ie leases. Those words are apt to include capital sums received as consideration for the use or exploitation of assets, title to which remains unaffected in their owner, referred to in the opening words of TCGA 1992 s 22(1), but are not apt to include capital sums received as consideration for a grant of the owner's title to the assets, whether in perpetuity, or for a term of years.'

It should be borne in mind that the basis of the taxpayer's appeal was that, if the receipt of the consideration could be deemed to fall within TCGA 1992 s 22(1) (d), as a 'capital sum received as consideration for use or exploitation of assets', then it was outside the general provision in TCGA 1992 s 28 (time of disposal), ie the date of the contract, because section 28 is subject to TCGA 1992 s 22 (which gives the time of disposal as the time at which the capital sum is received).

The decision of the judge was therefore whether the development value received should be tied to the disposal of the two leases, or whether it could somehow fit within the definition (as consideration for use or exploitation of assets). Since it was undoubtedly additional consideration for the two leases, his decision is not surprising. His comments on licence/profits are very brief.

He merely draws a distinction between licences/profits, where the asset title is unaffected in the hands of the owner, as opposed to leases, where there is fundamental effect on the grantor's rights, which no longer extend to the land. He does not look at the difference between licences and profits; nor did he look at the different type of licences.

In the context of selling the mineral rights that attribute to a piece of land, difficulties arise.

Leases, licensing and profit à prendre

14.35 Is the right to take a substantial amount of minerals from the land really treated in exactly the same way as a mere licence, say, to walk across a field? In the first case, there is a permanent effect on the land that could turn from being useful agricultural land to a water-filled pit. It would be surprising in those circumstances if it were not treated as a part disposal, because part of the value would have gone once the mineral content had been mined. According to Megarry and Wade's *The Law of Real Property*, there are many types of 'profit' ranging from shooting rights to pasture rights to mineral extraction rights. The latter is called a 'profit in the soil'. It may exist either as 'appurtenant', ie attaching to a piece of land, or 'in gross', ie as an independent right granted to an outsider, not the holder of the land.

In the former case, it is capable of 'reservation' ie mineral rights can be excluded, or 'reserved' from a sale of that land. This seems to indicate that a disposal of mineral rights is capable of being a part disposal, particularly if the grantee is the lessee of the surface, as is the case in the treasury arrangement. There seems to be a legal difference between the situation where a stranger is permitted to enter the land, take some sand and leave (with no restriction to the landlord's rights), and the situation where the lessee of the surface has the right to occupy that surface, build mining works and extract minerals to the exclusion of others, including the landlord.

Most profits fall into the former category hence, presumably the comments of Mr Justice Rattee in *Chaloner v Pellipar* that 'The grant by a freeholder ... of a ... profit leaves his rights to the land unaffected ...'. He was clearly envisaging the first category of profit above. If you start with a field and then, for a period of years have a mining works which is operated for the benefit of the mining company, then no one could say that your rights to enjoyment and use of the land are unaffected. The judge was merely saying that licences and profits could be examples of assets falling within TCGA 1992 s 22, while leases could not. He did not consider exhaustively all the types of licences and profits, because he was only concerned with whether the granting of a lease was a part disposal or a capital sum derived from an asset. The only explicit reference we have at present, differentiating between leases, licences, and profits under the same heading, implies that they are taxable under TCGA 1992 s 22 (the catch-all for taxing capital sums, even if there is no capital asset acquired by the purchaser).

Approach of HMRC (the tax Inspector)

14.36 Then, to add to the basic legal problems, it is necessary to address the Inspector's development of the judge's comments above, to the effect that 'the profit deriving from the granting of the licence [this] would not appear to be an asset used in the farming business'. The Inspector covered himself by saying that, whether or not the granting of a licence counts as a part disposal (which it needs to do in order to qualify for business asset taper relief) depends upon the wording of the licence. This implies that, if the licence grants rights to the exclusion of the landlord, then it might qualify as a part disposal. The danger point is that this might make it a lease and, if so, we might have income tax problems under ITTOIA 2005 s 284. There could also be drafting problems turning a licence into a lease, although, interestingly, Matthew Hutton in an article on TaxationWeb (www.taxationweb.co.uk/tax-articles/capital-taxes/farming-structures-myth-grazing-licences-are-good.html) says 'Many so-called grazing licences are not licences at all, because they grant exclusive possession and therefore become tenancies (*Street v Mountford* [1985] AC 809). Very often, a so-called 'grazing licence' will amount to a short farm business'. Licences in force prior to 1 September 1995, when the Agricultural Tenancies Act 1995 took effect, became exclusive on that date by operation of the law (see **14.20**). We should be aiming to have such an agreement which:

- does not fall foul of the income tax rules for leases (note that the definition of lease in ITTOIA 2005 s 307(1) includes any tenancy); and

- transfers part of the value out of the land to the extent that it counts as part disposal without falling foul of existing precedents, ie licence/profits *à prendre* are generally not part disposals.

Reverting to the question of whether the Inspector is correct in saying that the asset from which the capital sum is derived, in the case of a licence, is the licence itself, it is interesting to see in *Tax Bulletin* Issue 61, on the subject of capital sums derived from assets, that 'the question will often be whether the sum derives from the asset itself, or from a right to take action for compensation or damages'. In the case of the removal of minerals from land, if a company took minerals without permission, and then paid compensation, Extra-statutory Concession D33 would deem the underlying asset to be the land, in which case ER would be available if the other conditions are met.

If the Inspector is correct, a prior agreement for the company to take the minerals before entering the land renders the capital gain ineligible for ER.

The summary is that mineral royalties captured as a capital gain can benefit from the 18% and/or 28% rate as opposed to the 40% or 50% rates of income tax. Where sums are substantial, planning is worthwhile.

PART DISPOSALS AND SMALL PART DISPOSALS

Part disposal rule

14.37 Statement of Practice D1 issued by HMRC states that where part of an estate is disposed of, for example the sale of a field, HMRC will accept that such part disposal can be regarded as a separate asset and any fair and reasonable method of apportioning the total cost will be accepted by them. This cost is then deducted from the original cost or March 1982 value. (See **5.45** for Red Book ruling.)

HMRC are not, however, forced into using the part disposal basis: the estate may still be treated as a single asset. However, a decision will normally have to be made on the timing of the first disposal out of an estate and then use the same basis for subsequent sales, etc.

The advantage of the part disposal rule is that there can be short-term benefits in reducing the chargeable gain by being able to allocate a higher base cost against the gain, which can be very beneficial. However, like all the disposals that have been discussed, it is the interaction with other reliefs and the interaction of future disposals and the interaction of what future tax reliefs will be.

Part disposal rule – interaction with CGT reliefs

14.38   The decision as to whether or not the part disposal rule applies must depend very heavily on the current and future plans of the farmer/landowner. The interaction of ER is a very interesting question here. Do 'part disposals' qualify for the relief?

Issues to be considered are as follows:

- Death is not a chargeable event, ie there is no CGT payable on death and so short-term CGT benefits should be weighed against long-term tax-planning aims.

- 18% and/or 28% are favourable rates, the best 'pure' rates since 1965 when CGT was introduced but not as good as the previous effective BATR rate of 10% even with all the 'tainting'.

The timing of disposals will be important when looking at this area of tax planning. The part disposal rule gives the tax practitioner and the landowner some degree of choice over what base cost can be used. There will be scope for timing of reliefs.

Small part disposal rule

14.39   Another element of the part disposal rule is that known as the small part disposal rule and the use of this cannot be challenged by HMRC. Under TCGA 1992 s 242 the transferor may claim that the sale of land does not constitute a disposal where the following conditions are met:

- the consideration does not exceed £20,000;

- the consideration does not exceed 20% of the market value of the entire holding at the time of transfer; and

- the consideration for all transfers of land made by the taxpayer in the year in question does not exceed £20,000. In this instance the sale proceeds would be deducted from the base cost.

Once again, both tax planning and tax calculation in relation to disposals of land are not straightforward and there are some factors which could influence the decision-making process surrounding the disposal. These would include the use of annual exemptions which might give this rule no advantage between husband and wife.

Small disposals –still relevant after 6 April 2002?

14.40   Of particular concern must be the small part disposal of land advantage given under TCGA 1992 s 242. Under this provision, proceeds from a small part disposal of land used to finance new ventures can be maximised by taking advantage of the relief. The transferor may claim that the sale of the land does not constitute a disposal where the conditions as set out above (see **14.39**) are met.

If a piece of land were to be sold, for example by a husband and wife trading together, there would be a clear need to check the use of the annual exemption for CGT. There could be strong advantages in not claiming the relief so as to secure a higher base cost for future use. Again, this is not an exact science, as it would depend what the future use of the taxpayer's base cost will be. As death is not a chargeable event, some would argue that the effect on the future base cost is irrelevant. However, some taxpayers who intend to make a further disposal would have to look at how they could use the base cost, how it would interact with future tax planning, and a number of combinations arise.

This shows what a complex time the tax planner faces in advising clients. There are many clients who have fallen into the habit of needing to make business decisions very quickly demanding almost immediate, over-the-telephone, advice: 'Do I buy now?', 'Do I sell now?' and so on. It will be a practical point for the practitioner to make sure that the client realises that, with the complexity of the CGT reliefs (in spite of the reform), there is no such thing as a quick over-the-telephone answer. From a practice management point of view, this highlights the need for the tax practitioner to document the choices clearly. Ultimately, the decision on which action to take rests with the taxpayer, and all options must have been thoroughly explained to him, and documentary evidence of this will be required. This additional paperwork adds costs to the process, which should be built into the fee structures.

FARMLAND DISPOSALS – TRADING IN LAND?

Alternatives available

14.41   With the acute housing shortage and the large demand for development land, farmers have in the last decade turned to land sales and building development for survival. As mentioned in the introduction, the tax planner must ensure that these are taxed in the most efficient way. With the 50% rate of tax on profits over £150,000 from 6 April 2010, there will be an increased need to protect against being caught in this way.

Property transactions have a very high unit cost and, therefore, there is scope to look at individual transactions rather than the whole. Also a very large profit on a single transaction could arise giving HMRC a great incentive to try to tax the profit as trading rather than capital because, there are CGT reliefs to lose, such as annual exemption, roll-over and now ER if the asset is treated as a trading activity.

It is possible for a gain arising on the disposal of land to be taxed under one of three headings:

1   CGT (see **14.42**).

2   'trading in land' (see **14.43**).

3   ITA 2007 s 756 – 'artificial transactions in land' (see **14.45**).

The VAT position on the disposal of land is dealt with in Chapter 9. The tax implications of selling land for development should be considered before the sale is agreed because if the gain is not subject to CGT any contemplated relief such as ER (subject to the "part or whole" of the business conditions) or roll-over would be lost, and this could destroy the whole economic purpose of the sale as approximately only 50% to 60% of the proceeds would be left. The whole matter should be planned now and the status of all land and future transactions reviewed.

Capital gains tax

14.42   A gain on the disposal of land will be taxed under this head where it can be demonstrated that the taxpayer is not dealing in land. Likewise, it will be taxed under the CGT provisions provided that the anti-avoidance legislation of ITA 2007 s 756 does not come into play. This classification is generally the most advantageous with all the generous CGT reliefs eg the 18% rate from 6 April 2008 and the 18% and/or 28% rates from 23 June 2010 (see **1.3**).

Trading in land

14.43   It can be argued that if the farmer/landowner carries out any work to the property to promote development or sale other than by just obtaining planning permission, then he is trading in land. It is possible that if a farmer/landowner makes frequent disposals or buys to sell on he could be caught under the trading in land provisions. Trading was defined in the Taxes Act as including 'every trade, manufacture, adventure or concern in the nature of trade'. This does not really define trading at all and, therefore, the so-called 'badges of trade' have been formulated. It is not necessary to show that all badges of trade are present for an activity to be assessed as a trade; however, a profit-seeking motive at the time of acquisition is the most persuasive, which is often confirmed by the existence of other badges.

Let us look at what makes up the trading emblems known as the badges of trade.

1   Motive: this is classically illustrated where land has been acquired for the purposes of resale. The land has not been acquired as fixed capital but rather as stock in trade and this will usually be confirmed if there is a short interval of time between the acquisition and sale. File notes and documentation should support the capital disposal motive, not the trading motive. Document also that the land has been used for dedicated farm purposes or diversification purposes.

2   Trading interests in a similar field: is the taxpayer involved in similar ventures that have been admitted as trading or do other capital disposals in the light of the current disposal connect the transactions as trading after taking account of the other badges?

3   Frequency of transactions: a number of similar transactions may indicate a continuous activity. Transactions normally treated as of a capital nature in isolation, acquire the characteristic of income due to the frequency of the transactions. This would apply to a farmer who sells a number of areas of land over a short period of time. Again, it would be looked at 'in the round'. Was this merely a disposal of long-held farmland in a number of transactions or were there frequent disposals of newly acquired sites which scarcely saw a farm animal or a plough?

4   Circumstances of acquisition: it is difficult for HMRC to demonstrate that the sale of land acquired by gift or inheritance amounts to an adventure in the nature of trade, as intention of resale will not necessarily be in mind at the time of acquisition. Again, can it be shown it was acquired to improve the farming trade?

5   Subject matter: is it genuine farmland? Has it been farmed or stored for resale? This badge of trade tends to be unhelpful in land cases since land can be acquired as an investment, own occupation and resale. Links to motive are relevant here. Was it bought as farmland as well as being farmland?

6   Time interval: holding the land for a number of years may point to a lack of profit-motive when the land was acquired. However, this factor is not considered conclusive by HMRC. In *Cooksey and Bibbey v Rednall* (1949) 30 TC 514, the taxpayer successfully argued that there was a lack of profit-motive, but the case still went to the High Court even though the land in question had been held for 15 years.

7   Supplementary work: this applies where work is done to the property to make it more marketable (eg in cases of development) or where the taxpayer actively takes steps to find purchasers. However, there may be circumstances where cash needs to be raised as soon as possible. The more development work carried out the more likely the need for trading clarification.

8   Method of finance: the purchaser may have purchased the land with the assistance of a loan that has been made on terms requiring repayment upon resale. This gives a clear indication of intention as demonstrated in *Turner v Last* (1965) 42 TC 517. It is one point among many.

The tax planner must ascertain what the intention is on acquisition. Of crucial importance is the acquirer's intention at the moment of the acquisition of the land: see *Simmons (as liquidator of Lionel Simmons Properties Ltd) v IRC* [1980] STC 350, in which Lord Wilberforce said: 'Trading requires an intention to trade: normally the question to be asked is whether this intention existed at the time of the acquisition of the asset'. In land transactions, the moment of acquisition is defined as the moment of exchange of contracts for purchase and not the moment of completion. The simple task of obtaining planning permission does not constitute development but buying farmland with a view to development profits could. This consideration is reviewed further in **14.45**.

Tenant's disposal of superior interest in land

14.44   Where a tenant buys and immediately resells a superior interest in the land he occupies (usually his landlord's freehold), it may be possible to argue that the transaction amounts to an adventure in the nature of trade. This is so whether the buyer is a residential, commercial, industrial or agricultural tenant. The consideration of agricultural tenancies is looked at in Chapters 11 and 15.

In order to quantify the profit relating to the purchase and sale of the freehold, the market value of the tenancy at the time the freehold was acquired must be established. The tenancy is then treated as if it were appropriated from fixed assets to trading stock thereby invoking TCGA 1992 s 161 (*Bath and West Counties Property Trust Ltd v Thomas* [1978] STC 30).

This market value constitutes the 'consideration' on which the capital gain is computed. It also constitutes a deduction in the computation of the profit.

The basic trading principles apply in determining whether the transaction is a trading transaction. Common features of such transactions are prearranged or early sales and funding of the purchase to be reimbursed from the proceeds of sale. Such transactions merit close scrutiny to see whether a trading argument is appropriate.

The HMRC argument is that:

- such transactions involve two separate assets – the tenancy and the freehold;

- the tenancy is a capital asset and any gain on that asset will be a capital gain;

- the freehold was not acquired with the intention to retain but to sell at profit;

- the freehold was therefore never part of the taxpayer's capital structure and is not consequently a capital asset;

- it is the profit on the freehold alone that HMRC wish to isolate, and tax as the profit of an adventure in the nature of trade; and

- that profit is part of a marriage of profit which is generated when the tenancy and the freehold merge.

ARTIFICIAL TRANSACTIONS IN LAND

Definition

14.45 Further to the consideration of farmland sales not being caught as capital gains, developers are usually caught under the terms of ITA 2007 s 756, which encompasses cases where: 'land is developed with the sole or main object of realising a gain from disposing of the land when developed'. The aim of this section is for HMRC to prevent property-dealing profits being treated as capital.

It has been said that some farmers and landowners enjoy 'growing houses' more than growing crops and after one genuine disposal they start to 'trade' in land. The purpose is to prevent property-dealing profits being disguised as capital. The circumstances are clear and are likely to be kept to two situations:

- the disposal of shares in a property company (*Yuill v Wilson* [1980] STC 460); or

- where a UK resident passes the opportunity to make a trading profit on UK land to an overseas company.

The scope of ITA 2007 s 756 is broad and catches transactions which have little or no element of artificiality; therefore the avoidance can be accidental or unwitting by the landowner. With the current shortage of houses, there could be farmers and landowners who are caught in these provisions.

The rules apply in the following circumstances:

- land is developed with the sole or main object of realising a gain from disposal later;

- land is held as trading stock; or

- the land or any interest that has its value derived from it (eg shares in a landowning company, interests in partnerships, etc) is acquired with the sole or main object of realising a gain on disposal.

In order for ITA 2007 s 756 to apply, a gain of a capital nature must result. Section 756 means that the gain could not be chargeable as income under any of the Taxes Acts if it is trade. If a trade exists, the sale will be caught in the trading in land provisions.

A farmer who sells land confident that any tax will be sheltered under the provisions of CGT relief could be caught for the 50% income tax rate as opposed to the 18% and/or 28% tax rates of CGT.

In summary, the disposal of land by a farmer can fall into three taxable activities:

- a genuine capital gain;

- trading in the development of houses (a property developer);

- a capital gain that is developed with the sole purpose of realising a gain and is therefore an 'artificial transaction in land'.

'Slice of the action' schemes

14.46 One of the most common applications of ITA 2007 s 756 involves 'slice of the action' schemes. These schemes involve the landowner selling surplus land to a developer, receiving a fixed sum, followed by future contingent payments based upon the success of the development. The developer himself will be trading and will, in effect, be passing some of the trading profits on to the former landowner. The receipt will be of a capital nature in the landowner's hands and accordingly will be caught by ITA 2007 s 756, as a trading profit has emerged in a capital form. HMRC's authority for treating additional payments in this way can be found in *Page v Lowther* [1983] STC 61. The fixed sum, however, will remain chargeable to CGT. It is the contingent payments that must be taxable as trading profit.

ITA 2007 s 756 cannot be invoked where the landowner could be charged under trading profit – refer to the 'badges of trade' to see if it is pure trading.

ITA 2007 s 756 cannot apply in respect of the disposal of a main residence, which is exempt from CGT (TCGA 1992 s 222), or would be if it were not for TCGA 1992 s 224(3) regarding residences acquired wholly or partly for the purpose of realising a gain from the disposal.

Non-resident company

14.47   Other schemes that evoke ITA 2007 s 756 are normally intentional rather than unwitting. A common device involves structuring what is, in essence, a trading transaction in land in such a way that the gain is realised by a person who is not within a charge to UK income tax. This can be done by diverting profits into non-resident companies, as was the case in *Sugarwhite v Budd* [1988] STC 533. It was held that a person who provides the opportunity of making a gain to someone else (who is non-taxable) could be taxed under ITA 2007 s 756.

First intention date

14.48   When ITA 2007 s 756 applies, the gain is taxed for income tax purposes as income arising when the gain is realised, but there is a restriction of the charge (ITA 2007 s 756). The effect is that the gain attributable to the period before the intention to develop the land was formed is excluded. Any gain that has arisen while the land was being used as a capital asset is chargeable to CGT, not under ITA 2007 s 756. This requires the land to be valued at 'the first intention date'. The amount chargeable under ITA 2007 s 756 will normally be the difference between the total proceeds (ie fixed sum plus contingent payments) and the market value of the land at the 'first intention date'. The latter is used as the disposal proceeds in the CGT computation.

The 'first intention date' is a question of fact.

Advance clearance procedures

14.49   A formal HMRC advance clearance procedure is available in respect of transactions potentially falling within ITA 2007 s 756. This can be made before or after the relevant transaction. However, it is rarely used in practice since disclosure puts HMRC on notice, and there is a tendency for Inspectors to 'play safe' if there are any doubts, knowing full well that an enquiry can be raised once the tax return has been submitted.

Freehold reversion – purchase by the sitting tenant

14.50   This has been effectively looked at: see **14.44** – Tenant's disposal of superior interest in land. A sitting tenant will want to acquire the freehold reversion from the landlord in order to unlock the marriage value. What are the tax implications if the tenant sells part of the freehold after acquiring the reversion? Has he entered into a trading transaction or will he be able to use the shelter of CGT?

The answer to this will often depend on how the acquisition is financed. A common arrangement in these circumstances will be the provision of funds in the form of a bridging loan. The loan will be conditional on its being repaid shortly after the purchase and the lender will usually expect that there is a willing buyer of the freehold land already lined up. The transaction is likely to be viewed as trading.

This will result in the tenancy being appropriated from fixed assets to trading stock (TCGA 1992 s 161(1)), which will represent a deemed disposal at market value for CGT purposes. This same value will then be deductible in computing the income tax profit.

However, the deemed disposal of the tenancy could give rise to significant gains (especially if the tenancy was not in existence on 31 March 1982). However, the tenant can elect for no capital gains to arise (TCGA 1992 s 161(3)) and the value of the tenancy acquired as trading stock will be such that it produces neither a gain nor a loss on appropriation. This would avoid valuing the tenancy where it has commenced after 31 March 1982.

Diversification into the trade of property developer

14.51   It may well be that the farmer/landowner wishes to diversify into the trade of property developer. The diversification 'option' of the farmer developing the land himself is dealt with in Chapter 6. Development can be an investment operation and it can be a trading activity. It depends whether it is intended to retain or sell the property. If the intention is to try and obtain a rental income from the property, then it is an investment. The IHT angles of the investment have already been looked at (see Chapters 5 and 13).

OPTION AGREEMENTS

Timing and business usage

14.52   In a lot of cases the farmer will sell his land to a professional developer, and this will be classed as a CGT disposal.

However, the possibility of progressive and deferred sales and the use of option agreements should be considered. In the nature of things, developers are often only too ready to defer completion of transactions, and this readiness needs to be taken advantage of in terms of tax planning.

If a series of options are entered into with the sole aim of obtaining CGT annual exemptions, then the basic principles of *Ramsay*, with extension by *Furniss v Dawson*, cannot be overlooked, ie the Inspector will be very aware of general anti-avoidance rules.

So as to avoid the restriction of roll-over, ensure that land over which a client has granted an option to a developer does not stand unused, or becomes incapable of use because it is inaccessible as a result of work that the developer has started on adjacent land. This can happen during the construction of motorways or other developments. All the problems raised in the book on the failure to qualify as a business asset apply in this case. CG61020 sets out the position that HMRC accept that roll-over relief on replacement of business assets is available in respect of a grant of an option over land by reference to the underlying land, though the land has to be occupied as well as used for the purposes of the claimant's trade to qualify.

It may be prudent to preserve photographic or other evidence of farming use of the land right up to the day when the option is exercised.

Deferred consideration may fail to qualify for roll-over relief.

When does the option qualify for CGT?

14.53   An option is not a part disposal of the underlying land over which the option is granted (TCGA 1992 s 144). The grant of the option is the disposal of a separate asset. In terms of the option itself, because it is not a part disposal, it does not matter how long the underlying land has been held by the person granting the option. In a straightforward situation where the option is never exercised, capital gains tax arises on the grant of the option.

Once the option is exercised, the disposal created by the grant of the option is cancelled (TCGA 1992 s 144(2) and (3)) and the sums received for both the grant and the exercise of the option are aggregated in one disposal at the time of the exercise.

This is an area of complexity and must be given close consideration where the top income tax rate of 50% exceeds the top CGT rate of 28%.

Exercise of option

14.54   If the option is subsequently exercised, the original grant and the subsequent exercise are treated as a single transaction (TCGA 1992 s 144(2)) (see **14.53**).

The treatment of the consideration paid for the option is as follows: the grantor of the option adds the consideration for a 'put' option to the sale proceeds; alternatively he deducts the consideration for a 'call' option from the acquisition cost.

The case of *Mansworth v Jelley* [2002] EWCA Civ 1829, [2003] STC 53 established that the market value rule applied not only to the grant of an option but also to the disposal of the asset subject to the option once it was exercised. This had the consequence that on exercise of the option the application of the market value rule to the grant of the option was ignored (as was the price actually paid, if any, for the grant). FA 2003 amended this interpretation for options exercised on or after 10 April 2003 by inserting TCGA 1992 s 144ZA. From 10 April 2003, if the market value rule is applied to the grant of the option, the subsequent exercise of the option does not undo that application of the market value rule. Instead, on exercise, the disposal proceeds for the asset transferred (and the acquisition cost for the person acquiring it) are calculated by aggregating the market value of the option when granted with the amount actually paid under the terms of the option when the option is exercised. Again this emphasises the need for all farmers/landowners who hold option rights or are thinking of entering into an option agreement to review the overall tax position.

PROBLEMS OF DEVELOPMENT – ALTERNATIVE LAND USE

14.55 The question of protecting hope value from IHT is looked at in Chapter 5 (**5.33**). The question of developing land as a rural initiative is first looked at in Chapter 6 (see **6.38**).

The question of sheltering development profits from tax was looked at in Chapter 10 as the tax advantage can attract the 'reluctant farmer' into the farming world in order to take advantage of the tax relief (see **10.8–10.10**).

Planning consent for residential development may be difficult to obtain, but in terms of the value involved, this may be the most substantial category of diversification. There is all the more reason to review the tax consideration. James Cleary explains the process of obtaining planning permissions in Chapter 3.

Commercially, it may be beneficial to retain some right over the land in order to keep some control over future development. Overage is looked at in **14.5** and **14.6**. Ransom strips or covenants can be used to protect the landowner. Ransom strips result in part disposal rules (see **14.37**). Covenants are a capital asset and so again result in a part disposal. Their value will be difficult to ascertain, and so will have negligible cost.

Sale of land to a developer – not trading in land

14.56 As set out in **6.38**, a farmer who has owned land with no intention of selling does not become a property developer just because he takes steps to enhance the value of the property to the developer who might want to acquire the land (*Taylor v Good* [1973] STC 383).

Development is not defined by statute. HMRC interpretation is any physical adaptation or preparation for a new use of land (see BIM60460).

The increase in value created by planning consent, representing the difference between agricultural value and development value, can raise problems if matters are not thought through first.

The development by the farmer himself of houses for sale will be an adventure in the nature of trade as a developer or property dealer. The question of whether or not there is a trade is dealt with at **14.41**.

There are circumstances where it must be accepted that the trade of property developer has started and the eligibility to CGT reliefs ceases. As mentioned previously, this must be planned accordingly.

Land – compulsory purchase

14.57 Where land is compulsorily acquired, it is common to find that payment may be made for land, which is conveyed, and for diminution in value of adjacent land, which is retained by the farmer (see **1.18**). The CGT consequences are different.

The date of disposal is usually the date upon which the acquiring authority went into occupation (but would be the contract date if earlier) but the price payable is often not finally settled until some years later. This can make planning difficult, but the first approach would be to seek to eliminate liability under the small part disposal rules – in particular those applying to disposals to authorities having compulsory purchase powers (TCGA 1992 ss 242 and 243). If the disposal falls outside the criteria for exemption, then consideration should be given to the availability of roll-over relief.

The severance payments are regarded as part disposals under TCGA 1992 s 22, with the timing of the disposal being the date on which each payment is received. As the total amount payable is often spread over a number of instalments, the ability to exempt the gain under the small disposal provisions is increased. Again, if these provisions do not cover the position and there remain gains outside the annual exemptions, roll-over relief is available.

Owner of tenanted land with development value

14.58 The disposal of tenanted land will qualify for CGT rates of 18% and/or 28% but it is doubtful it will qualify for ER. It would probably be possible to offer an incentive to procure a surrender of the tenancy. Such a transaction should not be entered into without the help of a lawyer.

The Lands Tribunal case of *Bairds Executors v IRC* [1990] SVC 188 did confirm that a tenancy had a value, but gave no guidance as to how the value should be ascertained. HMRC's approach had broadly been to regard one-half of the difference between the tenanted and the vacant possession values of the freehold as being the value of the tenancy.

REINVESTMENT RELIEF AND ENTERPRISE INVESTMENT SCHEMES (EIS) DEFERRAL RELIEF

Deferral relief

14.59 Chapter 8 on incorporation looks at EIS. Farming does not qualify as an EIS trade, nor does property; however, some diversification activities might (see **8.16–8.19**).

In reality the EIS deferral relief in other projects could be of use to farmers wanting to shelter their gains via the deferral option.

As mentioned in Chapter 8, EIS might not be considered relevant to this book, as farming and market gardening are not qualifying trades. VCT can also be considered.

As announced in the coalition government Budget on 22 June 2010, to comply with EU state aid rules, a number of changes are required for venture capital trusts (VCTs) and enterprise investment schemes (EISs).

For VCTs there will be a change in the definition of eligible shares and the minimum holding of such shares will rise to 70% from the current 30%.

Company shares will be excluded from qualifying for VCTs and EISs if the company is an 'enterprise in difficulty'. The current rule that a company must have a qualifying trade carried on wholly or mainly in the UK will be replaced with a requirement that the company must have a permanent establishment in the UK.

Legislation is in inance (No 3) Act 2010 Sch 2 but no date has yet been set for implementation. The new eligible shares rule will not affect funds raised by VCTs before the implementation date.

Cottages and retired farm workers

14.60   Farm cottages occupied by a retired farm worker under a protected occupancy, under the Rent (Agriculture) Act 1976 or equivalent provisions of the 1988 Housing Acts, did not qualify as business assets for CGT taper relief purposes, because they were not considered to be in use for the purposes of the farming trade. The new flat rate of 18% and recently increased to a top rate of 28% for CGT disposal could therefore be attractive for some farmers and landowners.

Property valuations – the Red Book

14.61   The 'Red Book' is looked at in Chapter 5 (**5.45**).

Those instructing valuations, including CGT base values in 1982, should understand that Royal Institution of Chartered Surveyors (RICS) members are now required to do this in a formal structure under the 'Red Book' and cannot, under professional rules of the Institution, simply give an estimate. This will not, of course, prevent landowners indicating that they might wish to sell, have a number of agents running around and putting forward valuations, which will be used 'illegally' (see **19.30**).

It is a common trap to overlook the circumstances, which existed in March 1982; if the farm was then subject to a tenancy, its value at that time would be very considerably discounted below the vacant possession value, and thus a large gain might arise. The same point may apply to farm cottages where they were occupied in March 1982, and even more forcefully to the shares in a company to the extent that they are in minority holdings.

It is considered that for discussions with the District Valuer (DV), the RICS Red Book valuations are necessary for property values for IHT and CGT land and property disposals.

Indexation relief

14.62   Indexation relief ceased to be effective from 6 April 2008.

DIVERSIFICATION – GIFTS TO FAMILY MEMBERS

14.63   The bold step of gifting all or part of the farming enterprise now is looked at in Chapter 5 – protecting assets (see **5.8**).

There will be cases where as part of the diversification process it may be timely to make gifts of land or buildings to other family members, as part of a planned programme of succession.

Suggested action may be to put the assets in the same hands as the son/daughter who is going to carry on the new diversified business; or the timing may reflect a belief held by the client that the current generous IHT regime, including potentially exempt transfers, and APR at 100%, cannot last forever. This has been looked at in Chapter 13.

Other angles which need to be looked at are:

- CGT (see **14.26**) hold-over relief;

- IHT the 'mere asset' rule and now ER the whole or part of trading activity;

- possibility of a 'failed potentially exempt transfer' (see **13.18–13.24**);

- gifts with reservation of benefit (see **5.11**); and

- SDLT.

PROPERTY TRANSACTIONS IN GENERAL

14.64   As stated in **14.1**, it is probably this chapter that will be read the most. There is an inescapable fact facing farmers – whilst incomes drop, property values increase. This, together with the emphasis on the reluctant farmer (see Chapter 10), ie the landowner who can embrace business tax reliefs through farming – makes the whole question of property tax relief very relevant. Whether it is the protection (as set out in Chapter 5) or the disposal (as set out in this chapter), the subject is complex and with potentially large tax reliefs at risk. The aim of this publication is to help consider the alternatives for both protection and planning.

HMRC APPROACH TO TAX AVOIDANCE

14.65   It is hoped that the approach of this book throughout has been to use legitimate tax planning, with the emphasis on 'planning ahead to use the tax reliefs efficiently'.

Tax avoidance remains a strong theme for the government. It had already announced legislative changes to target various widely marketed tax mitigation plans, eg certain film partnerships, gilt strips and deficiency relief. FA 2004 announced further measures, such as attacking companies acting through partnerships. In addition, it brought in new disclosure requirements to make accountancy firms provide details to HMRC certain to be defined 'schemes and arrangements'.

The behaviour-based penalty regime was introduced by FA 2007 Sch 24 from 1 April 2008. FA 2008 Sch 40 extended the behaviour-based penalty regime introduced in FA 2007 Sch 24 to IHT.

At a practical level, the HMRC approach to IHT enquiries has moved from 'benign' to 'battling'. It has been said that enquiries into IHT liabilities on farming estates are certain post 1 April 2009.

Areas of the IHT account that HMRC have been known to look at closely following the submission of IHT 400 are as follows:

- under-valuations where there are no IHT reliefs available;

- over-valuations where there are reliefs and the high value could benefit tax relief in the future, eg base costs for CGT;

- incorrect claims for reliefs, eg BPR where there is no business carried on for gain, where there is an investment business not a trading business (IHTA 1984 s 105(3)), APR ensuring strict restriction to agricultural value and the occupation rule applies.

An example of a complexity of valuation is the quantum of hope value (the difference between market value and agricultural value) of potential development land at the date of death. The PRs have a responsibility to obtain a quality valuation that shows a well-researched review of potential hope value. It is considered that the quality of the valuation is more important than the *number* of valuations.

Farmland and redundant farm buildings could result in property development gains for farmers and landowners who will seek 'exotic' tax-planning schemes and arrangements not covered in this book – beware! (See **19.3**.) With the drop in development land values from 2008 it might be argued that these gains are a planning point for the future.

THE SET-ASIDE SCHEME – LAND DISPOSALS AND CGT

14.66   From 1 January 2009 there is no longer any requirement for farmers to set aside land (see **2.4**).

The fact that land has been set aside will not affect the basis of computation of any gains arising when some, or all, of the land is disposed of. Where the set-aside land is left fallow, HMRC take the view that farming nevertheless continues on the land and that the set-aside receipts are income of the farming trade. This is so even where the whole of the arable land of a farmer is set-aside. The farmer remains in occupation of the land and is obliged under the rules of the scheme to maintain the land in good agricultural condition by performing certain acts of husbandry – sowing and cutting a clover crop, maintaining drainage, hedges, fences, etc. This is sufficient to constitute the continuation of 'farming' for the purposes of ITTOIA 2005 s 9(1) and ITA 2007 s 89.

If the set-aside land is put to some use other than a farming trade, then the farming tax reliefs could be lost. If a new activity commences, the question has to be whether the new use amounts to a use in a trade, which qualifies as a business asset.

Chapter 15

Farmland and buildings – the letting activity

Julie Butler

- **Surplus farm property and land letting opportunities**
  This is possibly the most significant form of farm diversification in terms of income stream and profit. For income tax purposes ensure that the interaction of trading and property income is considered and that maximum expenses are claimed. The further IHT impact of the *Farmer* case has been looked at in great detail in Chapter 13 as well as the *Earl of Balfour* case.

- **Furnished holiday lets (FHLs)**
  This was potentially a very tax-efficient form of diversification for the farmer/landowner. The basic tax planning is looked at in Chapter 5. FHLs are treated as a separate diversified activity in Chapter 6. However, the proposed changes to the rules from 6 April 2011 have major implications. Is this a letting activity (FHL), or a business activity (FHB)?

- **Farm business tenancies (FBTs)**
  These are looked at in depth in Chapter 11.

- **Grazing rights, tenancies and licences**

  Again these are looked at in depth in Chapter 11 following the *McCall* case.

- **VAT time bomb for partial exemption**

  The supply of land (which includes farm buildings and cottages) is an exempt supply for VAT which causes problems of partial exemption.

FURNISHED LETS

History

15.1   One of the first forms of diversification for the farming industry has been the letting out of 'redundant' farm cottages. Traditional farming units contained a large number of cottages for farm workers but, as farm machinery improved efficiency and fewer workers were required, so more and more cottages became available to let out. In addition, various redundant traditional farm buildings originally designed for smaller equipment have been converted into residential accommodation, which has the potential of being let out (or sold for development, see Chapter 14).

In the current climate rental income is at a height where many landowners and farmers are looking to maximise their income from property. The planning permission angles are set out by James Cleary in Chapter 3.

The IHT position is explained in detail in Chapter 13 (see *Farmer (Farmer's Executors) v IRC* [1999] STC (SCD) 321 and *Earl of Balfour*).

Tax treatment – when can trading status be achieved?

15.2 There are cases when letting income can be treated as farming income (see **12.6**).

BIM41015 indicates when HMRC will allow rents to be included in the computation of business profits. The object is to avoid the need to apportion outgoings on accommodation partly used for business purposes and partly let. The circumstances are as follows.

- The accommodation must be temporarily surplus to current business requirements. That is, it must have been used or intended to be used in the business.

- The individual premises must be partly used for the business and partly let. The treatment cannot be applied if a whole building is let, as there would be no need to apportion expenses.

- The rental income must be comparatively small.

- The rent must be in respect of the letting of surplus business accommodation only and not land.

Where rents have been included as farming income, however, this does not mean that the properties will be regarded as assets of the business for CGT (eg for roll-over), or as agricultural property for IHT.

The general position with regard to rents received from farm cottage letting is that they are assessed as letting income separate from the main trade of farming. The exception is FHL – see **15.34–15.36**. The letting income should be included in the main farm accounts and the management of the properties incorporated in the management of the farm accounts (see *Farmer (Farmer's Executors) v IRC* [1999] STC (SCD) 321 at **13.25–13.45**) for the IHT benefit to be achieved. It is essential that the letting is included in the main farm enterprise.

In sorting out the division between trading and letting income, the income and expenses must be deducted in the business tax computation. As mentioned previously the income should be integrated in the accounts. It is imperative to claim the correct expenses against the correct source of income. There are tax-planning implications where there are trading tax losses brought forward. Advantages in maximising 'trading' profits and minimising letting income can be looked into. The tax position of each individual, partnership or limited company is different, but the planning implications of expenses allocation should be considered.

There can be valid reasons to have separate rental accounts, but the impact of *Farmer* needs review and these are better dealt with as 'enterprise' accounts.

VAT TIME BOMB FOR PARTIAL EXEMPTION

15.3   Whilst VAT is the subject of Chapter 9 it is impossible not to mention it in relation to farm letting activity.

Do farmers and landowners understand an exempt supply? Above all, do they understand a partial exemption calculation? It would appear that very few farmers and landowners carry out their VAT partial exemption calculations correctly. Indeed, many do not even realise that they are partially exempt traders. A decade or two ago, the farming VAT Return was a simple affair. Agricultural outputs are zero-rated, so there were virtually no output VAT or exempt supplies arising from diversification and the maximum input VAT could be claimed, subject to minor debates about the private use of telephone and the dreaded 'scale charge' for motor vehicles. The only other problem was 'blocked' input tax on non-business activities.

How times have changed. The majority of farmers have moved away from the pure trade of farming and into the 'land and property' sector. The implications include not only charging VAT on standard rated supplies but also restricting input tax claims to take account of exempt supplies (the 'partial exemption' calculation), not to mention consideration of the 'option to tax'. Many farmers have not enjoyed a VAT inspection for some time (in some cases, as long as ten years) and there could be a potential problem of VAT arrears – a VAT time bomb?

The first step must be for the farmer to list all the supplies made by the farm and note any which are standard rated or VAT exempt. So what qualifies as standard rated? Examples are income from holiday cottages, caravan and camping pitches, from parking and sporting facilities and from selling the right to fell and remove standing timber. The farmer must then ensure that VAT is charged and accounted for on all standard-rated supplies. But more complex and serious problems are likely to arise when the farm generates substantial VAT-exempt income.

As farm workers have disappeared, their cottages have been re-let. Likewise old agricultural buildings, such as pig sheds and dairies which are no longer needed, have been converted and let out for residential use. Except in the case of holiday lets, residential lets are an exempt supply for VAT. Often the farm income has grown with the residential lets, but the input VAT on the expenses of the whole enterprise has been reclaimed. What of consideration for partial exemption?

It is quite normal for a 1,000-acre farm to have say ten surplus cottages. Many farms have completed conversions of old farm buildings which can result in a greater income from lets than from farming. Often it is only the letting income which ensures that the overall enterprise is profitable. Unless an 'option to tax' is made, commercial lets will also be an exempt supply.

The basis of calculation is as set out below.

Calculating the input tax restriction

15.4   Where a farm is making exempt supplies via letting income, the farmer must remember that the legislation denies relief not only for input tax directly attributable to the exempt supplies (eg input tax on the cost of repairs to a let residential building), but also for a proportion of the input tax suffered on the 'mixed costs' of the farm – the 'overhead expenses' which relate to both taxable and exempt supplies. Under the 'standard method', input tax on 'mixed costs' is allowed in the ratio of taxable sales (zero and standard rated) to total sales. Accordingly, where a high proportion of the farm income is VAT exempt, an equally high proportion of the input VAT on 'mixed costs' will be disallowed.

The key here will be careful analysis of the input tax incurred and its allocation between taxable and exempt activities. In exceptional circumstances, an application to use a 'special method' could be considered, but the benefit to be gained is unlikely to be enough to make this worthwhile.

Easement for smaller businesses

15.5   However, many smaller farms will be able to benefit from the easement which allows a trader to obtain full VAT recovery where the 'exempt' element is relatively small. This is fully explained in VAT Notice 706 Partial Exemption (December 2006).

Conversely, if the annual recalculation shows that the farmer's exempt input tax is within the *de minimis* limit taking the year as a whole, the trader will be treated as fully taxable for the whole year. Any input tax he did not claim on a VAT Return during the year because he was above the *de minimis* limit for that quarter (or month) may then be recovered.

This easement does not affect the treatment of 'blocked' input tax (eg on cars and business entertainment), which is always non-recoverable.

Partial exemption annual adjustments (which are correctly carried out and entered in the farmer's VAT account for the correct period) are not errors and do not have to be notified to the local VAT business centre under the voluntary disclosure procedure. However, the farmer should remember that a trader cannot use the annual adjustment to correct actual errors, such as input tax incorrectly treated as exempt when in fact the goods or services were used to make taxable supplies from the outset. Errors such as these should be corrected in accordance with the guidance in Notice 700/45 How to correct VAT errors and make adjustments or claims.

Clawback and payback

15.6   In principle, input tax is allocated to taxable or exempt supplies according to the use the trader intends to make of the relevant purchase. However, paragraph 11.3 of Notice 706 emphasises the problem for the farmer. To quote: 'The land and property sector is an area where it can be particularly difficult to establish what your intentions are when you receive supplies. [For example] a supply that would otherwise be exempt may become taxable if an option to tax is made and notified to HMRC …' Accordingly, to avoid distortions, a system of 'clawback' and 'payback' applies:

Input tax relief claimed will be clawed back where:

- the farmer has claimed input tax on goods or services because he or she intended to use them in making taxable supplies but in the event used them, or formed an intention to use them, in making either exempt supplies or both taxable and exempt supplies; or

- the farmer has claimed input tax on goods or services because he or she intended to use them in making both taxable and exempt supplies but in the event used them, or formed an intention to use them, in making exempt supplies only; and

- in either case the change of intention occurs within six years of the beginning of the period covered by the VAT Return in which the original intention was formed.

If 'clawback' applies, the farmer will be required to recalculate the input tax he has claimed in the past tax periods and repay any amount over claimed. The farmer must do this on the Return for the period in which the use occurs or the revised intention is formed. The farmer's recalculation must be carried out using the partial exemption method the farmer used when making the original claim to input tax.

Conversely, 'payback' arises where:

- the farmer has not claimed input tax on goods and services because the intention was to use them in making exempt supplies but in the event they were used, or the farmer formed an intention to use them, in making taxable supplies or both taxable and exempt supplies; or

- the farmer has not claimed input tax on goods or services because he or she intended to use them in making both taxable and exempt supplies but in the event used them, or formed an intention to use them, in making only taxable supplies; and

- in either case the change of intention occurs within six years of the beginning of the period covered by the VAT Return in which the original intention was formed.

If 'payback' applies, the farmer should write to the local VAT business centre applying for a sum equal to the under-claimed input tax to be repaid. When the local VAT business centre has confirmed the amount to be repaid, the farmer can enter this in his VAT account as an under-claim and include it in his next VAT Return. When the farmer calculates the amount under-claimed, he must use the partial exemption method used when making the original claim to input tax.

Action to be taken by the farmer

15.7   So, the farmer, having come to terms with the consideration that 'partial exemption' might apply to his business, now has to look at what action he can take.

Many farmers did not have a long-term plan to move into the land and property VAT sector. Many have been aware of the partial exemption rules, but have been unaware of the possible advantage of 'payback'. By contrast many farmers have been aware of the disallowability of input VAT, but find it all too complicated and are just awaiting the next VAT inspection, when the helpful official from the VAT office will tell them how much extra VAT they owe and advise them on how to move forward with partial exemption calculations. There must be a better way!

Cottages held outside the trading activity

15.8 Many farm cottages are held outside the trade of farming, the rent being shown directly on the farmer's self-assessment Tax Return as income from land and property. There are no apparent VAT problems – but what of the loss of potential IHT relief? The case of *Farmer's Executors* [1999] STC (SCD) 321 comes to mind (see Chapter 13). A Special Commissioner held that 22 let units (cottages and premises for small businesses) were eligible for IHT BPR because they were part of the wider farming business – included in the farm accounts, organised from the farm office etc.

Horse liveries

15.9 Are horse liveries letting income or a business that provides a service? The VAT position is complex.

Livery yards obtained a potential boost when VAT charged to clients with minimum service (Business Brief 21/2001) was deemed to be exempt. However, it comes with the downside of the 'exempt' supply – not being able to claim back input VAT and the possible complexities of partial exemption. This can cause large problems when the livery yard is part of a diversified farm.

This brief seems a contradiction to the basic principle of the grant of right over land, for the supply of land is exempt. However, 'full' livery by definition means that the service is not ancillary to the supply of land. Full means a horse being 'fully' looked after. The result is that there is a variance in the interpretation of 'full'. In many establishments, DIY and part liveries are treated as exempt, but full liveries are charged standard-rated VAT as it is considered that by definition the volume of the services provided do not fulfil the basic principle of exemption criteria.

Problems can arise in deciding whether schooling and breaking in are provided. If the yard is mainly a specialist breaking yard, then any supply relating to breaking in will be standard-rated and the provision of livery services will be ancillary to this and therefore standard rated. On the other hand, if the main purpose of the yard is livery, with schooling or breaking as an add-on, then the entire supply will be exempt.

The farmer's long-term plan

15.10 It is essential to produce a full list of all property included in or linked to the VAT registration. A 'property audit' should be carried out, to consider not just VAT, but also IHT, capital gains tax, income tax, corporation tax, SDLT and National Insurance contributions. Such an audit is necessary, not least because many farmers are unclear as to who owns what and why.

This should be an opportunity to review not just partial exemption but the 'option to tax' and the full VAT position on the interaction of land and property with the trading activity of farming. With the 'VAT attack' on shooting there is scope to incorporate shooting rights and property leases. And a final point: have all rights, licences and general casual letting been checked for the correct documentation and VAT treatment? The rural world is changing.

Capital allowances and wear and tear allowance

15.11   No capital allowances are available on machinery or plant (eg furniture, fixtures and fittings) let for use in a dwelling house. For example, if a house is let furnished, no capital allowances are given on the furniture (wear-and-tear/renewals allowances are available instead). However, where furnished holiday lets (FHLs) are treated as if a trade then capital allowances are available on items of furniture etc (see **6.13**).

Capital allowances are available for machinery or plant used or provided for use for the purpose of a letting income business and are deductible as a business expense.

Expenditure on furniture etc that would otherwise be disallowed, qualifies for wear-and-tear allowances calculated on 10% of the rents less any expenditure that the landlord meets which would normally be the tenant's responsibility, eg water, council tax etc.

The wear-and-tear allowance is intended to cover furniture and furnishings, and fixtures of a type which, in unfurnished accommodation, a tenant would normally provide for himself (eg cookers, washing machines, dishwashers). It only applies to furnished residential accommodation (not commercial/ industrial property where capital allowances are available). Additionally, the accommodation must be fully furnished so that the tenant could occupy the accommodation without necessarily having to provide any of his/her own furniture etc. Wear-and-tear allowances cannot be claimed in respect of qualifying holiday lets (as capital allowances will be available).

Renewal basis

The principle

15.12   As an alternative to the wear-and-tear allowance, the cost of the renewal of furnishings, fixtures etc, may be claimed. The conditions that must be met are:

- There should be no deduction for the original expenditure (disadvantageous for long-life assets).

- No claim should be made for the cost of any improvement element (a more expensive item does not necessarily constitute an improvement).

- The old asset should be definitely discarded before renewals allowance on its replacement is due; the old asset cannot be kept as a reserve.

Renewal of fixtures that are an integral part of the building

15.13   The landlord can claim the cost of renewing fixtures which are an integral part of the building which would not normally be removed by either tenant or owner if the property were vacated or sold (eg baths, washbasins, toilets). Expenditure on renewing such items may be treated as expenditure on repairs in addition to the 10% wear-and-tear allowance.

One estate election

15.14   The 'one estate election' allowed an owner-occupier of a mansion house to deduct excess allowable expenses over a notional rent against rents received from other properties on the estate (ICTA 1988 s 26).

Note, however, that the one estate election has been repealed as from 2001–02 (from 1 April 2001 for companies).

Rent-a-room exemption

15.15   Rent-a-room applies to income from providing furnished residential accommodation in the owner or tenant's main residence. This applies whether the rent would be assessable as trading or rental income. It can, therefore, apply to bed and breakfast accommodation but not where any part of the residence is let out as unfurnished (eg let as office accommodation). (See ITTOIA 2005 Pt 7 Ch 1; PIM4000 et seq.)

The scheme is for qualifying individuals and does not apply to companies or partnerships. However, it can apply when individuals have the income jointly (eg husband and wife where there is no partnership).

It is not necessary for the residence to be the individual's only or main residence throughout the whole of the basis period. Occupation as the main residence at some time during the basis period is sufficient.

Gross annual receipts of £4,250 are exempt from tax under the scheme which includes additional services eg meals as well as rent. Where receipts are in excess of £4,250, the taxpayer has a choice of:

● preparing an income and expenditure account and being taxed on any profit; or

● being assessed on the excess gross rents over £4,250 with no relief for expenses being available.

An election is required for the latter, which must be made within one year after the 31 January following the relevant tax year. Once an election is made it remains in force until it is withdrawn. The time limits for a withdrawal are the same as for the election. It is, therefore, possible to apply or disapply the exemption on a year-by-year basis.

Business property relief (BPR) – let property

15.16   So what is the inheritance tax position on let property qualifying for BPR? This is discussed in great depth in *Farmer (Farmer's Executors) v IRC*

[1999] STC (SCD) 321 (see Chapter 13), but not all landowning situations meet the criteria established in this case and each situation must be reviewed in depth. The case that preceded *Farmer*, or set the foundation was *George*. Please also see Chapter 13. The *Earl of Balfour* case has added further hope for BPR on let property.

BPR – the importance of George

15.17   *IRC v George (Executors of Stedman)* [2003] EWCA Civ 1763, [2004] STC 147 went to the Court of Appeal and is now an authority when letting income (eg site fees) needs to be made more robust by services provided. In common with many other cases, *George* concerned a caravan site on which several activities were conducted. These included a residential park of caravans owned by their residents on which site fees were paid, and profits made from the supply of utilities; a club and bar open to all; storage facilities for touring caravans; an administration office; let property; agricultural grazing land subject to licences; and commissions from an insurance agency and from sales of caravans. It had been a feature of previous cases that services provided in connection with any lease or licence were part of letting and hence an investment activity. It was an important finding of the Court of Appeal in *George* that the characterisation of additional services or facilities depended upon the nature and purpose of the activity.

The importance of additional services or facilities

15.18   Thus, in *George* these additional services or facilities were not of necessity investment activities. They were not of necessity incidental to a letting. This was important because it meant that the supply of utilities to the residential caravans was not of necessity an investment activity ancillary to the site lettings. The approach favoured by the Court of Appeal in *George* when considering a multi-faceted business was to consider the nature of the whole business in the round. In an observation that will provide much comfort to many diversified rural businesses, Lord Justice Carnwath observed 'I find it difficult to see any reason why an active family business of this kind should be excluded from business relief, merely because a necessary component of its profit-making activity is the use of land.' A subsequent Special Commissioner's decision which followed the principle laid down in *George*, this time in the context of a property rental and development company, was *Clark v IRC* [2005] SpC 502.

The judgments in *Farmer* and *George* have important implications for the majority of family farming businesses. Both judgments emphasise that it is possible to secure valuable BPR on let property. The *Earl of Balfour* case must also be considered.

There is no doubt that the letting out of property is currently one of the most profitable uses of assets available to the landowner and farmer. However, as with all areas of diversification, the tax efficiency and implications must be fully considered. The short-term income advantages must not be taken without fully protecting the income tax, IHT and CGT advantages (see **13.51**).

VAT

15.19 Rents from holiday accommodation in buildings, huts, caravans, houseboats or tents are standard rated for VAT provided the accommodation is advertised and held out as such. Holiday accommodation advertised or offered at lower rates during the off season can be treated as residential accommodation, where it is let for that purpose for more than four weeks, and the property is situated in a holiday resort where trade is clearly seasonal. In such cases the whole let, including the first four weeks, is an exempt supply. The 'season' in such resorts would normally be expected to be at least from Easter to the end of September.

It is generally understood that despite the review of the FHL legislation post 5 April 2011, the VAT on holiday lets will remain at the standard rate.

BED AND BREAKFAST

15.20 The situation where the farmer runs a bed and breakfast as a positive diversified activity has been dealt with at **6.16**. It can be a clear and separate diversified activity.

The whole activity of bed and breakfast is only likely to amount to a trade where the owner remains in occupation of the property and services are provided substantially beyond those normally offered by a landlord. The key factor for assessment as trading income, and therefore greater chance of BPR, is the provision of services. For longer term lets, HMRC tend to argue that there are two sources of income: one of rent (letting income) and the other relating to the provision of services where significant, and including meals (trading income). However, the landlord will usually not be in occupation of his own property in these cases – the tenant will. HMRC Technical Note of 9 December 2009 on the withdrawal of FHL rules from 2010–11, together with their Property Income Manual, is a helpful source of information on this subject. The supply of bed and breakfast accommodation is standard rated for VAT purposes.

On the basis that the activity of bed and breakfast is a trading activity, then the assets involved should be eligible for BPR at 100%.

COTTAGES LET RENT FREE TO FARM WORKERS

15.21 Vacant cottages, surplus to the needs of the farming business and let under assured shorthold tenancies, need to be treated as letting income and the expenses thereof identified and claimed in the letting business.

There are potential problems in claiming full deductions for expenses in respect of cottages let to farm workers either rent free or at a nominal rent, but HMRC Help Sheet 251 offers valuable guidance on claims that can be made in this type of situation. Further guidance may be found in HMRC's Property Income Manual.

The farm worker has the advantage of tax free job-related accommodation with regard to benefit in kind, provided it meets the criteria. The allocation of expenses is a big issue for all letting income and trading income interaction.

LANDLORD WITH DEVELOPMENT VALUE

15.22   The most intense action by the landlord to remove the tenant could arise when there is a potential development value on the land he owns. Where vacant possession is acquired and there is a disposal of the whole interest at a later date, liability may arise on trading income as an adventure in the nature of trade, but HMRC have indicated that they would not mount an attack under ITA 2007 ss 756 and 765 (see Chapter 14).

If the landlord makes a capital payment to the tenant, the latter will be liable to CGT in the hands of the tenant. In computing the tax, deductions will be due for expenditure by the tenant on improving etc the land and any buildings surrendered with the tenancy (see later for details).

If the landlord pays nothing for the surrender, the whole of the tenant's assets will have been lost or destroyed in the act of surrender and it may be that a loss will arise for CGT in the hands of the tenant. On the other hand, if the landlord and tenant are connected persons, it may be that HMRC will seek to infer or substitute an 'arm's length' price as consideration for the surrender with consequential effects on the capital gains tax computation (TCGA 1992 s 17), but hold-over relief may be claimed. If, exceptionally, the tenant pays the landlord, the payment will fail to be treated as expenditure incurred in the disposal of an asset, so, presumably producing a loss.

THE TENANT ACCEPTS COMPENSATION

15.23   The tenant's position will differ if what he receives is not a payment for the surrender of his tenancy, but compensation in respect of disturbance under the Agricultural Holdings Act 1986 ss 60 and 63. Such payments are intended to reimburse the tenant for the loss or expense suffered in having to quit. Up to one year's rent can be claimed with proof of loss and up to two years' rent if particular proof can be provided. These receipts are not derived from an asset and therefore no liability arises. Similar treatment is accorded to comparable payments of up to four years' rent made under the Agricultural (Miscellaneous Provisions) Act 1968, as compensation for surrendering the tenancy on a notice to quit from the landlord or on a notice of entry served by a local authority.

Payments of this class are made where land is required for private or public development or for other non-agricultural purposes and the tenant would be entitled to compensation under the Agricultural Holdings Act 1986 ss 60 and 63. This receipt is wholly exempt from income taxation and CGT (*Davis v Powell* [1977] STC 32).

The question arises as to the taxation treatment where a tenant does not serve out a period of notice following the receipt of a notice to quit, but instead enters into a surrender agreement with his landlord. In the past, HMRC have taken the view that in such circumstances the surrender agreement broke the chain of causation, so that the tenant was not quitting in consequence of the notice to quit, but in consequence of the surrender agreement. HMRC's view was that payments made by the landlord were not statutory compensation and that the whole of such payments were chargeable to CGT.

Compensation to tenants for milk quota on the termination of a tenancy is also now regarded as within the scope of CGT. The Agricultural Holdings Act 1986 Sch 1 paras 1–4 impose liability on landlords to pay compensation to tenants for milk quota on the termination of a tenancy.

CAPITAL GAINS TAX POSITION OF THE TENANT

15.24   The tenant should consider his CGT position. The surrender of an existing tenancy for consideration is the disposal of a capital asset for CGT purposes. The tenant could therefore become liable to CGT where he surrenders the old tenancy, either where he is connected to the landlord, or because the bargain with the landlord is not considered to be a bargain at arm's length. In either case the tenant will be deemed to receive the open market value of the tenancy as consideration (see TCGA 1992 ss 17, 18).

The CGT reliefs available to the tenant range from principal private residence relief on the element of the farmhouse to roll-over relief into another asset.

The question is whether an existing family farming tenancy should, in the light of the existing reliefs, be brought to an end. That is inevitably a more difficult question, because the answer may depend upon the precise advantages and disadvantages being secured under an existing structure, the tax costs of making a change and the issue of what new structure should be substituted for the old.

For the tenant's disposal of a superior interest in land see **14.44**.

INCOME FROM GRAZING LICENCES

15.25   This is looked at in more detail in Chapter 11.

A person who owns farmland which he lets for grazing will be treated as carrying on a farming trade if certain criteria are met. The CLA has a recommended form of agreement for the grant of a 'right of herbage' which meets these criteria and has been approved by HMRC. If the criteria are met, the income will be taxed as farming trading income, CGT roll-over and hold-over reliefs will be available and APR for IHT will be available on the land and also the farmhouse where appropriate (see Chapter 4).

As explained in Chapter 11, the case of *McCall (as Executor of Mrs McClean deceased) v Commissioners of HMRC* [2008] STC (SCD) 752 and Court of Appeal (Northern Ireland) GIR 7387 [2009] explain the vulnerability of grassland letting in order to achieve BPR in addition to APR.

Non-trading status can apply with grazing rights, unless the landowner:

● cultivates, sows and establishes the grass crop (ie he is responsible for the grass crop);

● harrows and rolls the grass as necessary;

● fertilises the grass crop in spring and through the season as necessary.

It is important that the owner should cut or spray all weeds to prevent seeding and the owner must do any mowing that may be required for whatever reason.

In the *McCall* case above it was noted that the grass grazed had not been sown or grown in the manner of a crop. There were no acts of husbandry commensurate with growing the grass as a crop and accordingly no occupation for the purpose of husbandry.

The grazier must also covenant not to mow or cut the grass and the owner must do any hedging (see **19.11**), fencing and ditching needed and any other work of a proprietary nature.

If the landowner manages to achieve this, he should then be deemed to be a trading farmer with paramount occupancy, and therefore eligible for not only the APR available on the land, but also the APR on the farmhouse, subject to the problems associated therewith (see Chapter 4). The period of occupancy could then also be reduced. There is also greater potential to claim business expenses and qualify for CGT relief.

Historically, many written and unwritten tenancies have evolved (see Chapter 11) within farming partnership and farming arrangements between members of the family, and these could jeopardise the tax shelter that the farmland should provide. Likewise, diversification could move towards the claim for BPR and not APR and again jeopardise the claim for APR on the farmhouse.

LICENCES TO HORSE OWNERS AND A PROFIT OF PASTURAGE

15.26   Consideration must be given to farmland let to horses for grazing.

A licence is a simple form of agreement between landowner and horse owner, and is used typically to permit the horse owner (non-exclusive) use of land for grazing. The use of simple licences (and *profit à prendre*) are, in most cases, better limited to situations where the proposed arrangement is of short duration and relates to grazing only for private recreational horses.

If the licence purports to grant the horse owner exclusive occupation of the land, that will be fatal to it being construed as a tenancy (it is of the essence of a licence that the licensee is not granted exclusive rights of occupation). Furthermore, to avoid the risk of a licence being construed as a tenancy by the courts, the licence should not:

- use the language of landlord and tenant (eg use of the expression 'rent'); or

- impose tenant-type obligations (eg for hedging and ditching (see **19.11**), maintenance and repair).

The danger to the landowner of a licence being construed as a tenancy is that the horse owner may have conferred on him rights which the landowner never intended the horse owner should have the benefit of; this is particularly so if what purports to be a licence, is subsequently determined by the courts to be a business tenancy.

A *profit à prendre* is a right to take something from the land, which in the case of animals is grass by grazing (a 'profit of pasturage'). It is in the parties' (and particularly the landowner's) interest that the granting of a profit of pasturage should be documented by deed. A profit of pasturage comprises an incorporeal rather than a corporeal hereditament and, accordingly, no tenancy of land arises. The animal owner does not acquire exclusive possession of the land and, indeed, the landowner is treated as remaining in possession of the land, and remains free to exercise all rights over it (including granting rights to third parties), which are not inconsistent with the right of pasturage granted to the animal owner.

This arrangement can be attractive to landowners who wish to be treated (commonly for tax reasons) as continuing to farm the land (ie by growing a crop of grass on the land). As with licences, the deed granting the *profit à prendre* (to be treated as such) must avoid language or terms which infer any exclusivity of occupation on the part of the horse owner, or seeks to impose tenant-type obligations on the horse owner. Again, as with licences, all responsibility for care of the animal will lie with the animal owner (although the prudent landowner will maintain public liability insurance in respect of his land). Legal advice must be taken on all these matters.

HORSE LIVERY – TRADING STATUS OR INCOME FROM LETTINGS

15.27   The whole area of equine tax is dealt with by the author in her book *Equine Tax Planning* (Bloomsbury Professional). The issue of equestrian business is dealt with as a separate diversified activity in Chapter 6 (see **6.24** and **6.25**).

Trading status will usually apply where an element of care is provided by the stable owner, eg feeding, mucking out, putting out to graze, arranging for veterinary and farriery services etc. However, this may not be so sustainable where the stables are merely rented out as rental income for DIY livery, where the horse owner has exclusive use of the stable. There may be a mixture of DIY and non-DIY activities with trading status being secured on the basis that both activities will usually also involve a supply of feed to the stable owner (by the fact that the horse will be put out to graze in any event). It will, therefore, be necessary to consider each case on its own facts. BPR should be available provided that the stable rent is not the main activity. The businesses of riding schools and horse trekking will be assessable as trading income. These are again looked at as a diversified activity in Chapter 6 (see **6.26–6.29**).

WAYLEAVES AND RECEIPTS FOR GRANTS OF EASEMENTS

15.28   These are no longer received net of income tax and the gross receipts can normally be left in the farm trade tax computation, as (with effect from 2005 under ITTOIA 2005 s 22) they constitute farm income by concession.

An easement is the right to use, or to restrict the use of, the land of another person in some way. A wayleave is the right to use a defined area of land for purposes unrelated to its primary use (BIM55220). Landowners may receive payments from electricity and gas concerns, or other similar undertakings, for easements in connection with cables, pylons etc on or over their land. The types of payment which may be made include:

- yearly payments for easements;

- single lump sum payments for grants in perpetuity or for a specified number of years;

- yearly or lump sum payments for disturbance arising from the erection of pylons, relaying of mains etc.

  '… any element of compensation received for temporary loss of profit, or for damage to crops or to reimburse revenue expenditure on the repair of damage to land or buildings falls to be included as a receipt taxable [as] trading receipts.' (BIM55220)

In certain circumstances, the tax planner might try to organise a capital receipt taxable under the CGT regime and benefiting from the annual exemption for CGT and the 18% CGT rate effective from 6 April 2008 together with 18% and 28% rates from 23 June 2010.

Costs of reinstatement of land

15.29 Where there is expenditure on repairs of damage to land or buildings etc covered by the compensation payment, this will be an allowable deduction if the compensation is chargeable to income tax. Where a lump sum payment is regarded as capital, any corresponding expenditure should be excluded from the trading income computations.

QUOTA LEASING

15.30 Quota is being phased out by 2012.

Most types of quota can be leased by one farmer to another for a fixed period, usually a year. In particular, there has been a very active market in the leasing of milk quota. The essential difference between leasing and sale is the temporary nature of the leasing arrangement, with the quota reverting back to the original owner at the end of the agreement. This leads to a difference in the tax treatment. Payments for quota leasing are allowable expenses in the farmer's accounts. Similarly, receipts from the leasing of quota which is temporarily surplus to the requirements of a particular activity carried on by a farmer may be regarded as part of the farming trading income.

The tax consequences of selling or leasing quota should be considered when looking at the commercial alternatives. Chapter 7 deals with the capital position concerning quotas.

AGISTMENT

15.31 A 'contract of agistment' is an agreement whereby the landowner (in this context referred to as 'the agister') agrees to take in someone else's animals to graze on the agister's land for a fee. The horse owner in such an arrangement obtains no tenancy or interest whatsoever in the agister's land, and no part of the agister's land is designated for the purpose of the arrangement. Under such arrangements, the horse(s) are returnable to the horse owner on demand. It is important that the contract of agistment expressly provides that the agister will have a lien on the horse(s) until any monies owing under the contract are paid, otherwise the agister will not be entitled to retain a horse until the horse owner has paid his debt to the agister.

COMMON LAW LETTINGS – HORSE AND PONIES KEPT FOR PRIVATE AND RECREATIONAL PURPOSES

15.32   The conventional grazing agreement to an individual or individuals in respect of ponies or horses kept for private recreational use will usually be a tenancy under common law. It is essential (for the tenancy to be treated as a common law letting) that the proposed tenancy is not for a horse owner's use in connection with a trade or business. There is, however, a catch for the unwary in that a landowner granting a tenancy to a group of people, such as a riding club, may unwittingly create a business tenancy. The definition of business in the Landlord and Tenant Act 1954 s 23(2) includes 'any activity carried on by a body of persons, whether corporate or unincorporate'.

A common law letting for a fixed period will simply expire at the end of its contractual term without any special notice provisions. Periodic common law tenancies, however, require termination by notice, the relevant period of notice being dependent on the type of periodic tenancy.

Notice required for differing periodic tenancies

Type of periodic tenancy	Notice required
Weekly	One week
Monthly	One month
Quarterly	One quarter
Year to year	At least 6 months (the expiry of the notice period to coincide with the end of the tenancy year)

It is worth noting that a common law tenant has no right to compensation for improvements to the property let, unless provision for such is written into the tenancy agreement.

FARM BUSINESS TENANCIES (FBTS)

15.33   FBTs are dealt with in Chapter 11 on legal agreements. FBTs have featured throughout the third edition. They are looked at in Chapter 11 with regard to tenancy alternatives and feature in most chapters.

The Agricultural Tenancies Act 1995 introduced a new regime for agricultural tenancies by the introduction of FBTs. There was a recognition that increasingly there was a need in the agricultural industry for a more adaptable form of tenancy that could accommodate farmers' wishes (or indeed economic need in many cases) to diversify farm activities into areas outside traditional farming ones.

The essential elements of an FBT are that:

- it must have commenced after August 1995, and the property which is the subject of the FBT is used for business;

- the character of the property must be wholly or primarily agricultural – or notices must have been exchanged between landlord and tenant before the tenancy is entered into, stating it is intended to be an FBT;

- FBTs for fixed terms of two years or less expire at the end of their contractual term (without the need for service of notices);

- FBTs from year to year or fixed terms longer than two years run on until either the landlord or tenant serves notice to terminate (of at least 12 months). In practice, this may mean that a notice with a notice period of between 12 and 24 months has to be served, as the expiry of the notice must coincide with expiration of the relevant tenancy year.

Subject to complying with the requirements of Part III of the 1995 Act (which relates to landlords' consent to improvements) tenants' improvements can qualify for compensation. Improvements in this context can be both tangible and intangible (eg planning permissions). In essence, the compensation the landowner may have to pay for qualifying improvements equates to the increase in the letting value of the property at the end of the tenancy as a result of the improvements.

FBTs may be suitable where, for example, the land in question is to be used as grazing ancillary to an equestrian business (eg a riding school), or where the land use is diversifying out of an agricultural use. At the moment, there is no substantive body of case law to give guidance as to the extent to which land use can diversify out of an agricultural use, and the tenancy remain an FBT within the ambit of the 1995 Act. Accordingly, in the equine context the terms of an FBT need to be very carefully thought out, and in many cases the preferred route may be the creation of a business tenancy contracted out of the provisions of the Landlord and Tenant Act 1954 ss 24–28. Chapter 11 looks at the IHT disadvantages of BPR on hope value and APR on the farmhouse. There is also concern regarding entrepreneurs' relief for CGT.

FURNISHED HOLIDAY LETS (FHL) OR FURNISHED HOLIDAY BUSINESS (FHB) – THE QUESTION

15.34   FHLs are looked at in detail in Chapter 6 as a diversified activity. The loss situation is also looked at in Chapter 12. We now look further at the question of letting or business.

What are the rules that apply to FHLs until 5 April 2011?

The property does not have to be in a tourist area, but the pattern of lettings must satisfy three conditions (ITTO1A 2005 Pt 3 Ch 6):

1   The property must be available for commercial letting as holiday accommodation for at least 140 days a year.

2   It must actually be let as holiday accommodation for at least 70 days a year.

3   It must not normally be let for a continuous period of more than 31 days to the same tenant in seven months of the year and those seven months include any months in which it is actually let as holiday accommodation.

The government consultation document issued in July 2010 proposes that in item 1 the availability for commercial letting is extended from 140 days to 210 days. It also proposes that in item 2 the actual days let increases from 70 days a year to 105 days a year.

FHL – THE BUSINESS

15.35   The IHT guidance is found in IHTM25278 which states:

'In the past we have thought that business property relief would normally be available where:

- the lettings were short term, and

- the owner, either himself or through an agent such as a relative, was substantially involved with the holidaymakers in terms of their activities on and from the premises.

Recent advice from Solicitor's Office has caused us to reconsider our approach and it may well be that some cases that might have previously qualified should not have done so. In particular we will be looking more closely at the level and type of services, rather than who provided them.

Until further notice any case involving a claim for business property relief on a holiday let should be referred to the Technical Team (Litigation) for consideration at an early stage.'

See further **6.14**.

FHB – INVOLVEMENT WITH THE TOURIST

15.36   The tax-planning confusion rests with the fact that the FHL rules only apply to income tax and CGT and the extent of the involvement with the tourist. The tax relief post 6 April 2010 is helped if there are lots of services provided, eg 'the meet and greet', organising car hire, cleaning and laundry, supply of basic food for the fridge etc. The owner can subcontract out these services. The important point is the extent of the involvement with the holidaymakers, even if this is handled by an agent. The key is to ensure that there is a contemporaneous record of the services provided. Further examples are visits to the cottage with local maps and guides to historic attractions and organising the maintenance of the property before, during and after the period of let, including gardening.

In order not to fall foul of the new rules and IHTA 1984 s 105(3), greater evidence of the provision of practical services to genuine holidaymakers will help.

Other relevant factors might be:

- the cottage is located in a tourist area;

- the property is marketed professionally;

389

- small business rates are paid;

- the cottage is awarded a rating by the English Tourist Board or equivalent;

- public liability insurances are paid on the property;

- the operation of the business is commercial and profits are made and tax paid accordingly.

FHL – WORRIED ABOUT S 105(3)?

15.37   The BPR position is set out in **6.13–6.15**.

When claiming BPR on FHLs, one is more than likely going to meet opposition by HMRC and you need to be prepared to fight. Fortunately, there is plenty of internal guidance in the IHT manuals that actually supports the claim. One of the more interesting texts can be found at IHTM25277 (Caravan Sites and Furnished Lettings: Hotels, Bed and Breakfast and Residential Homes), for example:

> 'IHTA84/S105 (3) will not usually apply to these businesses in view of the level of services provided. This has been recognised by the courts who have distinguished these businesses from mere exploitation of land. In *Griffiths (Inspector of Taxes) v Jackson* 56 TC 583 at page 593, Vinelott J observed:
>
>> "The distinction between a hotelier or a lodging house keeper, on the one hand, and the owner of a property who lets furnished rooms and provides services is no doubt in practice a narrow one, more particularly in these days of self-service hotels and motels, but the principle is clear and in the present case there can be no doubt on which side of the line the taxpayer's activities fall."
>
> Only in cases where it is clear that IHTA84/S105 (3) applies should you pursue it. Any doubtful cases must be referred to the Litigation Group before an entrenched position is taken.'

The *Farmer* and *Earl of Balfour* cases provide some hope of a defence against attack under s 105(3). Does the remaining business meet the criteria (see Chapter 13)? Is this the time to consider whether the farming unit is overloaded with investment assets (and this includes FHLs that do not qualify as FHBs)?

LETTING TO SEPARATE BUSINESS

15.38   As mentioned in Chapter 6, many diversified activities take on a separate legal entity, eg the limited liability company (see Chapter 8). The owner of the land will let the land (buildings) to the new business. But what of preserving IHT reliefs?

The points raised throughout this chapter hopefully set out the tax position of letting farmland and buildings to the diversified activity, but integrated into the main business to ensure IHT protection – see Chapter 13.

Chapter 16

Divorce and farming

Michael Gouriet, Antonia Mee and Patrick Bidder
(Withers LLP)

- **The impact on the farming community and land owners of the case of *White v White***
  Review of the court's approach to the division of assets on divorce and consideration of the implications of *White v White* and subsequent cases.

- **Divorce issues of particular relevance to farming cases**
  Consideration is given to liquidity, valuations, deferred charge/postponed interest and property acquired prior to, or inherited during the course of, the marriage.

- **Protecting the assets**
  The chapter considers ways of protecting assets, for example, by use of pre-nuptial agreements and trusts. Consideration is also given to the preservation of confidentiality.

- **Tax implications**
  An overview of tax considerations surrounding a divorce including income tax, capital gains tax (CGT) and inheritance tax (IHT). The chapter also reviews the tax treatment of maintenance payments, business partnerships and the availability of tax allowances.

NOTE FROM THE EDITOR

16.1   As the main theme of this book is the protection of assets for the farmer and the landowner, it would be incomplete if mention was not made of the potential issues and pitfalls that can arise for farming and land-owning families when a marriage breaks down. It is a particularly complicated subject, with asset values going through turbulent times and income unpredictable, and there is no-one better than the family law specialists at Withers LLP to comment on this area of the law which has seen significant developments over recent years and in doing so to highlight the cases that are of relevance to farming; to consider how assets are divided on divorce (with particular consideration of the impact of the well-publicised House of Lords judgments in *White v White*, *Miller v Miller* and *McFarlane v McFarlane* and other relevant cases); to look at possible ways of protecting assets with trusts and pre-nuptial agreements; and to consider the various tax implications.

Michael Gouriet has extensive knowledge on and experience of the financial ramifications of divorce. He is ably assisted by others in the family law team at

Withers, including Antonia Mee. They have the added advantage of immediate access within the firm to leading experts specialising in trust and tax law and agricultural, commercial and residential property, all of whom have a wealth of experience in dealing with and advising on land-related issues. Michael is particularly well placed to produce this informative chapter.

Michael and Antonia also wish to thank Patrick Bidder, a trainee at Withers LLP, for his help in updating this chapter.

INTRODUCTION

16.2   This chapter will look at the potential impact of divorce on a farming family, steps which might be taken to reduce the impact of a divorce, and tax considerations arising on divorce. It is instructive to consider the general approach of the Family Court to the division of assets on divorce before looking at various issues which are likely to be of particular significance in farming cases.

DIVISION OF ASSETS ON DIVORCE – THE COURT'S APPROACH

16.3   On divorce, the Family Court has a very broad discretion to make appropriate financial provision between the parties as it sees fit. When considering what orders to make, the court has to take into account a number of factors prescribed by the law. These are set out in s 25 of the Matrimonial Causes Act 1973 (MCA 1973) as follows:

'The court has a duty in deciding whether, and how, to exercise these powers, to have regard to all the circumstances of the case and to give first consideration to the welfare of any child of the family under 18. The court shall, in particular, have regard to:

(a)   the income, earning capacity, property and other financial resources which each of the parties to the marriage has or is likely to have in the foreseeable future, including in the case of earning capacity any increase in that capacity which it would in the opinion of the court be reasonable to expect a party to the marriage to take steps to acquire;

(b)   the financial needs, obligations and responsibilities which each of the parties to the marriage has or is likely to have in the foreseeable future;

(c)   the standard of living enjoyed by the family before the breakdown of the marriage;

(d)   the age of each party to the marriage and the duration of the marriage;

(e)   any physical or mental disability of either of the parties to the marriage;

(f)   the contributions which each of the parties has made or is likely in the foreseeable future to make to the welfare of the family, including any contribution by looking after the home or caring for the family;

(g)   the conduct of each of the parties, if that conduct is such that it would in the opinion of the court be inequitable to disregard it;

(h)   the value to each of the parties to the marriage of any benefit (for example, a pension) which, by reason of the dissolution or annulment of the marriage, that party will lose the chance of acquiring.'

16.4   The basic guidelines found in s 25 of the MCA 1973 were originally introduced in 1969, and have not changed substantially since. One important statutory development has been that since the mid-1980s the courts have had a duty to consider whether or not in the circumstances of the particular case a clean break can be effected between the husband and wife so as to terminate their respective financial dependence on the other.

The interpretation by the courts of the statutory rules has developed significantly over the last three and a half decades. In the early 1970s, the tendency was to award one-third of the joint capital and of the joint income to the financially dependent party (usually the wife), leaving the breadwinner or wealth-holder (usually the husband) with the lion's share of the assets.

This gave way in the 1980s to a propensity of the courts to seek to meet the reasonable requirements of the wife (or financially weaker party) in terms of both capital and income. The motives were sound, but the effect was that the more money there was the less equal the settlement. This was particularly so in cases where there were sufficient resources to enable a husband to pay a capital sum to his wife by way of a clean break in settlement of her maintenance claims. By reference to what are known as 'Duxbury tables' (which make actuarial assumptions as to life expectancy, capital growth, income yield and inflation), the courts can calculate the level of lump sum which a wife would need in order to meet her income requirements for the rest of her life – assuming that she will draw down on the capital as well as the income produced so that at the end of her life expectancy that sum would be exhausted.

A fundamental flaw in this approach was that it appeared to penalise the long-serving wife since the younger the wife and the shorter the marriage the higher the Duxbury award, whereas the older the wife and the longer the marriage the lower the Duxbury award. This sometimes led to wives concocting large inflated budgets to boost their claims.

In October 2000 the House of Lords was given its first opportunity to consider the exercise of discretion and the interpretation of the statutory criteria set out in s 25 of MCA 1973 since the legislation was introduced. The case which came before the House of Lords (*White v White* [2001] 1 AC 596) involved a farming family.

White v White

The facts

16.5   Martin and Pamela White had married in 1961 when he was 24 and she was 26. They had three children. At the time of the hearing before the House of Lords they were in their sixties. They both came from farming families.

Following their marriage they formed a farming partnership pursuant to an oral agreement between them. At the outset each of them contributed a similar amount of capital (£1,884 from Mrs White and £1,135 from Mr White).

In October 1961, Mr and Mrs White acquired the former matrimonial home (Blagroves Farm with 160 acres) for £32,000. This was mainly borrowed on mortgage but supplemented by what was effectively a gift of £14,000 from the husband's father to the young couple jointly. In 1974 Mr White's father released his loan of £14,000. Initially, this was reflected by an increase in Mr White's partnership capital account but ten years on Mr and Mrs White's capital accounts were merged into a single joint capital account.

Various land purchases over the years saw Blagroves Farm expand to 339 acres (acquired by the parties through the partnership).

In April 1971, the opportunity arose to acquire the Willett Estate which was largely tenanted by Mr White's father. It was a joint purchase by Mr White and his brother at an advantageous price reflecting their father's tenancy and with the aid of an advantageous mortgage. The three brothers farmed separate portions of the Willett Estate individually. Mr White's portion was Rexton Farm which was, effectively, farmed by the husband and wife partnership together with Blagroves Farm as a single unit. Both farms were dairy farms.

In 1993, the White brothers entered into a deed of partition of the Willett Estate so that in place of joint ownership of the whole each brother took his individual share – Mr White taking Rexton Farm, which was then registered in his sole name.

After 33 years of marriage the wife left Blagroves Farm in August 1994 and petitioned for divorce in December of that year. Her financial application followed in March 1995. That came before Bristol County Court in September 1996.

Judgment in the High Court

16.6   The judge (Holman J) determined that the net total assets amounted to £4.6 million made up as follows:

- approximately £185,000 in the sole name of the wife;

- approximately £1,730,000 in the sole name of the husband;

- £1,343,000 being the wife's share of the assets held in joint names; and

- £1,343,000 being the husband's share of the assets held in joint names.

The judge identified two fundamental issues:

1   whether the wife should be entitled to fulfil her desire to continue to farm; and

2   whether in a case such as this it would be right to make a net transfer of assets from the wife to the husband.

On contributions the judge made the following finding:

'Each party contributed a great deal of effort to this marriage and to the welfare of the family. Within the home it was the wife who primarily brought up the children. I am also quite satisfied that she worked hard in all sorts of ways on the farm.

I am quite satisfied that the husband has been a hard working, active farmer. In truth this was a marital and also a business partnership in which, by their efforts and commitment, each contributed to their full for 33 years and any attempt to weigh the respective contributions of their effort is idle and unreal.'

However, having regard to financial needs, he said:

'In my judgment it would be unwise, and not justifiable on the facts of this case, to break up an existing, established farming enterprise so that the wife, at 61, can embark much more speculatively, on another. Her claim has strong emotional, but little financial sense.'

The judge focused on the wife's reasonable requirements and assessed that she needed £425,000 to purchase and equip a house and he capitalised her income needs (by reference to the Duxbury tables) at £555,000, thereby giving her a total of approximately £980,000. He concluded that it was justifiable in this case that the wife should receive a lesser lump sum than the paper value of the assets currently in her name.

He recognised that the wife's share on his judgment would amount to only 20% of the whole. He said:

'I acknowledge that a final result which accords to this wife only one-fifth of the total wealth seems low in proportion to the length of the marriage and her contributions. That is, in part, a result of the well-known paradox that the longer the marriage and hence the older the wife, the less the capital sum required for a Duxbury type fund. But one-fifth is not so low as to be manifestly wrong or unfair.'

Mrs White, who had contended that her contributions to the marriage and the length of it should result in an equal division of the assets, appealed to the Court of Appeal.

Mrs White's Appeal to the Court of Appeal

16.7   The Court of Appeal concentrated on the wife's legal entitlement. Thorpe LJ said that the dominant feature of the case was that the parties traded as equal partners and that had the partnership been dissolved by the death of either of them the extent of the estate of the deceased partner would have been established according to the law of partnership. He said that equally, the wife was in law entitled to her share on dissolution of the partnership by mutual agreement. He concluded that in his opinion once the financial worth of each of the parties had been determined on the immediate dissolution of the existing farm partnership the next issue was to decide whether or not the Court should exercise its powers to increase or reduce the parties' respective shares.

Thorpe LJ raised the pertinent question that if it was reasonable for the husband to be able to continue farming in a worthwhile way, why was it not equally reasonable for the wife to require to be able to continue farming in a worthwhile way?

The original judgment of Holman J was set aside and the wife was awarded a lump sum of £1.5 million (up from £795,000) in addition to her own assets of £185,000.

Appeal to the House of Lords

16.8   Both Mr and Mrs White were unhappy with the ruling of the Court of Appeal. They both appealed to the House of Lords. Mrs White sought an equal share of the assets contending that the correct starting point was equality of entitlement. Mr White sought to reverse the Court of Appeal's decision and restore the order of Holman J.

The House of Lords took the view that the approach of the Court of Appeal in focusing on the parties' respective entitlements under the partnership was not the correct approach.

Principles

16.9   The guiding principles which emanated from the House of Lords judgment in *White v White* [2001] 1 AC 596 were as follows:

- The court must consider each and every s 25 (MCA 1973) factor. There is no hierarchy in those criteria. In certain cases some of those criteria will carry more weight than others depending on the circumstances of the case in question.

- The court must look to achieve a fair outcome. In seeking to reach that objective there is no place for discrimination between a husband and wife and their respective roles. There should be no bias in favour of the money-earner and against the home-maker and child-carer.

- Before reaching a firm conclusion, a judge should check his tentative views against 'the yardstick of equal division'. There is no presumption of equal division but as a guide, equality should be departed from only if, and to the extent that, there is good reason for doing so.

The House of Lords rejected the judicially developed concept of 'reasonable requirements' and held that there was nothing in the statutory provisions or in the underlying objective of securing fair financial arrangements to say that the available assets become immaterial once the wife's financial needs are satisfied. In the leading judgment, Lord Nicholls asked, rhetorically, 'where assets exceed the financial needs of both parties why should the surplus belong solely to the husband?'

Although the House of Lords did not agree with the approach which the Court of Appeal had adopted in reaching its conclusion, their lordships did not alter the resultant figure (£1.5 million), as this was within the ambit of what a court might reasonably award and therefore the result could not be challenged on the ground that it was plainly wrong. The Court of Appeal had taken into account all of the available assets and the significant contributions made by the husband's father. The House of Lords found no ground to interfere with the Court of Appeal's exercise of discretion.

Since *White v White*

16.10   The House of Lords decision in *White v White* [2001] 1 AC 596 provoked huge debate and raised many questions about its application in a variety of circumstances. The glass ceiling of 'reasonable requirements' was demolished by the House of Lords. The touchstone became 'fairness'. As was acknowledged by Lord Nicholls at the start of his judgment in *White*, the concept of fairness is in part a subjective one.

> 'Everyone's life is different. Features which are important when assessing fairness differ in each case. And, sometimes, different minds can reach different conclusions on what fairness requires. Then fairness, like beauty, lies in the eye of the beholder.'

Following *White* there were a number of cases where the principles enunciated by the House of Lords have been applied. It is instructive to reflect on the more influential of those cases as follows:

1   *Cowan v Cowan* [2001] EWCA Civ 679, [2001] 2 FLR 192. In this case the total assets amounted to approximately £11.5 million, mainly due to the husband's business success, and the parties had been married for over 30 years. The husband had invented the (now ubiquitous) plastic bin liners/bags on a roll, and it was his success which gave rise to the parties' wealth. The Court of Appeal assessed that the husband and wife had equal needs in terms of capital and income amounting to £3 million. The Court of Appeal justified the unequal division of the surplus of £5.5 million as to 25% to the wife and 75% to the husband giving him a total of £7.1 million and her a total of £4.4 million, on the basis of Mr Cowan's 'stellar' contribution to the creation of their wealth notwithstanding that all of the assets had been built up during the marriage. Overall, the wife received approximately 38% of the total assets.

2   *H-J v H-J* [2002] 1 FLR 415. This case involved a marriage of approximately 25 years and total assets of approximately £2.7 million. On appeal Coleridge J held that the wife should have 50% of the net assets. He based his decision on the fact that fairness often dictated that there should not be a departure from equality, otherwise one party might feel that his or her contribution to the marriage has been undervalued. The judge also emphasised that when the sums involved were easily sufficient to meet the needs of the family, the courts should not involve themselves in unnecessary and costly forensic analysis.

3   *G v G (Financial Provision: Equal division)* [2002] EWHC 1339 (Fam), [2002] 2 FLR 1143. The parties had been married for over 30 years and the family assets totalled approximately £8.5 million. The wife had not worked during the marriage. She had cared for the four children and looked after the home while the husband had created their exceptional wealth. Coleridge J awarded the wife 50% of the family assets as the wife's contribution had been of equal importance to that of the husband's.

4   *Lambert v Lambert* [2002] EWCA Civ 1685, [2003] 1 FLR 139. The Court of Appeal acknowledged that it may have been too restrictive on the wife's entitlement in its earlier judgment in the case of *Cowan v Cowan* (above). Lambert involved a marriage of 23 years and two

grown-up children. The assets (amounting to approximately £20 million) had all been generated during the marriage by the husband's business success. The wife had not worked outside the house since very early in the marriage.

In the leading judgment, Thorpe LJ held:

(i)   It is unacceptable to place greater value on the contribution of the breadwinner than that of a homemaker as a justification for dividing the product of the breadwinner's efforts unequally between them … the nature of the contributions are intrinsically different and incommensurable.

(ii)   The danger of gender discrimination resulting from a finding of special financial contribution is plain, since there is no equal opportunity for the home maker to demonstrate the scale of her comparable success.

(iii)   Special contribution remains a legitimate possibility but only in exceptional circumstances.

(iv)   A finding of equal contribution will not necessarily lead to an outcome of equal division, since other considerations under the Matrimonial Causes Act 1973 s 25 may justify departure from equal division on the facts.

A major impact of the decision in *Lambert* has been to quash the opportunity for the majority of divorcing spouses to argue exceptional contribution. That concept does, however, remain alive for those who can validly claim to have made an extraordinary contribution (eg in the cases of *Sorrell and Charman* referred to below).

5   *GW v RW* [2003] EWHC 611 (Fam), [2003] 2 FLR 108. In this case, the marriage lasted 12 years. There were two children (aged five and two). The husband had brought into the marriage assets worth approximately £475,000 and on divorce there were total assets of approximately £12 million. The husband had built up the assets entirely from his remuneration as a financier in the City of London. The judge in that case awarded the wife 40% of the total asset base and he identified two reasons for this departure.

(i)   First, the duration of the marriage was not of a sufficiently substantial length to warrant an equal distribution. However, after *Foster* and *Miller* and *McFarlane* (see below), the length of the marriage will no longer necessarily justify a departure from equality.

(ii)   Second, the husband had brought to the marriage a developed career, an established earning capacity which was unmatched by any comparable contribution by the wife and his assets, which had grown significantly (by about £2.4 million) during a two-year period of separation in the middle of the marriage. In saying this, the Judge attributed a capital value to the personal capacity of the husband to make money in his field, which he brought to the marriage. This approach has since been rejected by the Court of Appeal in *Jones v Jones* [2011] EWCA Civ 41.

6   *Foster v Foster* [2003] EWCA Civ 565, [2003] 2 FLR 299. The parties
     who were in their early thirties and had no children had been married
     for only four years. Each had been employed throughout the marriage
     (with the wife earning considerably more than the husband). As a
     result of property dealing and development, the parties had amassed a
     considerable amount of capital during the short marriage. The wife's
     financial contributions towards the acquisition of the properties had been
     significantly larger than the husband's.

     The District Judge sought to return to each party what he or she had
     brought into the marriage (as well as any post-separation contributions
     which he or she had made towards outgoings on the properties) and then
     divide the profits made during the marriage equally between the parties.
     This resulted in the wife having 61% and the husband having 39% of the
     total assets. Following a successful appeal before a Circuit Judge, the
     Court of Appeal reinstated the District Judge's order.

     In the leading judgment, Hale LJ said that just as there should be no
     discrimination between spouses on the basis that one was a breadwinner
     and the other a homemaker, there was no justification for discriminating
     between spouses on the basis of differences in income. Both may work
     equally hard but in jobs which are unequally remunerated. In this
     case, each spouse had made financial contributions towards the assets
     accumulated in the joint enterprise, and there were no considerations,
     such as the housing needs of the parties or the needs of children to justify
     anything other than an equal division of the profits of that joint enterprise.

     On the question of length of marriage, Hale LJ said 'the duration of the
     marriage will obviously be relevant in cases where one party's earning
     capacity may have been seriously affected by a long period devoted to
     homemaking and child rearing, but … where a substantial surplus had
     been generated by their joint efforts, it could not matter whether it had
     taken a short or a long time to do so'.

7   *Sorrell v Sorrell* [2005] FLR 497. This was a marriage of 32 and a half
     years. At the time of the hearing the husband was 60 and the wife was
     59 and a half. The parties had three grown-up sons. The wife had always
     been the homemaker and the husband the breadwinner. The family assets
     were approximately £75 million net of tax. The main issue was whether
     the yardstick of equality should be departed from on the grounds that the
     husband's contribution was exceptional, as the main asset was shares in
     a company the husband had built up.

     The wife wanted a clean break and a 50/50 division of the assets. She
     went into a full account of her contribution as wife and home maker. The
     judge held that she had tried to over-egg the pudding in this respect. The
     husband had admitted that she had made a full contribution.

     The judge considered the case of *Lambert*, which emphasised that the
     court must be cautious, but special contribution does still 'remain a
     legitimate possibility but only in exceptional circumstances'. He said
     that the real issue in this case is whether the husband has established
     that he made a special contribution in exceptional circumstances. The

judge concluded that the husband's genius was the generator of most of the family fortune. It would be unfair not to recognise this. The judge awarded a 60/40 split of the assets in the husband's favour.

Miller and McFarlane

16.11

1   *Miller v Miller* and *McFarlane v McFarlane* [2006] UKHL 24. These two cases were heard simultaneously in the House of Lords on 24 May 2006. They set another touchstone in the interpretation of s 25 of the Matrimonial Causes Act 1973. The main judgments were handed down by Lord Nicholls of Birkenhead and Baroness Hale of Richmond.

2   In the case of *Miller* the marriage lasted just under three years. When they separated the husband was aged 39 and the wife was 33. There were no children. At the time of the marriage the husband was a senior fund manager with Jupiter Assets Management and the wife worked in public relations earning £85,000 a year. At the time of the financial court hearing on divorce in October 2004, the husband's assets were worth approximately £17.5 million, plus whatever value could be attributed to his shares in New Star (estimated at between £12 million and £18 million). The wife was awarded a capital sum of £5 million. The judge considered that a key feature of the case was that the husband gave the wife a legitimate expectation that she would, on a long-term basis, be living on a higher economic plane. That philosophy was accepted by the Court of Appeal as was the judge's reliance on the husband's misconduct (in having an affair) as being a counter balance against the brevity of the marriage.

When the case reached the House of Lords, these two concepts were quashed. The husband's conduct was not found to be conduct which it would be inequitable to disregard and thus should not sound in the financial award. Further, the ruling at High Court level that the wife had been given a legitimate expectation of living on a higher economic plane was rejected by Lord Nicholls in the House of Lords, who said that it did not fit with the notion that both parties were free to end the marriage.

The Court of Appeal had held that the award of £5 million was within the generous range of permissible awards. The House of Lords upheld the amount of the award on the basis that there had been a substantial increase in the husband's wealth during the marriage, to which the wife was entitled to share. Her award represented approximately 1/6th of the overall assets at the time of the hearing and less than half of the wealth accrued during the marriage. It was held that it was appropriate to take account of the husband's efforts in generating the business assets prior to the marriage and during what was a short marriage.

3   *McFarlane.* The parties were in their mid forties. They had been married for 16 years (with two years' prior cohabitation) and had three children (aged nine to 16 at the time of the hearing). Early in the marriage the wife qualified as a solicitor and the husband as a chartered accountant.

On divorce they were able to agree an equal division of the accrued family capital (approximately £3 million). However they were unable to agree how the husband's annual net income of approximately £750,000 should be divided. Although the wife's income needs were assessed at around £120,000, she was awarded £250,000 a year to reflect her needs, obligations and the contribution she had made over the years of the marriage. On appeal to the High Court, the wife's annual maintenance figure was reduced to £180,000 per year. On further appeal, the Court of Appeal reinstated the original District Judge's order of £250,000 but limited it to a term of five years, on the basis that the wife could save the surplus income above her needs to provide for a clean break.

4   On appeal by the wife to the House of Lords, her maintenance order of £250,000 a year was reinstated on a joint lives basis without a term.

5   The wife was also granted £20,000 per annum for each of her three children until they reached the age of 23 or finished university.

6   In 2009, the wife applied to vary the order for periodical payments for herself and the children. Charles J held that the amount and structure of any increased award should be guided by:

(i)   the application primarily of the need principle to identify surplus income over and above either party's need; and

(ii) an application of the principles of compensation, need and sharing to determine how that surplus should be applied between the parties.

Having assessed the husband's income, Charles J decided that it was appropriate to increase the payment to each of the children to £25,000 pa. He also increased and restructured the payment to the wife by awarding her, until May 2015, 40% of the husband's yearly net income up to £750,000, 20% between £750,000 and £1,000,000 and 10% of any income above £1,000,000, in anticipation that there would be a clean break at that point (coinciding with the husband's anticipated retirement), but leaving the door open for the wife to extend the maintenance term if she required.

Principles arising from the House of Lords in Miller and McFarlane

7   The Law Lords agreed that there were three strands which should be considered on all claims for financial provision on divorce.

(i)   Needs – it being recognised that needs are likely to be the start and end of the search for fairness in cases where there is insufficient income/capital to be divided.

(ii) The novel concept of compensation was introduced by the House of Lords – the purpose of which is to redress 'any significant economic disparity arising from the way the parties conducted their marriage'. If compensation is applicable it could be paid as income or as capital depending on the available resources.

(iii) Sharing the financial fruits of the partnership. Lord Nicholls observed that when parties marry they commit themselves to sharing their lives and they live and work together. Marriage is a partnership of equals. He said that when their partnership ends each is entitled to an equal share of the assets of the partnership, unless there is a good reason to the contrary. He also held that a short marriage is no less a partnership of equals than a long marriage.

8   It was held that Mrs McFarlane was entitled to compensation for giving up her career to look after the home and bring up the children which put her at an economic disadvantage. Baroness Hale said that the wife was entitled to a share in the very large surplus of income on the principle of *sharing* the fruits of the matrimonial partnership and on the principle of *compensation* for the comparable position which she might have been in had she not compromised her own career for the sake of the family.

9   It was accepted by the Law Lords that not all property would be treated in the same way and the distinction was drawn between matrimonial property (being property acquired during the marriage through common endeavour) and other property (such as that brought into the marriage or acquired by inheritance or gift during the marriage). The Law Lords have indicated that the duration of the marriage (as well as needs) would be highly relevant to the question of whether or not non-matrimonial property should be divided.

10   Lord Nicholls said that in the case of a short marriage claimants should not necessarily be entitled to a share of the other's non-matrimonial property and that that may be a good reason for a departure from equality. However, he went on to comment that for longer marriages the position in relation to non-matrimonial property is not so straightforward as although it represents an unmatched contribution made by one of the parties it would be counter balanced by the length of the marriage and the way in which the parties had organised their finances.

11   The judgment in the *White* case remains valid – namely that the nature and value of the property, and the time when and circumstances in which the property was acquired, are among the relevant matters to be considered, but in the ordinary course the fact that assets may be classed as non-matrimonial property can be expected to carry little weight in a case where the claimant's financial needs cannot be met without recourse to that property.

12   Lord Nicholls went on to say that the parties' matrimonial home (even if brought into the marriage at the outset by one of the parties, usually has a central place in the new marriage so should normally be treated as matrimonial property for this purpose). The writers' view is that would very much depend on the nature of the property and the circumstances in which it was acquired. If, for example, it is a property which has been in the family for generations, it would be inappropriate for the equal sharing principle to be applied to it.

13   The Law Lords did, however, appear to be at odds over the constitution of matrimonial and non-matrimonial assets. Lord Nicholls is clear that the yardstick of equality should be applied to all matrimonial property (being all assets made during the course of the marriage) whatever

the character of the property and whatever the length of the marriage. However, Baroness Hale indicated that where business or investment assets have been generated solely or mainly by the efforts of one party (particularly in a marriage of short duration) that may justify departure from the yardstick of equality of division. Lord Mance agreed with that saying 'non-business-partnership, non-family assets may not be subject to the equality yardstick with the same force, particularly in the case of short marriages'.

14 Aside from the uncertainty over the composition of 'matrimonial assets', the judgment in the House of Lords in *Miller and McFarlane* gave rise to uncertainty on other points, including whether 'special contributions' remained a valid reason for departure from equality. Lord Nicholls said that exceptional earnings were to be regarded as a factor pointing away from equality of division when, but only when, it would be inequitable to proceed otherwise. On the other hand, Baroness Hale indicated that a special contribution should only be allowed to influence the result where it can be clearly shown that there is such a disparity in the respective contributions to the 'welfare of the family' that it would be inequitable to disregard it. This was addressed in the Court of Appeal case of *Charman* (referred to below).

Since Miller and McFarlane

1 *S v S (Non-matrimonial property: conduct)* [2006] EWHC 2793 (Fam)

The husband had brought substantial assets into the marriage; the total net assets were over £7 million and he had earned considerable sums of money as a chartered surveyor; the wife had given up work before the marriage and there were two young children. The marriage had lasted less than eight years. There had been considerable tension, including domestic violence by both parties in the course of the marriage and the husband had eventually been sentenced for assault occasioning actual bodily harm against the wife.

It was held that the properties which had been brought into the marriage as investment properties were to be treated as non-matrimonial property, whereas a pension portfolio was to be treated as matrimonial property because it had been liquidated and re-formed using the husband's professional skill and judgment as a property expert. The matrimonial property had a total value of about £6 million. Because of the husband's substantial financial contribution, it was appropriate to depart from the yardstick of equality and to award him 60% of the matrimonial property, although he was also ordered to pay the wife's significant debts. It was not accepted that the yardstick was to be applied to the total assets, rather than to the matrimonial property alone. The husband's conduct, although bad, was not so exceptional as to be taken into account on the financial division.

2 *Charman v Charman* [2007] 1 FLR 593

The parties had been married for 30 years and had two children who were 20 and 24. The wife had looked after the children whilst the husband had built and enjoyed a very successful career in insurance. At the time of the hearing the family's wealth amounted to approximately £131 million, of which £56 million was held in the husband's sole name, £8 million in the wife's name (represented primarily by the former matrimonial home) and £68 million was held in a family trust (the Dragon Trust). The husband argued that the assets in the Dragon Trust were a dynastic trust and should not be part of the family pot to be divided. He asked the court to award the wife a sum of £20 million. The wife sought a 55/45 division of the assets, conceding that there should be some recognition for the husband's special contribution.

The judge included the assets in the Dragon Trust as part of the assets to be divided. The wife was awarded £48 million representing 36.5% of the assets.

The husband appealed to the Court of Appeal saying that the judge had erred in regarding the assets of an offshore discretionary trust as being 'financial resources' of the husband and therefore wrongly included in the computation of the parties' assets. The husband said that the judge in the High Court should have asked himself whether or not, if the husband requested the trustee to advance him the whole or part of the trust assets, the trustee would be likely to do so, and should have answered that question in the negative.

The husband also contended that the judge made insufficient allowance for his special contribution.

The Court of Appeal did not accept the husband's contention that the assets of the Dragon Trust should be left entirely out of account because they were deposited in a 'dynastic' trust for the longer term benefit of members of his family. Therefore, all of the trust assets (amounting to approximately £68 million) were regarded as a resource available to him.

The Court of Appeal decided that the judge had approached the departure from equality in the correct manner. The basis of the decisions in *White and McFarlane* was that the court should apply the sharing principle not just to part but all of the property. The method by which the judge had allowed for the husband's special contribution was not flawed. The judge's endorsement of a departure to 63.5/36.5 in part reflected his view that the husband's assets were laden with greater risk. Where a special contribution was established the departure from equality should not be less than 55/45 or more than 66.6/33.4.

3   *Rossi v Rossi* [2007] 1FLR 790

This case comments on the constitution of matrimonial and non-matrimonial property, in particular how to deal with assets accrued after separation of the parties. The parties married in Italy in 1964 and separated in around 1978, however the wife continued to run an antiques business that she and the husband used to run together.

The Deputy High Court Judge dismissed the husband's claims for ancillary relief and other orders, but set out the following principles:

For the purposes of establishing the matrimonial property in respect of which the yardstick of equality will apply, the value of assets brought into the marriage by gift and inheritance (other than the former matrimonial home), together with economic growth on those assets, should be excluded as non-matrimonial property.

Assets acquired or created by one party after (or during a period of) separation may qualify as non-matrimonial property if it can be said that the property in question was acquired or created by a party by virtue of his personal industry and not by use (other than incidental use) of an asset which has been created during the marriage.

If the post-separation asset is a bonus or other earned income, then if the payment relates to a period when the parties were cohabiting then the owner cannot claim it to be non-matrimonial. Even if the payment relates to a period immediately following separation the judge said he would himself say that it is too close to the marriage to justify categorisation as non-matrimonial. The judge agreed with Coleridge J when he pointed out that during the period of separation the domestic party carries on making her non-financial contribution but cannot attribute a value thereto which justifies adjustment in her favour. The judge said he would not allow a post-separation bonus to be classed as non matrimonial unless it related to a period which commenced at least 12 months after the separation.

The non-matrimonial property is not quarantined and excluded from the court's dispositive powers. The court will decide whether it should be shared and, if so, in what proportions. It will have regard to the reality that the longer the marriage the more likely non-matrimonial property will become merged or entangled with matrimonial property. By contrast, in a short marriage case non-matrimonial assets are not likely to be shared unless needs require this.

4   *H v H* [2007] EWHC 459 (Fam)

This was the first reported case following *Miller and McFarlane* on the vexed issue of a spouse's entitlement to a share of the other's substantial future income in 'big money' cases where the capital assets enable a clean break.

The husband and wife were married for 20 years. They had four children (aged between nine and 18). The husband worked throughout the marriage for a bank. The wife worked on and off as a teacher.

The parties agreed that there should be a 50:50 split of the capital assets which amounted to approximately £25 million. What they were unable to agree was how the husband's post-separation income (in particular) his bonuses for 2005 and 2006 (of approximately £2.3 million each) should be treated.

The judge rejected as arbitrary the suggestion in the cases of *Rossi* and *S v S* (referred to above) that a post-separation bonus should only be classed as matrimonial property (and thus to be divided equally) if it related to a period up to 12 months after separation. The judge seemed to follow the steer from Lord Mance in *Miller and McFarlane* in deciding that the yardstick of equality of division should not apply with the same force to assets acquired after the breakdown of the marital partnership and prior to determination of the financial issues.

The judge held that 'the principles of fairness, equality and non-discrimination required that the wife should receive an additional award to reflect her contribution over the years of the marital partnership that has resulted in the husband's enhanced or greater earning capacity (and is a fruit or product of the marital partnership)'.

However, some comfort can be gleaned from this by the high-earning spouse, as the judge went on to say that a husband's level of earnings and his earning capacity are mainly based on his talents and energy and only a small part of his future income comprises an 'enhanced earning capacity' to which the wife has contributed and which can properly be said to be a fruit or product of the marital partnership to which she should be entitled to some share.

The judge decided that the correct approach was to 'ease the wife's transition to independent living' and in doing so took account of the disparity of economic positions which would arise in the years ahead. As a result of the magnitude of the husband's ongoing income, the judge awarded a one-off award of £1.4 million which was equivalent to a combined total of one-third of the husband's 2005 income, one-sixth of his 2006 income and one-twelfth of his 2007 income.

There was concern amongst practitioners that the judgment in *Miller and McFarlane* might be interpreted to justify an entitlement to a significant ongoing share in future income even in cases where there were sufficient capital assets to achieve a clean break. The case of *H v H* appeared to adopt a restrictive approach to this.

5   *P v P* (also known as *SP v LP*) [2007] EWHC 2877

The parties in this case were married for 24 years, with three children aged 23, 21 and 18 at the time of the trial. The husband was a senior managing director of JP Morgan Chase and an executive director of JP Morgan Cazenove. The parties separated in 2005.

At the time of the trial the husband's stated intention was to leave JP Morgan after his 2007 bonus and enter a new business venture. During the marriage, the parties had acquired three properties:

1   a home in England worth £3.4/£3.5 million;

2   a house in South Africa worth £1.4/£1.5 million; and

3   a flat in London worth £3.5 million.

The husband had also set up trusts during the marriage and, in oral evidence at the trial it was clear that they were available to meet the needs of the husband, the wife, and the children whilst they were in education. In total, the assets in this marriage comprised £2,790,000 of liquid cash, £1.825 million of potential shares, £5.83 million in trusts, employee benefit trust sub-funds of £7.74 million and a pension worth £392,000. There were also trust assets that could come in to being in the future. There were, in total, £16.8 million assets and £1.825 million potential assets. The husband's income in 2005 had been £2.5 million and in 2006 it was £4.5 million. He was also about to release shares which would realise £992,000.

The main issues in this case were the extent to which the wife's award should reflect the increase in wealth after their separation and how the award should be affected by the husband's future earning capacity. Also, an issue arose as to whether contingent deferred assets should be shared in kind and what level of award was necessary to meet the wife's reasonable needs.

Moylan J aimed in his judgment to apply consistently the principles taken from *Miller*. However he emphasised that the speeches in *Miller* did not replace s 25 of the Matrimonial Causes Act 1973. He agreed with Baroness Hale in *Miller*, in that 'it can be assumed that the marital partnership does not stay alive for the purpose of sharing future resources unless this is justified by need or compensation'. This promoted predictability and a clean break. However, Moylan J stated that it was not necessary to draw a clean and precise boundary between matrimonial and non-matrimonial property because *Charman* had made it clear that the sharing principle was not confined to matrimonial property. Rather, the extent to which assets were non-matrimonial property meant that there was more reason for departure from equality. However, such a departure was still a matter for the judge's discretion.

Moylan J took into account the fact that significant wealth had been made since separation and the husband's significant earning capacity.

He also concluded that the wife should keep the £1.4 million South African house and the £3.4 million former marital home (in trust but the capital would be available to her). The combined assets transferred to the wife would be £4.8 million, to which would be added a £3.5 million capitalised income fund on a clean break basis, thus bringing her financial claims to an end. The wife would therefore retain £8.4 million with the husband retaining £8.3 million.

The wife's award was ultimately larger because of the potential deferred shares that the husband would receive at a later date. It also took into account the husband's position, his significant earning capacity (from which he would continue to accrue capital) and the wife's need. The wife would not receive anything further therefore there would be an ultimate imbalance in the husband's favour. This was justified due to the wealth the husband had accrued post separation.

6   *S v S* [2008] EWHC 519 (Fam)

This case involved an 11-year marriage between an investment banker husband who earned £193,000 to £343,000 a year and a wife with an earning capacity of approximately £15,000 a year. The parties had split their time between a flat in London and a farm in Gloucestershire where they kept horses. On divorce, the parties had agreed that there were assets of £2.8 million, which included the sale proceeds of both properties and pensions. The husband had expressed a desire to leave the country and to retrain, as he was concerned that he might be made redundant. The wife claimed she needed to be rehoused in a property with enough room for keeping her horses. She sought a joint lives maintenance order with payments of £56,000 per annum. The husband argued that a smaller property would be sufficient for the wife and that she should be forced to put the horses out for livery. He offered periodical payments for five years.

At first instance the District Judge found that the husband was likely to leave London in three years but that it was impossible to predict this with certainty. He, therefore, found that a joint lives award would be fairest and ordered that the husband pay £50,000 per annum to the wife with the opportunity for both parties to come back to court were the circumstances to change. He ruled that it was fair for the wife to live in the same way that she had for at least two years previously and should be allowed a large enough property to keep the horses.

On appeal Sir Mark Potter found that it was impossible to predict when the husband would leave the country, which was critical to his future income. He therefore concluded that fairness demanded a joint lives order as opposed to a fixed term of periodical payments.

Sir Mark Potter made it clear that as long as the husband continued in his role as an investment banker, the order was appropriate but if he decided to move then the parties would need to return to court to review the spousal maintenance. The judge recognised the importance of the horses to the wife. The District Judge had been right to allow the wife to maintain her standard of living by allowing her a property large enough to maintain the horses. However, he emphasised that if the husband was made redundant or if he expressed a desire to retire, the 'horses would become an unjustifiable extravagance and the wife should plan accordingly'.

7   *H v H* [2010] EWHC 158 (Fam)

The husband and the wife were married in 1987 and had three children, two aged 19 and one aged 14. They separated in March 2007 and their divorce was finalised in June 2008.

The assets in the marriage comprised the former marital home of £11.1 million, bank accounts of £14.3 million (£13.4 million in the wife's name) and £232,503 in life policies. The husband also had trust interests of £26 million, a pension of £600,000 and surplus cash in his business of £17 million.

In an open offer letter to the wife's solicitors, the husband informed them that he had implemented the following arrangements:

- a transfer of the former marital home, free of the mortgage, to his wife. This was accompanied by a schedule claiming the home was worth £21 million;

- a transfer of £7.234 million in cash to his wife;

- a transfer of life policies worth £106,815 to his wife.

The letter claimed that such arrangements would take the wife's wealth to £34 million, the total value of the party's wealth being £101 million. It was argued that such an arrangement was based on the judgment in *Charman*, but the letter acknowledged that there might be issues with the value of the husband's business and the value of the former marital home.

It later transpired that the husband was in possession of a letter from Savills indicating that the house was worth £17.5 million. This letter was only revealed after the hearing and the husband was criticised by Munby J for keeping it concealed. Ultimately, there was a significant difference in the value of the assets between the March 2008 offer and the date of the final hearing. The former marital home was in fact worth £11.1 million as opposed to £21 million, the trust assets were worth £26 million as opposed to £20.6 million and the business surplus cash was worth £17.5 million as opposed to £8.5 million. All of these discrepancies were to the disadvantage of the wife.

However, Munby J refused completely to reopen the division that had been implemented by the husband's letter. He held that a readjustment was, however, required because there were assets available to the husband that had not been included in that division. Munby J was, therefore, faced with determining what lump sum should be paid to the wife.

One key issue in this case was the approach the court took to the valuation of the husband's business. This is discussed further below.

Munby J concluded that the husband's interest in the business was a future income, and, therefore, a s 25 factor. It was not a capital asset and, therefore, was not to be shared. However, the wife was entitled to share in actual capital assets of the business and the additional surplus cash which had accrued since March 2008. The wife was therefore awarded an additional lump sum of £7.5 million.

8   *Vaughan v Vaughan* [2010] EWCA Civ 349

In this case the parties were divorced over 25 years ago. The marriage had lasted 13 years and there had been no children. The wife, aged 66, appealed against a decision that the husband, aged 71, was under no obligation to continue to make periodical payments to her or provide her with a lump sum in lieu of maintenance. Originally, the parties had entered into a deed of separation followed by a divorce. The husband had remarried and had purchased a new home in joint names with the second wife. His second marriage had lasted for approximately 25 years.

At first instance, when calculating the husband's future annual income, the judge had halved the value of some of the husband's financial interests, including his private pension to reflect the interest of his second wife. It was also held that considering the first wife's own liquid capital, including her recently received inheritance, were the wife to 'amortise' her capital, converting it into income, she would be able to meet her annual needs and adjust to the immediate termination of the payments without undue hardship.

However, in the Court of Appeal Wilson LJ criticised the judge at first instance because on a second marriage a spouse should take the other subject to all encumbrances, including the other's obligations to a previous spouse. Although no priority should be given to the first wife there should definitely be no priority given to a second wife. Wilson LJ, therefore, held that the husband was still obliged to make periodical payments but capitalised the periodical payments order.

9   *B v B* [2010] EWHC 193 (Fam), [2010] Fam Law 905

In this case the parties had been married for 13 years and had three children. The capital assets were worth £15m. The husband was a trader who received significant annual bonuses. The parties separated in 2007. The main issue for the Court to decide was how the husband's bonuses should be treated as part of the clean break (ie in circumstances where the wife would receive a lump sum and no ongoing spousal maintenance). The judge awarded the wife a £7m lump sum and 15% of all net sums representing deferred payments for the husband's bonuses up to 2009. The Judge found that, as a general principle, sharing ends at the conclusion of the matrimonial partnership. To award the wife one half of the assets as at the date of the trial would give insufficient weight to the husband's post-separation contributions. However, there is no fixed approach to post-separation bonuses and this may not be the last decision on the matter.

10   *Robson v Robson* [2010] EWCA Civ 1171, [2011] EMLR 13

This was a 21-year marriage and the parties had two children aged 20 and 17. At the time of the final hearing, the husband's capital assets were valued at £22.3m (which included an Oxfordshire stately hall and estate valued at £16m mostly inherited by him before the marriage) and the wife's assets were valued at £343,500. In the High Court the Judge had ordered the husband to pay the wife a lump sum of £8m and periodical payments of £140,000 a year until the lump sum was paid in full, whereupon there would be a clean break. Child maintenance was £15,000 a year per child. The case went to the Court of Appeal. The Court of Appeal endorsed the High Court judge's view that the parties had spent extravagantly during the marriage, largely from the husband's inherited wealth from his late father. The husband's case that the estate was part of a dynastic plan to pass wealth on to the next generation was rejected. The Court of Appeal agreed with the High Court that the parties should live less extravagantly post divorce and found their spending during the marriage extravagant and reckless. Essentially, the Court of Appeal was saying that the capital fund from the hall and estate which had been inherited had been used by the parties primarily as an income resource during the marriage and so neither could complain if the same was again used in this way to measure and provide for their future accommodation and maintenance needs on divorce. The wife's award was reduced by 10% and she received a lump sum of £7m in addition to her own assets.

11   *Kremen v Agrest* [2011] EWHC 2571 and 3091 (Fam)

This was a preliminary issue in financial proceedings upon divorce between a Russian financier and his wife. They lived in a £4m home on a golf estate in Weybridge, Surrey. The husband had disposed of a £2m mansion in Surrey (which was the sole asset of a BVI company, which had been owned by the husband but which he had subsequently sold, first to another gentleman (which sale was found to be a sham) and then to the current owner). The Court of Appeal upheld the High Court judge's decision that Mr Agrest had done his best to divest himself of any assets which could be the subject of a claim by Mrs Kremen and the sale of the BVI company was ordered to be set aside.

The impact of White v White

16.12   The case of *White v White* [2001] 1 AC 596 and the cases decided since then reflect a sea change in judicial treatment across the whole range of ancillary relief cases. Judges and practitioners alike are focusing on percentages and, in particular, what in the circumstances of each case is a fair percentage distribution and whether or not there are any particular factors (such as need or exceptional or unmatched contribution) by one party to justify a departure from equality.

The decisions of the family courts since *White* have meant that in general where resources exceed needs, wives (particularly those in long marriages), can now expect to be awarded a substantially larger share of the parties' combined wealth on the dissolution of their marriage than previously. Unless there are good reasons to depart from this course, the development of case law since *White* clearly suggests that the value of assets generated during the marriage should be divided equally. However factors such as liquidity (or lack of it) and inherited wealth (discussed below) may affect this principle.

OTHER ISSUES OF PARTICULAR RELEVANCE TO FARMING AND LAND-OWNING CASES

Liquidity

16.13 The main difficulty created by farming cases is the illiquidity of assets, since capital is usually locked away in the form of land, livestock and machinery. Also, generally, income yield is relatively modest. In the pre-*White* era it was often difficult to provide adequate compensation for an outgoing spouse as the court set its face against breaking up a business which would have an adverse effect on the livelihood of the parties.

A good example of this was the case of *P v P (financial provision: lump sum)* [1978] 1 WLR 483, where the farm had been purchased shortly after the marriage by the wife's father, which he eventually conveyed to the wife. The farm was run down at the time when it was acquired and the husband put in a great deal of effort in improving the farmhouse and the land and building up a successful farming business, which the husband and wife ran as partners. On divorce, the husband was awarded a small lump sum of £15,000 payable in three instalments of £5,000. His appeal was dismissed by the Court of Appeal as the wife would have to bring up the children and, therefore, she should be allowed to keep the farm in order to derive an income from it. The largest capital sum that she could reasonably be expected to raise from the farm business without being obliged to sell it was held to be £15,000. As the sum of £15,000 would satisfy the husband's principal requirement of a home, that was held to be a practical and realistic figure.

It was a similar approach and similar outcome (one party being allowed to continue farming at the apparent expense of the other) which led Mrs White to appeal on the first instance decision of Holman J (as related at **16.7**).

There have, however, been cases in the past where the courts have decided that the farm should be sold: for example, *Moorish v Moorish* [1984] Fam Law 26, where it transpired that the farm had been seriously mismanaged by the husband.

Alternatively, courts have directed that part of the land (or livestock) be sold where it does not seriously affect the viability of the business itself: for example, *S v S* (1980) *The Times*, 10 May. In that case it was directed that three smaller farms should be sold in order to provide a lump sum for the wife. The main farm unit was retained as a viable one to permit the husband to continue farming.

Various cases since *White* have addressed the difficult issues of liquidity and unrealisable assets when carving up resources on divorce. These include:

1   *N v N (financial provision: sale of a company)* [2001] 2 FLR 69

This case concerned a 14-year marriage with three children and total net assets of approximately £2,575,000. There were substantial liquidity problems in that the vast majority of the family wealth was represented by the value of the husband's business interests in two companies and various partnerships. The only immediately available funds amounted to approximately £200,000.

The husband argued for a substantial departure from equality whereas the wife argued for 50%.

In his judgment, Coleridge J stated that:

- The accrual of assets after separation might be a relevant factor if the increase was referable to specific contributions on the part of the husband rather than the effects of inflation, increase in land prices or general market forces. However, the significance of that factor would be diminished by the continuing contributions of a non-financial nature (such as looking after the children) made by the wife after separation.

- The division of the assets would be based on the value of the assets at the time of the hearing.

- Most significantly, the judge decided that the wife should not be prejudiced on the grounds of liquidity but acknowledged that the husband should be given a realistic period of time in order to effect an orderly realisation of assets.

This judgment represented a significant deviation from past practice. Whereas, prior to *White* the courts were reluctant to order a sale of a business or land which produced income, post-*White* the courts will do so if there is no alternative way of achieving a 'fair' outcome between the parties as regards the division of assets.

It was noteworthy, however, that in *N v N*, the business which the court directed should be sold (over time) was not the husband's main business.

Where the business is the sole source of income for the family, the court will look at ways of protecting that income source insofar as possible, by considering alternative ways of raising capital to meet the other spouse's needs and entitlement without selling the whole (such as borrowing against the assets; sale of part of the business or land if parts can be hived off without undermining the validity of the business).

2   *Wells v Wells* [2002] EWCA Civ 476, [2002] 2 FLR 97

This case involved a 17-year marriage with two teenage children. For the majority of the marriage, the husband's business (which he had run successfully for 13 years or so before marrying the wife) had provided a good standard of living for the family. At the time of the divorce, the business had become less successful and was running at a significant loss. The judge at first instance concluded that given the precarious state of the business (and the limited trading in the company) it was not possible to put a precise value on the husband's shares. He awarded the wife approximately £1.3 million out of the approximately £1.8 million liquid assets, leaving the husband with £510,000 and his business.

The Court of Appeal reduced the wife's award by £190,000. It concluded that had the marriage survived, the family would have shared adversity as it had formerly shared prosperity. It was unfair for the husband to carry all the risks and the disadvantages of the shares in the company, and therefore, the judge's allocation of the risk-free realisable assets was not fair.

The Court of Appeal gave the wife the right to apply to the court in the event of a sale of the husband's shareholding within five years from the date of the order.

3   *Parra v Parra* [2002] EWCA Civ 1886, [2003] 1 FLR 942

The marriage in this case lasted 22 years and there were two teenage children. At first instance, the judge had divided the total assets (amounting to approximately £2.5 million) 54%:46% in the wife's favour. She was to receive a lump sum in return for her half share in the family business (in which the husband and wife had been equal shareholders) and its premises. There was a significant issue over the value of development land owned by the business. As the land was to be developed by the husband in the future, the wife was granted a claw-back of half of any increase in the value of the development land in the event that it was subsequently sold.

The Court of Appeal held that the division of assets for which the parties had themselves elected should not be adjusted by judges on the ground of speculation as to what each might achieve in the future. In this case the parties had been joint owners of the company and the land and the former matrimonial home had been acquired by their joint efforts. There was no justification in the circumstances for a departure from equality. They reduced the wife's award so that the outcome was 50:50.

The Court of Appeal also went on to say that the imposition of a claw-back provision should be exceptional, as it was inconsistent with the clean break objective. However, in this case such a charge was justified as, although the windfall was a remote prospect, its scale would be great and, therefore, the charge achieved parity (albeit at the expense of a clean break between the parties).

4   *F v F (Clean break: balance of fairness)* [2003] 1 FLR 847

This was a 28-year marriage with two adult children. The wife had not been employed outside the home. The husband had established his own company in which he owned 94% of the shares and through which the family's wealth had been generated. His annual income was £450,000. The husband's shareholding in the company was valued at £2.8 million. The other major asset was the former matrimonial home worth £650,000 and the husband's pension worth £468,000.

The husband argued for a departure from equality by reference to the illiquidity of the company. Singer J noted that the husband's suggested solution would give the wife only 25% of the assets and that would not be fair.

The judge held that on the evidence, it would not be possible for the husband to raise an additional lump sum (of £550,000 to £600,000) which would be required to achieve a clean break without his selling the company. That was not an outcome which the wife was suggesting should be imposed on him. Therefore, instead of a clean break, the husband would continue to pay maintenance to the wife. This would mean that she would share in the results of the company's performance until such time, if ever, as emerging liquidity enabled a clean break to be achieved upon a basis that was fair in the circumstances then prevailing.

The judge said that if liquidity had been no object (and broad equality the outcome) the wife would have received far more capital than was presently available. The judge commented that the reality was that the husband would be trading with and making profits from capital which (in the absence of a liquidity problem) would fairly have been the wife's. It was difficult to see how the imposition of a maintenance obligation in return for use of that capital could be unjust.

5   *R v R* [2003] EWHC 3197 (Fam) [2004] 1 FLR 928

This was a farming case in which the marriage had lasted 14 years. There were two children, who by the time of the hearing in the High Court were aged 20 and 17, and were in full-time work. The husband was a potato farmer who ran his farming activities through a long-established family company.

The farm was situated on two sites. The husband lived in a farm house on one site which was rented by the family company under an agricultural tenancy with about 500 acres of land. On the other farm site, the family company owned the property, which comprised a farmhouse and a second large house, in which the wife lived with the two children, two cottages and 380 acres of land.

The husband owned 6.18% of the family company and he had a vested interest in remainder in relation to 5/8ths of the shares held by his late father's executors on trust for his mother for life. When he came into possession of his full shareholding, it would amount to 39.5% of the company, and he would become the largest single shareholder. The other shareholders were members of his family.

The husband's gross income from the company for the year most recently ended was £41,309 per annum. He also received benefits in kind of substantial value. The husband had liquid assets of about £41,000, and he had three personal pension policies.

The company-owned house in which the wife lived had a value of over £600,000. She paid no rent and the company paid a number of the running expenses. Among the benefits in kind for which the husband paid tax was the benefit of that occupation, which was charged to him at a very low value. The wife had illiquid assets of £9,000 and a one-third interest in a block of shares in a small trading and property company run by members of her family. Dividends amounting to £9,600 per year were declared on the shares. It had long been the practice of the wife and her two sisters, who were the other joint holders of the block of shares, to waive receipt of the dividends in order that their parents should receive them instead.

The case was first heard in the county court in May 2002. The children were still at school at that stage. The District Judge found that the contributions of the husband and the wife were, though different, nevertheless equal, although it was important that the vast bulk of the capital in the family was represented by shares which had come to the husband by gift and inheritance. The wife needed a home large enough, albeit perhaps only for the next few years, to accommodate the children, even when they were working.

The husband had made an offer during the hearing for the company to buy the wife a home, mortgage-free, for £200,000, to be occupied by her during her lifetime; a lump sum amounting to virtually all the husband's liquid capital, namely, £30,000 and periodical payments for the wife and the children in the global sum of £15,000 per annum.

The District Judge made the following order:

- the company should provide £200,000 for the purchase of a home for the wife for life (including supplementary terms whereby, for example, the wife might call on the company to sell the first home and buy an alternative one);

- the husband should pay periodical payments to the wife and the children at the rate of £15,000 per annum.

The husband was to pay a lump sum of £110,000 to the wife within 28 days of the date of the order. This was on the basis that, from the point of view of fairness, the wife should have more capital than was offered by the husband and that the husband could readily afford £110,000. After deducting the wife's capital net needs and her costs that would leave her with about £75,000 for investment.

The District Judge made an earmarking order in favour of the wife in respect of 50% of two pension policies.

The husband appealed to the High Court. The High Court judge held that:

- In terms of the lump sum, there is good authority for saying that the onus is on the husband to establish that he cannot borrow upon the security of his shares both in possession and in remainder. The husband had approached various lenders since the first hearing. The husband's accountant and an accountant instructed on behalf of the wife agreed that the husband's shares would not be accepted as security for a loan. The order for the husband to pay a lump sum of £110,000 could not therefore stand.

- In terms of the main factors relevant to provision for the wife, the court had to make a decision as to whether the company should purchase a property for the wife to live in for her life or whether a property should be purchased in the wife's own name with a very substantial mortgage, paid for by the husband. The judge found that the present cost of reasonable accommodation for the wife was between £250,000 and £275,000.

- The husband's income could reasonably be increased to above £60,000 per annum gross and the judge worked on a figure of £38,350 net per annum. The judge placed a value of at least £20,000 per annum gross on his benefits in kind. The husband's maintenance needs were £9,600. The wife's maintenance needs were £16,000. The wife was earning £6,552 from her hairdressing work.

The High Court judge made the following order:

- The wife would choose a property at a price of about £250,000.

- The wife was awarded £6,500 to purchase a new car.

415

- The wife was to obtain a 20-year repayment mortgage, guaranteed by the husband, annual instalments on which would be £19,343, payable by the husband. He would pay them as the second part of an order for a lump sum payment. The first part would provide for the initial payment of £30,000. The second part would provide for him to pay 240 further monthly instalments, over 20 years. The reason for this structure is that, unlike periodical payments, the lump sum payments would endure even if the wife remarried. The husband's estate would be bound in the unlikely event of his death within the 20-year period.

- The husband's obligations under the lump sum order would be secured by the wife holding a first charge over his shares in the company, both those in possession and those in remainder.

- The husband would pay periodical payments to the wife at the rate of £8,000 for one year from the date of her likely move into her new home and at £6,000 per year thereafter during joint lives until her remarriage or further order.

The judge said that the wife's contribution as a wife, a mother and a homemaker was no less valuable than if it had been directly, as opposed to indirectly, productive of income for the family. The judge found that the husband's shares had substantial value, which his family could unlock for him. The company could, if so minded, properly buy back the husband's few shares in possession at a price which, net of tax, would have yielded him £155,000. Referring to the case of *Thomas v Thomas* [1995] 2 FLR 668, the judge said that this would be no more than, '… judicious encouragement to third parties to provide the maintaining spouse with the means to comply with the court's view of the justice of the case'.

6   *P v P (inherited property)* [2004] EWHC 1364 (Fam) [2005] 1 FLR 576

This was a 19-year marriage. There were two children, a boy, who was 18 and a girl, who was 16. Both had special needs which meant they were a year behind in their schooling.

The husband and the wife were both farmers. They had spent their entire married life farming a hill farm in the north of England. The farm had been in the husband's family for four generations and he made representations that farming was his whole way of life, stating that he wished to die on the farm, 'preferably in harness'. The family assets were £2,501,356 net. These were held as to £2,105,610 by the husband, £70,678 by the wife and the remaining £325,068 by both of them jointly.

The four most important assets were the farmland, vested in the husband, with a net value of £1,746,900, the husband's interest in a mineral lease which had a net value of £67,700, the farm business, which was a partnership with assets worth £325,068 and shares that the husband and wife held in a local farmers' cooperative worth in total £250,840 net (husband) and £3,675 (wife). The parties also had a number of bank accounts, pension funds and other investments.

The family's income had been modest and they had lived frugally. They had been drastically affected by the BSE and foot and mouth crises. The wife was, at the time of the hearing, unemployed as she spent a lot of time caring for the children. There were doctors' reports stating that it was necessary for her to be at home until the children were settled in school, which by the time of the hearing they were. After separation, the wife moved to the south of England with the children and they lived in a rented property. At the time of the hearing, the wife was unemployed and cared for the children in a rented property in the South of England. The children attended private schools and the total sum needed to meet their future school fees was £95,000.

As well as running the house and looking after the children, the judge said that the wife had played a significant part on the farm. She undertook hard physical work, kept the books and also supplemented the family income by her work as a farming journalist. She had lent the farming partnership £40,000, which was used to renovate the bungalow on the farmland. The judge held that the wife's contribution was to the family income and family life. It was not the acquisition of the capital assets.

The wife sought an award in the alternative of a lump sum of £938,000 (representing approximately 40% of the assets).

Throughout the course of the hearing the husband agreed to pay the children's maintenance in the sum of £4,000 per annum and the school fees. It was also agreed that the wife should keep her car and retire from the farm partnership.

The areas in dispute were the wife's capital and income claims. The wife sought £360,000 for a house and £27,750 a year in income for herself (albeit this included a sum for food and holidays for herself *and* the children). In order to meet her claims, the wife suggested that the husband could sell the farmhouse; he could realise his interest in the mineral lease; he could sell his cooperative shares or even sell the bungalow on the farmland. The husband raised difficulties in relation to each of these suggestions.

The judge held that the husband, if he wished to keep the farm, whilst still meeting the wife's proper claims, would need to adopt a more realistic approach to the need to release capital. The judge considered the factors in s 25 of the Matrimonial Causes Act 1973 in light of *White*. Taking the emphasis from that case, the judge said that the objective must be to achieve a fair outcome, not discriminating between the husband and wife and their respective roles. He also referred to the case of *Lambert* stating that 'a finding of equality of contribution may be followed by an order for an unequal division because of the influence of one or more of the other statutory criteria as well as the over-arching search for fairness'. He also referred to Thorpe LJ's comment in *Parra v Parra*, 'I am of the opinion that Judges should give considerable weight to the property arrangements made during marriage'. The judge commented that the farm business was put into the parties' joint names whereas the land and the other tangible assets were retained in the husband's sole name.

In relation to inherited property, the judge referred to the judgment of Lord Nicholls in *White*, who said that, 'this factor is one of the circumstances of the case. It represents a contribution made to the welfare of the family by one of the parties to the marriage. The judge should take it into account. He should decide how important it is in the particular case. The nature and value of the property, and the time when and circumstances in which the property was acquired, are among the relevant matters to be considered.'

The judge in this case said that sometimes, the fact that certain property was inherited, would count for little. On other occasions, the fact may be of greater significance. Fairness may require quite a different approach if the inheritance is a pecuniary legacy that accrues during the marriage than if the inheritance is a landed estate that has been within one spouse's family for generations and has been brought into the marriage with an expectation that it will be retained *in specie* for future generations. However, the judge said that the reluctance to realise landed property must be kept within limits.

The judge in this case held that the proper approach was to make an award based on the wife's reasonable needs for accommodation and income. He applied the approach adopted by Bennett J in *Norris*, not because of any principle that this was the approach to be adopted in farming cases, but because in the particular circumstances of this case that was the approach which most closely accorded with the over-arching requirement of fairness, having regard to all the circumstances but in particular to:

- the fact that the family assets consist primarily of a farm which had been in the husband's family for generations and there was an expectation that it would be retained *in specie*;

- the farm business was put into the parties' joint names but the land and other tangible assets were retained in the husband's full name;

- the fact that any other approach would compel a sale of the farm, with implications little short of devastating for the husband; and

- the fact that this approach would meet the wife's reasonable needs.

The judge said that, to give the wife more than she reasonably needs for accommodation and income, would tip the balance unfairly in her favour and unfairly against the husband. However, he rejected the husband's arguments to limit the wife's claim to the amount of the husband's free capital. He awarded the wife:

- a lump sum of £400,000, representing the cost of a new property;

- a further sum of £175,000, being a capitalised maintenance figure on an annual income need of £10,000;

- the husband would pay maintenance for each child in an agreed sum of £4,000 and the children's school fees.

The aggregate lump sum of £575,000, when added to the wife's existing assets of £70,678, represented a little over 25% of the family assets.

7   *P v P (Financial relief: illiquid assets)* [2004] EWHC 2277 (Fam) [2005] 1FLR 548

The husband was 48 and the wife was 46. They had been married for nearly 25 years. The parties had two adult children who were financially independent. The assets were £2.875 million.

The husband worked for a company which had been in his family for generations and which had grown into a profitable car business. The wife had worked as a full-time secretary before their first child and part time after their second.

The wife sought a clean break. She wanted to retain the matrimonial home, which was worth £615,000, free of mortgage, plus a lump sum of £1.1 million (payable in three tranches over the following 15 months). The husband contended that a clean break was not possible because the most valuable asset in the case, which was his interest in the family companies, was illiquid.

The judge held that:

- It would have been of more assistance to her if there had been one jointly instructed expert instead of two experts to value the family companies with an abundance of material. It would have been significantly cheaper and better if one expert had been instructed to report on an unbiased basis to the court.

- Taking into account the case of *Wells* (referred to above), the judge said that she had taken into account the need to share the copper-bottomed assets fairly, whilst ensuring that both parties also have a fair share of risk-laden assets. The judge held that in this case the copper-bottomed assets obviously included the former matrimonial home, the policies and pension schemes and also the cash which could be extracted from the companies over the following 20 months. Both accountants considered that the funds could be removed without damaging the ability of the companies to trade and expand.

- Although the family had about £2.5 million in assets this was not a big money case, as there was no great surplus of funds over needs.

- The shares in the company were to be divided between the parties to achieve broad equality.

- Parties should take into account the erosion of family assets by legal costs, which meant that those funds were not available for other important long-term needs.

Considering the s 25 criteria, the judge found that the parties needs were £2.45 million. That was virtually the total capital in the case. Not all that capital was liquid so the income which the husband earned would have to be divided whilst the parties waited for the companies to be sold in the mid term.

The judge found that during the marriage each party made equal but different contributions. The husband's father and his brother had been the founders of the business, which factor merited consideration but did not entitle the husband to a greater proportion of the assets in this case, given the parties' actual needs. The judge referred to Lord Nicholls in *White* who said that, whilst inherited assets might be placed in a special category, they might have to be invaded if there was a need to do so. The company was in its infancy when the parties married. The real value of the company was founded on the franchise which was obtained in 1977, after the date of the marriage. It was the husband and his cousin who were really responsible for making these companies ultimately successful and valuable.

8   *D v D & B Limited* [2007] EWHC 278 (Fam) [2007] 2 FLR 653

This was a 35-year marriage. The wife was the homemaker and the husband the sole breadwinner. The matrimonial home was worth £2.143 million net.

The pension was worth £1.77 million net. There were art pieces worth £1 million. The husband was a 100% shareholder of a holding company which had a number of subsidiaries, some of which were incorporated abroad in the USA and Uganda. The success of the business was largely due to the personal relationships and reputation the husband had developed over the years. One of the issues in dispute was the valuation of the companies. A joint expert was instructed to value the husband's business interests and to examine his ability to obtain capital from his companies to meet the wife's claims. It was held that in order to get a fair distribution of wealth when a private company is one of the assets of the family, the court has not to focus solely on the valuation and liquidation of a company but must consider a range of potential issues. Even though the parties wanted a clean break, the sale of the asset and a division of its proceeds might not be fair. Commercial alternatives should be considered, for example, the ability of the company lawfully and sensibly to finance one or both parties.

9   *H v H* [2008] EWHC 935 (Fam) [2008] 2 FLR 2092

The marriage in this case had lasted from 1990 to 2005 and there were two children, 10 and 13. The husband's business as a chef had run for 33 years. The wife had valued the parties' total wealth at £7.8 million including a £5.3 million valuation of the business and was seeking 50% (£3.8 million) plus school fees and maintenance of £12,000 per annum for each child. On the other hand, the husband valued the business at £1.7 million leading to a total asset valuation of £4.2 million. He sought a sale of the former marital home and a payment of £1.3 million to the wife, a school fees fund of £260,000 and a further £300,000 lump sum to the wife to affect a clean break.

The key issue was the dispute over the valuation of the business. Both parties had used experts who applied the method of calculating 'maintainable earnings', and a multiple to arrive at a capital value. The wife's expert had applied a multiple of nine whereas the husband's expert had applied a multiple of six.

With regard to the approach to valuations, Moylan J emphasised that the court was engaged in a broad analysis, not a detailed accounting exercise. The purpose of valuations was to assist the court in testing the fairness of a proposed outcome, not to ensure mathematical accounting accuracy. To determine an award based solely on a business valuation that may not be more than a broad guide was unsound and potentially unfair. However, Moylan J did go on to conclude that a multiple of 6.5 should be applied due to evidence that had been given of similar transactions and it should be applied to future maintainable earnings of £725,000. This gave the business a valuation of £2.5 million net with no liquidity. Therefore, the total capital of the parties was assessed at £4.79 million. Going forward H's net annual income would also amount to £280,000.

Moylan J also ruled on how assets should be divided. They should not be divided into pre-marital and marital, rather there should be 'a global assessment of the fairness of the award'. Having looked at the s 25 factors Moylan J concentrated on the need and sharing principles. He argued that *Charman* had made it clear that the sharing principle applied to all the parties' property. This was easy to apply if there had been a clean break but more difficult in a case like this.

He concluded that the wife should be given £1.5 million which represented 32% of the entire capital (albeit 67% of the non-business wealth). The wife was also awarded periodical payments of £60,000 per annum and £20,000 per annum for the children. The wife's shares in the restaurant business were transferred back to the husband.

10   *D v D* [2010] EWHC 138 (Fam)

In this case the husband and wife had been married for 17 years and separated in 2003. There were two children, both of whom were at university. The husband was a farmer and the wife a manager at an early learning centre. The farm, which was a family asset of the husband's, had been incorporated and at the time of the hearing, the husband owned 85.65% of the shares. His mother owned the balance. These shares had been transferred to the husband through gift between 1977 and 1994. In 2009, on his father's death the husband had become the only director responsible for the day-to-day running of the business.

The husband had moved out of the marital home in 2003 and had purchased a home for *£499,000 using £160,000 and a mortgage.* The wife remained in the marital home.

The husband argued that the farm should be left out of any ancillary relief claim due to the fact that it had been gifted/inherited, therefore any division of assets should only be based on the need principle. The shareholders' funds in the farm had increased dramatically from £256,506 on cohabitation to £6,256,608 at the time of separation and were worth £6,398,919 when the parties came to trial. The former matrimonial home was worth £975,000. Acquisition of land by the parties during the marriage had led to a further amount of £5,015,247. With regard to income, the husband's salary had been £395,250 in 2003 but was only £80,000 in 2010. The husband had not drawn down all his salary and bonus from 2005 as the farm's profits had reduced dramatically. The wife on the other hand had a salary of £36,000 which had reduced to £10,000 by 2010.

Charles J emphasised that the principle of need might have a large, informative and sometimes determinative part to play in assessing whether there should be a departure from equality and how much that departure should be. However, an assessment using all the s 25 factors (listed at **16.3** above) should be carried out in every case. He clarified that a fair departure from equality could result in a 100%/0% split. It was possible that the fact that assets were inherited or gifted and had been in the family for generations could lead to such an approach. However, merely because they were inherited or gifted did not necessarily lead to this conclusion and one must still look at all the circumstances.

In this case, Charles J said that it could not be said that the asset base and the farm business could be equated to that which had been inherited, created and passed on by a previous generation as the husband had in this case acquired it through a gifted shareholding. However, the fact that it had been formed by various gifts of shares should be taken into account when assessing what the wife's fair award should be. Charles J said that an assessment of whether a clean break was fair was not confined to a consideration of capital values but should also have regard to the nature of the assets, the difficulty in valuing them and how they had been treated by the parties during the marriage. In this case the farm had been at the centre of family life as the family business, therefore, the husband should not be forced to sell the farm and a clean break award should not be given.

Charles J set out the principles that had led to his decision. The husband should be allowed to continue farming through the company and the value of the company should be judged in the present, but also in the light of its prospect as an income source that would increase in profit and value. He also gave weight to the fact that this had been a long marriage. In conclusion, Charles J awarded the wife the former marital home, £1.5 million and maintenance of *£44,000 per annum*.

Valuations

16.14 Whereas in the pre-*White* era the court was resistant to applications for expensive and detailed valuations in cases where the business (as the source of income for the family) was not going to be sold, now the value of the farm business assumes a far greater significance whether or not any part of it is to be realised. The value needs to be ascertained to enable the court to assess whether or not the outcome is a fair one.

When looking at valuation, first consideration has to be given to the structure of the business: for example, whether it is sole proprietorship, partnership, company, subject to share farming or contract farming schemes.

Consideration then needs to be given to the ownership of farm assets: for example, if the assets are owned by a company then consideration has to be given to the size, ownership and structure of shareholding and whether or not control is affected by relationships with family or third parties.

If the assets are held in trust then the trust instrument needs to be considered as to the identity of the trustees and beneficiaries; the powers of the trustees and how those powers have been exercised in the past; as well as the timing of the creation of the trust and the purpose for which it was established.

Other issues to investigate include:

- Whether or not the land has vacant possession and, if not, what the tenanted values might be, whether or not the existing tenancies are valid and are capable of assignment and whether the tenancy is a protected one under the Agricultural Holdings Act 1986 (which may give it a significant value). If the tenant is a limited liability company the tenancy value is likely to be high which would have a detrimental impact on the value of the freehold.

- The value of livestock, farm machinery and equipment needs to be determined and consideration as to whether or not any part can be sold without materially affecting the business once ownership has been established. For example, equipment may be shared or leased.

- The timing and saleability of growing crops and harvested crops (considering also actual and projected yields) and whether or not income is awaited on crops already sold.

- The value of milk quota.

- The value of government grants or subsidies.

- Whether any quota belongs to the owner of the land or the occupier (if different), for example a tenant who farms the land or a farming partnership or company.

- As a result of the mid-term review of the farm subsidy system, a one-off allocation of single farm payment entitlements was made to farmers in 2005. The new scheme replaced the old subsidy system and works as follows:

  – Ownership of an entitlement allows an annual claim for payment to be made against that entitlement by the farmer.

  – The monetary value of an entitlement will vary between claimants and from year to year. Most entitlement payments have both a flat rate regional component and an element based on the farmer's subsidy claims in the years 2000 to 2002. The historic element reduces annually and at the time of writing makes up only a small part of the payment.

  – Where land is being divided between parties, entitlements can be transferred either with or without land. In theory, the transfers can take place at any time. However a farmer can only claim payment against an entitlement if he owns it on 15 May in any year. Also, the entitlements must be matched against hectares of eligible land.

  – At the time of allocation some farmers obtained entitlements from the national reserve, set up mainly to deal with hardship situations. Restrictions apply to the transfer of these national reserve entitlements.

  – In order to be eligible for the single farm payment the farmer has to observe various cross-compliance obligations which include the keeping of records for soil management and, in nitrate vulnerable zones, use of manure and fertilisers. Spot checks may be made by the Rural Payments Agency at any time, and so before agreeing a transfer of entitlements copies of these records should be obtained from the outgoing farmer.

  – The current single payment system is due for reform in 2012.

- Farmers claiming under the single farm payment scheme also have to comply with various statutory management and environmental regulations. The single farm payment may be affected if the regulations are not observed.

- Whether or not there is value in timber or minerals.

- Whether the farm or any part of it has development potential (residential or commercial development including the sale of surplus farm buildings and conversion of those into houses or industrial units), having regard to local development plans.

- Whether or not revenue of the farm business can be increased, for example, by the letting of land under farm business tenancies or cottages (as, for example, holiday cottages).

423

Consideration also needs to be given as to the type of expert to be instructed in assisting in valuation (chartered and/or rural surveyors or farm management consultants) and whether or not such experts should be instructed by the parties jointly so as to minimise the cost of each party having their own expert valuers. Disagreements between experts will necessarily increase the matters in issue and thus the costs and extend the court's time for the hearing of expert evidence and adjudication. The appointment of joint experts is encouraged by the courts.

Although valuations are required to enable the court to carry out its function, in the case of *White v White* [2001] 1 AC 596 Lord Nicholls (in the House of Lords) made it clear that where parties are in business together there should be a broad assessment of the financial position and not a detailed partnership account. He said there did not need to be a full and detailed investigation in order to assess precisely each party's proprietorial interests. Specifically, with reference to the *White* case, Lord Nicholls commented as follows:

> '... If a strict valuation of the parties' shares on a dissolution of the partnership were needed several disputes would have to be resolved: disputes about the assets and liabilities of the partnership, a dispute about the value of the milk quota, and a dispute over the proper interpretation of the somewhat obscure retirement provisions in the partnership agreement. I do not think any of these differences need to be resolved.'

One effect of the case of *Charman v Charman* [2007] 1 FLR 593 is that there is likely to be a change to the court's approach to ascertaining the value of a spouse's interest in a company. In that case there were two valuations of the husband's shares, options and warrants referable to the insurance company, Axis (held personally by the husband and in trust), carried out by the accountancy firms KPMG and PWC. KPMG valued these at £53 million and PWC valued them at £73. KPMG had valued the assets by reference to their 'fair market value', that is, the likely proceeds of their immediate, ordinary sale on the basis of what a hypothetical purchaser would pay for them if able to buy them subject to their existing restrictions, which involved heavy discounts. The approach of PWC, however, was to tailor the valuation to the profile of the husband and to identify the 'economic value' of the assets. PWC sought to discern how and when the husband would be likely to set about any such disposal of the assets. In the High Court, the judge preferred the approach taken by PWC and this view was endorsed by the judges in the Court of Appeal. The effect of this is that the relevant valuation exercise appears to have inclined towards value to owner (which is subjective) as opposed to the more objective open market value, and that shift could have serious implications for owner managers in particular.

1   *A v A* [2006] 2 FLR 115

The parties in this case were married for 22 years. The assets were the matrimonial home (£626,000 net), two endowment policies (£41,000) and each party had a pension (husband of £192,000 and wife of £125,000). Furthermore, the wife had a 25.37% shareholding in a company founded by her father, who was the majority shareholder.

Two expert accountants carried out valuations of the wife's shareholding. However, the difference in their valuations created a bracket of £1.7 million to £800,000. Both were experienced valuers in their field.

The main point of interest in this case is that the judge held that, in matrimonial financial cases, the court needed to take a business approach to valuations to avoid the difficulties encountered in valuations. The relevant issues were that the diverse benefits of a controlling interest in a private company means a shareholder might fight hard to keep the company rather than accept a capital sum based on the commercial value of the interest; it is difficult to predict the future of a company; there may be a lack of an open market; there is a difference in the value of shares in the hands of a controlling shareholder and a minority interest shareholder; and there may be problems in raising finance to buy out a shareholder.

It was also recognised that there was an inherent difficulty in valuing private companies with the potential unfairness arising from a 'snapshot' valuation of a company, as there could be large differences between different valuations based on an accountant's view as to the prospects of the company and what multiples and discounts should be applied (where there is no open market for its shares).

The judge ordered the matrimonial home to be transferred into the husband's name, with a charge of £125,000 over it in favour of the wife, with the sale delayed for just over five years (when the youngest child would reach 16), and the sale proceeds to be split 87%/13% in favour of the husband.

2   *H v H* [2010] EWHC 158 (Fam)

See **16.11** for the facts of this case.

The husband possessed a 25.5% share in his business and surplus cash. It was agreed by both parties that the shares were unsaleable; however it was necessary to decide on an 'economic value to the husband' by reference to his ongoing right to receive distributions. Both parties employed experts and both experts approached the valuation of the business in a different way. The wife's expert estimated that the husband would work for a further 15–25 years and applied a capitalisation rate of 30%–20% of the business and therefore valued the husband's interest at between £52.1 million and £78.2 million. However, the husband's expert estimated that the husband would work for a further 15 years and applied a 40% figure to maintainable distributions and argued that the husband's interest was only worth £4.2 million to £11.8 million.

Both experts were criticised by the judge; the wife's for only taking a simple average of the entire life of the business and, therefore, not taking into account a later downturn of business, and the husband's expert for merely relying on a six-month period which unduly emphasised the downturn. The judge concluded that, as he found the husband's expert to be more persuasive, no reasonable person would pay £52.1–£78.2 million for the business.

Deferred charge/postponed interest

16.15   Depending on the circumstances of the case it might be appropriate, in order to achieve fairness, to give one party a deferred charge over part of the land or property. Inevitably, this would prevent a clean break between the parties but it has been a solution which the court has been prepared to consider in the past. For example, in *Webber v Webber* (1982) 12 Fam Law 179 the wife was awarded a 25% share by way of a charge on the farm business which was to vest in her on the husband's sixty-fifth birthday; the charge was to lapse in the event of her remarriage or death. Also, the deferred charge route was followed in *Robinson v Robinson* (1982) 4 FLR 102, CA.

Alternatively, the court might be prepared to consider adjourning the financial application if there was a realistic prospect of the farm (or part of it) being sold or one party being bought out by business partners (eg *Davies v Davies* [1986] 1 FLR 497).

Although the deferred charge was a tool rarely used in the 1990s, it is one which is likely to be increasingly employed in the post-*White* era in the quest for fairness, particularly for example in cases where capital is limited and has to be used as a priority to rehouse the wife and children during their minority. For example, in *Elliott v Elliott* [2001] 1 FCR 477 the husband was given a charge in his favour for 45% of the equity in the wife's new home which had been purchased from the proceeds of sale of the former matrimonial home. The Court of Appeal held that that charge should be redeemed upon the youngest child reaching 18 or completing full-time education. Alternatively, where there may be future value in an asset such as land with development potential – for example *Parra v Parra* [2002] EWCA Civ 1886, [2003] 1 FLR 942 (referred to at **16.13** above) in order to achieve fairness the court may apply a charge in favour of the other spouse against the retained property.

The court adopts a flexible approach in exercising its discretion and in an appropriate case it may take account of the assistance of third parties. For example, in *B v B (Financial Provision)* [1990] 1 FLR 20, the court was informed that trustees would co-operate with the husband to enable him to raise money from farmland held in trust.

Further consideration will be given to the use of trusts at **16.17**.

Property acquired prior to the marriage or inherited during the course of the marriage

16.16 In contrast to certain countries (such as New Zealand), the basic rule is that there is no distinction in the matrimonial *legislation* in England and Wales between:

1 inherited property and property owned before the marriage on the one hand; and

2 matrimonial property on the other hand.

However, as explained above in the *White* case and reaffirmed by the same judge in *Miller* and *McFarlane*, Lord Nicholls suggested that inherited property should not necessarily be treated in the same way as 'marital property'. He said that property which had been acquired by way of an inheritance by one spouse should be one of the circumstances of the case to be considered by the court. It represents a contribution made to the welfare of the family by one of the parties to the marriage. The judge had to take it into account. He should decide how important it is in a particular case. The nature and value of the property and the time when and circumstances in which the property was acquired, are among the relevant matters to be considered. However, in the ordinary course, this factor can be expected to carry little weight, if any, in a case where the claimant's financial needs cannot be met without recourse to this property.

Since *White*, the following cases have shed further light on the issue of inherited wealth:

1   *M v M (Financial provision: valuation of assets)* [2002] Fam Law 509.

This was a case heard in the High Court of Northern Ireland in relation to a marriage which had lasted 17 years. The husband had inherited business interests and what became the matrimonial home from his father. The wife had brought up the four children. The total assets at the time of the hearing were approximately £3.7 million of which £2.16 million represented business assets. The judge decided that in order to reflect the value of the business and the house that the husband had inherited, £400,000 should be deducted from the assets of the family and allocated to the husband before the process of division took place (together with a further £100,000 for potential capital gains tax). The remaining assets of approximately £3.2 million were allocated as to 45% to the wife and 55% to the husband.

This approach has been criticised in various commentaries on the basis that a deduction from the resources available for division prior to the division of the assets was not what was intended by *White*.

2   *H v H (Financial provision: special contribution)* [2002] 2 FLR 1021

In this case, the parties had been married for approximately 30 years and had two children. On divorce the wife sought £2.9 million of total assets of approximately £5.8 million – contending that fairness dictated that she should receive half of the assets.

Peter Hughes QC (sitting as a District Judge) treated the parties' inheritances differently. The wife had inherited shares in the family business on the death of her father in 1990. These shares had been gradually realised over the years. Some of the money was used to buy carpets and curtains for a property. Much of the remainder was invested by the husband on the wife's behalf and formed part of her current investments.

The husband had inherited around £80,000 on the death of his father in 1990 and that money was used to purchase a property. In addition, the husband had approximately £380,000 in the US which he had inherited some years previously from his grandmother and a great aunt. Further, the husband was likely to benefit from inheritance on the death of his mother (who was 87). As regards the latter, the judge decided that fairness to the wife did not require him to take into account the husband's future inheritance prospects.

Whereas the husband's inheritance from his father had gone into the family pool (approximately £80,000), in contrast his US inheritance (approximately £380,000) had always been kept separate and apart and had not been drawn upon. The wife's inheritance had formed part of the parties' resources and the husband had played an instrumental role in its realisation and investment. The judge decided that the husband's US inheritance should be left out of account so that the total assets were reduced by £380,000 before division. The wife was thus awarded £2.75 million representing half of the total assets excluding the husband's US inheritance. As the other assets inherited by the parties had been used during the marriage the judge held that it was not appropriate to make similar deductions. He took the view that it was possible to strike a balance that was fair to both parties by disregarding the US inheritance.

3   *Norris v Norris* [2002] EWHC 2996 (Fam), [2003] 1 FLR 1142

The marriage was of 23 years duration and there was one adult child. At the time of the hearing, the wife's assets, including the former matrimonial home in which the husband had transferred to her his share after separation, and chattels which she had inherited from her family, amounted to approximately £3.7 million. The husband's assets amounted to approximately £4.2 million. The husband had set up a company in IT recruitment of which the wife was a director and shareholder. The company's profitability was affected by the economic downturn in the early 1990s and during that period the wife lent it various sums from her inheritance. Subsequently, the turnover increased significantly and the company was later sold. The husband received £4.5 million for his shareholding and the wife £2.25 million for her shares.

In addition to her domestic contributions, the wife had made financial contributions throughout the marriage from her inherited wealth. She had contributed to the purchase and improvement of the home, the child's education had been funded from a gift from her mother, and she had lent money to the company during its years of difficulty. The wife claimed an exceptional contribution.

Bennett J decided that the totality of the wife's contributions, both domestic and financial, could not be characterised as exceptional and did not justify a lump sum bringing her assets to more than one half of the joint assets.

The judge noted that many wives who are financially able may contribute to the purchase and improvement of the marital home, the child's school fees and the company which the other spouse runs. In this case, the wife was a shareholder and so it was in her own interests to assist the company. In any event, she had received her husband's share in the matrimonial home and she had also received a very good price for her shares on the sale of the company.

There was considerable debate in the case as to whether or not the wife's inherited assets should be quarantined. Her existing inherited assets (aside from those which she had lent to the company and for improvements on the house), including valuable chattels, amounted to approximately £375,000. These had been inherited from her mother during the course of the marriage (some 10 years or so prior to separation). Much of the debate centred upon the meaning of Lord Nicholls's judgment in *White* on inherited property (referred to above). Bennett J agreed with the husband's counsel in deciding that the binding part of Lord Nicholls's speech on this point was that: 'It [inherited property] represents a contribution made to the welfare of the family by one of the parties to the marriage and the judge should take it into account'.

Bennett J said that if he was wrong and Lord Nicholls did enunciate a guideline that in general inherited property ought to be excluded, then in his judgment he was not saying that it was an immutable or fixed principle. Whether the guideline (if there was indeed such a guideline) should be applied in any particular case must depend upon the facts and upon the court's assessment of fairness in each case.

Bennett J disagreed with the approach adopted by Peter Hughes QC in the case of *H v H* (referred to above) by which some inherited assets had been left out of account before division of the assets. Bennett J reminded himself that the Matrimonial Causes Act 1973, s 25(1) provides that the court is under a duty to have regard to all the circumstances of the case and under s 25(2) to various particular matters, one of which is: '... property ... which each of the parties in the marriage has or is likely to have in the foreseeable future'.

Bennett J concluded that in his judgment the court is required to take into account all property of each party. That must include property acquired during the marriage by gift or succession or as a beneficiary under a trust. He said that merely because inherited property has not been touched or does not become part of the matrimonial pot is not necessarily a reason for excluding it from the court's discretionary exercise.

Bennett J held that in this case, if the inherited assets of the wife were to be taken into account as part of her contribution to the marriage and the family (which in his judgment they should be), then there was no reason to exclude them from the wife's assets when performing the discretionary exercise of distribution. 'To do so would mean the wife could have her cake and eat it.'

Furthermore, the wife was able to preserve the balance of her inherited monies because the husband was earning a very good income which maintained the family and therefore, there was no need for recourse to her inherited funds. As regards the wife's chattels which she inherited from her mother, they were hers and she was capable of selling them and turning them into money if she chose to do so. Accordingly, they should be taken into account.

In summary, Bennett J included the value of the wife's inherited assets as part of the overall resources (rather than excluding the value of them before division of the other assets). Further, he did not accept that the wife's financial contributions (by way of her inheritance) amounted to an exceptional one which would justify a departure from equality.

4   *H v M* [2004] EWHC 625 (Fam), [2004] 2 FLR 16

This case involved a different inheritance point from the three cases referred to above. The marriage lasted 14 years. There was one child. The total assets amounted to approximately £1.2 million. Mrs Justice Baron held that the jointly held assets should be divided equally and each party should retain their respective business, pension and personal assets which were broadly similar. One of the primary issues in the case was whether or not a farm which had been inherited by the wife's mother (having been in her family for some time) and which was run by the wife's parents as a chicken farm should be left out of account as contended by the wife.

The farm had been transferred to the husband and the wife in 1992 in order to protect the property from the potential bankruptcy which the wife's parents faced at the time. The family was reluctant to see the farm sold as it was the only home which the wife and her sisters had known as they had grown up. A mortgage was taken out in the joint names of the husband and wife. This was tied up with borrowings on other assets in joint names and also with the wife's overdraft on her jewellery business.

The wife's parents continued to run the farm operation from which they received a salary. The mortgage was paid through the profits of the chicken business.

The mortgage on the property made it clear that the parties were legal and beneficial owners of the property.

However, the wife sought to argue that there was a constructive trust in favour of her parents under which they had a beneficial interest in the farm.

The judge held that the wife's parents did not have any beneficial interest arising under a constructive or a resulting trust. The judge held that the husband and wife had a joint interest in the property and that the value of it would be taken into account (subject to a discount owing to the agreement that the wife's parents could continue living in the property for the remainder of their life) as part of the overall resources for division on divorce.

5   *G v G* [2009] EWHC 494 (Fam); [2009] 2 FLR 795

This was a relatively short marriage with one child, although involving several years of pre-marital cohabitation. The wife had no real earning capacity, whereas the husband was a broker with a complicated remuneration package. He was entitled to borrow from two employee benefit trusts. The husband was originally ordered to pay interim maintenance of £7,500 per month but it transpired that the husband had hidden investment funds into which discretionary bonuses had been paid.

Singer J held that the correct approach was to evaluate available assets as at the date of the hearing and considered their nature and provenance. If the assets were derived from pre-marriage acquisition, from an intra-marriage gift or inheritance, then, subject to the needs requirement, fairness might dictate that they be left wholly or partially out of the dividing exercise. Also, the judge must use his discretion to decide when the 'clock should stop', when a spouse continued to accrue savings or wealth from earnings or elsewhere after the marriage.

Three recent decisions of Charles J have sought to shed light on the court's approach to inherited wealth.

The case of *D v D* [2010] EWHC 138 (Fam), referred to in **16.13** above is another example of a case in which the fact that assets had been acquired before the marriage was taken into account in assessing the fairness of the wife's award, and the amount by which the award should move away from an equal division of assets.

6   *N v N* [2010] EWHC 717 (Fam)

The parties in this case married in October 1978 and separated in May 2007 with four children. The inherited asset in this case concerned the husband's shareholding in a company, REC, which was incorporated by his father in 1946. REC owned a property, S Hall, which had been in the husband's family for some time, as well as a portfolio of land and other buildings. The husband held a 49.46% shareholding in REC which had been gifted to him (primarily following the marriage) and increased by company buy-backs following the marriage. The other shareholders comprised two discretionary trusts for the benefit of the parties' children and their eldest child respectively, the husband being the effective donor of the shares owned by the other shareholders.

The family moved into S Hall in 1987 and the company granted the husband a 50-year lease over the property at that time. The sale proceeds of the family's previous home were spent on decorating and other work at S Hall. It was common ground that the wife had put a great deal of work into S Hall.

The assets in the case totalled approximately £16 million of which £12 million represented inherited assets.

Charles J held that in applying the sharing principle and deciding on the extent to which there should be a departure from equality, the court should not only look at the assets as a composite whole but should consider the extent of the departure in relation to the particular inherited assets in question. Assets may be subject to 100:0% division, however, this is likely to be appropriate only where it would not be fair to expect that asset to be sold or given a cash value, or where the asset cannot be shared. For example, he awarded the husband 100% of inherited photograph albums on this basis. On the other hand, some chattels that had been inherited by the husband were divided equally as they had been used by the parties as an aspect of the matrimonial home.

Charles J held that the buy-backs had been funded from the proceeds of sale of properties owned by REC since its inception, ie inherited funds rather than the use of profits created by the work and business decisions of REC's management and the husband's input. The buy-backs, therefore, supported a departure from equality. They were attributable to inherited wealth rather than to the husband's endeavours, and were, therefore, not matched by the domestic support given to the husband by the wife and the marital partnership.

In conclusion, the wife was awarded a housing fund of £2.5 million, £400,000 to cover moving costs, liabilities and her costs and a Duxbury fund of £2.4 million, giving her a total award of £5.3 million which was approximately 33% of the total assets.

The writers believe that the approach adopted by Bennett J in *Norris* and more recently by Charles J in *J v J* [2009] EWHC 2654, *D v D* and *N v N* is to be preferred to the approaches taken in *M v M* and *H v H* (referred to above) in that all assets (whether inherited or not) should be taken into account (rather than being deducted from the pool of assets prior to division). Whether or not the inherited property should result in a departure from equality will depend upon the circumstances of the case. Relevant factors will include the circumstances by which the property was acquired, to what extent it has been used during the course of the marriage and the extent of the other resources available for division.

In the circumstances of a particular case, the court may well decide that it is in the interests of fairness that the spouse who came into the inheritance be allowed to retain it provided that no prejudice is caused to the other spouse in doing so. It may be possible, therefore, to employ this argument to seek to retain a farming business where it has passed down generations of the same family in seeking to minimise the other spouse's claim to it. The retention line of argument might also be assisted where there is a child of the family who is already involved in the farm or undergoing training in farming, providing, once again, that that argument does not cause prejudice to the non-retaining spouse's needs.

In *White*, Lord Nicholls said that a parent's wish to be in a position to leave assets to his or her children would not normally fall within the statutory criteria of financial needs (under MCA 1973, s 25), either of a husband or of a wife. He added, however, that that wish is not wholly irrelevant to the section 25 exercise in considering all of the circumstances in a case where resources exceed the parties' financial needs.

A principal concern for farming families on divorce is that, since the case of *White* and the cases which have followed it (eg *N v N* at **16.13** above and *Norris v Norris* above), in contrast to the past, the issues of illiquidity and inherited property are not likely to prevent the sale of the farm (or part of it) if to do so would obstruct a fair outcome between the spouses. It is likely to prove much more difficult to resist the argument that there has to be a sale (or part of it) in order to raise the requisite funds to meet the financial claims of the other spouse unless there are cogent reasons for not selling (such as the ability to satisfy the claim from other resources, a relatively short marriage or the fact that the farm has been in the family for generations) and provided that those reasons do not cause prejudice to the other party. The argument against realisation becomes more difficult to sustain when regard is had to the amount of capital tied up in the farm proportionate to the income produced by it.

7   *K v L (Ancillary Relief: Inherited Wealth)* [2010] EWHC1234 (Fam)

This was a marriage of over 20 years and the parties had three children, who lived with the wife. Thirteen years before the parties met, the wife had inherited substantial assets, mainly shares in a family company. The parties had lived off the income from those shares during the marriage and neither had worked. They had spent relatively modestly during the marriage though. The assets to be divided were £57.4m and the issue was as to what lump sum the husband would receive. The husband sought £18m but the wife offered him £5m.

The judge found that a lump sum payment of £5m was appropriate. The most relevant points were that the assets were inherited 13 years before the parties met, very little recourse was made to them in capital terms and their value grew through passive growth rather than skilful management by anyone. These were good reasons to depart from the yardstick of equality in the wife's favour. The wife's shareholding had remained her own as a discrete asset which had never intermingled with any of the husband's assets and there had never been any discussion about putting the assets into joint names. The wife's offer gave the husband more than four times the annual income than he had initially sought in his budget and met his reasonable requirements. The pursuit of fairness with an eye to the concept of sharing did not dictate that the Court should take further money from the wife's pre-marriage inheritance so as to enhance the husband's post-divorce financial circumstances.

8   *Jones v Jones* [2011] EWCA Civ 41

This is a Court of Appeal case involving a 10-year marriage. The husband's business was the main asset and had been in existence since around 1986 (10 years before the marriage). It was a company which supplied specialist gases and associated equipment to the oil industry in the North Sea and the husband had worked in that industry since he was 15 and had considerable expertise in this area. The parties had a very good lifestyle during the marriage. They had a castle in Scotland as their main home as the husband's business was based in Scotland. In 2001 they purchased another home in Buckinghamshire where the wife and daughter went to live as the daughter was educated in England and the husband lived there with them every weekend. In 2007, 16 months after separation the husband sold his company for £32m gross (£25m net). In the High Court, the judge found that it was appropriate to depart from equality in favour of the husband to reflect the increase in value of his business since the separation, which could be attributed to his management decisions and experience. The judge found that 60% of the net proceeds of sale of the company in 2007 represented what the husband had brought into the marriage in 1996, even though the parties had agreed that the company was worth £2m at the date of marriage. This placed a capital value on the personal capacity of the husband in 1996 to make money in his chosen field ie capitalising the husband's earning capacity at the date of the marriage and proceeding to treat it as a non-matrimonial asset.

The Court of Appeal was critical of this decision. The capitalisation of earning capacity at the date of marriage was rejected, which overruled the case of *GW v RW* [2003] EWHC 611 (Fam), stating that this was not a function of the divorce Court.

The difference in this case between some cases involving a company is that the sale proceeds were known so the Court of Appeal felt it might be appropriate to first divide the pots into matrimonial and non-matrimonial assets (whereas if the valuation of the company is a guideline and not yet crystallised then it might be appropriate to look at overall outcomes before doing a division of assets into matrimonial and non-matrimonial pots as a cross check).

The Court of Appeal attributed an initial value of £4m to the company at the date of the marriage (on the basis the husband received an offer to purchase the company for between £6m and £7m a year after the marriage). It also allocated an allowance for 'passive economic growth' between the date of marriage and the date of sale which the Court of Appeal said was as much non-matrimonial as its value at the date of the marriage. The Court of Appeal found therefore, taking into account this passive growth that this gave a figure of £9m to the company as its value as a non-marital asset. Therefore, a figure of *£16m* (being the difference between the value of the non-matrimonial company (£9m) and matrimonial company (£25m)) was to be divided equally between the parties. (Lady Justice Arden on the tribunal rejected the application of 'passive growth'.)

9   *N v F* [2011] EWHC 586 (Fam)

In this case, the same approach was adopted as in *Jones v Jones* (above). This was a 16-year marriage and there were two children. At the date of the marriage the husband's assets were worth £2.1m. On divorce the total family assets, including the husband's pre-acquired wealth, were worth £9.7m. The main issue was as to how the pre-marital wealth should be treated.

The judge said that the approach to pre-acquired wealth remained fact-specific and discretionary. However, pre-marital contributions are an unmatched contribution made by one of the parties. The likelihood that contribution would be shared between the parties increased with the length of the marriage.

The judge's approach was that the court must first decide whether the existence of pre-marital property should be reflected at all. This would depend on the length of the marriage and whether the assets had been mingled with the parties' marital assets. If the pre-marital property is to be taken into account and kept separate, a decision must be made as to how much of that property should be excluded. This would depend on whether there has been much mingling of the property and also whether passive growth should be taken into account. The rest of the matrimonial property should be divided equally. The fairness of the award would then be tested by the overall percentage technique. In this case the judge excluded £1m from the pot of assets to be divided equally. This meant the wife was left with 44.7% of the total assets. This high percentage was due to the wife's needs and if these had been less, the judge said he would possibly have excluded more of the pre-marital property and possibly all of it.

PROTECTING ASSETS

Trusts

Generally

16.17   Although in some circumstances a trust may be a useful device to seek to protect family wealth from a divorcing spouse, the Family Courts do have jurisdiction to vary or look straight through certain types of trust on divorce. (Chapter 17 explains the creation of the trust, the administration and the tax treatment.)

Ante-nuptial or post-nuptial settlements

16.18   Trusts which constitute an ante-nuptial or post-nuptial settlement of property for the purposes of MCA 1973 are capable of variation by the court on a financial application within the context of a divorce. To be capable of variation there has to be a nuptial element to the settlement, but the word 'settlement' is given a wide meaning.

The settlement has to be upon the husband or the wife or both in the character of spouses – with reference to their married state. However, even in a long-standing family trust, where there is a power to appoint a life interest to a spouse on a beneficiary's death and that power is exercised, the trust may become (albeit inadvertently) a post-nuptial settlement capable of variation on divorce.

One example of the court's approach on variation of an ante-nuptial settlement is the case of *E v E* [1990] 2 FLR 233. The husband's father was paymaster throughout the marriage and provided funds to set up an offshore discretionary trust to hold shares in a Panamanian company, which in turn held the title to the matrimonial home. The property was worth £1.25 million at the date of the hearing. The husband, wife and the children were members of the class of beneficiaries and the husband's father was protector. The powers of the trustees were only exercisable with the consent of the protector. Ewbank J varied the settlement by removing the husband's father as protector, removing the trust company acting as trustees and granting the wife £50,000 outright from the settlement, with a life interest in £200,000 from it and the remainder to the children. The award to the wife in that case may have been higher had she not abandoned the children and engaged in serial adultery.

Where possible, therefore, in order to seek to maximise protection any settlement of property on trust should be made well outside the context of marriage. It would be more difficult on a divorce to argue that a settlement of property should be excluded from consideration if the settlement or re-settlement of assets took place when the marriage was in prospect or during it. Also, if the class of beneficiaries is broad it is likely to be more difficult to link the settlement with a particular marriage. That would be all the more so if the class of potential beneficiaries specifically excludes any prospective spouse but includes future generations of the family creating the trust.

Other trust interests

16.19 Even if the trust in question is not an ante-nuptial or post-nuptial settlement capable of variation (within the matrimonial legislation), where a spouse has an interest under a trust that interest will be taken into account when assessing the resources of the parties.

Both parties have a duty to give full and frank disclosure of their financial means, resources and other relevant circumstances within divorce-related financial proceedings and that duty to make full disclosure includes the valuation of any interests in a trust.

Following the demolition by the House of Lords in *White* of the judicially imposed glass ceiling of reasonable requirements, which had previously restricted a spouse's financial claim on divorce, the value of one party's trust interests could prove to be a very significant factor in assessing the overall resources and deciding what is a fair outcome in a particular case. The party with the trust interest will not necessarily be expected to realise the trust assets (as that would necessarily depend on the nature of the trust interest, the level of control the spouse has over the trust assets and also on what other assets are available). However, the presence of trust interests may result in a greater proportion of the non-trust assets being distributed to the other spouse. The financially weaker party (and his/her lawyer) will usually aim to maximise the value of assets available for division.

Trustees may be joined to divorce proceedings. They may be asked to explain the practice of distribution, or to produce accounts, deeds and records of distributions which the court considers may be necessary for the purpose of dealing fairly with a financial application.

1   *T v T (joinder of third parties)* [1996] 2 FLR 357

In this case, the husband had transferred his interest in the business which he had set up to a Jersey trust of which he was a beneficiary. His spouse was also a beneficiary. When the wife applied for an injunction against the trust, the husband argued that he had no effective control over the trust assets.

The trustees' application to set aside the court order was refused and it was held that there were various benefits of enjoining the trustees. Those benefits included assisting the court with discovery and the provision of evidence; assisting the enforcement of any financial order; and the obtaining of a mirror or supplementary order in Jersey if required.

It is important that trustees are separately represented so that they can seek to minimise the allegations that they might be 'in the pocket' of the husband or wife (as the case may be).

The courts are particularly suspicious of discretionary trusts in the context of divorce. Every judge will have heard many times the arguments of wealthy spouses who say that a trust is wholly discretionary and entirely beyond their control when in fact it has been utilised as a personal cash fund or credit facility for the duration of the marriage. If the trust has advanced money regularly or on request, this situation will be assumed by the courts to continue in the future, even though the beneficiary may only be one of a class of discretionary beneficiaries.

2   *Thomas v Thomas* [1995] 2 FLR 668

This case is interesting for the way in which it afforded judicious encouragement to third parties to provide a spouse with the means to comply with the court's view of justice in the case. Here, the majority of the husband's wealth was tied up in a shareholding in a family company whose policy it was to pay relatively low salaries to directors and plough the profits back into the company. There were heavy charges to the company on the family home to cover a mortgage, a bank guarantee covering contingent liability to Lloyd's as well as loans for Lloyd's losses. Lord Justice Glidewell reached the following conclusions:

'(a)   Where a husband can only raise further capital, or additional income, as the result of a decision made at the discretion of trustees, the court should not put improper pressure on the trustees to exercise that discretion for the benefit of the wife.

(b)   The court should not, however, be "misled by appearances"; it should "look at the reality of the situation".

(c)   If on the balance of probability the evidence shows that, if trustees exercise their discretion to release more capital or income to a husband, the interests of the trust or of other beneficiaries would not be appreciably damaged, the court can assume that a genuine request for the exercise of such discretion would probably be met by a favourable response. In that situation if the court decides that it would be reasonable for a husband to seek to persuade trustees to release more capital or income to him to enable him to make proper financial provision for his children and his former wife, the court would not in so deciding be putting improper pressure on the trustees.

In relation to the facts of the present case, I would apply these principles to the family company as if it were a trust, and the shareholders (the husband, his mother and brother) the trustees.'

The court is not obliged to limit its orders exclusively to resources of capital or income which are shown actually to exist. The court can draw inference from a spouse's expenditure or lifestyle or from his inability or unwillingness to allow the complexity of his financial affairs to be investigated in a way necessary to ascertain his actual wealth or the degree of liquidity of his assets.

As in *Thomas v Thomas*, the court may make assumptions about funds being made available to the beneficiary which would have the effect of making the beneficiary bankrupt if the trustees refuse to co-operate.

3   *Browne v Browne* [1989] 1 FLR 291

This was another case in which the court seized on the practice of distribution. The court made an order in the husband's favour, which the wife could only meet by drawing from a trust of which she was a beneficiary. The reason for this order was that the pattern of distributions was such that whenever the wife requested a distribution for almost any purpose, sums were advanced. On that basis Butler-Sloss LJ concluded that the wife in effect had immediate access to the funds. The fact that the trustees objected to future distributions (which would in effect pass to the husband) was not held to be decisive.

4   *Mubarak v Mubarak* [2001] 1 FLR 673

This case also threw third-party interests into the spotlight. As a result, the court may be more reluctant to look through trust arrangements where there are genuine third-party interests. In that case assets were kept out of reach of the wife by being held in trust through underlying trading companies. In the context of enforcement proceedings where the husband had not complied with the court order to pay a lump sum to his wife, the court ruled that to attack the trust by lifting the corporate veil would prejudice the interests of the third parties involved. The court did say, however, that it would have no hesitation in attacking the trust structure if it had been set up or used as a sham or a device with the intention of diminishing the claims of the other spouse.

5   *TL v ML & Others (Ancillary Relief: Claim against assets of extended family)* [2006] 1 FLR 1263

This was a marriage of six years with one year prior cohabitation. The husband was 36 and the wife 33. There were two children aged seven and four, who after the separation lived with the wife in her parents' home in Vienna. The total assets of the parties amounted to approximately £560,000. During the marriage the parties had lived in a spacious mansion flat in London, which was held in the husband's brother's name. They enjoyed a high standard of living. The husband's family was very wealthy and he worked in the family business in London, receiving money for his services more or less as required.

In matrimonial proceedings the wife claimed that the husband was the beneficial owner of the former matrimonial home. She further contended that the husband was also the beneficial owner of the assets held by two offshore companies. Finally she argued that the court should include the 'bounty' that the husband was likely to continue to receive from his parents and that her claim should be ordered on the basis that his parents be 'judicially encouraged' to make funds available to the husband to meet her claim.

The judge held that a dispute with a third party must be approached on exactly the same basis as if it were being determined in the Chancery Division (as opposed to the discretionary exercise undertaken in a financial relief dispute between spouses). That third party must be joined to the proceedings at the earliest opportunity.

The judge held that the property was registered in the names of the husband's brother and the evidence showed that the wife fully appreciated that he was the owner of the property. It was clear that the wife's case regarding the ownership of the property was a fabrication.

He further held that the evidence clearly established that the money in the company's bank accounts was used by the husband's parents to support themselves and their children. The husband's expenditure out of the first account did not denote ownership of the assets in that account and it was clear that the payments into the account came from sources other than the husband.

In terms of the 'bounty', the judge held that if the court was satisfied on the balance of probabilities that an outsider would provide money to meet an award that a party could not meet from his absolute property, it could make an award that applied pressure on persons who had historically provided bounty. However, if it was clear that the outsider, being a person who had historically supplied bounty would not, whether reasonably or not, come to the aid of the payer, the court would not make such an award. In this case, on the evidence, funds belonging to the husband's parents could not be included in an assessment of the husband's resources.

6   *Minwalla v Minwalla* [2005] 1 FLR 771

In this case, the wife was concerned that the husband was trying to suppress the extent of his wealth and she obtained a worldwide freezing order, extending to his interest in a Jersey-based trust. The husband asserted that the freezing order should not apply in relation to the trust on the basis that he was not a beneficiary. The judge, Mr Justice Singer, followed the judgment of Mr Justice Coleridge in *J v V* (Disclosure: Offshore Corporations) 'and held that 'the suppression of assets is not of course behaviour that of itself enhances an award. But the non-disclosing spouse does make himself vulnerable to adverse inferences being drawn against him'.

The judge concluded that the husband had ample resources to satisfy the wife's modest financial plan and rejected the assertion that the husband had no beneficial interest in the trust. There had been complex and voluminous documents that supported the contention that the trust effectively belonged to the husband and this was supported by the way in which he treated the trust assets 'with utter disregard for any but his own wishes, decision making and – in short – total control'.

The husband had written two letters of wishes, both dated 22 September 1998. Each letter incorporated different directions. One was to regard the husband as a principal beneficiary during his lifetime and thereafter one-third to his widow and two-thirds to his four sons. The second letter omitted any reference to himself as principal beneficiary and stated that on his death the fund should pass to his sons. The judge accepted the wife's contention that these differing letters were in existence to enable a dishonest selection to be made in the event of a divorce.

The judge concluded that 'the husband never had the slightest intention of respecting even the formalities of the trust and corporate structures that had been set up at his direction. His purpose was only to set up a screen to shield his resources from other claims or unwelcome scrutiny and investigation'. The judge concluded 'where it appears that an offshore trust had been woven together to create a shroud designed to bury the husband's resources from view, but the husband himself pierced that veil as and when it suited him, a court exercising the ancillary relief jurisdiction would strain to see through the smoke and would set the structure aside so as to treat the resources as his. This is what the parties, trustees and directors should expect.

7   *A & A and St George Trustees Limited and Others* [2007] EWHC 99

This was a 17-year marriage. The husband was 64 and the wife 59. There were no children of the family, but both parties had children by previous marriages. The assets were about £2.7 million. There were three family companies. The most relevant for the purposes of this case was HDC, a company set up by the husband's father. The husband held 23% of the shares in this company, the wife had 22.98% of the shares, the husband's son had 0.02% of the shares and 54% of the shares were held by the trustees of two separate trusts (34% of which were in a discretionary trust created by the husband's parents, and 20% in a discretionary trust set up by the husband's brother.) The beneficiaries of both trusts were the children and remoter issue of the husband's parents, ie it was not a closed class. Both trusts were governed by English law. The trustees of both trusts were professional accountants in Jersey, under a vehicle called St George Trustees Limited.

The principal issues in this case were that:

- The wife claimed that the trusts were a sham so, in fact, the husband owned 77% of the shares in HDC because he was 'de facto the controller and beneficiary of the trust'. She said that the reasons for the shares initially being placed in trust was because the husband was divorcing his first wife at the time and he wanted to portray himself as a minority shareholder, there were 'passive trustees' and there were no letters of wishes for some time. There was a long discussion about the list of principles and doctrines in relation to sham. The judge referred to the case *In the matter of the Esteem settlement (Abacus (CI) Limited as trustees, Grupo, Torras SA and Culmer and Al Sabah and four others* [2004] WTLR 1 whereby, 'in order for a trustee to be a sham, both settlor and trustee must intend that the true arrangement is otherwise than as set out in the deed'. If the trust had been a sham, it would be void. However, the judge concluded that a trust which is initially not a sham cannot subsequently become a sham. In order to be a sham all the trustees and beneficiaries had to have joined with the requisite intention. In this case, not all the beneficiaries were ascertained so this was an impossibility. If the trust was previously a sham, it could be genuine now if the current trustees were not party to the sham at the time of appointment.

- The second issue was in relation to whether the shares in the trust should be treated as available to the husband. The court referred to the case of *Thomas v Thomas* above, and said that if it decided it would be reasonable for the husband to seek to persuade the trustees to release more capital or income to him to enable him to make proper financial provision for his children or former wife, it would not be putting improper pressure on the trustees. It would come down to whether the wife could demonstrate that, if asked, the trustees would be likely, immediately or in the foreseeable future, to exercise their powers in favour of or for the benefit of the husband. The court could encourage but could not compel the trustees. It was found that, in this case, there was no history of any distributions, the husband was only one of a number of beneficiaries and there was no money to extract.

The judge felt that HDC was a family asset. It had been a longish marriage in which the wife had played a full part. The parties had made an approximately equal contribution so there should be an equal division of assets.

8   *Charman v Charman* [2007] 1 FLR 593

The facts of this case have been referred to above.

From a divorce and trust perspective, this case represents a significant step in the trend on the part of the English courts to look through trusts (especially self-settled trusts) and treat them as a resource of the settlor regardless of other beneficial interests in the trust fund. In a departure from the previous importance placed on the pattern of distributions, the Dragon Trust was considered to be a 'resource' of the settlor (the husband), despite the absence of such a track record of regular distributions. The husband in this case was not assisted by a letter of wishes requesting that the trustees regard him as the principal beneficiary. The existence of such a letter of wishes is likely to increase the prospect that a court will view the trust as a 'resource' of the settlor. Also, the retention by the settlor of the power to remove and appoint the trustees may encourage the court to view the trust as a 'resource' available to the settlor. In *Charman*, it was said 'the husband's power to replace the trustees was indicative of the likelihood of advancement'. This reflects a departure from established trust law principles that the power to replace trustees is fiduciary and cannot therefore be exercised lawfully in response to a refusal by a trustee to accede to a request for a distribution. The operation of replacement trustee powers by an independent third party might offer the settlor a stronger argument against the inclusion of trust property within the matrimonial property available for distribution between the parties on divorce.

9   *Mubarak v Mubarik* [2007] EWHC 220

The husband, aged 49, and the wife, aged 48, had married in 1983 and moved to Kuwait. The husband's jewellery business had prospered and the husband had set up branches in Hong Kong, Paris and London. In 1994 the husband had incorporated a holding company in Bermuda which owned the shares in the subsidiary company referred to in this case. In August 1997, the family moved to London. However, before the move there had been a corporate restructuring of the company, transferring the majority of shares owned by the husband and wife into the company save for 11,000 and 1,000 still owned by the husband and wife respectively. On this transfer, the purchase price had not been paid, therefore the company still owed a liability of £35 million to the husband and wife.

The company's assets included the former matrimonial home. In September 1997 the husband and wife, as settlors, set up a discretionary trust governed by Jersey law. The beneficiaries in this trust were the husband and wife, their children and any future children. The husband had the power to add and exclude beneficiaries and to appoint and remove a protector or trustees. The protector in this case was the husband's father who had the power to remove any trustees and whose consent would sometimes be needed for the exercise of trustee's powers. The husband and wife transferred their shares in the company into this trust, but not the debt that they were owed by the company.

In 1998, the husband left the former matrimonial home and proceeded to exclude the wife from the beneficiary class under powers given to him in the trust. Following this the husband wrote two letters of wishes to the trustees. In September 1997 he wrote that the trustees should consult the husband on all aspects, including administration, distribution of income or capital to either the husband or wife and expressed a wish that if the husband died the trustees should hold it equally for the benefit of his wife and children. However, on 8 July 1998 he deleted his wife from the previous letter and wrote that the trustees should hold it merely for the benefit of his children, were he to die. Soon after writing this letter, the wife commenced divorce proceedings against the husband.

Originally Bodey J ordered the husband to pay the wife a lump sum of £4.875 million and additional periodical payments until that lump sum was paid. However, the husband continually failed to make payment. The wife, therefore, tried to enforce the payment in England and in Jersey in numerous hearings in both the High Court and the Court of Appeal. Finally the wife applied to the Family Division seeking:

- to set aside her exclusion as a beneficiary by reason of a deed of exclusion dated 20 April 1998;

- to satisfy the transfer of shares in the company to the trust; and

- an order under the Matrimonial Causes Act 1973 to vary the terms of the trust so as to require the trustees to pay to her an amount equal to the amount owed by the husband to the wife under the Bodey J order.

On 30 March 2007 Holman J varied the terms of the trust and required the trustees to pay to the wife an amount equal to the balance owing under the lump sum ordered by Bodey J. This amounted to approximately £7.6 million, including costs. Under the Judgments (Reciprocal Enforcement) Jersey Law 1960, an English judgment can be registered in Jersey and, therefore, is enforceable if it is a final and conclusive judgment, one in which a sum of money is payable and the English court has jurisdiction for the purposes of the statute. However, a judgment exercising a power under the MCA 1973 to vary a trust was not one to which this act applied. Furthermore, in most cases the trustees would not have submitted to the English jurisdiction. However, overseas judgments could also be enforced under customary law if a debt or definite sum of money was owed and the overseas court had jurisdiction over the judgment debtor.

The High Court of Jersey explained in this case that there are two types of variation. First, a variation of a trust could involve the altering of a trust deed by varying its terms, ie adding a beneficiary that the trustees could not have added under their powers. This was called an alteration. Secondly, the court could vary it in a way that the trustees could have varied it themselves under their powers, ie one could vary a trust to say that a beneficiary under a discretionary trust should get the amount absolutely. The latter did not include a departure from the trust deed. Although the Jersey court did not have a general power to alter the terms of a trust as there was no reason in principle why the court should assume a power to override the express intentions of a settlor, the Jersey court held that when the variation is of the latter class the Jersey court might give a direction to achieve the objectives of the English law. However, this was a matter of discretion in each case. In this case it was an alteration; therefore, there was no jurisdiction. However, it was concluded that in this case all the beneficiaries could alter the trust under the *Saunders v Vautier* principle (ie, if all the beneficiaries consented, they could direct the trustees to transfer the trust to them, enabling them to alter the trust). Also, the Jersey court was allowed to approve alterations as it was for the benefit of minors and/or children. This case emphasises the different routes by which the Jersey courts might give effect to an English judgment.

10   *Bin Hashem v Al Shayif* [2008] EWHC 2380; [2009] 1 FLR 115

The husband and wife had married in England and moved to Saudi Arabia, with the wife giving up her job to do so. When relations broke down the wife moved back to England and forced entry into a flat owned by the family company. This company was incorporated in Jersey and the husband owned 30% of the shares with the remainder to the husband's children. The properties owned by the company were used as places to live on family visits to England. The children did not object to the wife's occupation of the flat as long as the husband met the outgoings and on reconciliation the husband visited the wife in England.

The wife sought a divorce and ancillary relief. The court held that the marriage was bigamous and therefore void. The husband refused to engage in ancillary relief; therefore, it was unclear what wealth the husband possessed. The court found that he was worth many millions.

Ultimately, the wife was awarded approximately £7 million. It was held that the company was the beneficial and legal owner of the properties as it was not held on trust for the husband. Any advances the husband had been given were loans and this was inconsistent with any beneficial interest on his part by resulting trust or otherwise. The fact that the husband had control and decided on the direction of the company did not mean the company was not beneficially holding the assets.

Nor was it held that the husband was the beneficial owner of the children's shares. This was for the reason that otherwise no shares would have been allotted to the children let alone in the specific differing proportions.

In relation to the investment property that the company possessed, there had been no post-nuptial settlement within the meaning of s 24 of the Matrimonial Causes Act 1973 as the parties' use of the property had been too temporary to constitute continuing possession. There had also been no nuptial character to this use. However, in relation to the flat occupied by the wife on the original breakdown, this was a settlement the court did have jurisdiction to vary. The provision of a home for the wife had a sufficient nuptial element and it had been intended to make continuing provision for an undefined period. It was emphasised that the court's discretion to vary a nuptial settlement under s 24(1)(c) of the Matrimonial Causes Act 1973 is unfettered and unlimited, however, the judge must remember that the court should only do enough to do justice between the parties. The court should be slow to deprive innocent third parties of rights under a settlement.

Munby J concluded that, due to the wife's use of the flat as a home for six years and the fact that she remained there for two years after possession proceedings, justice would only be done by requiring the company to give the wife two months' notice. This judgment reminds us that the court must consider not only whether a settlement is nuptial in character, but also what properties are comprised in it and reminds us that the court must exercise its discretion.

11   *PCJ and ADC and (1) VJW (2) DJH (3) Stephen Howard Woolfe (4) Philip James Tostevin* [2009] EWHC 1491

This case again involves the question of whether a husband's interest under a trust was a resource of the husband for the purposes of s 25(2)(a) of the Matrimonial Causes Act 1973.

The trust arose out of a will made in 1973 by the husband's late father, comprising securities worth £220,000, chattels and landed estates worth between £4 million and £6 million. It was on trust for the testator's widow for life and on her death to her four children as trustees in common in equal shares of whom the husband was one. There were no powers under the trust to vary the beneficiaries' entitlement or pay, apply or appoint anything for the benefit of any of the children. The only powers the trustees had in relation to any beneficiaries were to pay the whole or any part of the trust fund to the widow and a power of advancement. It could, therefore, only be varied by the beneficiaries under the *Saunders v Vautier* rule.

Munby J emphasised that there was a large distinction between the relationship of fiduciary and beneficiary and the relationship of donor and donees. There were no powers to give to the husband any money without the consent of the widow. It could not, therefore, be said that the husband's interest under the trust was a 'resource' in which he had any significant realisable value at the time of the hearing. However, the question was whether it was nonetheless a resource he was likely to have in the foreseeable future. He referred to the case of *Charman* and the question of whether a trustee would be likely to advance capital immediately or in the foreseeable future to the husband.

In making his judgment Munby J considered several factors. First he considered that the widow's life expectancy was 15 years, second that there was a speculative prospect of a *Saunders v Vautier* arrangement to vary the trust, and finally, that there was a distinct possibility that the trustees would exercise their powers under the will to advance the money to the widow. He therefore concluded that in 15 years' time the husband could expect to receive his quarter share subject to the possibility that the trustees might deplete it by making advances to the widow. These would not, however, encroach upon the value of the family estate. The question was whether the husband's interest fell under a financial resource which he had or was likely to have in the foreseeable future. If so, the court could make an immediate order in favour of the wife if the judge decided that the money was likely to come into effect on the death of the widow. There was certainty that the money would fall in and that it would be of a significant value, however, it was not certain when this would happen and what the amount would be.

In concluding that this interest should be considered a financial resource, Munby J said that, 'this was very close to the outer extremity of what can properly be considered a financial resource which the spouse is likely to have in the foreseeable future'. However, in this case it was and Munby J based this on the fact that it had vested and, although it was liable to be divided in part or in whole, the likelihood was that the husband would still obtain a significant amount of money. However, Munby J emphasised that his decision would have been different if the chance of obtaining the money had been slightly less or the life expectancy of the widow had been slightly longer.

12   *R v R also known as SR v CR* [2008] EWHC 2329; [2009] 2 FLR 1083

The husband and wife in this case had been in a relationship for 20 years from engagement to separation and were married in 1988. There were three children under the age of 18. The husband was the discretionary beneficiary of various trusts belonging to his father, as were his brothers and sisters. The husband had been given lump sums from these trusts to pay for his unsuccessful business and an unsustainable lifestyle of the family. At trial the father gave evidence that he would give no more money to the husband and would oppose any distribution to him from the trusts. However, in a letter of wishes the father had made it clear that he wished his four children to share equally from the trusts on his death and the trustees said that they might benefit the husband notwithstanding the father's stance. In particular the husband's debt to the trust might be taken off his future apportionment and the husband might be provided with rented accommodation and a modest living allowance.

The assets in the marriage were worth £7.5 million, the majority of which had come to the marriage from the husband's family, which was inadequate to maintain the lifestyle of both parties and the husband suggested that it should be divided equally. On the other hand the wife applied for a sum in excess of £7.5 million arguing that the husband could expect to receive a large amount of money from the trust and that the father's reluctance was not genuine, but merely to avoid his son's money being transferred to her.

Singer J held that the courts could not put improper pressure on the trustees to make distributions but could make an ancillary relief order that encouraged the trustees to allay the husband's needs by putting him in a position where he needed the trustees to make a distribution. However, this order should only be made if the requisite assistance was anticipated as forthcoming. Therefore, one must look at what the trustees were likely to do, which was complicated by the father's attitude. However, the trustees would only pay regard to the father's attitude and were not bound by him.

Again the *Charman* question of whether the trustees would be likely to advance the capital immediately or in the foreseeable future to the spouse should be posed.

It was held that the husband did not control any disposition but there was a reasonable expectation of further money being made available to him in the short/medium term and this forseeability should be taken into account. On the facts it was held that the husband and father had misrepresented that his 25% share (at least $23 million) would remain settled on the father's death when in fact it was likely that his quarter share would come to the husband outright and in the not too distant future. It was also held that the trustees would certainly not disregard the father's attitude if the father was to decide that the husband should be given a distribution as was likely.

It was held that the marital assets should be divided as to £6.25 million to the wife (to meet her income and capital needs) and £1.6 million to the husband on the basis that he was likely to receive significant sums in the future from trust (in particular on his father's death).

The cases of *Minwalla*, *Charman*, *Mubarak* and *R v R* all demonstrate how influential letters of wishes can be in the divorce court.

Pre-nuptial agreements

16.20

1   *Radmacher (formerly Granatino) (Respondent) v Granatino (Appellant)* [2010] UKSC 42

In this highly publicised case, the Supreme Court held that the Court should give effect to pre-nuptial agreements which are 'freely entered into by each party with a full appreciation of its implications unless in the circumstances prevailing it would not be fair to hold the parties to their agreement'. The parties (French and German) had entered into a marriage contract prior to their wedding in 1998 which provided for a separation of assets and no financial provision in the event of a divorce. They separated in 2006 after eight years having had two children. During the marriage the husband had been working as an investment banker earning as much as £330,000 per annum, however, at the time of their English divorce the husband had left the bank and was studying for a PhD at Oxford. His earning capacity as a researcher was approximately £20,000 net per annum. In contrast, the wife owned shares in the family company worth approximately £50 million and had further assets of approximately £55 million, all of which she had inherited before the marriage. Her net annual income was approximately £2.6 million.

On divorce in England the husband claimed £9 million but the wife sought to uphold the pre-nuptial agreement. When the English High Court first considered the case, whilst not completely enforcing the pre-nuptial agreement, its existence was acknowledged to be a feature of the case which circumscribed the husband's award. However, the court decided that it was manifestly unfair that no financial provision had been made for the husband. It was influenced by the fact that a marriage contract was the cultural norm for both of the parties and it would have been valid and enforceable in Germany (where the wife was from and where the agreement was executed), and in France (where the husband was from). The husband was awarded £5.5 million (which would give him an annual income of £100,000 for life and allow him to buy a home in London, where the children could visit him).

The wife appealed and the Court of Appeal reversed the decision of the lower court. It held that any reform in this area was for Parliament and not for the court. This was particularly the case as the Law Commission was discussing the issue. However, the belief that pre-nuptial agreements were void was increasingly unrealistic, as it did not sufficiently recognise the rights of autonomous adults to govern their financial arrangements by agreement in an age when divorce was commonplace. The court warned against England and Wales being isolated from the laws in other EU countries and the wider common law world. Therefore, pending the Law Commission report, it was held that judges should give weight to the marital property regime into which parties had freely entered. This was part of the wide discretion that judges had to achieve fairness in financial proceedings.

The husband received his English home on loan only, to be returned to his former wife when the children reached the age of 22. In addition, his capital fund was re-calculated not to provide an income for life, but simply for the duration of his time as carer for his daughters. It was acknowledged that at the time the pre-nuptial agreement was signed, there was no financial disclosure, no independent legal advice and no translation of the document from German. However, the Court of Appeal held that the husband was a man of the world who knew what he was signing. Therefore, the absence of the usual contractual safeguards were held not to be determinative.

The husband appealed to the Supreme Court. The Supreme Court had to decide what principles should be applied in considering what weight should be given to an agreement between parties made before the marriage. The Supreme Court dismissed the husband's appeal by a majority of 8:1. In the summary of the case prepared by the Supreme Court, it was stated that three issues arose in relation to the agreement in this case for the Court to consider:

1. *Were there circumstances attending the making of the agreement which should detract from the weight which should be accorded to it?* Parties must enter into an ante-nuptial agreement voluntarily, without undue pressure and be informed of its implications. The question is whether there is any *material* lack of disclosure, information or advice.

2. *Did the foreign elements of the case enhance the weight that should be accorded to the agreement?* In 1998, when this agreement was signed, the fact that it was binding under German law was relevant to the question of whether the parties intended the agreement to be effective, at a time when it would not have been recognised in the English courts. After this judgment it will be natural to infer that parties entering into agreements governed by English law will intend that effect to be given to them.

3. *Did the circumstances prevailing at the time the court made its order make it fair or just to depart from the agreement?* An ante-nuptial agreement may make provisions that conflict with what a court would otherwise consider to be fair. The principle, however, to be applied is that a court should give effect to a nuptial agreement that is freely entered into by each party with a full appreciation of its implications unless,

in the circumstances prevailing, it would not be fair to hold the parties to their agreement. A nuptial agreement cannot be allowed to prejudice the reasonable requirements of any children of the family, but respect should be given to individual autonomy and to the reasonable desire to make provision for existing property. In the right case an ante-nuptial agreement can have decisive or compelling weight.

Applying these principles to the facts, the Court of Appeal was correct to conclude that there were no factors which rendered it unfair to hold the husband to the agreement. He is extremely able and his own needs would in large measure be indirectly met from the generous relief given to cater for the needs of his two daughters until the younger reaches the age of 22. There is no compensation factor as the husband's decision to abandon his career in the city was not motivated by the demands of his family but reflected his own preference. Fairness did not entitle him to a portion of his wife's wealth, received from her family independently of the marriage when he had agreed he should not be so entitled when he married her.

The Law Commission is embarking on a consultation in 2010/11 on pre-nuptial agreements with a draft bill anticipated in 2011/12. Whether or not statutory change will be passed in due course to make pre-nuptial agreements binding will depend on the political will in Parliament. However, the Supreme Court has sent a clear message in its majority decision in this case that the judiciary supports law reform in the area of nuptial agreements. Even Lady Hale, dissenting from the majority view, stated that 'the law of marital agreements is in a mess. It is ripe for systematic review and reform'. The Law Commission is due to report in 2012, having sought the profession's views and it should make detailed proposal for legislative reform. The Government indicated support for the concept of pre-nuptial agreements in a consultation document produced in November 1998 entitled *Supporting Families*. Safeguards proposed in the consultation paper, which, if found to apply, would render any such agreement not binding or less binding, included:

● the existence of children;

● the absence of legal advice at the time of signing;

● the lack of financial disclosure at the time of signing;

● when signed less than 21 days before the wedding;

● if there is significant injustice; and

● where agreement would be unenforceable under contract law.

Therefore, if parties to a marriage wish to have pre-nuptial agreement, then in order to give the agreement as much persuasive weight as possible in the event of a divorce the following factors should apply when the document is prepared:-

● each party must take separate independent legal advice;

● there must be full and frank disclosure of the assets and resources available to each party, including any trusts of which either party is a beneficiary;

- the agreement should be executed as far in advance of the wedding day as possible, so that neither party can subsequently claim they were under undue circumstantial pressure to agree terms;

- the agreement must be fair, ie within the general sphere of what a court might award each party in the event of a divorce; and

- there should be evidence of genuine negotiation of terms to avoid a challenge on the basis that the 'agreement' was in fact simply a dictat from the financially stronger party to the weaker.

Generally, where there is significant wealth disparity going into the marriage and/or the likelihood of significant inheritance or trust interests falling in during the marriage, it is in the interests of the financially stronger party to have a pre-nuptial agreement, particularly in the early years of a childless relationship.

Post-nuptial agreements

16.21   The status of post-nuptial agreements was thrown into the spotlight in December 2008 when the case of *MacLeod* came before the Privy Council. Until this case, if a couple entered into an agreement whether before or after their marriage to regulate their financial affairs in the event of a divorce, such an agreement would be contrary to public policy and thus not binding on the court. The case of *Radmacher v Granatino* (above) has overtaken the case of *MacLeod* but the latter case still has some points of interest.

1   *MacLeod v MacLeod (Pre-nuptial Agreements)* [2008] UKPC 64

In this case, the husband had derived much of his wealth prior to the marriage and had doubled it during the marriage. When living in Florida, the parties had executed a pre-nuptial agreement on their wedding day which would have been binding had they been divorced in Florida. They moved to the Isle of Man and had five children during a ten-year marriage. During the marriage, they entered into two post-nuptial agreements. The second was over a 14-month period of negotiation (during which time their fifth child was born) when the marriage was already breaking down. The agreement gave the wife capital of £1.8 million, but on divorce she claimed £5.5 million.

The judges in the Isle of Man High Court found that there had been proper financial disclosure, independent legal advice, no undue pressure and emphasised the 14-month period of negotiation. Furthermore, various parts of the deed of variation had been implemented. The wife was, therefore, held to the structure of the deed and pre-nuptial agreement, but allowed a substantial additional sum for housing paid outright to her rather than in trust. The husband then lost his appeal in the Isle of Man Court of Appeal.

The Privy Council held that the court could not change the fact that pre-nuptial agreements are contrary to public policy, therefore, not binding in a contractual sense. If this were to be changed then it was for Parliament and not for the judiciary. However, the court took the view that post-nuptial agreements are very different. In the case of *Radmacher v Granatino* [2010] UKSC 42 the Privy Council's decision was overruled in regards to the distinction between post-nuptial agreements and pre-nuptial agreements. It was acknowledged that although the agreement may have lacked generosity of provision for the wife (being much less than she could have expected had there been no agreement), there was no basis for interfering with it. The fact that the agreement was finalised just 12 months before they separated was highly influential.

Therefore, the public policy objection to post-nuptial agreements has been removed. Such agreements can now be binding on the English family court and thus can be upheld as valid contracts. However, this does not automatically mean that all post-nuptial agreements will be binding, as the court retains its discretion and overriding power to vary terms agreed between spouses. Therefore, certain safeguards should be observed. The terms should be recorded in a deed, both parties should take independent legal advice, there must be no undue pressure exerted on a party to sign and both parties should comply with their duty of disclosure.

The next question was what weight should be given to a post-nuptial agreement in ancillary relief proceedings.

The Privy Council stated that it would expect the statutory provisions for the validity and variation of maintenance agreements to be the starting point. Parliament had laid down circumstances where an agreement relating to a couple's property and finances during and after the marriage could be varied by the court. At the same time, Parliament had preserved the parties' rights to go to the court for an order governing the financial arrangement on divorce. It would be odd, therefore, for Parliament to have intended for the approach to post-nuptial agreements to be different in ancillary relief claims from the variation of maintenance agreements. Therefore, the same principles should be the starting point in both. The court would, therefore, look for a change of circumstances which would make the post-nuptial agreement manifestly unjust and would check whether it provided sufficiently for any children.

The Privy Council held that the post-nuptial agreement was valid and enforceable but the arrangement for the division of assets on separation was still subject to the court's powers of variation. In this case there had not been a sufficient change in circumstances; however, it was held that the post-nuptial agreement had not provided sufficiently to accommodate the children. The wife, therefore, received a larger financial award for the children. However, it was held that the High Court in the Isle of Man had been wrong not to accede to the husband's request that the wife and children's housing needs be catered for by a trust fund as opposed to a lump sum. The effect of the Isle of Man order had been to make further provision for the wife as opposed to the children therefore the husband's appeal was successful.

Proceeds of crime

16.22　Any party going through a divorce needs to be aware of the Proceeds of Crime Act 2002 (POCA) which came into force in 2003. This Act makes it an offence (s 328) for a person to become involved in an arrangement that he knows concerns 'the acquisition, retention, use or control of criminal property by or on behalf of another person'. However, a person is protected from liability under that provision if he makes an 'authorised disclosure' and obtains the 'appropriate consent' from the NCIS (National Criminal Intelligence Service).

The Act also introduces offences of tipping off if notification of a party might prejudice an investigation.

The primary purpose of the Act is to curb money laundering. However, criminal property is widely defined as constituting a person's financial benefit from criminal conduct, which is conduct that constitutes an offence in the UK or elsewhere. This may often present itself in the non-payment of tax. The law imposes an obligation on professionals (such as solicitors, barristers and accountants), as well as the parties involved to notify the NCIS where that person knows or suspects the facilitation of the acquisition, retention, use or control of criminal property by or on behalf of another person.

This case of *Bowman & Fels* [2005] EWCA Civ 226 concerned information which had come to the attention of the solicitors for one of the parties during legal proceedings. The information caused the solicitor to suspect that the opposing party's client had engaged in money laundering many years previously and in respect of a minimal amount. The solicitor informed NCIS of this in accordance with s 338 of POCA 2002 without informing the opposing side's solicitors. When NCIS were unable to provide authorisation to proceed with the litigation prior to the trial date, the case had to be adjourned.

The central issue considered in the appeal was whether s 328 of POCA applied to the ordinary conduct of legal proceedings or any aspect of such conduct, in particular whether it applied to any step taken to pursue proceedings or obtaining a judgment or settlement. The Court of Appeal considered whether lawyers are obliged to make any disclosures that are in breach of legal professional privilege to NCIS at all, and if so, under what circumstances.

The court ruled that (i) Parliament did not intend the conduct of litigation to be a form of money laundering within the meaning of s 328; and (ii) questions of legal professional privilege do arise when a solicitor discloses to a third party external to the litigation, in this case NCIS, documents revealed to him through the disclosure process. Therefore s 328 should not be interpreted as overriding legal professional privilege and is not intended to cover or affect the ordinary conduct of litigation by legal professionals.

It is understood that legal privilege would not be a defence if the intention behind the arrangement has criminal purpose.

Bankruptcy

16.23

1   *Hill (1) & Bangham v Haines* [2007] EWCA 1012

This case was heard in the Chancery Division of the High Court. The respondent wife and the bankrupt husband were married and were joint legal and beneficial owners of a property in Worcestershire called Strudges Farm. The wife issued a divorce petition on 25 April 2003. She commenced ancillary relief proceedings on 15 May 2003 seeking orders including a property adjustment order. The Family Court made an order for the husband to transfer to the wife all his interests in the property, to pay nominal periodical payments and for the application of a lump sum order to be adjourned. The judge in the

Chancery Division found that it was clear from the judgment in the Family Court that there was a substantial risk that the bankrupt would be made the subject of a bankruptcy order and if he was that this might affect an order made by the Family Court. The Family Division judge, adjourning the lump sum order, said that this was to 'guard against [the] eventuality that the husband will go bankrupt in the near future and the possible consequences to the wife of the trustee and the bankruptcy seeking, as he may, to impugn the transfer of the Mercedes and house to the wife'. For that reason the judge kept the wife's lump sum order alive.

On 31 March 2005 the husband made himself bankrupt on his own petition. On 24 May 2005 the appellants, Hill & Bangham were appointed trustees at a creditors' meeting. On 22 September 2005 the District Judge executed a transfer of the Property on behalf of the bankrupt.

The bankrupt's total liabilities were £132,000. The property had been sold and the wife had preserved one half of the net proceeds (£120,000) in a fund that was available for transfer to the appellants if they were successful. The land which had not been sold was held in the wife's sole name.

The trustees in bankruptcy had made an application to a District Judge for the transfer of the property to be set aside on the basis of s 339(i) of the Insolvency Act, 'where an individual is adjudged bankrupt and he has at the relevant time … entered into a transaction with any person at an undervalue, the Trustee of the Bankrupt's estate may apply to the Court for an order under this Section'.

The judge in the Chancery Division had to consider the appellant's case that the property adjustment order made in this case did not involve the wife giving consideration at all and therefore it was a transaction at an undervalue.

The judge held that the court retained discretion to make such order as it thinks fit for restoring the position and allowed the appeal in favour of the trustees in bankruptcy.

This case has now been successfully appealed in the Court of Appeal.

The wife argued that the judge had been wrong to hold that only the release of a pre-existing right or cause of action was capable of constituting consideration for s 339(3)(a) of the Insolvency Act 1986. Also he had been wrong to focus his attention on the compromise agreement and not the relevant transaction. Further, a party to an agreement compromising an ancillary relief claim gave consideration in money or monies worth. It was held that the wife had given consideration and that it was in money/monies worth. Its value was not less than the value of consideration provided by the bankrupt. There was, therefore, no question of exercising any discretion under s 339.

CONFIDENTIALITY CONSIDERATIONS

16.24   In the Court of Appeal judgment in the case of *Clibbery v Allan* [2002] EWCA Civ 45, [2002] Fam 261, [2002] 1 FLR 565, the court considered the issues of privacy and confidentiality in family proceedings. Miss Clibbery and Mr Allan were not married, but had a relationship for about 14 years. When the relationship ended, Miss Clibbery applied to the court for an occupation order in respect of one of the properties owned by Mr Allan which they had occasionally used. Her application failed, and she approached a national newspaper which later published an interview with her and extracts from Mr Allan's sworn statement to the court.

Mr Allan obtained an injunction against further publication of details of or documents from the hearing, but this injunction was overturned. The following points arise from the case.

- There is a fundamental 'implied undertaking' or duty to the court to the effect that 'a party who seeks discovery of documents gets it on condition that he will make use of them only for the purposes of that action, and no other purpose' (Lord Denning MR in *Riddick v Thames Board Mills Ltd* [1977] QB 881, CA). This implied undertaking applies even where documents have been read out in open court.

- There is, however, no duty of confidentiality between unmarried partners, save for the general 'implied undertaking' referred to above in relation to documents disclosed under compulsion.

- No subsequent publication of information is allowed in a case that concerns children.

- In divorce-related financial proceedings, the implied undertaking applies and covers information disclosed 'before, during and after the proceedings', including that disclosed voluntarily. However, questions remain about whether the implied undertaking applies before divorce or ancillary relief proceedings have been commenced and, therefore, if confidentiality is likely to be a concern, an express undertaking to that end should be considered.

On 27 April 2009, new rules came into force whereby accredited members of the media were for the first time permitted to attend hearings in the county courts and the High Court in most family court hearings. Separate provision was made for hearings in the Family Proceedings Courts.

The press still cannot attend conciliation appointments (in children cases), financial dispute resolution (FDR) hearings or any hearings in adoption and placement proceedings. However, it can now attend private Children Act proceedings (unless combined with adoption or placement proceedings), issues resolution hearings and any interim hearing. The press can attend hearings in ancillary relief proceedings other than an FDR or a first appointment hearing treated as an FDR hearing, hearings for non-molestation and occupation orders and forced marriage protection orders.

However, at any stage, the court may exclude the media representative or direct that media representatives shall not attend the proceedings or any part of them. There also remain restrictions on what the media can report.

1   *D v D* [2009] EWHC 946 (Fam) [2009] 2 FLR 324

This case concerned a husband's request to exclude the media from the proceedings on the ground that he felt he could not give full and frank evidence about his financial affairs in front of the press. This request was rejected as there was nothing exceptional about the case warranting the removal of the media's right to attend. The real issue was that he was worried the media might report the case rather than attend.

Whether anything could be reported was to be dealt with at a later stage and the media would apply to report or the parties could seek to stop publication.

Therefore the existing reporting restrictions applied.

2   *Spencer v Spencer* [2009] EWHC 1529 (Fam) [2009] 2 FLR 1416

At an ancillary relief hearing, at which the press were present, an application was made by both sides for an order that the media be excluded from the hearing altogether. Both parties relied on paragraph 5.4 of the Practice Direction of 20 April 2009, which expands on the grounds for excluding the media under rule 10.28 (4) (b) ie where justice will be impeded or prejudiced. This rule could be satisfied for example if the discussion of finances would betray price-sensitive information or if witnesses refused, giving credible reasons, to give evidence in front of the media. In particular, the parties argued that there was a significant risk that witnesses in this case might not give full and frank evidence in front of the media as there were allegations of conduct on both sides.

Munby J held that despite the interest of the public in this case and its high media profile, the proceedings were typical of normal financial proceedings. There was no great point of law or principle involved. However, although the public interest was not engaged by the subject matter of the case, there was a public interest in the media being able to attend hearings in general which transcended the subject matter of the proceedings.

Munby J made it clear that there should be no extra protection afforded to celebrities and rejected the parties' arguments relating to the risk of witnesses not being able to give full and frank evidence. The application to exclude the media failed in this case.

3   *X (A Child), Re* [2009] EWHC 1728 (Fam) [2009] 2 FLR 1467

Child X was the subject of contact and residence proceedings, which were started in 2007. She is the daughter of a male celebrity and lives with her mother, who is well known in the press as a result of her relationship with him.

Following the amendment to the Family Proceedings Rules with regard to media attendance, the press were proposing to attend future hearings. Previously all hearings had been in private with the parents also being bound by undertakings to the court not to disclose any information concerning the proceedings except to their legal advisers. They had also agreed not to give or permit interviews concerning the arrangements for X's upbringing.

Following a fact-finding hearing in March 2009 where the court heard evidence of an intimate, emotional and sensitive nature concerning X from CAFCASS officers and in light of manifest media interest outside the court, the judge, in anticipation of her judgment and on the joint application of the parties, made an order for reporting restrictions to be applied to the case until X's eighteenth birthday.

The matter was referred to the High Court following the rule changes on 27 April 2009 and the intention of media representatives to attend the hearings.

The President of the Family Division, Sir Mark Potter noted that private law cases concerning children of celebrities were no different from those involving children of anyone else in principle; however, in practice the press interest and danger of leakage to the public of confidential information was more intense. He emphasised that r 10.28 of the Family Proceedings Rules provided that the court must be satisfied that any exclusion is necessary and the burden is with the party trying to seek the exclusion. In deciding, the President made it clear that the court should have regard to the nature and sensitivities of the evidence and the degree to which the watchdog function of the media may be engaged or whether the media's interest in the proceedings lay merely in the public's curiosity as opposed to the public interest.

The President held that the press should be excluded in this case in the interest of the welfare of X. The matters being discussed in court were not in the public domain and the attendance of the media would constitute a betrayal of trust built up already between the child and psychiatrists.

TAX IMPLICATIONS

Income tax

16.25   Since 1990/91 spouses and, where applicable, civil partners (see later), have been (in almost all respects) subject to independent taxation. This means that each is entitled to a personal allowance regardless of their relationship status. The basic personal allowance in 2010/11 is £6,475 (£7,475 in 2011/12).

The basic personal allowance increases to a maximum of £9,490 in 2010/11 (£9,940 in 2011/12) for those 65 to 74 and £9,640 in 2010/11 (£10,090 in 2011/12) for those 75 or over (the age-related allowance), depending on the level of the person's adjusted net income. For 2010/11, if the person's adjusted net income is over £22,900 (£24,000 in 2011/12), the age-related allowance is reduced by £1 for every £2 of income above £22,900 (£24,000 in 2011/12). The biggest effect this can have (where the adjusted net income is below £100,000) is to reduce the allowance to the level of the personal allowance for a person under 65.

From 2010/11 the basic personal allowance is reduced in respect of taxpayers with an adjusted net income of over £100,000, by £1 for every £2 above the £100,000 limit, notwithstanding the taxpayer's age. This can reduce the basic personal allowance to zero.

Income tax is payable on a person's taxable income after certain deductions including the personal allowance. In 2010/11 the tax rates for earned income and pensions are:

- basic rate (20%): £0–£37,400 (£0–£35,000 in 2011/12);

- higher rate (40%): £37,401–£150,000 (£35,001–£150,000 in 2011/12);

- additional rate (50%): over £150,000 (over £150,000 in 2011/12).

For 2010/11 the tax rates for dividend income are:

- dividend ordinary rate (10%): £0–£37,400 (£0–£35,000 in 2011/12);

- dividend upper rate (32.5%): £37,401–£150,000 (£35,001–£150,000 in 2011/12);

- dividend additional rate (42.5%): over £150,000 (over £150,000 in 2011/12).

For 2010/11 the tax rates for non-dividend savings income are:

- starting rate for savings (10%): £0–£2,440 (£0–£2,560 in 2011/12);

- basic rate (20%): £2,441– £37,400 (£2,561– £35,000 in 2011/12);

- higher rate (40%): £37,401–£150,000 (£35,001– £150,000 in 2011/12);

- additional rate (50%): over £150,000 (over £150,000 in 2011/12)

If a person's taxable non-savings income is in excess of the starting rate limit, the 10% starting rate for savings is not available for that person's savings income.

Married couples' allowance, child tax credit and working tax credit

16.26 Until April 2000 the married couples' allowance provided some tax relief to married couples. However, on 6 April 2000 that allowance was abolished, except for those couples where one spouse was born prior to 6 April 1935. Since 5 December 2005 the married couples' allowance also applies to civil partners, where one partner was born prior to 6 April 1935. For couples married before 5 December 2005 the amount of the allowance depends on the income of the husband. For couples married on or after 5 December 2005 and civil partners, the amount of the allowance depends on the income of the spouse or civil partner with the highest income (a couple who married before 5 December 2005 can jointly elect to be treated as if they had married on or after 5 December 2005). In 2010/11 the married couples' allowance reduces the tax bill by up to 10% of £6,965 (£7,295 in 2011/12). The allowance is reduced if the husband (marriages prior to 5 December 2005) or higher earning spouse or civil partner (on or after 5 December 2005) has income above £22,900 (£24,000 in 2011/12), but it cannot be less than the minimum amount of £2,670 at 10% in 2010/11 (£2,800 in 2011/12).

The child tax credit (CTC) is a payment to support families with children. Working tax credit (WTC) supports people who work but earn low wages whether or not they have children and is intended to top up low wages. Ascertaining eligibility for CTC and WTC can be complicated and the applicable rates and thresholds can be subject to change from time to time, so appropriate advice and up to date information should be obtained where relevant.

Tax treatment of maintenance payments

16.27 The basic rules are, broadly, as follows:

- Maintenance payments between spouses and civil partners generally have no tax consequences for either the payer or the payee. They are not treated as taxable income in the hands of the recipient [Income Tax

(Trading and Other Income) Act 2005 (ITTOIA 2005) s 727(1) and s 729(3)]. No tax relief is available to the payer unless either party was born prior to 6 April 1935 (in which case the payment is a 'qualifying maintenance payment' provided certain conditions are met), when limited relief is available (by way of a reduction in the payer's income tax liability at the rate of 10%, on a maximum amount of £2,670 in 2010/2011 (£2,800 in 2011/12) (Income Tax Act 2007 (ITA 2007) s 453 and s 43).

• Neutral tax treatment of maintenance payments referred to above applies whether the payments are made to a spouse or to a child (although a payment made directly to a child cannot be a 'qualifying maintenance payment').

Business partnerships

16.28   If spouses or civil partners are in a business partnership together, the breakdown of the personal relationship may well also result in a breakdown of the business relationship leading to its termination. If the business ceases altogether, the normal income tax rules for the cessation of a business will apply.

If the business continues there are separate rules for retiring and continuing partners.

The retiring spouse or civil partner is treated as if he or she had ceased trading on the date of retirement and the profits are apportioned to that spouse or civil partner in accordance with the profit-sharing agreement of the partnership (ITTOIA 2005 ss 202 and 203)

The continuing spouse or civil partner is taxed on the basis that his or her business continues. Profits accrued prior to the other spouse's retirement are apportioned in accordance with any profit-sharing agreement whilst the profits arising subsequently accrue and are taxable to the person continuing in business (who may become a sole trader).

Capital gains tax

General

16.29   As with income tax, as spouses and civil partners are subject to independent taxation they are each entitled to an annual exemption (£10,100 in 2010/11; £10,600 in 2011/12) on chargeable gains. Capital gains tax (CGT) payable is computed separately for each spouse or civil partner without reference to the CGT liability of the other. In tax year 2010/11, the CGT rate for gains arising from 6 April 2010 to 22 June 2010 rate is 18%. On and after 23 June 2010 the CGT rate applicable to an individual's gains which are not eligible for entrepreneurs' relief is 18% up to any unused amount of the individual's income tax basic rate band, and 28% for other gains (ie higher rate tax payers pay CGT at 28%). This remains the position in 2011/12. Gains of trustees and personal representatives accruing on or after 23 June 2010 are also taxed at 28%. This remains the position in 2011/12.

Allowable losses of one spouse or civil partner may only be deducted from that person's deductible gains and unrelieved losses may only be carried forward and relieved against future gains of the same person.

The key event for CGT purposes when a relationship breaks down is not the date of the divorce but the date when the couple cease to be living together.

Under Taxation of Chargeable Gains Act 1992 (TCGA 1992) s 288, spouses and civil partners are considered to be living together for CGT purposes unless they are separated under a court order or a deed of separation or are separated in circumstances where the separation appears to be permanent. It is possible for a couple to live separately even under the same roof (*Holmes v Mitchell* [1991] STC 25).

Whilst spouses and civil partners are still living together a transfer of assets between them will be deemed to be on a no gain/no loss basis. During the balance of the tax year in which they separate any such transfer will also be on a no gain/no loss basis (TCGA 1992 s 58).

The recipient takes the transferor's cost base as the acquisition cost for any subsequent disposal. On the eventual disposal of the asset the recipient is then taxed on the total gain over the combined period of ownership since the asset was first acquired by the transferor spouse or civil partner (or 31 March 1982, if later).

Spouses and civil partners remain connected persons for CGT purposes following separation. Transfers between connected persons are not regarded as transfers at arm's length (TCGA 1992 s 18). This means that, unless the no gain/no loss rules apply as mentioned above, where an asset is transferred between spouses or civil partners the market value at the date of disposal will be the deemed consideration when computing the capital gain made by the transferor spouse or civil partner. Chargeable gains can therefore arise on gifts of assets or on sales at an undervalue. If a loss accrues on such a disposal the loss can only be set against gains made on the transfer of assets between the same connected persons.

Assets which are transferred following a divorce or the dissolution of a civil partnership, when the parties are not longer connected, are sometimes treated by HMRC as transferred at market value (eg, where consideration cannot be valued) and sometimes treated as transferred for an actual consideration.

The date of transfer between spouses or civil partners is important, but ascertaining the date can be complex. HMRC accept (see Capital Gains Manual (CG22410) that the date of disposal of a transfer which is not made under a court order is the date of the contract (or the date of transfer if there is no earlier contract). HMRC consider that if the transfer is made under a consent order before the decree absolute, the court giving effect to an earlier agreement between the parties, the date of disposal may be that agreed by the parties, in certain circumstances (CG22423). However, HMRC consider that if the transfer is made by a court order (not being a consent order) before the decree absolute, the date of disposal is the date of the court order (CG22423). Likewise if the transfer is pursuant to a court order made after the decree absolute, the date of the disposal is the date of the court order (CG22420), even where the court order is a consent order which gives effect to an earlier agreement.

As mentioned, this is a complicated area and professional advice should be sought as to the timing of disposals and the deemed consideration for the disposal, in order to minimise potential CGT liability. Chapters 4 and 14 look at property disposals and CGT.

Transfer of the matrimonial home

16.30 On a divorce or dissolution of a civil partnership, the family home is usually transferred between the parties or sold.

A house which has been occupied by the owner as his or her main residence throughout the period of ownership will be wholly exempt from CGT (TCGA 1992 ss 222–224). This is known as the principal private residence (PPR) exemption. The last three years of ownership will be treated as a period of occupation even if another main residence has been acquired in that period.

If there have been periods of non-occupation during the period of ownership then only the appropriate proportion of the gain will be exempt.

Often it will be the case that on the breakdown of a marriage or civil partnership one party will leave the family home whilst the other remains in occupation. If the departing spouse or civil partner transfers his or her interest in the property to the remaining spouse or civil partner within three years of having left the property, his or her gain will be covered by the PPR exemption. This exemption from CGT will apply even if the departing spouse or civil partner has acquired another property in the meantime. The exemption will also apply if the property is sold rather than transferred.

A more detailed analysis of the PPR exemption and the extent to which it may apply to a farmhouse and its surrounding land and buildings is considered in Chapter 4 (Protecting the Farmhouse).

If the spouse or civil partner who has an interest in the former family home has left the property more than three years prior to the transfer or sale of his interest in it, further relief may be available under TCGA 1992 s 225B (this relief used to be set out in Extra-statutory Concession D6). It applies, broadly speaking, if the departing spouse or civil partner leaves the property which was his only or main residence, and later disposes of his share to the spouse or civil partner who remains in occupation under an agreement made in connection with the dissolution of their marriage or civil partnership or a separation order or a court order granting a divorce or the dissolution of the civil partnership. The property must have continued to be the only or main residence of the spouse or civil partner in occupation and the transferor must not have elected for another property to be his main residence in the meantime. If a new house has been acquired consideration should be given to the CGT consequences of electing which one should be treated as his main residence.

Section 225B applies only to the transfer of, or of an interest in, the family home to a spouse or civil partner. It does not apply where the home is sold to a third party.

Deferred charge or postponed interest in the home

16.31   As indicated above, in order to achieve fairness between spouses and civil partners in the post-*White* era it may be appropriate for the departing spouse or civil partner to retain an interest in the home to be realised at a later date, for example, when the youngest child reaches a certain age or completes full-time education. This may be done in one of two ways: by a deferred charge or a postponed interest.

1   *Deferred charge.* The home is transferred to the remaining spouse or civil partner (assuming that it is not already in that person's sole name) subject to a charge in favour of the departing spouse or civil partner (either for a fixed sum or a percentage share of the proceeds). At the date of transfer if the PPR exemption (with s 225B relief if applicable) is available then there will be no CGT payable by the transferor.

   However, the ongoing CGT position is different depending on whether the charge is for a fixed sum or a percentage share of the proceeds.

   If the deferred charge is for a specific amount of money (eg £50,000) then it is, arguably, to be regarded as a debt within the meaning of TCGA 1992 s 251 and there may be no chargeable gain on the repayment of that charge to the departing spouse or civil partner (TCGA 1992 s 251). Income tax may be charged on interest paid or rolled up in respect of the loan.

   However, where the deferred charge is represented by a percentage or fraction of the value of the property it is arguably not a debt within the meaning of s 251, as the amount cannot be ascertained until the date of repayment. It is likely that the increase in value between the date that the charge was created and the date that it is repaid will, therefore, be subject to CGT on the spouse or civil partner who has the benefit of the charge, subject to any reliefs or exemptions.

2   *Postponed interest.* An alternative to a deferred charge is where the home is retained in (or transferred to) the joint names of the spouses or civil partners or to trustees on their behalf. This is known as a 'Mesher' order. HMRC regard a 'Mesher' order as a settlement and the CGT consequences are generally favourable. The initial transfer into joint names or to trustees will usually be exempt under the PPR rules for the spouse or civil partner remaining in occupation and also for the departing spouse or civil partner.

   When the date of realisation of the interest is reached the trustees are treated as selling the property and reacquiring it for themselves as bare trustees (TCGA 1992 s 71). The trustees will be able to claim the PPR exemption on the deemed disposal assuming that the remaining spouse or civil partner has continued to live in the property under the terms of the settlement since the original order was made (TCGA 1992 s 225).

   However, owing to the change in the taxation of trust interests brought about by the Finance Act 2006, these 'Mesher' type arrangements where a trust interest in the home is created for the departing spouse, will in future carry inheritance tax consequences (see below under the section on inheritance tax).

Transfers of business assets — hold-over relief

16.32 As mentioned above, the timing of transfers between spouses or civil partners is crucial.

If the transfer can be made before the end of the tax year of separation the transfer will be made on a no gain/no loss basis and no immediate CGT will arise on the transfer. In contrast, transfers made after the end of the year of separation are chargeable to CGT.

A disposal of an asset which is not a bargain at arm's length is treated as a disposal at the open market value and the donor is deemed to have received the market value of the property even if he has received nothing in return for it.

It may be possible for such a gain to be held over where the disposal is a gift of business assets (TCGA 1992 s 165) or is a gift to a relevant property trust (TCGA 1992 s 260), provided the trust is not settlor-interested for CGT purposes.

HMRC's CG67192 indicates that, while the transfer of assets between spouses or civil partners after the year in which they separate but before the final divorce or dissolution of a civil partnership will usually be regarded as made in exchange for a surrender of rights by the donee (which could be regarded as actual consideration which would restrict the availability of hold-over relief (TCGA 1992 s 165(7))), where the transfer is made under a court order, hold-over relief will not be so restricted. As a result, transfers of certain business assets which are eligible for hold-over relief will be free from any immediate CGT consequences if made pursuant to a court order. The transferee spouse or civil partner will inherit the transferor's base cost for the purpose of CGT on any future disposal of the assets.

Generally speaking, business asset transfers which are not made under a court order and which are transferred after the tax year of separation will continue to be treated as immediately liable to CGT. Exceptionally, this may not be the case where the parties can show that there was a substantial gratuitous element in the transfer and that the amounts transferred were substantially more than the transferee spouse or civil partner could reasonably have expected to have received under a contested court case (see CG67192).

The assets to which hold-over relief will apply are as follows.

- Unlisted shares in a trading company (AIM-listed investments are not listed for these purposes).

- Shares in a trading company in which the transferor spouse or civil partner holds at least 5% of the voting rights.

- Any assets or interest in assets used in a trade, profession or vocation carried on by
  - the transferor (either in his sole name or in partnership);
  - by any company in which that person holds at least 5% of the voting rights (the transferor's 'personal company'); or
  - a member of a trading group of which the holding company is the transferor's personal company.

- Agricultural property which would qualify for agricultural property relief under IHTA 1984 s 115.

As mentioned, the CGT payable on the transfer or sale of shares to a spouse or civil partnership outside the tax year of separation but before the dissolution of the marriage or civil partnership is referable to the difference between the cost (or deemed cost) of the shares and their market value at the date of sale.

Where the couple own shares in a company, if the company has sufficient financial resources, it may be able to buy back one spouse or civil partner's shares. This would normally be treated as an income distribution for tax purposes. There would also be a capital gain as the shares are being disposed of to the company. To the extent that an amount has already been charged to income tax, this should be offset against any CGT payable. It should be noted, however, that income tax and CGT are only relevant to the extent that the buy back price exceeds the original subscription. An asset, as opposed to cash, could be distributed by the company in which case there may be a gain arising on the asset in the company based on the asset's current market value and on which corporation tax might be payable.

If the company does not have the financial viability to effect a share buy back, a bank might lend on the security of the company's assets and forecast cash flows. The non-exiting spouse or civil partner could form a new company that takes out a loan that is used to acquire the entire issued share capital of the original company. The loan is used to pay cash for the departing spouse or civil partner's shares and the non-exiting spouse or civil partner exchanges their shares in the original company for shares in the new company. The bank loan is subsequently repaid out of future profits of the original company, which is now a wholly-owned subsidiary. CGT will potentially be charged on the departing spouse/civil partner (entrepreneurs' relief may be available if certain conditions are met and the company is a trading company).

A company could be split in two if it has two or more businesses or separate investment and trading activities in which each spouse or civil partner has an ongoing interest. Two new companies could be formed, to which the businesses are separately transferred on liquidation of the existing company. Each spouse or civil partner would have a 100% interest in one company. There are special tax rules applicable to demergers which potentially allow demerger transactions to be undertaken without triggering any tax charges in relation to the demerger events themselves. But it should be noted that there is no specific demerger type exemption available in relation to stamp duty land tax (SDLT) and so a demerger could still have immediate tax consequences for a business and its proprietors if a significant part of the business's value was tied up in UK land and buildings, unless it was possible to structure the demerger as a transaction which fell within the scope of the separate SDLT provisions relating to company reconstructions or acquisitions of business undertakings. Where the company only has investment activities, the liquidation demerger route will not be tax effective.

Tax indemnity

16.33 It is important to note that where potential CGT issues exist as a consequence of transfers made in connection with a divorce or the dissolution of a civil partnership, the recipient spouse or civil partner is likely to seek tax indemnities and it may well be appropriate for the transferor spouse or civil partner to give such indemnities.

As the provision of such indemnities is likely to impact on the structure of a financial settlement it is important that they are not overlooked in negotiations.

Inheritance tax

16.34   Whilst the parties are married or in a civil partnership, any gifts made by one to the other (whether during lifetime or on death) will be exempt under IHTA 1984 s 18. That exemption is limited to £55,000 if the recipient spouse or civil partner is not domiciled or deemed domiciled for inheritance tax (IHT) purposes in the UK but the transferor spouse or civil partner is so domiciled or deemed domiciled. The exemption for gifts between spouses or civil partners is not conditional on the couple living together and, therefore, it will apply to gifts made after separation but not to gifts made after the dissolution of the marriage or civil partnership.

Changes brought about by the Finance Act 2006 (referred to below) mean that the IHT advantages of setting up trust structures for spouses or civil partners and children on a divorce or the dissolution of a civil partnership are now more limited. HMRC usually accept that a divorce settlement is covered by s 10 of IHTA 1984 which excludes from a charge from IHT a transfer made at arm's length which is not intended to confer any gratuitous benefit. That overrides the exemption for potentially exempt transfers (PETs) and there is, therefore, usually no risk of an IHT charge if the transferor dies within seven years.

The payment of maintenance (for a spouse or civil partner or for children) is specifically exempted from IHT (IHTA 1984 s 11) and will not be regarded as a transfer of value provided it is for the maintenance of the other party and is made on the occasion of the dissolution of the marriage or civil partnership, or is for the maintenance, education or training of the child no later than the year in which the child becomes 18 or ceases full-time education or training.

Other payments to or for a child will normally be PETs and there will be no IHT liability unless the transferor dies within seven years after the date of the gift.

Other forms of relief from IHT (in particular agricultural property relief) are considered in detail in Chapters 4, 5 and 13.

As indicated above, it is essential that specialist advice is sought in order to ascertain and seek to minimise the potential adverse tax consequences which may arise in connection with a divorce.

The Finance Act 2006

16.35   The effect of this Act has been covered in detail in Chapter 7. The commentary in this chapter is limited to examples where the Act may affect couples in the process of a divorce or the dissolution of a civil partnership.

Prior to the introduction of the Finance Act on 22 March 2006, it was not uncommon for trust structures to be used where one party's needs in terms of accommodating the children of the family were significantly greater than the other's. This necessitated the retention of the majority of the capital to provide a home for one party and the children until the latter finished education at which point the property could be sold and the other party could receive a share (see the section on CGT above under 'postponed interest').

As already described in Chapter 17, non qualifying interest in possession trusts established on or after 22 March 2006 are now subject to the same IHT charges as relevant property trusts. However, as stated above, most transfers or payments under a court order on divorce are covered by ss 10 or 11 of IHTA 1984 and are thus exempt from the initial entry charge of 20% on the value of the assets transferred into trust. However, the 10-yearly charge of 6% on the value of the trust assets and the exit charges (of up to 6%) will (in contrast to the pre- 22 March 2006 position) now be payable. This can cause serious cashflow problems where the trust assets are illiquid (as, for example, where it is the family home which is settled). In this case it is normal for cash to be settled as well with a view to meeting the tax and possibly other expenses while the trust continues, or for the order to oblige one party to meet the tax out of his own resources.

The usual structure of a Mesher order (usually to provide housing for a mother and children until the children have completed their education) is affected by these charges. The extent of the charges depend (amongst other things) on the value of the property and the ages of the children at the time of the setting up of the trust. As mentioned, an alternative to the protection of the departing party's interest in the property through a trust structure is by way of a deferred charge. However, if, as would be usual, this is in percentage terms, it would be subject to CGT (see the comments above). Parties negotiating a dissolution settlement with that sort of structure in mind will now have to consider the alternative potential CGT and IHT implications.

There are other considerations for the settlor contemplating the setting up of a trust for a child as part of an overall settlement on a divorce or the dissolution of a civil partnership, where, for example, the wife receives the income (and thus has an interest in possession) until the child turns, say 25, when the child then becomes entitled to the capital. This could give rise to serious tax implications for the settlor, for example:

- When the assets are settled on trust, there will be no IHT on the value of the assets going into trust because it is a financial settlement pursuant to divorce and thus exempt under s 10 of IHTA 1984. The trust will, however, be subject to the new IHT regime in terms of exit charges and 10-year charges.

- If the trust is funded by cash there will be no CGT. However, there may be CGT liabilities if other assets, such as quoted shares or a shareholding in a property company are settled on trust.

- If part or all of the capital of the trust was to revert to the husband if the child died before reaching the age at which the trust would vest, the value of his interest in the asset would remain in his estate for IHT purposes and, by retaining a future contingent interest in the asset, the settlor could potentially be subject to a pre-owned asset tax charge and the trust would also be 'settlor interested' for income tax purposes.

The Civil Partnership Act 2004

16.36   This came into force in 5 December 2005. Two people of the same sex may now enter into a civil partnership by signing a civil partnership document in the presence of a registrar and two witnesses. A civil partnership can be terminated on the grounds of nullity, or by either party bringing an action for dissolution (on the same facts as divorce except adultery), or legal separation or applying for a presumption of death order. It brings with it provision for financial claims on dissolution. The ancillary relief provisions correspond to those made in connection with divorce, that is, orders for periodical payments, lump sums, property adjustment orders, variation of settlement, sale of property and pension sharing. The same factors are taken into account pursuant to Sch 5, para 21(2) as those set out in the Matrimonial Causes Act 1973 s 25. Parties entering into civil partnerships may enter pre-partnership agreements, which although not binding on the courts, will be one of the factors to be taken into account. Whilst there are no reported cases as yet, it is expected that the matrimonial case law will provide precedent for determination of financial applications on the breakdown of a civil partnership.

Michael Gouriet

Michael Gouriet has been with Withers LLP since 1993 (where he did his training), moving into the firm's family law department on qualification in 1995. He was made a partner in January 2002. Michael advises on all aspects of private family law with a particular emphasis on the resolution of financial issues on separation and divorce (including those involving farms and landed estates). Many of the cases he advises on feature international elements.

Michael has had various family law articles and commentaries published – both in the national press and in legal journals. He has lectured on family law issues in the UK and abroad, and he has also appeared on TV and on radio.

Michael is a fellow of the International Academy of Matrimonial Lawyers.

Antonia Mee

Antonia Mee qualified in 2001 and spent three and a half years at Kingsley Napley before moving to Withers LLP in April 2007. Antonia specialises in all areas of private family law including financial settlements arising from divorce and separation.

Patrick Bidder

Patrick Bidder is a trainee solicitor at Withers LLP and, at the time of updating was sitting in his family law department seat.

Note: The information and comments contained in this chapter are for the general information of the reader and are not intended to be relied upon in relation to any particular circumstances. For particular applications of the law to specific situations, the reader should seek professional advice.

Chapter 17

Trusts

Judith Ingham and Imogen Davies
(Withers LLP)

INTRODUCTION

17.1   The law of trusts is one of our greatest exports. Jurisdictions across the globe have adopted the concepts of equity with enthusiasm and vigour. Many of the world's trust laws follow the English model, a model which has been revised, extended and adapted over the years to suit particular needs and different markets.

It is from a common law base that the law of trusts has developed in England and Wales. Its roots lie in the concept of the 'use' which, as long ago as the fourteenth century was used as a means of avoiding restrictions on the alienation of land. Trusts still offer opportunities for tax-efficient estate planning for landowners and farmers. A trust can control the devolution of a large parcel of land, but a discretionary trust set up to receive the death benefits payable under a life policy can also secure significant inheritance tax savings.

The law of trusts is contained in legislation and case law, the principal statutes being the Trustee Act 1925, the Settled Land Act 1925, the Variation of Trusts Act 1958, the Perpetuities and Accumulations Act 1964, the Trusts of Land and Appointment of Trustees Act 1996, the Trustee Act 2000 and the Perpetuities and Accumulations Act 2009.

Whilst statute governs the structure of a trust and the duties of trustees, the trust is above all a creature of equity and as such is ruled by equitable principles. These are founded on a distinction between legal rights and equitable interests. Where property is held in trust, the trustees have the legal rights of ownership over the property, but the beneficiaries on whose behalf the trustees hold that property enjoy the equitable interests. Trustees must administer trust assets in the best interests of the beneficiaries and must have regard to the nature of the beneficiaries' interests, balancing the interests of those presently entitled with those of future beneficiaries, such as the unborn.

Trustees are subject to stringent duties and responsibilities and risk personal liability if they fail to carry out their duties in a proper manner. The Trustee Act 1925 contains the principal duties and powers of trustees but those powers are usually extended specifically in the trust instrument. The Trusts of Land and Appointment of Trustees Act 1996 and the Trustee Act 2000 further enhance the duty of trustees to consult and act in accordance with the wishes of beneficiaries, and widen trustees' powers of delegation.

THE CREATION OF A TRUST

17.2   A trust can be created by deed during lifetime, by an oral declaration, or by will. Certain formalities are required to establish a trust.

The individual wishing to create the trust (the 'settlor') must demonstrate an express intention to do so and, where land is involved, that intention must be evidenced in writing. The asset subject to the trust must be vested in the names of the trustees and put under their control. The trust only becomes operative when the property is vested in the trustees. Very often trusts are established with a nominal sum of, say, £10 with other property being added in due course when the formalities necessary to transfer that property have been complied with.

Different types of property have different formalities to achieve an effective transfer, for instance chattels vest on delivery, shares must be re-registered into the names of the trustees and a transfer of legal title to land must be effected by deed.

The trust itself must comply with the three certainties:

- words;

- objects; and

- subject matter.

It must be clear from the wording that the settlor intends to establish a trust. The individuals for whose benefit the trust is intended (who are called 'the objects') must be ascertained or ascertainable, and the property subject to the trust and the beneficial interests in it must be certain.

In addition to satisfying the three certainties, the trust must not infringe the rule against perpetuities and, where it continues to apply, the rule against excessive accumulations (see below for the changes made by the Perpetuities and Accumulations Act 2009). These rules were designed to ensure that property cannot be tied up in trust indefinitely. Under the rule against perpetuities, all the interests under the trust must vest, ie cease to be contingent, within the perpetuity period (which is commonly the same as the trust's specified 'trust period'). If this is not the case, the trust will be void.

The Perpetuities and Accumulations Act 2009, which took effect from 6 April 2010, made changes to the rule against perpetuities. For trusts created before 6 April 2010, three possible perpetuity periods were:

- a period based on the life of someone alive at the date the trust instrument takes effect plus 21 years;

- a period based on the lives of members of the Royal Family; or

- 80 years (this was the period most commonly incorporated into modern trust instruments as it had the advantage of certainty).

Following changes made by the Perpetuities and Accumulations Act 2009, all new trusts created on or after 6 April 2010 will automatically have a 125-year perpetuity period, whether or not the trust specifies a different period. However, it is possible for the settlor to choose a shorter trust period. It should be noted that the 125-year perpetuity period does not apply where, after 5 April 2010, a new trust is created in the exercise of a special power of appointment or power of advancement, if the instrument which created that power was made before 6 April 2010. In practice this means that it is not possible to extend the life of a pre-6 April 2010 trust by transferring its assets to a post-5 April 2010 trust which has the new longer period.

For trusts created before 6 April 2010, alongside the rule against perpetuities was the common law rule against excessive accumulations of income. This reflected the principle that the trust assets were intended for the benefit of certain individuals and the ability to have the use or enjoyment of the income at some point in time was an essential part of this. Although under the Law of Property Act 1925 and the Perpetuities and Accumulations Act 1964, there were several ways to limit the period during which income could be accumulated, the majority of pre-6 April 2010 trusts provided that income could not be accumulated for any period longer than 21 years from the date of the trust. The rule against excessive accumulations of income still applies to trusts made before 6 April 2010, but in light of the Perpetuities and Accumulations Act 2009, the rule does not apply to trusts made after 5 April 2010. This means that income can be accumulated in such trusts for 125 years (but the rule continues to apply to new trusts created after 5 April 2010 made in the exercise of a special power of appointment or power of advancement, if the instrument which created that power was made prior to 6 April 2010).

THE CHOICE OF TRUSTEES

17.3   The office of trustee involves the assumption of onerous duties and obligations. Individuals may be appointed or a corporate entity or trust corporation. In general there is no limit to the number of trustees although the maximum number permitted to hold a legal estate in land is four and for administrative convenience it is usually preferable to appoint no more than this number. There is also a limit of four trustees where a trustee is added (and no trustee is replaced) using the statutory power of appointment.

A sole individual trustee may act, but will not be able to give a good receipt for the proceeds of sale or other capital money arising from the sale of land. If individual trustees are appointed it is therefore usual to appoint at least two. A corporate trustee can act as a sole trustee but (unless a sole trustee was appointed at the outset and will be able to give a valid receipt for capital monies) must be a trust corporation if it is to act alone. In practice only corporate entities with substantial capital backing will be eligible for designation as trust corporations.

The Trusts of Land and Appointment of Trustees Act 1996 has eased the rule that a retiring trustee could only be discharged from his office if two 'individuals' remained in office after his retirement. Under the 1996 Act, a retiring trustee can be discharged if two 'persons' or a trust corporation remain as trustees.

The settlor may choose to appoint trustees resident in the UK or outside the UK. The residence of the settlor, trustees and the beneficiaries, the domicile status of the settlor and beneficiaries and the location of the trust assets will influence the tax regime which applies to the trust.

The English court will accept jurisdiction over a trust where there is a proven connection with the jurisdiction. The location of the trust assets in England and Wales or the residence of the trustee or beneficiaries in England and Wales will usually be a sufficient connection. Even if the trust assets, beneficiaries and trustees are not in England and Wales, the English court may still accept jurisdiction if the trust is governed by English law. Moreover, the English Family Division may assume jurisdiction over a foreign law trust on the basis that one of the parties to ancillary relief proceedings has an interest in the trust assets or has been able to access the trust assets as a resource. In these circumstances, the Family Division may vary the terms of the trust.

TYPES OF TRUST UNDER ENGLISH LAW

17.4   There are a number of ways of categorising English law trusts. One way is to distinguish between trusts with and trusts without an interest in possession. The distinction affects, in particular, which income tax regime applies. The definition of an interest in possession is the 'present right to present enjoyment of the trust property' (see *Pearson v IRC* [1980] 2 All ER 479) and a trust with an interest in possession is therefore one in which one or more beneficiaries has such an interest.

An interest in possession can take a number of forms, the most common being a right during life to enjoy the income arising from the trust assets. This is commonly called 'a life interest'. A beneficiary may also acquire such an interest when, for example, he is given the exclusive right to occupy a trust property. A beneficiary with an interest in possession is called 'the life tenant'.

Another way of categorising trusts which is used for inheritance tax purposes is to distinguish between trusts with a 'qualifying interest in possession' and trusts without a qualifying interest in possession (most such trusts being called 'relevant property trusts'). Broadly speaking, the life tenant of a qualifying interest in possession trust is deemed to own the underlying capital and a charge to inheritance tax arises on his death.

Since 22 March 2006, the only qualifying interests in possession that can exist are, broadly:

- Interests in possession that were in existence on 22 March 2006.

- Transitional serial interests. A transitional serial interest is an interest in possession which could, for a limited period after 21 March 2006, be created from an interest in possession in existence at that date. A transitional serial interest may still be created to arise on the death of a life tenant, if the new life tenant is the previous life tenant's spouse or civil partner.

- Immediate post death interests. This is a type of interest in possession which takes effect under the will or on the intestacy of the former owner of the assets.

- Certain disabled persons' interests.

A common type of trust without a qualifying interest in possession is the discretionary trust. The trustees have complete discretion to determine when and if a particular beneficiary should be given an absolute or limited interest in some or all of the trust assets. Limitations can be put on the trustees' discretion, but as a rule it is often preferable to give the trustees wide unfettered powers to apply the trust assets in the interests of some or all of the beneficiaries as and when they think fit. Notes of wishes from the settlor can, however, provide helpful guidance to the trustees.

In addition to the standard discretionary trust, inheritance tax legislation allows for certain other types of non-qualifying interest in possession trusts. These include the following:

- Trusts formerly known as 'accumulation and maintenance (A&M) trusts', which were flexible trusts for persons aged under 25 which benefited from favoured status for inheritance tax purposes. Following extensive changes made in Finance Act 2006, A&M trusts which were in existence on 22 March 2006 now fall within three categories:

  ○ A&M trusts which were restructured before 6 April 2008 so that the beneficiaries receive capital on or before the age of 18 (known as an 'outright-at-18' trust). If the beneficiary does receive capital on or before 18, there will be no inheritance tax charge.

  ○ A&M trusts which were restructured before 6 April 2008 so that the beneficiaries have a right to capital on or before the age of 25 (known as an '18-to-25' trust). If the beneficiary receives capital after the age of 18 then, broadly, there will be a charge which accumulates each year after the beneficiary's eighteenth birthday (at a rate of 0.6% each year), to be paid when the beneficiary receives the right to capital, on the value of the assets at that point.

  ○ A&M trusts which were not restructured in one of the above ways before 6 April 2008. These have become subject to the relevant property regime.

- Most interest in possession trusts created after 21 March 2006 during the lifetime of the settlor.

- Charitable trusts.

- Certain trusts for the disabled.

- Trusts for employees.

THE TAX TREATMENT OF TRUSTS

17.5   It is helpful when looking at tax, to consider the three stages during the life of a trust:

- the creation of the trust;

- the continuance of the trust; and

- the termination of the trust.

It should be noted that the taxation of trusts is a complex area and the information set out below is merely an overview. Reference should be made to a specialist text for a detailed account of the issues. Unless stated otherwise, the information below deals with trusts created during a settlor's lifetime.

Creation of a trust

Capital gains tax

17.6   The creation of a trust requires the transfer of property from the settlor to the trustees. This will be a disposal by the settlor for the purposes of capital gains tax, which may or may not give rise to a chargeable gain. That said, certain types of property (principally business and agricultural property) can qualify for hold-over relief if made to a trust that is not settlor-interested

('settlor-interested' for capital gains tax purposes means a trust from which the settlor, his spouse or civil partner, or his minor child who is unmarried and not in a civil partnership, can benefit). Where a settlor transfers such assets to trustees and elects to hold over the gain, the trustees will take the assets at the settlor's base cost and no charge to capital gains tax will arise on the disposal by the settlor. A similar relief can be obtained where the settlor passes any type of property to trustees and the transfer gives rise to an inheritance tax charge (or would do but for inheritance tax exemptions and reliefs such as agricultural and business property relief). Such reliefs are important to landowners and farmers. See further Chapter 13.

Inheritance tax

17.7   Since 22 March 2006, the creation of most lifetime trusts results in a transfer of value by the settlor for the purposes of inheritance tax. A transfer to a relevant property trust (such as a discretionary trust or a non-qualifying interest in possession trust) is an immediately chargeable transfer, with inheritance tax presently being charged at 20% unless the value transferred is within the settlor's nil rate band or other reliefs such as agricultural or business property relief are available. There will also be an additional 20% charge if the settlor dies within seven years.

The creation of a disabled person's trust is treated as a potentially exempt transfer if the settlor is not the disabled person, rather than an immediately chargeable transfer. If the settlor is the disabled person, there is no transfer of value.

In all cases, unless it is specifically intended, care must be taken to ensure that the settlor does not retain any benefit in the property transferred. If the settlor does retain a benefit the transfer will fall foul of the 'gift with reservation of benefit' rules and the assets in the trust will be treated as still comprised in the settlor's estate for inheritance tax purposes.

Continuance of a trust

Income tax

17.8   Trustees are treated for income tax purposes as a single person distinct from the persons who are trustees of the trust from time to time. The type of trust and whether or not it is settlor-interested (see below) determines the income tax treatment.

Interest in possession trust

17.9   Where a beneficiary has an interest in possession in the trust property, the trustees must account for tax on trust income at the basic rate (20% in 2010–11 and 2011–12) and on UK and qualifying foreign dividend income at the dividend ordinary rate (10% in 2010–11 and 2011–12, the tax credit attaching to the net dividend meeting the trustees' basic rate liability). The life tenant is entitled to credit for the tax paid by the trustees. If he does not pay tax, he can reclaim the tax paid by the trustees (although he will not be able to reclaim the tax credit on a dividend). If he is a higher or additional rate taxpayer, he will have further tax to pay. However, if the trust is 'settlor-interested' (for income tax purposes this means the settlor or his spouse or civil partner can benefit under the trust) or payments are made for the benefit of the settlor's minor unmarried child who is not in a civil partnership (this is often called a 'parental settlement'), the settlor and not the income beneficiary will be taxed on trust income at his own rates (with credit for tax the trustees have paid).

Non-interest in possession trust

17.10   If there is no beneficiary with the right to trust income, the first £1,000 of income is taxed at reduced income tax rates. Income over £1,000 is taxed in the hands of the trustees at the trust rate (50% in 2010–11 and 2011–12 or 42.5% on dividends).

Where income is distributed to a beneficiary, the trustees have to pay 50% on the grossed-up value of the distribution (less any amount available from the trustees' 'tax pool'). If the trust is neither settlor-interested nor a parental settlement, the distribution is treated as the beneficiary's income and taxed at his rates with credit for the tax paid by the trustees.

If the trust is settlor-interested, the income will be treated as that of the settlor and taxed at his own rates, although he will get a credit for tax paid by the trustees. If the settler pays tax at a lower rate than the trustees, he must pay over to the trustees any amount repaid to him by HMRC (repayment includes a set off tax of tax borne by the trustees).

Trustees must keep adequate records of their running of the trust so that they are in a position to produce accounts on request by the beneficiaries. The cost of preparing these accounts is borne by the beneficiaries.

Trustees are generally under a duty to file annual tax returns where chargeability to UK tax exists, although in certain circumstances HMRC may dispense with the need for trustees to submit returns where income is mandated directly to a life tenant (but HMRC will not permit this in some cases, for example, where the trustees have made chargeable disposals for capital gains tax purposes or where the trust is settlor-interested).

Similarly, where a trust is dormant, for instance a trust established to receive the death benefits payable under a policy of life assurance, HMRC may be willing to dispense with the need for annual returns on application by the trustees, but this will usually only be on the basis that the trustees undertake to submit returns as soon as the proceeds from the policy are received and chargeability to tax therefore arises.

Pre-owned asset tax

17.11   Finance Act 2004 introduced a charge to income tax on pre-owned assets. Separate regimes exist for land, chattels and intangible property comprised in settlor-interested trusts. 'Intangible property' is defined as any property other than chattels or interests in land.

The charge applies to benefits received or after the 2005–06 tax year. The government's aim was to catch individuals who disposed of assets in a way which removed the value of the assets from their estates for inheritance tax purposes whilst they continued to benefit from the assets in some way. The rules are complex but essentially there is an annual income tax charge on an individual who at any time during a tax year occupies land or possesses or uses other assets where one of the following conditions is satisfied:

●   the disposal condition – at any time after 17 March 1986 the individual owned the chattel or an interest in the land (or other property the proceeds from the disposal of which were used to acquire the chattel or the interest in land) and the individual disposed of all or part of his interest in the chattel or land (or other property); or

●   the contribution condition – at any time after 17 March 1986 the individual directly or indirectly provided any of the consideration used by another person to acquire the chattel or the interest in the land (or other property the proceeds of disposal of which were used by another person towards the acquisition of the chattel or the interest in land).

Certain categories of transactions are excluded from the scope of the rules, eg a transfer to the individual's spouse. There will also be exemptions from charge, eg where the aggregate of the chargeable amounts in a given year does not exceed £5,000. Individuals to whom the charge applies are able to elect to be subject to inheritance tax gift with reservation of benefit rules as an alternative to paying the charge.

A formula is set out for calculating the chargeable amount in each case based on the rental value (as defined) of land, or interest (at the prescribed rate) on an amount equal to the value of the chattel. In calculating the chargeable amount, payments made under any legal obligation in relation to occupation/use may be deducted, but not, in relation to chattels, payments for insurance, security, etc. The chargeable amount is also adjusted to take into account any cash consideration given for the initial disposal. The charge on intangible property does not follow the pattern set for land and chattels and does not rely on any concept akin to occupation, possession or use. The provisions are concerned with any intangible property (including cash) held in trust if it is or represents property settled by the individual after 17 March 1986 on terms such that income from the property (if there were any) would be treated as income of the settlor under the settlor interested charging provisions in the Income Tax (Trading and Other Income) Act 2005. There is no need for there to be any income, nor for there to be any benefit to the individual for a pre-owned assets charge to arise. The basis for calculating the chargeable amount in relation to intangible property relies on a notional rate of interest.

CGT

17.12   The trustees are treated as a single and continuing person distinct from the persons who are trustees of the trust from time to time. In 2010–11, for gains accruing before 23 June 2010, trustees pay capital gains tax at the rate of 18%, and for gains accruing on or after 23 June, trustees pay capital gains tax at the rate of 28%. The rate of gains accruing to trustees in 2011–12 is 28%. The annual exemption from capital gains tax is set at one-half of the exemption available to individuals, but trusts made after 6 June 1978 by the same settlor share one annual exemption. Chargeable gains made by trustees are calculated in the same way as for individuals.

It should be noted that trustees are deemed to dispose of trust assets when a person becomes absolutely entitled to all or part of the trust assets as against the trustees (ie on a distribution of assets from a trust). This is considered below at **17.14.**

IHT

17.13   During the continuance of a relevant property trust, legislation provides for two occasions of charge to inheritance tax.

- The ten-year anniversary charge entails a charge to inheritance tax on each tenth anniversary of the date the trust commenced. The formula for calculating the charge is complex and will usually necessitate taking professional advice.

- The exit charge arises whenever trust assets cease to be 'relevant property' within the definition in the legislation. This is broadly when the property ceases to be held on relevant property trusts, for instance if a beneficiary becomes absolutely entitled to it. As with the ten-year anniversary charge, the calculation of the exit charge is complex and professional advice is usually necessary.

The combination of the ten-year anniversary and exit charge is designed to ensure a full charge to inheritance tax on the trust assets once each generation.

Before 22 March 2006, interest in possession trusts did not suffer the inheritance tax charges outlined above during their continuance because the life tenant was deemed to own the underlying capital with the result that a charge to inheritance tax arose on the beneficiary's death. The inheritance tax treatment of interest in possession trusts in existence on 21 March 2006 continues, broadly, as before. However as mentioned, most interest in possession trusts created on or after 22 March 2006 will not be 'qualifying' interests in possession and the property will be subject to a ten yearly and an exit charge when capital is paid out to beneficiaries. There is no inheritance tax charge when the life tenant dies. Immediate post-death interests, disabled persons' trusts and transitional serial interests are among the exceptions to this. The beneficiary under these types of post-21 March 2006 interest in possession trusts is deemed to own the underlying capital in the trust property.

Termination of a trust

CGT

17.14 For capital gains tax purposes, trustees are deemed to dispose of trust assets in certain situations:

- When a beneficiary becomes absolutely entitled to all or part of the trust assets as against the trustees, whether on a distribution or in the event that property ceases to be settled property on the death of a life tenant and some other person becomes absolutely entitled. The trustees are deemed to dispose of the property at market value. However, for deaths on or after 22 March 2006 there is no chargeable gain provided the interest in possession is one where the life tenant is deemed to own the underlying capital in the trust property.

- When the trustees of another trust become absolutely entitled to all or part of the trust assets as against the trustees.

- In respect of deaths on or after 22 March 2006, in the limited situations where a life tenant is deemed to own the underlying capital in the trust property, where an interest in possession in trust property ends on the death of the person entitled to the interest, but the property remains settled. In such circumstances, the trustees are deemed to dispose of the assets at their market value and to reacquire them at market value, however no chargeable gain arises (except to the extent that any gain was held over on the creation of the trust).

Where a chargeable gain arises on the termination of a trust, in certain circumstances, hold-over relief may be available to defer the charge arising.

IHT

17.15 The termination of a relevant property trust will result in a charge to inheritance tax (an exit charge) unless reliefs or exemptions are available.

For deaths on or after 22 March 2006, the termination of a qualifying interest in possession during the life or on the death of a life tenant results in a charge on the whole of the capital of the fund, subject to, in the case of lifetime terminations, the potentially exempt transfer regime if the settlement ends. There is no charge where the life tenant or his spouse or civil partner beneficiary becomes entitled outright.

USES OF TRUSTS

17.16 What role can trusts play in modern day life for landowners and farmers? Trusts are an obvious vehicle for controlling devolution, securing succession and ultimately maintaining estates or farms as single viable entities. The availability of business and agricultural property reliefs may mean that landowners and farmers are not subject to inheritance tax or capital gains tax on the creation of a trust, and that thereafter the trustees are not liable for such taxes during the course, or on termination, of a trust (although such reliefs may not survive indefinitely and the rates of relief may change. In this regard it should be noted that on 3 March 2011, the Office of Tax Simplification recommended that IHT should be reviewed and that any such review should include a review of the taxation of trusts).

Trusts can also play a major role in ensuring tax-efficient pension provision, life assurance and school fees planning. By restricting the value of assets transferred to trustees within available exemptions, such as the inheritance tax nil rate band, and utilising the spouse/civil partner exemption, generous provision can be made for future generations during lifetime at little or no tax cost.

Judith Ingham

Judith Ingham is a partner in Withers LLP Wealth Planning practice group and head of Withers Zurich office. Judith focuses on tax, trust and estate planning work for individuals and trustees.

Imogen Davies

Imogen Davies is a professional support lawyer in Withers LLP London office. Imogen advises members of the Wealth Planning and Estates, Succession and Trusts practice groups about new developments of law relating to trusts and tax planning.

Note: The information and comments contained in this chapter are for the general information of the reader and are not intended to be relied upon in relation to any particular circumstances. For particular applications of the law to specific situations, the reader should seek professional advice.

Chapter 18

Wills

Robert Brodrick, Partner
(Private Client Department, Trowers & Hamlins)

- **Plan a will effectively**
  You can achieve tax savings with a well-drafted will. Intestacy must be avoided at all costs – land is a very valuable asset that must be protected.

- **Finance Act 2006**
  Understand the implications of the Finance Act 2006 changes to inheritance tax and how they affect wills.

- **Understand the transferable nil-rate band**
  This chapter looks at specific examples of saving tax.

- **Tax exemptions and reliefs**
  Ensure that you take advantage of all the exemptions and reliefs that are available.

- **Avoid disputes**
  Historically, farming families have wasted unnecessary time and professional fees in disputes as a result of intestacy and badly drafted wills.

- **Manage the client's affairs in the event of mental or physical incapacity**
  Few farmers retire and land always needs to be managed to protect against incapacity.

NOTE FROM THE EDITOR

18.1　　Many farmers and landowners die 'intestate' – without a will – and this not only causes huge problems for the family, but also makes winding up the estate more complicated.

These are times of change for farmers and there is no better time than now to review asset ownership and the tax efficiency of current arrangements. A complete review has to incorporate the drafting of wills for all the family. In this chapter Robert Brodrick, a partner at Trowers & Hamlins LLP who specialises in advising the owners of landed estates, sets out why a will is not just an 'evil necessity' but is also a useful tax-planning device. He covers areas such as how to hand assets on to the next generation tax free, how to make the most of tax reliefs, as well as how best to deal with personal possessions and funeral arrangements.

It is a practical approach to a subject that so many clients are loath to embrace. It ties into the theme that the affairs of the farming/landowning family have to be looked at 'in the round'. One aspect of tax planning is not enough and all good tax advice must incorporate a review of wills.

Although the chapter is not exhaustive, it deals with the main points to consider when planning a will. It also addresses the changes to inheritance tax brought about by Finance Act 2006 and how these affect wills.

INTRODUCTION

18.2   There are many reasons why people should make wills, but the principal ones are tax and succession planning. Unlike most European countries where there are strict rules of succession (known as forced heirship) which restrict the way in which you can leave your estate, people in England and Wales have testamentary freedom which means that they are free to dispose of their assets as they wish on death (although there is a mechanism for close relatives who were financially dependent on the deceased to make a claim under the Inheritance (Provision for Family and Dependants) Act 1975 if the deceased makes inadequate provision for them under the terms of his will). (Scotland has slightly different rules that favour spouses and close family members and give them a right to inherit movable assets, eg personal possessions and bank accounts.)

One of the most visible effects of testamentary freedom is that landowners have been able to protect the integrity of their properties, hence English farms and landed estates have largely been kept together where, in other countries, forced heirship would give rise to successive divisions of the property amongst siblings. This is why, for example, vineyards and farms in France are often so small and have such disparate ownership.

INTESTACY RULES

18.3   Without a will, you have to rely on the intestacy rules, which set out how a person's estate is to be distributed in the absence of any other direction; sometimes a person can die partially intestate (eg if they left a will that made pecuniary legacies but did not deal with the residue) and the intestacy rules would govern the distribution of the part of the estate not dealt with by will. Although this may not be a problem in the context of a simple, low-value estate where the deceased left no surviving spouse or children, for anyone with an estate that includes land (or any other illiquid asset) who is survived by a spouse, the intestacy rules are likely to be very unsatisfactory: they will almost certainly mean that the surviving spouse has to share the land with children or other relatives of the deceased, which may force the land to be sold in order to achieve a workable division of the deceased's estate.

The limits that apply under the intestacy rules were amended so that the new limits apply for all deaths on or after 1 February 2009. Where a person dies intestate with a surviving spouse and children, the intestacy rules allow the surviving spouse to receive a 'statutory legacy' of £250,000 (assuming the estate is worth more than this amount) and any personal chattels, with a life interest in half the remaining assets. The children will inherit the remaining half share of the assets on statutory trusts (ie dividing the assets equally between them and giving them a right to inherit at 18). Where there are no lineal descendants, the surviving spouse's legacy is increased to £450,000 plus a half share of the rest of the estate outright – the remaining half share is divided between the deceased's closest surviving relatives.

Example

Henry is married to Harriet. Henry owns a farm worth £900,000, and shares (worth £300,000). Henry dies intestate on 1 May 2010. They have no children, but Henry is survived by his brothers Hector and Humphrey (their parents both having pre-deceased him).

Under the intestacy rules, Harriet is entitled to:

●   a statutory legacy of £450,000; plus

●   a half share of the rest of the estate (ie £375,000).

As his closest surviving relatives, Hector and Humphrey are entitled to share the remaining half share of Henry's estate on the 'statutory trusts'. Their share is £187,500. However, the shares are not worth enough to satisfy their entitlement of £187,500 each, so part of their entitlement must come from the farm.

There is a further complication in that the share of the estate passing to Henry's brothers exceeds the 'nil-rate band' of £325,000 which means that, unless the farm qualifies for 100% relief, there will be tax to pay.

As Hector is in the process of setting up a new business he needs cash, and he is likely to push for a sale of the farm. If Harriet had sufficient funds of her own, she could buy out her brothers-in-law, but she does not.

If Henry had written a will leaving his estate to Harriet, he could have avoided leaving his widow in a very difficult situation.

It is worth pointing out that when a person gets married, their will is automatically revoked and unless they re-write their will (or sign a codicil to 'republish' their earlier will), they will be intestate. On the other hand, divorce does not cause automatic revocation – instead, the divorced spouse will simply be treated as having pre-deceased the testator.

WHAT OTHER MATTERS NEED TO BE CONSIDERED WHEN PREPARING A WILL?

Guardians

18.4   Where a couple have children it is important to decide who should take care of them in the event of both of the parents dying. In the absence of an express appointment of a guardian (eg in a will), it will be left to the court to appoint a guardian for any children under the age of 18.

Legacies

18.5   It goes without saying that the intestacy rules do not cater for people choosing to leave legacies, either pecuniary or 'specific' (eg a particular item), to friends or family, nor do they allow gifts to be made to charity. Where a person dies owning a farm, it is not only his family who are likely to be affected, but also his employees, and it is quite common to see these people remembered in a person's will, often with the proviso that the gift is only to take place if the individual is still in the deceased's employment at the date of his death.

Gifts can be made either 'free of tax', in which case the tax (if any) will be borne by the residuary estate, or 'subject to tax', in which case the recipient of the gift will have to pay tax on it at the rate of 40% to the extent that the value of this and other gifts exceeds the nil-rate band (see **18.8**).

Funeral wishes

18.6   Many people want to leave specific directions dealing with their funeral, cremation or burial arrangements and, although a testator has no power to dispose of his own body, any request included in a will is likely to be adhered to by the executors. If there are any religious or other reasons why burial would need to take place very shortly after death, it would be more sensible for these wishes to be stated elsewhere, as people generally store their wills either at a bank or in a solicitor's strongroom and it can take several days (and the production of a death certificate) before the will can be released to the executors, by which time it may be too late.

Funeral instructions can either be included in the will, or, where the instructions are particularly detailed, they can be set out in a side letter (which would usually be left with the will addressed to the executors). Funeral wishes can range from the simple request for the deceased's ashes to be scattered in a particular place, to the more esoteric. For instance, those who have a fear of being buried alive can include a clause requesting the executors to arrange for the deceased to be given a medical examination prior to burial to guard against 'premature burial'.

Personal possessions

18.7   The best way to deal with personal possessions is by way of a letter of wishes. The will should direct that the deceased's personal possessions be left either to the surviving spouse or to the executors to be distributed in accordance with a letter of wishes, or in the absence of any letter of wishes or specific instruction, to be distributed at the discretion of the executors. This makes the will extremely flexible and allows the executors to rectify any oversights (eg failure to include a godchild) by giving them an item that belonged to the deceased.

It is important to bear in mind that distributing personal possessions in this way may give rise to tax, so if there are particularly valuable items, it would be better to leave them to the surviving spouse (so that they qualify for spouse exemption) and leave it up to him or her whether to follow any letters of wishes – for inheritance tax (IHT) purposes, the surviving spouse would then be treated as inheriting all the personal possessions and to the extent that any are handed on (eg to godchildren) he or she would be treated as making a gift for IHT purposes, which would be a 'potentially exempt transfer'.

EXEMPTIONS AND RELIEFS

18.8 There are several exemptions and reliefs that need to be considered.

For instance, for the 2011–12 tax year the first £325,000 of a person's estate is taxed at 0% and can therefore be given away tax free to a beneficiary who would otherwise be chargeable. This is usually referred to as the nil-rate band because, although it is subject to tax, the rate of tax is nil.

The nil-rate band is now transferable between spouses and civil partners so that any un-used part of the nil-rate band of the first spouse to die can be used by the surviving spouse on their subsequent death, providing the death of the second to die occurs on or after 9 October 2007. It does not matter when the death of the first spouse (or civil partner) occurred. In calculating the amount of the nil-rate band available for transfer, any chargeable transfers made in the seven years before the death of the first spouse to die will eat into the nil-rate band in the normal way and so reduce the amount that is available for transfer.

Where an unused nil-rate band is available, each person may use a maximum of two nil-rate bands on death. This means that if a person has been widowed and remarried, it is important they use the nil-rate band of their deceased spouse before they die or on death, as this cannot be passed to the new spouse along with their own nil-rate band and used on the second death.

Gifts to spouses and charities are also exempt from IHT, although where the surviving spouse is non-UK domiciled and not deemed domiciled, the spouse exemption is limited to £55,000.

Certain assets also qualify for relief from IHT: the most significant are agricultural property and business property (dealt with in Chapter 13 in more detail).

Tax-efficient wills

18.9 It is very important to make sure that advantage is taken of all exemptions and reliefs that are available, and although there will be no tax to pay if an individual leaves his entire estate to his spouse or civil partner, on the spouse/civil partner's subsequent death there is likely to be more tax to pay if the first to die has not made full use of his allowances.

In the past, before the introduction of the transferrable nil-rate band, clients were always advised to divide ownership of their assets to ensure that they were both able to make a gift of the full nil rate band, and each will would include a gift of the nil-rate band to a discretionary trust or to adult children/ other non-exempt beneficiaries to avoid wasting the nil-rate band on the first death. All of this has now changed because in most cases it is preferable to take advantage of the transferable nil-rate band.

Wills that contain a gift of the nil-rate band to a discretionary trust do not need to be changed, as the discretionary trust can always be transferred to the surviving spouse within two years of death (taking advantage of Inheritance Tax Act 1984, s 144). The effect of this will be as if the entire nil-rate band had been left to the surviving spouse at the date of death with the benefit of spouse exemption, so that the full nil-rate band (less any lifetime gifts and legacies that need to be taken into account) is available on the second death.

Where the gift of the nil-rate band is to individuals, the will may need to be amended if the testator wants to be able to take advantage of the transferable nil-rate band, because the only way of doing this after death would be by way of deed of variation which will require the legatees' agreement and this may not be possible (eg if they are minors).

Using the transferable nil-rate band means that married couples no longer need to consider setting up sophisticated debt/charge schemes to ensure that the nil-rate band is not wasted on the first death. Couples should, however, still consider whether it is in their best interests to use the transferable nil rate band or whether they have assets that may go up in value significantly in the future which could be passed down to the next generation tax free as part of a nil-rate band gift.

The other point to consider is whether the nil-rate band is likely to increase significantly in the future. If the nil-rate band is put up to £1 million and the transferable nil-rate band remains unaltered, a married couple will be able to pass £2 million to their children tax free which would take the vast majority of estates outside the scope of inheritance tax. Some people suggest leaving a small portion of the nil-rate band unused on the first death so that a proportion of the transferable nil-rate band is still available on the second death, just in case the nil-rate band is put up significantly.

A point to watch is that where a married couple own property as joint tenants, it will pass automatically to the survivor by right of survivorship, and would not pass in accordance with the terms of the will. In order to include jointly owned property the joint tenancy should be severed. This is very easy and can be done simply by writing a letter of severance to the other joint tenant. Where a couple own property as tenants in common, it is advisable to record the fact not only by registering a restriction against the title at HM Land Registry, but also by declaring a trust specifying the shares in which the property is held.

Another common pitfall is to overlook other reliefs. For instance, as mentioned in Chapter 13, agricultural property is usually capable of qualifying for relief from IHT on death (provided that it was owned and occupied by the deceased for two years prior to his death for the purposes of agriculture, or was owned by him for seven years prior to his death, but occupied by someone else for the purposes of agriculture). It would make much more sense for property that qualifies for relief to be left directly to 'taxable' beneficiaries (or a flexible trust), rather than left to the surviving spouse: the property may not qualify for relief on the death of the surviving spouse which would give rise to an unnecessary tax bill.

Likewise, certain shares and business interests are capable of qualifying for 'business property relief' (BPR), and these should ideally be left to a trust for the benefit of a class of beneficiaries, rather than simply given to the surviving spouse.

Residuary estate

18.10   Most married couples or civil partners leave the rest of their estate (commonly known as the 'residuary estate') to their surviving spouse or civil partner with the benefit of exemption from IHT. The surviving spouse or civil partner does not need to inherit the residuary estate outright. The exemption will still be available where a spouse is given the right to receive income from the residuary estate. This is because the IHT rules treat a person with an 'immediate post death interest' (eg a right to receive income from assets in a deceased's estate) as owning the underlying property for IHT purposes.

Immediate post death interest trust

18.11   Where people have children from more than one marriage there are rival concerns to consider. For instance, a man with two children by his first wife and one child by his second wife will want to ensure that his second wife is provided for, but will also want to ensure that his first two children are not overlooked. If he leaves his estate to his second wife outright, he is relying on her to 'do the right thing' and leave a third to each of his children, when her main priority may be to provide for her only child.

By giving the second wife a life interest, the husband effectively retains control over the devolution of his estate. His trustees can be given power to pay capital to the second wife, and she would have the right to occupy any property that formed part of the residuary estate. However, she would be unable to prevent the children from inheriting the estate on her death. In such a situation it is important not to underestimate the potential for conflict and great care should be taken when choosing executors and trustees. This is also a situation where it may be wise to consider using a nil-rate band discretionary trust, rather than rely on the transferable nil-rate band to ensure that the benefit of the nil-rate band is divided fairly.

How to hand assets on to the next generation tax free

18.12   Obviously, there is scope for IHT planning where a person's residuary estate is given to the surviving spouse on life interest terms, because, depending on the terms of the will, it should be possible for the trustees to take away the surviving spouse's interest in favour of other beneficiaries without an immediate tax charge. For IHT purposes, the surviving spouse would be treated as having made a potentially exempt transfer and, as the rules currently stand, would simply have to survive the transfer by seven years for the assets to fall out of account. However, to be effective for IHT purposes, the surviving spouse will have to ensure that they do not retain any benefit in the assets that have been given away. If the deceased's estate included a let cottage, this would mean that the surviving spouse could not continue to receive the rent.

For capital gains tax purposes, assuming there was an ongoing trust, there would be no 'disposal', so no immediate charge to capital gains tax.

There are other, more sophisticated, ways of saving inheritance tax where the deceased's estate includes relievable assets (eg agricultural property) and there are sufficient non-relievable assets available. In such a case, the relievable assets should be left – free of inheritance tax – to a discretionary trust, with the surviving spouse taking an immediate post death interest in the non-relievable assets. These assets can be swapped after the deceased's death so that when the surviving spouse dies, the assets in which she has an IPDI will again qualify for IHT relief and the non-relievable assets will not be subject to IHT assuming they still qualify for relief.

Other ways of dealing with the residuary estate

18.13 Where there is no surviving spouse, the residuary estate is likely to be subject to tax at 40% to the extent that it exceeds the nil-rate band and does not qualify for exemptions or reliefs. The residuary estate can either be left to one or more individuals outright, or on trust for their benefit. A trust is probably the most convenient way of dealing with a residuary estate that consists of land (or any other illiquid assets that are not easily divisible) that is to be held for more than one person (eg the grandchildren of the deceased). This is because a trust distinguishes between the legal ownership and the underlying beneficial ownership. In other words, although the land would be registered in the names of the trustees as the legal owners, they would hold it upon trust for the beneficiaries (who could be numerous) in accordance with the terms of the will. Following Finance Act 2006, any trust set up under the terms of your will will be subject to a special IHT regime that applies to trusts involving a charge to IHT on every ten-year anniversary of the testator's death (at a maximum of 6%) and a proportionate charge on assets leaving the trust between ten-year anniversaries unless the trust qualifies as an immediate post death interest, a bereaved minor's trust or a trust for a disabled beneficiary.

Immediate post death interest trusts are described in **18.10** and **18.11** above. For a trust to qualify as an immediate post death interest, a beneficiary has to be entitled to an interest in possession (ie a right to receive all of the income) in the trust assets from the date of the testator's death. Unless the beneficiary is the testator's surviving spouse, or the assets qualify for relief, there will be an IHT charge on the testator's death. The assets will then be treated as forming part of the beneficiary's estate for IHT purposes. This means that there will be an IHT charge on the beneficiary's death, unless their interest has been terminated more than seven years before they die in favour of another individual outright. For unmarried couples, particularly those with children, a discretionary trust is likely to be a better solution from an inheritance tax perspective, because this will avoid a second 40% IHT charge on the same assets on the second death. Although the assets in the trust will be subject to ten-year anniversary charges and exit charges, the survivor would have to live around 65 years before the assets were subject to a 40% IHT charge (on the basis of a 6% charge every ten years) and in the meantime the income can be distributed to other family members which may have income tax savings. After death, one or more beneficiaries can be given revocable interests in possession so that the income is taxed as the beneficiaries' income which should help to avoid the 50% rate that applies to trusts.

A bereaved minor's trust is also exempt from the IHT regime applicable to trusts provided the trust is established under the will of a deceased parent of the 'bereaved minor'. A person qualifies as a parent if they are a parent, step-parent or had parental responsibility for the bereaved minor. This definition excludes grandparents, and it is therefore no longer possible for a grandparent to leave assets in trust for their minor grandchildren without the assets being subject to the IHT regime applicable to trusts. For a bereaved minor's trust to qualify, the child must become entitled to the income and capital outright at age 18. In this case there would be an IHT charge on the testator's death, but the assets would not be subject to IHT whilst the beneficiary was under age 18 and there would be no charge on the beneficiary receiving the assets at age 18.

There is a hybrid version of the bereaved minor's trust, known as an 18-25 trust which allows the assets to stay in trust until the child attains age 25. To qualify, the child must become entitled to the income and capital by age 25. From age 18 the trust will be subject to the IHT regime applicable to trusts which means that there will be an IHT charge of up to 4.2% on making a distribution from the trust or on the beneficiary becoming entitled to the trust assets outright at age 25.

In most cases, parents will be prepared to accept a modest tax charge to ensure that their children do not get access to capital before they are mature enough to look after it responsibly. In such circumstances, a flexible will is probably the best approach which would give the trustees the ability to determine at what age the beneficiaries inherit. Any grandparent who is intending to benefit their minor grandchildren by will needs to review their arrangements in the light of Finance Act 2006.

Inheritance tax mitigation

18.14   It is worth emphasising that IHT does not distinguish between liquid and illiquid assets and, unless the assets qualify for relief from IHT, or pass to an exempt beneficiary (eg spouse or charity), IHT at 40% will be payable. In a typical family situation this means that on the death of the surviving spouse, the whole estate (except for assets that qualify for relief) will be subject to 40% tax. Therefore, where a person's estate consists of high value, or illiquid assets that are unlikely to qualify for full relief, it would be worth taking specialist advice at the same time as preparing a will to see whether there is any scope for lifetime planning that could help to avoid a large tax bill on death.

Agricultural Holdings Act tenancies

18.15   Where a person has an Agricultural Holdings Act tenancy, it is possible to include a nomination for a successor by will. Although this nomination is not binding, it can be persuasive where there is more than one possible successor.

For the landlord of any old AHA tenancies, it is worth investigating whether these can be converted into farm business tenancies so as to get the benefit of 100% agricultural property relief (as opposed to 50% relief which applies to old-style tenancies where vacant possession can not be obtained within two years of death).

Farming partnerships

18.16   If a person is a partner in a farming partnership, it will be important to ensure that the terms of their will are consistent with the terms of the partnership agreement, and that between them they set out what is to happen on death to the share in the partnership. Under normal principles of partnership law, a partnership will dissolve on the death of one of the partners. Most partnership agreements provide for continuation on a death, but care should be taken when deciding how to confer a right on the surviving partners to acquire the deceased's partnership share because this can give rise to tax consequences.

Carrying on the business of farming

18.17   Where a person owns a farm and the executors and trustees of his will are expected to carry on the business of farming, it is important to ensure that they are given an express power to carry on a trade. The statutory powers are very limited and although the executors would generally be able to carry on the deceased's business until it was sold, it would be advisable for them to be given wider powers. This is another situation where the choice of executors is likely to be important as it would be wise to choose executors with experience of farming and/or running a business.

SINGLE FARM PAYMENTS

18.18   It is worth noting that a single farm payment is 'personal' to the landowner and may therefore pass independently of a gift of agricultural property to different beneficiaries. Where your agricultural property and residuary estate are left to different people, you should consider including a specific gift of the single farm payment to ensure that any such payments are left to the correct recipient and not inadvertently separated from the land.

NON-TESTAMENTARY DOCUMENTS

Powers of attorney

18.19   When someone writes their will they should also consider whether they have appointed anyone to deal with their affairs in the event of their becoming unable to do so themselves. This could come about either as a result of old age or infirmity, or as a result of an accident or illness. In any of these circumstances a power of attorney is invaluable. An ordinary power of attorney is only effective for as long as the 'donor' of the power (ie the person granting the power) has mental capacity – as soon as the donor loses mental capacity, the power of attorney lapses. However, an enduring power of attorney (granted before 1 October 2007) (EPA) continues to work even if the donor loses mental capacity (which is just when it is most needed). From 1 October 2007 EPAs were replaced by lasting powers of attorney (LPA). There is a procedure for registering EPAs, which involves notifying various close relatives (to ensure that the EPA is not abused). An EPA granted before 1 October 2007 will continue to have effect but following the introduction of LPAs it is no longer possible to make an EPA. Once registered, the attorneys can continue to manage the donor's affairs without interference from the court. In the absence of an EPA or LPA it is necessary to appoint a 'receiver' to deal with the affairs of a person who is no longer capable of doing so themselves and this is a time consuming and bureaucratic procedure.

LPAs differ from EPAs in two important ways. The first is that it is not possible to use an LPA until it has been registered. Secondly, unlike an EPA, an LPA may extend to personal welfare matters as well as property and affairs.

Under an EPA/LPA the attorney stands in the donor's shoes and can do anything that the donor could have done himself. This extends to operating bank accounts. So, for instance, if the donor had been involved in an accident, the attorney could ensure that enough money was available in the right bank account to cover mortgage repayments and other bills which might otherwise not be paid.

Attorneys can also make gifts, but if you want your attorneys to be able to make gifts for tax-planning purposes (eg to use up surplus income or annual inheritance tax exemptions) it is important for the EPA/LPA to contain express wording. Otherwise such gifts may be held to be invalid.

Living will

18.20   Increasingly, people also write a living will (or advance directive) which sets out what should happen if they become terminally ill. Although not legally binding, living wills are becoming more common, and do carry a certain amount of weight, particularly if they are properly drawn up in consultation with the individual's GP (who should always be given a copy of the living will so that they know of its existence). The aim of a living will is to communicate a person's desire not to receive medical treatment designed to prolong their life in circumstances where they are suffering from a terminal illness or other 'intolerable condition' (eg persistent vegetative state), and are no longer capable of communicating their wishes. The living will also states who the individual would like to be consulted before any such decisions about their treatment are made. Obviously, this is very important for unmarried couples because an unmarried 'partner' would not automatically have the right to be consulted about medical treatment.

INSURANCE

18.21   If it is impossible to reduce the impact of IHT on death by making lifetime gifts, it is always worth considering insurance, provided that the benefit of the policy is assigned to a trust so that it does not form a party of the deceased's estate for IHT purposes and simply exacerbate the problem by creating more tax to pay. The topic of insurance is dealt with more fully at **5.24**.

Robert John Lee Brodrick

Robert Brodrick is a partner in the private client department at Trowers & Hamlins LLP. Robert is a trustee of a number of landed estates, and as well as acting for domestic landowning clients, he also has a large international tax and trust practice with a particular emphasis on the Middle East and the US.

Chapter 19

Miscellaneous – sundry planning points

Julie Butler

- **What's new?**
  This chapter includes a synopsis of the sundry key changes since the first and second editions of this book. It is hoped that these give a quick and easy to read guide. It also looks at how some of the 'breaking news' of the first and second editions is now dealt with in more detail.

- **Miscellaneous tax areas**
  The tax benefits available for farming and alternative land usage are extensive. This chapter aims to highlight different areas, which are not covered in earlier chapters. The direction is a quirky, fun chapter.

- **Land complexity**
  The traditional and alternative usage of land can present complex tax problems. The complexities of the taxation with the 'hidden taxes' of aggregates levy, climate change levy and landfill tax are considered.

- **Financial impact of diversification**
  The need for a business plan for diversification projects to ensure commerciality and impact on the whole farm enterprise is essential. The importance of checking the business plan to actual results is key.

ANIMAL OWNERS LIABILITY RULES

19.1   At the time of writing, the duty of the livestock owner arises under the law of negligence and the Animals Act 1971. The law since 1971 has been that liability for damage caused by animals can rest with the owner irrespective of fault or negligence. There have been many recent cases which have featured this.

The view of the judges has always been that the owners can insure against this liability – hence high insurance premiums. Currently strict liability (ie no fault liability) applies to owners of animals which cause damage.

All livestock owners must check the position as it relates to them and make sure they operate with maximum protection and insurance where appropriate.

This must present an opportunity for farming, equine and general agricultural organisations to warn members of the existing and future liability and not only to insure against that liability but also to try to guard against that liability. This presents huge opportunities for insurance companies to help define and explain the problems and above all help protect the risk through insurance.

Many animal owners are simply not aware of the law, although they are aware of the safe management of all livestock. There will be changes ahead – beware.

THE GREEN IMPACT

19.2   The green allowances as set out in **7.5** and enhanced capital allowances set out in **7.6** show how farmers and accounting firms are being used for the green direction, these allowances can present tax advantages and every Budget should be scrutinised.

DISCLOSURE OF USE OF TAX AVOIDANCE SCHEMES (DOTAS)

19.3   Chapter 14 mentioned new FA 2004 provisions particularly in relation to sheltering property development gains (see **10.15–10.16**).

The FA 2004 introduced the need to disclose avoidance schemes.

For VAT purposes businesses with supplies exceeding £10 million per year must disclose the use of schemes, which have 'certain of the hallmarks of avoidance'. The disclosure must be made within 30 days of the due date for the first VAT return affected by the scheme. Disclosure is not required where the promoter of the scheme has registered it with the Commissioners. Failure to disclose will give rise to a substantial penalty.

There has been concern amongst the farming community, moving towards diversification, especially property development, that these rules include the need to disclose any tax-planning schemes. Every tax-planning case could possibly be considered as some form of scheme by HMRC and should be reviewed on its own merits as to whether disclosure is required.

At the time of writing it is understood that transfers into Discretionary Trusts require disclosure under DOTAS.

LAND DRAINAGE EXPENDITURE

19.4   With the move towards alternative land use and changes, landowners need to consider the tax-planning opportunities for land drainage. There are clear opportunities to claim the expenditure as revenue but there are times when it should be treated as capital. This can be used to advantage in tax planning.

Business Income Manual at BIM55270 sets out the position:

'Land which in the past was reasonably well drained but subsequently becomes wholly or partly waterlogged because the maintenance of efficient drainage was uneconomic is sometimes made available for cultivation by the restoration of drainage or by re-draining. In such cases so much of the net expenditure incurred (after crediting any grants receivable) as restores the drainage to its effective state may be admitted as revenue expenditure in farm accounts. This excludes:

- any substantial element of improvement – for example, the substitution of tile drainage for mole drainage; and

- the capital element in cases in which the present owner is known to have acquired the land at a depressed price because of its swampy condition.'

With the SFP emphasis on land management, soil (see **1.25** and **1.26**) and cross-compliance conditions (see **20.17**), the grant opportunities of land drainage should also be considered.

ORCHARDS

19.5   In the current environment some farms are turning to fruit farming. This is looked at as a separate diversified activity (see **6.46**).

Regarding fruit farming as 'farming' for tax purposes (**1.4**), the crop of 'fruit' is on the 'negative list' for SFP (see **1.5**).

The move towards fruit farming is a diversification alternative for traditional farmers (but still farming for tax purposes in some cases). The tax-planning position on orchards is considered. This is set out in the Business Income Manual at BIM55275 as follows.

'The initial expenditure incurred by a fruit farmer on the planting, staking etc of a new orchard is disallowable as representing capital expenditure (see *IRC v Pilcher* (1949) 31 TC 314). After the trees have been planted, all subsequent expenditure on cultivations etc is allowable in full as a revenue charge (see *Vallambrosa Rubber Co Ltd v Farmer* (1910) 5 TC 529).'

The cost of setting up an orchard being treated as capital, not revenue, might influence the business structure.

The expenditure incurred by a fruit farmer on the grubbing up of an old orchard and the subsequent planting of new fruit trees (whether or not of the same kind) is normally allowable as a revenue deduction on a 'renewals' basis, provided that the replanting takes place within a reasonable time after the old orchard is grubbed.

Again, care in the identification (and justification) of expenditure as revenue rather than capital expense is important for maximising tax relief.

COST OF RECLAIMING SCRUBLAND FORMERLY UNDER CULTIVATION

19.6   At the time of writing more land for food production and diversification projects is scarce. Will more scrubland be reclaimed? The focus on diversification and maximising the utilisation of land will make some entrepreneurs look to the possibility of buying scrubland and converting it into cultivation. The Business Income Manual at BIM55265 sets this out as follows:

'Where land, which was under cultivation within a reasonable period in the past has been allowed to relapse into a wild state, the net expenditure incurred on clearing it for cultivation may normally be treated as revenue expenditure in computing profits for taxation purposes. However, where the present owner is known to have acquired land at a depressed price because of its uncultivated condition, the capital element of the expenditure should be disallowed.'

The entrepreneur landowner must be careful to see how the expenditure can be used most tax efficiently. Will this be farming expenditure? This will depend on the ultimate use of the scrubland – for farming or for a diversified project.

WORKING IN 'THE BUFF' – CLAIM FOR WORK CLOTHES

19.7   There is a long running debate – should clothes worn at work be allowed against a tax bill? The recent case of Sian Williams and the tax tribunal highlighted this point. There are a number of angles here. The employed question versus the self-employed required versus health and safety and exactly what is exclusively? Farming and diversified activities generally need clothing that provides protection.

Employed

To claim clothing as tax allowable the employed have to pass the HMRC test of 'wholly, exclusively and necessarily in the performance of employment duties'. It is important to look at the key word of 'exclusively'. Sian Williams claimed that because clothing was required by BBC bosses who asked for regular wardrobe rotation, the clothes were required for her employment. However, clothing such as that worn by Ms Williams could equally be used outside of the place of work and therefore did not qualify for tax relief.

There were many who were surprised that the case was taken to Tribunal, because the HMRC rules are so clear, and such people were not surprised by the outcome. If the claim had succeeded there would have been an opening of 'floodgates' of claims for 'city suits' by the employed which HMRC would fight with strength.

The self-employed

The HMRC legislation for the self-employed does not include the word 'exclusively'. The concept of 'duality' should also be considered.

Health and safety

The employer must provide their staff with correct and compliant health and safety clothes and equipment. When clothes fall into the category of being needed for health and safety compliance there is a distinct difference. The key for the self-employed is that where there is a health and safety element there has to be tax allowability. Record keeping will be of great importance ie to keep the documentation and record the use.

Sian Williams suggested to the Tribunal that HMRC had permitted other presenters to submit claims for clothing as tax deductible expenses and also suggested that her job was like that of an actor. Her legal team told the Tribunal: 'If the appellant wore the same clothes frequently when appearing on television she would lose her job. The appellant would be prepared to wear no clothing when performing her job but is required to do so by her employer.'

The Tribunal, which sat in Manchester in January 2010, rejected Sian William's claims that the clothes and haircuts were exclusively for work. It said: 'It is argued on behalf of the appellant that she does not need clothes for warmth as it is warm inside the studios, and that she would be prepared to read the news without clothes and only wears the clothes because her employer requires it … the Tribunal does not accept as realistic that she could perform her duties without wearing any clothes at all.' Apparently Sian Williams came to prominence as a presenter on BBC News 24, a job that she secured after standing in, while working as a producer, for a screen test wearing a man's jacket and without make up. There could be many who would argue that presenting the news in 'the buff' was not a bluff!

Perhaps some naked news presentation would emphasise the high cost of non tax allowable work clothing. The issues are clearly the difference between employed and self-employed status and protective clothing compared to decorative clothing.

AGGREGATES LEVY

19.8

- The aggregates levy was introduced from 1 April 2002. The levy is charged at a flat rate of £2 per tonne (£1.95 before 1 April 2009) on sand, gravel and crushed rock extracted in the UK or its territorial waters or imported into the UK. There are a number of exemptions and exclusions. The aggregates become liable to the levy when they are commercially exploited.

- The levy is subject to a phased introduction in respect of aggregates used to manufacture certain products in Northern Ireland, with the full rate applying from 31 March 2012. The relief, fixed at 80% of the full rate, will also apply to virgin aggregate, subject to certain conditions, including the implementation of environmental improvements.

CLIMATE CHANGE LEVY

19.9

- Climate change levy (CCL) was introduced from 1 April 2001. This is a levy on certain supplies of fuel for business. The current rates of levy, applying from 1 April 2009 are:

– electricity	0.470p per kWh
– natural gas	0.164p per KWh
– liquid petroleum gas used for heating	1.050p per kg
– any other taxable commodity (eg coal and other solid fuels)	1.281p per kg

- There are a number of exemptions and exclusions such as fuels supplied for domestic heating, for certain forms of electricity generation and, from 22 July 2004, energy products used to create new biofuels such as biodiesel and bioblend and from 1 January 2005, bioethanol and bioethanol blend.

- There is an 80% relief available for energy intensive facilities covered by CCL agreements.

- Energy derived from renewable sources is exempt from CCL.

- The current rates were not increased at 1 April 2010.

LANDFILL TAX

19.10

- Landfill tax was introduced in 1996 to encourage business and consumers to produce less waste and to promote recycling rather than disposal of waste in landfill sites.

- At the time of writing certain inert waste (such as bricks) is taxed at the lower rate of £2.50 per tonne (increased from £2 per tonne from 1 April 2008).

- All other waste is taxed at a standard rate of £40 per tonne for supplies made on or after 1 April 2009 (increased from £32 per tonne from 1 April 2008; to increase to £48 per tonne from 1 April 2010 and by a further £8 in each of April 2011, 2012 and 2013).

- The maximum credit that landfill site operators can claim against their annual landfill tax liability is 6.6%.

THE OWNERSHIP AND MAINTENANCE OF HEDGES

19.11 The fact that maintaining of hedges is part of the good agricultural and environmental conditions (GAEC) to receive the subsidy entitlement the single farm payment (SFP) makes it useful to review the legal requirements, as do the 'hedging' and 'ditching' requirement to prove trading status for grazing rights (see **15.25**) which is a key tax planning point.

The news that a man shot a neighbour recently in a dispute over a hedge highlights the fact that an understanding of the law relating to the ownership and maintenance of boundary hedges is important. The decision by two Welsh cattle farmers to take their dispute over responsibility for maintenance of a hedge to the Court of Appeal rather than spend the relatively small sum required to repair the hedge demonstrates that issues to do with hedges impact on the farming industry. They also impact on diversification and carry a host of tax implications.

So who owns a hedge? One of the best-known presumptions of English Law is that if a boundary is marked by a hedge and ditch, the boundary is on the side of the ditch furthest from the hedge. This is based on the theory that an owner wishing to mark his boundary digs the ditch on his own land, throws the soil on his side of the ditch and plants a hedge on top of it. This presumption needs to be treated with a great deal of caution for a number of reasons.

- If the owner of the land on the ditch side of the hedge carries out work to the ditch, he can acquire ownership of the ditch after 12 years. Landcare issues arise here (see **1.26**).

- All presumptions can be challenged/altered by any provisions in the title deeds or other extrinsic evidence.

- It has long been the practice of Ordnance Survey when preparing plans of a boundary marked by a hedge to draw the line on the plan down the middle of the hedge. If the conveyance or transfer of land is done by reference to an Ordnance Survey plan and/or Ordnance Survey numbers, the parties will be deemed to have adopted the Ordnance Survey 'boundary' and the presumption will be rebutted.

- Different presumptions apply if the hedge and ditch divide the land from waste or common land or the highway rather than land in private ownership.

Ownership of a hedge does not automatically bring with it an obligation to maintain it. There is no general rule that the owner of a hedge must maintain it unless he needs to do so to prevent his own animals straying.

What of GAEC? Sometimes positive obligations are inserted in conveyance requiring a particular person to plant and maintain a hedge. However, positive covenants do not generally run with land so as to bind subsequent owners. The impact of the GAEC on the SFP will be interesting. The whole issue of cross-compliance will be of interest – see **20.7**.

It has been argued in court that an obligation to maintain a hedge can develop if a person has carried out maintenance over many years. However, in the Welsh case cited above, the court found that no such obligation could arise unless the work was undertaken by one owner, after specific direction from the other. In that case, one farmer had maintained the hedge for 50 years but this was found to impose an obligation.

The right to cut a neighbour's encroaching hedge is based on the law of nuisance and the right of a landowner to abate the nuisance that affects his land. The courts have moved recently away from a statement of the law in 1895 that appeared to give the landowner free rein on the neighbours' hedge even if it resulted in the complete destruction of the hedge. In 2001, the court decided that this is not an absolute right and must be exercised in a reasonable way. In looking at the action a landowner takes the court is likely to ask a number of questions. Did the landowner approach the neighbour to ask the neighbour to undertake such work as was necessary before resorting to self-help? Was the work done after reasonable and careful consideration? Was there a sensible alternative?

TREASURE SEEKERS

19.12   The potential money that can be received from treasure seekers can be first in the form of a licence to search given to the seekers. Receipts from licences given to treasure seekers to search on farmland are, in strictness, taxable as non-trading income. Where, however, such receipts are comparatively small in amount no objection is usually raised by HMRC, in practice, to treating them as farming receipts within trading income. Secondly, there could be the actual finding of treasure itself and the farmer, landowner, land agent and tax planner should be aware of the current position.

Treasure trove belongs to the Crown, unless the true owner claims it. Treasure trove is money or coin, gold, silver, plate or bullion found hidden in the earth or in any other private place. The local Coroners Court has jurisdiction to hold an inquest under Coroners Act 1887 s 36 to decide if an object is treasure trove.

If the finding of the object is promptly reported, the Crown will repay the full value of the treasure trove to the finder as a reward if it wishes to retain the object. Alternatively, it will return the object to the finder and he or she is then free to dispose of it as they wish. The landowner does not have any rights as regards an object that is treasure trove.

If a found object is not treasure trove the person with the best title to it is its original owner. The owner may pay a reward to the finder but this is an *ex-gratia* payment and is not taxable. By way of contrast the following were found to belong to the finder:

- some bank notes found on the floor of a shop (*Bridges v Hawkesworth* (1851) 15 Jur 1079); and

- a bracelet found in an airport departure lounge (*Parker v British Airways Board* [1982] QB 1004, CA).

One other area that is of interest is the payment for protection of field monuments. Token payments received from the Environment Agency by an occupier for land used for arable farming or tree planting who undertakes to protect an ancient field monument on that land are to be treated as tax free and ignored for the purposes of income tax, corporation tax and capital gains tax.

RURAL DIVERSIFICATION IN FARMLAND THAT IS 'DESIGNATED NATIONAL PARKLAND'

19.13   Many parts of rural England have become designated National Parks. Should a farmer's land be situated in an area of English countryside that is designated National Park it is likely that planning policies (see Chapter 3) will favour activities such as tourism, crafts and catering over other rural diversification projects (see **1.9**).

The farmer and landowner face problems with planning issues, as it could be that the designation of 'National Parkland' followed on from the farm being in an area of outstanding natural beauty (AONB). Many consider that the restrictive planning policies could stifle the dynamic rural enterprises that are needed (see Chapter 6) to invigorate local economic activity, eg providing long-term employment and not low-paid seasonal employment.

NATIONAL MINIMUM WAGE – ACCOMMODATION PROVIDED IN RETURN FOR WORK

19.14   Private arrangements relating to the provision of rent-free accommodation in return for carrying out certain duties (eg farm work, caretaking, housekeeping or looking after animals) may mean that the recipient is also entitled to receive the national minimum wage (NMW) in respect of hours actually worked (see **1.15**).

Regardless of what has been agreed between the parties, the 'employer' needs to know that the employee could bring a claim for backdated pay. The value of the provision of the accommodation should be calculated so as to reduce the liability to pay NMW in money.

NMW is one of the facilities which needs to be taken into account regarding agricultural workers. In the event of any dispute, the whole NMW position can be renewed. If the accommodation does not come into the 'tax-free' category, the PAYE position must be calculated.

SPONSORSHIP AND THE DIVERSIFIED ACTIVITY – *MCQUEEN*

19.15 Good news for competitors! A tax case, *McQueen v HMRC* SpC 601, has ruled it is all about the winning – winning new clients that is. The decision in this case has resulted in a helpful result for those involved in commercial sponsoring of competitors of sports activities. In this case it was shown that the marketing advantage was not vague and uncertain but was clear and successful. There was evidence to demonstrate a direct correlation between sponsorship and the gaining of new clients.

In *McQueen*, the Special Commissioners considered an interesting claim for expenses relating to the sponsorship of a rally car which was of particular interest to the proprietor. There was nothing very surprising about the facts. Mr McQueen was rather a good rally driver and he chose to publicise his coach business by sponsoring a rally car which he drove with some success. The rally car was painted the colours of the coach business and was generally high profile – for example parked outside the business premises in Garelochhead and apparently not easily ignored in that part of Scotland.

The question was whether the expenditure on sponsoring the rally car was incurred wholly and exclusively for the purposes of the business, or whether there was a duality of purpose. HMRC argued that this was Mr McQueen's way of indulging his interest and the business purpose was incidental. No surprises there, either.

THE MARKETING ADVANTAGE OF *MCQUEEN*

19.16 However, the Special Commissioner decided that the whole of the expenditure was incurred for the purpose of benefiting the coach business by the promotion of the name and facilities it offered. The fact that it gave him satisfaction was merely a consequential and incidental effect of the expenditure. He concluded that Mr McQueen used his skill and enthusiasm for rally driving as the best means available for promoting his coaching business. Accordingly the expenditure was laid out wholly and exclusively for the purposes of the coach trade and was fully deductible.

This may seem like a surprising decision because many have tried and failed in this area before. One can understand a cynical tax Inspector looking sideways at such a claim. However, it seems that in this case, the marketing advantage was not vague and uncertain (which is often the position with marketing expenditure) but was clear and successful, the evidence demonstrating a direct correlation between the sponsorship and the gaining of new clients. It may be that in another case such a correlation would not be so clearly established but it certainly looks like a helpful decision.

BEWARE SPORTS COMPETITORS OF *MCQUEEN*

19.17   The Commissioner concluded that the expenditure had been incurred for the purpose of promoting the business and getting names and liveries into the public awareness. Although the taxpayer gained some personal satisfaction from competing in rallies, his preferred leisure activity was sailing rather than rallying and the private satisfaction of success on the rally circuit was an incidental benefit of expenditure, rather than its purpose.

Many argue that it is the purpose that matters, not the effect. In many cases although there has been a benefit for the business, the taxpayer could not demonstrate that the main purpose was anything other than private benefit. So the tough requirement for sponsorship-type arrangements is to be able to demonstrate a purpose (to promote the business) and show that the effect was a direct correlation to sales. There are many that argue that great caution must be taken with regard to this case.

HMRC are currently taking a very keen interest in sporting businesses (including horses) which do not produce a profit. This is especially the case where the proprietor has other income. The relevant legislation is now contained in ITA 2007 s 64 onwards. ICTA 1988 s 384 has been replaced by ITTOIA 2005 s 66. There are therefore two tests to be proven. One that the business is being carried on with a view to profit and two, that it is commercial. The business plan is being very carefully scrutinised.

'We are after the extreme cases in which expenditure very greatly exceeds income or any possible income which can ever be made in which, however long the period, no degree of profit can ever have been reached.'

CHANCEL REPAIRS

19.18   With regard to Chancel repairs the relevant case is *Parochial Church Council of Aston Cantlow and Wilmcote with Billesley v Wallbank* [2003] UKHL 37, [2004] 1 AC 546, which was decided by the House of Lords in June 2003. Mr and Mrs Wallbank inherited Glebe Farm in 1974. The farm had attached to it a liability to repair the chancel of the local church, about a quarter of a mile away. (The chancel is the area beyond the nave.)

Chancel repair liability dates back to the dissolution of the monasteries when many church properties passed into lay hands. Such properties benefited from a right to collect tithes and in exchange were burdened with a responsibility to repair the chancel. No doubt at one time the income was more than sufficient to cover the liability. Tithes were abolished in 1936 but chancel repair liability remained and, indeed, was reinforced by the Chancel Repairs Act 1932.

Mr and Mrs Wallbank knew of the liability attaching to the farm. The PCC presented them with a bill for repairs for £95,000. Mr and Mrs Wallbank decided to fight payment on the grounds it was arbitrary tax and breached the right to peaceful enjoyment of possession under the Human Rights Act 1998. Mr and Mrs Wallbank lost in the High Court, won in the Court of Appeal and have now lost in the House of Lords. The result is that the liability remains and is enforceable. What is the likely impact?

About 5,000 parishes in England benefit from the right to claim repair costs of the church chancels from individual landowners, so the liability is significant. Often the liability will attach to agricultural property. When buying, the action plan should be:

- enquire of the seller;

- check old title deeds if available;

- make a search of the public records office at Kew; and

- insure.

BIOFUELS – THE DEBATE

19.19   Having originally been presented as offering a natural, climate-friendly alternative to dwindling reserves of fossil fuels, biofuels started to be portrayed by some parties as 'a great green con', which would, it is considered, drive up food prices, contribute to poverty and starvation in the developing world, and cause untold environmental devastation without even – so the critics went on to allege – making any worthwhile contribution to reducing carbon emissions!

The 'food vs fuel' debate was under way (again) with a vengeance!

The above is a deliberately simplified account of how this issue has developed. This is actually an old argument that refuses to move on, having been thoroughly debated by academics since the late 1970s or for what seems forever. But it does raise many important questions, to which people in the UK and beyond will, quite rightly, expect proper answers.

These include:

- Will rising food prices caused by biofuels create poverty and starvation in the developing world?

- Can the UK produce enough crops to meet the likely demand for fuel as well as food?

- Will biofuels inevitably lead to damage to the environment, either in the UK or in other parts of the world?

- Can biofuels make a worthwhile contribution to combating climate change?

- And – a key question for farming organisations – will the impact of biofuels on animal feed prices have a damaging impact on the livestock side of the industry?

REASONS FOR DIVERSIFICATION

19.20 It is clear that both the need and opportunities for diversification will continue to increase whereas alternative land use was once rare it is now commonplace.

It is considered that the reason farmers diversified is:

- to raise income and increase profitability;

- to make better use of physical resources, eg barns too small for current machinery;

- to be in a position to maximise grants;

- to make better use of financial resources;

- to create more rural employment; and

- out of personal interest.

At the time of writing the price of corn is high but the fluctuations increase the attraction of diversification to underpin the uncertainty of pure farming.

FINANCIAL IMPACT OF DIVERSIFICATION

19.21 There are three broad categories of diversification:

- on-farm, agricultural diversification (alternative crops, exotic livestock enterprises, contracting);

- on-farm, non-agricultural diversification (tourism, retail, environment schemes, letting of farm cottages and buildings); and

- off-farm diversification (ranging from other self-employed business ventures to full or part-time employment).

There are four financial categories of impact of diversification:.

- Profitability – to identify past and present trends, present sufficiency and future requirements.

- Individual enterprise performance – to compare with standard figures: is there scope for improvement?

- Are any existing enterprises under performing or using up a disproportionate share of resources and should be restructured?

- Overheads – are they under control? Is there a sufficient margin to meet fixed-cost requirements and can diversification help with this?

There are many reasons for making a review of the existing farm business the start point:

- There may be opportunities for improvements within the existing business but this usually carries a lower risk than diversification.

- The new diversification enterprise may require the availability of capital to start up.

- Some restructuring of the core business may be needed before diversification can go ahead, eg incorporation (see Chapter 8).

Resources

19.22   When planning any diversification project it is imperative to review resources. Where land and buildings are concerned, it is worth considering (without being over simplistic):

- a map of the area;

- surplus land and buildings;

- any woodlands that could be developed and managed (see Chapter 6);

- any special designations resulting in either restrictions or opportunities that the land may carry;

- any special features that can be protected or upgraded;

- any buildings that have potential for other more profitable uses;

- the accessibility of buildings;

- any planning restrictions that apply (see Chapter 3); and

- if the land/buildings are rented, any tenancy restrictions that may apply (see Chapter 15).

When considering the location, thought should be given to its proximity to population, neighbours, other attractions, or potential business competitors. Location can be an advantage or a disadvantage:

- How easy is access to the property for the purposes of the business?

- How visible is the site?

Where finance is concerned this will relate closely to the financial review of the existing farm business:

- Is there capital available within the business?

- Are there under-utilised assets that could be sold to raise capital?

- What is the likely borrowing availability?

- What collateral is available?

- Are there grants available? (See Chapter 2)

The customers

19.23   Food chain reconnection was first looked at in Chapter 1. The diversification opportunity of shopping and the food sector has been looked at (see **6.33**). However, many of the diversification projects can be for a range of projects and products eg log sales, livery service, work shop letting etc.

Points to consider are the following.

- Is the market growing or declining?

- What is the local market?

- What are the key influences and usual terms of trade in the market and how are products normally sold?

- Who would buy the product and at what price?

- Where possible, seek independent third-party assessments of the market for the product.

- Contact relevant trade associations who will hold market information, eg regional tourist organisations, farm holiday groups, retail associations.

- Trade magazines can provide a good overview of current market issues by sector.

- Local business advisers will help.

Diversification opportunities and business risk

19.24   The diversification project must not put the main farming business at risk (see **8.2**).

Not all diversification enterprises will succeed. Research suggests over 30% of all new rural business start-ups fail within the first three years. Some activities carry higher risks than others. The key has to be the ability to adapt and change to the forces of demand.

The business plan

19.25   Every farm enterprise must have a business plan. If commerciality is questioned by HMRC either with regard to the claim for losses (see Chapter 12) or claim for IHT (see Chapters 5 and 13) then they will ask for sight of a business plan. Every diversification project must have a business plan. There is a tax angle here – if the future argument is that it is all one business (see *Balfour* **5.55** and **13.51–13.53**) then should the business plan be for one business with enterprise shown separately with the concept of one business? The business plan will:

- set targets;

- highlight problem areas;

- provide a basis for control of the project; and

- agree how it will be done, by when, and who will be responsible for it in the form of an action plan.

The business plan will draw together areas such as marketing.

- What is the product and where does it sit in the marketplace?

- Will sales be through direct sales, or through agents or wholesalers?

- Promotions:

  – advertising – why, when where and cost;

- public and press relations – this is a very cost-effective activity for small businesses but can be run in-house;

- packaging and labelling if appropriate;

- point-of-sale materials and marketing literature;

- personal selling;

- the terms of trade; and

- sales forecasts and projections with best and worse case situations.

- The local press might want to feature new businesses and new ideas:

- the new business set-up; and

- proposals for training and recruitment (see **2.6**).

The business plan will pull together the financial plan after all the research has been carried out.

- Capital requirements. This area is often underestimated. It is essential to be as accurate and realistic as possible.

- Profit and loss budget.

- Cash-flow forecast.

- Balance sheet forecast.

- The business plan must be checked to actual results on a regular basis.

TAX AND FINANCIAL ACTION PLAN FOR LANDOWNERS

19.26

- Produce a total map/plan of all land holdings (link to fixed asset schedule in accounts/personal holding). Check hedges/boundaries (see **19.11**).

- Produce list of all leases and licences – written and unwritten. Check tax status. (See Chapter 15.)

- Review all IHT availability – APR and BPR (see Chapter 5 and Chapter 13). Assess where APR suffers through agricultural value having to be used (see **13.2**).

- Consider entrepreneurs' relief (ER) and when this can be claimed effectively and through maximum members of the family.

- Consider woodland ownership and the potential of IHT deferral/compared to BPR/APR. Review interaction with farm activities, commerciality and tax status (see Chapter 6).

- Use the computerised Land Registration system for ownership to help control the above (see **19.23**).

- BPR audit to identify areas of weakness.

- Regularly update business plans in light of actual results.

Chapter 20

Single farm payment – the tax implications

Julie Butler

- **Single farm payments (SFP)**
  Single payment entitlements have become known as single farm payments (SFP).

- **Farm entitlements – the SFP**
  Review of the post 2013-CAP proposals.

- **Decoupling and modulation**
  Keeping land in good agricultural and environmental condition (GAEC), with emphasis on environmental compliance. Progressive siphoning of direct payments to fund agricultural environmental schemes and rural development initiatives have meant increased diversification and potential tax planning surrounding that subject is debated.

- **Tax planning surrounding the SFP**
- The potential CGT and IHT position of farmland and the impact of SFP are considered at a specific and at a general level. Looking forward to the 'CAP landscape'.

INTRODUCTION

20.1   Information about the CAP reform can be found at www.defra.uk/farm/capreform/index.htm.

The book starts with an explanation of the need to diversify. Chapter 1 and then Chapter 2 explain how this activity can be helped by the tax advantages and the EU and other grants. It is interesting to note that since the 2nd edition many of the original grant schemes are closed down and the main emphasis is on the SFP and environmental stewardship. It seems appropriate to finish the book with a final chapter on SFP. Chapter 1 explains the concept of the fiscal farmer at **1.12** and the SFP jargon at **1.17**. The book would have to start with an explanation of decoupling, partial-decoupling, naked acres, the national envelope and entry-level payments at the beginning rather than at the end.

The European Commission published its post-2013 CAP proposals on 18 November 2010. The reform has several competing objectives. Food security is key, along with environmental protection, climate change, and social and economic issues. A stated objective is to simplify the system; it seems to become more complicated than ever. Objectives need to be achieved with a smaller budget – still to be decided – spread more evenly around the Member States. For UK farmers it is likely to involve capping of payments for large farming businesses, the targeting of payments towards 'active' farmers (definition is still needed for active), and an overall reduction in funding. Member States have been responding to the proposals and the Commission will need to decide which, if any, it will listen to before issuing draft legal texts in July 2011. The negotiations and debate will start in earnest, with the proposals being formally debated and negotiated by Member States and the European Parliament. The final agreement is likely to be published in late 2012.

SINGLE FARM PAYMENTS

20.2 Single farm payments replace claims under all of the following schemes:

- arable area payment scheme (AAPS) (see **1.20**);
- set-aside (see **1.20**);
- suckler cow premium;
- beef special premium;
- slaughter premium;
- extensification premium; and
- sheep annual premium.

The SFP cannot move across Member State boundaries, nor can it move across internal UK boundaries. The unsubsidised sectors (such as roots and horticulture) will over time gain the same level of payments as their previously subsidised peers, providing a level playing field in the 'decoupled' world. The SFP has many of the characteristics of an annuity, subject to certain special conditions.

The intention is that a farmer receives payment under his SFP in each year from 2005 provided he can match his entitlement against hectares of eligible land (broadly, arable and permanent pasture, but excluding permanent crops, forests and land under non-agricultural use) which he has at his disposal for at least ten months ('the ten-month period'). A declaration that the farmer has the eligible land at his disposal will need to be made and submitted by 15 May in each year concerned. Once the claim has been made the farmer has much greater freedom than previously to farm as he pleases on his land, although in all cases he will have to keep his land in good agricultural and environmental conditions (GAEC), as defined by DEFRA according to the framework set in the EU regulations. Penalties can be imposed if the farmer fails to meet these conditions and indeed, further regulations concerning animal welfare, food safety and other environmental matters. These are known as the cross-compliance conditions (see **20.17**). Any SFPs not used over a period of three years are lost to the national reserve (see **20.3**). In the post-2013 CAP proposals the direction is towards 'active' farming, although at the time of writing 'active' is still to be defined.

'HISTORY BASED' OR 'AREA BASED'

20.3   The regulations provided for two methods that may be adopted by Member States (each state had to make a decision on which method to adopt before 1 August 2004). The two methods were described as 'history based', or 'area based'.

Under the 'history-based' method, the farmer's claim made in the three years 2000–02 (ie acres of arable area aid or set-aside, or headage for the livestock payments) formed the basis of the calculation of the SFP, which was then divided over the number of hectares that gave rise to the payments to yield SFP expressed as so many euros per hectare on so many hectares. One important ingredient of the 'history-based' method was that the claimant had to have a continuing business until SFP was allocated in 2005 (though there are special provisions that apply where a business has changed status, or merged or divided). The 'history-based' method also included special rules to allow for the following types of cases.

- Hardship cases (eg where production was depressed in the 2000–02 reference period through exceptional circumstances, such as being affected by the foot and mouth crisis), where it was possible to replace some or all of the reference years with other years.

- The establishment of a national reserve, by using up to 3% of the regional money and other shortfalls and contributions, which could then be used to fund the SFP for those farmers who might not otherwise have qualified (it is worth noting that SFP established from the national reserve must be used for a minimum of five years before they become transferable and any not used in any year are siphoned back into the national reserve).

- New entrants, who started within the 2000–02 reference period (who needed only average their payments over the period during which they were farming).

Under the 'area-based' method, each state was divided into regions and then the total money available under the scheme was divided by regional agricultural area to yield a standard payment to be made to each farmer in 2005 based upon his agricultural area in 2005. Clearly the 'area-based' method would favour less-intensive farmers (eg hill sheep farmers) rather than more intensive farmers, as compared with the 'history-based' method. The regulations partially recognise this redistribution compared with the 'history-based' method by allowing Member States who adopt it to introduce three separate levels of payment (for permanent pasture, for pasture grass and for other uses).

Land used to match entitlement must be at the farmers' disposal for a period of ten months for each year of claim, the 'ten-month period'.

The SFP thus calculated was then subject to deductions. As mentioned a one-off deduction of up to 3% is made to the national reserve. Further scaling back was allowed where the total SFPs exceed the total money available to fund them (more likely under the 'area-based' method). Deductions were made for what is termed 'financial discipline', ie to allow for reductions to be made to meet reductions in the total CAP money. This replaced the term digressively, and applies where the CAP budget ceiling was in danger of being breached between 2007–13.

SFP payments are made between 1 December of the year of claim and 30 June of the next following year (in the UK based upon the euro/pound, exchange rate as at 1 December prior to the year). This explains the vulnerability to exchange rate of the SFP and impact on farm budgets where there has been (and could be) a delay.

It might be questioned why this history features here but it helps to understand the 'backdrop' of the current need for the SFP and diversification.

THE TRANSITIONAL METHOD IN ENGLAND

20.4 Set out below is a presentation of the transitional method of allocating entitlements to decoupled support payments in England. The transitional method is essentially an area-based system, with transitional historic support added during 2005–11, ie this is the 'dynamic hybrid' referred to by Margaret Beckett all those years ago. During the transitional period of 2005–11, the SFP consist of two parts: one historic and one area based, as detailed below. The area-based proportion will increase over time as follows, to the point where the SFP will be 100% area based in 2012.

The transitional method of allocating entitlements to decoupled support payments

	2005	*2006*	*2007*	*2008*	*2009*	*2010*	*2011*	*2012*
Historic payment	90%	85%	70%	55%	40%	25%	10%	0%
Area-based payment	10%	15%	30%	45%	60%	75%	90%	100%

It was considered that the long period to 2012 allowed time for intensive or high subsidy receiving businesses to adjust. The farmer and tax planner must now look to the CAP reform post 2013. This could be a positive point for the tax planner and there is much planning moving forward.

- Historic payments ('history-based' method). As mentioned, the historic component was based on the average amount of support received by a farmer in the 2000–02 reference period (ie in the three years 2000, 2001 and 2002). Of this amount 90% was paid in 2005, tapering to 10% in 2011.

- Area-based payments. There will be two area-based payments in England. One within severely disadvantaged areas (SDAs) and one for all other areas. Most importantly, if a large area of land other than that included in the June census and other records comes into agriculture then payment rates will be lower than would otherwise have been anticipated, eg a large number of 'recreational' farmers, or perhaps farmers not helped by a land agent, are made aware of the scheme.

  A valid claim for support requires an area of entitlement plus a matching area of eligible land. All agricultural land is eligible with the specific exception of permanent crops, woodland and land used for non-agricultural activities. One acre of land can be used to validate only one acre of entitlement.

Land growing multi-annual crops such as asparagus, globe artichokes, rhubarb and fruit such as raspberries is likely to be eligible, as is land in short rotation coppice. All farmers, old and new must ensure they are maximising their claims.

THE FISCAL AND NON-FISCAL FARMER

20.5 This subject is dealt with in Chapter 1 under the heading the 'fiscal farmer' (see **1.12**)

For income tax purposes there are essentially three types of recipient that have been identified and the tax treatment is as follows:

- Farmer: ITTO1A 2005 s 9 (Schedule D, Case 1 as was).

- Non-farmer but trading in other activities: ITTO1A 2005 s 10 (Schedule D, Case 1 as was).

- Non-trader: ITTO1A 2005 Pt 5, Ch 8 (Schedule D, Case VI as was).

The 'farmer' is clearly someone who continues the trade of farming and receives the entitlement to the single payment. This entitlement is normally referred to within the farming community as the single farm payment.

The 'non-farmer' is someone who trades using the land as a business asset, but who carries out a different trade from farming (eg various diverse activities).

A non-trader is someone who has retired from farming and trading.

The existence of a trade is based on fact and the receipt of the SFP is not enough to justify a trade for tax purposes.

The recent BPR case of *Balfour* points towards the need for 'active husbandry' to achieve BPR and the post-2013 CAP proposals point towards 'active' farmers and therefore questions have to be raised over the original approach of the SFP of possibly just ceasing production. In reality this did not happen; corn and livestock prices became too good.

TAX PLANNING AROUND THE FISCAL FARMER

20.6 To be a fiscal farmer a person has to be the paramount occupier (see **11.33**) of land and be in occupation of the land wholly or mainly for the purposes of husbandry (ITA 2007 s 996) (see **1.3**). This tax definition for farming is set out at length in Chapter 1 and **1.12**.

HMRC have confirmed that in their view the payments are taxable.

The tax-planning consideration of ensuring the SFP is treated as farming income is established throughout the book.

Most recipients of payments will be fiscal farmers and will, accordingly have payments taxed as farming income. The main area of concern is whether HMRC will extend farming treatment to recipients of payments who are deemed farmers because their farming activity is not strictly from the occupation of land (eg fish farming in tanks). No view has been expressed to date but it is reasonable to assume that these cases will also result in the payments being farming income and in reality very few farmers ceased farming.

Many farmers could cease all production and just comply with GAEC and this may weaken arguments for both 'occupier' and husbandry. Is 'cutting the grass' husbandry for tax purposes? The key action point for farmers is to keep farming and do not let the tax status lapse. The author knows of very few cases where farmers have ceased farming, and see **20.13**, 'the need to keep trading.

SFP – farming income

20.7   It is possible, however, that minimum cross-compliance conditions may place in doubt whether the occupation of the land is wholly or mainly for the purposes of husbandry. What constitutes GAEC is clearly relevant to this consideration. In that case the purpose of occupation of the recipient will have to be reviewed carefully (and normally this will be by reference to the use made of the land). It is clearly possible that the main purpose of occupation could be other than husbandry (though still within minimum cross-compliance). Grazing by horses could prove to be an example as there is authority for the proposition that the activity of grazing is not husbandry (see *Wheatley (Wheatley's Executors) v IRC* [1998] STC (SCD) 60 and *Hemens v Whitsbury Farm and Stud Ltd* [1987] 1 All ER 430, CA), though this may in the end prove to turn on whether the occupier is mainly concerned with the supply of grass (ie offering it to any grazier, including grazing other than by horses) or whether the grazing by horses in part of a wider activity conducted.

SFP – the accounting treatment

20.8   The accounting treatment is based on the ICAS/ICAEW guidance issued in May 2005 (see www.icas.org.uk/site/cms/download/aa_singlepaymentguidlines.pdf).

The payment entitlement (PE) is described in this guideline as 'essentially receiving an intangible asset and it will be tradable when definitely established, say at the end of 2005'. The period to which an SFP claim relates is the calendar year from 1 January to 31 December.

In order to receive the SFP, the land must be kept in 'good agricultural and environmental condition' (GAEC), and 'cross-compliance' conditions must be met.

'Cross-compliance' conditions must be maintained for at least the chosen ten-month period. The ten-month period can commence at any time between 1 October prior to the year of the claim and 30 April within the year of the claim. If no specific period is taken, it is assumed to be 1 February to 30 November. The choice of the ten-month period was imperative for tax-planning purposes.

Failure to comply with the 'cross-compliance' conditions can result in a reduction of between 3% to 5%, building up to 15% for repeated non compliance. Any penalty arising from non compliance will be applied to the whole claim and not just the part relating to the non compliance. There will be clawback provisions.

SSAP 4 (Accounting for government grants) which explains accounting for grants, states that the grant should not be recognised in the profit and loss until the grant conditions of receipt are complied with. The recognition trigger should be the end of the ten-month basis period. The end of the ten-month period is not an adjusting post-balance sheet event and if the farmer retains the same ten-month period and year end, each set of accounts is the same. However, 2005 and 2006 were the difficult years in establishing the correct allocation of the payment.

The historic treatment of the SFP that might have evolved should be checked to the original guidance as some incorrect treatment might have become habit.

THE ENTITLEMENT – IS IT PROPERTY?

20.9 In principle, for unincorporated businesses the payment entitlement (PE) is an asset for capital gains tax (CGT) purposes and it is a business asset if it is charged to income tax under ITTO1A 2005, ss 9 or 10. The 'date of birth' for the PE with historic entitlement is 1 January 2005 for tax purposes.

The business PE will be eligible for rollover relief, holdover relief and entrepreneurs' relief, providing the specific CGT requirements are met.

The disposal of farmland (see Chapter 14) and the value of land of inheritance tax (IHT) purposes (see Chapter 13) has started taking account of the valuation of the entitlement and eligible hectares into the calculation.

The entitlement – inheritance tax

20.10 Chapter 24 (IHTM24254) of the Inheritance Tax Manual, provides guidance as follows:

Single Payment Scheme

'The Single Payment Scheme was introduced by the EU to replace a wide range of farming subsidies under the Common Agricultural Policy and break the link between subsidies and agricultural production.

The Scheme came into force on 1 January 2005. Entitlement to the annual Farm Payments was to be established by individuals who applied by May 2005, and once obtained such entitlement could be bought and sold in the open market, thereby acquiring a value.

The significance of this from an agricultural relief point of view is that:

Although entitlement could only be held by, and sold to, persons registered as "farmers", this definition could cover many who would not be 'occupying for the purposes of agriculture' for IHT. Therefore, mere entitlement to Single Farm Payments is no guarantee that s 117 IHTA is satisfied in respect of the residence of the holder.

...

Because entitlement to Single Farm Payments is not an "interest in land", and thus does not meet the definition of 'agricultural property' in s 115(2), agricultural relief will not be due on its value in any event.'

The June 2005 *Tax Bulletin* simply states 'the transfer of PE by someone who is not carrying on a trading business will not qualify for business property relief'. So if there is no trade, then there is no inheritance tax relief. That does go slightly against the 'tabloid' view of 'fat cat' farmers ceasing to farm, receiving a lump sum and being 'park keepers'. Land takes a lot of looking after and the best way of achieving that is via some form of farming both for practical and tax reasons. If alternative land use is pursued, then business property relief, will apply for inheritance tax purposes, which could put the agricultural property relief on the farmhouse at risk.

In summary, provided the entitlement is a business receipt and the farmland is a business asset used in the trade and owned for two years, BPR should apply.

The entitlement – VAT

20.11   The SFP is outside the scope of VAT. However, there are situations where VAT is payable, eg on the sale of the entitlement without land. If a farmer is not trading, a VAT deregistration will have to take place and there will be no opportunity to claim VAT. The whole issue of VAT is dealt with in Chapter 9.

TAX MARRIAGE BETWEEN LAND AND TRADING VEHICLE

20.12   The June 2005 special edition of the *Tax Bulletin* has explained at length the tax treatment of the single farm payment. All applications had to be made by 16 May each year and the subsidy scheme for farming is now decoupled from production and based on entitlement.

Historically, all farms have had a difficult marriage between the ownership of the land and the trading vehicle. In many small farms it is not even clear who owns what. Some trusts and limited companies have evolved over the years and there were debates as to who the single farm payment entitlement actually belonged to, who was the landowner, who the tenant and who was actually the farmer.

For tax purposes the previous production subsidy (see **20.2**) was linked by definition to production. The accounting and tax treatment was essentially to match the subsidy with the underlying trading treatment, therefore the subsidy was included in the accounts and tax computation of the trading vehicle which produced the relevant farm products. However, the entitlement now originates from the land and great care will have to be applied to make sure that they are allocated to the correct taxpayer.

The *Tax Bulletin* has also highlighted opportunities for tax planning for the adviser around the ten-month period that has to be achieved in order to receive the payment. Cross-compliance conditions have to be met for that period and the period can be changed. The end of the ten-month period is the trigger for the taxation of the single farm payment so tax planning can be introduced around its timing and the ten-month period could be changed to ensure that two entitlements appear in one accounting period.

The accounting guideline on this, FRS 18, as quoted by the *Tax Bulletin*, says that 'provided there is disclosure, two payments in one period could be acceptable'. This means that there could be some tax planning, for example, it could ensure that a loss-making farm became profitable and therefore gained protection for another five years of sideways losses under ITA 2007 ss 66 and 67 (see Chapter 12).

Clearly, now that the tax rules are known the action plan for the tax adviser has to be to meet with the farmer and ensure that the detail of the ten-month period is known and is planned for and the exact ownership of the entitlement is ascertained in relation to future accounts and Tax Returns and as we move towards post-2013 CAP proposals.

THE NEED TO KEEP TRADING

Do not give up farming

20.13   The June 2005 *Tax Bulletin* confirmed that the combination of collecting the SFP and ceasing to trade is very unattractive for tax purposes. This would result in the potential loss of BPR for inheritance tax purposes, entrepreneurs' relief and the other business capital gains tax reliefs of roll-over and hold-over, plus income tax treatment under ITTOIA 2005, Pt 5, Ch 8) with restricted claims for expenses as not qualifying under the 'wholly and exclusively' rule, no VAT registration and no claims for input VAT.

The scheme has moved farm subsidies away from production, on which they were previously based. It literally decouples the subsidy from production and moves it to 'entitlement'. In broad terms, the subsidy (or 'land management fee', which is the strictly correct term) is based on the area of land owned as opposed to the farm production. However, payments towards more active farming are proposed post-2013.

The theme of the *Tax Bulletin* is that if the recipient is a non farmer they will still be taxed under what was, and is, ITTOIA 2005 s 10 (previously known as Schedule D Case I) provided that there is a trade, even if it is not a farming trade. However, those who are not seeking to trade at all will have the subsidy taxed under Chapter 8 of Part 5 of ITTOIA 2005 (previously known as Schedule D Case VI). Herein lies the problem. If the subsidy is received not just by a 'non farmer' but by a 'non trader', then in principle the IHT on the land and the entitlement will not be eligible for IHT reliefs. So, essentially the IHT treatment will depend on the trading status.

The good news is that if the farmer continues to farm, then the entitlement to the single farm payment (the entitlement being an asset in its own right, separate from the land) will qualify for IHT relief (BPR).

The trading versus non-trading theme continues throughout the *Tax Bulletin*, mentioning that obviously if the farmer is not trading then they do not need to be VAT registered and therefore will not be able to make input VAT claims. Land and farmland that needs to be kept in good agricultural and environmental condition does take a lot of looking after, rather like an extremely large garden and the costs associated therewith would of course have input VAT. In addition, any expenses associated with the receipt of the income would have to be proved to be wholly and necessarily for purposes of the trade in order to achieve income tax reliefs and if there is not a trade, it could prove to be quite an onerous task for the tax adviser to justify the claim. The key problems here could be 'lifestyle expenses' such as motor expenses, farmhouse costs, etc. The recent tax cases and reports on CAP reform all point towards active husbandry and an active farming enterprise as one unit.

THE SFP AND WILLS

20.14   Wills are dealt with in Chapter 18 and the following notes are not intended to try and compete with that chapter, but instead deal with tax-planning ideas.

Quite often in drafting wills for farmers, solicitors are instructed to provide that farmland and farming assets are to be left to a specific member of the family, with residue of the estate to be divided amongst others. Leaving the farm like this, it is argued, enables the farming enterprise to continue and other members of the family to receive the benefit of non-farming assets.

Arable area payments and milk quota, being attached to or associated with land have passed historically to the farming member of the family. However, it seems likely that at least a proportion of the entitlement will be personal to the farmer and may not attach to the land in a similar manner. So, a significant amount of the entitlement might pass into residue unless specifically provided for in a will.

It is considered necessary for farmers to revise their wills to make sure their original intentions can be carried through; many solicitors are recommending an express provision be made in each will. Recent cases show the need to review the will regularly.

SET-ASIDE

20.15   Set-aside entitlements were allocated as a proportion of all of the land other than permanent grassland that was used to establish entitlements, including temporary grass, potatoes and vegetables. The area of land is defined according to the 2003 IACS claim.

Set-aside entitlements carry the same area-based payment per acre as all other entitlements, but only arable land managed as set-aside can be used to validate a claim using set-aside entitlement. With the 'active husbandry' considerations and prices of corn and livestock at the time of writing this is something that will disappear. However, land with conservation schemes, ie dedicated wildlife habitats, will still continue.

The CGT position on land disposals with set-aside is looked at in Chapter 14 at **14.66**. The IHT position of set aside is dealt with in **13.25**.

NATIONAL ENVELOPE

20.16   There was no transfer of payments into a national envelope in England. This could have transferred up to 10% of payments into a separate pot of money to fund environmentally friendly farming systems. Use of the envelope appears to be more likely in Scotland, to support forms of beef farming, and it is possible in Wales. Both administrations will be consulting further on use of the national envelope.

It is considered that this will help reduce complexity and it is understood that they cannot be reversed later.

'CROSS-COMPLIANCE' CONDITIONS

20.17 The concept of 'cross compliance' is that land managers (farmers) who are receiving financial support from the public are expected to comply with conditions to maintain good standards of environmental protection, public, plant and animal health and welfare. This will be in the form of two distinct areas: statutory management requirements and good agricultural and environmental conditions (GAEC).

GAEC is designed to encourage a level of good environmental management and prevent land abandonment. A major aspect will be a focus on soils with the inclusion of measures to prevent erosion, maintain soil organic matter and maintain soil structure.

SFP – THE ANNUITY

20.18 The single farm payment has been described as an 'annuity'. The cynics have described it as a 'redundancy payment', in the same way we could no longer mine coal and steel cost-effectively in the 1980s, no longer can we compete in the agricultural world marketplace. However, the SFP promotes freedom of production in the unsupported world. However, since writing the second edition farm profitability seems to have improved and it has not been the 'redundancy' payment some feared. At the time of writing farming profitability is hitting levels not seen for a decade which is very positive.

TAX DEFINITION OF FARMING

20.19 We go full-circle – back to Chapter 1. What is a farmer? What is husbandry? What is agriculture? Article 1 of the EU regulation describes SFP as an 'income support for farmers' but it is undoubtedly dependent upon land management and not husbandry. At **20.5** we looked at the 'fiscal and non-fiscal' farmer. What is the historic definition of farming, agriculture and husbandry for tax purposes?

- ICTA 1988 s 832(1) – Agriculture is defined as the occupation of land wholly or mainly used for the purposes of husbandry (see **1.3**).

- *Lean and Dickson v Ball* (1925) 10 TC 341 – 'for a business activity to be classed as farming it must be depend on the produce of land occupied by the person carrying on the activity' (see **1.3**).

- CAA 2001 s 362(1) – Governs the tax position on agricultural buildings allowances (ABA) and defines husbandry as follows: 'any method of intensive rearing of livestock or fish on a commercial basis for the production of food for human consumption and the cultivation of short-rotation coppice (FA 1995 s 154(3))'.

- For ABA purposes poultry farming and fish rearing are husbandry (see **7.12**).

- IHTA 1984 s 115(2) – Agricultural land is described as follows:

  'Agricultural property means agricultural land or pasture and includes woodland and any building used in connection with the rearing of livestock or fish if the woodland or building is occupied with agricultural land or pasture … and also includes such cottages, farm buildings and farm houses together with the land occupied with them, as are of character appropriate to the property' (see **1.6**).

- CAA 2001 s 361(1) – Agricultural land means land houses or other buildings in the UK occupied wholly or mainly for purposes of husbandry (see **1.6**).

- Article 2, *Farmer* (under the MTR of the CAP reform):

  'the production, rearing or growing of agricultural products including the harvesting, milking, breeding animals and keeping animals for farming purposes or maintaining the land in good agricultural and environmental condition.'

- IHTA 1984 s 24C – Land in habitat schemes is agriculture (includes land within conservation schemes and set aside) (see **13.25**).

CONCLUSION

20.20   The answer is that we need a clear definition of agriculture, diversification, farmer, fiscal farmer, non-fiscal farmer and environmental stewardship.

Chapter 24 has gone a long way towards defining what is agriculture and what is not. There are those who consider that this should be taken a stage further particularly with regard to the interaction of BPR and APR.

The way forward to protect both tax reliefs and future subsidies will be 'active husbandry' by the owners of the land, irrespective of the definition, the landowner must be actively involved in the farming enterprise.

Index

[References are to paragraph number]

515